# SPORTS

## IN

## NORTH

## AMERICA

# Volumes in This Series

# SPORTS
## IN
## NORTH AMERICA

## A DOCUMENTARY HISTORY

EDITED BY

DOUGLAS OWEN BALDWIN

VOLUME

SPORTS IN THE DEPRESSION

1930–1940

Academic International Press

2000

DEDICATION

*In memory of E. Dean Baldwin,*
*and to Riley Owen Baldwin and Cole Douglas Cantin*
*who didn't get to call her Baba.*

**SPORTS IN NORTH AMERICA. A DOCUMENTARY HISTORY**
**VOLUME 8. SPORTS IN THE DEPRESSION, 1930–1940**
**Edited by Douglas Owen Baldwin**

Copyright © 2000 by Academic International Press

ISBN: 0-87569-224-9

Composition by Janet Liles

Printed in the United States of America

*By direct subscription with the publisher*

*A list of Academic International Press publications*
*is found at the end of this volume*

www.ai-press.com

**ACADEMIC INTERNATIONAL PRESS**
POB 1111 • Gulf Breeze FL 32562–1111 • USA

# CONTENTS

# PREFACE

This volume comprises an extensive collection of some of the most important primary source documents pertaining to the development of sports in North America during the 1930s. Reprinted materials include newspaper and magazine reports and editorials, financial statements, first-person accounts, important rules and regulations, and descriptions of significant technological changes in the world of sports. All selections are reproduced as they appeared, except where extraneous material was deleted.

The Introduction provides an overview of the impact of the Depression on sporting activities in North America from 1930 to 1940. It examines contemporary views regarding the relationship between athletic activity, health, and societal values, as well as sports' perceived importance in combating the mechanization and regimentation of life. External factors such as government activities, attitudes towards leisure, and the role of the media in promoting sporting activities are also examined. Chapter One explores why athletic games were considered a reflection of national characteristics, and discusses the prevailing attitudes towards females and minorities in the sporting world. Except for the section on International Games, the remaining chapters examine individual sports and how their development reflected the major social, economic, and cultural themes of the decade.

This series defines sport as an activity that involves some physical skill (hence chess is omitted), involves competition (thus excluding such recreational activities as tumbling demonstrations and fishing), and possesses a national or regional organization (thus omitting hopscotch). Approximately fifty sports satisfied this criteria for the decade of the 1930s. In determining how to apportion space among sports the amount of national magazine coverage dictated my decisions—which meant that football received a disproportionate amount of space.

A documentary history is only as good as the available primary materials. For the 1930s, the pleasant problem was selecting the best documents for each sport from among a plethora of excellent sources. Every major newspaper had an extensive sports department that churned out from four to seven pages of daily sports coverage. Popular weekly and monthly journals included regular in-depth commentaries on athletics. Each sport had at least one magazine devoted to its concerns. The major sources for this volume were the popular and sporting journals. With so many sports to examine, extensive archival research was impossible. As the purpose of this series is to explore how sports reflect and shape societal values and behavior, rather than reporting which teams or individuals won the major sporting events of the decade, these sources provide the best accounts and critiques of the major issues of the day. Unlike more regional sources found in earlier volumes, most of the sources for this volume spoke to a national audience. Wire services, national columnists, movies, newsreels, and newspaper chains reduced regional differences. They also hurdled national boundaries. In 1929, for example, more than two million Canadians went to the movies each week, most of which were American films, and purchased fifty million American magazines.

In terms of sales, Saturday Evening Post was Canada's most popular magazine. A study of the best-known athletes in Canada in 1935-36, as judged by the headlines in two major Canadian newspapers, discovered that seven of the top ten athletes were American. Although ethnic and working-class views are not well represented in these middle-class publications, special care was taken to include documents written about issues relating to women and minority groups.

Prior to undertaking this project, Dean Sullivan surveyed the *Reader's Guide to Periodical Literature* for the most pertinent articles and generously gave me permission to use them. I then devoted a sabbatical to driving from Halifax, Nova Scotia, to Toronto, Philadelphia, Chicago, San Francisco, and San Diego in search of additional materials. Acadia University's interlibrary loan section helped fill in the missing gaps. The Bibliography lists the 60 magazines and 3 newspapers that formed the bedrock of this documentary history and specifies the major primary and secondary sources that informed the introductions to each chapter.

Special thanks go to the librarians of the institutions listed in the Bibliography for their assistance. My student assistants Krista MacKay and James Sedgwick spent many hours scanning documents into the computer and ordering materials on interlibrary loan. Dr. Thomas Spira provided his usual excellent expertise in commenting on the introductions to each chapter. Peter and Gail Kessler in San Francisco, Nellie and Paul Schneider in Chicago, Terri and Matt McCabe in Media, Pennsylvania, and my father in Toronto all provided accommodations and support during my journeys across the continent. Once again I wish to express my love and appreciation to my wife Patty. She eased my researches by ordering and photocopying pertinent articles. She typed many articles that resisted scanning on to the computer. Patty also proofread the manuscript. This book is dedicated to our two grandchildren, Riley Owen Baldwin and Cole Douglas Cantin.

# INTRODUCTION

The 1930s have many names, few complementary. The decade was termed "The Dirty Thirties," "The Bitter Thirties," "The Winter Years," "The Hungry Thirties," "The Depression Years," "The Nasty Thirties," and "The Ten Lost Years." When people think of this decade they imagine prairie dust storms so thick that it was difficult to see across the street. They remember long lines of unemployed people looking for jobs, and starving families waiting for food at soup kitchens.

When President Herbert Hoover was inaugurated in March 1929, he declared the American economy was "sound." There were warning signs of danger from Wall Street for some time. The stock market grew rapidly for much of the decade, and the prices for many stocks were now grossly inflated. Some sort of serious adjustment on the stock market was probably inevitable. It began on 29 October 1929. The average value of all stocks fell thirty-seven per cent in the next thirty days and the plunge continued. When the economy did not recover immediately, banks declared bankruptcy, public confidence ebbed, consumption of consumer goods fell, investments plummeted, and unemployment mounted. As the new decade began, the United States faced the worst economic depression in its history. By 1932, approximately one-quarter of the employable population was without jobs and the 1929 national income was halved. Unemployment peaked at from 12 to 15 million the next year. The economy began to improve in 1933, but the number of jobless adults hovered around eight million for the rest of the decade.

Canada experienced similar problems. At the height of the Depression, one-quarter of the non-agricultural work force could not find jobs. The average person's income was reduced by half. To save money, children went without socks, shoes and underwear. People stopped going to doctors, dentists, and hospitals. They wore patched clothes. Flour sacks were used for underwear, and cardboard filled holes in shoes. Young, unmarried men left home, climbed aboard boxcars and traveled the country looking for work, which was almost impossible to find. When an Edmonton "Five and Dime" store advertised for salesgirls, the next day hundreds of women formed a line that circled the entire block. Since there were only three positions available, there was a riot. Desperate men and women struck for better wages and working conditions or organized hunger marches and parades. When nothing seemed to work, many people joined left- and right-wing political parties.

The economic depression of the 1930s had a profound impact on athletics in North America. Sporting goods sales, which included firearms, playground equipment and yachts, declined from $58.3 million in 1929 to $25.3 million in 1933. Similarly, professional sports and college football suffered at the turnstiles in the first years of the decade. Many universities sought to economize by reducing their football schedules, decreasing coaching staffs, and eliminating minor sports. Many private golf and tennis clubs folded as people turned to less expensive sports such as volleyball, softball, bowling, badminton, table tennis, and basketball. The National Recreation Association's 1934 survey of the leisure pastimes of 5,000 people in twenty-nine cities concluded that financial exigencies limited Americans to "simple, inexpensive, quiet, and individual activities." The most popular sports were swimming with 2,976 participants and tennis with 1,841 participants, followed by baseball, basketball, golf, volleyball, soccer, and archery.

As the economy began to recover in 1933, so too did the popularity of athletics. Thanks partly to active advertising campaigns, sporting goods sales rebounded to $44.5 million in 1937 and to $64.8 million in 1939. Faced with declining revenues, spectator sports sought new, innovative ways to attract more customers. Pari-mutuel gambling boosted thoroughbred racing. Night games increased baseball attendance. Basketball eliminated the center jump after each basket. Football adopted more liberal passing rules to provide more excitement, and hockey modified its off-side rule to speed play. Skeet replaced trapshooting in popularity. America's Cup modified the rules to make the event more competitive. Golf experimented with a different ball and officials researched the best colors for billiard balls and tables.

Many sports promoted themselves by citing the movie stars participating in their sport, and Hollywood used the popularity of athletics to sell tickets. Boxing played a major role in movies such as "The Champ" and "The Prizefighter and the Lady." Football was featured in "Pigskin Parade," "Crowd Roars," "$1,000 a Touchdown," and

"Golden Boy." Films such as "This Sporting Age," "Kentucky," "Indianapolis Speed-way," and "Pride of the Blue Grass," used either horse or automobile racing to attract movie-goers. Baseball was the centerpiece of eight movies in the decade, including "Death on the Diamond" and "Girls Can Play."

Numerous commentators attributed the growth in participatory athletics, as opposed to spectator sports, to Americans' desire to escape, if only temporarily, from the growing mechanization and regimentation of life. James Rogers, Director of the National Physical Education Service of the National Recreation Association, complained that modern industrial society had turned Americans into robots who pulled levers, pressed buttons, and oiled machines, and were but "infinitesimal bits in the fabric of a mechanistic industry." Robbed of their creativity, he continued, workers needed to find expression for their creative powers in their leisure avocations. Other commentators noted that the country's emphasis on mass production had caused rigid standardization, dehumanization, and immense pressures to conform that encouraged people to turn to sports to escape the feeling of being an interchangeable part. The daily grind at the office or factory floor produced a longing for diversions. Sportswriter John Tunis explained in 1934 that "those distressed in mind, body, or estate are again discovering that an afternoon exercising in the open air is...a means of obliterating the world at large...." In a similar vein, author Bruce Bliven commented in 1932 that "America, like other Western peoples, feels an uneasy, increasing sense of insecurity in the modern world, where they [sic] seem more and more to be the puppets of great economic forces which are beyond anyone's power to control." This, he concluded, explained America's penchant for worshipping sporting heroes.

Some Canadians expressed similar concerns. A 1933 editorial in Maclean's, for example, claimed that as work became more mechanical and less active, incidents of nervous fatigue increased "from those poisons and disconcerting thoughts you accumulate sitting around...."

In the 1920s, most states made physical education a mandatory school subject. By 1930, the emphasis changed from play to the broader concept of recreation, including "carry over" sports that could be continued after graduation. As the Depression enforced idleness, what individuals did with their leisure time became a subject of national concern. Popular advice columns counseled Americans to relax and enjoy life. To many experts, participation in sports was a vital factor in the progress of civilization. The president of Lafayette College stated in 1931 that the "future welfare of America is as much dependent upon our use of leisure hours as our use of working hours." James Rogers told a conference of educators in 1940 that "The biggest problem facing America today is what will the people do with the new leisure which has been thrust upon them? The biggest problem facing education today is how can we best train and prepare for this leisure?"

Government policies also aided sporting activities. In accepting the nomination for president in 1932, Franklin Delano Roosevelt declared, "I pledge you, I pledge myself to a new deal for the American people." The term New Deal later became used to characterize his reforms during the 1930s. The first stage of the New Deal was primarily designed to promote the recovery of the national economy. The cornerstone of this attempt was the National Recovery Administration. Other programs in the first phase of Roosevelt's New Deal attempted to reduce unemployment through public works projects. The Public Works Administration spent millions of dollars employing laborers on a wide variety of construction projects from sidewalks to post offices. The Civilian Conservation Corps and the National Youth Administration provided training for young people by employing them to improve the nation's forests and recreational facilities. These and other make-work projects spent about $750 million for such athletic facilities as gymnasiums, ski trails, tennis courts, golf courses, baseball diamonds, parks, and skating rinks. Government employees built or improved 3,300 stadiums and 8,333 recreational buildings, constructed 5,898 athletic fields and playgrounds, and dug 770 swimming pools—and in the process stimulated athletics.

On a much smaller scale, Canadian governments promoted athletics. The Ontario Athletic Commission redirected its tax revenues from sporting activities to support selected athletic organizations and create a provincial training center. In 1934, British Columbia created the Recreational and Physical Education Branch of the Adult Education Division to provide organized activities for the thousands of young, unemployed men who were congregating in Vancouver's parks. By 1939, more than 150 recreational centers offered nutritional advice, keep-fit programs, and team and individual sporting contests. Two years earlier, the federal government provided limited funds for the provinces to establish youth training programs. New Brunswick, Manitoba, Saskatchewan, and Alberta used this money to develop their own versions of British Columbia's programs to stimulate public recreation and thereby strengthen the health and morale of the country's youth.

City and town councils, which considered athletics a good way for young people re-direct their restless energy, cooperated with these federal programs and trained local recreational directors who worked with YMCA, YWCA, Kiwanis and Lions clubs, American Legion, Boy and Girl Scouts, and church organizations in encouraging youth to exercise and play games.

Not every sector of society participated equally. Although the number of females interested in athletics increased, they still faced the barriers of male indifference and hostility. Many black athletes performed heroically during the decade, but most sports continued to prohibit them from playing against white opponents. Workers and other minority ethnic groups also found entry into mainstream athletics difficult. Revived by the Depression which caused many Americans to question capitalism, the Communist party denounced bourgeois sporting organizations that catered to pampered elite athletes and diverted attention from important economic problems. The Communist party called for full equality of blacks and sponsored counter-Olympics in 1932 and 1936.

Media coverage of sporting events was as central to the game as were the athletes themselves. In most cases, celebrated coaches and athletes owed their stature to the journalists who wrote about them, and who themselves became celebrities. "Whether situated in New York or Denver," stated The Nation in 1935, "the men in the sports department are often the best paid on the sheet and not infrequently they are the best writers....The Great Names who run columns syndicated over the country have an enormous influence, their thoughts are household words....These are the men who make America's gods."

A typical press box at a major college football game in the East accommodated 200 or more newspaper reporters, columnists, syndicated writers, spotters, and a radio announcer in two long rows of seats on the rim of the stadium. Several dozen telegraph wires connected the press box to various newspaper and wire service offices. The reporters generally wrote running play-by-play accounts of the game which went directly to the newspaper office for the early morning editions. The columnists sought a different slant to the game. To assist the radio announcers in calling the plays, some announcers employed a special electric box with a separate light for each of the 22 players on the field. When a play began, his spotter illuminated the light that corresponded to the player who was carrying the ball. When the play ended, the spotter did the same for the tackler.

Without the media's daily promotion and glorification of athletic events, sports would not have grown to such national importance as they did. Toronto hockey announcer Foster Hewitt, for example, received a letter from the former president of the Ontario Hockey Association in 1935 which claimed that his broadcasts had "made Canada's national winter game attractive to its followers everywhere. People in all walks of life and of all ages, who never before were deeply interested in this phase of athletic pastime, now concede hockey a large and intimate consideration in their pursuit of pleasures."

Newspapers counted on their sports pages to attract readers, especially men, eighty percent of whom admitted to reading at least a portion of the sports pages regularly. In 1933, the Toronto Globe announced that henceforth it would feature sports news more prominently, including illustrations and a daily sports cartoon. By the end of the decade, most large daily papers devoted from five to seven pages to sports and employed a large staff of reporters, columnists, photographers, and editors for this section alone. In 1936, for instance, the Boston Transcript sports department employed seven people.

In addition to reporting sporting events, many newspapers also promoted them. Arch Ward of the Chicago Tribune invented the annual All-Star Baseball game (1933) and the College All-Star Football game (1934). Other papers sponsored teams and athletic competitions. Edward Geiger, editor of the sports section of the Chicago American noted that it was the sports editor's job to boost circulation, and to do this he should promote various amateur athletic enterprises. In 1930, the American sponsored a softball league with 15,000 players, organized a local girl's track meet which attracted 1,200 entrants, and continued its sponsorship of a women's bowling tournament which had 3,700 participants that year.

Virtually every popular magazine included articles on sport, at least occasionally. In 1938, for example, News-week hired John Lardner to write a regular sports column, "The Spread of Culture," and Liberty published forty-four sports articles that year. According to The Writer's Monthly, by mid-decade there were approximately 1,500 trade magazines in North America and the market for fiction and non-fiction sports stories had grown rapidly since the beginning of the decade. Sport Story Magazine published articles on all the major sports, preferably with a college backdrop, including short stories, serials, and instructional pieces by well-known sports figures. Similar journals included Fight Stories, The All-American Sports Magazine, Ace Sports Monthly, and Dime Sports Magazine.

Although radio was becoming increasingly more common, newspapers remained the primary source of news and thus the major molders of public opinion. During the decade, some 250 daily newspapers ceased publication as the industry consolidated. To cut costs, newspapers began to rely heavily on wire service such as Associated Press. Most photographs came from one of four photography syndicates. As monthly and weekly magazines also became more national, a relatively small group of journalists controlled the news. John Tunis wrote regularly for Harper's, the New Yorker, the New York Evening Post, as well as for other journals, and published eighteen sports novels for juveniles. Grantland Rice, considered the dean of American sportswriters, wrote, on average, 3,500 words every day and his daily column was carried by about 100 subscribing papers. Young people memorized his words and coaches used them to inspire their teams. Grantland Rice's equivalent in Canada was Lewis "Lou" Marsh. When Marsh died in 1937, at the subsequent hockey game between the Maple Leafs and the Canadians the teams stood at center ice and the audience rose to honor the Toronto Daily Star journalist with a minute of silence.

Salaries for the leading sports journalists in 1935 ranged from $750 to $1,000 per week for the foremost columnists. Although many journalists lived like millionaires, traveled widely, and associated with celebrities, often they were restricted in what they could write. Since a big fight or a celebrated sports contest generally increased newspaper sales, sports editors expected their reporters to promote such events, even when they expected indifferent competition, especially common among prize fights. Also, if writers did not report favorably on the local team, they ran the risk of losing access to their major sources of information. Reporters who accompanied teams on the road and had their traveling expenses paid by the team were particularly vulnerable. In baseball, Commissioner Keneshaw Mountain Landis forbade radio announcers broadcasting the World Series from questioning either the umpires' or the managers' decisions. When Ted Husing criticized the umpires in 1933, Landis banned him from the booth for life. Other journalists thought nothing of putting themselves in compromising situations. Mike Roden and Lou Marsh, for example, acted as NHL referees and as judges in six-day bicycle races, Foster Hewitt was the Toronto Maple Leafs' publicity director, Henry Roxborough was a member of the AAU's publicity committee, and Myrtle Cook of the Montreal Star served on the Women Amateur Athletic Federation's executive. The Nation complained that only a handful of sportswriters "have any independence and still fewer possess the slightest degree of moral courage, or are willing to write of things as they see them and not as the customers want."

Except for newspapers aimed at minorities, sports journalism was a white preserve. Black athletes had to perform almost super-human feats to be recognized—and even then their accomplishments were minimized. Women's athletic accomplishments were also trivialized. The Women's Sportswriters' Association was formed in 1929, but the Depression made it especially difficult for women to participate. Even so, in 1936 there were two full-time women's sports reporters in New York and Boston, four in Philadelphia, one each in Baltimore and Washington, and a scattered few elsewhere. Several African-American women were also active sportswriters.

As in the United States, female sportswriters were usually current or past athletes. In 1928, Alexandrine Gibb of the Toronto Star became Canada's first female daily sports columnist. Other women sportswriters included Phyllis Griffiths of the Toronto Telegram, Myrtle Cook of the Montreal Star, Patricia Page of the Edmonton Journal, Ruth Wilson at the Vancouver Sun, Bobbie Rosenfeld at the Toronto Globe, and Gladys Gigg Ross of North Bay's Capitol News.

Sports owed much of its growing popularity in the 1930s to the radio. In the United States, the number of sets increased from twelve million in 1930 to forty million by

1940. In addition to home radios, there were sets in clubs, hotels, schools, taxicabs, and railroad cars. In 1940, more than five million automobiles had their own radios. In Canada, sales of radio receivers grew from 112,00 in 1933 to almost 350,000 six years later. Studies of the medium-sized city London, Ontario reported the proportion of homes with radios grew from sixty-nine percent in 1932 to eighty-seven percent five years later. The average American household listened to the radio three to four hours daily. Studies of how Americans spent their leisure time noted that almost every demographic group ranked radio listening highly. Radios were thus one of the most commonplace features of North American life.

In 1938, News-week noted that one index of the relative popularity of sports in America was the number of radio sets tuned to athletic events. Broadcasting officials, the magazine continued, estimated that sixty-four percent of all receivers listened to the Joe Louis-Max Schmeling fight that June, and that on an average fall Saturday, thirty-five percent of the country's radios were tuned to a football game. Two percent less listened to the 1938 World Series. By comparison, thirty-five percent heard Charlie McCarthy, America's leading radio show, and approximately thirty-two percent listened to President Roosevelt's fireside chats that year.

Radio's growing appeal was evident in advertising budgets. Between 1928 and 1934, total radio advertising expanded by 316 percent, whereas advertising in newspapers dropped thirty percent, and magazine advertising revenues declined by forty-five percent. Radio's possibilities soon became obvious. When Foster Hewitt announced on his Hockey Night in Canada broadcast that listeners could order a special Maple Leafs' program for ten cents, the following Monday more than 90,000 requests for copies arrived at the station. In 1939, Gillette razor blade company faced its lowest profits since 1915, its share of the market was down to eighteen percent, and there were now 3,000 rival companies. In a dramatic attempt to increase its profits, Gillette bought the rights to sponsor the 1939 World Series. Ford Motor Company had broadcast the previous three World Series, but its sales had remained stagnant. The gamble was a success, as more than four million razor blade sets were sold during the series.

Radio announcers were often stars in their own right. NBC's Graham McNamee was the first radio celebrity. McNamee used his baritone singing voice and variable pacing to convey the emotions of the game. By 1930, McNamee, who broadcast major prize fights, college football games and a variety of other sports and news events, was a household name. For him, accuracy was not as important as creating a drama. If he declared that the wrong player had the football at the beginning of the play, McNamee might have him lateral to the player who was actually carrying it. CBS's Bill Stern was just as loose with the truth. On his popular "Colgate Sports Newsreel," Stern deliberately created false stories for their dramatic effect. During one show, Stern reported that Abraham Lincoln summoned Abner Doubleday to his deathbed and said, "Keep baseball going. The country needs it." Other radio announcers such as Ted Husing and "Red" Barber were more objective.

On 17 May 1939, NBC took its van to Columbia University field to televise a football game between Columbia and Princeton. This was the first televised sporting activity. In June, television cameras covered the Max Baer-Lou Nova heavyweight fight. In August, NBC broadcasted a tennis tournament. The following month, two cameras, one equipped with a telephoto lens, televised a major league baseball game between

Cincinnati and Brooklyn. October 22, 1939, was the date of the first televised professional football game—Brooklyn Dodgers versus Philadelphia Eagles. So little attention was paid to television that many of the football players did not know their game was being televised. The following year, NBC televised its first hockey, basketball and track and field events.

Few people watched these early broadcasts on NBC's experimental station W2XBS, all of which took place in the vicinity of New York City. Prior to 30 April 1939, there were only about 1,000 sets, most of which were owned by RCA and NBC executives and engineers, and home receivers were not offered for sale. The audience, which included visitors to the RCA Pavilion at the New York World's Fair in 1939, probably numbered in the hundreds.

Reaction was mixed. The black and white screens were only from five to twelve inches in diameter and often unclear. Indoor boxing and early afternoon baseball games on sunny days were ideal. When the sun dipped below the stadium in the first professional football telecast, the screen became darker and darker and the announcer reverted to a play-by-play radio-type broadcast. Following the first baseball telecast, the New York Times media columnist complained that the players looked like little white flies, and the ball was difficult to see. "The televiewer lacks freedom," he wrote, "seeing baseball on television is too confining...." More encouraging was the reaction of the Sunday Times to the first televised professional football game. "Science has scored a touchdown at the kickoff of football by television. So sharp are the pictures and so discerning the telephoto lens as it peers into the line-up that the televiewer sits in his parlor wondering why he should leave the comforts of home to watch a gridiron battle in a sea of mud on a chilly autumnal afternoon." Earlier in the decade, major league baseball and some college football conferences had wondered the same thing about radio and temporarily banned radio broadcasts.

Most Canadians and Americans followed the exploits of Babe Ruth, Mildred "Babe" Didrikson, Bill Tilden, Lou Hudson, Sammy Baugh, Gene Sarazen, Byron Nelson, Howie Morenz, Lionel Conacher, Eddie Shore, Joe Louis, Hank Luisetti, Jesse Owens, Eleanor Holm, Buster Crabbe, Helen Wills Moody, Lou Gehrig, Jimmy Foxx, Barney Ross, and Don Budge. Behind these larger-than-life athletes, the games they played and the manner in which they played them, and how they were reported on by sports journalists, reveal some of the major social, cultural, and economic themes of the decade.

Chapter 1

## SPORT, CHARACTER, AND MORALITY

Sports provided perhaps the most widely read-about events and the most recognizable individuals in North America. Many Americans and Canadians believed that athletics reflected and shaped national characteristics. Psychologists claimed that nations as well as people had personalities. American sports, declared Esquire at the end of the decade, "was the expression of a people who love to fight, the symbol of a mass of self-made men, whose achievements and success are best expressed by the symbol of the man who is stronger and faster than his opponent." Competitive sports embodied America's will to succeed and to improve. "Our system," declared the editor of The Athletic Journal, "reflects the restless energy, the love of combat, the desire for success that characterizes the American people."

As the outbreak of hostilities in Europe became more likely in the second half of the decade, many Americans attributed their more peace-loving nature to the country's athletic system. Would Germany be in such a turmoil, asked Mark MacIntosh of Swarthmore College in 1939, "if its national physical education instead of being regimented gymnastics and military discipline was wholesome games and sports as in England and America?" Americans fought their battles on the gridiron, where they learned to respect the referees' decisions gracefully and to play by the rules. A nation that loves sports, claimed Canadian sportswriter H.H. Roxborough, "cannot revolt."

Sports were considered one of the foundations of a well-organized society. The positive character traits learned on the playing fields were transferred to the classroom, to the home, and to the business world. After examining the personalities of 20,000 young people, eighty noted psychologists concluded that team sports contributed most to the development of wholesome personalities. Athletics, noted Henry Roxborough, honed the mind, cultivated leadership, taught morals, and undermined racial and religious prejudice. In the first issue of Canadian Sports and Outdoor Life (Winnipeg, 15 October 1932), the editor claimed that, "sports are essentially healthy and clean, and those who love to read about sport and sportsmen are likewise healthy and clean themselves." That same year, the American Federal Office of Education's study of intramural and interscholastic athletics found that the following "traits of character" were most commonly mentioned as being developed through interscholastic sports: sacrifice, self-control, self-respect, honor, initiative, team play, loyalty, social mindedness, and courtesy. That was why the release of the 1929 report on intercollegiate sports by the Carnegie Foundation For the Advancement of Teaching that accused American universities of recruiting violations, caused such a nationwide furor.

In May, 1934, a male sportswriter noted in The Literary Digest that of the forty-five sports that newspapers regularly covered, there were only six that women would probably never be able to compete in with any skill. Significantly, these sports—boxing, football, ice-hockey, rugby, water polo, and wrestling—all stressed violent physical contact. Based on contemporary accounts, females were more sports-minded than ever before. Numerous surveys indicated that females particularly enjoyed tennis, swimming, basketball, golf, volleyball, bowling, skating, and softball. Everywhere they were throwing balls, shooting arrows, swimming channels, hitting home runs, jumping hurdles, galloping ponies, and scoring goals. And spectators came to watch—sometimes in larger numbers than attended similar male contests. The best female athletes became national celebrities.

When male journalists wrote about this "phenomenon" they invariably concentrated on the achievements of individual female athletes—Helen Hicks shooting a round of 72 in golf, Lorna Whittelsey skippering yachts, Stella Walsh running, Helen Wills Moody and Alice Marble hitting tennis balls, Floretta McCutcheon bowling, Eleanor Holm swimming, Sonja Henie skating, and Mildred "Babe" Didrikson excelling in virtually everything. Canadian sportswriters praised badminton player Dorothy Walton, golfer Ada MacKenzie, the Preston Rivulettes women's hockey team and the Edmonton Grads basketball players.

Some people viewed this "invasion" with alarm. Society expected women to look attractive, to move gracefully, and to be deferential. Life magazine, for instance, often featured young, attractive female athletes such as Sonja Henie on its covers. Participation in such "feminine" sports as tennis, skating, diving, and swimming long was permissible because they taught women to move gracefully, and Hollywood talent scouts attended swim meets and tennis tournaments to discover attractive actors. The fashions of the 1930s also emphasized "feminine" attire. The boyish, small-waisted and slim-hipped styles of the previous decade gave way to clothes that accentuated women's curves.

When females showed that women could achieve excellence in all types of sports, they engendered fear and suspicion among some men that women were invading male domains. Women's duty, declared many sportswriters, was to look beautiful. A Vancouver journalist wrote in the early 1930s that female athletes were "leathery faced Amazons with flat chests and bony limbs and walk like knock-kneed penguins." In his frequently quoted article in Vogue and reprinted in Reader's Digest in 1936, Paul Gallico pronounced that women should compete only in eight sports. In all other sports, he explained, they wore funny clothes, became out of breath and perspired, and their faces became twisted and contorted as exhaustion pitted their faces with ugly gray lines. "Masculine" contests, many males and females believed, developed grotesque muscles and scowling faces, and hindered women's marriageability.

The coach of the Edmonton Grads, Percy Page, simply noted that almost every one of his ex-players was married, and only one was not a mother. After columnist Andy Lytle wrote that female track and field athletes were "leathery faced," the coach of the Hamilton track team marched her entire squad to his hotel room at the national championships to refute his comments. And a women's softball team sent him a hatchet with suggestions on how best to use it.

A second approach to this "invasion" was to limit the sports females could play. Proponents of this view relied on the growing body of medical studies on gender differences which claimed that females were neither as physiologically nor as temperamentally strong as were males. Some doctors claimed that the physical contact incurred in some sports could lead to female neuroses and psychic damage. In a 1938 survey of college directors and high school teachers, the National Section on Women's Athletics for track and field divided females into two categories, the "feminine type" with narrow sloping shoulders, broad hips and short legs; and the "masculine type" with broad square shoulders, narrow hips and long legs. An overwhelming majority of the respondents to this survey replied that schools should select activities that appealed to the "feminine type" girls.

Believing that biological differences could not be ignored, many people sought suitable activities for women that would not cause undue nervous strain, endanger the reproductive system, or promote masculine characteristics. The Women's Division of the National Amateur Athletic Federation (NAAF) created its own parallel organization and modified men's sport to fit what it considered to be women's unique capabilities and needs. Competitiveness and body contact were proscribed. Gender-specific rules regulated space and time to create separate women's sports. Women's softball shortened the distances between bases and forbade sliding; basketball rules divided the court into sections and prohibited players from moving between zones; track and field meets did not include the discus or the pole-vault and women ran shorter distances; volleyball and badminton required fewer points to win; and female golfers teed off closer to the hole. In general, female rules limited physical touch and restricted the players' movements.

Under the motto "A Sport for Every Girl, and Every Girl in a Sport," women physical educators sought to foster a lifetime of participation by making athletics available to everyone. They stressed enjoyment over winning and participation in recreational sports which could be played after graduation. They also demanded termination of intercollegiate and interscholastic contests, an end to exploitation of female athletes for gate receipts, and doing away with elitist teams. Since these qualities were all typical of men's sports, the solution was to employ only female coaches, administrators, and referees. When a woman delegate to the 1935 meeting of the National Recreation Association claimed that ninety percent of "our difficulties" are caused by male coaches and officials, she received enthusiastic applause. Female physical educators were most successful in eliminating interschool competitions. In 1936, only sixteen percent of American colleges had varsity sports for women. The following year, a survey of the 170 largest American cities discovered that merely thirty offered interscholastic programs for girls.

As an alternative to interschool contests, girls participated in intramural games, sports or play days, and telegraphic meets. For sports days, females from different colleges joined together for a day of competition and socializing and the girls divided into teams irrespective of their schools. Frequently, scores were not kept and no special awards were presented. The more competitive women took part in telegraphic meets. The athletes performed their event at home and telegraphed the results to a central headquarters where all results were tabulated and a winner declared. Such meets were intended to reduce the strain of travel and decrease the anxiety of competition. By 1936, approximately seventy percent of women's colleges participated in play days and seventy-four percent held telegraphic meets.

In many ways, the new ideology was similar to the nineteenth-century doctrine of separate spheres. Distinct female rules ensured that men would not easily appropriate these programs, but shorter distances and playing times also implied "different from" and therefore "lesser than" male sports. On the positive side, female physical educators refused to accept the prevailing stereotypes of women as sex objects and developed their own definitions of womanhood.

As usual, American ideas influenced Canadian attitudes. American journals were widely read in Canada and many Canadian physical educators earned advanced degrees in the United States. This influence was especially true in Central Canada, where intramural play became more popular than interschool competitions, and several school boards, including Toronto's, eliminated interscholastic competitions for girls. At the University of Toronto, women who wished to take part in either intramural or intercollegiate athletics had to take a pre-competition medical examination. Participation in two or more sports required written approval. Perhaps because its leaders came from both the middle and working class and most female sportswriters supported competition, the Canadian Women's Amateur Athletic Federation (WAAF) was less restrictive than its American counterpart. In basketball, for instance, the number of females who played men's and women's rules at the end of the decade was about equal.

The black community provided a more favorable environment for female competitive sports. The black press sponsored women's basketball, softball, and bowling leagues and wrote approvingly of female athletes. In black colleges, female educators tended to cooperate with their male colleagues and generally endorsed interschool athletics. In 1939, for example, whereas only seventeen percent of white colleges scheduled intercollegiate female meets, seventy-five percent of the black colleges participated in them.

Despite the best efforts of the NAAF, industrial leagues, YMCAs, settlement homes, and community organizations also sponsored women's competitive sports. Except for the Amateur Athletic Union, these groups generally ignored the NAAF. In 1932, after surveying 232 of the country's best female athletes, the AAU reported that nearly every person was in excellent health and that these athletes believed that competitive sports benefited rather than harmed females.

For all blacks, athletic success took an extraordinary effort. Blacks generally earned lower wages than did whites and had fewer available recreational facilities. Thanks to the WPA, playgrounds for minorities increased from 361 in 1930 to 632 in 1937, although the equipment was of inferior quality. Those few blacks who could afford to attend white colleges had to excel to join the school team, and were never named to All-America squads. The Jim Crow laws in the South made many coaches leery of recruiting black athletes. Public facilities such as swimming pools, parks, hospitals, schools, hotels, buses, and restaurants were either forbidden to blacks or segregated. In St. Louis, black spectators had to sit in segregated stands if they wished to watch either the Browns or the Cardinals. In many Southern states, blacks feared lynchings, which numbered thirty-five in 1932. Colleges with black players had to plan separate travel, lodging, and eating arrangements for away games. Since most Southern colleges refused to play against desegregated teams, the coach either cancelled the game or benched his star black player. Then there was the possibility that his decision would anger his players, the alumni, and students.

The situation was worse in professional sports. Although white administrators denied the existence of a color bar, black athletes were barred from major league baseball, from most tennis and golf events, and, after 1933, from the National Football League.

When asked why these sports did not include black players, the answer invariably was that they were not good enough. As a result, blacks were forced to compete amongst themselves. The migration of blacks to Northern cities in the previous three decades made this possible. Crowded into ghettos, blacks developed a sense of community that supported black-owned newspapers, businesses, and sporting teams.

At the height of Joe Louis' boxing career, sportswriter Paul Gallico wrote in the New York Daily News, "Louis, the magnificent animal. He lives like an animal, untouched by externals. He eats. He sleeps. He fights. He is as tawny as an animal and he has an animal's concentration on his prey.... Is he all instinct, all animal? Or have a hundred million years left a fold upon his brain? I see in this colored man something so cold, so hard, so cruel that I wonder as to his bravery." This was one image of the black athlete. He was a savage animal not far removed from the jungle. At other times, blacks were depicted as lazy, slow-talking, frivolous, Sambos. The Harlem Globetrotters and barnstorming black baseball teams deliberately fit this stereotypical image.

As the decade began, most whites thought that blacks lacked stamina, courage, and physical skills. Joe Louis, Jesse Owens, and the success of black runners and jumpers in the 1932 and the 1936 Olympics exploded these beliefs. Now, the experts sought to explain black athletic superiority. Sportswriter Grantland Rice claimed that Louis' skills were "a matter of instinct with him, as with most of the great Negro fighters.... The great Negro boxer is rarely a matter of manufacture, like many white boxers. He is born that way." In other words, blacks were good athletes because of their naturally endowed physical skills, not through hard work, self-discipline, and other positive character traits. According to Dean Cromwell, head coach of the 1936 American Olympic track team, "it was not too long ago that his [black athlete] ability to sprint and jump was a life-and-death matter to him in the jungle. His muscles are pliable, and his easy-going disposition is a valuable aid to the mental and physical relaxation that a runner and a jumper must have." Blacks were thought to be better because they were closer to being "primitives" than were whites.

Just what anatomical advantages blacks possessed became a much studied topic. An article in the American Journal of Physical Anthropology for 1936 discussed skin types to argue that the Negro race was closer to primitive man than was the White race. Other researchers suggested that because Negroes rarely had angina, it proved that their nervous systems were not as highly organized. A variety of "scientific" studies concluded that blacks could endure higher temperatures, had larger nerve cells, possessed faster reaction times, maintained a lower blood pressure through "inward serenity," had thicker skin, smaller viscera, and larger nasal cartilages.

One of the more popular theories attributed black athletes' success in running and jumping events to longer heel bones and stronger Achilles tendons. Eleanor Metheny, a physical educator at State University of Iowa, took anthropometric measurements of white and black students and claimed she found that blacks had longer forearms and legs and narrower hips, which, she suggested, provided blacks with an advantage in throwing and jumping events. William Montague Cobb, the only black to hold a doctorate in physical anthropology prior to 1950, refuted such claims when he noted in 1939 that Jesse Owens possessed none of the anatomical traits which white researchers attributed to black athletes' success. Cobb pointed to the importance of the environment, although he also attributed black physical superiority to the genetic process of selection associated with the ordeal of slavery. See Chapter 20 for Cobb's article.

## THE PHILOSOPHY OF SPORT

[*John L. Griffith was a staunch supporter of capitalism and amateur sports. Prior to establishing The Athletic Journal in 1920 (it had 14,000 subscribers in 1939), Griffith coached football. This magazine, primarily for coaches in schools and colleges, featured in-depth articles on coaching, fundamental skills, athletic injuries, and rule changes. In 1935, one of his editorials reported—"Some time ago a college professor asked the Editor of this magazine the following question: 'Have you ever known an athlete who was a Communist?' The Editor was forced to confess that he did not know of a single outstanding athlete who was a member of the Communist party or who belonged to any of the various campus 'pink' societies." According to Griffith, "one of the best bulwarks that we have in this country today against the spread of subversive movement is the fighting, aggressive, self-reliant athletes who are found in our schools and colleges." In this article, he discussed how sports reflected the American character. John L. Griffith, "Athletics in a Time of Depression," The Athletic Journal (December 1932), 6-7.*]

College athletics should be adjudged not because of their physical or mental characteristics but because they tend to influence qualities of character that cannot be measured in a physical efficiency or intelligence test, and because of their effect on our attitudes, which means our philosophy of life. The peoples of each nation have their own peculiar philosophy of life; otherwise there would be no difference in the meaning of the words Americanism, Russianism, Japanism and the like. I am not insisting that all of the wisdom of the ages is contained in our American philosophy of life, but I do maintain that it is distinctly our own.

What has this to do with athletics? Only this: it is susceptible of proof that our American philosophy of life and our philosophy of amateur athletics are very much the same. How much the one has been influenced by the other no one can say. I suspect that since we take our athletics so seriously, our athletic idealism has to some extent affected our national attitudes. Certainly we have generally subscribed to such mottoes as "Play fair," "Hit the line hard but don't foul," "Don't alibi."

Someone has said that democracy is a complex athletic game. Certain it is that the nations that have had the greatest success in establishing "governments by the people" have been the nations composed of citizens who engaged in amateur athletics on a large scale and who believed that it was finer to be a champion in the games than a loser. Athens in her most prosperous days believed firmly in the democratic principles of government. At the same time the Greek people made far more of amateur athletics than we do. History records that at one time, when the Greeks were about to begin a set of games, a messenger arrived and reported that a large Persian army was marching upon Greece. The Greeks, however, were not disposed to let such a thing as a war with a foreign invader interfere with their athletic contests and spectacles. And so they sent Leonidas with a few other Greek citizens to hold the invaders in check until the games were finished. In due time the Greeks attended to the Persians. We would probably call that an overemphasis on athletics.

Mr. Samuel G. Blythe in a very interesting article recently in the Saturday Evening Post compared the American's demand for beer and sports with the Roman citizen's demand that their emperors provide them with free bread and circuses.

There is a vast difference, however, between the Greek and American ideal of amateur athletics and the Roman idea of entertainment that was expressed in terms of gladiatorial contests in which the fighting was done for the most part by slaves and captives.

Everyone who witnessed the Olympic Games that were so splendidly managed and promoted by the Los Angeles organizing committee this summer must have returned home not only with a more friendly feeling toward the peoples of all nations that were so spendidly [sic] represented by fine sportsmen and athletes but with greater pride in his fellow men. Sir Harold Bowden, Bart., Chairman of the British Olympic team, was quoted in the Los Angeles Times as saying:

"Everything has been extraordinarily well managed. I think a better spirit of real sportsmanship has reigned here than at any previous Olympic meet since the first in 1896.... I know we British return home with a glow of good feeling.... It will be increasingly difficult for misguided politicians to lead any nation into war after this."

Dr. T. Yanamoto, Waseda University professor, in charge of Nippon's track and field team, declared:

"We know you now. In sport the man is naked. His real character comes out, in victory or defeat. We get a clear picture of each other. We are face to face. We become truly friends in battle. There is brotherhood in this. Out Japanese men know your men now. We admire them. Japan is now closer to you. We will take back the word. No, we do not care what the statesmen may say: We know you now."

Under the capitalistic system, life is a series of competitions. Where in all of those competitions, however, except in athletics, do we guarantee a boy a fair start, an unimpeded path on which to run and a just award at the end of the race. Every possible precaution is taken in a foot race for guaranteeing the competitors a fair start. No one is permitted to throw obstacles in their way as they run, and each competitor may expect a just award at the finish of the race. Since the finish judges are human, moving pictures were taken of the finishes of the Olympic Games by way of guaranteeing that no mistakes of judgment would be made. When a man starts out in some of the other competitions of life he is not sure of having a fair start. It may be that he does not belong to the right clubs, or that he may be handicapped because of his race, religion, or color. None of these handicaps pertains when a boy enters an amateur athletic event. Sometimes in other of life's competitions a man finds combinations, obstacles or restrictions which make it well nigh impossible for him to succeed. If he is a contractor, for instance, bidding on a contract to be let in one of our large cities, even though he makes the lowest bid he perhaps will find that some competitor with political connections is awarded the job.

When a boy enters an amateur athletic event he is guaranteed an opportunity whereby he may put forth his best efforts and achieve whatever success is his due. The American's innate love of fair play guarantees such a competitor a fair field and no favorite. Perhaps we have a higher regard for the way in which our amateur games shall be played than we do for the way in which our other competitions shall be conducted. I have never heard of an attempt made to bribe a college football official, and one never hears even a suggestion from a spectator at a game that this or that football referee may have been corrupted by gamblers or by anyone else. We frequently hear it suggested that this or that public official has been guilty of accepting bribes.

One of the tenets of amateur sport is that each player shall respect the rights of his opponents. It is my duty in connection with my work as Commissioner of Athletics of the Big Ten Conference to receive each week during the football season reports from the officials regarding the games played each Saturday. Sometimes whole seasons will elapse without any adverse criticism on the part of the officials regarding the sportsmanship of the players....

President Coolidge once suggested that America did not guarantee any man a living but it did guarantee him an opportunity for making a living.

In athletics no boy is ever guaranteed a place on the team. If he is a man possessed of the necessary prerequisites of athletic success, which includes his ability to stand punishment, if necessary, like a man without cringing or whining, he is guaranteed a man's chance. There is a tendency today to want to make life easy, safe and fool-proof. Some people a few years ago objected because some of our ablest and strongest young men spend some time each fall in practicing and playing football. They thought it wrong for these boys to subject themselves to the hardships and rigors of this virulent game. During the War we were not inclined to take this soft attitude toward physical hardships. A great may of our young men in those days marched hour after hour, each carrying a rifle and a sixty-pound pack, and then perchance dug in or went into action. Football exemplifies many of the attributes of fighting and working, and it is only when we come in contact with a softening civilization that we listen to the prophets of senility and softness.

Today, whether we like it or not, we are working out the principle of the survival of the fittest. The weak will perish and the strong will survive. Some have perished who deserved a better end. This is always the case in times of stress and strain. After this crisis has passed, the men who are strong, the men with fighting hearts and with minds that think straight, will be in the forefront. These men will exemplify the rugged virtues of the race, just as football represents aggressiveness, endurance, quick thinking, yes, and fair play.

A man who has really learned the lessons taught on the athletic fields will not blame others for his mistakes. In athletics the name "alibier" is applied to the player who blames the officials or others for his defeats. Someone once called attention to the fact that in the fall of the year when the frosts come, the sound, healthy leaves on the trees turn to gold and the weak, sickly leaves turn yellow.

We have been passing through a period of adversity and many who have suffered because of their own mistakes have blamed the President or someone else for their disasters. The athletic type of man who does not growl but takes his blows standing up is not blaming his leaders during these troublous times. When we get into trouble, some people cry for help and others help themselves. Before Christ came into the world the Jews were tired of fighting. They were having a hard time; and so they looked forward to the coming of the Prince of Peace, believing that He would thereafter fight their battles for them; would ease their sufferings and would make their lives easy, safe and soft. When He appeared, however, He told them that He came not to bring peace but a sword. Apparently He wanted His people to realize that their troubles were largely of their own creation and that it would be better for them to help themselves. The men who today are blaming their leaders for all of their troubles, and who are sitting back waiting for some Moses to lead them out of the wilderness, are weaklings.

When I was a lad I was taught that it was a disgrace for a man to be so thriftless, careless and incompetent that he would need to spend his declining years in the poor house subsisting on other people. Today our country farms and poor houses are over-populated because we have been led to believe that if a man spends his earnings as he goes it is the duty of the government to take care of him in his old age. In athletics, men are taught not to depend upon the help of their team mates but to be ready to assist others when assistance is needed.

Much has been written and said by way of calling attention to the mistakes that have been made in connection with the administration of college athletics. The public expects that college athletics, like Caesar's wife, shall be above suspicion. Consequently, in the age of cynicism through which we have been passing, critical articles and books attacking college athletics have had a ready sale. The thinking man, however, knows that college football, for instance, is not moral but rather is an agency for good or bad depending upon the way in which it is taught, administered and played. So it is in like manner with books, the theatre and science; none of these is moral. There are good books and bad books; good plays and disreputable plays. The knowledge of chemistry may be employed by the thief in blowing a safe or it may be the means of safeguarding the health of a community.

Our amateur athletics are to be found very largely in the educational institutions of this country that are administering to the educational needs of some twenty-nine million boys and girls; young men and young women. School and college athletics are supervised by educators who as a class reflect the finest ideals and aspirations of the race. No wonder then that the philosophy of the playing fields is the philosophy of those who have helped shape the character of America and those who today are holding fast to American principles. When the historians of the future record the events of this period, perhaps they will see more clearly even than we can see now that our games and the manner in which they are contested have played an important part in shaping the manners, morals and philosophies of our people.

### PHYSICAL EDUCATION AND THE MACHINE AGE

[*In discussing the benefits of athletics, the sports editor of the Boston Telegraph reported in his column that a minister recently told him that sports were always uplifting—even something as sordid as a prize fight—and that he often illustrated his sermons with examples from the sporting world. "America's great love of sports activities," the editor concluded, "has been a fine outlet for our surcharged existence." The following address by the editor of the Journal of the National Education Association to the Annual Convention of the American Physical Education Association in Philadelphia in 1932 examines the themes of leisure and technology discussed in the Introduction to this volume. This publication, "the official magazine in the field of health and physical education," was intended for teachers, administrators and students. Joy Elmer Morgan, "Physical Education and the Machine Age," The Journal of Health and Physical Education (June 1932), 3-6, 37.*]

It is a privilege to share in this 37th annual meeting of the American Physical Education Association here in Philadelphia. It is in this very city that the National Education Association was organized in 1857. The 43 pioneer spirits who in that period of disunion came here to the scenes of the nation's birth to renew their devotion to the republic, laid the foundations for the greatest professional organization in the world. Today the National Education Association is helping more than 200,000 teachers to work at their problems. Largely as a result of the ideals and standards established through the association, the schools have been improved and extended....

Groups such as the American Physical Education Association are in a position to understand better than the rest of us the crucial significance of our heritage of physical vigor. May I suggest that because you are students of this special problem, because you hold positions of peculiar importance in the community you also carry obligations to interpret the significance of this heritage to your associates in the teaching profession and to the citizens of the community who determine our customs and our public policies. There was a time when physical vigor could be taken largely for granted. The necessity of war, the grim struggle with soil and climate made daily demands which exposed weakness and rewarded strength. The advantage of being strong was easily apparent. The constant association with soil, sun, and fresh air kept men close to the sources of their strength. It is no longer possible to take the mere fact of physical rigor for granted.

If we wish to maintain the accumulated vitality of the ages, we shall have to give some consideration to the ways of living necessary to preserve that vitality. Concretely this means that each of us must be an interpreter of the value of physical fitness. It means that you in contact with your classes, with your associates, with the homes you visit, in addresses before groups of which you are a member, in your writings, in your activities as a citizen, must make your influence felt; that you must exert a steady pressure in behalf of higher standards of physical wellbeing....

I should like this morning to suggest answers to three questions: First, in what ways is the machine age affecting our lives? Second, what changes should be made in our ways of life in order that we may enjoy the advantages of the machine age and avoid its dangers? Third, what can you personally do to improve conditions?

In the writings of Charles Dickens we get our first vivid picture of the **effects of the machine**. The textile mills take the place of hand weaving. People accustomed to the easy pressures and the simple ways of the small town and countryside are quickly herded-together in large towns without water supply, sanitation, police, or education. Under those conditions disease spreads, crime increases, the family tends to disintegrate, and there is a general sense of depression and social decay, reflected in the stirring narratives of Dickens' novels. Looking back upon that period, it is now plain that the worst fears were unfounded, that it was possible for humanity to adjust itself to the new conditions and to rise to a higher plane of well-being for all the people.

The present mechanical revolution is much more far reaching and pervasive than the changes which took place in the time of Dickens. The increase in machine power staggers the imagination. It discounts both the physical force and the skill of man in favor of the machine.

In the first place, it has shortened the working day and the working week, **giving an increased leisure.** I believe this increase in leisure to be much greater than is ordinarily realized. A century ago it was the custom for the entire population, even for children and old people, to work for long hours. Between that day and this we have freed the children from the necessity of toil for gain. We have in the schools of the United States today 30 million young people who, under conditions of an earlier age, would have been at work in the shops and the factories. We have added 5 millions of these to the schools within the past decade. Within the past century we have practically halved the length of the working week.

In the second place, the machine age has **raised the standard of living** until today people enjoy a variety of food, a beauty and comfort of clothing, a quality of housing, and a variety of transportation far beyond that of the earlier period....

A third effect of the machine age during recent years has been the further **concentration of population in cities**. Conditions, in these cities are vastly better than in the time of Dickens but they are still far below the standards which should be maintained by a civilized people. Already the tide is beginning to flow out of the cities. People are returning to the suburbs and to the land to seek conditions more favorable for themselves and their families.

A fourth result has been to **concentrate financial power** in the hands of fewer and fewer people and along with financial power goes the management of life itself....

A fifth effect of the machine is to change many of our people **from out-of-door activities** which tended to build up strong bodies **to indoor sedentary activities** which tend to weaken and destroy physical vitality. This is a fact of great mental and spiritual, as well as physical, significance.

You will be able to think of other ways in which the machine age is affecting our lives but these are the principal ones: increase the leisure, a higher standard of living, the concentration of population in cities, the concentration of financial and industrial power, and a change from active outdoor to sedentary indoor occupations.

Our next question is, **What changes should be made in our ways of life in order that we may enjoy the advantages of the machine age and avoid its dangers?**

Let us face the facts as they are. The machine age is here. We could not, if we would, turn back the hands of the clock. We may as well make a realistic analysis of our situation and set ourselves seriously to work to find ways of adapting ourselves to it....

**Preparation for leisure** is one of the major educational problems of our day. There has been a tendency to mechanize not only our work but equally our play. I believe that tendency to be inherent in the commercialization of recreation. I do not believe it can be corrected so long as the arts of recreation are left in the hands of those who would use them for private profit. The time has come when recreation for all must become as universal as education for all—when it must he thought of as one of the major phases of education for both children and adults. This means increased emphasis on physical education. It means you who are trained, will be better rewarded, and more fully appreciated by the public than you have been. Think what it would mean to America if we could have devoted to this great task of physical education one trained worker for every ten teachers in our schools so that there would he a mighty army of 100,000 devoted to this important phase of our life. I suspect that the services of this 100,000 would do to protect our national existence—even if war should come—than all the hundreds of thousands that constitute the forces of our peacetime armies and navies....

Already within our best schools are the beginnings of a new civilization. The school of tomorrow will be a community institution. Cities will he so built as to put at the center of each neighborhood the parks, the playfields, the school, the library, and the clubs. The school of tomorrow will be more generous and flexible than our traditional institutions. The public will absorb into its schools, activities now associated with the Y.M.C.A. and the Y.W.C.A, with social work, with art centers, with health preservation and with the movie, the dance hall, the bowling alley, and the golf course. The schools will he characterized by increased attention to three needs: first, they will give much greater emphasis to the relation between physical and mental health; second, they will give more time to educating for leisure; and third they, will include a comprehensive program for adults as well as for children.

Our people need to recognize more clearly, the relation of physical health to mental health—to the hygiene of our American life more particularly. They need to appreciate the importance of physical vigor to clear thinking....Some of the worst tragedies which afflict individuals today come from physical inability to stand life's strain. The whole "tempo of American life" as James Truslow Adams has expressed it, has been speeded up until owing to the number and variety of sensations and the constantly shifting environment—man is called upon to make a far greater number of adjustments to the world than was his remote relative in the caves and forests of Germany and Java. As a result there is a set of qualities which the spirit of our times does not encourage: poise, balance, steadiness, stability....

**The change from physical activity to relative inactivity** in many of our occupations has led to such measures as the exercising machines, the increase in Turkish baths and massage, and other substitutes for the purification of muscles through their own activity. The nationwide spread of the "daily dozen" and the morning exercises has been an attempt to offset the muscular decay that goes with indoor inaction. These are artificial substitutes for the real thing. The best effects of physical activity are lost when elements of interest, volition, and variety are lacking. It is through education, through the activities of such groups as yours, through a great increase in hiking, boxing, gardening, golf, ping pong, bowling, tennis, dancing, and horseback riding, that we shall find the natural correctives for the limitations of a sedentary life. It is of the utmost importance that through education and practice we establish, not for a few but for all, a reasonable program of physical activity. We cannot do this without changing the character of the physical education program in the school so that we shall develop there both the philosophy and the activities which will be useful in the years beyond the school.

**You can exert a steady pressure toward a more rational curriculum.** It is sheer nonsense to spend time teaching Latin to students who do not know how to care for their bodies. A curriculum which teaches higher mathematics to students who do not know how to play or to be happy is a form of foolishness. To do these things is simply to bring Latin and higher mathematics into disrepute and to create a distaste for scholarship and study which retards education.

The curriculum of the schools must be built around the needs of life and we cannot ignore the need today for more physical activity, for training in leisure, for an increased devotion to the fine arts of music, drama, human relations, gardening, and architecture....

## I DON'T LIKE AMAZON ATHLETES

*[The following article by popular Canadian sportswriter Elmer Ferguson represented the opinions of many North Americans. Women's role in sports, he believed, was to be graceful, sweet and beautiful—as they were in skating, diving, tennis, and golf. In all other sports, the effort, strain, and sweat involved was too physically and mentally taxing, produced ugly faces and bodies, and made them undesirable marriage partners. With such attitudes, it was unsurprising that most Canadian newspapers devoted less than ten percent of their sports coverage to female participation.*

*When Ferguson's article appeared, Roxy Atkins, secretary of the Ontario Branch of the Women's Amateur Athletic Federation, and Canada's premier hurdler, demanded that Maclean's publish her rejoinder. In the 15 September 1938 issue, Atkins noted that Ferguson had never attended a major women's athletic event and accused him of parroting the words of American writers such as Paul Gallico. Her rebuttal pointed out that many women's jobs created more strain and sweat than did athletics, and that while sports were irrelevant with how women looked, they promoted confidence and self-assuredness. Elmer W. Ferguson, "I Don't Like Amazon Athletes," Maclean's Magazine (1 August 1938), 9, 32-33.]*

I am speaking now exclusively to the girls, so you guys can turn to some other page for your literary nourishment and entertainment.

Well, girls, if you are listening (which I doubt very much indeed), I want to say that I am a much maligned man regarding the matter of girls in sport. I know that, as a result of your reading the girl sports columnists who have me continually on the pan, in the grease, out of the frying pan into the fire and vice versa, you must figure like this: "Why, this Ferguson is nothing but an old grouch. He doesn't want the girls to have any fun. He wants them to stay in the kitchen and cook for him, the glutton."

That is absolutely not true. I don't want to see the girls kept in the kitchen. Because, in the first place, men are far better cooks than women. All the better hotels have male chefs. In the second place, girls are entitled to all the fun they can get in this man's world.

Yes, girls, I know you think very hard things about me. You think: "He is just like all the men; besides which, he is so old-fashioned that he doesn't know that girl athletes were in the Olympic Games, and he thinks that woman's place is in the home, and all that stuff grandfather used to believe in."

Well, girls, it's not so. I think girls definitely have a place in sport, and don't let any character snatcher tell you anything different. In fact, on the matter of the participation of girls in sport, I'm your pal, and this isn't said with a significant passing of the hand across the throat. It's strictly on the level.

I never saw anything more beautiful in sport than this: A colored ice surface at the Montreal Forum, all painted with red tulips, yellow lilies, glowing roses and such. A lone blazing shaft of light, hitting on one spot, the rest of the great arena completely dark. Into the spotlight there suddenly whirls a figure of sheer glittering glory, of golden hair that blazes beneath the dazzle of the lights, of white skirt and trunks and shoes, and tight-fitting bodice, all covered with spangles that glow and glitter like diamonds, a figure that spins in rhythmic, swinging grace. I always had the idea that figure skating was a sort of sissy business, but that was a long time ago, before I'd ever seen or sensed what sheer beauty, what perfection of rhythm, what grace could be encompassed in the art by Sonja Henie, by a score of other girls who glide and pirouette and swing so sweepingly and beautifully around a glistening surface, without strain, effortlessly, a symphony of grace.

Girls have a place in sport. I knew that when I saw a graceful figure standing atop a high diving board, a girl whose physical perfection was enhanced by a clinging one-piece bathing suit of the sort some old fogies with nasty minds would bar as indecent, when such garb in reality removes all possibility of suggestiveness. The girl leaned forward, arms arched, and floated off the high board, coming down to the water like a great sea bird, a thing of infinite grace, to strike smoothly, without a splash, and go streaking into the depths, leaving hardly a ripple behind.

Girls have a place in sport. I knew it seeing Kay Stammers and the late Suzanne Lenglen gliding over tennis courts, slashing back drives. I knew it seeing Joyce Wethered or some other graceful girl golfer swing with precise rhythm and a certain power on a teed-up ball, though I've seen some ponderous females tramping the links who added nothing whatever to the scenic effects with their Clydesdale strides, dripping perspiration, stertorous breathing and blowsily flushed faces.

**WHY SACRIFICE FEMININE CHARM?**

That, indeed, is where I reach the dead-line. Sorry, but in girls' sport I can't go for those violent, face-straining, face-dirtying, body-bouncing, sweaty, graceless, stumbling, struggling, wrenching, racking, jarring and floundering events in which some girls see fit to indulge. Sorry again, but I like grace, sweetness, rhythm, freedom from sweat and freedom from grime among the girls. Of course, it's a matter of taste. Some of the boys may like to see the girl friend lumbering along from first to second in a softball game, hitting the dirt on her ear, and coming up with a lot of mud or sand ground into her visage. Probably there are some who are elemental that way. They may like to see the girls at hockey, a spectacle which I consider reaches the lower levels of competitive athletic entertainment after you've watched the grace and speed and certainty and skill with which males perform. They may like to see some nice girl bodycheck another and knock her down, half-stunned and breathless, though, in all truth, the girls in hockey skate in such rickety fashion, bobble along so uncertainly, that a good strong breeze will pretty nearly blow them off their stumbling feet, and bodychecks are just so much, wasted effort.

These boys, perhaps possessing some sadistic impulses which were not included in my natal make-up, may like to see their girl friends wearing that peculiarly bewildered and distressed look which girl athletes under strain always possess, that strain which so ill becomes them. They may like to see the girl friends in shorts up to their thighs, getting their legs rubbed and massaged by a professional trainer. I hope I'm not prudish on the matter of girls' legs, which at one time were considered no topic whatever for decent conversation, and were blushingly referred to as "limbs." The fact is that girls' exposed legs are no treat. The gay boys of the nineties who stood around the more exposed corners on windy days, trying to get a peek and extracting a naughty thrill at the sight of an ankle, were wasting their time. They got a kick—mentally, I mean—from a well-turned ankle because it was visually forbidden fruit.

But the truth is that the legs of most girls don't rate so high on exposure. They're prone to have queer blue marks on them, or lumpiness, or run to bulginess or something. They look more alluring covered up. But even so, darned if I understand a guy who feels no annoyance when some trainer or helper starts massaging the girl friend's legs in the better interests of promoting circulation, and right out in public too. Sorry, but I like a little delicacy, as well as sex appeal, feminine sweetness and such, among my girl friends. And I can't see that the more robust forms of athletics, such as sprinting, jumping, hurdling, heaving weights, sliding into bases, struggling weakly and gracelessly around armed with hockey sticks or crashing each other at basketball in a sweat-reeking gymnasium, are going to enhance any feminine charms, or those charms which I always did associate with femininity.

My contention is, in brief, that no sweet feminine, girl (and, I repeat, what male doesn't want girls to be sweetly feminine, and nice and sweet and frilly?) can be much good at the more robust forms of athletics. Those girls who excel in them very frequently look extremely unfeminine. Take the Galloping Ace, for instance—I'm not naming names but I'm thinking of one of the recent top-liners of sprinting—which is possibly the least revolting, at that, of the more strenuous sports indulged in by girls. And when I say take the Galloping Ace, I mean you take her; I'll take a cup of coffee. She can run 100 yards in better than eleven seconds, as indeed can many a schoolboy. Not that there's any sense comparing men and women on an athletic basis, for there isn't any comparison. But Ace is a big, lanky, flat-chested, muscular girl, with as much sex appeal as grandmother's old sewing machine, that we stuck up in the back of the attic. The sewing-machine and Ace both run well. So what?

I've seen some really pretty girl runners; at least they were pretty when they weren't contorting their comely faces out on the cinder track. There's Hilda Strike, for instance, and Myrtle Cook, and the little Halifax schoolmarm, Aileen Meagher, who has the muscled legs of a male sprinter but who is so feminine by instinct that she wears a bit of frilliness about her clothes out on the track. But my point is that these girls never could whip the big, masculine, flat-chested, leather-limbed and horselike-looking stars of the game, stars in point of speed. Many nice things were written of the pulchritude of the girls who made up the last Canadian Olympic team. Those pressing the case for girls' sport laid some great emphasis on the beauty of the team, emphasis which was well deserved, for they were a lot of beauties. But they didn't win anything. Beauty and success in girls' track and field sports don't go together so well. All of which goes to prove that a certain degree of masculinity is necessary to complete success in the realm of Violent Sports for Girls. And who wants masculinity in our girls?

**UNHEALTHY COMPETITION**

I said I'm your pal, girls, in the matter of sports activities, a real pal, because I'm advising you to stick to those sports in which you compete with a minimum of strain, a maximum of grace, beauty and rhythm; the sports in which you can compete with pleasure and success and still retain essential femininity, which includes no grime on your face. I mean, speed and figure skating, tennis, golf, swimming, and a few more in which neither grace nor dignity is sacrificed to face-straining and belabored effort.

It's for health too. Amateur sport in Canada to my mind knows no more sincere and diligent advocate than Dr. A.S. Lamb, of the Department of Physical Education at McGill University. The good doctor is another of the little heckled band (I mean the girl sports writers continually give us the bird) opposing participation by girls in violent sports, in which he coincides with the opinions of Dr. H.M. Abrahams of London, Olympic 100-meter sprint winner of 1924. This is Dr. Lamb's sensible theory:

"There is almost universal agreement that well-directed play and recreative activities are most beneficial, particularly to our youth. Play is, however, a two-edged sword, and misdirected activities and emphasis may be quite harmful. In well-directed play, activities should be utilized which appeal to the natural interests, which harmonize with age and development, and which have inherent values in the contribution they might make to better citizenship.

The nature, and characteristics of boys and girls differ very widely, and therefore care should be taken to foster activities from which the greatest benefits might be derived.

Nobody would wish to see a return of mid-Victorian fainting frailty and the traditional headaches of that era. There are numerous activities suitable for girls, and women, without the necessity of using those types of competition which call for such intensive concentration and effort as many which are now being promoted.

We need more, not less, activity for our girls and women, but let these be of the type that will be suitable to their physical and mental natures. Let us have more concentration upon the needy ninety percent instead of spending our time and energies upon the highly specialized ten per cent.

The tendency for girls to ape the activities of boys is regrettable. In most cases, it is physiologically and psychologically unsound and may be definitely harmful.

Play, recreation, competition, are just as essential for our girls as for our boys, but this must in no way be interpreted to mean that intensive competition with its excessive emotional and physical stresses is the type which should be participated in by girls and women."

That's the story, girls. The violent sports are no good for your looks, dignity, or health. Occasionally some writer comes out stressing the improvements of times and distances being made in women's sports, and hints that the day is coming when they'll equal the performances of males, which is a very stupid suggestion indeed, because they never will. But they usually omit reference to one athletic event—and to my mind the one that required the greatest courage and stamina in which a girl outdid all the men who tried it. This is the English Channel swim record established by Gertrude Ederle. She not only made the swim, but she broke the records of all the men. It was a great feat. But today Gertrude Ederle is an almost completely deaf and almost completely crippled woman. The water that penetrated her ears caused deafness. The strain of a performance for which no woman is fundamentally suited brought on other and more serious consequences. Perhaps that's why the enthusiasts for girls' sport don't mention Gertrude very often.

**DON'T BE RIDICULOUS**

Don't get out on the same field as the men, girls, if you wish to compete in the more violent sports. The comparison may be like most other comparisons—a trifle odious. The report from the last Olympics indicated that the feats of the girl athletes were not taken seriously. "There was a note of mockery in the applause," wrote Joe Williams from Berlin, of the women's events. And that sturdy critic, John E. Wray of St. Louis, penned this: "It would be better if they did not clog up the Olympic program with women's attempts at athletics, but either abandon them or hold games for women separately. Watching the pitiful efforts of some of the girls in field events, observers were inclined to feel the same way about the matter. In each event, one or two unusual specimens stood out above the rest. The grand average performance was incredibly bad."

Women say they don't wish to excel [sic] male records, and they never will, for they lack the power. And lacking power, they lack grace. The effort of a woman to struggle over five feet in the high jump is rather pitiful, after you have just seen a male athlete, with the superb grace that comes from power, soar over nearly seven feet. Women lack the grace of men in all track and field sports. Their efforts are labored, heavy. Kit Klein, great speed skater, a graceful and rhythmic performer on the steel blades, thinks that most sports make women look ridiculous. I chatted to her one day in her dressing room in a Montreal theatre. "Girls ought to stick to the things they do gracefully and without injury to bodies that never were meant for wracking, jolting sports," said Miss Klein. Of course, some of the girl writers put the blast on her, but I think she was perfectly right.

Organized sport, organized fun, for girl athletes—that's swell. I'm all in favor of it. But, girls, stick to the things you do gracefully, beautifully, with rhythm, without strain—in which category you can't put sprinting, hurdling, or heaving weights or javelins. That's a tip for you girls. It probably solves the whole mystery of man's slightly derisive and ridiculing attitude toward women in sport. The men want the gals to stay beautiful, graceful and sightly, not tie their bodies in scrawny, sinewy knots.

Leave the rough, tough athletics to the men. For if the girls think that running and weight-tossing are all right, it won't be long before they're into boxing and wrestling too. And why not? These sports are only other forms of athletics; and a few pioneers have already tried them both.

So let's close the whole argument on that horrible thought.

## THE CASE FOR AND AGAINST WOMEN'S INTERCOLLEGIATE SPORTS

[*The National Amateur Athletic Federation actively sought to spread its message. In 1938, for example, when the organization again attempted to eliminate women's events from the Olympic Games, its members organized forty-four state committee meetings, delivered nine radio talks, gave 127 speeches across the country, and wrote seventy-two newspaper articles on the topic. Publications such as Standards in Athletics for Girls and Women (1937), the Service Bulletin which, beginning in 1936, appeared six times a year for high school teachers, and Sport Guides which discussed coaching strategies, officiating, and sporting values helped disseminate the NAAF's views. The following article compares attitudes towards intercollegiate athletics between 1923 and 1930. The major deletions include the long list of colleges surveyed, attitudes towards interclass competitions, views on play days, and a few less pertinent statistics. Research Quarterly was published by the American Physical Education Association to keep its members abreast of current research in the fields of athletics, physiology, administration, and "character education." Mabel Lee, "The Case For and Against Intercollegiate Athletics for Women and the Situation Since 1923," Research Quarterly (May 1931), 93-127.*]

In the spring of 1923 the College Women's Section of the Middle West Society of Physical Education asked the writer of this article to present at its program a study of the situation of intercollegiate athletics for women, including the case both "for" and "against" such activities. At that time 50 colleges located in 23 states replied to the questionnaire sent out all over the country and the information gleaned was presented at this program and subsequently to the public, through the channels of various magazines and pamphlets.

During the summer of 1930 the Women's Division, National Amateur Athletic Federation asked that the study be repeated so that it might learn of the tendencies of the past seven years' growth and know the present situation. In response to that request, the following report is submitted.

## SOURCE OF INFORMATION

...Questionnaires were sent out to the Directors of Physical Education for Women in 154 leading colleges and universities of the United States. Replies were received from 98 colleges. (Only 50 replies were received in 1923.) Fifty-six directors failed to reply. The 98 directors replying represent 37 different states and the District of Columbia. (Only 23 states were represented in the replies of 1923.)

This study includes agricultural colleges, teachers colleges, state universities, privately controlled universities, women's colleges, co-educational colleges, junior colleges, and denominational colleges. It includes colleges of all sizes, with the enrollment of women students ranging from 52 to 9709....

## THE CASE—FOR AND AGAINST

A. Varsity Type of Intercollegiate Athletic Competition for Women (Varsity type involves the coming together of the teams of the competing colleges with each team representing its entire college.)

## I. EFFECT UPON WOMEN STUDENTS

a. Advantages to those who participate.

1. "In keeping necessary training rules they would acquire habits of hygienic living which should be of great value to them."

2. "Through contact with strangers as their guests or as their hostesses they would acquire a training in social values and a broadening of experience which cannot be approximated in playing games with none but home teams."

3. "Through the greater interest in intercollegiate games they would feel the more keenly defeat and victory so that their instructors would have an opportunity to drive home to them the lessons to be derived from defeat and victory more quickly and more sharply than in the case of intramural or interclass activities!"

4. "They would work harder, thereby acquiring better muscular control, co-ordination and increased vigor, also increased mental activity in quickened thought reactions!"

5. "They would acquire alertness, initiative, clear thinking, decisiveness, self-discipline to a much greater degree than they would through lesser interest in home activities."

6. "They would have opportunities to make contacts they would not otherwise have."

7. "It would give good players a chance to play good games."

8. "It is a wholesome pleasure."

9. "It broadens the vision of the girls."

10. "It creates an excellent test of sportsmanship and health training in order to succeed."

11. "The varsity type of individual needs opponents worthy of her calibre."

12. "It aids women to meet problems of competition in the business and professional world."

13. "It gives the girl with exceptional motor skill an opportunity for development and she should have this chance as well as the girl with the exceptional mind."

14. "It trains girls for later situations in life, physically and socially."

b. Disadvantages to those who participate.

1. "They would be apt to get more physical straining than physical training, showing the most perhaps in nerve fatigue."

2. "The emotional strain attendant upon such competition would be injurious."

3. "There would be ever present the tendency to take an active part in activities during the menstrual period for the sake of the trip and the honor of having played. Also the members of a team who can be the least spared by their team would be urged to keep secret their condition so the team would suffer no handicap through their absence, the desire to play the best players being so much more intense in intercollegiate games than it would ever be in a series of interclass or intramural games."

4. "The intensive training that would come with participation in these activities would lead to the neglect of other school work due to increase of interest in the activity or through physical fatigue from this intensive training, which would make the girl unable to give proper attention to the other work."

5. "The one idea to win at any cost would be bound to creep in, bringing in its wake the inevitable qualities of rowdyism, unless the activities and the players themselves are carefully supervised by competent and conscientious instructors."

6. "With the usual rush of college life there is no time that might rightly be given up for the intensive training intercollegiate activities demand."

7. "An undesirable newspaper notoriety would be sure to come to the girls; especially undesirable would be the mention of the fact that certain players are to be out of certain games, as is always the case when men players are out for physical disability of any sort."

8. "The sense of values of the players would become distorted as now happens in the case of men's athletics."

9. "The disadvantages so far outweigh the advantages that we should not even consider them."

10. "Girls are too high strung emotionally to participate wisely in such activities."

11. "The values, if any, when achieved are not worth the time spent to achieve them."

12. "They would make unfavorable contacts through the unfavorable publicity that would come with varsity competition."

13. "It is not a wholesome activity for a girl to enter judging from the experiences college men go through in their varsity competition."

14. "Membership on a varsity squad would curtail a woman's freedom to pursue the normal trend of college life just as it now curtails the freedom of a man who is on a varsity squad."

15. "A question which should not be ignored is that raised by certain members of the medical profession as to the bad effect of intense athletic participation on child bearing."

c. Disadvantages to those who do not participate.

1. "They may not get 'physical straining' but would be quite apt to get little 'physical training' through neglect if the teaching staff had to turn out varsity teams. It seems impossible that the 'many' would not suffer neglect for the 'few.' No school has sufficient staff or equipment to carry out a correct program for both the 'many' and the 'few.'"

2. "The many girls neglected are sure to be the very girls who need the most training for their physical welfare."

3. "They would not have their legitimate share of athletic and department funds spent upon their training, so high would be the expense of intercollegiate teams."
[Deleted "effect upon the teaching staff.]

### III. EFFECT UPON THE ATHLETIC ACTIVITIES THEMSELVES

a. Advantages.

1. "Intercollegiate competition would lead to more intensive study of the technique of the game and its possibilities."

2. "The type of playing demanded of a team prepared for such competition would raise the standards of interclass playing within the school."

3. "It sets an example of skill and thus encourages greater participation in the games."

4. "It gives a better idea of the purposes of sports."

5. "It creates higher standards of performance."

6. "It creates an excellent test of sports."

7. "Mass participation levels the best to mediocrity and unless other opportunity is given to the best, the best is lost."

8. "With proper coaching and officiating, intercollegiate athletic competition gives greater opportunity for fairer and more stimulating competition."

b. Disadvantages.

1. It would prevent the adaptation of the game to meet the needs of the average girl since the more intense interest would be in the game the stronger girl could play."

2. "It would limit the number actually playing the game since only a few can be chosen for teams."

3. "It would tend to produce 'fans' out of the majority, rather than players."

4. "It would lessen the field of interest in the activity through a lessening of the number that can be chosen."

5. "The highly undesirable commercialism of men's athletics would be sure to creep in."

6. "It would tend towards professionalism, a most undesirable thing."

7. "It would produce enemies for the game because of disapproval of the physical strain upon the participants."

8. "The entrance of women into the intercollegiate athletic world would take us still farther away from the goal physical educators seek—the goal of 'play for play's sake' and everyone on the field instead of in the grandstand."

9. "It would be sure to be conducted as is men's inter-collegiate athletic competition. Why do we think it would not be so conducted since there are so many men only too willing to step in and advise in that direction?"

10. "Even if it got started in an approved way, the situation would be sure to run away with itself and the whole thing would become like men's intercollegiate athletics—a highly undesirable thing."

11. "Athletic competition between colleges as it now exists in the field of men's athletics is unwholesome and a waste of time and energy. Why involve women in the same thing?"

12. "Intercollegiate athletics and strong general participation of students are incompatible."

13. "The college girl actually would not be interested in sports to the extent needed to carry on a successful intercollegiate program. Her interests can be sufficiently served in an intramural program."

14. "My experience at____ University teaches me that girls can be interested in large numbers in an intramural program without varsity competition to make a peak to the pyramid at the end of each season. We have been doubling and even tripling our intramural enrollment in many sports year by year for four years now, with the plea to come out 'just for the fun of it' as the only incentive. I am sure the majority of these girls would not come out for these sports if they thought it meant working up to varsity for they would not care to go into it so intensively. Many would feel they should not come out unless they were skillful at a sport if varsity play were the ultimate goal of the season and so we would lose the very girls we need most to reach. The appeal to come out 'just for the fun of it' reaches hundreds of girls the minute they know it is not to be intensive and is to be purely recreational."

15. "While a few girls on every campus may yearn for the notoriety varsity playing might bring them, the great rank and file of women students would greatly dislike being personally involved in the tedious work and physical straining of a varsity program. They wish for themselves play and fun from their physical activities, not the work and tedious confinement they see their brothers go through who are on a varsity squad. There are plenty of men students too who see these disadvantages in varsity participation and avoid being dragged into it personally. The epidemic of student opinion voiced in our college papers all over the country last fall (1930) will back up these statements."

**IV. EFFECT UPON THE COLLEGES SO INVOLVED**

a. Advantages.

1. "It would create a greater interest in the school's athletics on the part of the outside world."

2. "It would create a greater interest among the students."

3. "It hastens intercollegiate friendliness."

4. "It gives colleges a chance to know each other."

5. "It gives an increased respect for other colleges."

6. "It gives a broader perspective and criticism of one's own college as compared with other colleges."

b. Disadvantage.

1. Quoting one of the leading physical directors for women of the Middle West: "Men's athletic departments are struggling now with their difficult situation and are not as yet making much progress. In the present unhealthful state of public and alumni opinion, intercollegiate athletics for women would be subjected to the same pressure

from the outside as are men's, i.e., to make the game a good spectacle, to have a highly specialized team, so that it would be worth paying to go to see, and very likely, worth betting on."

2. "The handling of gate receipts and other business aspects of intercollegiate competition would tend to develop the director into a business manager rather than an educational expert."

3. "The gate receipts themselves would tend to develop extravagance in the department and the tendency to expend a disproportionate amount of money for the training of the few who earn the gate receipts."

4. "It would mean a reorganization of the physical education staff as well as its class work so that the intercollegiate squad could be trained separately, questions of eligibility could be passed upon and other intercollegiate matters could be properly dealt with."

5. "The desire to produce a winning team would tend to make students and faculty alike forget that the game should serve as a recreation for its participants as well as for the spectators. It is already a criticism of men's athletics by English observers that they take them too seriously and magnify their importance, forgetting on the other hand, the spirit of 'play for play's sake.'"

6. Quoting a prominent eastern director: "Most of us constantly see ways in which we could do more follow-up work, check up our procedures by more careful records and more study of those that we do keep, see ways of adapting work more carefully to individual needs, of stimulating intelligent effort in posture correction, in health habits, etc. Many of us are compelled to teach larger classes than permit of real instruction because we have not the floors or the staff to permit of organizing more classes. Attention to intensive competition would curtail the development of our departments in what to me seem more essential directions."

7. "My experience at____College where 400 students take part in the preliminary competitions and 200 compete on field day, and where Juniors and Seniors whose sport is entirely voluntary place a team in each of eight different sports on the field has intensified my belief that a general interest can best be obtained without intercollegiate competition. Our thirty-two different teams in the eight sports bring out this large number because no girl is a member of more than one team."

8. "It would be forcing something we are not properly organized to carry on."

9. "Our intramural program reaching over 2,000 women in a year's round of physical activities at____University would be sure to suffer if we were to organize for intercollegiate competition with its demand for winning teams. This would necessitate the giving of extreme attention to a mere handful of women and this in turn would call for failure of attention to these 2,000 and their activities, as things are now organized in our university and as they will probably be organized until the millennium comes due to the ever present shortage in staff and facilities."...

### E. WHY DIRECTORS HAVE CHANGED THEIR VIEWS ON THE QUESTION OF INTER-COLLEGIATE ATHLETICS FOR WOMEN

I. CHANGE FROM DISAPPROVAL TO APPROVAL

1. "Because there are more women coaches now, the rules are more unified and the public attitude is better." (This director is not having intercollegiate athletics however.)

2. "Sport conditions have changed, they are less emotionalized and games are not now over emphasized."

3. "Because of my experience with Play Days and because of the benefits derived from an extensive intramural program."

4. "Because I have had practical experience with intercollegiate athletics and have found none of the evils which I had drummed into me as a student."

5. "Because I believed without trying it out that intercollegiate athletics meant sports for the few with only the best participating. I find I was wrong. With an increasing intercollegiate program we have had an enormous increase in intramural and non-competitive sports.____Our varsity teams constitute a leader's group which coaches, captains and officiates for the lower teams. I doubt if the group would have the same incentive to meet for instruction, if they did not know that they were going to have their own matches as well as teach others, train teams and umpire games."

II. CHANGE FROM APPROVAL TO DISAPPROVAL

1. "Because of my observation of intercollegiate athletics and discussions of the problem."

2. "Because of the changing attitude toward play and physical education on the part of students and colleges."

3. "Because of my special training in the field of physical education."

4. "Because of my experience with intercollegiate athletics."

5. "Because of my observation of the great needs for training in sports of those who are inexperienced."

6. "Because I felt a stand 'for' was too radical."

7. "Because of an acquired interest in a concern for the effects of athletics on the body."

8. "Because of the changed attitude toward women in sports."

9. "Because of a more sincere study and closer observation. Such participation will not injure some girls—I do not believe it hurt me, but there are girls who played with me who are injured. If **one girl** is injured it doesn't pay."

10. "Because of National Amateur Athletic Federation's views."

11. "My original opinion was based upon the fact that I was a member of a varsity team. Since then the theory and practice of interclass and play day competition have shown themselves far more democratic."

12. "I am now against intercollegiate athletics in all sports of body contact but not against intercollegiate athletic sports such as tennis and golf."

13. "Because within the past eight years I have become a teacher and I see the teacher's viewpoint now."

14. "Because of my observations of intercollegiate athletic games and because of articles I have read on this question."

**F. ACTIVITIES USED IN INTERCOLLEGIATE ATHLETICS FOR WOMEN**

|  | 1923 | 1930 |
|---|---|---|
| Number of colleges reporting on intercollegiate athletics | 11 | 12 |
| Basketball | 11 | 8 |
| Tennis | 9 | 9 |
| Hockey | 7 | 8 |
| Swimming | 5 | 4 |
| Baseball | 4 | 3 |

| | | |
|---|---|---|
| Archery | 2 | 1 |
| Rowing | 2 | 0 |
| Handball | 2 | 0 |
| Fencing | 1 | 0 |
| Greatest number of activities used by any one college for intercollegiate athletics | 7 | 4 |
| Least number of activities used by any one college for intercollegiate athletics | 2 | 1 |
| Average number of activities used in the colleges for intercollegiate athletics | 4 | 2.72 |

## CONCLUSION

It is interesting to note the rising tide of condemnation of men's intercollegiate athletics. It has grown from a mild protest, voiced by a few in the study of 1923, to most emphatic statements of disapproval, voiced by a large number in this present study of 1930. There exists a great fear that once intercollegiate athletics for women gain a foothold, college women might become involved in the same athletic predicament of their brothers. The director who replies in the following strain seems to voice the opinion of the great majority when he says "I would approve of a program of intercollegiate athletics for women if it would actually be conducted as amateur sports should be conducted but not as men's intercollegiate athletics are conducted in this country." There is ever present the alarming thought that women might become involved in something equally undesirable. Directors for women seem to feel that these fears are not altogether idle fancies, judging from the pressure being brought to bear in yearly growing force from certain sources.

While one director writes "We 'stew' too much about organized recreation and sports. It is impossible to generalize for there are so many factors involved," yet another writes "the whole thought life of women is changing rapidly and its expression in activity is bound to change. The subject of athletics becomes one of the thought provoking questions."

The following quotations voice the opinions of many who replied in the same strain as did the writers of these lines.

"Intercollegiate athletics and strong general participation of students in athletics are incompatible."

"I have coached two teams each participating in one intercollegiate game per year. I feel they gained nothing from the games and as for 'college spirit' it was no better after the games."

"No group of players is so skillful that it is necessary for it to go outside its own college walls to find worthy opponents to play against. The skillful players can be cared for at home in an intramural program and can get all the strenuous playing they need and should have and the athletic needs of the other students can be cared for at the same time."

"Why have an intercollegiate program when all its advantages can be worked into an intramural program and all its disadvantages eliminated?"

"By the time every college has 90 or 95% of its women students participating in a sports program, then and not until then, have we a right to begin thinking in terms of intercollegiate athletics."

"The competitive element is already greatly overemphasized in all phases of our society. With the comparatively recent background which we have for women's athletics a country wide acceptance of the 'varsity' idea must necessarily be based on the poor standards of men. I do not believe we are in the stage of development which warrants a belief that this type of activity can be promoted to the extent that it will be beneficial."

"The only excuse I see for promoting a program of intercollegiate athletics for women would be in the case of a need to give certain women superior and intensive training so that they might be prepared to enter the world of professional sports for their life work after their college days. There is positively no other life situation that I can picture that calls for such athletic training. Thank goodness our colleges are not yet offering training for professional sport as a branch of their activities—at least not such training for women. May the day never come when our colleges lose all sense of proportion and throw to the four winds all educational ideals in regard to women's athletics as they have done in regard to men's athletics. Let us fight if necessary to keep our young women free to play healthfully and wholesomely. As a student I was captain of our varsity hockey team that played matches with two different colleges as "curtain raisers" to football games. As a young teacher I refereed many a shameful interscholastic basketball match. Any one, who has had such experiences and is interested in educational ideals and in creating in this world a spirit of friendliness towards others knows that there is positively nothing of value to gain in an intercollegiate program but that there is much of value to lose."

From a careful perusal of the questionnaires filled out, there seems to be a dearth of quotations to offer from the side that champions intercollegiate athletics for women. Those who are "for" seem quite content to cast their vote "for" with few remarks while a great many of those who are "against" seem eager to seize the opportunity "to speak out in meeting" for their side. Hence the few quotations to offer on the one side. But following are those that were offered.

"All of our intercollegiate contests are made social events and not sporting events as is the case with men's intercollegiate athletics."

"I approve of intercollegiate athletics in my case since conditions are ideal but I would not approve in most cases as conditions exist today." This director is in a woman's college where campus life is devoid of the "hurley-burley-rah-rah-circus-side-show" atmosphere of men's athletics and where the young women are not constantly distracted by "dates."

"I approve of intercollegiate athletics in the individual sports but not in sports of body contact."...

In the position of one who is presenting both sides of the question, the writer finds it necessary merely to present and to let the statements of those who are "for" and the statements of those who are "against" speak for themselves, and to let the figures in the statistics tell their own story of the situation as it stands today. Many of the suggestions, especially some concerning Play Days, will most probably sound utterly naive to most men and to some women but they prove how absolutely determined are the women of the physical education profession and, judging from the report of A.C.A.C.W. for 1930, how determined also are the women college students of today, not to permit women's athletics to follow in the footsteps of men's athletics. They are determined to keep them free of all taint of professionalism and commercialization—to keep them quite informal, entirely sane, and absolutely wholesome.

## WRITING ABOUT SPORTS FOR RADIO

[*As radio broadcasts became more popular, many large newspapers entered the business. By 1931 at least six Canadian newspapers were affiliated with radio stations, and by 1940, newspaper corporations owned almost one-third of all American radio stations. In addition to broadcasting live sporting events, radio also provided regular sporting news and commentary, the scripts for which were usually composed by professional writers. The Writer's Monthly provided a regular "Monthly Market Service" that reviewed the various fiction and non-fiction markets. The following article provided tips for prospective writers for radio sports reports. D.J. Foard, "Radio Sports Reviews," The Writer's Monthly (December 1936), 169-172.*]

Radio needs material badly, and the radio field is a wide-open market for the capable free-lance writer. Yet it must be recognized that it is difficult for a writer to establish himself definitely in this expanding area, because radio can consider only material specially designed for vocal production, and because it must have material of the highest quality.

One type of program, the radio sports review, offers the writer a great opportunity to write regularly for radio and, what is more, to realize a substantial profit for his work.

Most of the stations in this country are small, having power outputs of from five-hundred to three-thousand watts. But, regardless of how small a station is, it must have a sports program during the baseball season, for example, and it is usually written by an announcer, a control man, or some other employee on the staff. Because of the poor programs produced, a large number of listeners turn to the larger stations for sports news, which results in a substantial listener-loss to the smaller stations, so if any writer can produce a sports program that will attract listeners, his services will be welcomed by practically any low-or medium-powered broadcast station in the country.

Sports reviews are divided into two types, general and special. In the general type, the baseball scores and league standings are given first. Then follows news of racing, boxing and other sports. The program is filled out with bits of baseball or football statistics and "short-shots" about teams and players. The material for this filler copy is obtained from handbooks and yearbooks published by concerns such as the Sporting Goods Journal of St. Louis.

The special type of program is one in which a play-by-play account of a baseball or football game is included. In baseball, the scores and league standings of one league are given first. Then follows the play-by-play account of the game. This is followed by the scores and league standings in the league involving the game reported in the play-by-play account. The program is filled-out with news of other sports, "short-shots," or by the closing "commercial." The special type of program is slightly more popular than the general type, even though it involves the added expense of securing over the wire the data for the play-by-play account of the game in which most of the listeners are interested.

The sports review is usually a fifteen-minute program, but it should not run over fourteen minutes. This gives the announcer an adequate margin of safety and it will not matter if the program runs a few seconds short.

In preparing the sports review, the name of the program, the call letters of the station, the date and the name of the sponsor, should be written at the top of the first sheet. The copy should be double- or triple-spaced and the program should be neatly typed on a good grade of clean white paper.

To give you a general idea of the manner in which a radio sports review should be written, the following "sportscast" is reproduced. Note the heading. Note the paragraph marks at the beginning of each "item" for the announcer's convenience. Study the manner in which the copy is written for the ear rather than the eye:

HELLO FANS. We had a great day in baseball today. A lot of hard hitting, clean, fast fielding and some fine pitching performances. [The remainder of this sample sports report deleted.]

Throughout the baseball season, the sports review is broadcast daily. Immediately following the World's Series in the football season, with the big college games in which most listeners take a keen interest. During the football season, the sports review is usually broadcast twice a week, on Wednesdays and Saturdays, in the late afternoon or early evening.

Unlike the special baseball sports review, no play-by-play accounts of football games are included in the football sports review. Instead, the Saturday sportscast consists of the scores of most college games, with highlights on the performance of outstanding players and brief summaries of the deciding plays in the most important games of the day.

The Wednesday football sportscast usually includes the scores of professional games and interesting comment on the most important games to be played on the following Saturday. A popular feature to include in the mid-week broadcast is "picking the winner" of the most important games.

Practice writing sports review programs. When you believe you are capable of doing this work competently, prepare a complete "dummy" baseball sports review program. Take this to a local station and tell them that you would like to prepare their sportscasts throughout the next baseball and football seasons. If the station will not pay you what you think your work is worth, show your "dummy" program to possible sponsors and interest them to employ you to write a daily sports review to fill in radio time purchased by them. If you can write an acceptable program, and do not overestimate the value of your work, you can find a ready market and regular employment in a steadily expanding field. If you want to write for radio, you can't afford to miss this opportunity.

## SPORTS JOURNALISTS

*[More than 130 radio stations in North America broadcast the Max Baer-Joe Louis fight in 1935 and approximately 1,000 newspaper reporters attended the prizefight. One journalist, who could not get a seat at ringside, dictated his story into a tiny ultrashort-wave set that conveyed his words directly to the newspaper office. United*

*Press assigned several reporters to the bout—Stuart Cameron dictated his blow-by-
blow account to a Morse telegraph-operator, another reporter composed the main lead,
two men stayed by the fighters' dressing rooms, and another scrutinized the celebrities in attendance. The final copy was distributed to the United Press' sixty-five bureaus
across the country, where it was rewritten for local appeal and sent to 1,300 subscribing newspapers.*

*According to most contemporaries, the best sportswriters included Grantland Rice,
Paul Gallico, Frank Graham, Damon Runyon, Ring Lardner, Westbrook Pegler, William McGeehan, Stanley Woodward, Dan Parker, John Kieran, Joe Williams, John
Lardner, Henry McLemore, Alan Gould, Heywood Broun, Arch Ward, Gene Fowler,
John Tunis, and Canadians Lou Marsh, Henry Roxborough, Dink Carroll, Leslie Roberts and Ted Reeve. These are the men who provided the bulk of the documents for this
volume. The following article outlined the growth of sports writing in the twentieth
century and discussed some of the best-known sports journalists. Stanley Walker, City
Editor (New York, 1934), 115-116, 122-124, 127-133.]*

As a distinct branch of American letters, sports writing has existed only since about
that period which Mark Sullivan, the Bat Nelson of political writers, has called the Turn
of the Century. In its infancy it was a lonely orphan. Then came an era of luxuriant
verbiage, when a spade could be called a spade. Later the art had its period of disil-
lusionment and debunking, a period which still hangs on, sometimes as a healthy attitude and sometimes as mere exhibitionism. Today the art seems to be maturing, and
in the larger cities it shows signs of producing a department of the newspaper distinguished by intelligent reporting and writing—the ancient, simple test of newspaper
excellence.

The sports page once was the poor relation. It was read principally in barber shops
and barrooms to supplant the Police Gazette. Publishers and managing editors knew
it was necessary, but they didn't like it. Now the sports pages are second only to the
general news pages in importance; indeed, on some days they may be more important.
The clientele is wider; it handles more sports and finds its readers among ping-pong
players, duck shooters, hikers, fishermen, bowlers and fencers. It is genteel, sometimes
too genteel; fortunately some sports writers retain enough of the old beer, beef and
beans flavor to ward off anemia.

It is not now a skimpy sports page, but a sports section. The space daily devoted
to sports has more than doubled in the last fifteen years. The Sunday sections may run
to twelve pages. It is, rightly, a department to which newspapers devote brains and
money. Even more attention should be paid to headline writing and editing.

The character of the writers has changed. With a few scholarly exceptions, sports
writers used to be rather unlettered chroniclers (muggs) writing for an audience of their
own kind. Now much of the writing is done by college men, aimed at readers who are
college students or college graduates. The boys who thirty years ago aped the late
Charley Dryden, who probably deserves to be called the real father of modern sports
writing, have dropped out or learned better. Too many of them were bankrupt in imagination and had to resort to tricks when something more than monosyllables was demanded. After Dryden, such men as Lardner, W.O. McGeehan, Hughey Fullerton,
Damon Runyon, Grantland Rice, to name only a few of the signposts, brought to the
business a grown-up judgment, some sense of proportion, a gentlemanly taste and even
some literary quality....

The sports writer today is supposed to be not only a fair writer but an informed reporter, educated in his game, acquainted with its background, personalities and politics, if any. He is a specialist. To name only a few, such men in New York as Stanley Woodward on football and rowing, Will Wedge, Edward T. Murphy and Frederick G. Lieb on baseball, Harry Cross on a half-dozen subjects, Hype Igoe on boxing, William J. Macbeth and Henry V. King on racing, Fred Hawthorne on tennis and William H. Taylor on yachting, may not be great writers, but they do know their materials. One of the last of the really great baseball reporters, who understood baseball better than most players knew it, and who wrote classic English even when explaining the most technical points of the game, was the late William B. Hanna, a grumpy journalist but a great one. He hated trees, but he knew sport.

In sports writing, and in the attitude of writers toward sports, there are two fairly definite schools, sometimes defined as the "Gee Whizz!" and the "Aw Nuts" wings. Grantland Rice, perhaps the most popular and respected gentleman ever to write sports, came out of the South long before the war bearing an unusual equipment—he had a good education, he was a poet at heart, and he had genuine, almost fanatical love for sport. His career probably has been the most successful of all sports writers, although he, like Dryden, set an example for many a young man, who, seeking to be a word-painter, loaded his pop-gun with red paint and fired at the rainbow.

Rice wrote much poetry, some of it good; much of his prose was poetry too. His leads sang of sunsets which displayed the colors of the victorious college football team, which was an advantage, because except on rainy days the crimson of Harvard or the blue of Yale may be found in the late afternoon sky. A football team in a desperate stand near the goal-line reminded Rice of the French at the Marne, the Spartans at Thermopoylae or Davy Crockett and his boys at the Alamo. A fighter like jack Dempsey, a former hobo, might carry the hammer of Thor or the thunderbolts of Zeus in his right fist ("maulie" or "duke"). A half-back, entering the game belatedly to turn defeat into victory, would remind Rice of Phil Sheridan at Winchester. Walter Johnson, Washington pitcher, was the Big Train roaring through. There were ghosts there too, strange but lovable visitors from that Valhalla where all good sportsmen go, hovering about in the dunight [sic], advising the gladiators and making themselves useful around the place....

It was about twenty-five years ago that the late Ring W. Lardner went to work on the myth that sports characters were glamorous—kind to their families, courageous in all circumstances, possessing healthy minds in god-like bodies. He began his "You Know Me Al" stuff, which pictured the typical ballplayer, a stupid, stingy, gluttonous, noisy, cruel lout. It is said that when George Horace Lorimer, editor of the Saturday Evening Post, received the first Lardner story he refused it because he didn't believe a ballplayer could be so dumb. But Lardner went on, bitterly, though he liked sports. At the end of "Champion," his short story of the prizefighter Midge Kelly, he summed up the public attitude against which he and all other honest debunkers have had to fight—the whole story of hollow ballyhoo and false writing:

"Suppose you can prove it," the sports editor would have said. "It wouldn't get us anything but abuse to print it. The people don't want to see him knocked. He's champion."

McGeehan was another debunker, though at heart a sentimentalist. No amount of build-up could convince him that a yellow or inept fighter was a potential champion. Nor could he see any resemblance between a fourth-rate sports event and the second siege of Troy. He was among the first to belittle Carnera's farcical knockout tour of the United States. He emphasized the professional character of almost all sports; while other writers might speak of "fans" and "sports lovers," he called them "customers." He coined many nicknames. James J. Johnston, the fight promoter, was "the Boy Bandit." Wrestlers were "pachyderms" and Jack Curley, the impresario of wrestling, was their "mahout." Boxing was "the manly art of modified murder." Baseball was the "ivory industry" and the club owners were "ivory traders."

In his exposures of papier-mache gods, and in his allusions to the intricate financial and political system controlling sports, McGeehan relied mostly upon sarcasm. Other debunkers, notably, John R. Tunis, showed how the "gate" was the dominant influence in all sports, and that no amount of romantic flapdoodle could change that truth. It is still hard to make the sports writers, even some of the grizzled ones, admit that all is not beautiful and clean.

A recent trend, and a healthy one, is away from the sports cartoon. Burris Jenkins, Jr., sports cartoonist of the New York Evening Journal, which has an incomplete sports section from a technical standpoint but an excellent one as a circulation builder, is one of the few whose stuff is worth printing. The average sports cartoon is without humor or point. When the Giants win a National League pennant, that fact will not be more vivid to the reader by a drawing of a burly ballplayer striding over the remains of a bear (the Cubs). A favorite, moth-eaten motif before a big game is to draw the teams as their symbolic animals or reptiles, such as the Yale bulldog, the Princeton tiger or the Army mule, glaring and snorting, while a weak-chinned half-wit labeled "Gus H. Fan" stares at them goggle-eyed. Silly business.

Newspapers in many cities have excellent sports pages, though often filled with too much syndicate material, but the best ones are in New York. In general, a paper's sports pages seem to be in keeping with the rest of its character; the Times's are made up exactly like the news pages, with conservative headlines, plenty of facts, usually thorough, and very dull; the Herald Tribune's usually contain all the facts, written by experts, but they often are erratic with stories of unusual competence beside a childish essay; the American's are bright, well-illustrated, carrying a little of nearly all the main events, but they are incomplete; in the afternoon the Sun's pages are authoritative, sober, a bit ponderous and probably the most satisfying in the city; the World-Telegram has some good stuff, but, like the rest of the paper, it often is written with a futile straining for effect.

The sports columnist is a natural development. Sports lend themselves admirably to personal comment. From Rice's original "Sportlight" to the most modern of the younger Addisons and Swifts, the column has enhanced or disfigured the sports pages. The fault to be found with the worst ones is that they attempt to conceal their lack of knowledge behind a jerry-built structure of wisecracks; the best ones are likely to become tired or bored. There were days, in the last years, when even McGeehan, whose "Down the Line" was one of the soundest of all columns, was actually hard to read.

Perhaps the most scholarly columnist writing sports in New York is John Kieran of the Times. He is the most erudite of them all. He has a usually harmless tendency to burst into poetry, and his humor is not often high-pressure, but he knows his business. He has had to file off the "I" on his typewriter to conform to the impersonal style of his paper, but he loses little by that, even in interviews ("And what did Mr. Simmons have to say about the claim that he was all washed up?" "Nuts," said Mr. Simmons.") The matter is thus disposed of....

Another popular afternoon columnist is Bill Corum of the Evening Journal, who fits perfectly into that paper's somewhat showy but always eye-filling sports policy. Corum, a bouncing, laughing man about town, is interested principally in fights and horses, but he has an excellent groundwork in other sports. Like many another, he is sometimes careless with his details.

John Lardner, son of Ring, who does a syndicate column which is printed in New York in the Post, has the equipment to become one of the greatest. With a background of general news reporting, which many sports writers miss, and with a genuine interest in sports, coupled with a restrained style, he is attracting a following. He is young, but his outlook is sane, and he is better informed on technical matters than many sports writers twice his age.

Joe Williams, the sports editor and columnist of the World Telegram, is an expert of sound experience, but his stuff is uneven. A few years ago his column contained some high-class foolery, and on some days he told a narrative, or expressed an opinion, which was easy to read. Now he has become somewhat more editorial, and battles for reforms. His ideas, even when they make dull reading, still show the workings of a mind that is alive and inquiring.

The liveliest columnist, who realizes that it is possible to possess an education and still avoid a limping style, is Paul Gallico of the morning tabloid, the Daily News. He could be as lyrical as Rice or as literary as Kieran if he wanted to, but he slugs along with a simple, pliant vocabulary which makes him the ideal man for his spot. When he spits on his hands and cuts loose with invective, he is positively alarming. He puts on a vaudeville act, but it is in good taste.

Another tabloid columnist, Dan Parker of the Mirror, is generally underrated. The peculiar circulation of the paper, among odds and ends of curiously assorted strata of humanity, has led him to invent low-brow jokes for his readers, a practice known among sports writers and others in New York as "gagging for the goose trade." But there is nothing wrong with his ability, either as a sports analyst or a writer. He would he at home, once he got his bearings, on the most conservative paper. He knows the rackets and has courage. He endeared himself to a few collectors of curiosa when he defined "Gloober's Disease," at that time a relatively little known affliction, as "spots on de vest."

The Calvin Coolidge of columnists is George Daley, sports editor who a few times a week writes a resume of the doings of the athletes and the horses for the Herald Tribune....

Damon Runyon, veteran general reporter, is consistently good in the New York American, even when he sounds a little like Birsbane. He is one of the best of the stylists, and he knows all the rats and all the heroes. He is by nature so kind-hearted, or it may be that he has a streak of the promoter in him, that he somtimes goes off balance over a prizefighter like Floyd Johnson or "Napoleon" Jack Dorval. Or he will hang medals on Herbert Bayard Swope, New York's new Racing Commissioner....

One of the best minds to attempt the sports column in recent years was Westbrook Pegler, who in 1933 was hired by Roy Howard as a counter-irritant on the discussion of general affairs to Heywood Broun on the World-Telegram. His sports stuff was sometimes highly amusing, although often, unfortunately, he wrote of matters of which he knew little. This scheme of shocking the reader can be effective, but if carried too far it comes to be regarded as mere show-off.

Are sports writers today really tougher in their attitude, more honestly realistic, than those of another generation? It has been debated hotly. The truth probably is that the attitude itself is old, as witness the early Lardner and the early McGeehan, but that more of the modern writers are tough. The tough attitude has merit, for there is a tragic tendency in sports to lose all sense of proportion and to live completely within the boundaries of sports.

The sports department is an attractive place for any man who feels an urge to write of sports and the people of that world. If he doesn't, he'd better stay out of it. There is considerable truth in the public belief, fostered partly by the motion pictures, that the sports writer, taking one week with another, has a pretty easy time of it—certainly easier than is the lot of the average writer on general news.

Chapter 2

## AERONAUTICS

The transcontinental and intercontinental flights of Charles A. Lindbergh in the 1920s, and of Amelia Earhart in the 1930s, popularized aeronautics. Hitherto regarded as undependable and dangerous flimsy crates of bamboo and canvas, airplanes now attracted national attention. Cross-country derbies, aerobatics, and air races captivated large audiences and further stimulated interest in flying. The sudden emergence of air races and the accompanying huge cash prizes resulted in a flood of new pilots. More than 500,000 people watched the ten-day National Air Races in Cleveland in 1929. The popularity of the sport was illustrated by the number of specialized magazines about air racing, including Airway Age, Aviation, American Air Racing Society Newsletter, Aero Digest, Popular Aviation, and Western Flying, and the creation of the Professional Racing Pilots Association and the Aviation Writers Association.

Cities vied with each other for the privilege of hosting the National Air Races. When Cleveland received the rights to stage the National Air Races from 1931 to 1936, race organizers built a grandstand that seated 50,000 and an administration building to provide a similar atmosphere to the Indianapolis 500 and the Kentucky Derby. Regional air races sprouted up around the country in the first years of the decade. In 1932, the Chicago Tribune sponsored the American Air Races. Miami, Fort Lauderdale and Cincinnati organized annual air exhibitions. In 1933, the American Air Race Association operated air shows in cities such as Fort Worth, Oklahoma City, Tulsa, Omaha, Chicago, and Kansas City. Air shows sometimes included street parades, and many communities closed schools and stores early so everyone could watch the festivities. "Air carnivals" usually incorporated altitude contests, glider exhibitions, parachute jumps, stunt flying (aerobatics), speed races around pylons, formations flown by military planes, spot landing contests, "efficiency races," speed dashes, derbies flown from one city to another, and various races based on different engine displacements. When the city of Miami held its third annual air races in 1931, additional events included a Goodyear blimp contest, in which the slowest blimp was the winner, a mock battle that pitted dirigibles and bombers against attack planes and anti-aircraft batteries, and a bomb dropping contest in which military pilots destroyed a miniature city built at one end of the airport. Prizes for the day's activities totaled $7,550. This was the Golden Age of aviation.

The National Air Races, which commenced in 1921, was the most prestigious event. Initially, it lacked spectator appeal, as watchers only witnessed take-offs and landings, and, in the case of transcontinental races, either one or the other. This changed in 1928, when Clifford and Phillip Henderson took control of the National Air Races and commercialized it. The next year, the National Air Races featured head-to-head competition. The following year, in Chicago, the event attracted 200,000 spectators. Airplanes took-off abreast, flashed around pylons, and crossed the finish line in front of the grandstand. To make the planes more recognizable in the air, each was painted in distinctive colors. The National Air Races continued through the decade and was held in Cleveland every year except 1933 and 1936, when Los Angeles hosted it.

The most written-about race was the Bendix Trophy, which was established in 1931 for the fastest flight between Los Angeles and Cleveland. When the race was hosted on the West Coast, the planes departed from New York. Planes could fly non-stop, refuel in flight, or land to refuel. This race was usually run in two segments, with competitors flying from California to Cleveland to claim the trophy and then continuing to the East Coast to complete the transcontinental crossing. In 1931, the winner completed the trip in 9 hours and 10 minutes. Eight years later, the fastest time was 7 hours and 14 minutes. The record for the east to west run improved from 11 hours and 30 minutes in 1933 to 8 hours and 58 minutes in 1939. Despite slower speeds in the mid-decade races, average speed increased from 233 mph in 1931 to 282 mph in 1939. The second most prestigious event was the Thompson Trophy. Both races were speed events, but competition for the Thompson Trophy was on a closed course, which gradually expanded from 100 miles over a twenty-lap course in 1930 to 300 miles and thirty laps in 1938. It was in these two events that Jimmy Doolittle, Roscoe Turner, Steve Wittman, Frank Fuller and Jim Haizlip made their reputations. Roscoe Turner captured the Thompson Trophy race in 1934, 1938 and 1939, while finishing third in 1932 and 1937. He also won the Bendix Trophy in 1933, came second in 1935 and third in 1932.

Interest in the National Air Races gradually declined during the decade due to the impact of the Depression, the decreasing novelty value of flight, and the lack of new designs—which was the lifeblood of the sport. Initially, thanks to large cash prizes, more specialized aircraft soon dominated the National Air Races and by 1931, conventional planes had no chance of winning. Military pilots and planes also lost out to the newer designs and more powerful engines, and by 1931 there was only one separate event for military planes. The 1930 National Air Races took place over ten days and included forty-nine separate events and seven derbies. There were races for every type of aircraft, from small single-seaters with motorcycle engines to trimotor planes. Gradually the number of events declined. The Los Angeles National Air Races in 1933 took place over four days. The next year, slower races and the derbies were eliminated. In 1937, but eleven closed-course races were held, and in 1938 there were only three races over three days.

As with automobile racing, the promoters emphasized the improvements their sporting events brought to the industry. The advertising brochure for the 1932 National Air Races claimed the event would be "another milestone in aeronautical progress. Again this outstanding international sports classic will serve as the rendezvous of the industry. The stimulus this year's project will give to aircraft research and development is inestimable. From the technical knowledge it will produce, greater material benefits will accrue." Air races were called "flying laboratories."

The National Air Races was supported by the larger corporations. Oil companies and aircraft-related manufacturers sponsored pilots or provided free engines for their advertising value. Bendix Aviation Corporation sponsored the Bendix Trophy in hopes that the event would develop faster and more economical cross-country trips. Cleveland Pneumatic Tool Company donated the Louis W. Greve Trophy for planes with engines under 550 cubic inches in order to focus attention on airframe design and pilot skills. Prize money was apportioned to encourage faster and more efficient aircraft. In 1930, American Cirrus Engines organized and sponsored the $25,000 All-America Flying Derby to demonstrate the possibilities of long distance flight by light airplanes. The only requirement was that the competing aircraft be powered with an American Cirrus or American Ensign engine. Eighteen pilots flew 5,541 miles from Detroit to New York City, to Texas, to California, and back to Detroit. For greater press coverage, overnight stops were mandated at eleven cities. This event established the practical value of several construction design forms for which only experimental evidence was available.

During the decade, gyroscopes to keep planes on course, radio altimeters to determine exact height, two-way radio communications, and lighter and more durable alloys made flying a safer enterprise. Improvements included full-cantilever monoplanes, faster wing curves, dependable retractable landing gears, better fuels and lubricants, cowlings, surface stall characteristics, metal strengths, propeller designs, flutter, and countless other engine improvements.

The Depression both helped and hindered aviation in Canada. Faced with huge deficits, the government slashed its aviation budget. Although membership in private flying clubs remained steady from 1932 to 1935, it languished far behind the 5,233 members in 1929. Another drawback was the lack of wealthy individuals willing to offer huge cash prizes for noteworthy achievements. In the US, the total purse for the Bendix Trophy Races rose from $17,500 in 1931 to $24,000 eight years later. Similarly, an American offered $2,000 for the longest flight by a glider. There were no separate prizes or contests for Canadian gliders and as a consequence there were few glider clubs north of the border. On the other hand, by 1935, government relief workers had built 114 intermediate or emergency landing fields exclusive of municipal airports.

The early successes of female pilots owed much to the efforts of Amelia Earhart. In a field where women were considered spectators, Earhart regarded flying as a career. In 1929, Earhart became the first president of the Ninety-Nines Women's Aviation Organization, which sponsored races and aerial shows to prove that flying was safe and that women made excellent pilots. Earhart also sponsored a "hat-of-the-month" contest to stimulate cross-country flying. The member who flew in to the most airports won a Stetson. Earhart emerged as a household name in 1932 when she became the first woman, and the second person, to fly solo across the Atlantic. Three years later, Earhart became the first person to fly solo across the Pacific Ocean—from Honolulu to Oakland, California. Later that year she soloed from Los Angeles to Mexico City and back to New Jersey. In 1937, while trying to fly around the world at the equator, which would have been the longest single flight ever made, she and her co-pilot disappeared over the Pacific Ocean.

At the beginning of the decade, most males did not think women were skilled enough to race against men and they established women's-only events. Soon, there was the Annette Gipson All-Woman Air Race, the Women's International Free-For-All, the Dixie Derby in Washington, D.C., and Dayton's Women's National Air Meet. The National Air Races also created separate contests for women. In 1933, women were allowed to compete in the Bendix Trophy Race, but Florence Klingensmith's fatal crash that year provided an excellent excuse to again exclude women. When it soon became evident that women's cross-country times were similar to men's, women were readmitted to the Bendix Trophy Race in 1936. That year, Louise Thaden and Blanche Noyes won the race and two other women finished second and fifth. In 1938, Jacqueline Cochran won the race from Los Angeles to New Jersey.

### THE VALUE OF NATIONAL AIR RACES

[*The National Air Races discussed in the following document by the General Manager of the event took place from 23 August to 3 September 1930. The forty-four races included a women's derby, parachute jumping, dead stick landing, balloon bursting, glider duration, soaring duration and spot landing. There were also races for various-sized engines, the Marine Corps, the National Guard, the US Navy, and amphibian aircraft. Prior to the Air Races, five cross-country air-derbies commenced for prizes totaling $40,000. This article discusses the importance of such sporting events in the evolution of the aviation industry. Clifford W. Henderson, "The Value of National Air Races," Aero Digest (July 1930), as quoted in S.H. Schmid, Truman Weaver, The Golden Age of Air Racing Pre-1940 (Random Lake, 1991), 106.*]

"Why the National Air Races?" is a question sometimes asked, not only by laymen, but by members of the aircraft industry as well. Such skeptics see in the annual air pageant only a circus ballyhoo event, a publicity parade for a few prominent pilots and members of the aeronautical industry, and spectacular exploitation of the air arms of the various services—Army, Navy and Marine Corps. The doubters see in the audiences attending chiefly a mob of ghoulish-minded yokels out for thrills from the hair-raising nature of events by which they will be impressed with the Dangers of flying rather than its genuine offerings of Safety, Convenience and Speed.

Had such pessimists dominated the automobile industry cars today would be expensive, slow and more dangerous to operate. It was on automobile speedways that the high-compression engine was evolved, that such important refinements as four-wheel brakes proved their place as standard equipment. Much of the speed, safety and convenience in the present development of the automobile may be traced to the motor speedways.

The National Air Races are performing the same function for aeronautics. When the tapered-wing job made its bow in the transcontinental derby of 1928, other contestants protested against the radical design. Two years later we find the clipped wing jobs universally popular in the medium-priced airplane field, for the increased speed offered.

The airplane owner with the lowly OX job which is entered in an event must pay strict attention to his streamlining. In working out his own problems, he is using his brains for the good of the whole industry.

In the 1929 air races one so-called "Mystery Ship" was the sensation of the show. It provided competing manufacturers with a new standard of speed to eclipse—194 miles an hour for a commercial job. Boots to reduce the wind resistance on landing gears, cowlings to accomplish the same purpose with engines, both were evolved principally through lessons demonstrated at the air races.

The 1930 races may be depended on to bring forth several "mystery" ships, which will make their bow at Chicago. The public will see them and other manufacturers will adapt from them those advances in design which most impress them.

In the field of power similar developments will be in evidence. The adaptation to commercial jobs of the supercharger, which in the past has been confined to service planes, is assured. The Diesel aircraft engine will be demonstrated in its present advanced refinement, and fliers who are familiar only with the high-compression gasoline engine may inspect and compare its performance in the air.

The Women's Air Derby of 1929 is chiefly responsible for publicizing the fact that women as well as men may fly. That race event is deemed the greatest single stimulus to the enrollment in flying schools of several hundred women student-pilots in the ensuing six months and the advance of scores of girl fliers from private pilots to the highest license class—transport pilots.

The National Air Races truthfully may be described as the laboratory of the aeronautical industry. In them and from them, engineering and aerodynamic problems, safety, comfort, speed, all are advanced. Everyone interested in aeronautics, from the greenest pilot to the manufacturer, must profit by attendance.

Let us analyze the race audiences. In the first place, every race is marked by months of activity before the event opens. The race unfailingly arouses wide civic interest in the city where it is held. All the civic and fraternal bodies are educated and enthused in the whole broad subject of aviation. These groups are made air-active, as well as air-minded.

Although it is true that many laymen are primarily attracted to the grandstands in search of thrills, all unconsciously absorb some basic knowledge of flying. They see the airmen and airwomen they have been reading about for years and see that they are flesh and blood, essentially no different from themselves, that fliers are not necessarily super-beings. They listen to shoptalk among these fliers. They acquire a real foundation for further interest.

And last but not least is the international publicity deriving from the event. No other industry in America can command the front pages of every newspaper in the United States and Europe for ten successive days. Such education of the reading public is simply unpurchasable. Such publicizing is the result in part of the evolution of the races. This affair has progressed from highly technical starts and finishes, which the public found confusing, to race horse starts and other features of great exhibitions which have established precedents on race-tracks and motor speedways. The races recognize new public interests in aeronautics, lighter-than-air, gliding, every phase of the entire field.

Every class of race has one free-for-all event. That is the wide open invitation to the industry to improve and advance aircraft design. It is opportunity for the large and small manufacturer, the inventor with radical ideas, to demonstrate before an expert, as well as a lay audience the thing he has to offer. That fact alone is justification for the air meet. That's the Why of the National Air Races!

## AIR RACES. CLEVELAND SKIES HUM

*[The cheapest airplane in 1934 was the International Aircraft Heath at $1,095. The purchaser usually waited several weeks for delivery and was required to take a long and expensive course in flying. This article notes that Jimmy Doolittle flew actress Mary Pickford to Cleveland to open the National Air Races, but fails to note that Amelia Earhart had earlier refused to fly Pickford to Cleveland to protest the exclusion of female pilots from the Bendix Trophy Race. "Air Races. Cleveland Skies Hum with Aviation's 'Big Event,'" News-week (8 September 1934), 23-4.]*

Just as baseball fans have the World Series, racing fans the Kentucky Derby, so United States flyers have their annual meet—the National Air Races. These opened for a four-day session in Cleveland Friday of last week.

Out over viaducts spanning the murky Cuyahoga, tens of thousands of Clevelanders fought through traffic snarls to reach the Cleveland Municipal Airport. For those who paid from 50 cents to $2.50, race officials had a record display. Hangar space was, as reporters put it, "at a premium." From Germany had come 30-year-old Gerd Achgelis and his stunting Focke-Wulf plane. From England had come Flight Commander R.L.F. Atcherly, British ace who once won the Schneider Cup for the Royal Air Force. Dozens of parachute jumpers stood by, eager to risk their necks for $50 a day.

**Planes:** Two of the nation's premier racing plane designers have died since last year's contests in Los Angeles. Jimmy Wedell, designer and builder of the Wedell-Williams racer, dove to his death in a Louisiana swamp last June. Z.D. Granville rode one of his Gee Bee "death crates" to his end in South Carolina last Winter.

Though the men are gone, their planes looking like fat little sections of sewer pipe which have sprouted vestigial wings, were destined to ride again.

On hand in a Wedell-designed plane was Col. Roscoe Turner, famous for his blue tunic and fawn-colored trousers. He has the same Wedell-Williams racer in which he streaked across the country last year to win the Bendix Trophy, $6,050, and a new speed record.

Another Wedell-plane flyer was Doug Davis of Atlanta who rode the dead pilot's famous '44" in which Wedell set the world's land-plane speed record of 305.33 miles per hour.

Most promising of the Granville color carriers was Lee Gehlbach, famous speed pilot, who roared into Cleveland in a tiny Gee Bee racer. Most of these planes were expected to whiz around the pylons in sickening vertical banks at a speed of 300 miles an hour—about half the rate of a .45 automatic bullet.

**Bendix Trophy Race:** For the pilot who could travel the 2,042 miles between Los Angeles and Cleveland in the shortest time there were prizes totalling $10,000. Although Russell Boardman was killed in this race last year when he made a bad landing at Indianapolis, the Bendix is not essentially a dangerous race.

The only real danger arises when pilots have to put their tiny crates down for fuel. Landing a Gee Bee at from 80 to 100 miles an hour is no child's play. A field bump the size of half a brick will toss the ship 30 feet in the air.

Slated to fly out of Burbank, Calif., airport on the long grind to Cleveland were six pilots. A leaky fuel tank kept out of the race Col. Roscoe Turner, generally conceded the best chance of winning. Motor trouble held two others back.

The first of the three remaining pilots off the field was Douglas Davis. At 3:20 A.M. his Wasp motor yanked his little Wedell-Williams into the air. Buffeted by winds and drenched with rain, the Atlantan spent 9 hours, 26 minutes getting to Cleveland where he was awarded a $4,500 prize.

Second place went to John (Red) Worthen, 25-year-old Pine Bluff, Ark., pilot who also flew a Wedell-Williams. On finishing the race he said: "Hell, I didn't find Cleveland and I've been flying over Lake Erie for half an hour..." Last of the three pilots to finish was Lee Gehlbach whose Gee Bee made a ten-and-a-half hour crossing. Hard luck hounded him all the way. In Des Moines he had to stop to have a loose motor cowling removed.

Somewhat disappointed by the slow time, also the lack of contestants, Vincent Bendix, Indianapolis manufacturer, then offered a $3,500 consolation prize to any flyer who would establish a new transcontinental record from California to New York via Cleveland. Dapper Roscoe Turner obliged by whizzing across the land in 10 hours, 2 minutes, 51 seconds—a bare 2 minutes and 39 seconds less than his record-making flight last September.

**Thompson Trophy Race:** While the long, grueling Bendix race is the most interesting to the aviation industry the Thompson Trophy Race is the one for the spectators. Watchers see Bendix racers only once—when they land. They see Thompson racers a dozen times as they flash by stands on their laps in the 100-mile, closed-course race.

Knowing that the planes are capable of 300 miles an hour (they must go 225 to qualify) spectators sometimes wonder why average speeds are usually about 250 miles an hour. Sometimes they blame pilots for lack of nerve.

Only the nerviest can enter this equivalent of the seaplane's race—the Schneider Trophy Race. They cannot maintain top speed because of frequent turns. As it is they get dangerously light-headed when the frightful centrifugal pull on the turn draws blood from their brains. They must make lightning decisions while their planes are a bare one-quarter of a second's traveling time off the ground. Of all former Thompson Trophy winners only one was still alive—Jimmy Doolittle, who last week flew Mary Pickford from Chicago to Cleveland.

This year's running of the classic added to the list of tragedies. Doug Davis, flying the same old Wedell-Williams '44" which three days before had won the Bendix Trophy Tace, recklessly tore around the pylon on the backstretch of the course at what proved a breakneck speed. He was on the seventh lap, well ahead of the field. After making the turn he tried to straighten out, but he was going too fast. The tail of his plane tore loose, and he side-slipped into the ground at nearly 300 miles an hour, killing himself and reducing his plane to match-wood.

Roscoe Turner won the first prize of $4,500 with an average speed of 248.129 miles an hour, 4 1/2 miles an hour slower than the race record made by Jimmie Doolittle in 1932. Roy Minor came in second to win $2,500. J.A. Worthen got $1,500 for third place.

**Promoters:** In the early days air races were random, haphazard affairs. With no minimum requirements to bar entrants, almost anyone with a plane stood a chance of getting a prize after likely contenders had crashed. The idea of building special race planes was unheard of. Then, in 1928, came two brothers from California: Clifford and Phillip Henderson.

Persuading the National Aeronautic Association to give them charge of the National Air Races, they began to jack up requirements. Today a stock model plane would have no chance of winning any important events. Clifford, 38, is the master showman of the team; Phillip, 40, is the business man, who sees to it that the races keep out of the red.

The brothers are both "small town boys." Both have a religious fervor for their races which "we stage for the advancement of aviation." First of the pair to become aviation conscious was Clifford. In 1911 he saw an air meet at Dominguez, Calif.

Not until 1928 did he commercialize that interest. Then he persuaded Phillip to abandon the automobile business and seriously take up aviation promotion. Their meets, staged all over the United States, have been phenomenally successful. Few have earned money. The reason is that brother Phillip would rather plow back his earnings. When the till gets full, he offers more prizes, stages more events.

Thus the great National Air Race of 1930 made a bare $2,500. The following years it lost a tiny sum which backers had to make up. Last year, the meet just about broke even.

This year the Henderson brothers discovered a dangerous threat to profit; Farmers surrounding the Cleveland race course staked off their fields into parking lots and put up signs: "Park Here and See The Races." Quietly Phillip Henderson installed twelve miles of canvas fence. Ranging between eight and fourteen feet in height, it cut off the potential farm-parkers' views of planes until the planes were 500 feet in the air.

## STOP PICKING ON US RACERS

[*By mid-decade, air racing lost its novelty, and hard times limited funds available for experimentation. In 1939, several top pilots retired from racing for the more secure life of commercial flying. The author of this article designed, built and raced his own planes. In 1939, he won the Greve Trophy race with record-setting speed of 263 mph. Below, he outlines several of the major reasons why air racing declined in the second half of the decade. Art Chester, "Stop Picking on Us Racers!" Popular Aviation (December 1939), as quoted in S.H. Schmid, Truman Weaver, The Golden Age of Air Racing Pre-1940 (Random Lake, 1991) 523-525.*]

Just before the National Air Races each year, there is a pilot's meeting. The opening shot at this meeting is usually something like this:

"Boys, this is going to be the meet that will determine the future of air racing in this country. There are some who claim you contribute nothing to commercial aviation, the CAA has a critical eye on you, you have two strikes on you already and one slip on your part, one infraction of the rules or one spectator hurt and air racing is done for!" or words to that effect.

As a race pilot, I am tired of being on the defensive, tired of being threatened, intimidated and scared into believing that air racing has no rightful and useful place in the aeronautical picture in this country. The National Aeronautics Association, which is the governing body for competitive events in this country and professes to be looking out for our interests, has been asking us to give them some good, sound arguments they can use to prove that air racing has served some useful purpose. Whether the following arguments serve that purpose or not, they are the sentiments of one who has been racing for 10 years—and they do help get a load off my chest.

First of all, why all this antagonism towards air racing? Is it true that the CAA looks with disfavor on racing? If so, why? We race pilots try hard to stay within the CAA rules and, to my knowledge, there have been no flagrant or intentional violations of

these rules. There has not been a single spectator hurt by a civilian racing plane in years
of racing. It is true that we do have crashes—fatal ones too—but the number is not out
of proportion in view of the highly experimental nature of most racing ships and the
abuse to which they are put.

Why are the commercial interests in aviation bucking racing? We are told that
manufacturers and especially the airlines would like to see air races abolished, apparently because of the unfavorable effect a crash in full view of the public would have
their business. It is my contention that the public is not so unthinking as to let a racing plane crash scare it out of flying the airlines. If seeing big headlines and pictures
in the papers of an airliner splattered against a mountain top does not scare the layman
from flying, the lines have nothing to fear from racing, even if all the race ships pile
up in front of the grandstands.

Why must air racing justify its existence by contributing something to commercial
aviation? Why can it not be conducted as an attraction or amusement, the same as horse
racing, speedboat, auto or yacht racing? Many thousands of dollars are spent in building yachts, for instance, to compete in the annual yacht races and, although I fail to see
where it contributes anything to commercial navigation or is of public benefit, it is
looked upon as a perfectly good and sensible sport—which it is. Air racing is certainly
more spectacular and thrilling and, with the ever-increasing speeds obtained and with
more ships competing, it will be even more so. If racing ship owners and pilots were
not so harassed, there would be more of them, competition would be keener and the
races better.

However, I claim that air racing does contribute to the development of faster airplanes. Manufacturers claim they derive nothing from races. Certainly if you put nothing into it, you derive nothing. Admittedly, racing has not contributed as much as it
might have for the reason that, for a good many years, all special racing ships in this
country have been built by private individuals like myself and financed by their own
rather meager funds. We depend, in part at least, upon prize winnings for our livelihood and if we do accidentally stumble unto something that will enable us to fly five
or ten miles an hour faster, we are not inclined to broadcast it to an unsympathetic
industry. Despite this, some builders have taken a small four cylinder engine, normally
rated at 100 to 150 hp, and built planes around them that flew as fast as 270 mph. Not
an imposing speed these days, until stacked up against the results of some of our pursuit ship manufacturers in trying to get high speeds with 10 or 15 times the horsepower.
After all, a pursuit ship is not a great deal different from a race ship and I doubt if there
are more than one or two single-engined pursuit ships in this country today that will
do much more than that at sea level.

One cannot build and develop a ship with so much speed, using so little engine,
without learning a great deal about both planes and motors. Consequently, if our manufacturers have not learned anything from air racing, it is because they have not taken
any part in it and have not availed themselves of the opportunity it has presented. Had
they, for instance, as a part of their development or experimental work, built or helped
to build, an entry for the races each year they would have learned a great deal that they
could apply to their commercial and military models. Not to be overlooked, too, would
be the international publicity if they won and the possibility of regaining some of the
expense involved.

Plane manufacturers would first of all have found that no great speeds can be obtained with big radial engines, no matter what kind of a washtub they wrapped around

them. They would have called on the motor makers for more streamlined engines suitable for high speed work. Uncle Sam would not now be five or six years behind in high-speed engines suitable for pursuit work. They would have called for smaller, more compact units putting out greater power per cubic inch of piston displacement, inline engines—liquid cooled perhaps—anything but big radials five or six feet in diameter. This was well demonstrated in 1937 when S.J. Wittman, in a none-too-good-looking but very efficient ship with an obsolete inline V-type liquid-cooled engine, showed his tail feathers to the field for 17 of the 20 laps of the Thompson Trophy Race. Failure of an accessory forced him to slow down and give way to radial engined ships with two or three times the power. These in turn were overtaken by a ship with an even smaller inline type engine.

We American race pilots took a lot of razzing when, in 1936, a Frenchman came over and trimmed us so easily and completely. This should not have been surprising in view of the fact that we Americans had in our ships nothing more than pepped-up commercial engines. Even today, we must be content with taking a stock commercial engine, increase the speed and power output, reinforce it here and there and call it a racing engine. We try to run them just below the point where they will fly to pieces. We can put in heavier cylinder studs, stronger pistons, pins and other small parts, but when it comes to making stronger crankcases, crank-shafts and other major parts to withstand the added loads imposed by the increased power developed, our limited funds make it impossible. Racing against us, the Frenchman, Michel Detroyat, had a combination of plane, motor and propeller, each of which was developed especially for racing by large manufacturers who were financially able and willing to do this as a part of their development or experimental work. Who can deny that they benefited by these efforts as did Rolls-Royce of England (in their development of engines for the Schneider Cup racers) and Fiat of Italy by Mussolini's yen for copping the world speed record a few years ago?

Meanwhile, we were so thoroughly sold on the radial engine that, as late as the fall of 1937 when the writer went to the NACA at Langley Field to learn if anything new had been developed in the cowling and cooling of inline types of air-cooled engines, they frankly admitted that nothing had been done up to that time. They were just starting a series of tests along this line, but so far were able to determine only that a 145 hp engine of the inline type, with the conventional cowling had as much drag as a 450 hp radial with the NACA cowling and said that they believed, that the gain of an inline type over the properly-cowled radial was negligible. We now learn that one of our latest pursuit ships, with an Allison inline engine, is 45 miles faster than the same ship with a radial of equal horsepower. Quite a gain, I would say.

Our motor manufacturers have done a fine job of developing good, reliable radials. The NACA has done wonders in reducing the drag of these big brutes by developing very efficient cowlings, but it seems that other countries have put forth an equal amount of effort on another type of engine, basically a more aerodynamically correct type, and have gotten better results in ultimate performance of their airplanes, at least as far as speed is concerned. After all, speed is the chief virtue of the airplane. In airplane, automobile and speedboat racing, European creations have been taking a large part of our American prize money an trophies lately—too large, in fact. Is it not because in those countries the manufacturers of the corresponding commercial and military counterparts undertake the development of these creations instead of individuals as in this country? And, are not the results reflected in the performance of their commercial and military products?

It is significant that, so long as our Army and Navy participated in racing, we held a good share of the world records and were at least equal to, if not ahead of, other countries in motor development. Likewise, our pursuit ships were as fast or faster than any in the world. Since the Army and Navy quit their racing activities and the demand for extreme speeds was not there, our plane and motor manufacturers naturally turned their efforts to the slower and less exacting requirements of commercial enterprises. However, it is the struggle for extremes that brings the average to a higher level in any line of development.

Had our plane manufacturers gone in for air racing they would have learned too that, along with the inline type of engines, more suitable propellers would have to be developed. Propellers without a foot or two of round shank next to the hub, churning up the air right at the "entering edge", messing up the air flow over the fuselage and contributing little or nothing to the thrust. Then, too, it is likely that the windshields on some of our military ships would not look so much like steel bridges with plastics wrapped around them. Take a look at the new Heinkel pursuit which made such a remarkable speed record recently, and you will see a nice smooth curved shield similar to those used on some of our race ships for years....

The disinterested and somewhat contemptuous attitude of the manufacturers towards air racing and its present and potential accomplishments is quite incomprehensible and discouraging to we racing plane builders and pilots. The races have suffered from lack of more entries recently. In addition, throwing this scare of the possibility of air racing being done away with entirely, certainly does not encourage the building of more race ships. It requires an investment of at least $8,000 to $10,000 to build a racing airplane in the smaller of the two classes now being raced. The unlimited class requires even more. This year all indications were that we would have only the National Air Races at Cleveland from which to realize a return on our investments. We had another race scheduled earlier in the year, but it was called off, ostensibly because of a war scare. Actually, it had all the earmarks of this same sinister opposition, working from the inside. It seems very short-sighted on the part of those responsible and I fail to see where anyone was benefited thereby. It seems selfish in that, in some cases, this opposition is in the form of personal dislike for certain individuals engaged in racing activities. There are others, now definitely opposed to racing, who were themselves at one time prominent in racing activities but who have apparently now grown old and sour.

The National Air Races, in spite of a very successful meet in 1938 with an ever-increasing gate, cut the total prize money down this year by $17,000. The race management wanted the 397 cu. in. class of race reinstated this year and had a sponsor for it, while the NAA wanted a 50 hp race. The net result was no race at all and the $17,000 reduction in our prize money. This was done in spite of the wishes of the Professional Race Pilots chapter of the NAA, of which all the race pilots and plane owners are members and who were all with the race management in this case. We have wondered lately just who is closest to the heart of the NAA, the race pilots, the race management or other commercial interests.

Unless we are able to change this antagonistic attitude of the industry towards air racing, enlist the participation of the Army, Navy or our manufacturers and get more support instead of discouragement, I am afraid air racing is doomed to die. It is an interesting and potentially constructive and useful endeavor, if only our commercial and military interests would recognize the opportunities it offers and spend a small part of their appropriations for development work in this way. Certainly, it is not deserving of the ill will and intolerant attitude of the industry which now prevails.

### SOARING

[*Motorless flight first became an organized sport in 1929. Growing interest in gliding was reflected by the addition of motorless flying events to the regular race schedule in the National Air Races. In the 1930 event, because of the lack of hills near the Curtiss-Wright-Reynolds airport in Chicago, an automobile tow launch provided flight impetus for each entrant. Gliders were classified in three categories according to the extent of their wing surfaces. This article discusses the different events and their dangers in the 1939 National Soaring contest. Arthur Lawrence, "The Best One Yet," Soaring (August 1939), 2-3, 13.*]

Bob Stanley's flight from Elmira, to Harrisburg brought to a close the most successful National Soaring contest yet held. During the meet, nine silver "C" awards were won, and the first three golden "C"s to be made in the United States were recorded. The American altitude record was exceeded some seven times, and the figure raised to nearly three times the previous one, with an altitude of 17,264 feet by Bob Stanley. The meet record for distance was broken by the winner of the contest, Chester Decker, with a goal flight of 233 miles to Atlantic City, N.J. The two seater altitude and distance record for this country also went by the board when Lewin Barringer flew 101 miles and attained 6,560 feet in the Airhopper's Schweizer on separate flights.

Among the more spectacular incidents were two thunderstorm flights by Bob Stanley. Bob is one of the small number of high ranking soaring pilots in the United States with an instrument rating, and consequently, is one of the few who have attempted to fly into the raging interiors of these mountainous clouds. On both flights he was forced to leave the cloud because his instruments iced up. His first attempt left his ship with a broken seat and set of loosened control cables. Later during the meet, he again rode a storm to 17,264 feet above the point of release or over 20,000 feet above sea level, to better his previous altitude mark and make what will be the new American record...

Among the more lucrative prizes was an award to the first pilot to reach the airport at Norwich, N.Y. On the first favorable morning most of the pilots named that as their goal, among them, Decker and Stanley. Merboth was first off, then Decker, and later Stanley. Gradually Stanley overtook, and finally passed Decker, and set out to catch Merboth. He entered a cloud and, upon emerging, spied a sailplane far ahead. With a desperate burst of speed, he closed the gap between them, and was amazed to recognize Decker again in the lead. Although neither of them knew it, Merboth had strayed off his course. By this time they could see their goal 20 miles away. They began to dive toward the field, at well over 100 miles per hour, neck and neck. As they skimmed over the fence, and landed without slackening the terrific pace, there was not a spectator who could determine the winner. Both pilots and all witnesses agreed that it was a dead heat.

A new feature of the Meet this year was the inauguration of the National Sailplane Derby, sponsored by Richard duPont. This event, the first speed trial ever included in a national meet, provides a prize for the fastest time turned in on a goal flight to a certain point which will be selected before each National Soaring Meet. The goal this year was Harrisburg. On the last Sunday of the meet, Bob Stanley again took the spot light when he borrowed the IBIS from Bob Platt (who bought it from the Soaring Society) and made the 125 miles in four hours and 19 minutes, to wrest the $1,000 award at the last minute from Chester Decker.

We could go on indefinitely telling interesting and thrilling experiences. However, let us look for a while at some of the significant results.

Taking contest performances first, the storm flights on instruments deserve to be considered as the most outstanding advance of the year. Credit goes to Bob Stanley for showing the way. His background and experience as an instrument pilot enabled him to make a systematic study of this type of cloud flying, and his reports to be published in this and later issues of SOARING, will be poured over by the rest of us with avidity.

The fact should not be lost sight of that the cloud flights made at Elmira—30 flights from 5,000 feet up to 17,264 were recorded—were the outgrowth of two prior meetings held on June 27 and 28, when our good friend B.L. Wiggin of the U.S. Weather Bureau talked of meteorology fundamentals and led the discussion on cumulo-nimbus clouds. Wolf Hirth's contributions were most valuable, as were points brought out by Stanley, John Robinson and other pilots.

Fortunate were the less experienced pilots on avoiding trouble. They realized their limitations, and stayed out of difficulty vowing, no doubt, to return another year with good instruments and as much instrument training under their belts as they could afford. Udo Fischer's experience may have served as a warning though Udo used his head like a veteran.

Unfortunately, for us we saw very little of Chet Decker during the contest. He certainly went to town on distance, piling up the greatest mileage total in history for a like period—1,149 miles. When one considers that in 16 days Chet made 10 distance flights—his longest 233 to Atlantic City and five of them over 100 miles—that really is something. He worked hard for the Championship and we all feel that he earned it.

Another fellow who deserves recognition is Warren Merboth. He flew Richard duPont's famous old Bowlus-duPont Albatross last year for the first time and made his Silver "C." Built in 1933, it is a slow cross-country craft when compared to more recent designs. Yet Warren placed third place on contest point with it this year making a total of 823 miles on nine cross country flights and was second on distance with a flight of 202 miles to Roosevelt Field on July 2nd.

Many of the Group II or "C" pilots did a lot of concentrated flying off Elmira Airport, which was used simultaneously with Harris Hill. The Randolph Meeker and the Chicagoland winches were used almost continuously during the contest with highly satisfactory results. Tows in excess of 800 feet enabled pilot after pilot to connect with thermals, reach clouds and soar cross-country.

The significant fact about the airport flying is that it conclusively proved what has been realized by many in the past, that one does not need hills in order to soar. Flat country, with a large enough area for launching is even better under light, variable wind conditions when thermals are good. Another point might be brought out while on the subject of soaring from low-altitude starts over flat country. Pilots have learned, as a result of the airport work not to give up too readily on cross-country flying. Richard duPont was one of the first pilots to employ the technique of winding a sailplane into a tight spiral when caught with only a few hundred feet of altitude over a likely field, frequently stirring up a thermal and climbing several thousand feet. More pilots did this same thing this year with gratifying results.

Two-place sailplanes are very definitely on their way in. Jay Buxton's Transporter was in the air with passengers almost continuously during the pre-contest period, and the crack-up on the afternoon of June 23rd was tough on everybody. The accident occurred in a cross-wind take-off from Harris Hill, when a down-gust caught the left wing and the glider rolled over. The winch crew, fearing trouble, cut the power, and the ship stalled, turning on its back. Essery would have shown us a few things, but it had to be left to Lew Barringer and Don Hamilton, as pilots of the two Schweizer sailplanes, to carry on. Lew's new American altitude record for a flight with a passenger was 8th highest for the contest out of a total of 138 altitude flights to exceed the minimum requirements. Lew made a 45-mile trip on that flight and Don took Dr. Eastman Jacobs 35 miles to Towanda. On another occasion, Don played around with some clouds for four hours with J. Arnot Rathbone in the rear seat. [The discussion of the people involved in the meet, including the Army Air Corps observers and the Civil Aeronautics Authority, has been deleted.]

Just how significant the Decennial celebration Soaring Contest has been to the future of the Soaring movement in the United States, time alone will demonstrate. We can all agree that it was a fitting climax to the ten year that motorless flight has been called an organized sport in this country, and everyone who shared in making it successful can be proud of his contribution. Most important of all, and in keeping with the spirit of the contest and of our sport, we all had fun. Let's have an even better one next year.

Chapter 3

# BASEBALL

In 1932, an article in the New York Evening Post declared that "Old man depression finally has caught up with baseball. Except in a few small leagues, the bat-and-ball industry did not really feel the hard times until this year." Major league gate receipts fell from an all-time high of $17 million in 1929 to $10.8 million in 1933, and attendance declined from 10.1 million in 1930 to 6.3 million three years later. "The man who thought he was laid off for a few weeks two summers ago," the Evening Post explained, "in many cases still is unemployed. Whereas in July, 1930, it was a case of scaring up four bits for a bleacher seat at the Stadium, now it is a matter of getting enough for a cheap meal." Tickets were a luxury. Total major league profits dropped from $1,462,000 in 1930, to $217,000 in 1931, to losses in the next two years of $1,651,000 and $290,000, before profits of $566,000 returned in 1935.

One reason for the continued interest in baseball in 1930 was the increased number of runs and homers that year. The National League made the ball livelier, and both leagues lowered the height of the stitches on the ball to make it harder for pitchers to get a good grip on their breaking pitches. As a result, six National League teams averaged over .300 and Louis Robert "Hack" Wilson batted .356, slugged 56 homers, and drove in 191 runs. The following year, the stitches were raised and a coarser cover made for greater wind resistance. As a result, in the National League, which had adopted the most severe changes, homers dropped from 892 to 492 and 21 percent fewer runs were scored. In 1933, both leagues adopted the more lively American League ball.

Whereas some people wondered what could be done to attract more customers, Commissioner Keneshaw Mountain Landis argued that attendance would improve as the economy recuperated. As a result, the league initiated few changes. Rather than reduce ticket prices, the owners announced in January 1932 that prices would remain the same as they were for the previous two decades. In mid-1932, when Congress imposed a tax on seats worth more than 40 cents in mid-1932, only a few clubs promised not to pass the tax on to their customers. Instead, clubs reduced salaries. Judge Landis and the president of the National League took voluntary pay cuts after the 1932 season.

Players' average salary declined from $7,500 in 1929 to $6,000 in 1933, before returning to $7,300 at the end of the decade. Babe Ruth experienced the largest drop in income. His salary fell in successive years from $80,000 in 1930 to $70,000, $52,000, $35,000, and to $25,000 in 1935—Ruth's final year. In 1931, more than two dozen players earned more than $20,000 annually, but by 1936 less than a dozen ball players earned that much. After an abortive hold-out for $40,000 in 1938, Joe DiMaggio settled for $25,000. Other cost-cutting measures included reducing the maximum number of players per team from 25 to 23 in 1931 and hiring player-managers to save a salary. Player-managers in the 1930s included Rogers Hornsby, Bill Terry, Joe Cronin, Frankie Frisch, Mickey Cochrane, and Gabby Harnett.

Some clubs traded or sold their best players. The Athletics sold Lefty Grove, Mickey Cochrane, Jimmy Foxx, Al Simmons, and Jimmy Dykes. The Depression separated rich from poor teams. Large-market clubs such as the Yankees and the Cubs could afford the best players, while smaller-market teams such as the St. Louis Browns and the Philadelphia Phillies had to part with their higher salaried stars. The New York Yankee payroll in 1937, for example, was approximately five times as large as that of the St. Louis Browns', thanks in large part to attracting 1,850,000 fans compared to the 200,000 spectators who attended Browns' games. Led by Yankee owner Jacob Ruppert Jones, the major leagues vetoed a suggested profit-sharing plan—visiting teams earned only twenty-one percent of the gate. In the American League, the Yankees won five pennants and Detroit and Philadelphia captured two each. Chicago and St. Louis each earned three National League pennants.

Landis was proven correct—by mid-decade, fans flocked back to the stadiums as the economy improved. In 1937, attendance reached near nine million. Promotional events helped. Clubs adopted "ladies day," or provided musical entertainment and free presents. Lower-priced concessions were another draw, as was allowing fans to keep balls hit into the stands (1930), installing loudspeaker systems, permitting players to talk to the spectators, and providing each player with a uniform number (standardized in 1932). In Cincinnati, Larry MacPhail outfitted the players in red uniforms, forced cigarette girls to wear satin pants, and hired usherettes.

At 8:30 on the evening of 24 May 1935, President Roosevelt pulled a gold switch in the East Room of the White House and 400 miles away more than one million watts turned on 634 lights in Crosley Field, Cincinnati, enabling 20,422 fans to watch the Reds play the Phillies. Although most journalists and club owners opposed night baseball, new Cincinnati owner Powel Crosley, Jr., who sold radios and refrigerators, wanted to make the Reds profitable and keep his name before the public. The team had finished last each year from 1931 to 1934, and the previous season the Reds averaged fewer than 3,000 customers per game. The National League owners reluctantly voted to let Cincinnati play seven night games—one per visiting team, but only if the visitors agreed.

Night games were played as early as the 1880s, but were conducted mainly to demonstrate the technical proficiency of a particular lighting system. In 1929, the Kansas City Monarchs employed a portable lighting system. The following year, night baseball made its debut in Des Moines, Iowa. This Western League game between the Des Moines Demons and the Wichita Aviators attracted national attention. The lighting system cost $20,000, but the minor leagues desperately needed to boost sagging attendance. By 1934, most of the sixty-seven minor league parks which operated after dark reported increased revenue and night baseball became a fixture in the minor leagues.

The major leagues were more skeptical. Most club owners and journalists considered night baseball to be a sacrilege. The Cardinals' decision to try night ball, one owner declared, was "a cowardly surrender to commercialism." The Yankee's general manager said it was "a wart on the nose of the game." Sportswriters worried about finishing their stories in time for the early-morning editions. Players complained about the effect of the lights on their eyes, making errors, becoming injured in the cooler night air, and confused training routines. "You never know when to eat," complained one player. But night games attracted larger audiences than did day games and the owners tended to make more money from concessions. Night lights also allowed the parks to be used for many different kinds of events. The major leagues thus gradually installed elaborate lighting systems.

The inauguration of the All-Star game in 1934 and the creation of the Baseball Hall of Fame—with its annual inductions—also promoted interest in the game. To "reseed baseball pastures," the American League sponsored three baseball films that included lessons from the greats of the games. "Batter Up!," "Play Ball," which cost $25,000, and "Take Me Out to the Ball Game," which General Motors filmed for $50,000, were shipped free to any club, school, or league that requested them. In 1937, twelve million people saw at least one of these films, which were viewed as far away as Canada, Australia, New Zealand, and China.

Similar to the introduction of radio broadcasts and night games, these promotional films, the All-Star game and the Hall of Fame were all adopted reluctantly by major league baseball. Sportswriter Arch Ward of the Chicago Tribune convinced reluctant owners to hold an all-star game in conjunction with the 1933 World's Fair. Although it was to be a one-time event, when more than 47,000 fans came to Chicago's Comiskey Park, the All-Star game became an annual competition. For the first two All-Star games, major league managers and the fans shared in the selection process, but from 1935 the managers chose the teams. The Baseball Hall of Fame owed its existence to two residents of Cooperstown who sought to use the myth that Abner Doubleday had invented baseball in their town in 1839 to promote tourism to the area.

Each year, beginning in 1936, the Baseball Writers Association of America selected candidates. At the official opening of the Hall of Fame Museum in 1939, twenty-six players were inducted into the Hall of Fame. Ty Cobb led the balloting with 222 of 226 votes. Babe Ruth was second with 215.

The media was crucial to baseball's success. John Tunis wrote in 1934 that baseball was kept alive by the evening papers which gave the game twice as much publicity than to any other sport. Four years later, The American Mercury (June) claimed that sportswriters provided a "chronic over-emphasis" on baseball. Reporters had to serve two masters—baseball and the newspaper. If their writing seemed like advertising copy for the ball clubs, it was because they identified with baseball and believed that if baseball did well then the paper would benefit from increased circulation. "That baseball interests have trained the large dailies to stand on their heads and jump through hoops," wrote The American Mercury, "is nothing short of astounding." In 1936, an unidentified baseball owner stated in Liberty that he paid the expenses for twelve newspapermen to report on the team's progress during spring training and to travel with the team during the season. Although the reporters cost him $38,400 that season, the owner considered it money well spent because it kept the goodwill of the city's sports editors.

Radio broadcasts, which began in the 1920s, were easier to control. More American families now had radios than either automobiles or indoor plumbing, and at the beginning of the decade, radio stations did not pay clubs for broadcast rights. Following a decline in attendance, club owners met in 1931 to consider a league-wide ban on local radio broadcasting, but eventually left the decision to the individual clubs. In Chicago, five stations carried Cub games. The three New York-based teams agreed to a five-year ban on radio broadcasts beginning in 1934. Some teams refused to allow broadcasts on Sundays and holidays—normally the best-attended games. Teams that shared the same city agreed not to carry radio accounts of one team's away game if the other team was playing at home. In 1934, the Cardinals and the Browns banned radio broadcasts of their home games.

Eventually, major league baseball realized that radio broadcasts helped to sustain fan interest in smaller towns and villages and for those not normally able to attend games. Just as important, when radio stations realized they could sell commercial time during the games they were able to pay the clubs for broadcast rights. In 1937, for instance, four Chicago stations paid the two Chicago teams $21,000 each for broadcast rights. Three years earlier, Judge Landis negotiated a deal with the Ford Motor Company that gave Ford permission to broadcast the World Series from 1934 to 1937 for $400,000. By 1936, every team but those based in New York broadcast at least some of their games. In 1939, Brooklyn secretly negotiated a deal with General Mills to sponsor Dodger games for $70,000 and refused to renew the radio ban. This forced the Giants and Yankees to allow broadcasts of all away games. Unlike the journalists, few radio broadcasters traveled to away games. Instead, they recreated these games for the listeners using the concise information provided by wire over Western Union Telegraph, taped crowd noise, and inventive reporting. Some broadcasters, such as Red Barber, became local celebrities. Commissioner Landis reserved the right to select the announcers for World Series and All-Star games.

In 1934, Baseball Magazine initiated a "Write Your Congressman" campaign to persuade the federal government to commit some of the "public money now being so lavishly given for recreational purposes" to the construction of baseball diamonds. The magazine's argument illustrated the prevailing attitudes towards "the National Game." Baseball Magazine wrote every Senator and Congressman stating that baseball promoted the "cardinal virtues of the nation"—team play, discipline, and sportsmanship. It developed clean-minded, clear-thinking citizens, while acting as a powerful instrument for combating juvenile delinquency. The American Legion supported a junior baseball league because the game taught sportsmanship and was thus "a good thing" for the American people. The committee in charge of American Legion Baseball was labeled the National Americanism Commission. In 1939, in an article entitled "It Isn't Cricket," Baseball Magazine noted that whereas cricket was leisurely and social, baseball was fast and combative, which made baseball teams "marvels of efficiency." President Roosevelt lent his support to the game by appealing to the American people shortly after his inauguration to support baseball as a sign of national confidence. When the economy began to improve, Roosevelt claimed that "major league baseball has done as much as any one thing in this country to keep up the spirit of the people."

The campaign to permit Sunday baseball in Pennsylvania employed similar rhetoric. Thanks to the growing secularism of society, when Boston allowed Sunday ball in 1929, only the two Pennsylvanian major league teams forbade Sunday play. Baseball Magazine argued that instead of reducing the number of people who went to church, Sunday baseball would encourage people to see the bright side of life and live happier lives. Pirate President William Benswanger stated in 1934 that "Sunday ball will mean much to the moral life of our community. Due to the closed Sunday, Pittsburgh long has been noted for Sunday drinking and gambling parties with their attendant evils all because of lack of public entertainment. Sunday ball will serve to overcome this condition to a very great extent, much more, possibly, than one can conceive." Mired in debt, Pittsburgh and Philadelphia hoped to benefit financially from Sunday games, as did hotels, restaurants, and transportation companies. In the 1933 referendum, the urban vote in favor of Sunday baseball overwhelmed rural opposition.

Baseball offered a brief escape from the misery of the Depression. Until his retirement in 1935, Babe Ruth remained North America's most popular athlete. Commenting on his 1930 salary of $80,000, which exceeded President Hoover's by $5,000, Ruth quipped, "I had a better year than he did." Two years later, Ruth hit the famous "called" home run in Wrigley Field in the third game of the World Series. Even without the Babe, the Yankees continued to win, capturing five pennants and finishing second three times, with Lou Gehrig, Frank Crosetti, Tony Lazzeri, Joe DiMaggio, Bill Dickey, and Vernon "Lefty" Gomez.

In 1934, Lou Gehrig captured the triple crown—batting .363, with 49 homers and 165 RBIs. Just eight games into the 1939 season, Gehrig removed himself from the lineup after playing a record 2,130 consecutive games. Later that year he became the first ball player to have his number retired. Lefty Gomez was the best pitcher in the American League. He won the pitching triple crown in 1934 and 1937 with the most victories, strikeouts, and the lowest Earned Run Average (ERA). Robert "Lefty" Grove led the league in ERA seven times during the decade and won 175 games. With power pitcher Carl Hubbell, Johnny VanderMeer's consecutive no-hitters in 1938, and "Dizzy" Dean and the St. Louis Gashouse Gang, it was an era of colorful and competitive baseball.

Success on the ball field often generated local pride and optimism. On another level, businessmen continued to promote baseball as a way of deflecting labor unrest. Many firms believed that company-sponsored teams helped to unify a heterogeneous work force, promoted company loyalty, advertised the firm's name, reduced absenteeism, and lowered the labor turnover rate. Similarly, baseball officials argued the game converted new immigrants into good Americans. Baseball, they claimed, illustrated the American dream that anyone could succeed if he was moral and worked hard. Ethnic leaders often felt baseball provided a visual symbol of ethnic accomplishments and identity. In reality, clubs sought ethnic ball players to promote attendance. New York teams, for instance, wanted Jewish players to appeal to the large Jewish population, just as other teams sought Italian players. It worked. Italians honored Tony Lazzeri and Joe DiMaggio with special days at Yankee Stadium, and, as historian Peter Levine has shown, Hank Greenberg not only helped demolish stereotypes about Jewish physical weakness, but also illustrated that Jews could be Americans without sacrificing their ethnic identities.

Contemporary studies indicated that major league ball players tended to come from Pennsylvania, California, Texas, Missouri, Ohio, and New York. Oakland, San Francisco, St. Louis, Pittsburgh, Cincinnati, Los Angeles, Philadelphia, and New York City produced the most major league players. A growing percentage of major league players were second-generation southern and eastern Europeans. One journalist noted that such Italian players as Ernie Lombardi, Gus Mancuso, Frank Crosetti, Tony Lazzeri, Cookie Lavagetto and the DiMaggios, "take to baseball quicker than they take to spaghetti."

Despite racist slurs, baseball accepted all peoples—except blacks. Segregation, taken for granted in every walk of life, remained a barrier for blacks. The issue of allowing blacks to play the "national game" was rarely discussed in white papers, which almost totally ignored the Negro Leagues.

In the early years of the Depression, black teams, especially those in cities with white major league teams, struggled to prosper. The Eastern Colored League folded in 1928, and its replacement, the American Negro League, lasted only one year. The National Negro League (NNL) failed in 1931. Two years later, William "Gus" Greenlee, the numbers king of Pittsburgh and the manager of light-heavyweight boxing champion John Henry Lewis, convinced numbers racketeers in Harlem, Newark, and Baltimore to help rejuvenate the NNL. The numbers racket was generally a black-run business that provided jobs and credit in the black community. Bettors wagered as little as a nickel on any number between 0 and 999. If this number coincided with the last numbers on such impossible to fix figures as the volume of stock market transactions for the day or the betting handle at a racetrack, then the lucky number paid off at around 600 to 1. Since the real odds were much higher, the racketeers had an enormous amount of capital to invest in black-owned businesses such as the NNL.

By 1940, the NNL teams included the New York Black Yankees, the Baltimore Elite Giants, the Pittsburgh Homestead Grays, the Newark Eagles, the Philadelphia Stars and the Cuban Stars. The Negro American League, which began in 1937, included the Chicago American Giants, the Toledo Crawfords, the St. Louis Giants, the Memphis Red Sox, the Birmingham Black Barons, the Kansas City Monarchs, and the Cleveland Bears. Both leagues used the same equipment and rules as the major leagues.

By the late 1930s, the Negro leagues were the largest black-owned enterprise in America. This success owed much to migration north that began in the mid-1920s and continued to flow into Chicago, Cleveland, Detroit, and New York, helping to make baseball an integral part of ghetto life in the north. The players earned good money and held esteemed positions in the community. As black baseball prospered, the clubs employed white booking agents to rent major league parks and attracted fans from all social backgrounds. The society pages of prominent black newspapers carried stories about opening day and who attended. The most important game, and one of the highlights on the social calendar, was the annual East-West All-Star game which commenced in Chicago's Comiskey Park in 1933.

At the conclusion of the regular season, the best players often barnstormed around North America. Staying in colored hotels or private homes where available, or sleeping and eating in the bus, the ball players participated in about 130 exhibitions a year, which was approximately how many games they played in a regular season. Supported by stars such as Satchel Paige, Josh Gibson, Buck Leonard, and Cool Papa Bell, Negro teams often defeated major league barnstorming teams, frequently drawing favorable comments from their white counterparts. With his blazing fastball and unusual personality, Satchel Paige occupied the center stage of black baseball and a legend of epic proportions grew around him. The Negro leagues played a more flamboyant game than did the major leagues. The Saturday Evening Post wrote in 1940: "Negro baseball is much more showmanlike than white baseball. Negroes never play deadpan ball—their baseball is to white baseball as the Harlem stomp is to the sedate ballroom waltz. They whip the ball around without looking where it lands, and woe to the receiver if he isn't there instinctively. They play faster, seem to enjoy it more than white players."

As the document "Wendell Smith Preaches Unity" illustrates, the black press supported the Negro leagues and were often zealous advocates of integrated baseball. Led by sports editor Wendell Smith, the Pittsburgh Courier favorably compared black to white ball players and privately implored major league clubs to hire black players. White society, baseball officials usually replied, was not prepared for integrated baseball.

Minor league baseball was particularly stung by the Depression. From twenty-five leagues in 1929, only sixteen leagues survived the 1931 season, and many of these leagues had fewer teams. The following year, the Eastern League, the Three-I, the Cotton States, and the Inter-State circuits folded in mid-season. In desperation, the minor leagues elected Judge William Bramham as president of the National Association and gave him sweeping powers akin to those of Commissioner Landis. Bramham commenced a series of fundamental reforms. To place the leagues on a more solid footing, Bramham insisted that all owners put up a guaranty deposit equal to one-half the team's monthly payroll. He established a promotional department to provide feature stories and information for the press, and encouraged night baseball.

Some commentators credit Frank Shaughnessy, general manager of the Montreal Royals in the International League, for saving minor league baseball. At the beginning of the decade, the team with the best record during the season became the league's champion. Unless the league played a split season, there were no playoffs. Under the Shaughnessy plan, four teams in an eight-team league qualified for post-season play. Since this system helped to sustain interest longer into the season, attendance increased. The International and the Texas leagues adopted the Shaughnessy playoffs in 1933, and most other leagues quickly followed suit. By the end of the decade, minor league baseball was stronger than ever and paid attendance reached record levels. In 1938, for instance, 15,500,000 people watched National Association games, and five years later almost twenty million came to the ball parks.

One way for minor league teams to avoid insolvency was to become the property of major league clubs. Although Branch Rickey of the Cardinals started to build a farm system of minor league clubs in the previous decade, the 1930s witnessed the full-scale construction of the farm system. Since the Depression reduced minor league salaries to approximately $300 per player, major league clubs could more easily afford to purchase more minor leaguers. A second factor in the rise of farm systems was the 1930 decision to restrict the AA League draft only to those players who had completed a minimum of four years play at that level. This allowed major league clubs to protect their players from the draft for a reasonable length of time. Branch Rickey led the way. He hired scouts and held tryouts around the country. By 1940, the Cardinals owned thirty-two clubs and had working agreements with eight others—involving over 600 players. Other teams soon built their own farm systems. To keep top prospects in the draft, some organizations resorted to the illegal practice of secret working agreements with minor league clubs, or signed players to undated contracts. Judge Landis, opposed to the farm system, attempted to stop such practices by fining the offending teams and granting free agency to wronged players.

Canadians also loved baseball and most newspapers included comprehensive coverage of major league baseball. Each province had an extensive system of leagues from age groups, schools, churches, YMCAs, community, industrial, inter-urban, to interprovincial and semi-professional. The local team was often a source of civic pride, and according to historian Colin Howell, baseball was synonymous with small-town life. St. Stephen, New Brunswick, was the Yankees of the Maritimes, winning seven senior titles during the decade. But, since the Maritime teams rarely played clubs from central Canada, there was no way of determining the best Canadian team. Instead, the Maritimes tested themselves against teams from New England. This orientation reflected the Maritimes sense of political alienation from the rest of Canada.

Several black teams barnstormed extensively throughout Canada. The Boston Royal Giants played approximately three hundred games against Maritime teams in the 1930s. Other popular teams included the Zulu Cannibal Giants and the Ethiopian Clowns who painted their bodies and played-up the prevailing racial stereotypes. Black communities in the Maritimes and central Canada organized their own teams that played exhibitions against white teams. Although segregation was illegal in Canada, black players were often refused accommodations and were seldom admitted into white leagues. As the decade progressed, inter-racial play became more common.

In 1931, Virne Beatrice "Jackie" Mitchell became the first female to sign a minor league baseball contract when she joined the Double-A Chattanooga Lookouts. Later that year, the seventeen-year-old pitcher struck out Babe Ruth, Lou Gehrig, and Tony Lazzeri in an exhibition game before a sellout crowd of 4,000 and dozens of sportswriters. Several days later, Commissioner Landis voided her contract, declaring that baseball was "too strenuous" for women, and banned them from professional baseball. In 1934, Babe Didrikson pitched in several exhibitions against major league teams, and later that year appeared in approximately two hundred games around the country with the House of David barnstorming baseball team.

Thanks to ladies' days at the park and to radio broadcasts, many women followed baseball in the 1930s. Sometimes, so many women turned up for ladies' day that there weren't enough seats for paying customers. To avoid this possibility, some clubs limited free passes, or asked women to appear in person a few days prior to the game to collect their free passes.

Many managers considered wives a hindrance because they gossiped about other players and caused dissension within the team. In a 1936 article in Liberty magazine, the wife of Joe Cronin, Boston Red Sox manager and niece of Washington Senators' owner Clark Griffiths, wrote that baseball wives were both a necessity and a handicap. Wives insured their husbands ate properly, stopped smoking, went to bed early, and didn't play poker into the wee hours of the morning. Some wives acted as their husband's business manager and helped him save for the future. "A woman must coddle, fondle, cajole, flatter, and solace a husband-ballplayer," she declared, "but never irritate him while he is in a slump."

## BASEBALL'S FINANCES

[*In 1936, the average seat cost about one dollar. Of this amount, two and a half cents paid officials and umpires and the visiting team received twenty-two and one-half cents. Rain on opening day or a holiday could cost the owner as much as $40,000, and an injury to a star player would require an additional expenditure to replace him. In 1936, an unidentified major league owner listed his revenue at $745,000 and his expenses at $578,000.*

*The following article examined baseball's role in society; "the average player" and his climb through the minor league farm system; the owners' attitudes, expenses and profits; the players' lifestyles; the different styles of managing (which was omitted); and the likes and dislikes of the typical spectator. "Big League Baseball," Fortune (August 1937), 37-45, 112, 115-116.*]

Drop in these days on that arch pessimist, the baseball owner—who is always looking out of the window for signs of rain or expecting to hear that his ace pitcher has broken his wrist—and don't be amazed if he greets you with something that almost resembles a smile. It's hard to look worried and anxious knowing how much faster the turnstiles are clicking off attendance in 1937 than they did in 1936, or have done in any season for years. The only solid explanation seems to be that 1937 is running ahead of 1936 generally; but baseball's mystic sense vibrates, all the same, with the hunch that the game itself has taken on fresh allure and is nearing the peak of another cycle, as it did in 1920 and 1929. After all, the past few years have seen some hot races and close finishes, some spectacular performers like Dizzy Dean, Carl Hubbell, Joe DiMaggio, Bob Feller; some refreshingly mad teams (with a method in their madness) like the Gashouse Gang from St. Louis; they have lapped up huge publicity from the growth of the farm system, the fireworks of the All-Star Game in midseason, the unfamiliar glare of night baseball. Lumped together, such factors should make baseball "mysticism" pretty safe for underwriters.

Indeed, baseball has always come back: neither scandals nor depressions have killed it off. Not idly have you heard it called, once or twice, The Great American Game. It continues to flourish, not only because it magnificently brings out the average American's most healthful instincts, but also because it quite harmlessly brings out his most psychopathic ones. Sport has always helped to satisfy man's killer instinct, but someone actually had to be butchered to make a Roman holiday, and unpleasant things still happen to horses and bulls and men to make a Spanish or a Mexican one. Baseball is a far better safety valve. It subsists on purely vocal massacre: "Kill the umpire!"—and it purifies the blood by no costlier purge than yelling, swearing, sarcasm, and now and then a pop bottle. Dangerous steam is worked off in terms of innocuous sweat, and metaphorically your fan sweats as hard as your ballplayer—because he **is** your ballplayer. In no other game does a spectator engage in such intense vicarious participation, being now the player, now the manager, now the coach, now the umpire; hence in no other game is there so much rage when things go wrong, so much jubilation when things go right. The Great American Game, unlike the great British one, doesn't make a fetish of fair play; it makes a fetish of success. Accordingly, in grandstand and bleachers heroes die like flies. Grandstand and bleachers tirelessly pump new cynicism, endlessly mint new wisecracks, showering all their affection on the man of the moment, all their contempt on the man of a moment ago.

For baseball's paradoxical soul lies in its hooting and cheering alike out of the same deep well of rabid partisanship. In the end, all the national characteristics displayed by fans are swallowed up in their local pride. They forget they have paid money to see men perform for money in the money making interests of still other men. While the game is on, the fair name of Washington, the civic honor of Pittsburgh, the eventual fate of Chicago hang in the balance. Safety valve, business, amusement, sport—baseball is all of these; but more than any of them, it is imaginary ownership—something that belongs, as much as his hat or his home, to the fan. Of the approximately 8,000,000 persons who paid to see major league games last year, the overwhelming majority, you can bet your boots, went because they wanted to see **their** team win.

That is why, though big-league baseball may be an industry, an individual team is something more than a business. Baseball is idiomatic, so to speak, not grammatical. There is no "typical" big-league club. Each one is a complex of varying elements—of the atmosphere of its particular city, the policy of its particular owners, the ideas of its particular manager, the personalities of its particular players, the location of its particular ballpark, the number of victories to its credit, the degree of vehemence among its fans. Every major-league club stands in relation to the fifteen others as a theme in music does to fifteen variations. [The section on baseball's farm system has been deleted.]

**THE BOSSES**

Even Barney Dreyfuss, it is told, always asked, "What was the score?" before he asked, "What was the gate?" And now and then men acquire ball clubs out of civic interest: Powel Crosley Jr. took over the Cincinnati Reds, and a group of businessmen have taken over the St. Louis Browns, chiefly to prevent their franchises from going to other cities.

True enough, Colonel Ruppert saw the New York Yankees as a darn good investment. And true again, Fan-Owner William Wrigley Jr.'s son P.K., to whom the Chicago Cubs descended at his father's death in 1932, treats baseball as a straight business though he likes the game as a sport as well. (P.K. along with J. Louis Comiskey and Horace C. Stoneham, belongs in a special category of owner—what might be called the Second Generation Man, or the Man Who Has Baseball Thrust Upon Him.) Aiming at steady volume, he is using the merchandising methods on baseball that he uses on gum. He has taken advertisements, in midwinter, in the newspapers; he has plastered Chicago's El with baseball posters; he has attempted to advertise the Cubs in taxicabs; he has arranged with Western Union to open a ticket agency in some hundred-odd of its Chicago branches; he has put the club on a budget, which in 1936 was only $1,000 out of the way. Possessing the money for a long-pull experiment of this kind, he may eventually **create** baseball fans as well as tempt those who already exist. But outsiders and other baseball men think that Wrigley is a step ahead of himself; say emphatically, moreover, that his policy could work only in a very large city like Chicago or New York.

The mixed sentiments of most baseball men have created a somewhat anomalous industry. The eight clubs in each league, in terms of putting on a show, are like partners; in terms of assembling a cast, like competitors. Yet actually they are neither. They do not really pool their finances, although they support a common organization; they do not really pit their finances against one another, although they are rival bidders in the market place. They are simply a confederation of businesses dependent upon one another for existence but militantly independent in their operations. Baseball, perhaps the most publicized commercial activity in America, is perhaps the most secretly operated. As President of the Wm. Wrigley Jr. Co., P.K. Wrigley can stalk a rival gum company; but as President of the Chicago National League Ball Club he is pledged by the rules of the game not to stalk another club. (What he **happens** to hear is another matter.) The proper analogy for a big league is an interfraternity association. The members stand ganged up against the outsider, but each has his own grip and password.

But the secrecy inside baseball is nothing compared to that displayed toward the public. Shushing has become the byword of the industry. It is not beyond the realm of possibility that some clubs keep their players' salaries in code. Most clubs won't tell you how much money they make or lose, though they will sooner tell you what they lose than what they make. Peculiarly yet logically enough, what causes this secrecy is the extremely public nature of the game itself. Just because every fan regards his team as a personal possession, he subconsciously disputes the owner's right to it. For an owner to make too much money seems calculating—the reverse of public-spirited. Turn back your profits, yell the fans, into the ball park, cut the price of seats. So the shushing goes on, every club has its pet secrets, the Giants won't give out even a lump sum on players' salaries, the Cubs won't breathe their attendance figures, the Pirates won't say what percentage of the stock Mrs. Barney Dreyfuss owns.

But there's nothing quiet about how a club gets its revenue. Listen, first and foremost, to the slapping down of bills and jingling of silver at the ticket booths. Listen, again, to the crunching of peanuts and crackling of popcorn in the stands. Listen to the radio booming out home games—which Wheaties (General Mills) or Mobiloil (Socony-Vacuum) or some other firm pays to broadcast, and which most clubs take advantage of. The Giants, Yankees, and Dodgers, who do not, insist that broadcasting hurts the gate. Notice, at the majority of ball parks, the screaming billboards on the fence. Some clubs, like the Chicago Cubs (Only advertising at Wrigley Field consists of two Wrigley Gum imps perched on top of the four-story-high scoreboard.) refuse to "mutilate" their park fences; but as an indication of possible returns, Charles A. Weber, the Cubs' business manager, says he would gladly pay Mr. Wrigley $25,000 for the privilege of reselling the space. Your club owner also gets revenue from scorecard advertising; from renting out the park for prize fights, football games, rallies, and the like; and, finally, from selling players.

Of what he pays out, the largest amount goes into players' salaries. For all sixteen clubs, salaries this year are reported to be in excess of $3,200,000—roughly half of total operating expenses. Individual payrolls differ considerably: the Yankees, probably baseball's highest-priced team and including baseball's currently highest-paid player (Lou Gehrig, $36,000), will cost this season around $370,000; the Pirates, by no means baseball's lowest-priced team, will cost around $200,000.

For a breakdown of annual expenses, the Cubs for 1936 offer a good example of a higher-bracket club. Omitting concessions, plant depreciation, and reconstruction costs, and omitting any expenses in **buying** players, total operating costs came to $644,000. Of this $74,000 went into fixed charges, such as taxes and rent; $177,000 went into supplies, equipment, spring training, traveling expenses, and publicity. The remaining $393,000 went into direct labor of all kinds, that is, ground crews, ushers, and office force as well as players. Office force absorbed just $33,000; Wrigley himself draws a salary as President.

As for profit and loss, they run a fairly extensive gamut. Over the two-year period 1933-34, the Cubs lost $430,000; over the two-year 1935-36, they made $198,000. Last year nine of the sixteen clubs made money, two lost it, one broke even—and the remaining four won't say what they did.

Without divulging the business of one club to another, the league offices act as clearinghouses and registry bureaus regulate and supervise umpiring. Club owners or their representatives meet several times a year to approve the playing schedule; make, modify, or rescind the laws; agree upon new tactics or questions of policy. Each year sees one or two changes: this year, for example, it was voted to begin and end the season a week later than usual, since there is more likelihood of encountering rain and cold weather in April than in late September and early October. Next year, the modern "lively" ball will be stripped of some its zoom....

**THE CROWD**

...The Cubs' park, hard by a well-to-do residential section, draws a tremendous number of women fans. Many are steady customers; many more are simply Ladies' Day faithfuls who get in free. Ladies' Day at Wrigley Field is so popular that the Cubs now have to limit their passes to 20,000, which sometimes isn't enough to go around. At Wrigley Field you might also once have seen Al Capone surrounded by his henchmen. Or another gangster named Bugs Moran who (while the papers ran huge headlines reading Where Is Bugs Moran?) was sitting day after day in the ball park. The Sox park is in the heart of an industrial center, near Chicago's large Negro belt. (Negroes are fair fans.) The two clubs play up the rivalry for all it is worth, but it is probably less intense than they make it out to be and certainly less today than it once was. Most parks are in industrial centers, or in or near lower-class residential sections. This is far from a draw-back, for most real rooters are workers and white-collar people. Navin Field in Detroit, however, is close to the center of town; Forbes Field in Pittsburgh lies next to lovely Schenley Park; and the Bee's park in Boston is close to fashionable Brookline.

Though population is an immense asset, it is not an infallible yardstick, for there are naturally good baseball towns and naturally bad ones. Probably the best major-league city is Brooklyn, with Boston and Detroit the next best, and New York and Chicago good because of their size. Rated the poorest are St. Louis and Philadelphia: they become **ennuye** even of pennant winners (probably one reason why Connie Mack had twice to break up his highly successful but expensive Athletics). Last year the Browns in St. Louis showed what a poor team in a poor town can look forward to: their total paid attendance for seventy-seven home games sagged to 93,000. The record high is around 1,500,000, achieved by the Yanks in 1928 and perhaps equaled by the Cubs in 1929 and 1930.

But in the main, so far as packing in the crowd goes, it's not where the team plays, but how. It's a winning team that makes the fans hoarse and the owner rich. And if it isn't a winner, as Joe McCarthy puts it, you could install armchairs and serve a free lunch at the end of the sixth inning, and the crowd still wouldn't come. Next to a winning team comes a close race: the fans want a fight as well as a finish. And after that comes personality on the ball field, whether in individual players or whole teams. Babe Ruth was a legend for the provinces; the Gashouse Gang from St. Louis tilts the road gate today partly under the heading of vaudeville. (Best drawing cards on the road are the Yankees and Tigers in the American League, the Giants and Cardinals in the National.)

But a winning team in a close race, all tricked out with glitter, can still come to grief. On crucial days the skies may open and the rain descend. Or injuries may cripple a team all rarin' to go, as they did the Tigers last year, with Cochrane and Greenberg out of the line-up.

Finally, general economic conditions can mow down the most enthusiastic crowd in the world. The depression, reaching its baseball nadir in 1934, cut into gate receipts everywhere, although at the very beginning, when idle men still had money in their pockets, it boosted the gate a little. Pittsburgh, for example, with a team that finished second in both 1932 and 1933, was both years in the red.

But one part of any crowd can snap its fingers at depressions—the part that gets in free. The pass gate always does well. There are Boys' Club Days at every park, Ladies' Days at every park but the Yankees'. And there is a long line of such people as stockholders, politicians, clergymen, newspapermen, and a "friend of a friend," who slide through on "pink slips." New York and Chicago have particularly heavy free lists; last year, all told, the Cubs had 309,000 unpaid admissions....

### BASEBALL AND SOCIAL DEMOCRACY

[*The following document discusses the variety of nationalities that played major league baseball during the decade. It also illustrates the prevailing belief that baseball helped promote social democracy and assimilate players of different nationalities. James M. Kahn, "America's International Game. There is Just as Much Opportunity for the Foreign Born Player in Baseball as There Is for the Native Son," Baseball Magazine (November 1939), 534, 569.*]

America is the land of opportunity, and nowhere is this incontrovertible fact more pronounced than in sports. Many young men have found the sports arenas the stepping stones to fame and fortune. Baseball in particular is full of them.

While baseball is our national sport, it might well be called America's International Game, for the opportunities which it offers certainly aren't limited only to native sons. Thumbing over the rosters of the big league clubs, one encounters many foreign born athletes who have become stars in the big leagues. At least five foreign countries are represented in the big leagues today by players born in them.

Starting with the champion Yankees there is Arndt Jorgens, the old reliable understudy to Bill Dickey, who has just rounded out ten years of faithful service with the New York club. Arndt is a native of Oslo, Norway, and came to this country when a child. He lives in Chicago now, but still adheres to one Scandinavian custom, anyway. That is, his taste for smorgasbord, that wide assortment of appetite-tempting delicacies which invariably grace the Scandinavian boards on festive occasions.

Canada has two solid representatives in the hard punching George Selkirk of the Yankees and Jeff Heath of the Indians. Selkirk was born in Huntsville, Ontario, and Heath in Fort William, in the same province. Joe Krakauskas, the Washington lefty, is another Canadian. He was born in Montreal.

Cuba, of course, of all foreign countries, has always had the biggest non-native representation in the big leagues. Many have risen to real stardom who came to America from the Pearl of the Antilles, most notably the incomparable Senor Adolfo Luque. He not only had an abundance of stuff with which to fool the batters, but he was a real fox when it came to outthinking the hitters, and no one who has ever heard it will forget the Senor, getting ready to out-smart a batter with a half-speed ball, exclaim:

"I zink I throw now a change of space!"

The current Cuban representative in the playing ranks is the Senators' unpredictable Estalello, while another Spanish-speaking teammate of his who was born outside of our borders is Alexandro Carrasquel, who comes from Venezuela. Of course, there still remains on the coaching lines of the St. Louis Cardinals the inimitable Senor Mike Gonzales, author of the immortal report on a young prospect: "Good field-no hit!" He is a native Cuban.

These are the players who today grace the big league rosters who actually were born in foreign lands, but there are few nationalities, indeed, which are not represented by players born here of foreign parentage. Once there even was an Oriental touch to our occidental game, though not for long, when Buck Lai, an infielder who was part Chinese and part Hawaiian, had a brief tryout with the New York Giants.

Buck was a real speedster whom many minor league fans of the old Eastern League will remember. He could run like a deer, and more than once scored from second base on the squeeze play.

One of the oddities one encounters in considering the varied nationalities that have contributed players to the big leagues is that, while there have been a great many ballplayers of Italian descent who have made good, not one was born in Italy. There never has been a native born Italian in the big show, though virtually every team at one time or another has boasted an Italian star.

The big Italian population in California has contributed the majority of its ballplayers, though one section of the country holds no exclusive rights on Italian players. It is merely that most of them have come from there, as well as the most celebrated of them all, Joe DiMaggio.

It would be interesting to know just how wide an influence Ping Bodie had on this preponderance of California-Italian ballplayers. Ping was one of the first well-known Italian big leaguers. He was a rotund and jolly fellow, built along the generous, though squat lines of Tony Galento. He wasn't a great ballplayer by any means, but he was a great character, and he had plenty of opportunity for his fun-loving proclivities while Babe Ruth's roommate on the Yankees of the early '20s.

Ping came from San Francisco, and was a hero when he returned there in the fall, very much as he was a popular and familiar figure in the big league cities during the season. Undoubtedly he gave the impetus to many an Italian youngster's ambition to become a big league ballplayer, too, particularly in California. Ping could sting the ball hard, and after they saw what he could do the Yankees certainly were always much interested in Italian ballplayers.

Well they might have been, for all big league clubs they have had the best luck with their Italian rookies. Tony Lazzeri, Frankie Crosetti, and DiMaggio formed an Italian triumvirate through a couple of pennant-winning years which was the envy of every manager in the big show. Now the Yanks appear to have come up with another Italian prize in the person of Marius Russo, who showed himself to be a capable lefthander during the campaign just closed. Russo, incidentally, is a New York lad and not one of the numerous Californians.

However, there are plenty of Pacific Coast Italians sprinkled around, among them Dolph Camilli, Cookie Lavagetto, Ernie Lombardi and Joe Marty, besides the DiMaggio boys and Crosetti. Zeke Bonura and Lou Chiozza are a couple of players of Italian descent who first saw the light of day in Louisiana, while Tony Cuccinello hails from Long Island City in New York, and Phil Cavarretta from Chicago.

In assimilating players of innumerable national backgrounds into the single pattern of our American game no one group has become proficient at any one particular job. That is, no one particular nationality has produced good outfielders, while no other has sponsored good outfielders, or pitchers or catchers. There are ballplayers of all nationalities in all positions.

However, it is odd once again, in contemplating the ballplayers of Italian descent, that they have become proficient in every position, but have produced very, very few pitchers. This may only be a coincidence, but it is noteworthy just the same to consider that Russo is about the only hurler of any prominence now on a big league club who is of Italian extraction.

### WENDELL SMITH PREACHES UNITY

*[Minority sportswriters such as Frank Young of The Chicago Defender, Sam Lacy of The Baltimore Afro-American, Ed Harris of the Philadelphia Tribune, and Wendell Smith of The Pittsburgh Courier comprised the entire sports section of their respective newspaper and thus covered every sport. Wendell Smith is generally considered the best black sportswriter of his generation. Smith arrived at the Courier in 1937 after graduating from West Virginia State College. An initiative to integrate baseball was already underway at the Courier, but Smith brought his own vision of an American society where ability, skill and character were the sole measures of a man.*

*Smith grew up in Detroit. He was a good athlete and pitched for an integrated team in the American Legion. When a scout informed him that he was good enough to play professional baseball except for his skin color, Smith decided to become a sportswriter and work towards integration. In the following article, Smith appeals to his readers to act together to end the color bar by refusing to attend major league games. Wendell Smith, "A Strange Tribe," The Pittsburgh Courier (11 May 1938) as quoted in Jim*

*Reisler,* Black Writers/Black Baseball. An Anthology of Articles from Black Sportswriters Who Covered the Negro Leagues *(Jefferson, North Carolina, 1994), 36-38.*]

Why we continue to flock to major league ball parks, spending our hard earned dough, screaming and hollering, stamping our feet and clapping our hands, begging and pleading for some white batter to knock some white pitcher's ears off, almost having fits if the home team loses and crying for joy when they win, is a question that probably never will be answered satisfactorily. What in the world are we thinking about anyway?

**NOT WANTED**

The fact that major league baseball refuses to admit Negro players within its folds makes the question just that much more perplexing. Surely, it's sufficient reason for us to quit spending our money and time in their ball parks. Major league baseball does not want us. It never has. Still, we continue to help support this institution that places a bold "Not Welcome" sign over its thriving portal and refuse to patronize the very place that has shown that it is more than welcome to have us. We black folks are a strange tribe!

**MARKING PROGRESS**

Negro baseball is still in its infancy. In the last 10 years, it has come a long, long way. Gone are the days when the players having the most knives and razors won the ball game. Gone are the days when only one or two good players were on a team. Now, their rosters are filled with brilliant, colorful, dazzling players who know the game from top to bottom. Negro teams now have everything the white clubs have. Except of course, the million dollar ball parks to play in, parks that we helped to build with our hard earned dollars. Nevertheless, we ignore them and go to see teams play that do not give a hang whether we come or not.

Sounds silly, doesn't it? Well—it's true! Despite the fact that we have our own teams and brilliant players, the most colorful in the world, mind you we go elsewhere and get a kick out of doing it. Suckers! You said it brother!

**NO ENCOURAGEMENT**

They're real troopers, these guys who risk their money and devote their lives to Negro baseball. We black folk offer no encouragement and don't seem to care of [sic] they make a go of it or not. We literally ignore them completely. With our noses high and our hands deep in our pockets, squeezing the same dollar that we hand out to the white players, we walk past their ball parks and go the major league game. Nuts— that's what we are. Just plain nuts!

**FROM DIXIE**

Listen! if any one of us wanted to talk to one of the ballplayers whom we've been spending our hard earned dough on, screaming and hollering, stamping our feet and clapping our hands for, we'd probably be ignored. If he did speak to us, it would probably be a disrespectful salutation. Such as "Hello George," or "What ya' say Sam." Or maybe even worse than that. Oh, he wouldn't eh! That's what you think. Don't forget that he comes from Mississippi, Georgia, Texas or any other place you can think of below the Mason-Dixon Line. And he's white! He looks upon us as something the cat brought in. Even though he is playing ball in a northern city, making northern money, he still looks upon us that way. He's a leopard and you know what they say about their spots. You can't change em.

**TOUGH FIGHT**

We have been fighting for years in an effort to make owners of major league base-ball teams admit Negro players. But they won't do it, probably never will. We keep on crawling, begging and pleading for recognition just the same. We know that they don't want us, but we still keep giving them our money. Keep on going to their ball games and shouting till we are blue in the face. Oh, we're an optimistic, faithful, prideless lot—we pitiful black folk.

Yes sir—we black folk are a strange tribe!

**THE COLOR BAR**

[*Throughout the decade, black baseball teams criss-crossed the country in overcrowded buses. In 1938, the Homestead Grays played 210 games. Their home park was Pittsburgh's Forbes Field, but they had to dress at the local YMCA. The American Communist party sought to end discrimination as did a few sportswriters such as Shirley Povich in Washington and Bill Roeder in New York.*

*Like the athletes they covered, black sportswriters were also subject to racial dis-crimination. The large number of barnstorming games that each team played made it especially difficult to report on their activities. Ed Harris, the author of the following scathing article against baseball's color ban, soon became the paper's managing editor. Ed Harris, "Abstract Reasoning," Philadelphia Tribune, 6 August 1936, as quoted in Jim Reisler, Black Writers/Black Baseball. An Anthology of Articles from Black Sports-writers Who Covered the Negro Leagues (Jefferson, North Carolina, 1994), 149-151.*]

**The asininity of race prejudice**, as practiced by the so-called "superior groups," is shown up by the feeble reasons advanced by its proponents for its existence. To the intelligent man, the theory of discrimination defeats itself by its own arguments.

In last week's issue, there was reprinted a column by Jimmy Powers, sports editor of the New York Daily News, in which he wrote about some of the letters he had gotten in relation to his favorable stand on Negro players in the big-leagues.

The piece de resistance of the whole batch, came from a fan who raised the old familiar cry of **"Would you want your sister to marry one?"**

Now that my friends, is a product of deep thinking, of a careful association of all the factors involved in the case and the resultant conclusion. Nothing but a brilliant man could have reached a decision whereby he felt that marriage and ball playing were related.

Powers triumphed, "No, but at the same time, I wouldn't want my sister to marry Bill Terry, Ty Cobb or Bill Klem, they're too grouchy." His reply was eminently cor-rect and of a squelching variety.

Every objection recorded by Mr. Powers in his column could not be intelligently upheld. There was the usual cry that other ballplayers wouldn't associate with them, that fans in southern towns wouldn't stand for it, that Negro players were inherent gamblers and roisterers.

In my more or less frail association with big-league players in the American and National set-ups, it is my conclusion that very few of them spring from what might be termed "the best homes." In fact, as far as I'm concerned, quite a few of the boys could go down to Cat-gut Alley and not be noticed in mixing with the natives. The mass of ballplayers are like the mass of the American people, the very common and very ordinary. In company with them, quite a few Negroes might rightfully feel superior.

As for the conduct of fans in southern towns, it might be said that there are but few in the big leagues. Cincinnati, St. Louis and Washington are the towns. In Cincy and St. Louis, the sports' fans are used to seeing Negro athletes playing in company with whites. Quite a few of the football teams have had colored stars cavorting up and down the gridiron. I have yet to hear of any mob violence because some prejudiced white became infuriated at seeing a colored star play with the white boys.

As for Negroes being gamblers and roisterers, it would do some of the self-appointed critics good to view the behind-doors scenes when some of the big league boys get together in a quiet game of "bones" or poker. And the late, lamented Rube Waddell and the still-living but unfortunate Grover Cleveland Alexander never took any Sunday School prizes as models of propriety. The idol of present-day baseball, Babe Ruth, very nearly shut himself out of a manager's job by leaving behind him a history of irresponsibility and carefreeness.

The argument simply doesn't hold water.

The president of the National League, Ford Frick, put his stand in writing and said that except for ability, moral character and the like, there were no bans against any player in his league. This is all very ethical and abstract, but yet has nothing to do with Negro players, as Mr. Frick does not hire the athletes.

Some manager with guts and vision might precipitate things by signing up a colored player and seeing what would happen. It would clarify things a great deal. We would get some sort of decision, pro or con, instead of a lot of theories.

I have an idea that with the addition of Negro stars to the roster, that the turnstiles would start clicking regularly again. And I think that lots of baseball managers are of the same opinion. But baseball owners are notorious for their dislike of change. They like to hold onto the old things and not acquire newer methods. For instance, night ball. Cincinnati is the only team that has had the vision to install a light system and they have made money.

But, do the rest of the owners admit this? No. They bellow, "It is only a fad...It wouldn't last." That's what they said about the auto.

But, like all men, I live in hopes. Some day, someone will surprise the baseball world and sign a couple of good colored players. And the baseball world will be surprised to find out that after the initial interest and excitement, that the Negro will be accepted as part of the club and the world will go its way. Like lots of things, anticipation is much greater than realization.

### THE NATIONAL GAME

*[In 1934, major league baseball distributed a questionnaire to 115 university presidents, mayors, school board members, company presidents, and YMCA and Boy Scout leaders. The tabulated results of the eighty-six responses disclosed that most Americans believed that baseball helped to improve the physical well-being and the moral standing of the country. In this vein, Baseball Magazine reprinted the following speech that*

*it hoped would be used at local celebrations for baseball's 1939 centennial—"Base-
ball is America's game, it epitomizes the American national spirit, the American temperament, fair play, sportsmanship, aggressiveness, clean, hard go-getting 'punch'....
America's battles are won on the ball diamond. All of us trust and devoutly hope that
our struggles will all be of the peaceful variety. In any case, baseball prepares young
Americans and young America for the battles of life–whatever they may be."*

*In the following speech before Congress to introduce a bill to commemorate
baseball's centennial, the Representative from Connecticut illustrates the values that
baseball was believed to instill. Note the references to the Bible and to the ancient
Greeks. Congressional Record, 76th Congress, 1st Session, Vol. 84, Part 1, 2 (February 1939), 1087-1089.]*

Mr. SHANLEY. Mr. Speaker and my colleagues. I rise to direct the attention of this
great House to the celebration that is scheduled for this year on the 12th of June in
Cooperstown, N.Y. It is the occasion for the one hundredth anniversary of baseball. I
have introduced a bill to commemorate this—not to make it a permanent national
holiday but to pay tribute this year—the centennial of our national pastime.

Baseball has created the American ideal of clean, hard play. Baseball is America's
game—American in origin, American in spirit, American in its appeal to player and fan.
Born 100 years ago, it grew to be the Nation's game, its favorite sport and spectacle.

Baseball demands skill, dash, and pluck, calm nerve in the face of crises. It has
perhaps contributed more than any other activity to the development of the American
temperament. Through its outlet for the energies and enthusiasm of player and spectator alike and in its teaching of hard play but fair, it has been the Nation's safety valve
and its insurance against excesses now prevalent among other nations abroad.

Any Biblical student will remember the exaltation of athletics from the Epistle to
the Corinthians:

"Know ye not that they who runneth in the race-ground, all run indeed, but one re-
ceiveth the prize? So run, that ye may obtain. And everyone who striveth for the mas-
tery restraineth himself from all things, and they, indeed, that they may receive a perish-
able crown: But we an Imperishable [sic]. I therefore so run, not as an uncertainty I so
fight, not as one beating the air but I chastise my body and bring it under subjection."

Every nation has realized to the fullest the training in fundamentals that sport installed among the ancients. The tales of valor of Spartan athletes are known to every
schoolboy. Mighty Homer himself has left us an immortal couplet: "For no fame may
a man win better the while he bath his life, Than from what his feet have accomplished
or his hands amidst the strife."

Someone has said that the Battle of Waterloo was won on the playing fields of Eton.
It might well be said that the historical military virtues of America's sensible discipline,
and leadership, were taught on the athletic fields of America. No troops during the
World War ever exhibited so much initiative as our own. We can well be proud of our
athletic prowess and the contribution it has made to America.

If divisions in religion in this country have forced toleration as one great student
believes and if the very confusion of our common law has taught us that our best safeguard is the independence and integrity of our judges we may well add that our principles of sportsmanship have never betrayed these manly virtues.

Shane Leslie, the Anglo-Irish author, has said that: "Modern sport, thanks to the
Celtic blend, keeps the mean between the torture of animals and humanitarianism. The

unwritten law of sport was gradually established that the pursued must be allowed a chance to escape. That big game have to be killed in the swamp rather than in the arena. The true sportsman prefers to miss a difficult quarry rather than slay an easy one."

With those great principles of sport he added a definition that a "sportsman is one who takes his chance when he ought and not when he can." He shall not aim at the sitting bird nor strike the fallen boxer. Baseball has these ideals.

American baseball develops good men. It instills in boys and young men the qualities for success in American life. Baseball requires virility, courage, sagacity, energy, and determination. Witness the brilliant array of statesmen, preachers, engineers, physicians, and merchants who have graduated from the ball fields of our town lots, schools, and colleges.

Baseball's hundred years of history provide as dramatic and as American a story as the struggles at the Puritans or the conquest of the West.

The chroniclers report that President Lincoln received notice of his nomination while playing baseball with the neighborhood men and boys.

Afterward there came the Civil War to interrupt peacetime baseball, but the game, a hardy infant, continued in wartime on tented fields and behind the stockades of Army prison. Both Union and Confederate troops were playing the game. Here it became truly American, for, according to Army tradition, the soldiers of both forces laid aside their arms while a series of games was played between picked teams from the Union and Confederate Armies—yes sublimely, typically American.

With the demobilization of the Blue and the Gray the soldiers headed homeward, carrying baseball to the farthest corners of America. It caught on everywhere. Baseball teams sprang up in every town and village and each team was loudly and proudly supported by its home folks.

Here in Washington the interest of our Presidents and Vice Presidents is known to everyone.

The saga of American baseball is a thrilling part of our national history, an integral section of our development as a people and a power. Courageous, far-sighted Americans took the game abroad to show the world, and from those visits mutual benefits have been derived.

The National Baseball Centennial Commission, created to honor the one hundredth anniversary of the birth of our national game, has attracted some of the greatest figures in this country. I am privileged to cite the roster of the national commissioners who are lending support to this great national birthday celebration: [This list of notable sportsmen, military people, educators, and businessmen has been deleted.]

This honorable commission is now directing the Nationwide sweep of baseball centennial celebration. Every hamlet, village, town, and city of this Nation will be made conscious of the greatness of our national game. Radio, motion pictures, and the press will all tell the story of baseball's century of achievement.

On June 12 the greatest stars of today from the 16 teams of the 2 major leagues converge upon little Cooperstown to honor the stars of yesterday. There on this day the National Baseball Museum and Hall of Flame will be dedicated to the everlasting glory of our Nation. A cavalcade of baseball will be presented to again tell the story of America's past century and the part played in these tenscore years by baseball. We here even in these trying days should do our share.

Throughout the entire world today American baseball is the personification of sportsmanship, team play, fair play, and Americanism. Behind the bivouacs of the Civil War, on every peaceful Main Street, hard by the lethal cannon in Flanders Fields, and in huge sun-flooded stadia baseball brought everliving hours of thrills and pleasure and relaxation to countless millions. The printed page and the spoken word over the radio have given the game a following through history unrivaled in sport annals.

For a hundred years it has been America's pastime—and passion. For a solid century it has brought despair to Mudville, joy to Middletown. This year Uncle Sam is giving a gigantic birthday party to baseball. It Is everybody's game, everybody's party. Let all America rejoice and thank God for a game that for 100 years has built Americanism. Let this Congress pay official tribute to our national game by naming June 12 as National Baseball Day.

But it is the day we celebrate that concerns us. From that colorful epochal figure, A.G. Spalding, in his immortal classic, America's National Game, I am taking an account of the early annals of the game. I ask unanimous consent to extend and revise my remarks at this point and include this famous version.

I quote from the book: "I have no intention, in this work of reopening the discussion which waxed so warm a short time ago, as to the origin of the game. It would be an act of disloyalty to the commission that was appointed at my suggestion in 1907, with instructions to consider all available evidence and decide the case upon its merits, were I ever again to enter upon the details of the vexed controversy—except in order to prove the righteousness of the verdict then rendered. It Is quite enough here to say that the commission referred to, after a long, thorough, painstaking investigation of all obtainable facts, unanimously declared:

First. That baseball had its origin in the United States;

Second. That the first scheme for playing it, according to the best evidence obtainable to date, was devised by Abner Doubleday, at Cooperstown, N.Y., in 1839. [Deleted concluding remarks of this commission.]

Thank you, Mr. Speaker and my colleagues. Let us honor all of them in this celebration, but, above all, let us commemorate the American spirit of baseball, our national game. (Applause.)

### BASEBALL'S FARM SYSTEM

*[The reserve clause system bound players to one team until that team sold, traded or released them. For four days each year, on the eve of the World Series, minor leagues clubs were at the mercy of the major league teams. By paying the draft price of $7,500 a major league team could purchase an eligible Class AA player. Class A-1 and Class A rookies went for $6,000. At the bottom, Class D players sold for $2,000. Next, the leading minor league teams drafted from the lower circuits. To avoid losing their players for such small sums, minor league teams sometimes sold their better players to major league clubs before the draft. This document outlines how some teams attempted to evade league rules, and Commissioner Landis' response to these tactics. Edgar Forest Wolfe, "Winter's Baseball Battleground—Is Player Monopoly Doomed? A Fighting Czar Declares War!" Liberty (28 January 1939), 23.]*

Baseball pennants are **not** won on summer playing fields, in the broad light of day and in full view of the fans. They are won on winter's baseball battlegrounds, behind doors that are closed to the public.

This winter a new battle rages behind those doors—a battle to destroy a system of baseball monopoly that has enabled the same three teams in each big league to monopolize all the pennants and the World Series for the past twelve years; a battle for which Commissioner Kenesaw Mountain Landis, who as a federal judge had plastered a fine of one million dollars on the Standard Oil Company for the same monopolistic tendencies, has forged new weapons.

With two of these—an edict forbidding the signing of players to "blind" contracts in which a club's name is subsequently inserted without the formality of registering these at headquarters until the club is ready to place them; and another, abrogating the contracts and making free agents of some ninety ballplayers whose future had been controlled either directly or indirectly through affiliated minor-league organizations by the St. Louis National League club—Landis fired the first shots in a new winter campaign against the whole system of player monopoly that defeats the purpose of the selective draft and in recent years has made scouting the minor leagues, formerly the happy hunting ground for big-league ball clubs, almost futile.

Take a look at the picture:

Recent investigations by the commissioner's office have disclosed the fact that, either through direct ownership or secret working agreements, a total of 191 minor-league clubs have become little more than subsidiaries to big-league teams. This means approximately 2,800 young ballplayers whose future services are made unavailable to any other team except as dictated by the "holding company" of this monopoly in player talent.

The St. Louis National League club led with thirty-one minor-league subsidiaries. The Cardinals thus had absolute control of more than 500 young ballplayers—and Section 1, Article 2, of the Major League Agreement provides that "No club shall have title to or **under its control** at any one time more than 40 players."

The Yankees have twelve minor-league clubs in leagues of various classifications: The Brooklyn Dodgers have twelve. Detroit has eleven. By recent acquisitions the St. Louis Browns have fourteen. Cincinnati has nine. Washington, Pittsburgh, Chicago White Sox, and Cubs have seven each. Cleveland and Boston Red Sox have six each. Giants and Boston Bees have four. Phillies and Athletics have three.

It is charged that one American League club has college coaches on its pay toll, in return for which they are to tie up all baseball players developed at these institutions for future service with the "chain farm" subsidiaries of the big-league club that pays them a salary.

Pacific Coast League clubs have lodged complaints with Landis, pointing to various baseball schools that big-league clubs through their minor-league subsidiaries have been conducting in their territory in violation of their territorial rights, thus raiding their natural source of supply and making the young players off the lots unavailable to any other ball club.

For the past two years the Cincinnati National League club, through its minor-league subsidiaries, has operated a chain of training camps over a territory of 2,500 miles of minor-league ground stretching from Phoenix, Arizona, to Seattle, Washington, in which a total of 600 boys each year have been coached in the rudiments of baseball—and all those who show promise have been tied up by these "blind" agreements that Landis is shooting at.

The St. Louis Cardinals, through their Sacramento minor-league subsidiary, have been conducting a baseball school at Sacramento, California. The Cardinals have also been holding baseball schools at Springfield, Missouri, Fort Smith, Oklahoma City, and other places, cornering all the promising sand-lot players in those sections in violation of the territorial rights of independent minor-league clubs.

The Brooklyn Dodgers have been holding training camps for young sand-lot and school players at Elmira, New York, where last spring 400 boys were tried out for future service with Brooklyn "chain farm" clubs in violation of the territorial rights of the Eastern League.

Thus colleges, schools, and sand lots have been raided to feed a monopolistic system of player control that governs the player's future from the lots to the big leagues, makes an open player market impossible, and puts the pennant races and the World Series permanently within the grasp of the few "holding companies" with the most minor-league subsidiaries to corner and retain control of the playing talent.

So Landis has taken the winter warpath against a growing evil that had sent its roots down deeper than he had ever suspected. Following his liberation of some ninety ballplayers from the St. Louis "chain gang," the commissioner fired a broadside at the other club owners in the following words:

"In connection with recent investigations, it appears that clubs have been signing players to blank contracts in which a club's name has been subsequently inserted and the player ordered to report to that club.

You are hereby notified that this practice is contrary to the rules and must be discontinued. Any player so signed will be declared a free agent and the club or clubs involved will be prohibited from having any dealings with such player. In addition, a fine of not less than $500 will be imposed upon each club involved for each offense."

As a result Commissioner Landis is definitely in the doghouse of certain club owners. And what happens on this winter's baseball battleground may well mean a drastic change in the future baseball picture—or it may mean the passing from the game of the man who left the federal bench to save baseball from itself.

### BASEBALL IN CANADA

[*Toronto, Montreal, Vancouver, and Winnipeg all hosted teams in international leagues, and Canadians were avid baseball players, yet in 1935, George Selkirk was the only Canadian-born player in the major leagues. The experts suggested several reasons for this situation—the game was not organized in schools and colleges, the summers were too short, there were few professional teams in Canada to provide suitable role models. The following document examines the state of baseball in Canada in 1937. Dink Carroll, "Can Baseball Come Back? Clubs Have Been Rejuvenated, New Leagues Started, But Baseball Still Needs More Canadian Players," Maclean's Magazine (15 May 1937), 23-24, 60-61.*]

Opening Day of the 1937 baseball season in Toronto. Bands blare, flags flutter, players parade, political dignitaries strut their parts. But the something extra which makes this opening different from all others is the spirit of thanksgiving in the hearts of the fans.

For the last decade or more, professional baseball has been fighting for its life in Canada. And what may prove to have been the turning point in this epic struggle, waged on a nationwide front, came in the Ontario city at the end of the 1936 International League season. Had the Toronto crisis had any other outcome, there is no doubt but what the game might have received its deathblow in this country. As it is—but let's set the film in reverse for a moment. A flashback of events will tell us much, and may help us to get a line on possible future developments.

It was one day late last fall when Toronto citizens first learned that the city was in imminent danger of losing its franchise in the International League. They had once been told, and up to then still believed, that their city was one of the best baseball towns in the North American continent outside the major leagues. But it seems they had been taking baseball too much for granted for too long a time. In the years that had elapsed since the club had had a winner, many old-time fans had acquired the habit of sitting at home and reading about the team's doings, instead of visiting the park and giving it their support.

According to reports, the club needed $35,000 cash right away to retain the franchise, and its officers had no idea of where it was coming from. Dan Howley, who had once been the very popular manager of a winning Toronto team, was anxious to get back in the picture as manager and part owner, and he was doing his best to raise the necessary funds. But day by day, as the wheel spun, no numbers turned up for Howley. And then suddenly, though it was the middle of the off season, the fans began to display a livelier interest in the welfare of the club than they had shown in more than half a dozen years.

**BASEBALL SAVED FOR TORONTO**

The New York Giants were the big menace of the moment. They wanted to establish a farm team in the International, top league among the minors, and they had secured a rental option on a beautiful stadium in Jersey City. Now they were in the market for a team to operate in their lovely new plant and they were bidding for the Toronto or Albany franchise, weak links in the International chain. When it was finally announced that they had purchased the Albany franchise, there was a sigh of relief from Toronto. But immediately a new threat arose to confront those who were interested in keeping the game alive in the Canadian city.

Joe Cambria, the voluble Latin who had just disposed of his Albany interests to the Giants, thought he'd like to stay in baseball. And why not? Mr. Cambria, whose real business is running a steam laundry, had only been in baseball a few years, but in that brief time he'd broken off the sugar in large chunks. It was said that he had bought the Albany franchise originally for a meagre $5,000 and then, the very first year he operated it, sold $15,000 worth of players. Now he had just sold his Albany holdings to the Giants for a sum reported to be in excess of $50,000 and thought he'd like to buy the Toronto franchise if he could get it for $35,000, which he's been told was the price. You can't lose money that way, and if you were Mr. Cambria you'd be reluctant to quit too. So there he was, all ready with the dough.

Meanwhile, in Toronto, a couple of young lawyers met in a business office and began to talk about this and that. They were both red-hot baseball fans and they'd both been reading the papers. They felt rather badly over what they were certain was bound to happen. "What's the matter with this town anyway?" one of them asked. "Both amateur and professional baseball have had tough going for years. Now it looks as if they're going to have to sell the club to a city about one third this size."

"If things get too stale this summer," the other answered ironically, "we can always go watch a few girls' softball games. But it wasn't always like this."

They talked on, recalling summers they had spent together on Hanlan's Point off Toronto's waterfront, when the Maple Leafs played all their games there. They remembered how they had thrilled to the towering home runs big Tim Jordan used to belt into the bay. They remembered the flashy base running of Bill Bradley around third base, the marvelous pitching displays of little Dicky Rudolph. Then they recalled how they used to saunter past the Bay Tree Hotel at night, where the ball players lived when the team was at home, holding their breath and hoping to catch a glimpse of some of those glamorous figures off the diamond. Baseball was a great game and it had had a long and glorious tradition in Toronto. It had sunk to its present low level because the fans would not support a losing team, and its owners could not afford to gamble even one more season. But should the game be allowed to perish when a few thousand dollars might save it? Both these men thought not.

One of them was Don Ross, son of a former Lieutenant-Governor of Ontario, and he was in a position to do something about it. He got in touch with Dan Howley right away, and together they went to call on some prominent investment bankers. In no time at all they had more than the amount of money needed, the ominous shadow of Joe Cambria and his sackful of foreign gold had been dissipated, and the new-deal-for-baseball movement in Toronto was on.

**NIGHT GAMES HELP**

The happiest man in baseball this spring must surely be Dan Howley. The last man to lead a Toronto team to a pennant, he left the club when it fell upon evil days. But since then he has not been particularly happy or conspicuously successful. He had sad managerial experiences with the St. Louis Browns and the Cincinnati Reds—clubs which have broken the hopes and shattered the spirits of some of baseball's wisest men. But Howley has always believed in the potentialities of Toronto as a big money-maker if given a hustling team, and he has kept bobbing up there year after year, always enormously interested in what was going on. Now he is again manager of the club, and this time he has a financial stake in it.

The new president is Don Ross, and the board of directors reads like the top sheet of eminents from Canada's income-tax lists. It includes Messrs. J.H. Gundy, Hon. W.D. Ross, Norman Urquhart, Fred J. Crawford, W.B. Milner and Percy R. Gardiner. Thus the club now is even more heavily backed than the Boston Gold Sox, which has only Tom Yawkey's ten-million-dollar lumber fortune behind it....

It's practically a sure thing now that baseball will come back with a bang in Toronto. Dan Howley has his own notions of how to attract and retain the loyalty of the fans. Last season, while the club was still battling for a play-off position, the St. Louis Cardinals recalled Si Johnson, the Leaf's best pitcher, who was their property and only with the Leafs on call. But the move angered the fans and lost the Leafs considerable patronage, and Howley wants to be free of these big league tie-ups. The Toronto club will try to make a deal with another club of lower classification, which it can use as a farm. It will have its own scout and will dig up and develop its own talent, which can't help but please the baseball-loving public. Already the fans have been writing in droves, offering suggestions on how to lure crowds into the park. Some think a more demure price list might help. Others ask for nothing more than a winning team. So the interest is there and, with plenty of new money in the club's coffers, everything will be done to convert it into action. And night baseball, which last year developed from a fad into a custom in the minors, is also going to help.

**MONTREAL'S TROUBLES**

What happened to professional baseball this past winter in Toronto has happened since the War in virtually every city and town in Canada boasting a professional team. But the crisis came sooner in most places, notably in Montreal, with the result that it is now fairly safe to predict that the game is on its way to regaining all its old popularity in this country. Let's look at the Montreal situation for a moment and see what has happened there.

Montreal also had once been a good ball town, but the War years so washed it up that its International League franchise had to be sold. In 1928, with everything commercial booming, a financial syndicate brought it back and also built a new stadium. Unfortunately, the depression came on too soon to allow this new effort a fair chance, though the team kept operating under the worst kind of conditions until 1932, when there was another show-down. This time another local group stepped in and saved the situation by buying the franchise exclusive of the stadium, which it rented on a pay-as-you-play basis. The new group then installed Frank Shaughnessy as business manager, because they wanted someone affiliated with the club who was a practical baseball man, and whom they knew and trusted. The club staggered along like that until the end of the 1934 season, when Shaughnessy told the owners something they had been trying for years to find out.

"To make a minor-league ball club pay," he advised them, "you've got to get a crowd in the park nearly every day, and you've got to sell players at a profit. The best way to do that is to spend some money and get a winning and colorful team together."

The owners took the elastic off what was left of the bankroll and let him go to market. He got the players he wanted, and the following summer he doubled in brass as field and business manager. By July the team was in first place and turnstiles leading into the park were clicking faster than in most major-league cities. By actual count, the Royals were outdrawing the Chicago Cubs, who were leading the race in the National League.

At the end of the season Shaughnessy disposed of several of his stars to major-league clubs. Jim Ripple, sensational outfielder, was sold to the New York Giants. Big Chad Kimsey, a pitcher, went to Detroit; and Pete Appleton, another pitcher, was bought by Washington. The club is reported to have finished the season with a credit balance of $80,000, a remarkable performance for an enterprise which had shown nothing but red figures for seven long, consecutive years.

A postscript on what went on in Montreal last summer shows how unexpected and rapid is the change in fortune of both clubs and individuals in the game of baseball. Though the team started the season well and was in first place at the end of May, Manager Shaughnessy was still trying frantically to plug the gaps left by the departure of his stars for the major leagues. But the other clubs ganged up on him and refused to enter into trades with him or even to sell him ball players outright. By midsummer the Royals had sunk into the second division where they belonged, and the fans, notoriously short of memory in any sport, were panning the man who only a few months before had given then their first pennant in more than a quarter of a century. Shaughnessy then quit in disgust. But his work of making Montreal baseball conscious had already been done and done thoroughly. For, while the team finished the season well down in the standing, it fared even better at the gate than it had the previous year.

There was general regret among baseball men over Shaughnessy's withdrawal. Johnny Ogden, manager of the Baltimore Orioles, even went so far as to make an indignant speech about it to the press.

"In Baltimore the fans booed Shag," said Ogden, "but that only meant they weren't indifferent to him. I wish they would boo all the managers. It would help the attendance. But there aren't many of them with enough color to make the fans feel one way or another about them."

Then, if ever, Shaughnessy's cup of bitterness seemed about to overflow. But, while his friends were still in the act of reaching for the crying towels, the office of president of the International League, one of the best executive jobs in organized baseball, fell open, and he fell into it without even the smallest lurch, so squarely did he land on his feet.

**A NEW PROFESSIONAL LEAGUE**

But so much for baseball in the East for a moment. Let's have a quick look at what's been happening to the game west of the Great Lakes. The old Western Canada League, which flourished for a good many years, produced many fine ball players. Some of them have made names for themselves in the big show: men like Oscar Melillo, who once played with Winnipeg; Mark Koenig, who was with Moose Jaw; and Babe Herman and Heine Manush, who are still remembered fondly by the fans in Edmonton. This league, which took in most of the large cities on the prairies, folded up back in the '20's. But the game is beginning to get a toehold again. Winnipeg now operates a franchise in the Northern League, along with Fargo, Moorehead and other cities south of the border, while there is talk of reviving the Western Canada League, though this project is still in the talking stage. Farther west, Vancouver enjoys baseball and is represented in the Western International League, which includes Seattle, Portland and several other large cities south of the international boundary.

Back East again for a look at the Maritime Provinces. Down there they have always been enthusiastic about baseball, though the only professional league in operation at the moment is the Cape Breton Colliery League. Glace Bay, New Waterford, Sydney and Sydney Mines all operate franchises in this league. There is much talk there also about a new league, which would include such cities as Saint John, Moncton and Bathurst, but this, too, has not advanced as yet beyond the talking stage.

The very newest professional league with Canadian representation is the Canadian-American in Eastern Ontario. Ottawa, Perth-Cornwall, Smiths Falls and Brockville all operate teams in it. They do not play a full schedule; it calls for only two and sometimes three games a week. But the league is in a very healthy condition and may conceivably grow into something much bigger than it is today.

Oddly enough, when and where professional baseball flourishes, there is an immediate pick-up in the amateur brand. Amateur baseball has had a new lease of life in and around Montreal ever since the International League franchise was returned to that city. When the Toronto Leafs have a winning team, the amateur leagues in Central and Western Ontario, as well as in the city of Toronto itself, take on new vitality. A larger section of the public becomes baseball-minded and more lads seem to want to play the game.

**CANADIAN PLAYERS NEEDED**

The thing that would help the professional game immeasurably in Canada would be the introduction of more Canadian players, just as it would help hockey considerably in the United States if more native sons were to emerge as N.H.L stars. The Toronto Leafs are well aware of this and, when the team left for its training camp in Florida this spring, three Canadian lads went with them. They are Bobby Porter, an outfielder, and Art Upper, a pitcher, both from Toronto's sand lots; and Dick Mitchell, a young catcher from Cobourg. They were joined in camp by Johnny Goodfellow, of Kingston, a brother of Ebbie, the Detroit Red Wings' great hockey player. Goodfellow had been in Florida for some weeks, attending Joe Stripp's baseball school. It is this kind of ambition that is going to produce some stand-out ball players, sooner or later, from the ranks of Canadian youth.

At the time of writing there is only one Canadian-born ball player in either major league. He is George Selkirk, of the New York Yankees, who was born in Huntsville, Ontario. John Heath, a twenty-one-year-old lad from Fort William, is attracting a lot of attention in the camp of the Cleveland Indians, and he may make the grade.

Speaking out of his thirty years experience in professional baseball, both here and in the United States, Frank Shaughnessy says the reason there are so few Canadian-born professional players is that there are no organized leagues in the schools and colleges. He thinks the short summers have something to do with this, but firmly believes that if baseball leagues are ever organized in our schools, as in hockey and football, Canada will straight-away begin to develop great ball players.

It requires no great leap of the imagination to see how the whole Dominion of Canada stands to benefit by a return of baseball to popularity in cities like Montreal, Toronto, Winnipeg and Vancouver. For Canada is by way of being the second greatest tourist attraction among the countries of the world today. Her annual income from the tourist industry is well over $200,000,000, which earns it a place in upper brackets as Canadian industries go. She is in the business of selling her mountain and lake and river scenery, and her summer and winter sports, to visitors from other lands. But to reach our playgrounds, visitors customarily arrive at and depart from our large urban centres, and usually have to spend some time in them. Instead of being content to rock along and look out the window at the large transient population in our big cities during the tourist season, we might be more gainfully employed in trying to anticipate and cater to their tastes. The vast majority of our guests are visitors from the United States, and baseball is their dish. We can't lose anything by having it ready for them.

Chapter 4

**BASKETBALL**

"If attendance figures mean anything," claimed *Spalding's Official Basketball Guide* for the 1939-40 season, "if the number of participants is significant, basketball has become the great American sport....Such figures as are available indicate an annual attendance for baseball (including professional games) of 30,000,000; for football,

40,000,000; for basketball (including high school games), 80,000,000, with more than 200,000 players participating." Thanks to the Public Works Administration, which constructed so many high school gymnasiums that it doubled the seating capacity for basketball games, basketball was played in approximately ninety-five percent of American high schools. Some of these new facilities were built to the highest quality and featured stands without obstructed views, electric clocks and scoreboards. Everywhere but in New England and Canada, basketball was the most popular winter sport. This was a far cry from the situation in 1930, when only a few hundred fans attended college games and the players were often football players trying to keep fit during the off-season.

Basketball was ideal for the Depression. It required little equipment and only five players to a team. This made it particularly attractive in smaller schools and urban areas. Basketball games provided a break from the hard times, and in small towns, in particular, the sport promoted community pride. The game also promoted ethnic pride, particularly among the children of recently-arrived immigrants from Eastern Europe in large eastern and midwestern cities. Here, Lithuanians, Jews, Serbs, Poles, and Russians participated in their own leagues. Teams and leagues were sponsored by lodges, fraternal orders, churches, the American Legion, ethnic clubs, and local factories and retail businesses. Following the game, the community often sponsored dancing, music and other entertainment. Settlement houses, social reformers and the YMCA promoted basketball among immigrant communities to help assimilate them into the mainstream of American life.

Jews, mostly from urban working-class neighborhoods, were the most successful ethnic group to take up the sport, and some sportswriters soon came to refer to basketball as the "Jewish" game. With success went anti-Semitism. Paul Gallico, sports editor for the New York Daily News, wrote in 1937 that the game appealed to the "temperament of the jews" because it placed a "premium on an alert, scheming mind...flashy trickiness, artful dodging and general smart aleckness...." Stanley Frank's 1936 book, The Jew in Sport, reflected similar stereotypes. The Spha, which was renamed the Philadelphia Warriors when it entered the American Basketball League, was identified and promoted as a Jewish team. Players such as Harry Litwack, Eddie Gottlieb, and Moe Goldman, who helped the Sphas dominate professional basketball in the East, became ethnic heroes. This was equally true for other ethnic groups. The Brooklyn Visitations and the Celtics were Irish teams. The Harlem Globetrotters (based in Chicago) and the New York Renaissance Big Five (the Rens) fielded blacks. Ethnic Chinese barnstormed as the Hong Wah Q'ues, and Olson's Terrible Swedes toured the midwest.

The best black college team was probably Baltimore's Morgan State College. But many black colleges could not afford a gymnasium. In the South, most black colleges played basketball outdoors. Black teams were excluded from tournaments organized by the AAU and from the Madison Square Garden double-headers. Lacking a basketball tradition, and with poorly balanced conferences, basketball was not a prominent sport in most black colleges. Northern white schools sometimes featured black players but seldom more than one at a time.

Before rules were standardized, intersectional games were common, and championship tournaments commenced, basketball styles varied widely from region to region. Court sizes varied and the rules were interpreted differently by each conference. The

East, which had small gymnasium courts, excelled in passing and ball handling. Western colleges generally had larger courts and employed long passes and elaborate strategies. The Midwest and Pacific conferences permitted more screens, which favored the offense, than did the East, which strictly enforced the blocking rule. The South allowed more body contact. The larger courts favored a running game, and it was at Purdue University, under teams captained by John Wooden and Ward Lambert, that the fast break was employed most successfully. Although this tactic attracted spectators, it was rare until the end of the decade.

Before the elimination of the center jump after every basket and the introduction of the 10-second rule, basketball was defensively-oriented, and "point-a-minute" teams (40 a game) were considered prolific scorers. Many of the best early teams were from New York—City College of New York, Fordham, Columbia, Long Island University, and St. John's University. In 1929-30, the "Wonder Five" of St. John's—four of whom were Jewish—held opponents to under twenty-one points a game. In its college career, the team used a controlled passing game to win eighty-six of ninety-four games.

In 1936, Stanford University played Long Island University in Madison Square Garden. Long Island, with its forty-three game consecutive win streak, was generally considered the best college team in the country. Stanford, which featured the one-handed shooting of Angelo "Hank" Luisetti, won 45-31. Luisetti scored fifteen points with his "unorthodox" one-handed shots and dazzled spectators with his behind-the-back passing and mid-air fakes. Luisetti scored fifty points in one game that year, and became a star in a game that previously featured teamwork and coaching strategy.

The one-hander eventually forced coaches to change their tactics. Because the favored two-hand set shot, with feet firmly on the floor, was easy to defend, coaches had devised elaborate weaves, and double and triple picks to free a shooter for the two-hander, which was often a dramatic moment in the game. The one-hander could be released quickly and seemed almost impossible to defend. Traditionalists feared it would destroy the patterned passing game, and coaches such as CCNY's Nat Holman sneered, "That's not basketball." But the one-hander grew ever more popular and contributed to the increase in scoring to a combined eighty points a game by the end of the decade.

Luisetti was not the first player to use the one-hand shot, but because he employed it in Madison Square Garden, and in such an important game, he captured the country's attention. The Long Island-Stanford game was part of series of double-headers at Madison Square Garden that pitted the best New York clubs against the top teams from across the country. By providing inter-sectional matches and spectator and media exposure, these double-headers, played before 18,000 fans, helped to transform college basketball into a national spectators' sport.

Edward "Ned" Irish was the driving force behind these games. According to Irish, the World-Telegram sent him to report on a local basketball game in 1929. When he arrived, there was such a crush of people waiting to get into the 500-seat gymnasium that he crawled through a window, tearing his pants, to watch the game. This lead him to ponder basketball's money-making possibilities. This potential was illustrated further by the success of New York's mayor, Jimmy Walker's benefit triple-header basketball games at Madison Square Garden for the Unemployment Relief Fund. In 1931 and 1932 these benefits attracted as many as of 15,000 spectators. Backed by the New

York Giants organization, Irish convinced Madison Square Garden officials to allow him to promote college basketball. In the first double-header in 1934 a standing-room only crowd watched Westminster beat St. John's and NYU down Notre Dame. Soon, the "Boy Promoter" was organizing a dozen double-headers, and in 1937-38, more than 250,000 watched basketball in Madison Square Garden.

These double-headers enabled the experts to compare teams from one region against another. The inauguration of the National Invitational Tournament (NIT) in 1938 and the NCAA national tournament the following year culminated in the crowning of a national champion. In the first NIT, which was sponsored by the Metropolitan Basketball Writers' Convention, only six teams were invited (Temple defeated Colorado in the championship game). Perhaps stung by the success of the NIT, by the sportswriters' attempt to usurp its powers, or angered by the number of good teams uninvited, the NCAA organized its own competition at Northwestern University in 1939. Oregon routed Ohio State in the final.

The growth of inter-sectional games during the decade required a common set of rules. As a result, rule changes characterized the decade. By 1937, most of basketball's 113 rules were either modified or formulated during the 1930s. Since many changes were revolutionary, coaches were soon either publishing instructional books or attending post-season seminars and clinics. Initially, the AAU, the YMCA, and the NCAA jointly established the rules, although each conference interpreted them to suit local styles of play. In 1936, the NCAA broke from the YMCA and the AAU and published its own rules for schools and colleges in the United States and Canada.

In 1930, big players tended to dominate the game. Following each basket and successful free throw the two centers lined up for a center jump. A team with the tallest center could often score repeated baskets without the opposition even getting a chance to score. During the play, tall players stood under the basketball where they could either block the opponent's shot above the rim or score themselves. In 1930, a 6 foot 5 inch player was rare, but by 1938 he was common. Since there was no time limit for shooting, games were low scoring and often boring. Rule changes throughout the decade sought to make the game more attractive.

The major changes included expanding from three to four time outs; allowing more substitutions and permitting them to immediately communicate with other players on the floor; dividing the court in half and requiring the ball to be advanced past mid-court within 10 seconds; forbidding players from standing in the foul lane with the ball for more than three consecutive seconds; penalizing players for touching the ball above the rim of the basket; allowing more personal fouls; reducing the circumference of the basketball by 2.5 inches and its weight by 2 ounces; and manufacturing an easier-to-handle laceless ball.

The most important rule change was the elimination of the center jump after every basket and successful foul shot. In December 1935, the southern division of the Pacific Coast Conference experimented with the elimination of the center jump. When the coaches of that conference reported that players and fans liked the new rule, that it increased actual playing time by from six to eight minutes, and that their players did not suffer undue strain, the 1937 National Basketball Coaches Conference voted 60 to 9 to eliminate the center jump. This was the beginning of "race horse basketball," what is now called "fast break basketball."

Lack of newspaper coverage and suitable gymnasiums retarded basketball's growth in Canada. Since youngsters did not take up basketball until high school, their hockey skills were far superior. Even so, basketball was a popular sport in Canada. By the end of the decade, Toronto Parks Playgrounds Basketball League had 123 teams and the Toronto and District Amateur Basketball Association comprised 213 teams. There were also church, YMCA, school, university and community leagues. In the Maritimes, basketball took second place only to hockey. New Brunswick teams, which competed in the United States, dominated the region. Acadia University in Nova Scotia experimented with placing the referee in the balcony. When the official wanted to stop play, he pressed a button which operated a whistle attached to a tank of compressed air and his assistant on the floor executed his orders. In such southern Alberta centers as Stirling, Magrath and Cardston, the Church of Latter Day Saints promoted basketball by organizing leagues and providing playing facilities. British Columbia dominated the national basketball scene, and the Canadian Amateur Basketball Association was pivotal in the growth of the game in Canada.

Professional basketball remained a minor sport during the decade. Numerous teams barnstormed around the country, often playing 175 or more games a year. As a promotional gimmick, a Jewish team, the House of David, all sported beards. A women's professional team, the All-American Red Heads, wore red wigs or dyed their hair red while competing against men's teams. The best barnstorming teams were the Original Celtics, the Rens, and the Harlem Globetrotters. At the initial "World Tournament," sponsored by the Chicago Herald-American in 1939, the Rens were victorious. The Globetrotters captured the title the following year.

Because of professional basketball's ethnic origins and working-class following, mainstream America tended to view professional basketball as slightly disreputable. Professional leagues suffered from a lack of good arenas, weak governing bodies, limited newspaper coverage, and unbalanced competition. Excluded from Madison Square Garden and many other large arenas, professional teams played in school gymnasiums, armories, and on theater stages. The American Basketball League (ABL), which folded after five years of play in 1931 and reopened in 1934, had franchises in New York, New Jersey, Philadelphia, Boston, Scranton, and Washington, D.C. The Midwest Basketball Conference—created in 1935 from a mixture of eighteen amateur and semiprofessional teams in the midwest—changed its name to the National Basketball League in 1937 to attract a wider audience. The NBL was largely a creation of the recreational directors of such large industrial companies as Goodyear, Firestone, Cleveland Midland, Wheeling Corrugated Steel, Pittsburgh Westinghouse, and Indianapolis U.S. Tire and Rubber. A few independents, such as the Buffalo Bisons and the Pittsburgh YMHA were also members. Small audiences and scheduling problems reduced the number of teams to eight in 1938.

The overwhelming majority of professional basketball players came from large urban cities (one-third were New Yorkers) and were of lower-class backgrounds. In terms of ethnicity, Jews, Germans, and Irish dominated. Race prejudice kept black teams from joining either professional league. Since salaries were low, most players held full-time jobs. Good college players could earn $5 a game for playing under an assumed name. The best teams were the Celtics, who played off and on during the decade, the Sphas, the Rens, and the Globetrotters. From 1932 to 1936, the Rens played 522 games against college, club, and YMCA teams and lost but forty-nine times. In one span of eighty-six days the Rens won eighty-eight matches.

Females also played basketball. In 1934, for instance, almost three-quarters of the high school girls in Des Moines, Iowa, stated that they liked it "very much." In addition to high school and college teams, women joined basketball teams sponsored by recreation centers, newspapers, municipalities, the YWCA, the Catholic Youth Organization, and various industries. A 1931 study of twenty-five industrial cities discovered that sixty-five different community organizations provided women's basketball. By 1936, an estimated one million females played basketball. Some companies were so competitive that they recruited employees based on their basketball talents rather than on their business skills. The Employers' Casualty Company in Dallas, for example, hired future Olympic and golf star Mildred "Babe" Didrikson to play basketball. Following her Olympic success in 1932, a promoter signed Didrikson to a $1,000 a month contract as the center piece in the barnstorming Babe Didrikson's All-Americans basketball team. Perhaps the best female player was Hazel Walker, who led her team to the AAU title in 1934 and was named an All-American eleven times. She played for several teams, including her own barnstorming Hazel Walker Arkansas Travelers.

There were three basic sets of rules for women's basketball. Colleges and many high schools used the Spalding Rules. These regulations divided the court into three separate areas, prescribed six players per team, restricted each player to her designated section of the court, and forbade players to keep possession of the ball for more than three seconds. As with men's rules, there were considerable discussion of and experimentation with the rules throughout the decade. In 1932, guarding was permitted on the vertical and the horizontal planes, thus making the game more skillful and exciting. All baskets from the field now earned two points. Six years later, the court was divided into two sections, and in 1939 players were permitted to reenter the game twice, rather than only once. The Spalding Rules were sanctioned by the National Section of Women's Athletics (NSWA), whose two guiding principles were avoidance of contact and undisputed possession of the ball once it was secured.

Philosophically, female physical educators rejected the male athletic model which gave priority to the best athletes and emphasized winning. Women, they believed, were psychologically and physically different from men. Male rules would endanger women's health and femininity, foster aggressive qualities, and cause nervous exhaustion. By confining women to a small section of the court, restricting the number of dribbles, and barring all physical contact while guarding, the Spalding Rules safeguarded the game for women. The elimination of male coaches and tournament play ensured that participation rather than winning was the goal.

As female educators gained control of women's college athletic programs, tournament play was replaced by play days and by non-competitive intramural games refereed by women. Women coaches replaced male coaches. Although fourteen high school state tournaments for girls were discontinued between 1931 and 1939 (some male coaches were quite happy to appropriate their funds), the campaign to suppress interscholastic girls' basketball was less successful. Small high schools, often lacking enough students for an intramural program, tended to favor interscholastic competitions. Basketball was also a popular game among students, their parents, and the community. A winning team brought publicity and a sense of identity to school and community. In Iowa, for example, women's competitive high school basketball flourished under male coaches and sponsors.

The AAU, which coordinated regional and national tournaments, promoted a different set of basketball rules. Also played by six players, the AAU court was divided into two, thus allowing more movement and active guarding. The difference between the two organizations is best illustrated by the women's uniforms. NSWA teams adopted bloomers with long stockings and middy blouses. AAU teams generally wore shiny, colored satin uniforms with high-cut pant legs similar to men's outfits. For added sex appeal, many AAU tournaments selected a beauty queen from among the players. The "lucky" women, who were nominated by their teammates, paraded before a panel of judges as part of the festival atmosphere of many tournaments. These beauty contests attracted sponsors and crowds, and helped verify the athletes' femininity. When the Employers' Casualty Company of Dallas adopted bright orange satin panties, the ensuing controversy increased attendance from 150 to 5,000.

Industrial teams usually played under men's rules with aggressive defense and high scoring. The greater attractiveness of these rules for spectators and players allowed the industrial leagues to withstand pressure from women educators who launched scathing media attacks on their male coaches and lobbied city officials and local businessmen to withdraw their sponsorship. The Chicago Evening American's annual basketball tournament regularly attracted more than 200 women's teams who played by men's rules. One of the best industrial teams was the Philadelphia Tribune Girls, which was sponsored by a black newspaper of the same name. Its leading player was tennis star Ora Washington, who became bored with winning her tennis matches so easily. Barred from AAU tournaments because of their color, the Tribune Girls played under boy's rules and captured eleven consecutive "Negro World Championships." The team toured the South in the winter and conducted basketball clinics.

The premier women's basketball team was the Edmonton Commercial Grads. From 1915 to 1940, the Grads lost only twenty of 522 games, including seven of nine from men's teams. In four Olympics they won all twenty-seven exhibition games, and in competitions for the Underwood International Trophy between Canada and the United States, the Grads took 114 of 120 matches from the best American teams and held the title from 1923 to 1940.

John Percy Page, the Grads' coach and ex-high school teacher for most of the women, emphasized physical fitness and the quick, short-passing game that employed a weave to free shooters. Unlike most teams, the Grads refused sponsorship and the players all worked as stenographers, bookkeepers, and sales clerks. Box office receipts paid the team's expenses. Page maintained such consistently stellar performances by developing a feeder system. At Page's McDougall Commercial High School the best players moved slowly through the school's junior to its senior teams, before joining the official feeder team, the Gradettes. Page insisted that his players all be "ladies first, athletes second"—which meant no smoking, drinking, and loud or vulgar language. The players were to be polite, respectful, discreet and sportsmanlike. Page replaced players by position, and in twenty-five years there were only thirty-eight Grads. The team disbanded in 1940 when the Royal Canadian Air Force appropriated the Edmonton Arena for the war. For several years, attendance was falling for lack of competition, and Page wanted to retire from coaching to pursue a political career.

## BASKETBALL—THE GAME THAT HAS EVERYTHING

[*The 1936 Olympics stimulated basketball's growth. The YMCA, the AAU, and college teams each conducted qualifying elimination tournaments for these Games. The final tournament consisted of the winning YMCA team, the winner and runner-up teams in the annual AAU championship, and the best five college teams based upon region. The American Olympic team included the seven men from the winning team, five from the runner-up team, and one each from the third and fourth placed teams. This article documents the growth of college and professional basketball during the decade. Yankee Stade, "It's Basketball Now—The Game that Has Everything," Liberty (5 November 1938), 37-38.*]

"Baseball is the only **real** ball game," the baseball fan said. "You can't deny that."

"I do deny it."

Then we were off.

What **is** the most important game?

Soccer football is—in more nations than any other game. And cricket is in some. And baseball, according to sports writers, is in some. But, as Mr. Roosevelt is so fond of saying, they are "thinking in the past."

Don't be misled by the big baseball-attendance figures in less than half a dozen big cities. The rest of the major-league clubs are dying at the turnstiles. Most minor leagues would disband tomorrow if it weren't for financial first aid from the few moneyed majors. College baseball incurs an annual deficit of $250,000. And don't take my word for it.

Ask the man whose business it is to sell bats and balls, mitts and masks. He knows. Ask the baseball magnates themselves.... Baseball schools, movies, pep talks, exhibition games in small towns, free admission for school children, radio interviews with stars, subsidies to semi-pro and semi-amateur outfits—all have been tried without any appreciable increase in the number of people who play the game, as distinguished from big-city crowds that just watch it.

**Meanwhile, between now and spring, 80,000,000 Americans will watch 60,000 teams play 1,500,000 games of basketball.**

On the attendance side, this is 30,000,000 more than see baseball games, 40,000,000 more than see football games, 50,000,000 more than see horse races or boxing matches.

This in spite of the fact that most basketball games are played in school, college, and Y gyms, where fans have to ease themselves in between the punching bag and the rowing machine and sit on the parallel bars.

In auditoriums where there are seats by the thousand, thousands fill them. In Indiana, where the game is hottest, crowds of 7,500 frequently converge on villages of 750. In New York, where basketball is just getting established, crowds of 15,000 to 18,000 in Madison Square Garden are the rule.

If the time comes when the game is played under floodlights in baseball stadia, the late Abner Doubleday, founder of baseball, will emerge from his dugout and throw away his bat. By the same token, if the game is regularly played in all movie theatres between features—as it already is played in some—show business will enjoy one of its biggest years.

Where basketball has it all over its rival games, however, is in the number of people who play it. Sixty thousand teams are rated good enough to play in public exhibitions. How many more teams there must be that play privately for their own amusement—and how many more unattached individuals who pick up an hour or two at the baskets, just as the golfer or the tennis player picks up a game on the fairways or the courts!

It is safe to say that the number of people who actually play basketball outstrips the number of people who play any other game in the U.S.—the home of baseball—by at least three to one.

Basketball's climb to the popularity tops would seem to be based chiefly on the fun that is inherent in the sport itself. This goes for players and spectators both.

Basketball has everything: the sharp physical contact of football and the prize ring, the mental and manual coordination of baseball, the intricate beauty of ice hockey, and the exciting speed of the horse race.

The last-named quality stands out.

"Heaving Hank" Luisetti, the "Slinging Sammy" Baugh of intercollegiate basketball—who hails from San Francisco—frequently scores a point a minute; in one game he made twenty-four points in exactly eleven minutes.

Not much chance for boredom, for players or watchers, in a game that goes as fast as that!

The conclusion is inescapable that more people play basketball, and more people pay to see it played, because they get more enjoyment out of it than they do out of any other athletic pastime. In short, basketball is the **real** ball game. [Section on early history deleted.]

The first national regulatory body, the Basketball Rules Committee, came into existence in 1934 and promulgated the national rules which are now universally accepted in the U.S. Since then the growth of the game has been phenomenal. Last year ninety-six per cent of all schools and colleges were playing basketball, and leagues, both professional and amateur, were operating all over the country.

Recognition of basketball by the general public, however, has been delayed until recently by the lack of seating capacity already referred to.

But all this is rapidly changing. The Big Ten colleges of the Middle West now have large arenas constructed especially for basketball. In the East, Pennsylvania built its Palestra; in the West, Leland Stanford built its Cracker Box.

Important games attracted important crowds. The press gave it space. Basketballitis became an epidemic. Personalities began to emerge.

There had long been successful and colorful coaches; but until uniform rules made intersectional contests possible their fame reached only limited areas. Finally, at the University of Nebraska, where Pop Naismith had gone as Professor of Physical Education, a great basketball mentor of national repute, "Phog" Allen, emerged as a trainer not only of players, but of coaches; and in 1930 one of his pupils, John Bunn, migrated to California, where, as basketball coach at Stanford, he became the game's best known figure.

Bunn's most notable contribution to basketball is the jumpless game. Instead of bringing the ball out to the center after each goal and tossing it up in the air for what is known as the "center jump," Bunn gives the ball at once to the team that has just been scored on for a toss-out from under its own goal.

This change adds even more speed to the game and between six and seven minutes of playing time. Also, it reduces the advantage that the tall player has always had over the short player. The jumpless game is now in the national rules.

The big U.S. universities are at last wise to the importance of the game from a financial standpoint. In most colleges basketball is the only sport besides football which pays for itself.

As the game increases in general public interest our shrewd graduate managers appreciate more and more the value of colorful personalities to draw a big gate. Already they are scouting the high schools and academies for players who are not poison at the box office.

In 1934 a new fillip was given to the intercollegiate game by a young New York sports writer named Ned Irish, who began promoting intercollegiate matches in Madison Square Garden. From the very first game, this professional promotion of an amateur sport proved itself a huge success.

To be sure, the game still suffers, as does football from the absence of a real world's series to determine the national championship. Such synthetic attempts as have been made to determine the champion team have only increased the confusion. Last year, for instance, Duke won the Southern, Dartmouth the Eastern, Purdue the Western, and Stanford the Pacific Coast Conference titles; yet the tentative effort at a world's series, staged by the Metropolitan Basketball Writers' Association in New York, did not bring any of these leading teams together.

All we know for sure is that skill in the game, like interest in it, seems to be very evenly distributed.

In the larger cities public-school athletic leagues, Catholic Youth Organizations, the Y's, and many Protestant churches support basketball fives and conduct tournaments.

So-called commercial and industrial leagues also flourish in the metropolitan areas. And as I write, politicians and retail liquor dealers are also going in heavily for the basketball-sponsoring game. Popular, too, are the intercity leagues composed of teams manned by outstanding ex-college players.

Avowedly professional clubs and leagues are also springing up in increasing numbers every year. For example, there is the American Professional Basketball League, which embraces principal cities in the East and Middle West.

Good players in the league sometimes earn as high as $1,500 a month, which may not compare with the top baseball salaries, but is not bad for a five-or six-months season.

As a result, the pro game is attracting more and more young college grads who are all dressed up and have no place to go.

On the whole, however, professional basketball is still in the barnstorming stage. Freak teams like the bewhiskered House of David, the Roller-Bearing Flashes (who play the game on roller skates), and the Harlem Hottentots perform to sell-out houses in competition with locally known fives.

The team captained by Jesse Owens, the Olympic champion, has cleaned up as a sort of olio between features in the movie houses.

Professional basketball offers a longer season than pro football does, and in the end should provide a larger income. Also, since it is played at night, the game enables its players to engage in business of their own during the day.

Another great advantage which the court game has over both baseball and football is the very general participation in it of women. Basketball is a strenuous game. But its strenuousness is of the quick-strength rather than the brute-strength variety. Quickness and resourcefulness are prime requisites. Into such a picture the woman athlete fits like a silk stocking.

In high schools the girls' basketball teams are almost as many and as popular as the boys'. In co-ed colleges the same situation prevails. And in colleges exclusively for women basketball is **the** major sport.

What the basketball craze, with its high entertainment value, its appeal to women, and its after-dark playing schedule, will do to the movies these winter nights, nobody can rightly tell.

With the development of floodlighted open-air arenas, basketball is also sure to cut into big-league baseball's summer take, because, although a game of vast activity, it can be played to advantage outdoors on the hottest evenings—and will be so played, I prophesy, within the next two years.

Then indeed basketball will have fulfilled its destiny. It will be **the** ball game, played by both men and women, appealing to both men and women spectators, enjoyed North and South, East and West, indoors or outdoors, all the year round!

## INDIANA MADNESS

[*In 1936, Time magazine estimated that 100 of the top 500 college basketball players came from Indiana. This article articulates the extent of Hoosier madness in the 1930s. Kyle Crichton, "Indiana Madness," Collier's (6 February 1937), 13, 38.*]

The state of Indiana is nuts. Politically it has always been slightly on the wacky side, but in that respect it has lots of competition. Where the matter shows now is on the subject of basketball, which has been made a state religion....

"The fathers watch their children in the cradles," a man told me later in Indianapolis. "The first time the kids lift their hands, they find a basketball in them. It may be a dirty trick but it turns out some swell forwards."

The colleges are strong in Indiana—with Purdue and Indiana University sharing the conference title last year, and with Notre Dame, De Pauw, Franklin, Butler, Wabash and Earlham having fine teams every year—but the real excitement comes in the high schools.

The Indiana High School Athletic Association—dubbed the Kingdom of Ihsaa by Bill Fox of the Indianapolis News—has 805 members and each has a basketball team. Since there are no classes (A, B and C classes as in other states), even the smallest teams have a chance for the state championship and often win it. In the old days, Wingate, with a population of 400, won the state title twice. In late years Montmorenci, with a population of 360, reached the finals. The largest city ever to win it was Muncie, with a population of about 46,000. No Indianapolis high school has ever won it and only one has been runner-up.

### THE STATE OF BIG GYMS

The seating capacities of Indian high-school auditoriums are beyond belief. When it is realized that the Palestra at the University of Pennsylvania seats 7,500 and is by far the largest college hall in the East and that the usual college auditorium capacity is about 1,500, one will get some notion of Indiana when it is learned that the town of Martinsville with a population of 5,000 has a hall seating 5,000; Muncie has a hall seating 7,000; and Vincennes can take care of 6,500. There are literally dozens of communities where the high-school gym seats more than the population of the town. Halls seating 2,000 and 3,000 are common.

The desire to win is so great that the luring and capture of high-school athletes has become a great problem for the association. Since it's against the rules for a boy to live in one town and play in another, they arrange that little matter by transporting the whole family.

There was a fine young player in a junior high-school team and several of the coaches saw him, they were telling me at Lafayette. His father drove a gasoline tank wagon and had no objection to a better job. One town offered him a job paying $125 a month and just when he was going to take that another offered him $150. The old man has the job and the boy is on the team.

A pitiful scene was enacted at the state finals of 1935 when Jeffersonville lost to Anderson in the last game. By some quirk no undefeated team has ever won the state championship. Jeffersonville had gone through the season victorious and the town was quite insane. When the crash came, the pistol fired, the game over...Anderson champion...Jeffersonville licked for the first time...The Jeffersonville fans stood stock-still with tears streaming down their cheeks, men, women and children sobbing as if they had lost a loved one. It rather epitomized Indiana basketball.

If there is proselyting [sic], there is also good common sense. Back in 1920-21-22, Griz Wagner's team at Franklin won the championship three times in a row. Since the boys were all entering Franklin college after graduation, the simplest thing was for Griz to go along, which he did. From being Franklin High School coach, he became Franklin College coach and the team went merrily ahead with its winning.

If there was ever need to worry about vital statistics in Indiana, the problem is simplified now. The age limit for high-school athletes is 20 and charges and countercharges fly thick around tournament time. It's a period for birth certificates, affidavits and sworn testimony.

An attempt is being made now to build up football as a high-school sport and ninety teams were engaged in it last year, but the state is still basketball heaven. The kids may be seen all summer long taking pot shots at a basket hung up in the back yard and many coaches have summer practice, and training twelve months in the year. The high-school season is limited to twenty games, starting November 1st. After that come the sectional tournaments, the regional tournaments, the semifinals and the finals. The semifinals are a development of last year, prompted both by an outcry which sought to limit basketball by state law and by the desire to allow more people to see the championships. In the old days the finals brought sixteen teams to the Butler Field House in Indianapolis (seating 14,833), but that didn't begin to meet the demand for tickets. It is estimated that 40,000 tickets could have been sold every tournament. As it stands, the general public is out of luck, the allotment to schools using up the supply. An additional 22,000 were accommodated last year by the four semifinal tournaments, with the final getting its usual quota of 14,833....

Around tournament time the furor is transcendental. The winning team in the championship will at the very least receive gold watches from the home-town patriots, and there have been instances where the winning players have each received an automobile as a memento of the great occasion. The rewards have ranged from that down through the gold watches to the sweaters and the usual gold basketballs, and it doesn't necessarily mean that the team has reached the state finals. Winning of the regional or sectional honors can do it.

## COLLEGE HUNTING GROUNDS

There is no question that Indiana turns out fine players. The state tournament is attended by college scouts from all over the Middle West, and the offers start coming for the players. Most of the young men prefer to stay in Indiana if they can manage it.

"The publicity is great," say the sports writers. "Why shouldn't they want to stay home where they're sure they'll be famous?"

On a checkup through the state it was found that an all-time Indiana high-school team would include such men as Johnny Wooden, formerly of Martinsville and Purdue, who is accounted the best of all. Bob Kessler of Anderson and Purdue was the freak shot who finished his college career last year with high scoring records. He was a left-hander who got his best results by hooking in a field goal while faced away from the basket. Stretch Murphy was the first of the extraordinarily tall centers, which are now a part of all successful teams. His career at Purdue was sensational. Among the new men Johnny Townsend, formerly of Indianapolis and now of Michigan, is topnotch.

"The best player I ever saw," pronounces Piggy Lambert of Purdue and utters a sigh of disappointment over having lost him for the old Alma Mater.

The best comparison of Indiana basketball with the rest of the country was given by Bill Fox of the Indianapolis News: "The best team of Indiana would find plenty of competition with the best team of any other state. The few best top teams would have the same trouble. But if you had twenty Indiana high-school teams playing twenty from any other state, or if you had forty teams playing, I think that the percentage on the side of Indiana would grow with every game added to the list. In short, the average quality of play will be higher in Indiana."

The game is raging all over the country, however, and I don't want to get into that argument. That's the Indiana story and until somebody can call them on it, the dispute can rage. I heard of great basketball teams in Iowa and Illinois, and Pennsylvania always had them. Back in the days of the Chicago Interscholastic Championship, some school in Colorado with a student body of nine boys and eleven girls was always coming down to the Stagg contest and making jokes out of the rest of the country. One year it was a mountaineer team from Kentucky which played out of doors at home and got their first basketball shoes when coming to Chicago. So it isn't well to be too cocky about the matter,

Without a doubt Indiana takes all records for number of contestants and ferocity of the competition. Somebody was telling me out there about a victory celebration which consisted in burning down a business block in the middle of town, but that is probably exaggerated. Mr. Trester, the commissioner, estimated a total of 9,372 players in last year's tournaments, which means that there were 781 teams of twelve players each. There were 64 sectional tournaments, 16 regionals, 4 semifinals and a final. It required a month for that competition to be run off and the papers were so full of it the Duke of Windsor was certainly fortunate in getting himself abdicated at another season. Otherwise Indiana would never have heard of it.

**HEARTBROKEN STEVE**

I missed the Frankfort-Logansport game, which was the hottest thing of the early season, with all seats sold a week before the game and reservations coming from as far away as Crawfordsville and Vincennes (150 miles), but I managed to get a glance at Frankfort against Lebanon. It was a walkaway for Frankfort but for an outsider the sight was astonishing. There may be spirit like that in other states but it couldn't be any higher. The score was 40-17 but for a time one would have thought the championship of the world was being fought out in the little Indiana town of Lebanon....

## WANTED. A COMMON CODE FOR BASKETBALL

[*In his 1931 presidential address to the assembled basketball coaches, L.P. Andreas of Syracuse University noted that hockey was a better spectator sport than basketball because it provided more excitement, and called upon his peers to put more action into the game. Earlier, a poll of college basketball coaches revealed that while seventy-five of 122 coaches thought that stalling was "smart basketball," a slim majority wanted stalling controlled. Two years later, teams were required to advance the ball across mid-court within ten seconds to put an end to stalling tactics. Other rule changes in 1933 eliminated the center jump after a successful free throw, and forbade offensive players from standing in the foul lane with the ball for three seconds or more. The latter change was made after the coaches screened a movie of violent lane violations at a rules' meeting. In 1936 the three-second rule was applied to offensive players not in possession of the ball. These changes led to faster-paced games with more passing.*

*The following document argued the case for more action and called for a uniform set of rules across the country. Although many people believed that the center jump after every basket should be eliminated to speed play, coaches generally opposed such a change. A 1931 survey of selected college coaches, for example, found that only nineteen of 116 coaches favored eliminating the center jump. Its supporters claimed the center jump provided drama, kept the game from becoming too strenuous for the players, and it was unfair to give up the ball in such a way. Gradually, feelings changed. Spectators wanted to see the losing team have a chance of rallying and disliked the fact that tall players dominated the game. The most important reason for the elimination of the center jump in 1937 was it might attract more spectators.*

*Researchers for The Athletic Journal put pedometers on a group of college players in 1931 and 1938. With the center jump, players averaged between two and three miles a game. Without the tip off, they averaged almost 4 miles a game. Stanley B. Frank, "Wanted. A Common Code for Basketball," The Literary Digest (15 December 1934), 42.*]

According to the strict letter of the rules, college basketball is essentially a non-contact game. Purist New England keeps as closely to theory as is humanly possible, and plays a game which is as lusty as touch-football. The South gives its young men more latitude in the business of hand-to-hand fighting, with a resultant quickening of the pace and spectator interest. The East, with the exception of the New England fundamentalists, interprets the rules with exuberant and enthusiastic reading between the lines, and probably plays the soundest basketball technically, certainly the fastest and most imaginative.

The Middle West and Far West place more emphasis on the physical aspects of the game, and sometimes come up with a pretty fair imitation of a water-front brawl.

There is a bird's-eye view of a game which probably is played by more people in the United States than any other sport, one which should be truly national in scope and one which, nevertheless, has developed as many sectional styles of play as there are characteristic idioms of speech.

### CRASHING MID-WESTERN GAME

Discrepancies making for varying styles of play spring from the interpretation of the code by working officials. The Middle West, for instance, says that basketball can and should be a rousing game involving crashing body-contact. Maybe it is right; the fans seem to like hell-for-leather tactics best. Crowds of 13,000 are not uncommon in the Big Ten Conference; New England, the cradle of the game, considers 1,000 a large attendance.

Bad feeling and impassioned oratory follow in the wake of intersectional contests, which rarely are fair tests of relative team-ability. All other factors being equal, the home team invariably will win because the visitors' attack is ruined by whistle-blowing, or their defense is riddled by tactics which they have been taught are gross violations.

A case in point: The University of Pittsburgh, always a high-ranking team, geographically belongs to the East, but plays typical Mid-Western basketball. Coach "Doc" Carlson's offense is based upon the use of screening—"pick-off," or block plays, as they are technically known. Pitt in its best years, has gone to New York and frequently has been given terrific battles by subnormal metropolitan teams, because local officials regard the pick-off as illegal. Conversely, a New York team makes an overnight jump to Pittsburgh, and considers itself lucky if it comes back in one piece, after absorbing severe body-punishment from the pick-offs featured by Pitt.

To repeat: Basketball is a non-contact game theoretically, but the rules agree that "it is obvious that personal contact can not be avoided entirely when ten players are moving with great rapidity over a limited playing space."

The number of basketball teams in operation throughout the country exceeds by far the combined total of organized football, baseball and hockey teams. And, perversely enough, the game's enormous popularity is one of the obstacles in the path of standardization. Three coaches, who teach different styles of play, exert a profound influence on every young basketball player at some time or other.

In the East, the head man is Nat Holman, coach at the College of the City of New York and the most dominant personality the game has ever known. He combines the talents and showmanship of Babe Ruth and the late Knute Rockne in the playing and coaching fields. He stresses the short-passing, fast-breaking offense most Eastern teams use. Dr. Walter Meanwell, of Wisconsin, has the largest following in the Big Ten and Middle West. Phog Allen of Kansas is the leader in the Big Six; his sphere of influence is wide-spread.

These three men have confined their coaching to their respective sections; they have not done the missionary work seen in football. Amos Alonzo Stagg and Fielding Yost, originally from the East, spread the gridiron gospel in the Middle West. John Heisman of Pennsylvania was a pioneer in the South. "Pop" Warner, Cornell '96, and Howard Jones, a Yale man, made the Far West the football power it is to-day. Basketball has never known such a common groundwork in coaching theory.

The rules, which lend themselves to all sorts of interpretations, can be blamed for contributing toward the division along sectional lines. The chief source of trouble seems to come from the fact that the code is worded negatively: It tells what a player shall NOT do rather than defines his legal rights in unequivocal terms.

Basketball is a game of swiftly changing situations. The action is so fast and spontaneous that individual players are largely motivated by instinctive reactions to conditions as they develop. When a referee is told he must be guided by "the apparent intent of the players," confusion is inevitable. Referees are not psychic.

**SPECTATOR DEMANDS ACTION**

The spectator definitely likes to see fast action. Just how much is the question. Last year, for instance, in a game between Notre Dame and Purdue, the huge number of fifty-two fouls was called; obviously too much whistle-blowing. Yet, if the harassed referee had not cracked down on the boys a fine Donnybrook would have followed in the natural course of events.

If the basketball bigwigs ever decide to choose arbitrarily the most satisfying and fastest version of basketball, it seems that the Eastern game would be the happiest basis for compromise. It is a significant fact that when college men started to play professionally, the Eastern stars made good in the American League—which gracefully died in 1930—while the men from Western schools found the pace too fast and tricky. The Original Celtics, unanimously conceded to be the best team basketball has ever known, was composed entirely of men who lived and learned the game in New York.

The trend to-day in basketball seems to be toward the elimination of the purely physical elements in the game with the purpose of giving fuller expression to imagination and technical skill. The Southern division of the Pacific Coast Conference will experiment this winter with the elimination of the center tap, which gives the tall man an advantage he may not deserve. The three-second rule on the pivot play also has the same idea behind it. The circumference of the ball, once thirty and one-half to thirty-one and one-half inches, has been reduced to twenty-nine and one-half inches to facilitate ball handling and passing, the basis of basketball.

Industry protests against a compulsory code. Basketball cries for regimentation. There is prestige—and money—to be made if a standard code can be evolved. Here is one infant industry which would welcome the removal of sectional suspicions and the introduction of strenuous cracking-down from people in the driver's seat.

## HEALTH ASPECTS OF WOMEN'S BASKETBALL

*[Many men agreed with the philosophy of the NSWA. In a much quoted article, sportswriter John Tunis described a girls' basketball game in which the players "pulled hair, hit one another viciously in the ribs with sharp elbows, tripped one another, tore one another's clothing, in fact did everything but play basketball." By the end of the decade, the NSWA successfully convinced most colleges to require medical exams for all female basketball players. The NSWA also created a committee to set standards for*

*referees and pressured female basketball leagues to employ these officials. The NSWA
was less successful outside college ball. In the following article, Marjorie Bateman,
Director of Physical Education for Women at Keene Teachers College, New Hampshire, outlined the NSWA's philosophy. "Health Aspects of Girls' Basketball," Mind and
Body: A Monthly Journal of Physical Education (April 1936), 21-24.]*

Every night during the basketball season for girls, onto hundreds of courts throughout the country, they come running, these slender, attractive young girls—sure footed
and graceful. Their faces glow; their eyes are radiant. They smile good-naturedly at
their opponents. The audience greets them enthusiastically. The game starts. The players leap, pivot, turn in the air with the ease, swiftness and grace of Russian dancers.
The ball snaps back and forth; bounces across the floor; twirls through the air and drops
into the basket. The crowd cheers wildly. The game goes on, through a quarter, and
then a half. Almost imperceptibly, the game changes. It is no more a ballet but a battle.
The players are now crouching, legs apart, bodies tense ready to leap in any direction.
Their eyes shift quickly from ball to opponent. A rush after the ball—two bodies crash
in mid-air and tumble to the floor. The radiance in their eyes has changed to an almost
insane glitter. The good-natured smiles are gone; faces are strained; sweat runs down
into the players' eyes; mouths are half open, gasping for breath. It is a fight, and from
the faces of the combatants, one would judge it to be a desperate fight with the stakes
high.

But a more important fight in girls' basketball is being waged, not on the courts,
but in doctors' and principals' offices, at educational conferences, and in the homes.
Should girls play basketball—is it harmful or beneficial? The "pros" say: "splendid
game for the development of health and character"—"basketball calls forth the best,
physically, emotionally and mentally, in a girl"—"in keeping training rules the girls acquire habits of hygienic living which will be of great value throughout life"—"basketball trains girls for the give and take of life."

The "antis" maintain "basketball, the sacrifice of the maidens"—"the slaughter of
the innocents,"—"one of the most atrocious crimes committed in the name of education." And there are well informed, intelligent people on both sides!

The spectator is inclined to agree with the "pros." He has watched the home team
through quite a few seasons. They're a healthy enough lot. Most of them rarely miss
a game out of the twenty or thirty played during the season. Of course, they're dead
tired at the end of a strenuous game and a few are pretty well worn out by the end of
the season. But it doesn't seem to hurt them. They keep training rules religiously; no
tea, coffee, cigarettes, pastry or late hours. Plenty of vigorous activity and clean, wholesome living—of course basketball is good for a girl. If some of these high school and
college girls who run around to late parties and dances, smoking and drinking, would
go out for basketball, they'd be a lot better off. And so the argument goes.

But what are the facts? What do authorities say on the subject? During the last ten
years the Women's Division of the National Amateur Athletic Federation has been
making extensive studies and surveys of girls' basketball—the rules used, the type of
physical examinations required, the number and length of practice periods, the number of games played during a season—to discover how basketball affects the health,
emotional stability and character of the girl. The studies were made by directors of

The whistle! They're off! The Edmonton Commercial Grads—World's Champions of All Champions in the history of competitive sports—sweep down the floor like a rippling chain of red lightning. And a crowd of thousands of fans bulges the Arena with roar after roar.

These nimble-footed sharpshooters are opposed by one of the most brilliant aggregations in basketball—the Tulsa, Oklahoma, Stenographers, the cream of all sharpshooters south of the international border.

The Grad are fighting hard, with all their skill, speed and determination. They want this game. It is the third in a best-three-out-of-five series for the international title and the Underwood trophy. The Grads want it out of a sheer love of good, clean sport and out of loyalty to that master mind, their coach, J. Percy Page.

The very roars of the crowd give answer to the question of whether or not a team of women athletes can deliver a brand of play which will satisfy fans who are used only to the very best. For many years, in many parts of the world, the Grads have adequately settled this question in the minds of sports lovers. Their fiendishness of attack, their ever-burning speed, their skill, and their utter sportsmanship have won for them a lasting spot in the hearts of countless fans.

In this series the Grads have perhaps the greatest handicap in all the years of their successful career. On the very eve of the series one of their star players has been seriously injured—Miss Mabel Munton, run down by a car. It has been a great shock. Miss Munton is a splendid guard.

Tulsa outweighs the Edmonton champs by an average of fifteen pounds, and outreaches them by an average of two inches. The Grads are fighting with their backs to the wall. The Tulsans want this game too—for they know that if they take it they stand a strong chance of annexing the next two and the series.

But the champions have that indomitable spirit which has brought them to the niche of fame. They likewise have on the side lines perhaps the greatest coach and trainer in the history of competitive sports—J. Percy Page.

When interviewed recently, Mr. Page spoke most modestly of his part in the Grads' successes.

"You see, it's like this," he said. "Odds seem to offer us a stimulant which brings out the best that is in us. When the Grads are up against the heaviest form of odds, they seem to have a reserve of fighting spirit and skill that is all the product of close co-operation, and friendly understanding throughout all the years of school and sports training."

In the first two games of this series the Grads just edged out wins. The third is the most critical game, for the weight and reach of the Tulsans is beginning to tell. Coach Page nods to a slender girl on the side lines—Noel MacDonald, the "rookie" member of the team, who is alternating with Miss Fry at center. Facing them is Miss Williams, the pivot of the Tulsans, an amazingly fast runner and deadly shot.

At the halfway mark the game is tied, with Tulsa turning on every atom of pressure. Miss MacDonald takes the floor and immediately opens a sizzling Grads attack. Noel whips the ball to Margaret MacBurney, who ducks the Tulsa guards and pivots, lacing a whirring pass to Doris Neale. Doris dribbles the ball a few paces, outfoxes a rushing Tulsan, tosses a pass over her head, which is caught by Noel, the brilliant rookie. Then follows a spectacle which brings the crowd to its feet. From nearly center floor this sparkling young member of the champs' team poises for the shot. It seems impossible that the ball can find that narrow basket from so far out when shot from such an angle. It drops—a magnificent field basket—to put the Grads two points ahead.

But Miss Williams of Tulsa strikes hard in a counterattack that seems no less brilliant than the Grads have staged. Again the score board teeters on an even balance. Again the Grads blaze through with a couple of baskets. There is no let-up to the speed of these girls.

Now Tulsa leads by four points! Radio announcers have lost their voices. The tongues of the crowd begin to lick lips parched with sheer excitement and expectancy. The clock is swiftly tolling off precious minutes. Gladys Fry, smiling regular center of the Grads, is forcing the play. Tulsa strikes back. The battle is ding-dong, highlighted by most amazing plays.

Coach Page glances quietly at the clock. He nods to Miss MacDonald, the rookie. The psychological second has come. The Tulsa star and her flashy associates have been pressing and have been pressed to the limit of physical endurance when Coach Page whips in the rookie of his team. Once more there is a sudden spurt of red. The Grads are away. Frantically the Tulsans attempt to break up the attack. But there is no breaking it.

In that terrible, dazzling combination attack the champs burn up the floor. The score is tied.

Miss Williams and Miss Walker, an aggregate of 295 pounds of physical fitness, lead a fierce attack. A referee is swept from the floor. But at the Grads' basket Doris Neale and Helen Stone come into the play with their unmatched checking. The ball whips to a Grads forward—MacBurney, who streaks for the Tulsa goal, only to pivot and whir a pass across to Noel MacDonald.

A breathless crowd sways, and then from thousands of throats bursts that avalanche of sound which marks the third straight win for the champs. What a win! What a series! Final score: Grads 48; Tulsa 41. In a blaze of glory the Grads have won for the twelfth consecutive time the international championship.

Thus was notched up for the Grads their 392d official game in defense of their many trophies and titles—and their 382d win. What a record for sports statisticians to chalk up in their books!

The Grads basketball team was first organized twenty years ago by Mr. Page, who is principal of the school at which the players have received their business training. But they begin their basketball training only after they are graduated from this school, the Edmonton Commercial High School. Meanwhile they commence to play when they first enter school, under Mr. Page's direction. There are, in all, four teams connected with the school. The fourth or senior team is known as the Gradettes, a brilliant aggregation of champions in their own right. From this team, coached by W. "Bill" Tait, operating under the general supervision of Mr. Page, the Grads find plenty of excellent material for their front string.

In 1915 they annexed their first title, the Alberta Provincial Championship, which they have retained, with the exception of one year—1920—for twenty years.

In 1922 the champs wrested the Dominion championship from the London, Ontario, Shamrocks. Since that time—thirteen consecutive years—they have successfully defended this title against all comers.

In 1923 the Grads met the famous Cleveland Favorite-Knits, claimants of the world's championship. They defeated Cleveland two games in a two-game series. On this occasion the Edmonton sharpshooters received, for the first time in its history, the Underwood trophy, and so cinched the international championship. Since then the Grads have played for, and won, this trophy against the cream of all basketball teams from the south of the international line.

Here are one or two pertinent questions put recently, with Mr. Page's answers.

QUESTION: Just how important is the application of psychology on your part in the training and coaching of the Grads? To what extent, if at all, is strict discipline necessary in the training and maintenance of your teams?

MR. PAGE: From the very commencement of the girls' associations with me as the supervisor of their school studies and their basketball activities, I seek to win their respect. I accept them as members of my own family and treat them as such, expecting them to give to me that respect and confidence and loyalty they would give in their own homes. We are therefore a large family, all growing up together in an understanding, loyalty, and friendship that completely does away with the necessity for any rigid form of discipline. The girls know exactly what I expect of them. They know that to stay with the family they must at all times so conduct themselves as to reflect credit on the whole. Any difficulties arising, and there have been extremely few, have been completely ironed out before they reached any serious proportions.

I place no restrictions on the girls' movements. At home or abroad, in the matters of diet, conduct, recreational diversion and so forth, there have never been any misunderstandings. In all my experience with the Grads I have never known a single member to smoke. Not that I have ever said, 'Don't!' My advice has been, at all times, to remember that as world's champions it is up to them to be ever conscious of the honor which is theirs. But they are not treated as small children, but as sensible grown-up members of my own family. I am happy to say that I number them all, past and present, among the very best friends I have ever had."

Off the basketball floor these champions are all hard-working business girls, stenographers in almost every case. They are perhaps the most strictly amateur organization in the whole world.

Let me give you a peep at each one of them. Miss Millie McCormack, once star flash with the front-string Grads and now official scorer, helped me meet them. I pass on Millie's introductions.

MARGARET MACBURNEY: Present captain of the team and world champion free-throw sharpshooter. Margaret scored sixty-one consecutive penalty shots to annex the above title. She has played nine years, scoring an average of 13.4 points a game. She is engaged full time as a stenographer in an Edmonton office. Is a good swimmer and an ace bowler.

GLADYS FRY: Genial center, who packs a permanent smile together with a wicked sizzling shot. Miss Fry is a graduate of Alberta University and is now a member of the university staff. She is a keen tennis player.

DORIS NEALE: One of the most dependable of the front-string Grads players; a guard who stops them. Doris can shoot with the best. She swims like a mermaid. Is employed as a stenographer by an Edmonton radio station.

ELSIE BENNIE: A former skipper of the Grads, one of the best known players, a guard. Elsie is employed as a stenographer at the Edmonton civic offices. She is an expert bowler and ice curler.

BABE BELANGER: Vivacious little brunette, one of the classiest little forwards ever seen in the game. Babe is also a stenographer in Edmonton.

HELEN STONE: A guard. She has a twin sister, EDITH, playing with her on the team. Both are stenographers. Edith plays at substitute forward position, and if you can tell them apart, go ahead.

MABEL MUNTON: One of the stanchest [sic] guards the Grads have ever had. Mabel is also a stenographer.

NOEL MACDONALD is the youngest member in point of service and the "hero" of the Tulsa-Grads games. Noel is one of the tallest members of the team; is still going to school, and when not playing basketball is a member of a topnotch baseball organization.

EVELYN COULSON and JESSIE INNES are two smart little ladies who complete the playing complement of the champs' team. Both have given some wonderful perfor- mances as alternates. Both are stenographers with city firms.

Mrs. J. Percy Page, wife of the coach, acts as chaperon to the team away from home.

On three different occasions the Grads have visited the Olympic Games—at Paris in 1924, at Amsterdam in 1928, and at Los Angeles in 1932. Unfortunately, basketball was not a competitive sport event at any of these games. But in both 1924 and 1928 a series of games, comprising fifteen contests in European centers, was arranged by the Federation Sportive Internationale, the world-wide governing body of women's athlet- ics. The Grads won all fifteen contests by overwhelming margins and were awarded the coveted title of World's Champions.

In all, the Grads have traveled well over 77,000 miles in defense of their many championship titles, visiting Paris, Lyon, Luxembourg, Strasbourg, Milan, Roubaix, and other European cities, and Cleveland, Detroit, Chicago, Windsor, Toronto, Winnipeg, Vancouver, and other points.

At one time they chalked up a record of seventy-eight consecutive wins in official contests.

I asked Mr. Page to recount the most thrilling high lights in their history. Listen in:

"We are back a few years, at Chicago, playing the worthy Taylor-Trunks," he said. "With but five minutes to go we are six points down. I nod to the team. The girls know what is wanted. We have our backs dead to the wall when I pass the signal to call on that last ounce of fighting reserve. We haven't even thought of a loss."

He pauses, his eyes dancing. "We pull out of that game five points to the good. And, then in our last series against Vancouver, at Vancouver, at three minutes to the final whistle we are four points down. That **is** a tough spot. On the face of it we are sunk.

But at the final whistle we emerge victors by a margin of five points."

And that, sports lovers will agree, is plenty of justification for pride on the part of any coach.

To show further the fighting reserve of these Grads girls, let me draw for you a more recent picture. Late last summer the Grads were billed to appear in exhibition games at Fort William, Toronto, Montreal, and Winnipeg. The day before their train left Edmonton, Coach Page received word that his captain and star forward, Miss MacBurney, had been injured and would not be able to accompany the team. It left without her.

Then at Toronto Miss Doris Neale, that great guard, was suddenly rushed to a hos- pital, where she underwent an operation. The Grads were to face a classy all-star team without the services of two of their most valuable players. None the less, they romped home with a win by a score of 49-12.

The scores for this entire trip follow:

| At | Fort William | Grads106 | Fort William 8 |
|----|--------------|----------|----------------|
|    | Winnipeg     | Grads 64 | Winnipeg 4     |
|    | Toronto      | Grads 49 | Toronto 12     |
|    | Montreal     | Grads 63 | Montreal 6     |
|    | TOTAL        | Grads 282 | opponents 30  |

Thus the Grads justify the claim which is made for them—Champion of All World's Champions in the history of competitive sports.


Chapter 5

# BRITISH BALL GAMES—CRICKET, RUGBY, SOCCER

Considering Canada's closer emotional attachment to Great Britain, it is not surprising that Canadians played more cricket, soccer, and rugby than their southern neighbors. In Canada, these British-associated sports flourished in private clubs, schools, and in areas comprising recent British immigrants. In both countries interest in cricket, rugby, and soccer, especially on a national scale, paled in comparison to that for North American football and baseball and to the growing popularity of golf and tennis.

**CRICKET**
Cricket was more popular in British Columbia and Ontario than elsewhere in Canada. On the west coast, where the highest proportion of recent British immigrants settled, cricket was part of the curriculum in public and high schools, and was taught in the Physical Education Department at the University of British Columbia. A system of feeder leagues kept the sport alive, and in 1938 there were fifteen teams in the province's senior league alone. In the Prairie provinces, the short school year, the harsh climate, limited facilities, and the smaller proportion of British settlers ensured that football and baseball triumphed over cricket and rugger.

In Ontario, private schools and exclusive clubs such as the Toronto Cricket Club were the strongholds of cricket. The province's leading private schools—Upper Canada, Trinity, Ridley, and St. Andrews college—which modeled themselves on the British public school system, competed with each other for cricket supremacy. Here, cricket was encouraged because it was thought to foster sportsmanlike conduct on and off the field; it taught team spirit and unselfishness, and instilled "an instinctive refusal to win unfairly." In contrast, the left-wing Canadian Forum noted in October 1940 "in the heads of the ageing governors of our endowed boys' schools…there remains the odd conviction that Canadian battles of almost any kind can also be won on the playing fields of Eton. Thus, cricket, a vestigial sport so far as Canada is concerned, is raised to a symbolic niche in these schools…and forced down the throats of helpless small boys like a dose of castor oil. In some of these schools, they are not even permitted to play baseball."

In 1937, Toronto supported more than fifty separate cricket teams in several leagues, and about a thousand junior players. Significantly, of the 503 players in the

Toronto Cricket League in 1931, 402 were British-born. The brief revival in the mid-1930s resulted from the adoption of matted pitches to off-set uneven ground of most pitches in Ontario and the philanthropy of a few British-born cricketers who supplied free equipment and instruction to younger players.

In Quebec, cricket was confined to the English in Montreal, who fielded three divisions of competitive teams and played for the Rubenstein Cup symbolizing the city championship. As elsewhere in Canada, Maritime newspapers regularly reported on the scores and standings of British cricket, soccer, and rugby teams, but cricket was more a participant's than a spectator's sport and the game attracted sparse crowds despite the creation of the Nova Scotia Cricket Association in 1934. Cricket's link to the British Empire and its emotional bond to the mother country ensured good press coverage.

In January 1934, The Literary Digest wrote, "like many other mysteries, cricket seems simple once it is understood. And once you understand it, you will have gained a real insight into the English character...." McGill professor Stephen Leacock noted in the June 1940 edition of Atlantic Monthly "That, of course, is the nice thing about cricket—the spirit of it, the sense of honor. When we talk of cricket we always say that such a thing 'isn't cricket,' meaning that it's not a thing you would do." These were the two themes in American press coverage of cricket in the 1930s. Although cricket all but disappeared from the American sport scene after World War I, American commentary on the game revealed much about contemporary American society.

**RUGBY**
In an article praising rugby in the November 1935 edition of Esquire, a Los Angeles rugby player noted, "It's really a relief to have one game where the kibitzers aren't forever scrambling the rules. As, I understand it, the rules of life aren't changed to suit the whims of the players, coaches or spectators either." A Princeton player stated, "I've had more fun and more exercise in one season of rugby than in three years of our game. It's the continual stopping and waiting of the American game that slows it up for players and spectators alike. In rugby, once started a game just flows. Anybody can carry the ball. You learn to think on your feet instead of memorizing twenty formulas." Rugby's reemergence in the United States in the 1930s was a direct reflection of the ills connected with American football. Promoted by such magazines as The Literary Digest, and by ex-British rugby players living in the US, rugby attracted many people concerned with the growing list of serious injuries associated with football, the sport's constant tinkering with the rules, the over-emphasis on winning, and the coaches' control of decision-making. This is the subject matter of "Rugby in America."

Rugby was a popular sport among undergraduates on the east and west coasts looking for an energetic sport that took skill, initiative, and did not entail much pressure. It was also favored by British immigrants and football players looking for exercise in the off-season. The New York Rugby Football Club, which was founded in 1929 by a group of British and American rugby enthusiasts, promoted rugby in the Eastern United States and introduced it to Yale and later to Princeton and Harvard. These universities joined with seven other Eastern colleges to form the Eastern Rugby Union and maintained an active schedule of games until the start of World War II.

Rugby, often termed rugger, was more popular in Canada, but, by the end of the decade it was supplanted by Canadian football everywhere except in the Maritimes. As with cricket and soccer, Canada's British connection ensured that it would be played in private schools and universities. Rugby quickly gave way to Canadian football in Ontario and the Prairies. It was not until 1933 in British Columbia that rugger was introduced into the school system. In the Maritimes, rugger leagues in the public schools provided training grounds for university and senior leagues. Regular crowds of up to 2,000 attended senior rugby games in Nova Scotia, and each year the best Maritime team challenged a rugby team from Montreal team for the McTier Cup. The Caledonia rugger team from Glace Bay, Cape Breton, was one of the dominant teams in the country during the 1930s. Sponsored by the Rugby Union of Canada, touring teams from Great Britain, New Zealand, and Japan sparked interest in the game.

## SOCCER

Soccer's revival in North America in the 1920s coincided with the influx of British and European immigrants before and after World War I. Unfortunately for the growth of soccer, the second generation often rejected this sport in its attempt to assimilate into North American society. In the United States, where soccer became known as "the immigrant sport," it flourished in the immigrant neighborhoods of large cities such as St. Louis, Chicago, Los Angeles, New York, and Philadelphia, where it inadvertently fostered acculturation through interaction with other nationalities and neighborhoods. The German-American Football Association, formed in New York in 1923, served as the model for other ethnic leagues.

Whereas these ethnic leagues often were semi-professional, the American Soccer League was American's first fully professional soccer league. Professional soccer was a working-class game that was concentrated in the north-east, where virtually every city newspaper had a soccer columnist who reported daily. Many mill towns and factories sponsored teams. Bethlehem Steel hired players from Great Britain and gave them factory jobs. The best team in the first years of the decade was the Fall River Marksmen. Thereafter, Keamy Irish won five league titles.

Soccer's largely immigrant composition precluded a national following—team names included the Prague Americans, the Philadelphia Germans, Queens Bohemians, and the New York Hispano. Because most Americans thought of soccer as a non-contact sport that was associated with elite British public schools, it was often considered an un-American sport. Hurt financially by the Depression, registered clubs declined from more than 200 in 1930 to eight in June 1941, and soccer disappeared from the public eye by World War II.

On the international level, the only major success of the US—which went largely unnoticed at home—was its appearance in the semi-finals in the 1930 World Cup. Poor showings followed in the 1934 World Cup and the 1936 Olympics.

Although the exigencies of the Depression forced the owners of professional teams to replace their more expensive players with semi-pros, soccer remained alive in the schools, especially for young women. Two studies of women's colleges in the 1930s discovered that approximately forty percent of them offered soccer instruction. By contrast, a 1938 study of boys' interscholastic games in 170 large American cities revealed that only twenty-five cities provided interschool soccer competition for grade twelve boys—ranking it just one step above fencing and three steps higher than ice hockey. Basketball and football interschool contests were each offered in 133 cities.

Men's varsity soccer, which sported seventy-five teams by mid-decade, was most popular in the East, where Penn State was the dominant team. Under coach Bill

Jeffrey's methodical, short passing game, Penn State boasted an unbeaten streak of sixty-four games between 1933 and 1940. In 1935 the team was unscored upon. Yale, Princeton, and Cornell also fielded competitive teams. By 1940, the west coast league comprised only four universities, and although Florida had no varsity soccer, the South had fifteen intercollegiate teams, centered in Maryland. In the mid-west, lack of opponents led to the demise of the soccer programs at Ohio State (1931) and Illinois (1935). In many universities, soccer's popularity was due to the involvement of foreign students and to those players who had learned the game in high school. As isolationist sentiments spread during the decade and immigration declined, colleges supplied the needed talent base.

The Dominion of Canada Football Association, founded in 1912, sought to boost soccer's popularity by organizing provincial championships and by encouraging British teams to tour Canada. Tours in 1931, 1937, 1938, and 1939 aroused great interest in the larger centers. The Connaught Cup was emblematic of the Dominion title. Although soccer was not a commercial success, the large number of church, mercantile, youth, YMCA, city, and provincial leagues attested to its popularity as a game. The Hudson's Bay Company, for example, fielded a team in Vancouver's Wednesday League. Toronto had an indoor soccer league, and Winnipeg introduced night soccer in 1932. In central Canada, the Intercollegiate Association Football Union arranged championships at junior, intermediate, and senior levels. It was played for the most part by former residents or descendants of Great Britain, who often selected club names that recalled the "old country," such as the Shamrocks, Celtics, or Sons of England. Soccer's popularity dwindled in the more nationalistic period following World War I. Although local newspapers provided extensive soccer coverage, this exposure was not translated into attention by the national magazines.


### CRICKET AND NATIONAL CHARACTER

[*In this indictment of American society, the author argues that sports reflect and shape national character. The seemingly mandatory description of the rules and play of cricket that appeared in almost every discussion of cricket was deleted. Robert H Hutchinson, "Then What is Cricket?" Harper's Monthly Magazine (December 1933), 59-68.*]

You sometimes hear an Englishman say, "It isn't cricket," and by that you know he is damning someone's conduct. The American may ask, "Then what is cricket? What is this game which has become proverbial? Have we anything like it in the United States?"

Let the reader be assured at the outset that this article is not an exposition of that extraordinarily tedious game which takes two days to play and which, judged by its soporific effects upon the spectators, has in it the properties both of an aspirin tablet and a lullaby. I know very little about cricket and I have seen only two games in my life, with a lapse of nearly a quarter of a century between, so that I can fairly claim to view the proceedings with the eyes of an average American. The first game I saw bored me to death; the second interested me intensely, for it gave me the challenge to find an American equivalent, something which holds so high a reputation that it has become the standard for decency of conduct in every walk of life. Whether a *bone fide* equivalent can be found in the United States I would rather leave the reader to say. If, however, after considering cricket as an institution, his reply should be that there is none, I would suggest that we may be on the eve of producing one; for it is a significant fact that cricket came into being, as a national influence, at a crisis in English history when politicians and judges were corrupt, when moral standards were low, and when the country was overrun with highwaymen, bandits, and the spiritual ancestors of the racketeer. With that perspective before one's eyes, cricket may take on a new and more interesting meaning.

I was recently invited to attend my second game by a friend.... The players, all in white, were standing about on the field, and I knew at once that the game was in full swing because practically no one moved.... Can this, a stranger would ask, after he had sat there for an hour or so, can this game, tedious and dragging as it is, however skilfully it may be played, be truly representative of English character—of the whole of English character? He would be constrained to answer "no"; for at football games and other sports in England you can witness as much speed and action and screaming enthusiasm as could be exhibited by any American collegians. Nor must it be forgotten that the English, for all their stolidity and slowness, have held recent speed records in the air, on the water, and on land. At the automobile show in London could be seen, two years ago, three peculiar-looking objects which were, at that time, the fastest airplane, the fastest motor boat, and the fastest racing car in the world—all English from stem to stern. For twenty years or so the **Mauretania** held the record for transatlantic speed, and England can boast of the fastest regular train service in the world, a sample of it being shown recently at the Chicago Exhibition. All of which would lead to the conclusion that the English are not slow when they feel like speeding up—that they are only *slow when they want to be.*

I would suggest that there is a good deal of significance attached to the italicized words, because they indicate an element of control in social life which is extremely wholesome. Is it not the very thing which we ourselves need?... Every school, as any headmaster will tell you, must allot some place in which the boys can romp and blow off steam, but it would not do to let sweet abandon run wild in every quarter; there should be at least one room—library, drawing-room, or chapel, perhaps—in which restraint and dignity rein and bestow their approval, as it were, upon the hilarity of other spheres. Boys instinctively recognize the value of this and they even like it; and the more they recognize it the more will they carry a measure of that restraint and dignity into other activities.

It would occur, then, to the American spectator at a cricket match that this game is the flywheel or governor of English sport, a kind of standard according to the spirit of which other sports are attuned. I say spirit advisedly, not rules, because that thing which is cricket—I mean the very essence of it—cannot be put into rules. Moreover, the English don't like rules: they prefer standards—practical, working standards which they can see with their own eyes. And standards they have many, for in England you may look into almost any department of life and you'll be pretty sure to find at least one unit there towering above all the others as a standard of high quality. The Rolls Royce, for instance, in the field of motor manufacture; the London **Times** in journalism, or **Punch** among the comics; the country squire, as a pattern of rural public spirit; Harley Street doctors; heads of the large joint-stock banks; judges, and those at the top of what they call the Services. In business, in politics, in the professions there is always a small group at the top by whose standards the conduct of others is rated. You may not own a Rolls Royce nor read the Times, and you may be bored—as many an Englishman is—by cricket, but you are constrained to recognize the value of these various standards as practical influences for good. For example, I was held up at a street crossing once by a policeman who asked me why I hadn't signalled that I wanted to drive straight ahead. I said I didn't know it was necessary to signal unless you wanted to turn right or left. He replied that it **was** necessary and added, "Rule or no rule, wouldn't it be more courteous to me and to the other drivers if you did?" He was right, and I was wrong, not because I had broken a rule but for the reason that I had failed to live up to a standard. But where did that cop get such an idea of courtesy? It would not be far wrong, I think, to say that he got it from one of those models aforementioned, and very likely from cricket.

These institutions, taken together, are what may be termed the higher conscience of the Englishman, and cricket might be defined as that part of his conscience which is deliberately and systematically handed down to the young. Whatever dross may exist in the lower strata of business, of journalism or sport, whatever derelictions of moral conduct the Englishman may permit himself or countenance in his neighbor, he will tolerate no tampering with the ideal, no trickery on the part of those in places of responsibility. High standards are the life-preservers of society; they keep people's heads above water when strength or spirits flag or when confusion sets in and, therefore, it is important that those life-preservers be kept in good condition.

...Among the gentlemen there may occasionally pop up some member of the titled nobility; but no man, either gentleman or player, has a ghost of a chance of representing his county unless his general character is deemed to warrant such representation— his **character**, please note, not his social position; for there is nothing snobbish about cricket. Thus the game is kept clean and uncommercial in every respect, and even betting is not permitted.... In this way the atmosphere which surrounds cricket is uncontaminated by any suggestion of gambling; and indeed I believe it when they tell me that no one does gamble on cricket, either professional or amateur. There are plenty of other things you can bet on if you want to.

So there comes to the spectator the realization that there is something hallowed, almost sacrosanct about cricket; and the explanation of this lies, I would suggest, in the fact that this game is not only an ideal, but that it is the putting **into actual practice** of that ideal....

Here, parenthetically, I should say that cricket among amateurs and schoolboys is not nearly so tedious an affair as it is among the crack players; a good game can be played in an afternoon, and no end of fun derived from it. I mention this to dispel any idea that schoolboys are forced to play cricket; they're not forced: they like it.

Think then, of the moral effect upon boys—young hero-worshippers that they are— of taking part in a game from which all petty disputes, tricks, and animosities have, by tradition, been eliminated, a game in which the idea is not merely to win and play well, but to hold your tongue and keep your temper no matter what happens, and under all circumstances to show that your gentlemanly self is not going to be turned into someone else's goat. As it is essential to practice batting to become a good batsman, so is it equally essential to practice gentlemanly conduct in order to become a gentleman, and this game offers an excellent opportunity. As soon as the boys put on those white flannel trousers they are dressed, not merely to play a certain game but to behave in a certain way. Consequently there is no trying to rattle the pitcher—or bowler, in this case—no loudly voiced opinions on the other man's playing, no slamming down of the bat as a protest against a doubtful decision; for to dispute a decision of the umpire is as unthinkable in cricket as to stand up in church and contradict the preacher in his pulpit. If players did that sort of thing the game would cease, by definition, to be cricket....

The parallel situation in America cannot but catch the attention. Our attempt to sweep away racketeers, corrupt politicians and judges, and to inject a new morale into the arteries of business is analogous to the evolution through which our mother country was passing at the very time when we were born....

It would seem, then, that we lack an institution in America similar to cricket in England, and we need it. We need it, not for the purpose of reforming our moral conscience, but because our moral conscience is being reformed and, therefore, seeks expression. As an idea is more exchangeable if it possesses a name, so is an ideal if it has an exponent, and the real value of cricket in England is that it fulfills these two desiderata. To import the game, however, into this country would be palpably absurd, and to pass a law reforming and remodelling baseball equally futile....

We are, like the English, a sport-loving people as contrasted, for instance, with the Continental or Oriental races. Our newspapers devote a great amount of space to the account of games and we are used to borrowing phrases from the lingo of sport, like "right off the bat" or "right from the word go" or "he's in the ring now" or "that's a knockout." We even speak of business as a game: "He's in the oil game now." For that reason there is a likelihood that our new conceptions of the moral law may be embodied in a game. But what game?

Certainly no one would want to prophesy, nor do I. All we have a right to say is that this game should embody two essentially important features: one, that it be played by groups of players, teams; and the other, that it can be indulged in by middle-aged, even elderly persons. The value of the first of these two is self-evident; the second deserves perhaps a word of consideration.

A game in which adults as well as younger persons can participate is naturally shared by a greater proportion of the population, and gains in dignity by the very participation of those older persons. The association of youth with age in sport, or the mere watching of elderly people playing, has a very salutary effect upon the young point of view; for age has less of the impatient, high-pressure desire to win, and is more inclined to play the game for pure fun. Taking victory and defeat philosophically, age can yet appreciate skill quite as much as youth.... Football and baseball unfortunately are games too strenuous for elderly people to play, though the latter might be modified, and indeed is, to suit the approach of arterio-sclerosis. Possibly, then, baseball may be our game, for it is a fairly old institution and has, therefore, the advantage, if not the dignity, of age; and every agency of control in society must have the prestige of years. But it must be painfully evident to everyone that no sport, in the public and professional exhibitions of which there can be whispers and suspicions of "throwing the game" can ever exercise a wholesome effect upon the people of that country in which it is a national institution. If men who play in the World's Series throw games, then why shouldn't the schoolboy do so too? And if he does it on the field, why not in the office as well when he becomes a man?...

I cannot help wondering, however, what the ideal sportsman of our near future will be like, and I venture to say he may be something of a cross between Bill Tilden and Bobby Jones, combining the zip and go of Tilden with the reliability, steadiness, and personal modesty of Jones. It is an unfortunate and perhaps significant fact that each of those men is a star in a game where group play has no place.

The ideal sportsman of our near future must be, then, not only typically American but typical of the best in America. I say this because I was much impressed when leaving the Oval by a portrait which hung in the principal room of the clubhouse; a lifesize portrait which, while it was the likeness of an actual player, since deceased, might be offered as the ideal type. It is of a man of about thirty-five or forty, and you see him, in batsman's rig, slowly descending the stairs of the clubhouse, drawing on his gloves in preparation to take his place at bat. In addition to a certain athletic grace in this figure, you are struck by the fact that it is the personification of poise, dignity, fairness, and gentlemanly bearing. This is not only a cricketer but a man who sees that the game of life is worth playing, and all the more so when played in a fair and friendly spirit. One could as easily imagine him "throwing" a game as throwing loaded dice for copper coins, and a sense of humor glimmering about the eyes assures you that he is not a god but a man. And the artist in this case did not miss his opportunity, for at the foot of the stairs and a little to one side he has portrayed a youth looking up at this player as he comes out to play the game. That, I thought, is what they mean, when they say "cricket." But what equivalent have we?

## CRICKET IN TORONTO

[*The Toronto Cricket Club (now the Toronto Cricket, Skating, and Curling Club) was a typical example of the wealthy, private, sporting clubs in Ontario. This excerpt from the Club's minute book reveals the large number of cricket tournaments and leagues available for the Ontario cricketer. Minute book of the Toronto Cricket Club for 1939. Baldwin Room, Metropolitan Toronto Reference Library.*]

### THE TORONTO CRICKET CLUB
### Report of the Cricket Committee for the year 1939

The cricket season of 1939 was again a successful one. The Club played thirty-four matches, won twenty-nine, lost three and two matches were drawn.

As holders of the John Ross Robertson Cricket Cup, challenges were received from nine clubs, seven from Ontario and two from Quebec. In the semi-final round we defeated the Yorkshire Cricket Club at Armour Heights and in the final match, played at Armour Heights on Labour Day, the Club defeated McGill Cricket Club of Montreal by 234 for 5 wickets declared to 93.

In the George B. Woods Memorial Trophy, we were defeated by the Yorkshire Cricket Club who eventually won the trophy, and whom we heartily congratulate.

In the Continental Life Section of the Toronto and District Cricket Council, the Club finished in first place, winning nine matches out of ten matches played.

The annual play-off for the Albany Club Cup took place at Armour Heights on Saturday, June 17th, (Garden Party), between the Club and a team representing the Hamilton District Cricket League who, in winning the match became the holders of the cup.

The winners of the Club batting and bowling averages for the season were as follows.

| Batting | Innings | Total Runs | Average |
|---|---|---|---|
| R.C. Dobson | 11 | 313 | 52.16 |
| Bowling | Wickets | Runs | Average |
| E.F. Loney | 66 | 407 | 6.16 |

Centuries

E.F. Loney—100 not out vs. Dentonia Park at Armour Heights, July 29th.

The batting and bowling averages for 1939 are herewith attached.

The Inter-Provincial match, Ontario vs. Quebec, was played at Armour Heights on July 1st and 2nd. The Ontario XI, under the Captaincy of W.E.N. Bell, were the winners.

Net cricket practises were held every Tuesday and Thursday evenings and the Toronto Junior Players were given the practising privileges one evening each week at our nets.

The financial statement of the Cricket Committee attached herewith shows an expenditure for the season of $160.16 as compared with $184.55 for 1938.

All of which is respectfully submitted.

Toronto

Chairman Cricket Committee

February 29th 1940

### RUGBY IN AMERICA

[*During spring 1934, The Literary Digest invited its readers to assist in establishing rugby in America and to "contribute to the financing of the matches which will be played by the Cambridge University fifteen against Yale, Harvard, Princeton, and an All-East team in April." The following article may be analyzed at two levels. On the surface, rugby is touted as an alternate to football, with its injuries, ponderous play, and its emphasis on winning. Note the many comparisons of football to warfare. At a deeper level, the author's dislike of football might be explained by its similarity to impersonal factory work, where managers controlled every facet of their employees' lives and reaped all the benefits. George Trevor, "Rugger Rises in the Land of Football," The Literary Digest (10 March 1934), 27, 31.*]

Doubtless the average American's definition of Rugby would run like this—"Oh, yes, you mean the game Tom Brown played in his school days." Every Yank reared on English B6 took his exercise vicariously when doughty Tom booted one into touch or as scrum half, ran hard for the corner. I'm afraid, however, that the ordinary run of the mill American knows almost as little about Rugby as the average Britisher does about our bone crunching game. Well, I won't be technical. The three primary points of cleavage that hit a partizan between the eyes are: 1. No interference (blocking) allowed in Rugby; 2. No passing the ball forward—that would outrage England's sacred on-side rule; 3. No continuity of possession guaranteed in Rugby to either side.

Those three negatives can't help staggering a Yank, particularly the first and last provisions. He admits that our forward pass is an artificial bit of tinkering introduced to open up the game. He could do without that, but blocking! Well, interference is "out" in rugger. Nobody runs ahead of the tackler to knock the latter for a loop. He'd be offside if he did and anyhow "cutting 'em down" isn't tolerated. We Americans think of the backs who don't happen to be carrying the ball on a given play as potential "blackjacks." The English think of them as potential ball carriers. Our idea is to throw a cordon of blockers ahead of the carrier; the Rugby scheme is to have confederates trailing the ball-toter's elbow, arranged in echelon, each one a few strides behind his predecessor and a bit outside for the purpose of free lateral maneuver. There's no such thing as "opening a hole" in Rugby because there's no defensive line to punch a hole through! Still more astonishing to Americans is the thought that neither side "owns" the ball until it is heeled or hooked out of the scrum, that queer turtle-back shaped pack of milling forwards, each set seeking to kick the ball back mule-fashion to a waiting halfback. Here's another shock for American football addicts weaned on the slogan—"hold the ball." That's just what you mustn't do after being fairly tackled in rugger. "Get rid of the ball quick!" is jolly good Rugby procedure—slip it to a confederate when you feel a tackler's arms tighten about your thighs....

No "continuity of possession" means no down field parades, slow yet inexorable, as in our Yankee game. On the contrary, Rugby resembles hockey in its kaleidoscopic swirl of action, its sequential ebb and flow of the tide. Once started, a game of rugger just "flows" like water poured from a bowl. Somehow it seems much more natural, instinctive, and casual than the highly synthetic, intense form of modified war that we call football.

Unquestionably Rugby is more fun for the player than is its American prototype. The ban on blocking would suffice in itself to make the English game a pleasanter recreational sport. Blocking—the physical operation of slinging one's body across an opponent's in such a way as to level him temporarily—is the very touchstone of American Football. Blocking is probably responsible for more injuries and far more unpleasant consequences than any other feature of the American game. Most boys loathe it....

Whether Rugby has as much crowd-appeal as our game is dubious despite the huge crowds that turn out at Twickenham. Certainly rugger is a far less satisfying sport to write about. You can chart an American football game for posterity as you would a famous battle, noting each detail for future surveys. Fancy trying to diagram a rugger match! As well try to chart the progress of the puck up and down a hockey rink!

Watching our American game you feel the grip of something as clearly chiseled as Greek Tragedy. Each team is operating according to a premeditated plan not of the boy's own making. In Rugby everything seems fortuitous and accidental. There's no rhyme or reason to the trend of events, no expert fencing for position by two rival armies; no gradual building up to a climax thrust, but instead a haphazard, crazy quilt patchwork of slanting puntings, oblique flank runs, and foot dribbling....

Altho rugger stresses team play it gives amazing free scope to personal initiative and individuality. Anybody can carry the ball and does at the most unexpected moments, something that should interest the utterly neglected Yankee guard and tackle.

Among the many charms of Rugby, the greatest is its delightful informality. For example, any group of youngish commuters out of New York or Chicago on the 5:15 could, if they had played rugger at various colleges, choose up sides on reaching their destination and organize an impromptu scrub game—no signals to learn, no assignments to master, nobody to knock down! They might be total strangers or soft in muscle—no matter as long as they had a love for the game and wind enough to sustain it.

Rugger is no pink tea party. It looks almost as rough as our game—sans the armor, remember—and allows no substitutions. If a man is hurt his side continues one short. There's an idea to make old Pop Warner's mane bristle. Say, I can read your thoughts— "why doesn't some Rugby fifteen deliberately try to cripple their opponents?" I guess the best answer to that instinctive question is that the game of Rugby means more to English boys than victory does.


### THE GROWTH OF RUGBY IN AMERICA

[*The following article details the growth of rugby in the US, while, at the same time, praising American ingenuity and athletic skills. Similar to the previous document, Buckner attributed rugby's popularity to the ills of American football—that section of the article is omitted. Robert Buckner, "Rugby in America," Esquire (November 1935), 90-91.*]

Rugby football is the fastest growing sport in America. In the East, with Harvard, Yale and Princeton as leaders, this fast, exciting game is now firmly established and is spreading rapidly to other colleges. A well-organized union, including teams of the New York Rugby Club, the French Sporting Club, the U.S. Marines of Philadelphia and the Irish Shamrocks, and supported by the excellent publicity of Literary Digest, is a conspicuous new feature of the Eastern sports scene.

In the Middle West the Illinois Rugby Union and the Missouri Valley Rugby Union are carrying the banner into schools, colleges and athletic clubs.

But it is in the Far West, under the direction of Harry Maloney, head of minor sports at Stanford University, that rugby has attained its greatest success in America. The California and Southern California Rugby Unions include well-trained and enthusiastic fifteens from Stanford, the University of California, the Olympic Club, San Francisco Blues, Pasadena A.C., Barbarians, Hollywood, University of San Francisco, U.C.L.A., San Jose State College and Lane Hospital.

Last year a Stanford-California team defeated the University of British Columbia 10 to 8, and a week later an All-Star California fifteen, inexperienced and outweighed by 200 pounds, swamped the crack British Columbia All-Stars, 14 to 3. Maloney, who coached two United States Olympic teams which won sensational victories over the French, is now planning a playing tour of Japan, Australia and New Zealand.

In 1933 the Yale Rugby Club sent a team which included two football captains, Bob Lassiter and Johnny Wilbur, to Bermuda, where they beat the British Navy fifteen.

Stanford is arranging a regular Eastern fixture with a combined Yale-Harvard-Princeton team for the American championship, and offers to foot the entire bill.

Rugby has caught on in America for many reasons, and the story behind its rapid growth is an interesting commentary on the ills and abuses of our present game of American football, which it may eventually supplant....

Rugby's return to popularity in America is due largely to Harold Cooper, an Englishman studying at Yale on a fellowship. With typical British obstinacy, and the help of Cecil Bullock, another English fellow, they established the game at Yale in three months' time. They wangled out of the athletic association a field which had been a dump heap, cleared off the tin cans and broken bottles, borrowed a few pairs of old football shoes and began to play. From that very humble beginning the Yale Rugby Club grew until in 1933 they sent their well-trained fifteen to Bermuda on its successful tour against crack British service teams.

The following year Cooper transferred to Princeton and established the game there. P. de Q. Cabot, who was at one time a member of the famous New Zealand All-Blacks, put the game on a solid basis at Harvard, and Big Three rugby began its promising career.

Visits to America by the Cambridge Vandals Club team, and the Cambridge University varsity team, attracted great attention and opened the eyes of sports fans, writers and players, to the beautiful smoothness and precision of the English game. Tennis, golf and polo are not a spectator's game from the point of view of popularity with the general public. A team-game with the action, speed and exciting body-contact which rugby offers, may provide the answer....

Whenever the subject of rugby arises in the company of American football players or coaches who are not familiar with the game, there is the inevitable story of the American Rhodes Scholars at Oxford. They will contend that this true story answers once and for all time the question of which of the two games is "superior." We think not. But the story is worth telling.

Among the Rhodes Scholars at Oxford in 1926-'27 there was quite a formidable collection of American football stars, including George Pfann, All-American quarterback at Cornell; Green, who had captained the Dartmouth team the previous year; Walter Brown, from Virginia, and several other ex-varsity players from the Middle West and the Pacific Coast. It would have been a fine squad in any man's college, but here at Oxford they were just a quiet bunch of individuals minding their business.

Some of their fellow-students (Australians, for the greater part, a very hearty and breezy people), overhearing Pfann and the other Americans talking about the sport, began to ride them, saying it sounded like a swell game for longshoremen in a dark alley, etc., a game without any technique or objective other than that of murder and mayhem. It was all very subtle, very insistent, and, after a couple of months, finally maddening.

The Americans bunched heads in a war council and came out of the huddle with an idea. They put it up to the Australians like this: We will play you, eleven men against fifteen—the first half American football, the second half rugby. We'll explain our rules to you; you explain yours to us. And give us a week to practice.

The Australians agreed instantly.... [The American team won the first half 47 to 0, and neither team scored in the rugby second half.] Since then, American football is a subject seldom discussed at Oxford. But the only conclusion to be drawn from that game is the one which has now been fully borne out in practice—that Americans adapt themselves quickly to the sport. [According to one astute American who loves rugby,] "the Englishman has on the whole subordinated the elements of skill in combination to the pleasantness of the sport, while the American has somewhat sacrificed the play-ability of the game to his insatiable struggle for success and his inexhaustible ingenuity in achieving it."

## RUGGER IN CANADA

[*Rugby supporters in Canada praised the game by comparing it to the presumed faults of football. Termed "rugger" in Canada, the game was still popular in schools and universities, although it was slowly being supplanted by Canadian football. Rugger's proponents exalted its Empire connections, the personal initiative required of its play-ers, its exercise component, the quick action and ease of play, and rugger's long tra-dition. Robin Merry, "Rah! For Rugger: The English Game with its open play and emphasis on personal initiative steadily gains in favour," The Canadian Magazine (December 1935), 17, 20, 48.*]

It was Balmy Beaches third down in their game with Sarnia on October 24th. Eleven thousand fans had turned out. The Varsity Stadium at Toronto was packed to the roof. Beaches were on the Sarnia twenty yard line and had only a yard to go. The line got ready for a kick and the ball came out to Ab Box. But instead of kicking, he ran. Bobby Porter and Art Upper were with him and there was a clear field on the Sarnia left end. Ab made for the hole but Sarnia were too quick for him and nailed him before he made a foot. All he had to do was toss a short lateral pass to Porter and there would have been no one to stop him scoring. Instead of passing, Ab Box had run straight into the defense. Why? Because the signals had called that play.

Now Bobby Porter and Ab Box are two players who seem to me to have very safe hands that can catch a pass anywhere and they could have got away with a play like that with very little danger of a dropped pass—and there was no one there to intercept. Yet Box didn't pass. And that serves to introduce my contention that all football players would be the better for playing a game that gave them passing practise. I suggest that these Ontario Football players give Rugger a whirl in the Spring, for I can guarantee that they will get plenty of running and plenty of passing practise.

Rugger is a game that appeals not only to the player but to the spectator. There are only two halves of forty minutes each with only five minutes at half time—when the players are not allowed to leave the field. There is no time out during halves and as no substitutes are allowed, an injured player is carried to the side of the field and the game goes on with one less. No water-boys or massagers are allowed on the field during the game.

Every season those in charge of Football go into solemn conclave to change the rules and try and devise ways and means of opening up the game, and only succeed in making it more intricate than ever for the players, the referee and the spectators. Rugger, on the other hand, is flourishing in Canada, the United States and all over the Empire and has never had a major change in the rules since they were first drawn up over fifty years ago.

That in itself is a testament that they must be based on sound principles.

If my figures are correct, there are more men and boys playing Rugger in Canada at the present time than there are playing Canadian Football. Quite apart from the schools and colleges, there are certainly more Rugger clubs than Football clubs. In Toronto alone for instance where Football is the most popular Fall sport there are outside the college teams only two major clubs, the Argos and Balmy Beach, while even two years ago there were ten Rugger clubs in the city.

Sports enthusiasts in Ontario very often forget that Rugger is played in all schools and colleges in the Maritime Provinces and that there are many clubs in Halifax, St. John, Glace Bay, Fredericton and Moncton. They sometimes forget too that in British Columbia, Rugger is far and away the most popular game. In Quebec Province, Montreal boasts four clubs not including McGill and MacDonald College Rugby clubs. Queen's and Toronto Varsity both have strong teams and in the West there is an even more striking picture.

In Winnipeg the schools took up the game and a couple of years ago there were thirty high school teams as well as several city clubs. In Regina, Calgary, Moose Jaw and Edmonton a Rugger player can always get a game, though because of the early winter, the season is held in the spring.

The New Zealand All-Blacks, now touring England are returning through Canada in January but they will only be able to play in British Columbia owing to frozen ground conditions in other provinces. But will we be able to send a touring side to New Zealand in the next few years—or to England, or to South Africa? Canadian Football is not played anywhere else but in Canada so the players cannot even get a tour across the line. But there are several Football players who should be able to make an All-Canada Rugger side if such a tour were in the offing.

Already Canada has sent quite a few teams both across the Dominion and to other lands. In 1926-27 Dalhousie University travelled across the Dominion to play in British Columbia and five years later the University of British Columbia sent a team to the East which incidentally won every game they played. In 1929 the annual Ontario-Quebec match was originated and has been played every year. Quebec won every game up to this year when Ontario at last turned the tide with a win of two penalty goals to one.

But the most ambitious undertaking of the Rugby Union of Canada came in 1933 when an all-star team visited Japan. The Japanese are crazy about Rugger and W.W. Wakefield's book "Rugger" is their Bible. They have studied all the text books on the theory and strategy of the game that they can lay their hands on and they play the finest, cleanest and headiest game in the world. It is likely that a Japanese team will tour Canada early next year.

One of the best things about Rugger is the simplicity of the rules. Once a man has learned the game—and it only takes a couple of games to get the idea—he can always get a game with a local team wherever he happens to be. "Rugger is like tennis", Earnest Pinkham, the brilliant Wing-three-quarter who played for Canada against Japan, once told me, "you can get a game when you feel like it, and if know the game, you can fit in with an unknown side with no preparation." That is probably why there is not more Football played than there is. So much preparation is necessary before the game in drilling the team to the various plays, that very few players can devote the time to it. At school and college, of course, it is easier to get the players together for practise but to my maybe biased mind, your best football years should be for ten years **after** you leave college. That may sound crazy to a Football player but it happens to be a fact in every other part of the Empire except central Canada....

A very interesting phase in the progress of Rugger on this continent, is the number of players who play both games. In the United States for instance, the game has made tremendous strides in the spring when star footballers take up Rugger. In British Columbia on the other hand several Rugger players took up Football and played mid-week games, playing Rugger on Saturdays. In one case in British Columbia, the whole backfield of one championship Football team was made up of Rugger backs.

I think that Football will never progress until they do away with the idea of leaning on coaches for all ideas. A team today is more often referred to by the name of the coach, such as "Lew Hayman's squad" instead of the "Argos". The coach may he able to pass on many tips gained from a wide and lengthy experience, but his presence is merely killing all originality in the players. Games are arranged on a blackboard and teams told exactly what to do long before the game is played. It is astonishing to me why players who are old enough to think for themselves, should tolerate such autocratic treatment. After all, the game is presumably amateur and played for exercise....

Another reason why I think Rugger will be played by many new players in Canada in the near future is because you get so much more exercise. I saw a recent Football game in which the head linesman was lame—the game was so slow he never had to run! With no substitutes, Rugger is a harder game to keep up the pace for two forty-minute periods.

A substitute in the old days of Football was one who was held in reserve in case a player was hurt because the signal system needs a full team for perfect operation. But the present method of using subs has degenerated into a farce. For instance when Argos were playing Montreal Winged Wheelers in Toronto on October the 26th, they had what amounted to a second team in reserve. On two separate occasions at least, ten new players walked onto the field and replaced every one except one of the backs. That to my mind is pretty far from the game being a test of stamina and if teams have to resort to such tactics to win games, there is not much future for amateur sport.

It is interesting to read that the Amateur Athletic Association is going to debate the question as to whether professionals will be allowed to play in strictly amateur games at their coming meeting in Halifax. The meaning of the word amateur is one who does not receive money in any form for playing games, apart from legitimate travelling expenses. It is difficult to understand therefore how such a question can even come up for discussion by this body. Rugger is definitely an amateur sport in the truest sense of the word and has the most stringent rules of amateurism in its rule-book. Rugger will always remain a game for the man who enjoys hard, fast physical exercise and it will not be many years before Canadian teams are touring abroad—if Footballers take up the game. If Rugger can teach them in its turn, to open up our Canadian game, then both will be better to play and better to watch.

### WOMEN'S SOCCER

[*Laura Huelster was an Associate Professor in Physical Education at the University of Illinois and Chairman of the Soccer Subcommittee for the Women's Rules*

*and Editorial Committee of the American Physical Education Association. The Edi-
torial Committee was established in 1917, and its soccer subcommittee began in 1920.
This document reflects the prevailing emphasis on participation and equality in sports
in schools and discusses the extent and reasons for the growth of women's soccer in
American schools, touches on why it was not more popular, and explains the differences between the rules for males and females. Laura J. Huelster, "The Growth of
Soccer for Girls and Women," The Journal of Health and Physical Education (September 1935), 39, 53.]*

For twelve years the problems of official soccer for girls and women have occupied
the attention of the Soccer Subcommittee of the Women's Rules and Editorial Committee of the American Physical Education Association, and during these years enthusiasts of the game have seen it grow in popularity and use. A survey which the 1934-
35 Committee made of the extent of the game in physical education school programs
for girls and women in the United States reveals these interesting facts. Of the 25,883
junior high school girls included in the survey, 40 per cent play soccer; 22 per cent of
the 59,905 senior high school girls play soccer; and of the 72,591 college women, 10
per cent participate in the game.

Why is soccer a growing sport for girls and women? First, because of the inherent
values of the game. We rightfully praise its peculiar emphasis on foot and leg skill, the
value of its team game experience, and its economical equipment. Physical educators
have so successfully stressed the educational and social values of team-game experience, and school boards have so successfully emphasized economical expenditures for
equipment, that no more need be said about these values. We do need new emphasis,
however, on sport skills as means of educating girls and women in the intelligent scientific use of the body in movement. Soccer skills demand efficient use of the thigh
joints and the necessity of balancing on one foot while using the other in a large kicking movement gives excellent opportunity to develop efficient balance throughout the
entire individual.

Soccer is also growing because of the policy of the Committee to keep the rules of
the game "as simple as possible so the game may be easily learned by the young girls
and still retain the interest of the older-girl." The soccer survey indicates that this aim
is being accomplished as the game is being played by junior high, senior high, and
college girls.

The first official soccer rules for girls and women were contained in the 1923-24
Guide, Athletics for Girls and Women. In her "Introductory," Helen Frost, Soccer
Chairman, stated that the following "changes from the men's rules had been tried out
and found satisfactory": the elimination of charging; allowing the arms to be folded
across the chest for protection against a swift-moving ball; a six-yard goal instead of
the eight-yard width; six yards uniform distance for the opponents on the plays which
the men ruled ten yards; a shorter playing field, and fifteen-minute halves, allowing
substitution of players....

In 1934, the Soccer Committee changed the value of the field goal from one to two
points, the penalty-kick goal still scoring one point. In making later changes in the rules
the Committee has added a policy to that announced in 1923. Not only should the game
remain simple, but the rules should give every possible justice to each member of the
team, and both teams on the field. To give a penalty-kick as much value as a field goal
placed too much emphasis upon the fouls made by defense players in their penalty area,

especially since no distinction is made in the type of foul or whether it was intentional or unintentional. This year another rule change is made which carries out this policy in relation to the corner kick. After the initial kick in this play, the defending team often had greater advantage than the opposing one. By placing the defending players behind the goal line, the attacking players are given greater opportunity, and still the opponents are in excellent defending position.

What more can soccer enthusiasts do to double the interest in the game during the next twelve years? In the soccer survey referred to in the first of this article, the majority of reasons given by teachers of physical education for not playing soccer centered around limiting conditions; such as, lack of playing space, lack of enough players to compose two teams, and lack of the teacher's knowledge of the game. The second largest number of reasons for not playing concerned the possible danger of injury to the player's toes, feet, and ankles. While we can only gradually make strides in increasing the number of playing fields and in securing sufficient numbers of players for teams, we can readily further knowledge of the game, and reduce the fear of injuries by facing facts about their possibility and reducing the conditions which contribute to their possibility....

A study made of rank classification of sports by degree of accidental hazard to college women ranks soccer eighth, below field hockey, basketball, and speedball, thereby classifying it in the low hazard group. The ankle is the joint most frequently injured in women, and this fact warns us of the necessity for precaution in costuming. The soccer survey shows the tennis shoe and romper suit to be the most popular costume. Eighty-one per cent of the 224 schools which answered this part of the questionnaire use tennis shoes, and 47 per cent use rompers. This is not a suitable costume for soccer, because players cannot enjoy the game to the fullest extent when so clothed. The toe protection given by low heeled rubber-soled oxfords, and the leg protection given by stockings, shin guards, or ski pants is necessary. Teachers of soccer need to be sure their players are suitably costumed for comfort and safety.

Chapter 6

## COMBAT SPORTS—BOXING, WRESTLING, FENCING

"There are neighborhoods in Chicago where a boy, to get by must be a man. One of these is the embattled terrain surrounding the corner of Bunker and Clinton Streets. It's back of the tracks, back of the yards...it's one of the toughest in a city that is famous for its toughness. Kids graduate from the cradle in this neighborhood, to inherit juvenile feuds that are as long lived as those from the Kentucky mountains. There is an eternal alliance between the Italians and Poles, augmented by a sprinkling of other Aryan nationalities under the general heading of Bohunks, which confronts the Jews in a never ending series of backyard battles. Boys graduate from these wars, upon attaining manhood. Some, having distinguished themselves as especially tough eggs, obtain the opportunity to do post-graduate work through membership in the Valley

Gang—one of the front entrances to gangsterdom. Some of the huskier ones become laborers. The smarter ones rise as high as bookkeeping jobs and petty clerkship, but seldom much more. It's what the social service workers call an under-privileged neighborhood....

The Bohunks outnumbered the Jew-boys five to one, and life, for one of the latter who fancied himself as a tough guy, seemed very long and none too merry." Such was the early environs, as described in the January 1934 edition of Esquire, of welterweight and lightweight boxing champion Barney Ross (Barnet David Rasofsky).

Boxing provided an escape from the slums and a means of advancement. Gyms and small clubs were filled with thousands of young men who dreamed of a professional career, with all the glamor and money it could bring. Approximately 8,000 men boxed as professionals during the 1930s. Since a preliminary bout paid $50 and even amateur boxers earned $5 a fight, boxing provided more money in less time than any other legitimate enterprise available for society's underprivileged. Heavyweight champions earned larger incomes than the most famous baseball players and the best paid football coaches. Primo Carnera, for example, collected more money for a single title defense than the President of the United States received for the entire year.

Boxing's practitioners came from the urban slum environment where young men from different ethnic backgrounds were constantly getting into fights to protect their honor or to save their lives. In places such as the Lower East Side of New York, Chicago's West Side, or San Francisco's Mission District, self-defense was a mandatory skill. Prior to the 1930s, boxers of Irish descent dominated boxing in the United States, but as the Irish moved up society's social ladder and as tens of thousands of immigrants arrived from central and southern Europe, first the Jews and by mid-decade the Italians provided the majority of boxers. During the 1930s, ten different Jews held at least one of the eight weight division titles. Historian Peter Levine has argued the success of Jewish boxers such as Maxie Rosenbloom, "Battling" Levinsky, and Barney Ross provided a source of ethnic pride, were symbols of Jewish toughness, and refuted stereotypes of the weak and cowardly Jew that anti-Semites voiced in their efforts to deny Jewish immigrants full access to American opportunities. Such symbols were especially important during the 1930s, when the Depression and the rise of Nazi Germany fueled American anti-Semitism. Prior to his first fight with McLarnin, Ross told a friend, "The news from Germany made me feel I was...fighting for all of my people." Ross' mother declared that after her son won, maybe Hitler will "learn something from it about our people. He should know that he can kill millions of us but he can never defeat us."

Boxers such as Jimmy McLarnin, Tony Canzoneri, and Barney Ross, who wore a Star of David on his trunks, became popular ethnic heroes who sought to prove the courage and manhood of their people and generated ethnic pride. Fight promoters took advantage of this situation to pit one ethnic boxer against another. The media labelled Barney Ross as "the Hebrew challenger" and Jimmy McLarnin was "the Vancouver Irishman." When Max Baer fought Max Schmeling for the heavyweight championship, Time's headline read, "Jew v. German."

The demeaning stereotypes used to describe the fighters from various ethnic groups illustrated the divisions within society. The Nation described Max Schmeling as an "oxlike, genial, stupid-looking German," and Time referred to him as the "sturdy, stolid German." News-week wrote that Max Baer defeated "bovine heavyweight champion"

Primo Carnera using lefts and rights "that would have done credit to any stockyard cattle-killer." The Literary Digest claimed that "one characteristic of Negro fighters is their inability to worry," and then described Joe Louis as "a large Negro boy with blown-out cheeks, fat lips, and an overdeveloped neck."

Despite such statements, compared to baseball and football, boxing was a relatively democratic sport for individuals seeking to escape the ghetto and achieve a measure of fame and fortune. Approximately 1,800 blacks fought professionally in the 1930s, including bantamweight champion Al Brown, middleweight title holder William Jones, and light-heavyweight John Henry Lewis. Henry Armstrong captured the championship of three different weight divisions, and Joe Louis became the most acclaimed boxer of the 1930s and 1940s.

In the early years of the decade, gate receipts declined dramatically due to a combination of unemployment, the retirement of popular heavyweight champion Jack Dempsey, lackluster boxers, and questionable fights. In the 1920s, five of Jack Dempsey's title fights grossed more than one million dollars, whereas the largest gate in the depression years for bouts not involving Joe Louis was $750,000 for the Sharkey-Schmeling fight in 1930. From 1930 to 1935, five different men held the heavyweight crown—Max Schmeling, Jack Sharkey, Primo Carnera, Max Baer, and James J. Braddock. The lifeless state of boxing's premier division was revealed in 1933 when The Ring gave its Most Valuable Boxer Award to Barney Ross and Tony Canzoneri, the first time a non-heavyweight won.

Max Schmeling won the title in 1930 when the referee disqualified Jack Sharkey for a low blow. In that year, eleven bouts, including two championship fights were decided by punches below the belt, and the New York World reported that the boxing fraternity felt that the vast majority of these winners took advantage of the rule that awarded the fight to the recipient of a low blow if he was unable to continue. To rescue boxing from the unpopularity created by the epidemic of such decisions, the New York State Athletics Commission ruled in 1930 that a low blow would result in the loss of a round, not the fight, and permitted boxers to wear special protective apparatus in the abdominal region. Despite initial opposition to this decision, by 1934 most state athletic commissions had adopted similar regulations.

For a short time, Primo Carnera reawakened interest in the heavyweight division. It was Carnera's physique that attracted the most attention. A giant of a man for his day, Carnera weighed 260 pounds, was 6 feet 6 and a half inches tall, had a size 19 collar, wore 23Z shoes, and reportedly had fists "the size of Virginia hams." Tailors didn't measure him, reporters joked, they surveyed him. Promoted by the press as "killer," "caveman," "the abysmal brute," and "Tarzan of the Apes," knowledgeable fight fans doubted his credentials. Carnera's handlers were associated with the mafia, and as News-week reported in July 1933, "after most of his fights there has been the stench of fouls and fixings." When Baer defeated Carnera in 1934, the division lost its attraction.

During the first half of the decade, the lighter weight divisions sported the most exciting boxers. In 1934, Barney Ross became the first boxer to hold the title of two different divisions simultaneously. Four years later, Henry Armstrong captured the feather, welter, and light weight championships. Fighters could be flamboyant too. Canadian boxer Jimmy McLarnin performed a forward somersault after knocking out his opponents.

Amateur boxing flourished during the decade. The American Legion, the YMCA, the YMHA, and the Catholic Youth Organization (CYO) all built rings and sponsored bouts. The CYO, which began in Chicago in 1930, sought to use athletics as an antidote to juvenile delinquency. The following year it initiated a city-wide boxing tournament that eventually spawned three members of the 1936 American Olympic boxing team. The CYO emphasized boxing because of its appeal to the urban poor and the publicity it generated. Under Bishop Sheil, the CYO promoted a sense of inclusion in society and recruited a wide variety of ethnic groups. Sheil established community centers in Japanese, Italian, and Puerto Rican neighborhoods. The CYO recruited Benny Leonard as one of its boxing instructors and competed against teams from the B'nai B'rith Youth Organization.

The Golden Gloves Tournament, which began in New York and Chicago in 1928, flourished during the Depression. In 1938, after six weeks of sectional preliminaries, the initial 8,000 boxers was reduced to 48 fighters. Approximately 18,000 Chicago residents came to the finals shouting "kill him!" "take that shine!" "use the right." Elsewhere, the Amateur Athletic Union sought to cure the many abuses in amateur "bootleg boxing."

Although college boxing also limited bouts to three rounds of two minutes each, the atmosphere was quite different. To encourage sportsmanship and mitigate the evils of professional boxing, college meets prohibited cheering during fights and instructed ushers to quiet the crowd. If there was too much noise the referee was empowered to stop the fight and announce, "the contestants are sportsmen: I ask you to be the same." The better boxing schools included the University of Virginia, Washington State, West Virginia, and Duke. Although dual meets attracted large crowds, some conferences refused to sanction the sport and the NCAA did not sponsor a national intercollegiate tournament until 1935 for fear that the notoriety successful college pugilists received would encourage them to become professional boxers. At the NCAA intercollegiate tournament in 1938, fifty-four fighters from twenty-one colleges participated.

Boxing was also popular in Canada. Following Sharkey's disputed victory over Schmeling in 1938, the Toronto Mail and Empire reported that its switchboard was jammed for hours "with the greatest barrage of protest calls in its history." In quantity of newspaper coverage, boxing ranked third behind hockey and baseball. Canada's premier fighter in the 1930s was welterweight Jimmy McLarnin, who Grantland Rice once termed the greatest pound-for-pound fighter in the world. Canadian sportswriters later voted McLarnin the best boxer of the first half century. Other notable Canadian fighters included Larry Gains, who captured the British Empire heavyweight title in 1931, and Lou Brouillard of Quebec who took the welterweight title.

Writing in The World, William Bolitho noted that a successful champion "must not only have the strength, the skill, the courage, he has to have a specially dramatic or heroic personality.... The heavyweight contender...must be material of folk-lore, like Dempsey, Carpentier, Tunney, Johnson, Jeffries—a gorilla-man, or a dude, or a terror, or a romance." Joe Louis (Barrow), the son of an Alabama sharecropper, was the story of boxing in the second half of the decade. Boxing was in need of a savior, and Louis' handlers trained him for this role. As the document "Joe Louis: Dusky Dynamite" illustrates, Louis sought to show white society that it had nothing to fear from him by playing the role of a God-fearing, Bible-reading, clean-living, modest young man.

Louis turned professional in July 1934. The following year he earned $350,000 by fighting fourteen times before almost 250,000 people. Millions more listened to his fights on radio or saw them on highlight reels in the movie theaters. For injecting new life into the heavyweight division, Ring Magazine named Louis Boxer of the Year and Associated Press voted him Athlete of the Year. Louis remained undefeated until Max Schmeling stopped him in 1936 before a crowd of 45,000. The following year, Louis knocked out James Braddock and became the heavyweight champion. Boxing's declining popularity, Louis' image, and the rise of fascism in Italy and Germany had provided the opportunity for the first black to fight for the heavyweight championship since Jack Johnson lost the title in 1915. Louis' rematch with Schmeling in June 1938 attracted 70,000 spectators to Yankee Stadium and grossed more than one million dollars.

Initially, the white media depicted Louis as a typical "sambo" who spoke in dialect, ate chicken, lacked intelligence, was lackadaisical, and fought like a savage animal. The Digest, for example, described Louis as "a shuffling, ex-Alabama pickaninny…[a] kinky-haired, thick-lipped embalmer." Cartoons frequently portrayed him as an ape with long arms, broad shoulders, and a narrow waist, and with big lips, white buck teeth, and frizzy hair. These negative images faded in the late 1930s when the media depicted Louis as America's representative against Nazi Germany.

The minority press devoted more attention to Joe Louis between 1935 and the end of the decade than to any other black. Although it also used color imagery to describe Louis ("the brown bomber," "the dark destroyer"), the black media did not quote Louis in dialect, avoided reference to jungle imagery, and depicted him as hardworking and clean-living.

After Louis defeated Carnera in 1935, "I started noticing some things I thought were strange," he later wrote in his autobiography. "A lot of Black people would come to me and want to kiss me, pump my hand. I thought they were congratulating me for my fighting skills. Now they started saying things like, 'Joe, you're our savior,' and 'Show them whites!'" As "Symbols of Black Pride" illustrates, Joe Louis became a positive inspiration to millions of blacks. Crowds packed his training camps to watch him spar. Despite the Depression, approximately one-half of the 45,000 spectators who watched Louis defeat Braddock were black. As it became obvious that Louis would win, they began crying and hugging each other, held hands, and winced with every blow Louis suffered. Those who could not be in the arena, listened on radio. After his victory over Carnera, and following every subsequent success, thousands of blacks poured into the streets to dance and celebrate. His every fight soon became a major social event.

Joe Louis was a hero who symbolized his people's trials and aspirations. Jazz singer Lena Horne remembered listening to one of his fights behind the grandstand during an intermission. "Joe was the one invincible Negro, the one who stood up to the white man and beat him down with his fists. He in a sense carried so many of our hopes, maybe even dreams of vengeance." In another moving story, Martin Luther King Jr. recalled being on death row with a prisoner when the poison gas pellet dropped into the container. As the gas curled upwards, the young black prisoner said—"Save me, Joe Louis. Save me, Joe Louis. Save me, Joe Louis."

Louis symbolized American values when he fought Primo Carnera and Max Schmeling. Prior to his fight with Carnera, the Associated Press wrote—"Little

Abyssinia and Big Italy war in the prize ring instead of Africa." American democracy, stated many newspapers, faced aggressive Italian fascism. Fighting Carnera at the same time as Mussolini was overrunning a defenseless Ethiopia, Louis received support from black and white America.

In 1938, the Nazis boasted Schmeling's victory over Louis would demonstrate Aryan supremacy. The NCAA, on the other hand, denounced the German fighter as an instrument of Hitler's oppression. American values and democracy were to meet German racism and militarism. Since nationalism was considered more important than color, and black America abhorred Hitler's racial doctrine, America united behind Joe Louis. At the White House, President Roosevelt felt Louis' biceps and said "Joe, we need muscles like yours to defeat Germany." On 22 June 1938, ninety-seven percent of the radio owners in New York, and sixty-four percent across the nation, listened as Louis knocked out Schmeling in the first round.

In 1938 The Literary Digest asked, rhetorically, why thousands of Americans, few having attended a prize-fight, avidly followed boxing—learning every detail about the their favorite boxers, their physical qualifications, their training and ring methods, and their histories. It concluded that, unlike sports such as baseball, football, and hockey, boxing's rules were simple. Most Americans, it argued, preferred to see bruising contests which offered the possibility of sudden annihilation. "However proud we are of our culture, our position in world civilization," The Literary Digest noted, "we seem to want a fight in which the sluggers trade punches toe to toe, absorb punishment with a smile, lunge, plunge, swing and hug."

The following extract from Time's description of the 1932 contest between Christopher Battalino and Billy Petrolle illustrates this point. "The ring canvas was spattered with blood. Reporters at the ringside held up newspapers to shield themselves. The referee had to wipe blood from his hands between rounds. But still the awkward, stooping little fighter advanced, his gloves now at his head for relief from the hammering it was getting, and now in furious, smashing action against the ribs and head of his opponent. The little fighter's flat nose, freshly broken, bubbled readily as he snorted for breath. His head rocked as punch after punch landed on it. But on and on he went, crowding, slamming, tearing in like a madman trying to whip a trip-hammer. Madison Square Garden, jammed to the eaves, thundered with bloodthirsty applause and excitement." "Boxing Not Dangerous" illustrates the argument boxing's defenders used against those people who decried such violence.

When Washington D.C. legalized boxing in 1934, it followed the lead of thirty-one states in placing boxing under commission rule. In the later half of the decade, the National Boxing Association, which was recognized by most state commissions, and Michael Strauss Jacobs fought for control over boxing. "Let's Clear Up Boxing," and "Jacobs: Am I a Menace to Boxing?" outline the ideas of both sides.

### WRESTLING

Amateur wrestling suffered from a lack of qualified coaches, space, and money. Some school districts refused to allow wrestling because of the stigma of professional wrestling, which was a booming entertainment industry in the interwar years, and the sport's competitive nature. Nevertheless, by 1932, some 800 high schools and 300 colleges offered either intercollegiate or intramural wrestling, and the 1938 NCAA Wrestling

Championships, which began ten years earlier, and concentrated on freestyle wrestling rather than Greco-Roman, attracted eighty-six contestants from twenty-nine colleges and universities. "National Collegiate Wrestling Meet" outlines the NCAA's stance on Olympic wrestling. The middle-west was the heartland of the sport and Oklahoma A&M usually had the best team.

Amateur wrestling in Canada also suffered from a lack of qualified coaches and publicity. Although some universities offered wrestling programs, the YMCA and company-sponsored wrestling clubs kept the sport alive during the Depression.

Wrestling proponents touted it as an ideal form of exercise that developed a symmetrical, well-rounded physique. It was natural for boys to want to try this ancient game that valued skill, speed, science, strength, and determination. In addition, wrestling taught courage and self-control, and inculcated self-confidence. It provided training for later life. The following story recounted by W.R. Wegner, the wrestling coach at Whittier Union High School, California, illustrates this way of thinking:

"John was coaxed out for wrestling by his chum during their freshman year in high school. He was a very thin lad (he weighed but 89 pounds) and he was timid. Apparently the family had a trace of tuberculosis, for his physique was in perfect condition to start the white plague. As he was such a backward chap, we took a little extra interest in him during practice. In our school tournament he was hopelessly beaten in the 95-pound class. But after four months of training he began to gain self-confidence. His parents reported that he was showing some interest in life other than in reading, that he was eating and sleeping better and constantly lived and talked wrestling, whereas, before he would not speak on any subject." John proceeded to gain weight, win tournaments, join several social clubs, and become a successful husky adult (Athletic Journal, January 1935).

## FENCING

Fencing also promoted itself as an ideal, all-around exercise. It sharpened the intellect as well as the eye. "A fencer to be successful," explained the Amateur Fencers League of America (AFLA), "must have more than technical perfection, speed and endurance.... He must match wits with the contestant with whom he crosses swords." The foil, the epee, and the saber constituted the three weapons of fencing. The foil was the most popular blade and was the favourite weapon of the beginner. It weighed less than a pound and its rectangular blade was blunted at the point with a button. The foil was a thrusting weapon, and since a touch by the point, in theory, would cause a cut rather than a serious wound, five touches were necessary to win. The point of the epee was burred and a sticky red liquid applied. A single smudge of red anywhere on the jacket, above the waist, constituted a touch. Since one successful thrust would cause a serious wound, the first fencer to score two touches won. The saber, a flat, double-edged blade, weighed five or six pounds and was used by the more advanced fencers. Because it was a slashing weapon, any touch counted and five touches won.

Fencing, an elite sport, had its home in New York, where most of the tournaments were held. The Intercollegiate Fencing Association, with teams at Army, CCNY, Columbia, Cornell, Harvard, Hamilton, MIT, New York University, Pennsylvania, Yale and Princeton, provided the majority of fencers for the AFLA, which had approximately thirty branches scattered across the United States and in the military academies.

## JOE LOUIS—DUSKY DYNAMITE

[*Joe Louis won the crown from James J. Braddock in 1937 and defended it twenty-five times until his retirement in 1949. Ironically, in Louis' battles with Carnera and Schmeling, symbols of Fascism and Nazism, the American media often portrayed the African American as a defender of the American way, even though blacks were still subject to discrimination and oppression. Earlier, the possibility that German fighter Schmeling might defeat champion Braddock persuaded the Non-Sectarian Anti-Nazi League, the NCAA, and the Jewish War Veterans to boycott their proposed title bout in 1937 at Madison Square Garden. A subsequent letter-writing campaign and picketing of stadiums suspected of wanting to promote the fight led to its cancellation. The result was a rematch between Schmeling and Louis. When Schmeling arrived in New York, hundreds of people picketed him and mocked him with Nazi salutes. The following two documents not only illustrate the prejudice of the times, but also reveal how the press presented Joe Louis to the public—as a clean living, non-threatening, modest boxer, who knew his place. Jimmy Powers, "Dusky Dynamite," Liberty (31 August 1935).*]

A Revealing Close-up of Joe Louis, the Sensational New Menace to the White Man's Supremacy in the Prize Ring.

A Whirlwind campaign unequaled in prize-ring history has brought the ominous shadow of Joe Louis, twenty-one-year-old Detroit mechanic, squarely across the doorstep of white heavyweight champion James J. Braddock.

Louis feints, weaves, crouches, and punches in a manner reminiscent of Sam Langford, Peter Jackson, Joe Gans. On his record, he is the best fighter his race has produced since Jack Johnson; and he is a terrific hitter with either hand, whereas Johnson's sole weapon of note was a right uppercut delivered in a mauling clinch.

Jack Dempsey and Gene Tunney both insist that Louis is Challenger No. 1. Jack grinned wryly when he saw the bloody hulk of Carnera smashed into the resin. "I'm glad I don't have to play catch with that baby," he said. Gene said, "Louis is such a good boxer and such a paralyzing hitter that all you have to do is make a wrong lead, one mistake, and—boom!—the fight's over."

Louis, if he continues his sensational pace through the autumn fights; will fight for the world title in the summer of 1936. Madison Square Garden controls Champion Braddock. A rival promoter, Mike Jacobs, has tied up Louis. But Braddock, confident that he can beat Louis, confided to this writer: "I'll give Louis a shot anyway. They say the gate will go to one million dollars. I'll fight anybody for that money!"

The secret of Louis's success lies in his sloping shoulders, loose muscles, strong legs, and short-coupled body. His fists are big, bony, and he can fire punches from any position. He is a beautiful boxer, sidling, swaying, bobbing, and weaving constantly. To top it all, he is a fine feinter. Feinting is a long-lost art. Louis revived it. He feints well with his head, shoulders, elbows, hips, and even his eyebrows.

Once he laces on his gloves, he is merciless. He hires the best sparring partners available, all colored men, and he whales them into unconsciousness. While training he wears a cold, deadly expression, the same fearsome glint Jack Dempsey had. During an interview he is alternately sleepy-eyed or sullen. He answers questions politely enough but he offers no information. If he does not wish to answer a question he stares at you. Only once in all the months that Promoter Mike Jacobs had business with him did Mike hear him laugh. Mike telephoned Louis to tell him his share of the Carnera gate was $44,636. There was a second of silence; then a low chuckle rolled into the receiver: "Boy," came the voice, "'at's pretty good for six rounds."

Louis has no ambitions other than the winning of the championship. He has no vices. He is phlegmatic. He has already built a $25,000 home for his mother, bought her a $3,000 automobile, and salted the rest of his earnings in annuities.

He neither drinks nor smokes. He dates no girls. "He's the eatingest and sleepingest darky I've ever seen," says his trainer. His press agent tried to put over the Tiger Flowers stunt of having him read a Bible before his bouts. Louis turned it down with "I'm a fighter—not an actor."

Between rounds in all his fights he stares intently at his enemy. "He watches his man like a dog waiting for the icebox door to open," was the way Dempsey put it.

Louis avoids white friends. "I figure," he says, "that if I did run around with 'em everyone would say, 'What is that bird busting in and pushing himself ahead for?' I don't want to give any one an excuse to say that. I'm going to make my people proud of me."

Louis despises Jack Johnson. He has had him thrown out of his camp, "Jack brought disgrace to my race. I intend to win the world title and bring credit."

The flaws in Louis's make-up are the mistakes of youth, such as his frequent circling clockwise into Carnera's right-hand arc, his temptation to drop his guard altogether when he has a man staggering, and his chin.

Louis has no concrete button. When he is tagged he drops to the deck just like the next one.

Johnny Miler, former Olympic amateur, nailed Louis seven times in an amateur bout and seven times Louis kissed the canvas. He arose and endured a beating. He has since improved immeasurably. His defense has tightened—but his chin is still the same glass chin.

Louis was an Alabama cotton-field pickaninny. His full name is Joseph Louis Barrow. Munn and Lily Barrow, his parents, were share-cropping farmers of Lafayette, Alabama. Joe's birthday was May 13, 1914. He was the lucky seventh of eight children.

Two years after his birth Pappy Barrow died. Joe's mother had down-home neighbors who had migrated to Detroit. They wrote glowing accounts of their prosperity. Mammy Barrow packed her brood into a battered bus and headed for this Michigan Mecca.

For a while it was tough sledding. The Barrows discovered that Woodward Avenue was not paved with gold. Meanwhile Joe Louis acquired a stepdaddy in one Patrick Brooks, a sober, industrious day laborer.

At twelve Joe had a part-time job as "assistant" on an ice truck. The Barrow-Brooks budget forced him out of school to learn the trade of cabinetmaking. He had a chum named Thurston McKinney, an amateur boxer. While training for a tournament Thurston's sparring partner became ill. Joe was drafted. His aptitude so impressed Atler Ellis, club instructor, that he persuaded the boy to continue the sport and gave him his first boxing lessons.

Shortly, at sixteen, Joe went to work in the Ford plant. Evenings he boxed the best amateurs in the neighborhood, club, city, and state tournaments. He scored forty-three knockouts in fifty-four bouts before he turned pro.

Joe was whipped four times as an amateur. His conquerors in the years from 1930 to 1934 were Johnny Miler, who decisioned him in his debut; Clinton Bridges, 1935 National light-heavyweight champion who recently turned pro; Max Marek, Notre Dame football player who beat Joe in the 175-pound National A.A.U. finals at Boston in '33; and Stanley Evans. Joe climaxed his amateur career by winning the 1935 National A.A.U. light-heavy title at St. Louis.

Two colored men, John Roxborough, Michigan graduate (his brother Charles is a member of the Michigan Legislature), and Julian Black, a Chicago insurance agent, manage Louis. Both were well-to-do when they came across him. Roxborough took Joe into his home and, to avoid litigation, became his legal guardian. When he turned pro, July 4, 1934, they placed him in Jack Blackburn's care. He says he owes everything to Blackburn.

A great colored lightweight at the turn of the century, Blackburn had fought Joe Gans, Philadelphia Jack O'Brien, and other headliners. He had fought four draws with Sam Langford! He offered to work for free if Joe Louis failed to make the grade. For four months he lived, slept, and ate with Louis. He taught him how to shift, how to move in under rights, how to twist his raking left hooks, how to feint, how to tie up men in the clinches.

"Joe is ready, boss," he announced to Roxborough one afternoon a year ago last spring. "And, boss, we got the best colored fighter of all time!"

Joe polished off a pack of palookas in Chicago and Detroit during the summer and fall of '34. All but two of his first seven professional fights ended in knockouts.

Blackburn craftily "stepped up" the caliber of the opposition. Joe kayoed Art Sykes in eight rounds, October 24, and a week later dusted off Jack O'Dowd in two. Blackburn took no chances of overmatching until the time arrived for the first "name" fight.

Stanley Poreda, who held a decision over Primo Carnera, was booked at Chicago. On the night of November 14 Louis flattened Stanley in one round!

Charles Massera, an able second-rater notches above Poreda, was next. Chicago gamblers, suspecting that Joe at last had overstepped himself, laid odds against him. Charley did start well when the two met in the Stadium November 30. He beat a two-fisted tattoo on Joe's stomach. He gouged his ribs, slammed him about the head. Joe weathered this attack and went out, wooden-faced and crouching, in the third round. His snaky left lashed out, his right found its target, and Massera fell with a brain concussion.

Blackburn then urged the two managers to negotiate a match with a smart speedy boxer. Lee Ramage of Los Angeles was brought to Chicago. It took Joe eight rounds to get to Ramage. His next opponent was the iron man, Patsy Perroni. The Italian was dumped four times, and at the end of the tenth Joe's soggy red glove was raised. This was in Detroit, January 5, this year.

Hans Birkie fought Louis in Pittsburgh on January 11. Joe went along with Hans until the last round, and then stretched him. Blackburn explained, "I told Joe not to stop Birkie until I gave the word. 'Go along with him and learn something,' I whispered. When the bell rang for the tenth I said 'Go get him Chappy.' He did."

Louis fought Ramage again, this time in Los Angeles on Washington's Birthday. Art Lasky was in the ring when Joe and Ramage were introduced. "I'll fight the winner!"

shouted Art melodramatically. Louis knocked out Ramage in the second round—as he had predicted. Art took the next plane to New York. He fought Braddock and was punched into obscurity in the bout that earned Jim his shot at Max Baer.

Joe and his entourage motored north, stopping at San Francisco to obliterate Red Barry. Then Joe signed to meet Natie Brown on March 28. The rugged Natie went the distance but took the cruelest beating of his picturesque career. Louis next picked up easy money in five soft bouts—and then came Carnera.

"I never told anybody this, but do you know how I was able to tell Carnera was ready?" Louis asked. "I punched him around the stomach for five rounds, softening him, letting him tire. When he came out for the sixth I saw he had planted his feet flat and spread them much wider than they were in the first round. 'Oho!' I said to myself; 'he's ripe!' So I started to pitch at his chin. He went down like an axed steer."

### SYMBOLS OF BLACK PRIDE

[*Black athletes were important symbols of black pride and success. Maya Angelou, a prominent black poet, singer, dancer, writer, and movie director, was a young girl when Joe Louis was at his peak. In this excerpt from her autobiography, which is set in Arkansas in the mid-1930s, Angelou recreates her experience of listening to the radio broadcast of the Louis-Carnera fight. Boxing was a natural for radio broadcasts and boxing promoters were experts at using the media to ensure large gates for boxing events. In 1939, Lou Nova fought Max Baer in the first boxing telecast. That year, the Senate legalized interstate commerce in prizefight films. Maya Angelou,* I Know Why the Caged Bird Sings *(New York, 1970), 111-113.*]

The last inch of space was filled, yet people continued to wedge themselves along the walls of the Store. Uncle Willie had turned the radio up to its last notch so that youngsters on the porch wouldn't miss a word. Women sat on kitchen chairs, dining room chairs, stools and upturned wooden boxes. Small children and men leaned on the shelves or on each other.

The apprehensive mood was shot through with shafts of gaiety, as a black sky is streaked with lightning.

"I ain't worried 'bout this fight. Joe's gonna whip that cracker like it's open season."

"He gone whip him till that white boy call him Momma."

At last the talking was finished and the string-along about razor blades were over and the fight began.

"A quick jab to the head." In the Store the crowd grunted. "A left to the head and a right and another left." One of the listeners crackled like a hen and was quieted.

"They're in a clench, Louis is trying to fight his way out."

Some bitter comedian on the porch said, "That white man don' mind hugging that niggah now, I betcha."

"The referee is moving in to break them up, but Louis finally pushed the contender away and it's an uppercut to the chin. The contender is hanging on, now he's backing away. Louis catches him with a short left to the jaw."

A tide of murmuring assent poured out the doors and into the yard.

"Another left and another left. Louis is saving that mighty right...." The mutter in the Store had grown into a baby roar and it was pierced by the clang of a bell and the announcer's "That's the bell for round three, ladies and gentlemen."

As I pushed my way into the Store I wondered if the announcer gave any thought to the fact that he was addressing as "ladies and gentlemen" all the Negroes around the world who sat sweating and praying, glued to their "master's voice."

There were only a few calls for R.C. Colas, Dr. Peppers, and Hire's root beer. The real festivities would begin after the fight. Then even the old Christian ladies who taught their children and tried themselves to practice turning the other cheek would buy soft drinks, and if the Brown Bomber's victory was a particularly bloody one they would order peanut patties and Baby Ruths also.

Bailey and I lay the coins on top of the cash register. Uncle Willie didn't allow us to ring up sales during a fight. It was too noisy and might shake up the atmosphere. When the gong rang for the next round we pushed through the near-sacred quiet to the herd of children outside.

"He's got Louis against the ropes and now it's a left to the body and a right to the ribs. Another right to the body, it looks like it was low...Yes, ladies and gentlemen, the referee is signaling but the contender keeps raining the blows on Louis. It's another to the body, and it looks like Louis is going down.

My race groaned. It was our people falling. It was another lynching, yet another Black man hanging on a tree. One more woman ambushed and raped. A black boy whipped and maimed. It was hounds on the trail of a man running through slimy swamps. It was a white woman slapping her maid for being forgetful.

The men in the Store stood away from the walls and at attention. Women greedily clutched the babes on their laps while on the porch the shufflings and smiles, flirtings and, pinching of a few minutes before were gone. This might be the end of the world. If Joe lost we were back in slavery and beyond help. It would all be true, the accusations that we were lower types of human beings. Only a little higher than apes. True that we were stupid and ugly and lazy and dirty and, unlucky and worst of all, that God Himself hated us and ordained us to be hewers of wood and drawers of water, forever and ever, world without end.

We didn't breathe. We didn't hope. We waited.

"He's off the ropes, ladies and gentlemen. He's moving towards the center of the ring." There was no time to be relieved. The worst might still happen.

"And now it looks like Joe is mad. He's caught Carnera with a left hook to the head and right to the head. It's a left jab to the body and another left to the head. There's a left cross and a right to the head. The contender's right eye is bleeding and he can't seem to keep his block up. Louis is penetrating every block. The referee is moving in, but Louis sends a left to the body and it's the uppercut to the chin and the contender is dropping. He's on the canvas, ladies and gentlemen."

Babies slid to the floor as women stood up and men leaned toward the radio.

"Here's the referee. He's counting. One, two, three, four, five, six, seven...Is the contender trying to get up again?"

All the men in the store shouted, "NO."

"-eight, nine, ten." There were a few sounds from the audience, but they seemed to be holding themselves in against tremendous pressure.

"The fight is all over, ladies and gentlemen. Let's get the microphone over to the referee...Here he is. He's got the Brown Bomber's hand, he's holding it up...Here he is..."

Then the voice, husky and familiar, came to wash over us—"The winnah, and still heavyweight champeen of the world...Joe Louis."

Champion of the world. A Black boy. Some Black mother's son. He was the strongest man in the world. People drank Coca-Colas like ambrosia and ate candy bars like Christmas. Some of the men went behind the Store and poured white lightning in their soft-drink bottles, and a few of the bigger boys followed them. Those who were not chased away came back blowing their breath in front of themselves like proud smokers.

It would take an hour or more before the people would leave the Store and head for home. Those who lived too far had made arrangements to stay in town. It wouldn't do for a Black man and his family to be caught on a lonely country road on a night when Joe Louis had proved that we were the strongest people in the world.


## LET'S CLEAR UP BOXING

*[In this article, Ambrose J. Kennedy, a Member of Congress from Maryland who sought to reform boxing, details the sport's ills and outlines his proposed changes. Ambrose J. Kennedy, "Let's Clear Up The Boxing Mess," Liberty (1 June 1940), 35-36.]*

As an ordinary sports-loving citizen, I am fed up with the fight game. My attitude is due to what happened recently to a boxer from my home city of Baltimore.

As a U.S. congressman, therefore, I shall introduce a bill at this session for federal supervision of professional boxing in the United States.

The wrong decision which started me on this fight track happened in Washington last September in the fight between Harry Jeffra of Baltimore and Joey Archibald, world featherweight champion. Jeffra won that fight. Thirteen sports writers said Jeffra won; none said Archibald won. But the decision went to Archibald, 2 to 1.

Above is a photograph of the moment. See that boy, deprived of his championship, crying against the ropes. That's his mother there, with the rosary held in her hands. They're the kind of honest clean-cut folks I'm fighting for.

Jeffra didn't ask me to help him, I went into this business on my own initiative. I have no tie-up with any promoter or fighter. My sole motive is sportsmanship, because, like millions of other people, I have always been interested in sports.

The District of Columbia Boxing Commission convinced me that the decision against Jeffra was an honest, though blundering error. My determination to clean up boxing was brought about not by that error but by the fact that there was no administrative or executive unit sufficiently co-ordinated and sufficiently powerful to bring about a return match between Jeffra and Archibald, after a decision unanimously pronounced wrong by thirteen sports writers and by the two D.C. boxing commissioners.

Naturally, I went first to officials of the National Boxing Association to inquire about a return match for Jeffra when Archibald would have to defend his title within the next six months. I was told that their executive board; consisting of seven widely distributed boxing commissioners had already voted that Archibald's next bout should be with Jeffra; and that Washington was open for the match. But the same officials told me also that Archibald's manager had hired a lawyer who threatened to sue the N.B.A. if Archibald were "forced" to box Jeffra. I was further informed that it would be difficult for the N.B.A. to enforce its ruling that Jeffra should be accorded a return match, since Archibald, to hold his title, could box in states not members of N.B.A. In other words, there is a field outside organized professional boxing in which the Jeffra return match ruling, based on the simple elements of sportsmanship and fair play, could be ignored.

Giving weight to the decisions of the National Boxing Association, founded twenty years ago for the specific purpose of "co-operation and uniformity" is a far-flung and important list of members, including twenty-nine states and the District of Columbia; the cities of Atlanta, Georgia; Miami Beach, Florida; Winston-Salem, North Carolina; Tulsa, Oklahoma; Portland, Oregon; and Montreal and Quebec, Canada; as well as Cuba, western Canada, Hawaii, Mexico, Puerto Rico, and Venezuela. Its affiliations include organized boxing in Great Britain, Italy, France, and Germany.

It will be noticed that New York, with its great Yankee Stadium, its tremendous Madison Square Garden, is on the outside. Counterbalancing all the organized sportsmanship in the U.S. is the New York money-power boxing monopoly, aided and abetted by irregularities and bad boxing practices made possible by the existence of other nonmember states.

The sports world recently was thrown into a furor by the charge that heavyweight Harry Thomas had thrown fights to Max Schmeling and Galento. It is to be noticed that these charges of fixed fights refer to bouts that did not take place in N.B.A. states but in New York and Pennsylvania. Other boxing states not members of N.B.A. are California, Missouri, and Washington, all of which are considering coming in, and Maine, which is expected to join next year. Michigan and Massachusetts are in suspension. The invitation to join is always out to non-N.B.A. states. These give as their reason for not joining: "The laws of our state require that the State Commission administer boxing"— a flimsy excuse, since the laws of all N.B.A. states that do belong also decree exactly that.

Senator Edwin C. Johnson of Colorado has joined with me in the effort to force a boxing investigation and will introduce in the Senate a companion bill to the one I introduce in the House. If we succeed in bringing these bills to hearing, the public inevitably will hear the same sordid tales of fenagling, hand-picking opponents, of championships that were not championships, that were revealed to me when I started a simple little one-man inquiry into the Jeffra-Archibald bout. Every schoolboy used to know the name of the world champion. Now he's somebody in New York, and somebody else in California, and still a third somebody over the rest of the continent. Let me illustrate some of the points that I expect this investigation to bring out:

By boxing over the weight, world champions can be defeated over and over again and still hold their championships, disregarding the challengers in their own class who are eager for matches with them. This does not apply to the heavyweight champion, who must defend his title everytime he steps into the ring.

Another championship situation that needs clarifying has at its roots several of the bad practices of boxing—the ridiculous proceeding of the declaring of a "world's champion" by a single state; the silly idea that a generally recognized "world champion" can refuse to box anywhere but in his home city; and the arbitrary assignment of a certain percentage of the gate that must be paid to the champion. The N.B.A. recognized Al Hostak as middleweight champion because Hostak, in a title bout, defeated Freddie Steele, who had been proclaimed champion in that class by the World Boxing Congress which met in Rome in 1938. But New York declared Ceferino Garcia middleweight champion. Both are good fighters, and should clarify the situation to make the Championship mean something. But Garcia, fighting under Jacobs, holds out for the champion's 87 1/2 percent and wants Hostak to take the challenger's 12 1/2 per cent, and also to fight him in New York. Hostak contends he is a champion himself, so why should he take the challenger's 12 1/2 per cent? And also that Garcia could come and fight in Hostak's home city of Seattle. Chicago and Jersey City want this match.

Both are N.B.A. cities. In the old days of the fight game there was a winner's and a loser's end, usually 60 per cent and 40 per cent; sometimes 75 and 25; sometimes winner take all. But now it all has to be advance guaranties. Why can't those fighters be sporting and meet in a neutral city; and the winner take the 37 1/2 per cent, the loser the 12 1/2 per cent?

Two champions, Henry Armstrong and Lou Ambers, fought for the lightweight title. Ambers won. Before they fought, both had to sign up to fight again for the welterweight title, when Ambers is not a welterweight at all. Well, Armstrong got sick, so he was excused from that fight; but he got well enough within a few days to fight again in Ohio. Maybe the promoter was really sick; fans who pay money do not like the same dish warmed over.

A champion should fight a logical contender. Two champions fighting each other certainly are adding nothing to the history of sportsmanship, except greediness for gate receipts.

Now we come to the place where the monopolistic promoter shows his system. A recent issue of Ring Magazine stated that Jacobs, New York promoter, absolutely forbade a bout between Henry Armstrong and Ceferino Garcia in California, and was quoted in news dispatches as saying: "That fight cannot take place unless I say so. I hold a contract for the exclusive services of both the fighters, and if and when such a fight is staged, you can bet your boots that Uncle Mike will promote it." Jacobs did go to California to promote the Joe Louis and Jack Roper fight; and he also went to Michigan to stage the Joe Louis and Bob Pastor fight. This in spite of the fact that Jacobs conducts his boxing under the rules of New York, which specifically state: "Financial interest in boxer or wrestler prohibited." Such tactics will kill boxing in the hinterland and the game will soon get sick in New York.

I expect the investigation also to go into such abstract but also important matters as the lack of general uniformity of scoring rules and the lack of co-ordination between states which permits the faker and the contract jumper to continue fighting.

New York uses the rounds system of scoring; that is, each fighter gets complete credit for each round he wins. Now a fighter may lose a majority of the rounds by the narrowest of margins, and still end by having his opponent out on his feet at the final bell—whereupon he loses the fight. That actually did happen in a fight between Art Lasky and Steve Hamas. Lasky left Hamas a completely beaten man, but the referee had to give the fight to Hamas because he barely won the most rounds. My State of Maryland uses the "Split Ten System," in which ten points are divided between the two fighters in each round. Most states use the "Ten Must System," in which the winner of each round gets ten points and his opponent a proportional number according to the showing he has made. Both of the latter systems are fairer.

One instance of how co-ordination controls the faker: in Virginia, an N.B.A. state, a fighter was suspended, and for all time, for lying down. He just ducked over into West Virginia, not at that time an N.B.A. member, to do his fighting. Now West Virginia also has joined N.B.A. and is now presenting the fighter to fight fans.

The deeper I have gone into this prize-fight problem, the clearer it has become that professional boxing needs a good house cleaning. It needs national co-ordination and co-operation—or championship titles will continue to mean nothing. A New York monopoly exists in boxing. Unless a challenger agrees to fight only for certain promoters, he won't get a title fight. The same interests control both fighters in a ring, fighting one against another. Fighters are paid in advance in order to tie up their services. There is a ridiculous practice of one state's recognizing an arbitrary "world" champion.

Certain sports writers have paid their respects to me. I will pay mine to them. Part of what we will investigate is the so-called agreement between newspaper writers and promoters.

Why don't they discuss in their columns men holding championships, though they have been defeated ten or a dozen times? There is nothing more disgusting than to pay money to see a fight on a newspaper build-up, only to find the fighter washed up, a stumble bum. Why, for instance, did they build up Harry Thomas as an opponent for Joe Louis? Thomas was a baseball catcher and even the better read boxing followers knew nothing of him. Why have they overlooked the fact a New York promoter can prohibit a fight scheduled to be held in California? And to the sports writer who remarked that other matters ought to take my attention, I will say that I have sponsored and passed more bills than any other member of Congress.

Several sports writers offer discouragement along this line: "Boxing as now conducted is a dirty business. Uncle Sam will soil his hands. The boxing gentry—a tough lot—want no investigator."

To this I reply that Uncle Sam has cured tougher guys than the boxing crowd, and as to covering up a bad mess, I like the saying in use in the Marine Corps: "Will you clean it up or sleep in it?" There remain, believe it or not, some men who do not relish "sleeping in it." Boxing as it is now run may not seem to some worth the saving. My answer is that, run as it should be run, it can rank in public opinion with any sport.

### JACOBS—AM I A MENACE TO BOXING?

[*Michael Strauss Jacobs learned the trade by assisting boxing promoter Tex Rickard. In 1934, Jacobs organized the Twentieth Century Sporting Club and soon became boxing's most dominant figure. Jacobs promoted Louis' fights for fifty percent of the proceeds and used his control over Louis, Rocky Graziano, Bill Conn, and other ranked boxers to make himself and Madison Square Garden the kingpins of boxing. In the following article, Jacobs responds to the charges laid by Congressman Kennedy in the previous document. Mike Jacobs, As Told to Jack Mahon, "Am I A Menace to Boxing? Controversy in Sportdom! A Much Criticized Promoter Strikes Back," Liberty (29 June 1940).*]

In the past six months I have been publicly accused many times of "ruining" the boxing game. Jack Dempsey accused me only a few weeks ago, and the National Boxing Association must agree with him, for they vacated two titles because I would not allow certain champions to fight the men they "designated." I have been called a monopolist and a boxing dictator and have been charged with "tying up" fighters by illegal contracts. One fighter, in a national magazine, said he would never fight for me because I was "wrecking the game." Big men in cities throughout the country say I am causing boxing's downfall by refusing to show champions outside of New York. They also charge that no out-of-town fighters can get a "break" from me in Madison Square Garden.

Now, I have been in show business for twenty-five years and actively interested in boxing for the past ten. I have taken all kinds of criticism and have been called many different names. While I've often lost my temper and threatened to make a reply which would certainly embarrass several of my critics, I have never done so. At this time, however, I think it is only fair to state my side of the case and let the public judge for itself.

Fight promoting is essentially show business—which, as any one knows, is really all a gamble. Champions are made—not born. They have to be developed over the years. It takes plenty of time, patience, setbacks, and hard cash. Boxing stars are built on publicity, just like stars of the stage and screen. Managers must have money to entertain, to pay their rent and feed their boys, to keep them out of trouble and to pay doctors' bills between fights. I have to supply that money. At the moment, I am owed approximately $110,000 by fight managers from coast to coast—and the figure is still climbing.

The 20th Century Sporting Club, of which I am president, is a corporation with approximately $14,000,000 worth of property on which to carry out its yearly schedule. Ticket takers, publicity men, office help, technical crews, traveling expenses, and those "advances" to fighters and managers must be written off each year, by shows at Madison Square Garden, the Polo Grounds, Yankee Stadium, and Long Island City Bowl, in New York, and by any out-of-town promotions I may try.

Last year I paid $496,000 in taxes to the state and federal government on my shows. That does not include the tax on the money earned by the fighters or the amount earned by the various charities, which shared in those fights. Does that look as if I am trying to kill boxing?

To protect my Investments and property certain business contracts are essential. When I see a fighter I think will develop into a champion, or at least a big box office attraction, I usually gamble on him. I stake him, offer him more money than he can get elsewhere, and try to build him up. I have no guaranty that he will make good for me. If my guess is correct and he develops into a title challenger, I demand that he sign, if successful, to defend that title exclusively for me. It is the only insurance I ask for advancing money and getting him a shot at the championship. Any theatrical agent who performed a similar service would certainly demand a similar contract. Yet because of these contracts I am accused of being a dictator and a monopolist.

Champions are the only fighters bound by such agreements. And the charge that I never let champions fight outside of New York is not only ridiculous—it's a downright lie. Henry Armstrong defended his welterweight title in no less than ten cities in 1939!

They were New York, Los Angeles, St. Louis, Minneapolis, Seattle, Denver, Des Moines, Cleveland, Havana, and London.

Ceferino Garcia made his first defense of the middleweight title in the Philippine Islands, and his second in Los Angeles against Henry Armstrong. There's an example of two fighters I promoted into champions fighting for a title under other sponsors thousands of miles from New York. Does that seem exactly like a tie-up?

Former lightweight champion Lew Ambers fought all over the country. Billy Conn has risked his light-heavyweight title in his home town of Pittsburgh and will risk it again in Detroit this summer. Joe Louis has fought in Detroit and Los Angeles and expects to fight outside of New York again this year. How, then, does the charge that champions are locked up in New York hold up?

Could it be that out-of-town promoters feel that, by blasting me, they can cover up less attractive cash guaranties and offers to these champions? Ambers and his manager, Al Weill, will readily admit they'll accept good offers anywhere; but when it comes to title fights they'll sound out New York first, for that is where the big money lies. Every other good manager has the same idea. Managers who have criticized me for years will break all speed regulations to my office once they find a fighter they think I can use. If they can get a title chance or a sizable cash advance, all past grievances are soon forgotten. If their fighter is beaten, they resume criticizing my methods.

When Jack Dempsey recently told some Kansas City newspapermen I was ruining the game by my monopoly, I wasn't greatly annoyed. I realize, now that Jack is out of boxing and is selling food and liquor, he has to keep his name in the headlines. The fact that I do not consider a certain heavyweight, in whom he has an interest, a good box-office attraction, might also have something to do with Jack's remarks.

Only a few weeks ago Al Hostak, the Seattle boy who claims the middleweight title, had his ideas on boxing published under the title, Why I Won't Fight for Mike Jacobs. Hostak said he wouldn't fight for me even "if he gave me the Empire State Building," because he did not approve of my methods, etc. He said his manager, Eddie Marino, had told him all about me, and that he was pledged to fight only for, Nate Druxman, the Seattle promoter who gave him his start.

I read young Hostak's piece very carefully. Either he is very naive or very dumb. Perhaps he forgets several conversations he, his manager, and Mr. Druxman had with me in Chicago only a few months ago. Perhaps he forgets how anxious his manager was to have him fight for me in New York if the proper terms were arranged.

Hostak was very willing to fight for the very sizable guaranty I offered him. The boy wanted to fight, but—in case he doesn't know it—the reason the match (with Garcia) never came off was because I refused to "deal" with Marino and Druxman. I offered to let the winner of such a fight make his first defense of the title in Seattle, provided, if Hostak became champion, he would then come to New York and defend it there. In order to prove Hostak's ability, I also asked that he have a tune-up fight in New York before the Garcia bout. Both Druxman and Marino refused to agree to this without other excessive guaranties.

All this was discussed in January, when I flew from Miami to Chicago to get my first look at Hostak. He was to fight Tony Zale there. When our final meeting, the day of the fight, broke up without any agreement being reached, I wished Hostak luck and warned him to be careful of Zale. That night Zale whipped him.

My chief objection to staging title fights outside of New York is a personal one. I like to run the show myself, have the headaches and take the loss or profits accordingly.

This is impossible when I move out of town. The police force, Chamber of Commerce, local newspapers and bankers think all they have to do is to ask and they can have as many complimentaries as they wish. You can't pay your bills with satisfied complimentary customers. I found that out in Philadelphia when I staged the Lou Nova-Tony Galento heavyweight elimination last September. It was a red-hot match. Several cities bid for it. One Philadelphia business man offered me a $150,000 check for the rights to the show. It was a good check, too; but, though I refused it, I was convinced Philadelphia was the spot for the fight.

So I promoted it there. The fight which was supposed to gross a quarter of a million dollars grossed exactly $69,906, which, less taxes, gave me $56,855 to pay off all expenses. There were almost as many customers there "on the cuff" as there were who paid their way in. How I wish I had taken that first check!

Then again, every place you go, you are under many obligations. I took Joe Louis out to the Coast to fight Jack Roper. Here too I was practically guaranteed a $200,000 gross gate. By the time I was through taking care of people "just had to be taken care of" the fight grossed $88,000. Louis' fights in New York have averaged over $335,000 gross, while in the last two years I've had shows between lightweights and welterweights which have drawn from $80,000 to $104,000. These figures should explain why I have to be sold a real bill of goods before pulling a "name" fight out of the big town.

The complaint that out-of-town favorites are denied a chance to fight at Madison Square Garden is another which will not stand up under close scrutiny. Where are the fighters working whom I supposedly ban? The answer is, they're not. A good fighter can get a chance very easily in New York. All I ask is that they fight good opponents, not handpicked second-raters.

The managers who talk the most about boycotts have repeatedly turned down bouts at the Garden. There are a few around New York right now who want main events for their boys without making them earn them in a preliminary bout.

All these complaints have found a welcome ear at the National Boxing Association, which has joined in the drive to "break the Jacobs monopoly." The N.B.A. every three months rates the first ten challengers for every crown in pugilism. It demands that champions defend their titles against the most favored members on these lists. That is all very well in theory. In practice, things don't always work out as planned.

This organization recently vacated Joey Archibald's featherweight title and Lou Ambers' lightweight title. Archibald lost his title because he refused to meet Harry Jeffra of Washington, who the N.B.A. felt was being unfairly ignored. In fact, Representative Ambrose J. Kennedy of Maryland demanded a federal investigation of boxing. Yet, a month or so after its proclamation, the N.B.A. suddenly abandoned Jeffra and decided that Pete Scalzo of New York should have first chance at Archibald.

When Archibald refused to abide by its confusing rulings, the board announced it had vacated his title. Though Ambers signed to defend his lightweight title against Lew Jenkins of Texas on May 10, he too was stripped of his robes because the great minds decided Sammy Angott of Louisville or Davey Day of Chicago rated such a bout.

This organization should content itself with its ratings and stop trying to make matches. If they know so much about fight promotion, why don't they stage an Archibald-Scalzo fight and gamble on its success?

I have often been asked if a czar of boxing would help the game. The idea has met with approval in some sections, and I understand Representative Kennedy is in favor of putting the sport under such an executive and also under federal control. I do not think it is a workable idea. Politics has no place in boxing.

A czar like Commissioner Landis is fine for baseball, where each club has its own organization and owns its property and players. We do not own fighters and there are different boxing rules in every state. Prizefighters appear and disappear much more rapidly than any other professional athletes. I believe it would be impossible for one man to rule them all.

I have been asked by many writers if Joe Louis is going to quit at the end of this year, and even told by some of them that he is. The doom not only of the heavyweight division but of my entire organization has been scheduled for that dread day.

Boxing is bigger than any one individual, and the 20th Century Sporting Club will live on, no matter who the champions are. And Joe Louis will retire only after he has been beaten or knocked out. And he won't quit then—until after I have staged a return match!

## NATIONAL COLLEGIATE WRESTLING MEET

[*The following report by R.G. Clapp, the chairman of the NCAA wrestling committee, outlines the growth of collegiate wrestling and its growing interest in eastern United States. R. G. Clapp, "Annual National Collegiate Wrestling Meet," The NCAA News Bulletin, 1 (1 May 1933), 2-6.*]

The Sixth Annual National Collegiate Wrestling Championships were held at Lehigh University, Bethlehem, Pennsylvania, on March 24th and 25th.

Question had been raised as to the advisability of holding this annual meet in 1933 on account of the prevailing financial conditions; therefore, a questionnaire was sent to the wrestling coaches of the institutions which had previously participated in our annual meet. The response to this inquiry was so encouraging that the Wrestling Rules Committee voted to hold the meet as usual. The soundness of this decision was fully confirmed by the size of the meet and by the general interest and enthusiasm shown by contestants and spectators.

In every respect this was the most successful meet which the Wrestling Rules Committee has conducted thus far. It was larger than any of the five previous National Collegiate meets, both from the standpoint of individual participants and number of institutions represented. The following tabulation shows the way the annual meets have gradually developed.

|  |  | INDIVIDUAL CONTESTANTS | INSTITUTIONS REPRESENTED |
|---|---|---|---|
| 1st Meet—Iowa State College | 1928 | 40 | 16 |
| 2nd Meet—Pennsylvania State College | 1929 | 61 | 25 |
| 3rd Meet—Ohio State University | 1930 | 79 | 29 |
| 4th Meet—Brown University | 1931 | 67 | 26 |
| 5th Meet—Indiana University | 1932 | 75 | 24 |
| 6th Meet—Lehigh University | 1933 | 86 | 30 |

This meet was also the largest from the standpoint of number of spectators and gate receipts. The somewhat limited seating capacity of the Taylor Gymnasium was taxed at all four sessions of the meet. The total receipts amounted close to $2400, which should allow nearly $2000 for refund on transportation expense of the visiting contestants and coaches. The meet was conducted in four sessions, two on Friday afternoon and evening and the remainder on Saturday afternoon and evening. The committee was somewhat startled at the announcement of the local manager at Lehigh University that no tickets would be sold for separate sessions of the meet, but only a blanket ticket good for all four sessions. The soundness of the manager's judgment is verified, however, by the fact that this year there will be between $600 and $700 more money refunded to the visiting contestants than in any previous National Collegiate Wrestling Meet.

From the standpoint of caliber of wrestling and closeness of competition, this was the best meet that we have ever held. Nearly every match was so closely contested that it was impossible to predict the outcome until shortly before the finish. In a fighting type of personal contest like wrestling, and especially where the matches are closely contested and hard fought, one would expect to find occasional loss of temper on the part of the participants, and yet in this meet not a single such case occurred and there was the best of feeling between participants at all times. This would seem to indicate that wrestling has a very marked effect in developing self-control to a high degree.

The 1931 and 1932 meets were conducted as invitation meets, open only to the winners and runners-up in the various college conference or wrestling association championship meets and to wrestlers of similar caliber representing institutions which were not members of such conferences or wrestling associations. On account of the possibility that the prevailing financial conditions might prevent many of the outstanding college wrestlers from participating in the annual meet, the Wrestling Rules Committee decided to make this year's meet an open affair, in order to insure a sufficient number of entries to make the meet a success. A post-meet check, however, showed that there were fully as many of the champions from different sections of the country as in any previous National Collegiate Wrestling Meet. [Deleted first, second, and third place winners, and their schools, in the eight weight classes.]

No team championship was awarded, because the committee felt that present financial conditions would not allow many institutions to enter full teams. Lehigh University was the only institution which was represented in all of the eight weight classes.

During the first few years the National Collegiate Wrestling Meets were held, institutional representation was confined almost exclusively to the Middle-West and South-West. The number of institutions representing the East has gradually increased, however, from year to year, and this year for the first time the number of Eastern institutions participating exceeded the number from the Middle-West and South-West. In this year's meet the East, including New England, was represented by 16 institutions. There were 11 from the West and South-West, and three from the South. The number of individual participants from the East has also gradually increased from year to year until this year there was an equal number (40) from the East and the West. The remaining six participants represented the Southern institutions.

Many faculty members of Lehigh University attended the meet. President Richards was an interested spectator, and he presented the medals to the winning contestants.

The caliber of wrestling in the National Collegiate Championship Meets has developed to such a high degree that only wrestlers of wide experience win National Collegiate championships. Generally speaking, therefore, these championships are won by seniors, and consequently relatively few champions appear to defend their titles in succeeding meets. This year two of the 1932 champions participated: namely, Robert Hess of Iowa State College and Joe Puerta of the University of Illinois. Hess successfully defended his championship, but Puerta was supplanted by Ross Flood of Oklahoma A.& M. College as the champion in his class.

As usual, the College Wrestling Coaches Association held its annual meeting in connection with the National Collegiate Wrestling Meet. 35 coaches and committee members attended the dinner meeting of the Association at the Bethlehem Club on Friday, March 24th. The meeting was given over to a discussion of matters of general interest to the college wrestling coaches....

The customary conference between the Wrestling Rules Committee and the wrestling coaches present at the annual meet gave the committee an opportunity to discuss thoroughly with the coaches the numerous suggested changes in the National Collegiate Wrestling Rules and to get the coaches' viewpoints on the same. Very few of the proposed changes were approved by the committee at its later meetings and those that were approved constituted only minor changes in the rules and had to do primarily with protection of contestants against injury and facilitating the running off of championship meets. The suggestion that we should adopt the Olympic Rules received little support either from the coaches or committee members, as this would mean the elimination, to a large extent, of "leg wrestling" which has been developed to a high degree in this country and which has added greatly to the popularity of college wrestling....

Intercollegiate wrestling continues to develop in a highly satisfactory manner. Perhaps this is best illustrated by referring to the recent Olympic competition. In 1928 and also in 1932 every one of the 14 members (7 representatives and 7 alternates) of the American Olympic Wrestling Team was a college or ex-college wrestler. In 1928 the American Team won one first place and one second, and failed to place in the team competition. In 1932 the American Team won three first places, one second, and one third, thereby winning the Olympic championship in the Free Style Wrestling. Of the seven members of the 1932 American Olympic Wrestling Team who actually participated in the Olympic competition, five were college undergraduates (or graduated in June, 1932). These five undergraduates won two first places, one second and one third. From the standpoint of number of participants in intercollegiate wrestling and interest on the part of the spectators, intercollegiate wrestling has improved during the past year in spite of the adverse financial conditions.

Mr. P.E. Wiggins of Columbus, Ohio, the new high school representative on the Wrestling Rules Committee, attended the meetings of the committee and presented a number of constructive suggestions for the developing of interest in wrestling among the high schools.

The Wrestling Rules Committee voted to recommend to the National Collegiate Council that the 1934 meet be held at Iowa State College.

## FENCING—ON GUARD

*[The following article illustrates the romantic nature of fencing for many of its followers. As with other sports of European origin, the US and Canada often benefited from*

*visits by touring teams or individuals. Although women are depicted solely as specta-*
*tors in this document, in 1929 the Intercollegiate Women's Fencing Association was*
*organized with teams representing Bryn Mawr, Cornell, New York University, and the*
*University of Pennsylvania. Arthur Mann, "On Guard! For Those Who Find Bridge*
*too Dangerous, There's a New Social Diversion—Fencing," Collier's (14 March 1936),*
*39, 67-68.]*

Pin the modern fencing fans down to a confession and you will discover that they
would substitute sword-swinging for contract bridge as a parlor pastime. Their reasons
for the change are many and somewhat logical.

First, they explain, a fencing bout requires only half as many players as contract
bridge. Secondly, the fencers can start in the parlor, but they don't have to remain there.
They can move out into the hallway and have at it, because the regulation fencing strip
is three feet wide and from twenty to thirty feet long. They can even fence up and
down the stairway and over balconies, thrusting, parrying and riposting as seen in the
screen thrillers.

**BUT WHAT ABOUT INJURIES?**

"Nonsense!" is the scoffing retort. "The hazards of fencing are nowhere near as
great as those encountered in the average mixed bridge game. Look-up the annual list
of casualties!"

And so the bull market in fencing is in full swing. It reached some kind of a high
mark recently when the world's greatest fencer, Aldo Nadi, a handsome, tall and willowy Italian, filled the grand ballroom of a New York hotel with a bejeweled and otherwise swanky group at admission prices that sounded as though Mike Jacobs had
something to do with the promotion. Tickets were five and seven dollars a copy, plus
tax.

New York City, of course, is the fencing center of the country. Most of the cham-
pionships are held in the East and won by members of the pioneer organizations, such
as the New York A. C., Fencers Club, J. Sanford Saltus Club, Salle d'Armes Vince, etc.
Many of the eastern colleges have strong swordsmen. The Amateur Fencers League of
America, formed forty-five years ago to control the sport, does its controlling from
New York and has the final say in the selection of the Olympic team.

But the American debut of this master swordsman from Italy brought out the fact
that all the big cities from coast to coast and as far south as Texas were clamoring for
his services as an entertainer, or an instructor, or both. It was surprising to learn that
peaceful communities which, you imagine, would encounter trouble opening a can of
sardines, have fencing clubs and have been at swords' points for years.

Boston, Detroit, Chicago, Washington, Dallas and Pacific Coast cities put in attractive bids to the Italian for early appearances. This indicated that Signor Nadi's visit here
would be a lengthy one. The offer from Cleveland, of $1,200 for a single exhibition,
indicated that his visit would be profitable as well.

Less imaginative humans are inclined to puzzle over the appeal of fencing, because
they fail to grasp its subtleties. They see no reason for wasting time with a blunt sword,
when it would be infinitely more effective to go out and slap somebody down with a
clenched fist.

No real fencer would stoop to conquer in that fashion. It smacks of prize-fighting,
or a Pop-Eye cartoon. It would be like getting out a sheriff's warrant and hauling your
enemy off to the jug.

In a fencing bout you can play your opponent into strategic positions, wear him down as a cat wears down a mouse before cracking its vertebrae—as a matador wears down the bull before the final thrust.

Swording is the oldest form of weapon combat since the Cenozoics quit throwing rocks at each other. The flashing steel blade brings a man closer to the thrill of medieval daring than any other form of quarrel. It is an ideal outlet for chronic hatred or sadism, because everything can be settled without giving or taking physical damage. It provides more satisfaction than initiation night at the lodge.

## THE HEIDELBERG SYSTEM

Modern fencers are well protected from injury. Their chests are padded and torsos covered with a heavy canvas jacket. They always protect their heads with a mask of heavy wire mesh, which makes them look like beekeepers who do not trust their bees. Very rarely does a modern fencer suffer injury, other than a dent or two in his ego.... [Deleted early history of fencing in Europe.]

## LIGHTNING FAST

In his first match here, Nadi fenced with George Santelli, United States open champion with the foils. It was an exhibition and hence no judges called the shots. The players acknowledged touches. It was a splendid exhibition, but hardly a quiet one, due to Mr. Santelli's constant acknowledgement of touches.

Here was the open champion of the United States fencing the greatest swordsman in the world, and that's exactly what they looked like. Santelli scored, but, had it been a real duel, he would have resembled a nutmeg grater at the finish, for Nadi pierced five and six times for each of Santelli's touches.

The Italian was overwhelming in every, way—strength, speed, footwork, grace, in parrying and on the riposte. His blade was quick and forcing at all times, plunging past the American champion's inadequate defense almost at will. Nadi wasn't even warm at the finish.

Later in the evening the international champion fenced with saber against John R. Huffman, American three-weapon champion, who finished third in the Olympic saber competition at Los Angeles.

Again it was one-sided. Nadi was not only quicker with his slashing touches, but they were infinitely more decisive. He would have made any Heidelberg corporation without suffering a scar.

## FENCING'S WATCHDOG

Aldo Nadi and his elder brother, Nedo, who exhibited in this country five years ago, are sons and pupils of the great Beppe Nadi, of Milan, now seventy-six years old. Papa Beppe in 1920 turned out an entire Olympic team that carried off practically every fencing honor in the games. Nedo was the shining star that year.

Aldo, now thirty-six, is heralded as greater than his brother in foils and epee, and at least his equal in the saber. It is his plan to find out what is wrong with American fencing during his visit here, accepting, of course, fees for his research. He is a great favorite in Paris, especially since the death of the great French champion, Lucien Gaudin. For Parisian instruction, Nadi receives from 10,000 to 15,000 francs a lesson.

Today in his tour of the big cities, Signor Nadi will find little wrong with American fencing, other than downright incompetence, which only time and competition can remove. He should have stepped into the fencing scene some forty or fifty years ago when titles and the prestige of "national" championship victories were handed out like political plums. [Deleted career of John Allaire]

Many actors take up fencing to keep fit, but, more important, to keep graceful, or get that way. Walter Hampden rates very high as a swordsman. His fencing in Hamlet was always something to see and hear.

Hampden has frequently come off the stage as Hamlet or Macbeth bearing cuts and scratches, despite his skill with the sword. It seems he used to have a leading man, Ernest Rowan, who could fence him to a standstill, and often did, regardless of how Shakespeare wrote the finish of Hamlet and Macbeth....

There are few better forms of exercise. Allaire never weighed more than 160, but he developed the legs and arms of a heavyweight. His legs are still firm. He quit competition when he reached the seventy-year mark, 1926. He fenced for a senior trophy and lost. Up until last fall he could still parry and riposte with anybody ten and twenty years younger.

Although fencing has been gaining popularity among women during the past ten years, it could take a big jump while Aldo Nadi is here. One look at this willowy, sword-shaped Italian, and many woman would willingly abandon contract bridge and its attending woes.

His chief hazard has not been supplied by our fencers, but by the social committees who insist upon writing a supper and grand ball into his appearance contract. It seem that the man has great appeal, and the tremendous possibilities of fencing as a social channel can be detected in the hope whispered by a fluttering dowager at Nadi's debut here.

"Imagine," she sighed as the wraithlike figure danced up and down the strip, "being hacked to death by such a handsome swordsman!"

Chapter 7

## FIELD SPORTS—LACROSSE, FIELD HOCKEY, SPEEDBALL

During the 1930s, lacrosse in the United States and Canada took different paths. Whereas field lacrosse grew in importance in the United States, it declined dramatically in Canada and was largely replaced by box lacrosse.

At the beginning of the decade, forty-four American colleges and thirty-one high schools offered men's varsity lacrosse, as did a variety of clubs and military schools. In general, north-eastern colleges dominated lacrosse. They often regarded it as a first-letter sport, which sometimes supplanted baseball as the major spring sport. The most powerful teams, Johns Hopkins, Navy, Maryland University, and St. John's, were based in Maryland. With strong lacrosse programs in Baltimore's two largest public high schools (Poly and City) and in almost all of its private high schools, the city provided the majority of the players. Other top teams included Army, Princeton, Syracuse, Mount Washington and Rutgers.

Faced with the growth in popularity of box lacrosse, the rules were changed in 1933 to make the game more wide-open and thus more appealing. The number of players per team was reduced from twelve to ten, the field was shortened from 110 to eighty yards (the next year it was lengthened to ninety yards, before it returned to eighty yards in 1940), and the space behind each goal was diminished from thirty-five to twenty yards. The game remained sixty minutes in duration, but was now divided into four quarters. Since the rules emphasized greater speed, protective equipment could be reduced and teams could save on costs. Faced with continued competition from box lacrosse, the American lacrosse association speeded the game even more in 1935 by eliminating face-offs when the ball went out of bounds.

Whereas the number of American lacrosse players had doubled in the previous decade, Canadian players declined by about one-third. In part, this was due to Canada's reliance on lacrosse as a club rather than as a university sport. Canadian rules, which allowed more "clouting," also had an impact on the game's declining popularity. Forced to wear heavy padding, Canadian lacrosse players tended to be slower and lacked the spectacular passing that had made it a spectator sport. The coup de grace was delivered by the short-lived professional box lacrosse (boxla) league.

Boxla was played either on a small field enclosed by boards, or indoors in a gym or arena. Its origins are unclear. A popular story at the time claimed that box lacrosse was introduced in Australia by former Johns Hopkins University lacrosse players and was attracting more than 20,000 spectators. A Canadian player, the tale continued, brought boxla home with him early in 1931. Since box lacrosse was unknown in Australia, the story was obviously false, and was probably circulated to promote the new game. Indeed, by the time the hoax was exposed, boxla was popular in Canada. Other accounts attribute the idea to several former lacrosse players in Montreal, one of whom became the first president of the professional boxla league in 1931.

National Hockey League owners in Montreal and Toronto were the architects of professional lacrosse. Looking for a way to earn money from their arenas in the off-season, the owners of the Montreal Canadiens, the Maroons, and the Toronto Maple Leafs created a professional boxla league. Frank Selke, one of the promoters, later recalled—"I was in it with Conn Smythe and the brand-new Maple Leaf Gardens. We argued that lacrosse would keep the gardens going in the summertime." In June 1931, four teams (later expanded to seven) formed a professional box lacrosse league.

To attract spectators, the league played night games in the spring and fall. The rules permitted a more physical style of play and the owners recruited professional hockey players such as Lionel Conacher, Nels Stewart, and Hooley Smith. With seven men per team, and substitutions on the fly, boxla emphasized speed and physical contact. Large crowds filled the stands. Interest in lacrosse was revived throughout Canada, especially in Ontario and British Columbia, and estimates placed the number of Canadian clubs at more than 300. The new league was so successful that the Canadian Lacrosse Association adopted boxla as the official game in September 1931, with the Minto Cup as the ultimate prize.

The following year, an international league was formed with two teams in New York City and one each in Brooklyn, Boston, Baltimore, and Toronto. To promote the game in the US, Smythe and Selke organized a charity exhibition match between the Montreal Canadiens and the Toronto Maple Leafs at Madison Square Garden in 1932.

The teams played in front of 8,000 spectators. Playing in baseball parks at night, international league teams attracted sparse crowds and folded in mid season. Amateur boxla leagues continued in the US, particularly in cities near the Canadian border, until about 1936.

In Canada, the professional boxla league ran short of funds and disbanded in the summer of 1932. Boxla continued on the amateur level, where the best senior teams competed for the Mann Cup. Ontario teams won the Cup eight times in the decade, and British Columbia captured it twice. Boxla was particularly popular in British Columbia, where more than 11,000 fans watched the New Westminister Salmonbellies lose the Mann Cup to the Hamilton Tigers. Much of Boxla's success in British Columbia was due to the efforts of the North Shore Indians who mesmerized spectators with their brilliant stick work and intricate passes, and their colorful shirts which featured a large image of an Indian head on the front. The North Shore Indians played before packed houses and received requests to play exhibitions throughout North America.

Women's lacrosse was played in a few private women's colleges in the United States in the 1920s, but it was not until 1931 that the Women's Lacrosse Association was formed. The following year, forty-one colleges, mainly in Baltimore, Boston, New York, and Philadelphia, joined the association. In 1934, a touring British women's lacrosse team promoted the game in the United States through exhibition games, demonstrations, and public talks. The following year an American team paid a return visit. Although lacrosse competed with hockey for the women's attention and suffered from a lack of coaches, women liked the game because of the continuous play and the fact that unlike hockey or soccer, players were not confined to one position. Educators approved of the game because it was played outdoors and, unlike in basketball, players tended to develop a natural upright running position.

Concerned with young women's health and reproductive systems, and bearing in mind that many parents were reluctant to allow their daughters to play lacrosse, the Women's Committee of the American Physical Education Association's subcommittee on Lacrosse, formed in 1934, shortened the length of the field and adapted rules to forbid physical contact.

**FIELD HOCKEY**

Women's field hockey also benefited from rule adaptations designed to make the game less strenuous, competitive, and dangerous. At Bryn Mawr College, Constance Applebee adopted British rules that forbid body checking, raised sticks, and shots on goal from outside the semicircle area in front of the goal, whereupon the United States Women's Lacrosse Association was formed in 1931. Although field hockey was just as competitive as lacrosse and basketball, female physical educators did not protest against it. Historian Susan Cahn has suggested that since few males played field hockey, the game was viewed as a female sport. Women organized, coached, and officiated women's interscholastic field hockey, unlike many other female sports which were controlled mostly by men. In addition, states Cahn, field hockey's "British roots and its association with elite institutions...fit the class and gender standards of physical educators [and thereby] escaped the criticism leveled at other strenuous sports."

In 1933, fifty-one of seventy-five women's colleges offered field hockey as part of their physical education program, with New England, followed by Middle Atlantic schools leading the way. More than 400 clubs sought to reach the national tournament sponsored by the US Field Hockey Association. By 1936, approximately 10,000 women played field hockey for nine weeks every fall. In Canada and the US, field hockey was largely a private school game. The cost of equipment (with cleats at $2.25, shin guards for $1.50, tunics for $8, and sticks at $7) no doubt prevented less well-off schools from adopting field hockey. Negative comments such as the following did not tend to encourage females to participate in the sport. "It has been said that if the women who play field hockey could get dates with men, the game would die out for lack of players." (News-week, October 1936)

Canada and the US both benefited from contact with other countries. In 1931, a Scottish team participated in the American national field hockey tournament and the US Field Hockey Association paid a reciprocal visit later in the year. Two years later, an all-star women's team toured Europe. In 1936, teams from Australia, Wales, England, Scotland, and South Africa played in a tournament in Philadelphia and then toured American colleges to further promote the game. In 1938, British Columbia initiated home-and-home games with an all-star team from Los Angeles.

**SPEEDBALL**
Speedball became one of the fastest growing sports for women. The sport originated as an intra-mural activity for males at the University of Michigan in 1921, but by the 1930s, it became almost exclusively a women's sport. In 1935, Spalding Athletics Library published the first comprehensive rules for women's speedball. Males played on a field measuring 360 by 160 feet. Women played on a much smaller field, the dimension varying depending upon the age group of the females. Speedball's rapid progress, especially in the mid-west and in intramural college programs, was due in part to the efforts of female physical educators who liked the fact that bodily contact was forbidden, that running was curtailed, that equipment was inexpensive, that anyone could play, and that it was beneficial for the students' neuro-muscular systems.

Speedball combined the catching and passing skills of basketball, the kicking and punting of soccer and football, and the drop-kick of football. The ball, which could be either a soccer ball or an official speedball, was advanced by kicking it to oneself or to another player. One dribble was allowed. Soccer rules governed kicked balls and basketball rules regulated thrown balls. A soccer goal counted 3 points, a completed pass from outside the 6-yard line to a teammate in the end zone was 2 points. A football-type drop-kick was worth 2 points, and a soccer-like penalty kick was 1 point.

### LACROSSE'S POPULARITY

[*This article describes the growth of lacrosse in the US and outlines some of the reasons for its popularity. The discussion of the how the game is played, disabuses the author's claim that lacrosse was replacing baseball. Lewis B. Funke, "Lacrosse Puts Ice Hockey on the Turf. Combining the Speed and Rough Play of Ice Hockey, Lacrosse Threatens to Replace Baseball as a Major Sport in Southern Seaboard and Eastern Colleges," The Literary Digest (14 April 1934), 28.*]

The heat of enthusiasm moved a sportsman to exclaim, "It has the dash of basketball, the crash of football, the soul-stirring action of hockey, the recklessness of polo and it is the fastest game on two feet." He had viewed for the first time the modern game of lacrosse, the game that preceded all games on this sport-loving continent.

Played for centuries in Canada and the United States, firmly entrenched at Oxford and Cambridge universities, popular in Ireland and Australia, lacrosse has been a fixture, since it was originated by the Indians when the sport was a mild form of war. Obviously our red cousins would hardly recognize the lacrosse of today as the baggatway they fostered on the plains—when entire tribes engaged for days over miles of terrain—but it retains the fundamentals of endurance, and agility, with coordination of mind and body predominantly important. In the East and near-South, lacrosse has had a permanent place on college and high school athletic programs because of its value as a complement for football and its personal appeal as a game providing spirited physical combat.

## GAME SPEEDED UP

Broken-field running, so thrilling to the spectator and important asset of the football player is just as vital in lacrosse. This is especially true this year with the use of Indian-tan for the cradling net of the "crosse," or stick, a much more pliant substance which has been substituted for the stiff clock cord of former years. This makes it easier for the player to run with the ball and as a result lacrosse will be even faster this season.

One of the sport's foremost protagonists is Glenn Scobie ("Pop") Warner. Long before he achieved his fame as a football strategist and developer of the double wingback formation, Warner learned of lacrosse's conditioning merits. Stationed at Carlisle Indian School and confronted by the necessity of deriving the most from a meager squad, he had to supervise the year-around conditioning of his men to enable them to withstand the rigors of a strenuous schedule.

He has attributed to lacrosse much of the credit for the famed "iron man" stamina which was the trademark of his Carlisle teams. It not only kept the Indians in training during the spring and provided relaxation following the football season, but it sharpened their minds: the speed essential to successful manipulation and finesse of stick handling impressed them as just a variation of their intricate football maneuvers.

To-day a new administration in the United States Intercollegiate Lacrosse Association presses its plans for the resurgence of the game. With the cooperation of the National Collegiate Athletic Association, lacrosse is gradually being propagated on a nationwide scale. The main hindrance to its spread—expense—now has been entirely eliminated.

Formerly the best lacrosse sticks were manufactured in Canada and heavy import duties usually made sale in this country a prohibited burden for athletic budgets. Now sticks can be manufactured in America of equal quality and at less than half the original cost. As in rugby, suitable apparel may consist of cast-off football jerseys, basketball pants, hockey gloves and any type of shoe. Thus the game is afforded a more democratic adoption.

Descended from a sport which once functioned as a means of settling tribal disputes without endangering the women, lacrosse has naturally undergone a metamorphosis. No longer is the object of the game to see how many men of the opposing team can be crippled. The sticks, however, have retained the shape that inspired the modern name given by the French Canadians when they first saw the game in action. The referred to it as: "La Crosse" the netted stick resembled a bishop's crozier.

Lacrosse is played by teams of ten men on a field of nearly the same dimensions as a football gridiron. The goals are similar to those in ice hockey and are placed ninety yards apart in the longitudinal center of the field. They are situated within an area eighteen by twelve feet known as the "crease." Twenty yards or more are allotted for playing space behind the goals.

Play is started by the "draw" of the centers in a circle in the middle of the field, corresponding to the face-off in hockey and the tip-off in basketball. From that moment what happens can not be charted. There is the sight of the elusive broken field runner, the mad pursuit, the crash of bodies and sticks. The side that has secured the ball as a result of the draw attempts to carry it toward the opponent's goal. The ball may be carried in the stick, "cradled" in the net, or thrown to another player of the same side, or if on the ground may be knocked or kicked.

Checking, which corresponds to tackling in football, may be practised upon a man actually in possession of the ball or within reach of it. Speed and concerted action are halted only for out-of-bounds and fouls which are divided into technical and personal categories, and the penalties are either a free throw for the opponents or suspension of the offending player from the game as in hockey.

**WIDELY PLAYED**

The Big Three, Yale, Harvard and Princeton, progenitors of practically all college sports, gave lacrosse its first impetus. Their success in propagating the game carried lacrosse to the greater universities of the country. To-day, after over fifty years of organized intercollegiate competition, the game is played at such major institutions as West Point, Annapolis, Johns Hopkins, Cornell, Dartmouth, Brown, Rutgers, Maryland, New York University, Georgia, Swarthmore, Pennsylvania, Williams, and Tufts.

Following the 1933 campaign a survey showed that over two hundred teams were playing the game and that in the South particularly lacrosse had established itself as a definite substitute for baseball. The diamond game has shown the signs of wear and tear below the Mason and Dixon line just as it has in the city high schools of the North. Maryland, for instance, has inaugurated lacrosse leagues, and senior pro teams may be seen in action over the weekends. There, at least, the baseball bat has been supplanted by the lacrosse stick.

### FIELD HOCKEY'S FIRST DECADE

*[Anne Townsend, President of the US Field Hockey Association, outlines the growth, purpose, and methods of her association in its first decade of existence. Anne Townsend, "The First Decade," The Sportswoman (May 1932), 7-9.]*

In the files of the United States Field Hockey Association is a modest two-page leaflet, headed "Report of the Organization of the United States Field Hockey Association," and beginning "On January 21st, 1922, at 3 P.M., a meeting was held in the auditorium of the Y.W.C.A., Philadelphia". Ten years ago last January, then, the U.S.F.H.A. came into existence. We have survived the first decade, and it seems a good moment at which to pause, to look back over the activities of the last ten years, and consider what we have accomplished.

Although no formal platform was ever adopted by the U.S.F.H.A., the Association was formed with a very definite purpose in mind—to organize, spread, and improve club hockey in this country. We have always welcomed schools and colleges to Allied Membership, and stand ready to help them in any way we can, but the U.S.F.H.A. functions primarily for the benefit of club players, for those who wish to go on playing after they have left school or college. We have attempted to build up an efficient organization in order to facilitate and encourage the formation of clubs, so that everyone who wishes to play club hockey may have the opportunity of doing so. We have tried constantly to widen our field of activity so that more people each year, in more localities, will be playing the game. And by regulating the rules in collaboration with the American Physical Education Association, standardizing the requirements for rated officials, offering coaching, exhibition games, and technical material, and encouraging the best kind of competition among our Active Members, we are always endeavoring to raise the standard of play.

Looking back to the time of the first Tournament, held in Philadelphia in November, 1922, we find that we had 4 Local Associations, 24 Active Clubs, and 65 Allied Members. At the present moment, April, 1932, our membership list includes 17 Local Associations, 91 Active Clubs, and 281 Allied Members. The growth has been slow, but very steady. Each year has seen an increase in the number of Active Members, and each new club means at least eleven new players!

Our first Tournament was an Inter-Local Association one, and teams from four cities were entered. The U.S.F.H.A. was then in its infancy, trying a new experiment, and everyone was a little uncertain as to how such affairs should be conducted. Players from the different cities knew each other very slightly or not at all, and styles of dress and of play were various and varied. But the National Tournament became an annual event, and until 1926 continued with intercity competition. By that time the U.S.F.H.A. had doubled its membership, and it was felt that each Section should hold its own Tournament, and send a Sectional team to compete in the National Tournament. The experiment was tried in 1926, and with one exception in 1930 when teams representing eleven Local Associations met in Philadelphia, the National Tournaments since then have been inter-sectional. Hockey Tournaments for club players are no longer in the experimental stage. The U.S.F.H.A. National Tournament is a recognized event, looked forward to by players and officials as a time for meeting friends, renewing acquaintanceships, exchanging ideas, seeing and participating in good hockey, and enjoying keen competition against sporting opponents. The improvement in general play is outstandingly evident, and seems to continue each year. Both on and off the field everyone seems to be having a good time. Contact with players from other sections improves our hockey, widens our interest, helps us in the solution of our local problems, gives us a more comprehensive idea of what the U.S.F.H.A. is doing, and inspires us with renewed enthusiasm for another year of hard work.

International competition began officially in 1924, when the 1923 U.S.F.H.A. team toured in Great Britain. But more than a year before the formation of the Association, a Philadelphia team had gone to England, and the next fall an English team paid a return visit here. Those first years of inter-national competition were in the nature of a rude awakening! They brought us the realization that as far as playing went, we were still in the primary department! But they brought us other things too, of even greater value, a standard of play towards which to work, friends who gave their time and energy to helping us improve and organize our hockey, and a feeling of kinship with British hockey which has grown stronger with the years. Since 1924 we have had teams from Ireland, England, and Scotland as our guests, and each visit has brought us new friends, stimulated and improved our hockey, and increased our admiration for the skill and sportsmanship of our British opponents. Now we are looking forward to sending a U.S.F.H.A. team to the International Tournament to he held in Copenhagen in September, 1933, followed by a tour in Great Britain.

The number of Committees under the U.S.F.H.A. has also grown with the years. Only one, formed for the purpose of organizing the activities of the coaches sent over by the English Association, has been discontinued. And in this connection, we cannot continue without expressing again our thanks to the volunteer English coaches who came over to this country and contributed their services to American hockey. At a time when we most needed help in developing our game, they gave invaluable assistance to the U.S.F.H.A. and what they did for our hockey can never be overestimated. We now have six very active Committees, carrying on different branches of hockey work. The Umpires committee organizes Local Umpiring Committees in the Associations, and in localities where there is no local Association, forms an Umpire Rating Center to carry on its work. Subject to the approval of the U.S.F.H.A. Executive Committee, it makes the rules in regard to the rating of umpires, fixes the fees for rated umpires, arranges for trials, awards National ratings, and tries in every way possible to help with local and national problems, and to maintain a high standard of umpiring all over the country. The Rules Committee receives and considers all suggestion for changes in the hockey rules, and meets annually with a committee from the A.P.E.A. to vote on proposed changes and make the final decisions as to the wording of the rules. The Committee on Technical Service issues each fall to all the Allied Members of the Association some kind of technical material which it considers will be of value to coaches and players. The Exhibition Games Committee was organized for the purpose of arranging exhibition matches on request, especially in localities where hockey is in the formative stage, when a group of experienced players can offer much help by demonstration and coaching. Our two newest Committees are the Committee on Membership, which explains itself, and the Committee on Equipment, which has just been organized. This last mentioned will attempt to answer the increasing number of requests received by the U.S.F.H.A. for used hockey equipment of any kind, to be used in schools which wish to begin hockey, but cannot afford to buy new equipment. The Committee, with a local representative in each Association, will collect from players as many discarded sticks and other equipment is possible, and distribute them where they are most needed. The work of all Committees grows in volume and scope each year, and all have important parts to play in the Association as a whole.

This is a very broad summary of the activities and accomplishments of the U.S.F.H.A. during the last ten years. We began in a very small way, and as national organizations go, we are not so big now! But progress and growth have been steady, which is always a healthy sign. We set out to organize, spread, and improve hockey, and a larger membership list, increased and more wide-spread activities, and a higher general standard of play, would seem to prove that we are at least headed in the right direction. But growth is not to be measured by figures and statistics alone. The question of the influence of an organization must enter into any consideration of its achievement. And influence cannot be computed in terms of figures, nor can any one person offer more than an individual opinion. But we know that we are reaching more hockey players every year, and that each year brings more wholehearted support and finer cooperation from our local organizations. We know that many who were opposed to the U.S.F.H.A. in 1922 have become its friends and supporters. And we believe that in the inter-Association, inter-Sectional, and inter-National competition sponsored by the Association we have helped to prove that competition for club players, imbued with the right spirit, is a very fine and worthwhile thing....

We believe in hockey as a game. We want it to be played as a game, a recreation, for the enjoyment to be had in it. We believe in its value, and each year we hope to see more people playing better hockey.

## SPEEDBALL FOR WOMEN

*[This article describes the early history of speedball and its growth as a female sport. Helen Barton's discussion also reveals the prevailing attitude of female educators toward adapting male sports to female needs and their desire for female coaches to teach female athletes. Helen M. Barton, "The Story of Speedball for Women. Its History and Latest Developments," The Journal of Health and Physical Education (October 1933), 38-40, 59.]*

High school and college girls today from Boston to San Francisco are enjoying the thrill of playing speedball. That drop kick for the bar, the fun of clever manipulation of ground balls, and the exhilaration that comes from matching wits in play and finesse are a few of the features that are winning more and more enthusiastic converts to the game. Ten years ago this was an unheard of sport in athletics for girls. This is indeed a "Century of Progress" in the field of athletics for women as well as in transportation and bacteriological sciences.

Speedball is a game with which physical directors and leaders of girls should become acquainted, if its possibilities have not already been probed. Its rapid development as a suitable game for girls and women speaks for itself. From its initial introduction into women's sports in the Middle West, speedball has gained popularity until it is now used by high schools, private schools, teachers' colleges, and universities from coast to coast. Although the original version was written for the play of men and high school boys, the evolution of the game has developed many features which make it adaptable to women's play, and also for the use of younger girls. The latest rules for the latter group indicate that accommodations to both physiological and psychological differences have been made, and that now the game is splendidly fitted for the participation of women.

### HISTORY OF THE GAME

The extent to which speedball has been utilized by coaches in girls' schools and colleges is not comprehended until something of its history and development is noted. The game was originated by Elmer D. Mitchell at the University of Michigan in answer to a demand for some sport for general student use which could be played during the fall season of the year. An autumn game which would take the place of the spring sport of baseball, and which would be played by men of average athletic ability, was the challenging situation that inspired the invention of this new game in the fall of 1921. Its reception was instantly popular with the boys of the intramural department. Proof of this is the fact that it was extensively transplanted in the next few years by graduate students and other means. Rule books also were printed because of the numerous requests for information that came from other intramural and physical education departments. State and city departments of physical education obtained permission to quote the rules in their bulletins to teachers. Many teacher training schools included speedball in their practice courses for specializing students. In this way the game became well known in the boys' curriculum of sports.

So much for the early development of speedball as a game for men. Girls and women, during the intervening years between 1921 and 1923 did very little with the new sport. Miss Alice Frymir, at that time of Battle Creek College, appears to have been one of the first women physical directors to actually experiment with speedball as a part of the regular college athletic program. The initial article on the subject, as far as can be found, occurred in The Cadet (Phi Delta Pi yearbook) for 1924, and called attention to the interest the girls at Battle Creek College were manifesting in the novel sport. About a year later in December, 1925, the publication, Old Gold of the University of Iowa, carried an article by Miriam Taylor in which the possibilities of speedball for girls were more widely discussed. The interest of the physical education department for women at that university seems to have been awakened very early in the history of the game. As a result of this early interest, many valuable suggestions and adaptations have been proposed which have helped to make the game more suitable for women's play.

A brief chronological resume of highlights in the development of speedball will indicate how, in the next few years, interest in the new game spread universally.

1928—October.—The Sportswoman, a magazine on topics of current account in the field of women's athletics, published an article by Miss Mildred S. Bruckheimer, entitled "Speedball, a Game for Women." This history of the game to date was concisely treated therein, and a helpful discussion for coaches upon speedball equipment, field markings, etc., as well as comment upon the interest of both junior and senior players in the game, were included in this number. Miss Bruckheimer, then of Mills College, California, was perhaps one of the leaders in her vicinity in promoting the play of speedball in her immediate locality.

1929—May.—The Sportswoman contained another write-up by Miss Bruckheimer, this time upon the "Technique of Speedball." Further use of the game as it developed in that section of the country brought out a need for definite technique practices which could be advantageously used by both beginners and advanced players. A few of the comments on form covered in this publication were the place kick, punt, drop kick, and practical suggestions for the improvement of the initial play at center when the game is started.

1929—October.--The Pentathlon, journal of the Middle West Society of Physical Education, published an article by Miss Elizabeth Beall of Wellesley College. The subject was "Practice Speedball Technique for Girls." Diagrams of plays to improve passing, kicking, and dodging maneuvers were well presented with accompanying hints for both coaches and players on the most recent technique developments. The more advanced type of play disclosed in this article points to the marked advancement in the game over comparable material of earlier publications.

By 1930 interest had become sufficiently marked to call for the inclusion of a section on "Speedball for Girls" in one of the Guide Books of the Women's Athletic Series by the American Sports Publishing Company. Speedball was incorporated in the Women's Soccer Guide which also includes a section on Fieldball. The first editor of the enlarged rule book was Miss Marian Knighton of Sarah Lawrence College and Miss Florence Huppich of Texas State College for Women edited the speedball section. In the few years that the game has been included in the Women's Athletic Series a number of important changes have been make toward clarification and adaptation of by women players.

**DIRECTORS' OPINIONS**

The recent attention given to speedball by the Women's Athletic Committee of the American Physical Education Association is very timely as interested teachers have long been seeking a clearing house for questions that have arisen as girls took up the game. In compiling this article information was requested from Mr. Mitchell regarding his knowledge of the early developments in the girls' game. In this interview he stated that while speedball was originally conceived as a boys game, he very early began to receive letters regarding problems that were arising as women teachers began to use the game. While glad to give advice whenever possible, Mr. Mitchell felt that it was imperative that women undertake the direction of developments in the girls' game.

The following extracts from letters, for example, show that women teachers in many sections of the country were making individual experiments with the game.

1929—March.—Miss Hazel Cubberley of the University of California at Berkeley developed with the assistance of her major students a wall chart showing in simplified and compact form the rules of the game. This helped to make the game more easily understood by girls who, for the most part, did not have the sport background to grasp new rules with the same readiness as boys.

1931—April.—Miss June McCann of Los Angeles, California, wrote that a controversy over a point of play had developed among her students. The question was, "could a ball be legally knocked from a player's hand or was this to be considered a transgression of the rules?" Such interest in the rules by coach and players indicated that the game was being viewed in the light of other major game experience (basketball, for example), and that, therefore, girls' rules needed to be differentiated from those of the boys.

1931—May.—Miss Marjorie Teitsworth, of the Belmont High School in Los Angeles, appealed for material by which her girls could measure their own advancement in self-testing forms of speedball technique. This communication marked a new development in the history of the game. Self-testing by students is not in demand unless their interest in their own progress in the game warrants it.

1931—October.—This date brought a note from Miss Elizabeth White of the University of Pittsburgh where the game had been very successfully used. Miss White added the idea of using field hockey as a game to familiarize her students with a major sport played on larger field dimensions than a restricted basketball court. The step from basketball (with which most girls are acquainted) to speedball, via hockey, trained the players in the use of greater areas.

1931—November.—Miss Marian Anderson of Northern Illinois State Teachers College compiled a form sheet of rule modifications for more improved play and in addition worked out more extensive material for individual tests and team relay practice.

1932—May.—Miss Katharine Carlisle of Utah State Agricultural College, Logan, Utah, told of her success with speedball in the West, and the excellent results she obtained by coaching with films of the game. The films were in two divisions, one touching upon general fundamentals of play and the other upon actual game play among the boys of Long Beach, California.

No doubt this marks one of the epochal steps in the coaching technique of speedball. Think of the very few years previous when Miss Alice Frymir was pioneering in the game at Battle Creek College!

1932—June.—Correspondence from Miss Miriam Taylor of the University of Iowa showed that experiments at that school had culminated in a set of mimeographed rules for the betterment of girls' play. These modifications, which had been carefully tested and worked out over a period of years by the Women's Physical Education Department, suggested changes in playing space, scoring, and several other points making for more enjoyment and better results on women's technique.

1933—April.—Miss Marie Phelan, Whittier College, California, with the assistance of the women major students in Physical Education, compiled an extensive study toward the end of clarification and simplification of the present speedball rules for girls. This was forwarded to the Chairman of the A.P.E.A. Women's Athletic Committee on Soccer, Speedball, and Fieldball.

Miss Blanche M. Trilling, who is always a loyal supporter of any movement for better womanhood, has expressed her interest in speedball as a suitable game for girls. Likewise Dr. Margaret M. Bell at the University of Michigan approves of the game as a general all-round sport for girls. Miss Laurie Campbell, of the same department, has contributed much toward adjusting men's rules to facilitate women's play. In the major department of physical education at the University of Michigan, speedball has been used since 1929. The junior and senior students have enjoyed it as a spring sport, however, instead of in the fall. At first, because of inadequate women's rules, Miss Campbell coached the game strictly according to the regulations set forth for the men. Over a period of four years the students and coach of the department have developed several alterations in the rules, namely:

1. Scoring should encourage a kicking game by girls, rather than the more natural throwing game. Hence, points made by kicking received a higher rating than thrown points.

2. Timing was changed to the regular eight-minute quarters of basketball play.

3. Obstruction as a foul used in hockey and soccer was introduced into speedball to promote better play.

4. Changes in follow-up plays after a penalty kick were worked out for the purpose of making speedball more congruous with other and better known sports for women.

This sketch of the major developments in the game of speedball from 1924 to 1933 indicates how expeditious the varying changes were and that the interest in it is becoming universal. It is a "coming" game in the field of major sports for women. Some of the latest developments in points of technique practice point to the fact that speedball will soon be used in junior high schools as well as colleges, although, of course, in a modified form.

**RECENT COACHING DEVELOPMENTS**

Speedball tactics demand the ability both to kick and catch a ball. (Note the suggested changes which have been made by physical directors to promote greater use of foot work among girls.) Observation of the play of girls will bring to light the fact that there is always present the desire and willingness to kick a ball. However, when it comes to receiving a ball to which impetus has been given by a kick, most girls appear to have an innate fear of the approaching object which unwittingly handicaps their play. On the basis of this observation a coaching program was tried out at State Teachers College, Clarion, Pennsylvania, the theory being that proper coaching can do much to eliminate this instinctive reaction. Once this disadvantage has been overcome the player will more readily respond to later coaching methods. [The discussion on skill development has been deleted.]

Chapter 8

# FOOTBALL—CANADIAN

The evolution of Canadian football during the 1930s reflected the spread of American culture into Canada and the exacerbation of regional differences between western and central Canada. When the decade began, the Canadian Rugby Union (CRU) consisted of twenty-nine senior teams, all of which were eligible to challenge for the Grey Cup. Since the beginning of the CRU in the late nineteenth century, university football was the backbone of the senior leagues, but city teams had gradually gained ascendancy in the 1920s. In 1924, Queen's University in Kingston, Ontario, was the last university team to win the Grey Cup. Ten years later, the Eastern Intercollegiate Union withdrew from Grey Cup play.

At the beginning of the decade, Canadian football was purely an amateur sport. Leslie Roberts wrote in the August 1931 issue of Canadian Magazine that college football was the sole major sport in which the amateur spirit prevailed and that its practitioners, unlike hockey and baseball players, later became useful citizens with respectable occupations. Other writers proudly noted that the 1929 Carnegie Foundation report praised Canadian universities for not overemphasizing athletics at the expense of the students' academic training. The Principal of Queen's University from 1930 to 1935 particularly detested "gladiatorial games," and refused to follow the University of Toronto's decision in 1932 to hire a full-time director of athletics (Warren Stevens).

Unlike American scouting tactics, expensive stadiums, athletic scholarships, overpaid coaches, training tables, recruitment of high school players, and rampant publicity, Canadian football was purely amateur. In the British tradition of Oxford and Cambridge, Canadian universities offered athletic training to cultivate character rather than as an end in itself. As University of McGill coach Francis Shaughnessy noted in his 1935 book, *How to Play Football*, football "will develop initiative, self confidence, physical courage and sportsmanship. These are the qualities he will need in his battle for success in the future!" The CRU's Constitution included a two-page explanation of sportsmanship—see "The Spirit of the Rules" in the Document "The Forward Pass."

Football players in the city senior leagues, which were not members of the Canadian Amateur Athletic Union, relied on their employers to grant them time off on game days. To prevent abuses, eligible players had to be in continuous residence from June of the year the season began. As the Depression deepened, senior football gradually became amateur in name only as the larger cities attracted American and Canadian players in search of employment—see "Introducing Tiger Cat Players.". Financed by an oil refinery, for example, the Sarnia Imperials captured the Grey Cup in 1934 and 1936.

Rule changes during the 1930s reflected the growing influence of American football. The major innovation of the decade was the adoption of the forward pass. Following two experimental seasons, the CRU adopted the forward pass for the 1931 season. Emulating American college football rules, a forward pass could be thrown only from a point at least five yards behind the line of scrimmage, and could not be completed inside the opponent's twenty-five yard-line. Initially, an incomplete pass was treated exactly as a kick and could be returned by the opposition, but when it soon became evident that some players could throw the ball farther than they could kick it, the rule was discontinued. Since the CRU feared the new passing rules might detract from the kicking game, passes were forbidden on third downs. The Canadian game only had three downs. Two consecutive incomplete passes brought a 10-yard penalty. Because of the punitive penalties for an incomplete pass, it took several years before the forward pass became more than just a weapon of surprise. In the 1931 Grey Cup game, for example, in which the Montreal Winged Wheelers defeated the Regina Roughriders 22-0, both teams combined for a total of twenty-three pass attempts and six completions.

In 1936, the CRU ruled that an incomplete pass thrown inside the twenty-five yard-line would result only in the loss of a down. An incomplete pass in the end zone still resulted in the loss of possession. Two years later, such incomplete passes resulted only in the loss of one down and fumbles out of bounds no longer brought a change in possession—which encouraged receivers to catch the ball and run it near the sidelines.

Other rule changes in the decade included moving the convert (via a drop-kick) from the thirty-five to the twenty-five yard-line, and then to the five yard-line the following year—at which time the scoring team could drop-kick, place-kick, run or pass the ball. About this time, the name "rugby football" replaced "rugby" and "touchdown" was used interchangeably with "try."

The forward pass paved the way for the import of American players. Since few Canadians were adept at throwing, having heretofore concentrated on the rugby-like lateral, and a proposal to bar Americans for two years to provide Canadians with the opportunity to learn this new skill failed, several teams recruited American football players. The first such player was Warren Stevens, a graduate from Syracuse University who had attended McGill University in 1931 to study hockey, which he believed would be the game of the future. That season, Stevens instructed the McGill team in the intricacies of the forward pass and, after accepting a position with a Montreal oil company, quarterbacked the Montreal Winged Wheelers to an undefeated season and a Grey Cup victory. The Winged Wheelers attracted such large crowds that their home games were switched to the more spacious Molson Stadium. For the first time, Montreal newspapers provided extensive coverage of the team's games, including discussions on the merits of the forward pass, complete with photographs of Stevens' passing technique.

As several of the documents reveal, reaction was mixed. Some commentators believed that the forward pass would open the game and appeal to spectators. In this age of speed and action, noted one sportswriter, the pass was a perfect fit. Other journalists argued it was just another example of "the insidious growth of the American rules in the Canadian game." They preferred lateral passing plays, the on-side kick, and sweeping end-runs to the "ponderous attacks" of American football. The Canadian game was steeped in tradition and national spirit, these defenders claimed, so it was "a pity to see us imitate the other fellow." Leslie Roberts, for example, protested that Canadians were "taking our cues from our cousins beyond the border, reconstructing our major games to appeal to the watcher rather than the players—because these games have become specialized branches of Big Business...."

In 1937, the introduction of pass blocking in the backfield, and the need for linemen to pull out of the line and either trap block or lead interference around the end, as in American football, further facilitated the transition to the use of American players. Likewise, as most teams hired American coaches to teach the new passing game, American recruiting flourished. Since these recruits were obviously receiving money under the table, and several players already were suspended in 1932 for playing professional football in the US before coming to Canada, the Amateur Athletic Union of Canada urged the CRU to impose residence rules.

When Winnipeg captured the Grey Cup in 1935, the CRU decided to limit American imports. Western teams first challenged for the Grey Cup in 1921, but met with no success. In Western Canada, especially in British Columbia, English rugby dominated the landscape and as a result high schools and universities did not produce the same caliber of players as did central-Canadian schools. The better players often moved to central Canada for employment in the larger centers. The long distances between football teams in the west further restricted competition. Central Canada's longer summers meant that the western representative in the Dominion final often had to sit idle for up to one month before making the long tiresome train trip to Montreal or Toronto.

In 1935, Winnipeg hired an American coach and recruited seven American players, including Fritz Hanson and Bob Fritz, to add to the two imports from the previous year. The team's salaries now consisted of one-half the total budget for the year. With only four Canadian-born players, Winnipeg captured the Grey Cup by defeating Hamilton 18-12, as Hanson rushed for more than 350 yards. "You should have been in Winnipeg that afternoon," stated a local magazine, "Radios set out in the snowy streets blared of Winnipeg's triumph to shouting, cheering crowds. Moviegoers bellowed thunderously as the news was announced in theaters." The team was the toast of the town, and Western Canada had won its first Grey Cup game.

The CRU, which was controlled by central Canadians, was unhappy with the way Winnipeg had created such a powerful team. In February 1936, the CRU ruled that no team could employ more than five imports and adjusted the residency requirements to make any player who had not lived continuously in Canada for at least one year ineligible to compete in the Grey Cup. In 1937, the west set the maximum number of imports at eight per team. The immediate result was that the western champion from Regina decided to default to the Sarnia Imperials in 1936 rather than compete without its five ineligible American players.

On a broader canvas, the import rule was symptomatic of western discontent with central Canadian economic and political policies that seemed to give no relief to high unemployment, low wheat prices, and crop failures. In addition to such protest movements as the On-to-Ottawa-Trek in 1935 and the success of the Social Credit and Cooperative Commonwealth Federation political parties, football was a way of expressing western hostility to perceived central-Canadian control. Within the CRU, east-west conflict arose over the forward pass, imports and residency requirements, the site of the Grey Cup, and blocking rules. "Pigskin Imports" outlines the regional differences.

In general, western teams favored the adoption of American football rules. Lacking competition, many prairie teams played exhibition games against American colleges, sometimes alternating between American and Canadian rules from half to half. Such games decreased resistance to American rules and provided information on prospective recruits.

Following the 1934 season, in which the CRU reversed its decision to alternate the site of the Grey Cup from east to west, the western teams adopted several new rules, including blocking up to five yards from the line of scrimmage instead of three yards; giving the team scored upon the option of kicking off or of receiving the kick instead of having to kick off; allowing unlimited substitution; and using the "pro pass" from anywhere in the backfield as in the NFL. A few years later, the west permitted blocking up to 10 yards down field. Whereas the west claimed that this rule would produce longer runs and more open play, central-Canadian teams argued that such a rule would favor the bigger players and would eliminate the lateral pass because everyone would be used to block for the ball carrier. Each section now played under separate rules, although the eastern regulations governed the Grey Cup.

Granting the west equal representation in the CRU in 1937 failed to solve the problem. While the west argued for "progressive changes" and accused central Canada of "conservatism," central Canadians charged that the west was plotting to Americanize the game. J. Lewis Brown, sportswriter for the National Home Monthly, wrote that "the West lacks something in national pride when they insist on foisting a hybrid game on their fans...." In February 1938, the CRU ruled that no team could compete for the Grey Cup unless it had played by its rules all season. A complete rupture was averted only when the CRU agreed to postpone this ruling until the 1940 season and western teams agreed to revert to CRU rules in all but the "pro pass" and 10 yards down field blocking.

Football, especially in western Canada, flourished during the 1930s. By the end of the decade, each stadium had floodlights, loudspeakers, and large scoreboards. In 1934, Maclean's Magazine acknowledged the growth of the game by initiating a yearly all-star football team. In the west, football was becoming popular in high schools and on sandlots. The Winnipeg team expanded from a one-man operation managed from home, with gate receipts of $136 in 1931, to a full-time assistant and more than $50,000 in revenue seven years later. The 1938 Grey Cup game attracted a record crowd of 18,778.

The outbreak of World War II in 1939 curtailed this expansion. Although the federal government urged the CRU to carry on as usual to bolster morale and "because, in Anglo-Saxon civilization, sport is an excellent training for war," the military appropriated the Ottawa Rough Riders' stadium and the militia assumed control of Montreal's football park. Each team felt the impact of enlistments. Regina and Winnipeg each lost one-third of its players. Edmonton suspended operations for the duration of the war. Despite the national unity fostered by the declaration of war, the two regions remained divided on the rules and the Grey Cup was suspended in 1940. At many universities, high schools, and military camps, six-man football was adopted for conditioning.

## INTRODUCING THE TIGER CAT PLAYERS

*[The following program for the 1939 Hamilton Tiger Cat football team provides an excellent profile of CFL players. It particularly details the age and size of the players, their early football training, and their occupations. "Introducing the Tigers of 1939," in "Agros vs. Tigers," Hamilton Amateur Athletic Association Program (14 October 1939), 37, 39 (Canadian Football Hall of Fame and Museum).]*

No.
21 William Mallard, inside wing, a product of local Junior Football. Age 31, weighs 237 lbs. and is employed at the Dominion Foundries and Steel Company, Limited.

22 Abraham Zvonkin, former Queen's University Middle Wing, graduated from Hamilton Interscholastic ranks, is 29 years of age also employed at the Dominion Foundries and Steel Company, Limited.

23 Leonard Wright, Outside Wing came to Tigers from Junior ranks. Len weighs 199 lbs. and has just passed his 22nd birthday. Works hard at the Dominion Foundries and Steel Company, Limited.

24 James Dunn, learned to play snap with many others in the local juniors, 28 years of age, weighing 180 lbs., has also played with Ottawa Rough Riders. Dominion Foundries and Steel Company, Limited, is his place of employment.

25 Theodore Manorek, came up from Junior ranks, played last season with Balmy Beach, plunging Half Back, weighing 184 lbs., and is 23 years of age. Also employed at Dominion Foundries and Steel Company, Limited.

26 John Agnew, another graduate of Junior Football, with Dundas Intermediates last year. Plays Outside Wing, is employed at the National Steel Car Corporation, Limited. Age 27, weight 173 lbs.

27 John Craig, the pride of Dundas, and son of Ross Craig, famous old-time Tiger. Jack was with Dundas last season, is a kicking and plunging Half Back, weighing 195 lbs. and his age is 26. Employed with United Gas and Fuel Company.

28 Harold Donald, also from Dundas, where he played Middle Wing last year, weighs 208 lbs., age 22. Employed at the Canadian Westinghouse Company, Limited.

29 Ivan Edwards, hails from Varsity, where he played at Outside Wing. Age 26, weighs 167 lbs., is Minister at the Kenilworth United Church.

30 Robert Isbister, Junior, came to Tigers from Toronto Argonauts. Bob is the son of the "Bob" Isbister, is a triple threat on the backfield. Age 24, weighing 198 lbs. Is an Auditor with Clarkson, Gordon, Dilworth and Nash.

31 George Mountain, 208 lbs., Inside Wing, came to Tigers from Junior Football, is a veteran at the age of 28. Is employed at the Dominion Foundries and Steel Company, Limited.

33 Reginald Wheeler, Middle Wing from Interscholastic Football ranks, weighs 195 lbs., and is 21 years of age. Employed by The Plak Company of Canada.

34 Leonard Onions, age 22, playing Flying Wing and plunging Half Back, weighs 170 lbs., came to Tigers from junior ranks. Works at the Dominion Foundries and Steel Company, Limited.

35 Michael Ozarko, formerly of Winnipeg, plays Middle Wing, weighs 180 lbs., is 23 years of age, and works at the Dominion Foundries and Steel Company, Limited.

36 George Pawley, a product of Dundas, where he played Outside Wing for the Bombers. Works at the Canadian Westinghouse Company, Limited, is 22 years of age, and weighs 180 lbs.

37 Robert Smith, good Utility Player with Tigers for several years, came up from Junior. "Skin" weighs 178 lbs., is 26 years old, and is employed by the National Steel Car Corporation, Limited.

38 George Stevens, graduate from Junior, plays Flying Wing, at the weight of 183 lbs., and is 21 years old. Employed at the Steel Company of Canada.

39 Alan Turnbull, graduate of McMaster University, where he played Outside Wing. With Tigers for the second season, weighs 167 lbs., and is 26 years old. Employed at Dominion Foundries and Steel Company, Limited.

40 Thomas Wood, Middle and Inside Wing, advanced to Tigers from the Junior League; weighs in at 187 lbs., and is 25 years of age. Works for the Steel Company of Canada.

41 George Wright, finally coming into his own as a kicking Half; 25 years of age and weighs 161 lbs. Stanley Works of Canada is his employer. Came up from Junior.

42 Hardy Awrey, also played in Junior, and Interscholastic Leagues; fits in as Catching Halfback; weight 175 lbs., age 21 years. Works for the National Trust Company.

43 Edward Jordan, hails from St. Catharines, played Intermediate also with Dundas; running Half Back. Weight 190 lbs., age 23 years. Employed at Canadian Westinghouse Company, Limited.

44 Edward Lane, weighs 190 lbs., plays Snapback and Secondary Defense, comes to Tigers from Junior League. He is 25 years old, and works at Proctor and Gamble Company of Canada, Limited.

45 "Mick" Magee, came to Tigers from Peterboro, where he played on the "Orfuns" O.R.F.U. team as Halfback. Weighs 170 lbs., and is 25 years of age. Employed by the Canadian Westinghouse Company, Limited.

47 Dillon Southwick, played last season with Tiger Intermediates as a Quarterback, weighs 160 lbs., and is 21 years of age. Employer is Masco Electric Company, Limited.

48 Norman Mountain, brother of George, plays Half Line or Outside Wing at a weight of 170 lbs. His age is 30 years. Graduate of Junior Football. Works for the Canadian Westinghouse Company, Limited.

50 Denis Whitaker, came to Tigers from Royal Military College, plays Quarterback, weighs 155 lbs., is 24 years old, and is a lieutenant in the Thirteenth Canadian Active Service Force.

51 Charles Waterman, young Snapback from last year's Junior League, is only 20 years old, and weighs 163 lbs. Employed at the Steel Company of Canada.

COACH: James Palmer has played for Argonauts of Toronto for 11 years. Employed by J. F. Hartz Company, Toronto.

## SPORTSMANSHIP IN FOOTBALL

[*This selection from the CRU's 1931 constitution summarizes the philosophy of this body. The following "unions" were affiliated with the CRU—Canadian Intercollegiate Rugby Football Union, Interprovincial Rugby Football Union, Ontario Rugby Football Union, Quebec Rugby Football Union, Western Canada Rugby Football Union, Western Canada Intercollegiate Rugby Football Union. Constitution and Official Playing Rules of the Canadian Rugby Union. Season 1931.*]

### INTENTION AND SPIRIT OF THE PLAYING RULES

While we believe that in general the sportsmanship shown by the players of Rugby Football has improved of recent years, it may not be amiss to say a few words for the benefit of those who are either just learning the game or those who have overlooked or neglected the preservation of the traditions of the game.

In order to maintain a high standard of sportsmanship in the game of Rugby Football, those actively interested in the management of the various clubs should seriously consider their responsibility, as the conduct of a team on the field reflects either to the credit or discredit of the club which it represents.

In some sports it is possible to attain reasonably high standards simply by the adoption and enforcement of rules, but this is not true in Football. There are so many men engaged in action, the action is so rapid and so constantly shifting, that it is impossible for any official to discover every possible infraction of the rules.

Probably no other game offers so many opportunities for a player or coach to use unfair tactics in an attempt "to win at any cost." Those guilty of using unfair tactics seem to fail to recognize that the first obligation of every football player should be to protect the game itself, its reputation, and its good name. He owes this to the game, its friends, and its traditions. There can be little excuse for any player who allows the game to be smirched with unsportsmanlike tactics, if the spirit of the club management is sound.

The Rules Committee has endeavored to prohibit and suitably penalize all forms of unfair tactics and practices. It has also, so far as possible, endeavored to remove special temptation or opportunity for unsportsmanlike play.

So far as the rules themselves are concerned, the Committee has endeavored to evolve a game that will prove attractive from a spectator's point of view and also give a light, skillful player an equal opportunity of successfully participating with a heavy player who may be less skillful.

For the benefit of those who are just beginning to learn the game and those who may be ignorant of what the proper standards are, we desire to publish, along with the official rules, the following suggestions:

### HOLDING

Holding is prohibited by the rules because it does not belong to the game of football. It is unfair play. It eliminates skill. The slowest man in the world could make a long run at any time if the rest of his teammates would hold their opponents long enough. The game of football is to advance the ball by strategy, skill and speed without holding your opponent. If your coach cannot show you how to gain distance without holding your opponents, dispense with his services. It is fair to assume that he does not understand the strategy of the game.

### SIDE-LINE COACHING

Coaching from the side lines is prohibited in the rules because it is considered unfair practice. The game is to be played by the players using their own muscle and their own brains. If, for example, an onlooker, having seen all the hands in a game of cards, undertook to tell one of the players what card to play, the other players would have just cause to object.

The sending in of substitutes for the purpose of giving information as to the following play is an unfair evasion of the spirit of true sportsmanship.

### TALKING TO OFFICIALS

When an official imposes a penalty or makes a decision, he is simply doing his duty as he sees it. He is on the field representing the integrity of the game of football, and his decision, even though he may have made a mistake in judgment, is final and conclusive, and should be so accepted. Even if you think the decision is a mistaken one, take your medicine and do not whine about it. If there is anything to be said, let your captain do the talking. He has that privilege according to the rules. You have not, therefore keep quiet and play the game.

### THE FOOTBALL CODE

You may meet players and even coaches who will tell you that it is all right to hold or otherwise violate the rules if you do not get caught. This is the code of men whose sense of honor is sadly lacking.

"The football code is different. The football player **who intentionally violates a rule is guilty of unfair play and unsportsmanlike tactics, and whether or not he escapes being penalized, he brings discredit to the good name of the game, which it is his duty as a player to uphold."**...

## PIGSKIN IMPORTS

[*Frank Shaughnessy was one of the most important figures in the evolution of Canadian football. A native of Illinois, he attended Notre Dame University, earned degrees in pharmacy and law, and coached at Clemson University before coming to Canada in 1912 to coach baseball. When Shaughnessy later moved to McGill University, he became the first professional Canadian football coach. At McGill, "Shag" established a residence and training table for the players, introduced the huddle in 1925, termed the "conference system," and advocated the forward pass as early as 1921—drawing complaints from Canadian stalwarts that he wished to adopt American tactics. He left McGill in 1928 to become a baseball scout for the Detroit Tigers and honorary coach of the Loyola University football team. In 1931, Shaughnessy returned to McGill to introduce the forward pass.*

*The following article by a former football player at the University of Toronto and McGill University examines the dispute over the forward pass, imports, residency requirements, and professionalization. Following the publication of Carroll's article, Michael Rodden, football coach of the Hamilton Tigers and the Toronto Argonauts in the 1920s, wrote a rebuttal in Maclean's Magazine (1 November 1936). Rodden preferred the running game and contended that coaches were devoting too much time to the pass. The forward pass, and the accompanying imports of "questionable amateur status," he wrote, had resulted in a decline in attendance. Although American players might be teaching the pass to Canadians, "it is more correct to say that they also deprive them of an opportunity to play in a Canadian national sport.... Had the pass been adopted and imports barred, scandals would have been avoided, the game would be amateur in reality as well as in name, Canadians would be able to participate in their own game, the crowds would be larger, the profits ditto...there would be vastly more thrills, and we would not have had the spectacle of seeing a United States-Winnipeg team winning the Canadian title at Hamilton last fall." Dink Carroll, "Pigskin Imports. Are We Heading Toward an All-American Canadian Football Team?" Maclean's Magazine (15 September 1936), 10, 47-48.*]

"He's away? He's in the open. Watch him go. There's nobody near him. Look at him run?"

"It looks like a touchdown."

"He's over. Hurrah! Hanson's over. Touchdown!"

"Hanson just scored a touchdown."

"Listen to that crowd cheer Hanson."

Hanson just ran eighty yards through the whole Hamilton Tiger team and scored a touchdown. Tigers'll never catch 'em now. Winnipegs are the new Dominion Champions. Some football player, that Hanson.

Sure, he's some football player. Just a year previously he ran through the University of Minnesota team, national champions of the United States, with the same ease that you saw him flash past the Tigers. He scored two touchdowns against Minnesota. Only a year previous he was an All-American. Well, maybe not All-American, because he played for the University of North Dakota, a rather unimportant little college. But he got All-American mention. Now he's All-Canadian. And how do you like that? Pretty well, it seems, from the way you yelled your head off every time he broke loose in that Dominion Final clash last fall between Winnipeg and Hamilton.

And what about the rest of that 'Peg team, the present Dominion champions, the first winning team from the West in thirteen long years challenging to lift the National title? Who are they and where do they come from?

Of the twelve men who started that game for the 'Pegs, only four were Canadian. The rest came from what is known south of the border as the Swede Belt—the Dakotas, Minnesota and Wisconsin—a section of the country which produces the best football material in the entire United States. Fritz, Marquardt, Hanson, Peschel and Perpich come from the Dakotas; Rebholz and Kabat from Wisconsin; and Oja from Minnesota. But nowadays you will find the same type of husky, fair-haired, sport-loving lad with the Scandinavian-sounding name on all our Canadian teams between the Great Lakes and the Pacific Coast. The West brought them in to lift that title, and they did.

The East, of course, started it all, this business of importing players from across the line. They started it back in 1931, the year the forward pass was first introduced into the Canadian code. They've kept it up, too. The key man on the Hamilton team which fell before the 'Pegs in that grand final game last December was Johnny Ferraro, who captained a Cornell University team a few years ago. Brock, the Tigers' snap, was a teammate of Ferraro at Cornell. Now shut your eyes and put your finger on the line-up of almost any Eastern team. It's a fifty-fifty chance that the name you've stabbed is that of a player from the United States, for there were plenty of them up here last year, and the chances are there'll be even more this year.

Is the presence of these United States stars on our teams a calamity to get all hot and bothered about, as some people seem to think? Must "drastic steps" be taken right away to save our Canadian game of football? Are our players in danger of being besmirched by professionalism? Should we kick the "foreigners" out and see to it that they don't come back?

Let's not do anything without first examining the subject a little and seeing if we can't find out the basic reasons for the presence of these "imports" among us. We may have to dig a little deeper than you think.

**SPECTATORS DEMAND GOOD FOOTBALL**

[Deleted discussion of rule changes in 1920s designed to produce more offensive football and thus to attract spectators.] When the forward pass was first drafted into our code, it was undoubtedly the intention of the Canadian Rugby Football Union that the play be learned by Canadians; it hadn't considered any development beyond that. But the Montreal Club in the Big Four, while realizing the possibilities of the play, could not take advantage of it because they had no passer. So, probably thinking in more or less of a straight line, they went out and got one. Warren Stevens, who had learned his football at the University of Syracuse, was the player they imported. The club had a very successful year, though that may be something of an understatement; the club really had a banner year. They won the Dominion title and they attracted huge crowds both at home and away, for everybody was anxious to see Stevens perform. The experiment was so successful that other clubs quickly followed Montreal's lead, and the next year the business of importing stars from the United States was on in earnest.

Some very funny incidents have happened since. We saw the University of Toronto, who had long declared their opposition to professional coaches, make a sudden wild grab for Warren Stevens and place him in complete charge of their athletic activities. Then there was the Masters-Carlston incident, when that pair of all-round athletes from the University of Pennsylvania played through a whole Big Four schedule with the Ottawa Club before it was discovered that they were professional baseball players. At the end of last season we witnessed the same kind of an exposure in the case of John Hilliard, the ex-Texas University star also with the Ottawa Club, only this time it was complicated by Hilliard's having played under an assumed name. But the highlight of all these antics was the strike staged by the Montreal Club's imports in mid season, last year. It was a little difficult for the club to explain what that was all about, but most people got the impression that it was a salary tangle, though the league was supposed to be operating on a strictly amateur basis.

Nobody wants to uphold sham amateurism, but there really hasn't been so much of it as you might suspect; the papers have overplayed it badly in the few instances when it did crop up. The O.R.F.U. has done no importing and neither has the Intercollegiate Union. Western Canada teams and the Big Four clubs have done most of it. But even in the old days jobs were always being found for football stars, which is all that has been done to date for most of the imports. It has been argued that these jobs would go to Canadians if the boys from the States weren't up here, but that works both ways; for there are certainly more Canadian lads making a living out of hockey in the United States than there are Americans making a living out of football up here, and a far better living, at that.

The Amateur Athletic Union of Canada discussed the importation question at its annual meeting a couple of years ago and resolved that the importation of players for Canadian football was undesirable. Their executive discussed the subject with governing rugby bodies, but right there they ran into a snag. The Dominion organization, which is called the Canadian Rugby Football Union, promised to and did enact legislation aimed at curtailing the practice of importing players; but the various unions over which the C.R.F.U. is supposed to have jurisdiction have never paid much attention to its edicts. They run their own show regardless of the C.R.F.U. This was never better demonstrated than this year, when the C.R.F.U. announced that all players to he eligible for a team must begin to reside in the city which that team represents by a certain date—and not one of the other unions recognizes that date. For example, the residence rule in the Big Four is June 1, while the date fixed by the parent union is somewhere around January 1. The C.R.F.U. date was fixed with imports in mind, but it does not look from this distance as if it's going to get much co-operation on the question from its member unions. That is the weakness of our football organization. But there may be a showdown by the time the play-offs roll around, for you may be sure the C.R.F.U. will try to exclude players from the playoffs who did not comply with its residence rule.

## CHANGE IN PUBLIC'S ATTITUDE

But let's get back to the game itself for a moment and see what basic effects the forward pass has had on it. It certainly has put an end to the era of low scores, of few first downs and many injuries, and the monotonous two-bucks-and-a-kick formula. The old, dangerous, close-packed style of play has given way to the fast, spectacular, open brand. The threat of the pass keeps the defense back and spread, with the result that end runs, spinners and line smashes are much more effective than they used to be. Scoring is more prolific, light teams now have a chance to ride over heavier opponents by taking to the air, no team is licked until the final whistle because it has the pass as a desperate, last-minute weapon of attack, and the spectator is having the time of his life because there is plenty to cheer about. [Deleted long list of American players.]

Then again, they've been doing something which most of their critics seem to have overlooked. They've been educating the youngsters who are just coming up, the boys in the high schools and on the sand lots, not only in the use of the pass but in the general science of football. Anyone who has ever played football, baseball, tennis, hockey, golf, or almost any sport, knows the value of having a good model to emulate. You can't learn how to play these games by reading books. You learn by watching the good ones, and Canadian lads won't find any better models among football players throughout the land than these same imports. The kids know this, and if you want to check up on it for yourself, all you have to do is stop at any street corner one of these evenings where there's a vacant lot....

The truth is that there has been a change in the public's attitude toward professionalism in sport. We said a while back that nobody wanted to uphold sham amateurism. That's true, but it's also true that the sport-loving public is indifferent about it. It's hard to say how, when, where or why this change came about, but maybe hockey had something to do with it. An official of one of the hockey unions said recently that there was no such thing as amateur hockey in Canada today outside the colleges, and it wasn't the bombshell he thought it was. The public does not resent the idea of hockey players being paid for their efforts; in fact, it seems to expect it. What is there to make anyone think the public's attitude toward football players would be any different? The answer is nothing; absolutely nothing. The people whom the public resent are the officials or executives behind amateur teams who might be getting something out of it.

But whatever happens, you and I want to get a real thrill out of our autumn Saturday afternoons, and we'll go to any game which promises good football, a lot of excitement or something in the way of novelty—which is going to make it tough for the reformers if the separate unions defy them.

## EAST-WEST PIGSKIN FEUD

[*This article outlines the on-going debate between central and western Canada over the rules. The word "east," referring to east-west issues, usually meant Ontario and Quebec. J. Norvil Marks, "Pigskin Feud. East and West Don't See Eye to Eye on Canadian Football Management, but it All Adds Spice to the Dominion Finals," Maclean's Magazine (1 October 1937), 23, 40-41.*]

Certain devotees of Canadian rugby have been wagging their heads sadly over the situation in the Dominion for the past ten years. Football, they say, will never come into its own until Western and Eastern exponents of the great autumn game manifest a little more brotherly love—a little more of the old give-and-take—until they bury the hatchet and smoke the pipe of peace.

"What Canadian rugby needs," they say, "is more unity and harmony. All this squabbling between the West and the East—it's bad for the game."

It is no secret in the world of sport that West and East do not see eye to eye on the subject of rugby football. But there are those who decline to view with alarm [sic]. It's healthy, they'll tell you. And natural. It is in the very make-up of a Westerner to break away from accepted tradition, just as it is bred in the Easterner to cling to the old order of things....

Differences over the rules; dissension over the importation of players from the United States; disagreements over the locale of the Dominion final, held in the East since the inception of the play-offs—these are the problems which have faced governing authorities of Canada's autumn pastime.

**WEST IMPROVES THE GAME**

Western unions have always taken the initiative in advocating rule changes in the Canadian code. It was the West that first adopted the forward pass, for many years a feature of American football. This drastic departure from orthodox rugby—until then inevitably consisting of two bucks and a kick—was frowned upon for some time by the more conservative Eastern authorities. Later, sensing the fact that the pass was responsible for a very considerable rise in spectator interest, and that the resultant game was speedier and far more pleasing, the East instituted the onside toss into its own code.

Running interference, designed further to open up the game and to give much-needed protection to ball carriers, then cropped up to result in more dissension between East and West. Carrying their radical changes to a further extreme, Western rugby moguls reached out and adopted running interference from the American college code of football. Longer runs featured ensuing games, fans and players alike expressing complete satisfaction with this departure from the old type of rugby. Eventually the East saw the handwriting on the wall, possibly traced there by enthusiastic Easterners who had witnessed games west of the Great Lakes, and adopted interference.

Then the question of importing players arose, further to complicate matters. Yielding to the demand of Eastern fans for skilled exponents of the forward pass, teams in the East went "below the line" and brought in brilliant American college stars. The resultant faster game aptly demonstrated the wisdom of such a policy.

Then too, these American all-stars were drilling the homebrews in every phase of the Canadian code, bringing to their tutoring the benefit of years of experience under some of the greatest football mentors in the States. It was generally conceded that Canadian youngsters would, in a few years, reap the benefit of this skilled teaching, by which time it should no longer he necessary to import players. Incidentally, it eventually happened that some of the American stars imported in earlier years, remained in Canada and qualified for the residence ruling which was later adopted by the Canadian Rugby Union.

Meanwhile, Western squads were coming East each autumn to participate in the Dominion final and were meeting with little success. Their failure to make much impression against mighty Eastern teams was attributable to several factors, primarily inferior kicking. On ground plays and passing attacks, Western teams were on a par with their Eastern rivals. Longer and more consistent booting by Eastern punters spelled the downfall of the West. Regina's Roughriders, led by the astute Al Ritchie, carried the Western banner into battle during most of the invasions. But even the craft and skill of a Ritchie could not offset the advantage in kicking possessed by the East. Eleven invasions failed.

**WEST WINS WITH IMPORTS**

The disadvantage of playing under slightly different rules, the long lay-off between the Western playdowns and the Dominion final, and the tiring train trip East—all played their parts in turning back those eleven invasions of Western teams into the Eastern strongholds.

Obviously something had to be done. Winnipeg blazed the way by importing practically an entire team from American universities. Bob Fritz, Bert Oja, Fritz Hanson, Gregg Kabat and Bud Marquardt were but a few of the galaxy of stars scintillating on the Winnipeg squad.

Carrying everything before them in the West, the Winnipegs departed for the East to meet Hamilton's mighty Tigers in the championship tussle for the Grey Cup, emblematic of Dominion rugby supremacy.

Paced by slim Fritz Hanson, the North Dakota flash, the Winnipegs crashed their way through to a decisive 18-12 victory over the Tigers in the Dominion final played in Hamilton on Saturday, December 7, 1935.... Surely, now that the Winnipegs were Dominion champions, the 1936 final would be played in the West under Western rules.

Then the Canadian Rugby Union went into action. Meeting in Toronto on February 29, 1936, the union moved to prevent further importations by the West, denied the petition of Western representatives for a Western final, drafted proposed rule changes into a considerably more conservative structure and then approved of the suggested changes.

To the motion of Western representatives that the Dominion final be played in the West in alternate years, the Eastern delegates objected strenuously. Late November weather on the prairies is not suited to football, was their contention. And yet, due entirely to protracted Eastern schedules, the Winnipegs had waited nearly a month before the 1935 final was staged in Hamilton.

Finally Eastern delegates partially acceded to Western demands and passed a ruling that the venue of the final should be decided each year by the executive of the Canadian Rugby Union, on which ruling body, Eastern representatives held the balance of power.

Then came the ruling designed to curb further importations of American players. Unless resident in Canada from Sunday, March 1, 1935, no American player was to be permitted to participate in the Canadian game. And in order to play during the 1936 season, American players must have resided in Canada for one year continuously prior to the opening of the season....

**NO PLAY-OFF LAST YEAR**

Completely disregarding the Union ruling on importations, Calgary and Regina, allied with Winnipeg in the Western Conference, looked over the field last autumn and went into action. Regina brought in practically an entire squad, while Calgary's Bronks, coached by Carl Cronin, who had learned his football under Notre Dame's immortal Knute Rockne, imported three stars from the States. One of these had played with the Calgary squad the previous season.

A very successful season in the West drew toward its close. Attendances were up everywhere, and for the first time in years all clubs were operating at a considerable profit. Upsetting the pre-season dope entirely, the Regina Roughriders copped the championship by beating the favored Winnipegs in the Western final. The stage was now set for the Dominion championship, Sarnia's Imperials having won the eastern playdowns.

Ruling that nearly the entire Roughrider squad was ineligible by not having complied with the residence ruling put into effect the preceding spring, the Canadian Rugby Union rapidly put the skids under the play-off for the Grey Cup. Regina, having but a shadow of a chance of winning from the powerful Sarnia squad without playing their imports from the States, defaulted to the Imperials, and for the first time in twelve years there was no championship tussle in the East.

**DOMINION FINAL LIKELY**

[Deleted prognostications for the coming season.] However, regardless of who represents the West, and who emerges from the Canadian final as victor, it is to be hoped that true Canadian sportsmanship will prevail at all times, and that East and West may continue to work together toward that ideal of all gridiron enthusiasts and performers—complete unity and amicability in the Dominion-wide operation of Canada's fall pastime.

Chapter 9

FOOTBALL—US COLLEGE

Following Clifford Russell's dismissal from the Louisiana high school football team in 1935 for breaking training rules, his father shot the coach and then turned the gun on himself. This was the era of "King football." With the falling leaves of autumn, boys everywhere turned to football. High schools mimicked university pep rallies, cheerleaders, victory celebrations, and outlandish outfits. The Chicago high school championships routinely attracted 120,000 spectators. In Sing Sing penitentiary, the inmates filled the stands to watch their team play outside squads, and a radio announcer provided the play-by-play to those confined to the hospital and death-row.

News-week reported that on an average fall Saturday in 1938, thirty-five percent of the nation's radios were tuned to a college football game. By comparison, that year's World Series attracted thirty-three percent of the market, and a similar number listened to the radio's most popular comedy, Charlie McCarthy and Edgar Bergen. Initially, colleges simply gave away radio rights, but as the broadcasts became more popular and radio stations sold advertising rights, schools and conferences demanded compensation. The drop in gate receipts at the beginning of the Depression led to conjecture that instead of attending the game and spending money on such items as food, drinks, souvenirs, and parking, people would listen to the game on radio. The NCAA appointed a committee to examine radio's effect on attendance, but its 1936 report was inconclusive. Some schools joined to ban radio broadcasts, and the Southern, Western, and Southwest conferences all prohibited radio broadcasts for at least a year.

Colleges in the Colored Intercollegiate Athletic Association and the Southwestern (Negro) Conference shared in football's popularity. For many blacks, success on the football field was a way of earning respect from a society that admired stamina, athletic skill, strength and courage, which many whites refused to acknowledge blacks possessed. Minority players needed extraordinary ability and a serene temperament to play for desegregated teams. At tryouts, players and coaches quickly tested their stamina, strength, and "courage." University of Michigan coach Harry Kipke, informed a national magazine that he ordered his veterans to pound a black candidate "without mercy" during practice, so that "if, at the end of the week he doesn't turn in his uniform, then I know I've got a great player." Unable to endure racial bigotry on and off the field at the University of Iowa, Ozzie Simmons quit the team. Colleges in urban areas in the north and west had more black players, but desegregated teams faced scheduling and traveling problems as many hotels and restaurants refused to serve blacks. Penn State forbade black and white roommates. Southern colleges usually refused to play desegregated teams unless the black players were benched. Such "gentlemen's agreements" were common. In the 1939 Cotton Bowl game in Dallas, for instance, Boston College agreed not to play Lou Montgomery against Clemson. Montgomery could sit with his teammates on the bench, but could not play, stay in the same hotel or eat in the restaurants with them. No matter how well they performed, blacks were denied conference honors, All-America recognition, and selection to the College All-Star team. They were often referred to as "dusky stars" by the mainstream media. All but the minority press ignored the racial abuse and discrimination in the sport.

College football rivaled baseball in the production of national heroes. Gridiron stars such as Sammy Baugh, Tom Harmon, Frank Albert, Don Hutson, Dixie Howell, Byron "Whizzer" White, Sid Luckman, Davey O'Brien, Nile Kinnick, and Jay Berwanger—the first Heisman Trophy winner in 1936—provided entertainment for students and alumni who filed into huge concrete or brick stadia built just for football. Black stars included Horace Bell (Minnesota), Jerome Holland (Cornell), and Kenny Washington and Jackie Robinson (UCLA). Winning teams attracted upwards of 80,000 spectators and added to the coffers of local merchants. In 1935, for instance, football fans bought five million dollars in tickets to the major games each week, spent another five million dollars on such items as meals, hotels, liquors, and the theater, and paid an additional million dollars on travel to and from the games. To aid the local economy, Miami, New Orleans, El Paso, and Dallas Chambers of Commerce hosted year-end bowl games (Orange 1933, Sugar 1936, Sun 1936, Cotton 1937) to rival California's Rose Bowl (1920).

After a decade of constant growth, 1930 witnessed a drop in attendance and the following year, Associated Press reported a ten percent decline in attendance, a fall of forty per cent since 1928. Although the football programs at Yale, Notre Dame and Southern California took in more than one million dollars annually, some universities, especially small private colleges, began to de-emphasize their athletic programs and cutback on traveling expenses. Most schools reduced admission fees. As the document, "King Football Answers the Depression" discusses, to attract more customers, schools eliminated as many "easy" games as possible and attempted to schedule natural state rivals and opponents of equal strength—especially early in the season. By 1933, turnstiles were clicking again. One Saturday, 453,000 fans attend sixteen important games. By 1935, attendance returned to pre-Depression levels. Two years later, News-week reported that based on paid admissions, football ranked behind only basketball and baseball. Financially, football's average ticket price of one dollar garnered the most money with forty million. Improvements in floodlights during the decade encouraged more than 1,500 high schools and 275 colleges to attract more spectators by offering night games.

When Notre Dame coach Knute Rockne died in 1931, The Literary Digest wrote "not since the death of Rudolph Valentino has there been such a high tide of post-mortem hero worship, and in this case it is the masculinity of the nation which has been stirred to its depths." The Detroit News felt that "the essence of Rockne's character was its complete masculinity, a circumstance calculated to set him apart in an age which has somehow lost the edge of an earlier national virility." Most people associated football with the American character. The president of Indiana University, Herman Wells, noted in 1940 that "there's something about it [football] that we like to associate with American qualities—its ruggedness and virility and aggressiveness." The vice-president of Ohio State wrote that "College football is based on a principle which is basically American—the principle of representation. It is enriched by all the loyalty and responsibility and unity of action that go with the fulfillment of that principle." Chairman of the NCAA, C.K. Hall, proclaimed in 1931, "In these soft days of movies, autos and mushy social weekends let's preserve in all its virility the ruggedest game we have left."

That the college coach was often better known to the general public than the university president was indicative of football's predominance. Illinois coach Bob Zuppke's stock reply to public appearance requests was, "My price is $200. You can't pay it, and I'm not worth it." College coaches such as Clark Shaughnessy, Howard Jones, Amos Alonzo Stagg, Pop Warner, Bob Zuppke, Fielding Yost, and Bernie Bierman were household names. Until his plane crashed in 1931, the 43-year old Knute Rockne, whose Notre Dame teams won nineteen consecutive games from 1929 to 1930, was the dean of football coaches. Studebaker Corporation, which paid Rockne $25,000 to give promotional speeches to its sales staff in South Bend, immediately named its newest automobile "The Rockne Six," which it proclaimed was "Forceful as Rockne himself was forceful; stirring as his influence was stirring...."

Coaching was an insecure occupation. Without tenure, young coaches were sometimes forced to desperate extremes to win games and establish a reputation. A national survey of secondary education in 1934 reported that when hiring a coach, high schools gave more weight to the applicant's football record than to his physical education background.

In a 1931 AP poll of eighty-one sportswriters as to how important skill, strength, strategy, and luck were for success in a given sport, football received fifty-seven votes for strategy, followed by baseball with only fourteen. The coach was the chief strategist. Not surprisingly, in the voting for the first college All-Star game, nearly three times as many people cast ballots for the coaches than for the players. Game films, blocking sleds and other training technologies, and extensive scouting systems added to the coaches' mystique.

The more successful coaches adapted to the plethora of rule changes that emerged to combat declining attendance and the growing number of injuries and deaths. At the beginning of the decade, most teams employed single or double-wing formations to better concentrate blockers at the point of attack. Offensives, especially in their own half of the field, were extremely conservative. With the ball on their own 20-yard line, a team often punted on first down, preferring to wait for the other team to make a mistake. The forward pass was usually considered a desperation move. "Making Football Safe" outlines the major rule changes prior to the 1934 season, and the reasons behind them, that resulted in the emergence of the passing game. During the summer of 1935, more than 500 coaches attended Colgate's coach Andy Kerr's camp to learn the intricacies of the forward pass. The offense was opened even wider in 1938 when it became permissible to throw two or more successive incomplete passes into the end zone without a penalty. At the end of the decade, Clark Shaughnessy used the T-formation at Stanford University to win the Rose Bowl.

Football's most serious problem was the sudden increase in fatalities. In 1931, the press attributed fifty deaths to football, which was double the previous high of twenty-five in 1925. Although this number was later greatly reduced, and new rules were implemented to make the game safer, the number of fatalities in succeeding years were thirty-one, twenty-four, twenty-five, and thirty. A 1932-33 study of thirty-eight college physical education programs discovered that in terms of injuries per 1,000, football had the highest rate of 87.9 followed by polo at 11.2. The resulting furor convinced some insurance companies to stop issuing accident policies to football players, and provoked heated debates on the merits of football. Hygeia, a popular public health magazine with a national circulation, repeatedly demanded better safety precautions and urged that football players receive regular physical examinations. In defense of football, the Yale Alumni Weekly declared in 1931, "The nation wants men who are fighters, who do not flinch at disagreeable work.... Sports, played hard against disappointment in the cold and in the rain are putting the steel fiber in character. They are building up the physical machine by rough tempering." Another college paper stated, "Football is no sport for the soft and the yellow. It draws on verve, determination, and common 'guts.'"

To counteract negative press reports, the college football establishment conducted several investigations into athletic injuries. A 1931 Coaches' Association study surveyed 147 colleges and concluded that only two fatal injuries occurred on university varsity teams and that they were accidental. Its analysis of 1,477 football injuries led to the rule changes discussed below in "Making Football Safe."

Since the NCAA seemed unconcerned that most fatalities occurred in high school games, the National Federation of State High School Athletic Associations left the NCAA rules association in 1930 and developed their own rules. Some school boards lowered eligibility from twenty to nineteen years; limited practice time to ninety minutes; outlawed spring football; classified leagues by age, height, and weight; limited players to four years of play; reduced the season to seven games; or required three weeks of football training before the season began.

The most innovative change was the adoption of six-man football, which coincided with the decade's love for small-scale games such as miniature golf, table tennis, and parlor baseball. Chester High School (Nebraska) coach Stephen E. Epler, with assistance from Don Gates and A.W. Larson of Fargo, North Dakota, invented six-man football. Because it featured a wide-open passing game in which every player could carry the ball or receive a pass, six-man football reduced injuries, saved on expenses, and appealed to schools with small enrollments and limited funds.

The release of Bulletin 23, American College Athletics, of the Carnegie Foundation For the Advancement of Teaching, was college football's Black Friday. After investigating 112 colleges and universities in Canada and the United States, the Foundation reported on 24 October 1929 that only 28 institutions obeyed the rules and accused the other schools of ruthless recruiting methods by alumni, coaches, and fraternities; of providing jobs, scholarships, and opulent living facilities to athletes; and easing athletes through courses. Although the Bulletin generally supported intercollegiate sports and noted there were fewer recruiting and subsidization of athletes than in the past, the report created a nation-wide tempest. Virtually every major newspaper in the country afforded it front page coverage. The New York Times headline declared, "College Sports Tainted by Bounties...One in Seven Athletes Subsidized."

Sportswriters such as John Tunis and Paul Gallico interpreted the Bulletin as a ringing indictment of commercialism in intercollegiate sports and accused university administrations of using football to gain national publicity at the expense of providing exercise for the bodies and minds of all the students. Athletic departments, whose programs were often supported by football revenues, fought back. The ensuing four years was a period of crisis for major football programs.

Beginning in 1930 and continuing for the rest of the decade the NCAA sought to devise regulatory codes for recruiting and subsidizing student athletes and affirmed its commitment to faculty control of the athletic program and to year-round coaching appointments. Although some conferences attempted to implement reforms, few conferences abided by NCAA codes of conduct as the association had no regulatory or judicial power.

At the core of the debate was the role of the university in society, and the place of athletics in this role. Virtually every newspaper and magazine in the United States commented on this issue. In its "Debate-of-the-Month Series," the Rotarian's October 1938 topic was "Should College Athletes Be Paid?" The next month the subject was whether college athletics were over-emphasized.

Several college presidents openly worried about football's growing influence on college life—what some commentators termed "stadium fever." Dr. James Angel of Yale stated, "I believe that any system which by its nature encourages proselytizing among boy athletes in the secondary schools is pernicious. I do not believe there is any obligation on the part of the college to furnish the general public nor even the alumni with substitutes for the circus, the prize fight, and the gladiatorial combat." Some schools placed athletics under more direct university control, waived admission fees, discussed reducing the number of games from eight or nine to five or less, and abolished the separate training table and pre-season practices, but most universities only paid lip-service to change. "King Football: The Vulgarization of the American College" presents the case for the elimination of varsity football.

Robert Maynard Hutchins, president of the University of Chicago, led the campaign for the elimination of intercollegiate football. Hutchins believed that sports for profit and public consumption had subverted the true goal of physical education—the training of the body. Believing that reform would not work, the university discontinued its varsity football program in December 1939. Other universities that abolished intercollegiate football by the end of the decade included Antioch, Loyola (Chicago), Reed, Emory, Clark, and De Paul (Chicago). The President of De Paul University stated, "I am convinced that for ninety-five percent of the schools in the United States, football is not serving its prime purpose in the education of the student body."

The public believed that college football players personified American virtues. Athletics were the proving grounds for the benefits of hard work, self-sacrifice, teamwork, courage, loyalty, self-control, and fair play. Football taught students to disregard pain in the pursuit of a desired goal, to subordinate their interests to the interest of the group, to work with others for the same goals, to expend one's last reserves of strength and courage, and to face defeat as well as how to win. The chief value of football, according to coach Louis Little of Cornell, was that it created situations in which courage and character were tested. In short, football made good citizens! In a 1934 survey of Iowa State graduates each alumnus asserted that athletics inspired courage and confidence and prepared the players for life after school. Two years earlier, a survey of Yale students revealed that eighty-four percent favored retaining the football program; ninety-five percent felt athletics constituted an essential part of a good educational program; eight-six percent said football developed courage; eighty-four percent reported it promoted determination; seventy-six percent believed it cultivated mental alacrity; forty-eight percent said it fostered unselfishness; and sixty-one percent said it produced leadership skills (Yale News, 13 December 1932). Coach Lou Little's report to the American Football Coaches Association provided the best defense against the claims of "over-emphasis." The statistical portion of this study is reprinted below.

Despite the academic debate on the merits of football and its commercialization, millions of spectators continued to flock to the games, or gambled their savings on either the local football team or on such perennial favorites as Alabama, Minnesota, Notre Dame, Southern California, or Morgan College. College football was a gambler's dream. Each week the major newspapers and weekly magazines printed their predictions for the major college games that Saturday. The most popular prognosticators were Grantland Rice, Associated Press, United Press, International News Service, Newsweek, and Paul Gallico. In the 1935 season, Rice had the best prediction rate of .686.

## KING FOOTBALL ANSWERS THE DEPRESSION

[*The Literary Digest was an avid follower of college football. This article discusses the impact of the Depression on attendance and the universities' decision to lower admission fees, foster local football rivalries and provide more competitive games for the fans. George Trevor, "King Football Answers the Depression," The Literary Digest (16 September 1933), 24, 33.*]

A few weeks ago, while stars twinkled above the gray outline of Soldiers' Field Coliseum, Chicago, some 60,000 enthusiasts clamored for admission, despite the muggy heat, to watch two all-star elevens representing the Mid-West and the Far-West put on an all-America football show under glaring arc lights.

The promoters of this midsummer night's madness misgauged the drawing power of their spectacle. They anticipated a crowd of about 30,000 persons—feeling that such a figure was high for a game which was so patently out of season. Just to be safe they printed 45,000 tickets. That liberal consignment was snapped up by football addicts who have been waiting impatiently since last December for another whiff of their favorite game. Pasteboards had to be improvised hastily. Those 60,000 thrill seekers were not disappointed. They saw a spectacular if somewhat unpolished struggle, with Harry Newman, Michigan's amazing point-getter, once again coming through in the pinch with a touch-down pass.

Football attendance figures for the entire nation fell off about 27 per cent last fall from the 1929 peak, but this drop may fairly be construed as reflecting the backlash of economic depression rather than any waning of public interest. As a matter of fact, gridiron gate receipts suffered less than most business balance sheets.

**TICKET PRICES**

The Hoover Commission on Social Trends reported that popular interest in football remained constant from 1920 to 1930. The sudden drop in attendance totals which began in 1930 and became more pronounced last fall coincides with the Market collapse and the general economic decline.

College athletic heads were slow to see the handwriting on the wall and reduce ticket prices to conform with shrunken budgets. The public is as keen as ever to watch this modern counterpart of the Roman gladiatorial show, but simply can not pay the price.

Yale, for example, packed the Bowl brimful for the Georgia game in 1931 when only a dollar per head was charged. Of course the gross intake may be greater when 25,000 persons pay three dollars apiece, but what is more bleak and depressing than vast expanses of vacant seats in a gargantuan concrete saucer?

Ticket prices are coming down decidedly this fall yet, unfortunately for John Doe, Yale '97, much of this saving will be off-set by the government amusement tax. John Doe, a typical graduate, has a wife and two children who show virulent symptoms of that contagious fall madness tabbed "footballitis Americanus." If he takes his family to four of Yale's major games it will cost him about $40 for tickets alone. New Haven is a good two hours motor or railroad ride from New York, but traveling expenses are negligible compared to the drain on his pocket-book for luncheon and then dinner at one of those Boston Post Road after-the-game dancing places. One Saturday afternoon's family outing at the Yale-Army game, let us say, will set him back around $30. That is a modest figure. Remembering that there are some 630 colleges in the United States capable of supporting a football team in the style to which it has become accustomed, you get a fair idea of the money spent by the public each fall on football and its concomitants.

**THE NATIONAL SPECTACLE**

For all its palatial stadiums—the thirty largest have a total seating capacity of 1,250,000 persons (excluding municipal arenas such as Soldiers' Field, Chicago)—college football is merely the tail that wags the dog. Parke Davis, football statistician, will tell you that there are ten high-school players for every college player; that high-school attendance figures exceed those of the intercollegiate gridiron by more than two to one; and that the scholastic arenas aggregate more seats than the collegiate coliseums. This won't surprise you much when you realize that every town in America has a high-school eleven, not to mention the private and secondary school teams. Despite its brief season, football has ousted baseball as the national spectacle if not the national game. Tho [sic] limited to ten weeks in the autumn, football outdraws baseball (with its six-month campaign) by a wide margin. Excluding sand-lots, the number of boys between the ages of twenty-four and fourteen enrolled on regularly organized football teams is greater than the number similarly affiliated with baseball nines.

The economic depression must inevitably be reflected in so wide-spread and popular a game, catering as it does to the entertainment of 10,000,000 people. Colleges accessible to large centers of population have been relatively less affected by the business debacle than such isolated outposts as Cornell, Dartmouth, Colgate and like. Community interest has sustained the University of Pennsylvania, for example, at something approaching boom-era box-office income levels. Generally speaking the Pacific coast has been less susceptible to the slump than the Atlantic seaboard, perhaps because of the phenomenal success enjoyed by the U.S.C. Trojans.

**IN THE WEST AND SOUTH**

...What of the football season now in the offing? Ticket prices, speaking generally, will he lower. You can see the Yale-Princeton game for $3.50 plus government tax—quite a drop from the five-dollar peak which prevailed during the piping post-war epoch. Back in the days of Pa Corbin and Hector Cowan, Yale-Princeton admission prices ranged from fifty cents to a dollar. As late as 1914, Big-three game tickets sold for two dollars. The overhead was much less in the prewar period of relatively small wooden stands, low-salaried or volunteer coaches, and restricted squads. Mortgage amortization and interest charges on the huge concrete stadiums are a nightmare to bedeviled graduate managers now that the customers have become budget-conscious.

Consider the amusing if embarrassing case of the New Orleans millionaire who advanced funds for a sumptuous college arena down Louisiana way and was forced to take over that white elephant when the athletic authorities couldn't pay the interest charges on the donor's investment!...

The problem confronting graduate managers is to fix ticket prices at a figure which will insure the maximum gate receipts rather than the biggest attendances. By reducing tickets unduly they might pack their stadiums and still make less money than they would from a smaller crowd at a higher tariff. Pacific coast prices have been cut about thirty per cent—the University of California selling a fifteen-dollar season-book for eleven dollars.

**DEATH OF THE PRACTICE GAME**

The economic ill wind has blown the so-called "practice game" evil clear out of the football picture. No longer will the lambs of the gridiron lie down with the tigers to be devoured for a cash guaranty. These remarks apply chiefly to the East, where it has been customary for the big college squads to spend several week-ends fattening on set-ups—the theory being that teams such as Harvard, Yale, Dartmouth, etc., must be developed gradually, and progress from a diet of cream puffs to raw meat.

Major elevens in the Middle-West, where the conference system is in vogue, are accustomed to pick on rivals their own size virtually from the season's start. Warmup games between badly matched opponents are extremely rare. Michigan, for example, tackles Michigan State, Cornell, Ohio State, Chicago, Illinois, Iowa, Minnesota, and Northwestern in rapid fire sequence.

Thanks indirectly to the depression, an Eastern Big Ten, patterned on Western Conference lines, will soon exist in fact if not in theory. Already, institutions of comparable educational standards, social rank, and athletic eligibility rules—such as Harvard, Yale, Princeton, Dartmouth, Brown, Cornell, Pennsylvania, Columbia, Army and Navy—comprise an unofficial "Big Ten."

In order to coax reluctant dollars out of hiding, Eastern schedule makers have booked up solidly with major games. Brown University, for instance, undertakes a man-killing assignment this fall by meeting Yale, Holy Cross, Princeton, Syracuse, Harvard, and Colgate on successive Saturdays!

Credit the depression likewise with an assist in the matter of patching up football feuds and reuniting traditional rivals. Army and Navy have already forgotten that squabble over the three-year rule. This fall, Cornell and Syracuse an ancient New York State rivalry will resume after a separation lasting a quarter of a century. Next year Brown and Dartmouth bury the hatchet, and Harvard smokes the pipe of peace with Princeton. Bill Roper's regime with its hard-bitten creed that "football is 90 per cent fight" has given way to a less pugnacious stewardship. Princeton can use the money that a second Big Three will draw....

The day when grads [in Harvard and Yale] were limited to two or four seats and threatened with blacklisting if they sold them to outsiders is gone but not forgotten. There will be no snooping through the stands by university agents this year in search of "aliens" who have bought their ticket from a speculator; no demands for personal signatures to compare with the name signed on subscription cards.

### FOOTBALL PUBLICITY GREATEST INDUSTRY IN THE UNITED STATES

[*This was the first issue of The Football News, whose editorial policy was that the "promotion of football as a sport will be uppermost in our minds as we publish this newspaper. The players are in the game because they love it. Few have ambitions to capitalize on their performances in the great drama of gridiron activity." In this article, McLemore, who was also a correspondent for United Press, bemoans the publicity raised for college football by its publicity agents. Henry McLemore, "Football Publicity Greatest Industry in United States, The Football News, 1 (14 December 1939), 11.*]

Agriculture once was the biggest industry in the United States, but it isn't anymore. It has been surpassed both in number of men employed and volume of output by the business of college football publicity.

For every bushel of wheat grown this year two bushels of brochures of football teams will be published, and for every bag of potatoes and every bale of cotton, there will be three mail bags full of gridiron dope run through the mimeographing hopper. I don't know how many farmers there are but there aren't half as many as there are publicity men at work spreading the truth and the untruth about the Woodcats, the Tigers, the Aardvarks, the Bisons, the Chipmunks, the Red Scourges, the Green Scourges, the Tornados, the Cyclones, and the heaven-help-me-everythings.

The postman doesn't ring twice these days. In fact, he doesn't even ring at all but has to kick on the door with his foot, what with his arms so full of the football literature he has to deliver. Three times a day the postmen arrive with their burdens and I am beginning to regret that neither heat nor snow nor rain nor gloom of day can stay the couriers from their appointed rounds. A few more days and this department is going to be forced to stage "Blackouts" so that the mail carriers can't find us and bombard us with the vital (?) football statistics of all the schools from Alfred and Bates to Yale and Xavier.

There is about as much variety in the football catalogues of the various schools as there is in a jar of peppermints. They all open up with a vivid paragraph listing the 1939 schedule, continue with a superbly written chapter listing the coaching staff, and then take your breath away with passages describing the seating arrangements of the stadium and the prices for the various games.

By this time the reader is so engrossed that he can't put the book down and plunge onward into such enthralling matter as letter men returning, letter men not returning, coach so-and-so's statement, 1939 manager, practice schedule, team physician, team trainer, team colors, team mascot, press box improvement, and how to reach the stadium from downtown.

Every one of the booklets I have read—and I am in the middle of my 2000th-has claimed at least two potential All-Americans for its eleven. By a hasty bit of multiplication I figure that no fewer than 15,000 potential All-Americans soon will be unloosed. This figure does not include St. Mary's estimate, which usually runs between ten and fifteen, according to the whim of that school's publicity chief when he sits down to glorify the mad men of the Manga....

## AMOS ALONZO STAGG TALKS ABOUT SPORTSMANSHIP

*[In November 1932,* Time *magazine declared "the role of football wizard is, on the whole, superior to any other in professional sport. Coaches get higher salaries than any other professional except a few baseball players. Their earning capacity is not determined by their age. They work only in the autumn and mostly in the afternoon. If they are successful they are rewarded by fame, authority and opportunities to act in cinema." Lou Little at Columbia reportedly earned the highest salary of the approximately 3,000 college coaches with $17,000. Howard Jones received $12,000, but earned one-third as much again from newspaper writing, cinema shorts, and his two books on football.*

*This article illustrates the esteem sportswriters held for the college coach and his role in promoting sportsmanship. Summarizing the article's laudatory description of Stagg—which is omitted—: Stagg came from humble beginnings. His first ambition was to be a minister. Stagg earned his way through Yale while playing baseball and football. Not a good speaker, he thought, "Why can't I do as much good as an athletic director as I could as a preacher?" In 1891 he became associate professor and director of the Department of Physical Culture and Athletics at the University of Chicago. As a coach, Stagg was an original thinker who designed, among other innovations, the direct snap to the running back. J.B. Griswold, "Born with It. Amos Alonzo Stagg Talks About Sportsmanship and Tells How to Acquire It," American Magazine (November 1931), 60-61, 133-135.]*

Next Saturday afternoon, as on last Saturday afternoon, in enormous concrete bowls throughout the country, mad mobs led by crashing bands and hand-springing cheer leaders will be roaring and singing and screaming. Before them will be twenty-two youngsters, just kids barely out of their teens, who, in their canvas armor, take on the form of seasoned gladiators. And as eleven smashes into eleven, the thousands in the stands will shout insanely such battle-cries is "Fight! Fight! Fight!" "Bust that line! Give 'em the ax!" "Twist their tails!"

Those twenty-two men are in there to battle until they have no strength left. Back from the side lines are eager substitutes, fists clenched, jumpy, anxious, tugging at the leash for a chance to enter the war.

And on opposite sides of the field sit the football coaches, the men who have trained these boy gladiators and who have sent them out to battle. Each coach has prepared his men, mentally and physically, to face the dangers of stout combat. He, and he alone, will shape their minds, as he has shaped their bodies.

Will they come out of it all better men—or worse? Let's look at a great football coach, inquire into his philosophy, and make up our minds whether we'd like our boys to play on his teams.

"Sportsmanship," said Amos Alonzo Stagg, "is a delightful fragrance that people carry with them in their relations with their fellow men." We were in the living-room of Mr. Stagg's modest home in Kenwood Avenue, Chicago. Around us was comfortable, old-fashioned furniture—a stately grandfather's clock in the corner, upholstered chairs with crocheted antimacassars. On the walls were wood etchings and Japanese prints. It might have been the home of a sheltered New England preacher in a tiny town miles from the whoop and the roar of football fanatics, except for a big, woolly University of Chicago football blanket, bearing proudly a huge C, that lay on the couch, touched by pillows with the same insignia.

On the walls were no photographs of groups of athletes, with a captain sitting stiff-backed in the center holding the ball. No trophies, no banners, no scrolls carrying the record of noble victories. Not a football in sight. Not even a photograph of the alumni banquet which celebrated the never defeated season of Nineteen Umpty-ump. Just a nice comfortable home for real folks; and out in front at the curb was a worn but stanch electric brougham, eight years old, in which later this amazing sixty-nine-year-old man was to take me scooting around trucks, trolleys, and gasoline cars, on a breath-taking ride to the University of Chicago, Stagg Field, and his football squad only a few blocks away.

Amos Alonzo Stagg is the oldest in point of service and oldest in years of all the American athletic coaches, and probably he has had a greater influence upon college athletics and athletes than any other man....

Alonzo Stagg is stocky and his bushy hair is gray. In spite of his sixty-nine years, he's only middle-aged. He plays tennis for an hour or more two or three times a week, and no "old" man can stand that sort of exercise....

It was here that he gave, at my request, his definition of sportsmanship quoted above. "A very few persons are born sportsmen," he went on, "and not even the foulest environment nor the most unhealthy teaching can drive sportsmanship from their blood. The great majority of boys and girls, however, learn their sportsmanship from others. Sometimes from their parents. Mostly, however, in these days of tremendous interest in college athletics, they learn it directly or indirectly from the coaches of college and school athletics. Few of us coaches realize the enormous responsibility that is ours.

The influence of the coach extends far beyond the boundaries of his campus. Youth loves to imitate what it admires. And the athlete's manners and morals—his sportsmanship—reflect the precepts of his athletic director.

The present generation of parents is not always holding up high ideals for the children to follow, and boys and girls are learning their codes of conduct elsewhere. They're going to the athletic field and the gymnasium for what they formerly got in the home. They're learning temperance, self-control, fair play, sportsmanship, courage, and the Golden Rule from athletes and athletic directors and coaches.

In the old days, the parents set a high example for their children to follow, but now—" He shrugged his shoulders, "instead of going to church to learn how to live, the youngsters nowadays go anywhere they want to. Thank God, they like to go to football games! And the fellows who play and the men who coach them must realize that, in no small way, by their actions they are preaching sermons and laying down rules of conduct for the coming generation.

Sportsmanship isn't a quality to be left behind on the gridiron after the crowd has filed out of the stadium. It's something you will find in every successful man and woman, in every person whose qualities you admire. The man who works in an office, if he would get along, must play the game like a worthy member of a good football team. The executive who gets the most out of his men, whose department shows a profit, whose superiors are slating him for a general managership, is the man whose code is quite like that of a competent coach."

I asked Mr. Stagg to write Ten Commandments for the football player and Ten Commandments for the coach.

"Here they are," he said. "They're codes of sportsmanship, and if a man obeys those codes in his businesslife, nothing can stop him."

### TEN COMMANDMENTS FOR THE FOOTBALL COACH
#### Or for the Business Executive

1. Be inspired by the vision of your opportunities. In your hands is far more than the reputation of the institution that employs you. To you has been entrusted the future of all those whose work you direct. You can make them or break them.
2. Make your conduct a worthy example. Don't drink intoxicants; don't gamble; don't smoke; don't use smutty language; don't tell dirty stories; don't associate with loose and silly women.
3. Be fair-minded. Deal justly. Bear no malice! Don't play favorites. Avoid politics. Shun graft, petty or great.
4. Harbor no hatred toward your rivals.
5. Don't be a swell-head in victory nor an alibier in defeat.
6. Stoop to no unfair practice. Try to win, with every ounce of energy that is within you—but win only by fair means.
7. Give rebuke with justice, and praise when it is deserved.
8. Diagnose each man's temperament skillfully so that you may prescribe accurately and properly to build his character and ability.
9. Be a sportsman and a gentleman at all times.
10. Whether fortune is good or fortune is bad, say a prayer of thanks each evening.

### TEN COMMANDMENTS FOR THE FOOTBALL PLAYER
#### Or the Man or Woman in Business

1. Keep your mind and body clean and alert. Practice self-control at all times.
2. Be true, square, and honest. Don't lie. Don't cheat. Keep your word. Don't be a tattletale.
3. Perform your own job just a little bit better than is absolutely necessary. Don't stagnate. Use your imagination. Don't become an automaton.
4. Help the other fellow. Work for the good of the team.
5. Don't complain, whine, knock, or gripe. If you are given a job, do it cheerfully. Never shirk responsibility. Always do your level best.
6. Don't be a grand-stander. Throttle your conceit. A swelled head will cut your career as short as though you had no head at all.

7. Don't be discouraged by failure. The man of average intelligence who has the courage to keep on trying will get farther than the genius who puts only half his heart into his work.

8. Always be a sportsman and a gentleman.

9. Develop courage, determination, perseverance, continuous interest, prolonged enthusiasm, and unbending ambition.

10. And say a prayer each evening.

Other coaches do their jobs well. Others invent new plays. But Alonzo Stagg has something more. He has the ability to transmit to his players that mysterious intangible something—a third wind, perhaps—that lifts men to the peak.

It is my guess that in Stagg this added power is a result of his rigid philosophy of life, his constant refusal to stray from the straight path of honest conduct, the old-fashioned code of our forefathers. [Next follows a laudatory summary of Stagg's career.]

"In athletics, or in business," he said, "you won't get far by teaching your men to hate your competitor."

If you imagine that Stagg's system of coaching turns out sissies, you need only talk to any man who has played against Chicago. In battle, Chicago fights grimly and shows no quarter, Stagg believes in attack, attack, attack!

"I teach my men courage and team play," Stagg told me. "I want them to accept responsibility and never to quit."

He is very proud of the business success of his boys. He keeps in close touch with most of them and he names one after another, important men in industry today, who were formerly members of his squads.

"Football has nearly reached its height," Stagg said. "But it will never go back. There is so much in the game, it develops such fine qualities in men, that college men will never lose interest in it. Seeing football games gives the spectators all the opportunities to appreciate and to learn the fundamentals of sportsmanship."

"This terrific urge to win," I asked: "You don't agree with some of the reformers who say it's low and unworthy?"

"Low and unworthy!" he exclaimed. "Low and unworthy, to want to win? Why man, isn't that what life's all about?"

## COACHES FACE PRESSURE TO SUCCEED

[*Similar to the previous article, Shaughnessy argued the coach was a teacher whose task it was to instill character, honesty, fairness, loyalty, and physical and mental courage in his players so they would be men when they left college to make their way in the world. While some coaches might be selfish and more concerned with winning than with the boys, this was not the norm. The following selection from this five-page article discusses the pressures many coaches were under to win. Clark Shaughnessy, "Don't Send Your Boy to..." Esquire (October 1935), 37, 177-178, 178a-b.*]

There comes a time in every coach's life when he finds himself in a losing streak. All the old tricks, ideas and methods that have won for him—just don't seem to work—and he just can't seem to get his team going. It isn't long before many people

wiser in football lore than he begin puckering their eyebrows and involving explanations and reasons, satisfactory to themselves, no matter how incorrect, for their team's
defeats.

No such explanations ever would be complete without the coach's shortcomings
getting a good airing. If he isn't too old, he's too young. If he isn't too tough on the
boys he is too easy, a poor disciplinarian and no leader. If he doesn't put enough fight
into the team, he is too cold, unfriendly and the boys don't like him and won't play for
him. If he is a good fighter and tries desperately to win, he is too emotional and excitable, and how can a person so highly strung and who does not have control of himself be expected to have control of the boys under him. It seems that no matter what
fault one clique finds with a losing coach, another clique finds just exactly the opposite fault. They don't stop with picking flaws in his football knowledge or tactics, but
go right on down the line. He may part his hair in the middle and look like a "sissy."
He may be guilty of occasional lapses in grammar, and therefore he's absolutely illiterate, and how can college boys respect a coach with such a poor education? Of course,
there are other more serious things too that suddenly come to life. It seems that a coach
may stay for years at an institution and as long as he is winning, his personal deficien-
cies are unnoticed, but just let him start losing and for some reason, all the personal
shortcomings that have been true all along and were never even noticed become of
paramount importance.... As long as he is winning—he is safe and he has nothing to
worry about. He can enjoy himself and entertain his constituents by "tackling football."
He might be too old, and then again, he might be too young, or too tough or too easy,
too excitable or too emotional, too much of a he-man or a "sissie." He might speak
incorrectly, grammatically and otherwise, and there might be a lot of other things
wrong, but as long as he is winning, everything is all right. In fact, the publicity department builds a sort of halo around such a winning coach and all his foibles, trivial
and otherwise, get to be looked upon as just the idiosyncrasies of a genius.

It isn't very long, however, after the inevitable losing streak starts before the coach
finds out that he is far from a genius—he is a bum—he never knew anything about
football and never will....

Not long ago at one of the prominent universities of the country a star player was
unfortunate enough to contract, during vacation time, a disease that made his participation the following fall dangerous to his life. This player was exceedingly popular
with the students, the alumni, the public and the press. His condition did not develop
until after practice had started. Wisely or not, the coach decided that he should he kept
on the squad but not used in any way that would jeopardize his health or endanger that
of any of the other boys. The object of this maneuver was to conceal from the public
what the real trouble was, because the nature of the disease was such that it would have
irreparably injured the boy's reputation if it ever got out. The failure to use this boy
in the games started the rumor that there was friction in the football squad and that the
coach could not get along with the men. Due largely to the absence of this player, the
team had a bad season, and the seed of discontent that was started in this way developed a movement to get rid of the coach; and once any movement of this kind develops, it usually gathers so much momentum that nothing but the dismissal of the coach
satisfies the wolves. This coach martyred himself to protect this boy....

This old timer [a former football coach] knew the pressure that was put on coaches
to win games. He knew of the necessity of holding their jobs, almost desperate in the

case of many of them with families. He had probably cut some corners himself, he had done a little proselytizing and taken a few chances to win games and hold his job. As an ambitious young coach anxious to be a big shot in the athletic world he hadn't thought much about these things. He hadn't had time during those early years to observe the harm to the boys that followed in the wake of such a policy. The alumni and even some of the administration of the institution that employed him, didn't worry about such things. Why should he? It was great while he was winning, but a series of defeats finally caught up with him, and he was put on the spot. He hadn't had the benefit of the advice of the famous old coach who told his protege to "talk football" while he was winning but to build character while he was losing. The inevitable happened—he lost his job.

He knew down in his heart that it hadn't been his fault that his team had been losing. As a matter of fact, he was a much better coach, and one who knew more football, after the experience of losing a number of games than he had been while he was winning. Still he had been fired. The unfairness of the thing galled him but did not embitter him.

He fortunately secured another position and perhaps due to this unhappy experience of being fired, or due to his increasing maturity, he gradually began to see another light—there must be something to football besides the mere winning of games. He discovered that these youngsters playing football were interesting, their problems and ambitions intriguing. He found that they turned to him for counsel and guidance if he encouraged them. He began to enjoy his coaching a lot more than when his only motive was to win games. Then a startling realization dawned upon him. The boys were playing better football. They seemed to appreciate his sympathetic interest in them. There wasn't any of the "take care of yourself at all costs" attitude on the squad. There was better teamwork. They won more games.

Years later after he retired from football he never forgot those experiences. No wonder when he had a son ready to go to college, he took so much pains to find an institution that he felt maintained the proper balance between education and athletics and which could give his son a well-rounded training.

## FOOTBALL SCOUTING

[*Innovative coaches employed game films to study their own players and scout the opposition. The University of Nebraska pioneered filming. It began in 1931 with just an ordinary 16mm. motion picture camera, but the players moved so quickly that it was not very useful. A slow motion attachment solved this problem. Later, a telephoto lens and a tripod allowed the photographer to abandon the side lines for the balcony at the top of the stadium. The following article on the growth of scouting illustrates the more scientific, businesslike approach that now dominated the game. Stanley B. Frank, "Secret Service of the Gridiron: The Work of Football Scouts, Once Frowned Upon, Now Is an Honorable Trade, Practiced in Most Stadia," The Literary Digest (17 November 1934), 38-39.*]

Football games are being decided these days, weeks in advance and in some cases, thousands of miles removed from the actual scene of the contests. Games are won and lost through the eyes of extremely knowing and observant young men, who sit in the stands of every stadium in the country, scribbling notes in little black books and drawing cabalistic designs and charts.

These bright young men are the football scouts, espionage agents who rank on a par with wartime spies for the accuracy and significance of their findings. The football scout is, in effect, a spy in enemy territory, but there is nothing underhanded in his methods or approach. The entire business is conducted on a strictly honorable basis.

The scout cheerfully announces his presence at a designated game by walking into the office of the graduate manager and asking for tickets to the game. He invariably is given his choice of locations, and usually chooses a seat behind the goal posts, where he can get a good, clear shot of the enemy's plays as they open up. Some scouts prefer to sit in the press-box, where they have more room to work, and can glean tips from glib newspaper men.

After the game, the scout may make part of his homeward trip with the team his own college is to play in the future, perhaps have dinner with the coach. If the scout is a bit hazy on a certain point, the rival coach may even supply the missing information—a very honorable profession.

Most scouts are assistant or freshman coaches during the week, then board trains or planes to keep their espionage engagements in all corners of the country. Some of them see their own teams play only once a season, in the last game on the schedule.

Even the most obscure schools have at least one scout and the larger ones employ a corps of three or four men. West Point, which always does things with military precision, makes use of the Army's flying facilities to send men all over the country.

Typical is the case of Gar Davidson, now the Army's head coach, who used to commute regularly between Cambridge, New Haven, South Bend, Palo Alto, Annapolis, Pittsburg, Chicago, and way-stations, in search of "dope" for Biff Jones.

Maintaining a thorough scouting system runs into important money, especially if a team plays an intersectional schedule. Fordham, for instance, recently had Earl Walsh in California watching St. Mary's and Ed Hunsinger in Texas giving Southern Methodist the once-over on the same Saturdays. Both scouts were back in New York on Monday with their reports for Jim Crowley, the head man. Fordham, incidentally, lost both games, which may or may not prove something.

**TRICK OF THE SCOUTING TRADE**

Espionage work in football is a highly complicated, technical business. Scouts concentrate on a team's offense, trying to analyze strong scoring plays so that they can suggest the rigging-up of a possible defense to the head coach back home. A good man has a photographic eye, can chart the assignment of every player in an intricate maneuver down to the most minute detail. All that, of course, involves the taking of a tremendous number of notes and diagrams. Others, like Arthur Sampson, who turned out an undefeated team at Tufts several years ago, and later, was the backfield coach for Lou Little at Columbia and Eddie Casey at Harvard, rarely put pencil to paper when out on an assignment. Yet Sampson, who never played football, can come back with a thorough report, which includes all essential data down to the color of the left halfback's eyes.

It is also the duty of the scout to note how a team "tips its mitt" through the unconscious habits of individual players. Does the star triple-threat back moisten fingertips before throwing a pass or does he hitch up his pants when he is going to run with the ball? Some linemen have the fatal fault of "pointing," giving away the direction of the play by shifting the position of their feet before charging. Then again, there are young backs—experienced ones too—who look toward the spot where they are to hit the line. All these things the good scout sees. If he muffs the "tip-off" signs, he doesn't hold his job very long.

A team's defense does not command more than the casual interest of the scout, for the very good reason that defensive alignments vary radically from week to week as each successive game brings new plans of operation into action. If a back, however, shows a marked weakness on covering passes, you may be pretty sure that most of the enemy's forwards the next week will be thrown into his sector.

## MAKING FOOTBALL SAFE

[*In the first years of the Depression, College football passed a series of rules designed to attract more fans and to counteract claims that the game was too dangerous. This article summarizes the first wave of changes and outlines the coaches' responses to them. The long lists of which coaches favored which rules is deleted. "Making Football Safe for the Men on the Gridiron," The Literary Digest (5 March 1932), 32, 34.*]

Football's face-lifting at the deft hands of the "plastic surgeons" of the rules committee is completed. And now the question arises: Was it worth while? Does the subject look any better?

The line of the nose, now, how about that?

And is the left eyebrow quite straight?

The operators have discharged the patient, and the family—the coaches and the sports-writers, who have to "live" with it—are busy sizing up the job and saying what they think.

Most of them praise (oh, with perhaps a few reservations) the six-rule changes, the most sweeping revision football has had since 1906.

The general opinion is that the rules committee, made up of E.K. Hall, William J. Bingham, W.G. Crowell, A.A. Stagg, H.J. Stegeman, D.X. Bible, Ray Morrison, C.H. Smith, W.0. Hunter, and W.S. Langford, did a good job.

But here and there, as we shall see in more detail later, there is hostility. Bernie Bierman of Minnesota, for example, thinks the changes "mostly a bunch of bunk."

The general meaning of the new rules is briefly summarized by Allison Danzig in the New York Times:

1. Equipment—Hard and unyielding substances used in the construction of protective devices must be covered on the outside with padding at least three-eighths of an inch thick.

2. Kick-Off—At least five players on the receiving team must remain within fifteen yards of the restraining line of the kicking side until the ball has been kicked, and the kick-off may be made by either a punt or a drop kick as well as by a place kick.

3. Blocking and Tackling—The flying block and tackle are made illegal. The player may leave his feet only at the instant of contact with his opponent. Penalty of five yards provided for infraction.

4. Substitutions—A player withdrawn from the game may return in any subsequent period, "time out" being charged against the team for the substitution.

5. Dead Ball—The ball now becomes dead the instant any portion of the carrier, excepting hands or feet, touches the ground, regardless of whether he is within the grasp of an opponent or not.

6. Use of Hands—Players on the defense are forbidden to strike an opponent on head, neck, or face, but may use palm of hands to ward off or push such opponent in effort to get to the ball or the carrier. Penalty for infraction is disqualification of the player and loss by his team of half the distance to the goal line.

The changes in the rules came about largely, it is generally conceded, through the public outcry against last falls football death-roll. In The Digest of December 26 forty fatalities were reported; and this number later rose to forty-nine. The previous high record was twenty.

Now we are assured that these figures are misleading. Said Mr. Hall, chairman of the rules committee, as reported by the Associated Press:

"An analysis indicated that the so-called fatality list accredited to football was more than 50 per cent entirely misleading and inaccurate, and that only twenty-one deaths can be at all properly chargeable to the game of football, and even three of these are in doubt. It is a conservative estimate to say that between 600,000 and 800,000 boys were participating in the game last season."

In an effort to place responsibility for the large number of injuries and deaths, a nation-wide survey of casualties in football was made and is said to have influenced the adoption of the new rules. This report, according to the New York Evening Post, "cited the lack of rigid enforcement of rules by officials, improper training, conditioning, and coaching of players, dangerous, equipment, and the indifferent treatment of minor injuries" as the causes for approximately half of the injuries and deaths....

Of course, it is impossible to arrange in neat groups the various reactions to the changes. Editorial comment is almost without exception favorable. As for the coaches and officials, some say yes, some no, and some both. What cleavage there is—and there is a good deal—is along logical lines, according to an analysis by George Trevor in the New York Sun. This cleavage, he says, "follows the particular system taught by each coach." Further:

"Broadly speaking, the Warner apostles are pleased with the drastic revision concerning arms and hands. Conversely, virtually all the disciples of the so-called Notre Dame school of coaching are bitterly opposed to the hobbling of hands on defense. They feel that the new rule will hamstring the Notre Dame type of "stand-up-and-fan-em-off defense," wherein the head is the target. Naturally they denounce this particular restriction."

Now, before you jump to an unfair conclusion, please remember this. Apostles of the Notre Dame defense technique, taken collectively, are as high principled a group of sportsmen as you can find anywhere in this broad land. They stood and they stand for clean football. It simply happens that the head-shoving type of defense which they teach— style inherited from Yale and Harvard by way of Chicago University—is susceptible of abuse."

The general type of these reactions you will find in this short series of thumbnail interviews gathered by the Associated Press and digested into one passage here:

Glenn S. "Pop" Warner of Stanford approved most of the modifications, but said he was opposed to the rule making the ball "dead" when any part of the ballcarrier's body except his hands or feet touches the ground. He pointed out that a player could break loose and run the distance of the field with no tackler near him, and yet, by slipping and falling down two yards from goal, would be deprived of a touch-down.

Hunk Anderson, head man of football at Notre Dame, sadly shook his head as he digested the new rule outlawing aggressive use of the hands on the defense. "The other rule changes made by the national football-rules committees are okeh," he said, "but I think the committee made a bad mistake in forbidding the aggressive use of hands. Do you know what will happen now if the officials vigorously enforce it? Why, there will be a premium on big fellows in football, more injuries than ever, and more football of the powerhouse variety."

The increasing importance of medical supervision in football was emphasized by Coach Marvin A. Stevens of Yale in voicing approval of the changes in football rules made by the national committee. "You will find that the long list of injuries and fatalities recorded last year were due to no little extent to the lack of medical supervision," said Stevens, president of the Football Coaches Association, and himself a physician.

Howard Jones, University of Southern California football coach, said he believes the new ruling on substitutions will speed up the game from the spectator's viewpoint.

"It simply means more and better whistle-blowing," was the comment of Bob Zuppke, University of Illinois football coach. "Rules put more responsibility on the officials, but I suppose that is a good thing. It can't be helped," he continued, "I like the new kick-off rule."

### NEW RULES AID THE PASSING GAME

[*The most important change to the college game in the 1930s was the new emphasis on passing. This article in News-week, which included a picture of a college football player on the cover, explains the reasons for the growth of the passing game. "Football. Aerial Game. Tricky Formations. A New Hysteria," News-week (3 November 1934), 17-18.*]

Some experts say football is undergoing the greatest revolution since 1906 when the forward pass was introduced on the gridiron. Last Saturday the country's 150 leading college teams completed half of their 1934 schedules, playing an ultra-modern game. Halfbacks, quarterbacks and fullbacks flung forward and lateral passes all over the field. Many observers felt the game looked more like basketball than football.

**CHANGES**: New rules encourage aerial plays. This year a team can try as many consecutive passes as it wants in midfield without being penalized. Furthermore an incomplete pass into an opponent's end zone no longer means the loss of the ball unless such a play happens twice in a row or on the fourth down.

The ball is six inches slimmer around the middle than last year—and far easier to handle. A large-handed back can heave it to a team-mate with the speed and accuracy of a shortstop whipping a baseball across the diamond to first base. Runners fumble less when tackled. Some players think the new ball is more catchable. Only kickers curse the streamlined pigskin, which refuses to spiral through the air unless booted perfectly.

Coaches like it. Lou Little (Columbia): "I didn't like it at first but I do now"...
Clarke Shaughnessy (Chicago): "It affords more accurate passing and cuts down wind
resistance"...Ossie Solem (Iowa): "I am heartily in favor of it."

**PLAY**: Most of the Southwest Conference teams—Rice, Arkansas, Texas Christian,
Baylor, and Southern Methodist—are displaying bizarre tricky formations. When running plays get under way the ball is tossed around the backfield as though it were a
hot potato. Sometimes it changes hands three or four times. Last Saturday Southern
Methodist's new tricks stunned the Fordham Ram.

In the east Coach Tom Hamilton's Navy, led by mercurial Buzz Borries (see cover),
is one of the most air-minded and shifty teams. Navy threw seventeen passes in each
of its last two games. Last year Navy seldom threw more than five passes a game.
Undefeated Princeton threw nineteen passes against Washington and Lee, sixteen
against Cornell last Saturday.

On the Pacific coast, "Old Man" Amos Alonzo Stagg, 72, is experimenting with a
variety of new plays. Although the team of his tiny College of the Pacific is not scoring many victories, this is only because of the superior man power of his opponents.
Coaches Claude Thornhill (Stanford), Bill Ingram (California), and Howard Jones
(Southern California) are sticking to the same moderately wide-open games they played
last year.

Only a few of the year's great elevens are still using rugged dynamite methods.
Pittsburgh and its sole conqueror, Minnesota, have kept their games successfully on the
ground.

**SPECTATORS:** Big-time football is probably back to stay if teams continue their
aerial maneuvers. Fans like to see the ball fly. Last Saturday more than half a million
people watched seventeen games. Mid-season prognosticators estimate that
$25,000,000 will be paid into football tills before the year is out. Jimmy Johnston,
Madison Square Garden's matchmaker, says boxing fans will contribute only a little
more than $3,000,000 to see their sport this year. Major League baseball customers laid
down about $10,000,000 last Summer, hockey addicts about $2,000,000 last Winter.

After a few years dulled by bad times and investigating reformers, football is once
more a national hysteria. Betting commissioners report that more wagers are being
made than ever. Sam Boston, pudgy New York bookmaker, never bets on football himself. But he makes a tidy living from his commission on the bets placed through him.

**OVER-EMPHASIS**: Athletic associations today are frankly vying for schedules that
will draw big crowds. To speed things up, referees are calling fewer penalties. Pittsburgh has $2,000,000 invested in a stadium, California $1,500,000. Michigan, Ohio
State, Illinois, Pennsylvania, Northwestern, Harvard, and Yale each spent about
$1,000,000 for their arenas. These must be paid for. Furthermore most universities
make football profits carry all other sports.

Star players are at a premium, regardless of race, color, or, in some cases, brain
power to meet scholastic requirements. Southern California, weeping because its team
is mediocre, charges rivals with "stealing" students. Last year, when Southern California was potent, the other universities on the Coast did the squawking. An editorial in
Stanford's daily publication last week urged leading colleges to come out in the open
and hire professionals on an above-board basis.

## DEATH BY FOOTBALL

[*Hygeia, which was established in 1923 by the American Medical Association to edu-
cate the general public on medical matters, led the fight for better medical supervision
of practices and games. In 1932, Alfred Parker argued that a too great desire to win
often placed the players in jeopardy. Seven years later, Parker discussed the changes
that had been made in the interim. Alfred E. Parker, "Revolution in Football," Hygeia
(November 1939), 984-986, 1022-1023.*]

...In the October 1932 issue of Hygeia appeared an article by me entitled, "Death
by Football." In that article an attempt was made to present a picture of the swelling
tide of criticism against a game that was causing so many injuries and deaths. In that
article I made an appeal for regulation of the game of football. Fortunately, that appeal,
and the appeal of hundreds of others in various sections of the country, did not go un-
heeded. The story of the revolutionary changes that have occurred since 1932 in the
administration of football is well worth telling. It was in 1932, in fact, that the National
Federation of State High School Athletic Associations [representing 27 states] adopted
interscholastic football rules which were used in the states of Illinois, Iowa and Wisconsin....

The game, as administered by the National High School Athletic Associations, is
still American football; but it is football adapted for miniature boys. And certainly one of
the objectives of the Interscholastic Football Rules Committee has been to plan the rules
so that injuries may be reduced to a minimum. In fact, the committee states that during
the last several years thirty-two measures have been adopted in the interests of safety.

Continuing their objective of making the game safer, the committee adopted a rule
for the 1939 season which permits a player to re-enter the game once during any quarter. This gives a coach an opportunity to remove a player for a short rest or for the
purpose of attending to a minor injury.

Proof of whether or not the high school football rules have improved the game for
boys is found in some of the answers to a questionnaire sent to high school coaches
in the state of Illinois. One of the questions asked was, "Have the rules decreased the
number of injuries?" All except two answering this question said "Yes," and they sub-
stantiated their claim by pointing to the fact that many dangerous features of the game
had been eliminated, such as flying tackle and the flying block. They also maintained
that rules regulating the kickoff, tackling, the forward pass, the returning of punts and
blocking had reduced injuries. Furthermore, the Illinois coaches called attention to the
fact that the high school football rules afforded the passer more protection; that less
piling up was permitted, and that, as a result of all this, sportsmanship had improved....

## SIX-MAN FOOTBALL

[*In this article, Stephen Epler explains his reason for inventing six-man football. Epler
later published* Six-man Football. A Handbook for Coaches and Players. *By the end of
the decade the rules allowed unlimited substitution of players and canvas-topped, rubber-soled shoes. Since several studies showed that most football injuries occurred*

*shortly after half-time and within the twenty-yard lines, half-times were expanded to fifteen minutes to allow time for warm-up, and a field goal was awarded 4 points. Equipment cost about $13 a man as compared to $30-40 in eleven-man football. Stephen E. Epler, "A New Deal for Football," The Journal of Health and Physical Education (October 1936), 507, 519-520.]*

In the fall, football permeates the air. College and high school teams are practicing, younger boys are playing on vacant lots, and older men in barber shops and elsewhere are talking football. Football is king. Little lads worship their football heroes and dream of the time when they shall be star backs, ends, or linemen. Football holds a thrill for young and old, for the girls cheering in the stands as well as the boys playing on the field. Love may capture the young man's fancy in the spring, but in the fall it is football.

How many boys have the opportunity of playing the game properly supervised? Because we live in a city where the high schools, and perhaps a college, have football teams, and because football talk fills the air and the sport pages, we suppose that every town has a football team and all boys have an opportunity to play. The truth is that over half of the high schools in the United States do **not** have football teams.

There were over 10,000 high schools in 1935 of a total of almost 18,000 high schools in the athletic associations of forty-five states that for some reason or reasons did not play football. Only 42.1 per cent of the high schools played eleven-man, interscholastic football in 1935. In compiling these figures, every state but Arkansas, California, and Massachusetts was included.

Most of the schools not playing football are small schools. There are a number of reasons why they do not have teams. Football is an expensive game. It costs money to equip a football player, and to equip twenty or thirty costs more than many schools can afford. Also, football is rough and boys do get hurt. If the boys are all big, and a big boy hits a big boy, usually both are able to "take it." But when a big boy hits some ambitious little youngster, he often damages more than his ambition. So small schools with a scarcity of large boys find the injury hazards rather high when they pit eleven of their boys, including some small boys, against another team. Boys, young and old, do like football. Six-man football is offered to give those boys now left out an opportunity to play. When we say football, we mean football. Blocking and tackling are not tampered with. The eleven-man rules are the constitution in the six-man realm, too. However, nine amendments were affixed to the constitution so the forgotten boy could have "life, liberty, and the pursuit of" football.

Six-man football does not tread on the toes of the old game, but offers this sport to the now football-less schools of the country. This is a wide field, since 10,191 schools of the 17,606 member high schools of 45 state athletic associations are untouched by the eleven-man game.

Football is serving some states very adequately. South Carolina has 160 of her 175 high schools (or 91 per cent) playing eleven-man football. New York and Rhode Island have over 80 per cent playing. The "Old Order" has not done so well by Maryland, where only 4 out of 176 high schools (less than 3 per cent) play football. In Indiana, just 90 of the 800 high schools are served by the eleven-man game. Kentucky likewise has 90 football high schools of a total of 563. Missouri has 712 high schools, of which 554 do not play football. In Vermont, 69 out of 95 high schools are non-football schools. Texas leads the states in three columns. She has the most high schools in her association, 2000; the most playing football, 551; and the most non-football high schools, 1,449....

The simplest and clearest way to describe six-man football is to say it is regular football played with six men on each team. Since the team is smaller, the field is also made smaller. In order to make the game more open, all players but the center are permitted to catch passes, and forward passes may be tossed from anywhere back of the line of scrimmage. Running plays are made more open by requiring a two-yard pass between backs before the ball is carried across the line of scrimmage. For schools short of funds it is recommended that the players wear basketball shoes. The other amendments merely clarify conflicts with the eleven-man rules caused by reducing the team and field size.

Six-man football is still an infant. It is less than two years old. It was conceived while the author was teaching in the Chester, Nebraska, High School. The first game was played at Hebron, Nebraska, September 26, 1934. In 1935, the first year after its initiation, the secretaries of state high school athletic associations reported 156 high school playing interscholastic six-man football in 10 states. Thus, in its second year, there is one high school playing six-man football for every 48 playing eleven-man football....

In conclusion, it is again emphasized that even in those schools having an eleven-man football team, only a small percentage of the boys play. Moreover, eleven-man football is used very little as an intramural sport. Six-man football is adapted for intramural use because of its team size, because it is relatively free from injuries, and because the boys like to play it.

**HARVARD FOOTBALL SUPPORTS ATHLETIC PROGRAM**

[*In his book defending college football, Barry Wood included the following financial statement of Harvard University's athletic department to prove that the football program supported the other sports at Harvard. "What would happen," he asked, "if football was abolished? It supports hockey, baseball, basketball, and track. Allows students to participate in boxing, squash, fencing, polo or wrestling." In addition, of the $400,000 in expenses, most of it went to the visiting teams as their part of the gate receipts. In reality, football was only profitable for the larger schools—such as the University of Michigan whose team netted $120,500 in the 1937-38 season. Many small liberal arts colleges conducted football operations at a loss. Income estimates in the popular press were often confusing. One source, for example, noted that in 1938 about ninety percent of college football programs lost money; yet another source reported that three years earlier, 750 college football teams brought in an estimated net profit of more than $14 million. Barry Wood,* What Price Football. A Player's Defense of the Game *(Boston, 1932), 148.*]

Committee on the Regulation of Athletic Sports
For the year ended June 30, 1931

| | Income | Expenditures |
|---|---|---|
| Baseball | 26,275 | 37,865 |
| Basketball | 3,130 | 8,799 |
| Boxing | 549 | 3,014 |
| Crew | 5,139 | 50,200 |

|  | Income | Expenditures |
|---|---|---|
| Fencing | 150 | 4,031 |
| **Football** | **891,932** | **404,711** |
| Golf | 1,982 | 4,193 |
| Hockey | 12,524 | 22,483 |
| Lacrosse | 677 | 8,231 |
| Polo | 772 | 4,000 |
| Soccer | 1,534 | 7,297 |
| Squash | — | 2,663 |
| Swimming | 573 | 9,339 |
| Tennis | 262 | 4,340 |
| Track | 15,681 | 45,567 |
| Wrestling | 1,303 | 7,187 |
| Miscellaneous | 5,302 | 8,190 |
| H.A.A. News | 48,110 | 45,820 |
| Sundry receipts: |  |  |
| Rentals, locker fees, etc. | 55,597 | — |
| Medical Department | — | 14,656 |
| General Athletic Activities: |  |  |
| Rowing, Physical education | — | 44,553 |
| General Expenditures: |  |  |
| Laundry, Boatshop, etc. | — | 19,153 |
| Maintenance and Operation of |  |  |
| Grounds and Buildings | — | 155,617 |
| Permanent Improvements | — | 43,208 |
| Administration | — | 65,821 |
|  | $1,071,498 | $1,021,946 |
| **Surplus** | 50,552 |  |

**KING FOOTBALL. THE VULGARIZATION OF THE AMERICAN COLLEGE**

[*The author of this article, who was dismissed from his job as editor of the college paper, the Columbia Spectator, in his senior year, believed that football had irreparably injured him. He demanded that football be banned as an intercollegiate sport. Football, he wrote, is a "Frankenstein threatening to throttle what is left of American education." In the following excerpts from his book, Harris refutes the contention that football builds character. Reed Harris,* King Football. The Vulgarization of the American College *(New York, 1932), 16-18, 22-28.*]

The football of the colleges today is a royal mess. It is the sore thumb of our educational system. Soreness there may be, and lots of it, in other sections of this mass of buildings, books and faculties called American education, but football remains the worst of the infections.

To me, college football as conducted these days is only a symbol for the super-materialistic, utterly hypocritical attitude which pervades administrations of the great universities and the tiny colleges. To put forth winning football teams, alumni, faculty, and trustees of the colleges will lie, cheat, and steal, unofficially. Officially, they know nothing of the sordid business behind the gigantic spectacles which are college football games....

I do not deny that many among the universities are making attempts to bring about some change in the situation—but their attempts are half-hearted, cautious and a disgrace to supposed upholders of intellectual honesty. One of the universities which has reorganized its whole athletic program still maintains a football coach at a salary of over $17,000 a year, a football training table which costs $10,000 a season, and similar idiotic misuses of university funds....

The average man playing football today finds it almost impossible to receive any real benefit from his college course. He must have eight or nine hours of sleep. He must pass hours in learning plays and signals for those plays. Three hours or more a day he must devote to the grueling work on the field. He must appear at certain stated hours for meals and eat prescribed food. Attendance at classes occupies most of the rest of his day, leaving only a short period following supper in which to study. Study, therefore, he can only indulge in as an occasional luxury. Coaches and trainers advise him to "live football" during the entire Fall season. He has little choice, for, after an afternoon of hard football, one's mind is usually in a state of lethargy out of which it is almost impossible to climb in order to indulge in any mental activity, let alone that specialized concentration which is study.

The football season lasts from two or three weeks before the opening of the college year to Thanksgiving Day. In the Spring of each year, special Spring practice is held at most of the big universities and football men are expected to report for this. During the off-seasons, gridmen are urged by their coaches to go out for other sports to keep in the unusual muscular condition which is necessary in modern football participation. All in all, the football man has very little time to devote to intellectual effort, if, indeed, he has any interest whatsoever in so doing.

The stimulation and occasional guidance of thought is, or should be, the goal of every college and university. Yet what educator will assert that football, as it is played today, is aiding the process? Modern gridiron practices cannot be condoned under the platitude concerning a "sound mind in a healthy body", for all too often the work of football men is so specialized that they become atrophied in other directions. Too often gridmen are mentally deficient when they begin their careers and later become physically incapacitated through injuries or overdevelopment of special muscles....

Soviet Russia, a young nation which, whatever else may be said about her, is searching the world over for the best technical methods and the best ideas, has recently begun stimulation of a program of competitive sports. Realizing that war spirit is developed by bodily contact games, and wishing sports for exercise rather than injury, Russia has barred football from her new athletic program, even though she has imported American baseball with enthusiasm. The official who made the announcement concerning the exclusion of football said that Russia saw no reason for killing off a number of her best young men each season in the pursuit of a sport which appeals in the first place to the least desirable emotions....

The argument so often advanced by proponents, that football furnishes good experience in discipline and courage, lacks conviction because the evils of the sport quite outweigh this possible advantage. Further, any team sport can furnish discipline. One does not need the offensive brutality of the average football coaching staff to learn discipline, nor does one need to experience the desire to murder in order to develop courage. If one desired to develop courage on this basis, it might be wise to join a modern criminal gang and shoot it out with an occasional policeman.

Another claim advanced for football is that its quarterbacks and captains develop leadership. But what kind of leadership? The same variety of leadership one expects from a sergeant, the moronic leadership of a man instructed as to what procedure to adopt on every occasion and allowed to use physical threats and the worst phrases of gutter language to enforce orders. Perhaps this instruction in leadership is valuable— if the "leader" intends on graduation to become a boss of a crew of stevedores....

The true spirit of learning in American higher education has collapsed, to be replaced by materialism of the grossest sort. This change, unnoticed a few years ago, is now prompting the intelligent portion of America to demand a complete change in the college system. Everywhere experiments are being conducted frantically in an attempt to redeem "higher education" from its obviously low state. But even in some of the experimental colleges the god of materialism and his supporting genius, King Football, continue to hold sway, leering down upon the absurd faculties and administrations, which take all but the most immediate means to bring about change in their educational system. But the day of ruthless gods and despotic kings is gone everywhere and surely in America. Why then should the fight for the survival of the American educational system be completely bogged in gridiron mud?

## A STATISTICAL STUDY OF COLLEGE FOOTBALL PLAYERS

*[In introducing the debate in the* Rotarian *in 1936 on whether college athletics (read football) was over-emphasized, the editor noted this problem "is hotly discussed on many an American university college campus every fall...." Warren Piper, a businessman and founder of Chicago's Interfraternity Club, wrote the "yes" section. He argued that college "football is a public spectacle, commercialized to the point where it is rapidly becoming a large industry." It was "a monumental sham of hypocrisy, falsehoods, and misrepresentation." Since less that two per cent of the eligible students even tried out for the team, "bridge, golf, ping pong, poker, and even crap-shooting are more truly college games than football, because more students actually participate in them."*

*In reply to such criticisms, the American Football Coaches Association distributed a questionnaire to more than 400 colleges and universities. The first 200 replies were given to a research assistant for the National Bureau of Economic Research to tabulate the results. Included below are the conclusions drawn from this study and the statistical data compiled from the questionnaires. Tables of indexes, probable error, and coefficients of variability are deleted. Lou Little, "Report of Special Committee," The Athletic Journal (March 1932), 14-18.]*

...It is the opinion of the Committee that the information obtained from the questionnaires indicates that football is not overemphasized. That it may be overemphasized in some institutions we do not deny, but to condemn the game because too much attention is paid to it in a few institutions is manifestly unfair and unjust. It would be just as sensible to condemn a religious or political institution in its entirety because some official was lax in the performance of his duty. Of course, there are those who stoutly maintain that the sole function of the college is the exclusive attention to things scholastic. But in the opinion of this Committee those who entertain this notion view the purpose of collegiate life very narrowly. Collegiate training and collegiate experience means more or should mean more than mere scholastic endeavor. It should develop to the fullest possible degree that which we call self or personality. For after all, personality is the key to a successful life measured in terms of usefulness, achievement and happiness.

In making this statement your Committee has not the slightest intention of belittling the scholastic side of college life.... But the library, study hall and classroom are not the only collegiate agencies or means that make for the development of personality. Extra-curricular activities along with other agencies contribute to this end and among these extra-curricular activities is football. Football, we believe, tests a boy's capacity and tends to increase his self-confidence. It brings out and develops in him qualities of leadership—leadership which is self-confident, creative, independent and aggressive. The game makes for mental alertness, poise and self-control.

Those of us who have played the game know what it does in developing a spirit of co-operation and fair play. Friendships of everlasting duration are formed. But these benefits are familiar to you all.

There can be no denying that football is a popular game, and therefore attracts outside interest over which neither we nor the college or university official have direct control. We should, however, guard against the evils that from time to time threaten the game. To put it differently, our chief concern should be to see that football remains a vital cog in the largest education of the students who participate in the game....Stripped of the glamor that goes with the crowds, over which we have no control, football is one of the natural outlets of the college student.

Committee:
Louis Little, Chairman, Columbia
Charles Bachman, University of Florida
Alvon McMillan, Kansas Agricultural College
Noble Kizer, Purdue University
Paul Schissler, Oregon Agricultural College

## APPENDIX, CONTAINING STATISTICAL TABLES

From the replies sent in, all the figures relative to each sport are abstracted on separate sheets. Then all the figures listed on the "football sheets" are added up and a total is obtained: the same is done for all the other sports. The totals for each sport are divided by the number of colleges that have reported that particular sport and an average (or arithmetic mean) is thus obtained for each one.

The next step is to compare the averages. The sports are listed according to the magnitude of their averages; so that one can easily see which is the largest, the second largest and so on, as well as the place occupied by football....

**TABLES I & II**
**NUMBER OF HOURS DEVOTED TO PRACTICE**
**AND LECTURES DURING THE SEASON**

| Place | Type of Activity | Average No. of Hours | No. of Colleges |
|---|---|---|---|
| 1 | Student publications | 241 | 95 |
| 2 | Crew | 186 | 6 |
| 3 | Dramatics | 132 | 92 |
| 4 | Lacrosse | 122 | 17 |
| 5 | Debating | 111 | 95 |
| 6 | Football | 109 | 200 |
| 7 | Basketball | 108 | 183 |
| 8 | Track | 106 | 155 |
| 9 | Water polo | 102 | 16 |
| 10 | Gymnastics | 102 | 51 |
| 11 | Baseball | 101 | 127 |
| 12 | Swimming | 100 | 51 |
| 13 | University band | 97 | 109 |
| 14 | Glee club | 90 | 116 |
| 15 | Golf | 87 | 48 |
| 16 | Wrestling | 85 | 49 |
| 17 | Boxing | 84 | 50 |
| 18 | Hockey | 76 | 21 |

**TABLE X**
**LENGTH OF DAILY PRACTICE: IN HOURS**

| Place | Activity | Average No. of Hours in Season | Average No. of Hours out of Season |
|---|---|---|---|
| 1 | Golf | 2.15 | 2.07 |
| 2 | Dramatics | 2.09 | 1.12 |
| 3 | Baseball | 1.96 | 1.60 |
| 4 | Lacrosse | 1.85 | 1.69 |
| 5 | Football | 1.78 | 1.71 |
| 6 | Basketball | 1.70 | 1.60 |
| 7 | Hockey | 1.68 | 1.33 |
| 8 | Student Publ. | 1.67 | 1.56 |
| 9 | Crew | 1.61 | 1.50 |
| 10 | Debating | 1.59 | 1.27 |
| 11 | Univ. Band | 1.53 | 1.73 |
| 12 | Wrestling | 1.53 | 1.44 |
| 13 | Boxing | 1.46 | 1.50 |
| 14 | Glee Club | 1.46 | 1.51 |
| 15 | Track | 1.44 | 1.12 |
| 16 | Swimming | 1.35 | 1.15 |
| 17 | Water-Polo | 1.33 | 1.00 |
| 18 | Gymnastics | 1.28 | 1.27 |

**TABLE XIV**

**NUMBER OF MEN WHO REPORTED AT THE BEGINNING OF THE SEASON**

| Place | Activity | Average No. of Men | No. Colleges Reporting |
|---|---|---|---|
| 1 | Gymnastic | 108 | 41 |
| 2 | Crew | 84 | 6 |
| 3 | Glee Club | 59 | 94 |
| 4 | Univ. Band | 58 | 92 |
| 5 | Football | 56 | 219 |
| 6 | Lacrosse | 56 | 21 |
| 7 | Track | 50 | 165 |
| 8 | Dramatics | 46 | 69 |
| 9 | Baseball | 39 | 139 |
| 10 | Boxing | 39 | 49 |
| 11 | Student Pub. | 37 | 62 |
| 12 | Basketball | 36 | 198 |
| 13 | Swimming | 36 | 64 |
| 14 | Wrestling | 33 | 56 |
| 15 | Water Polo | 27 | 11 |
| 16 | Hockey | 26 | 23 |
| 17 | Debating | 24 | 81 |
| 18 | Golf | 21 | 55 |

**TABLE XVI**

**NUMBER OF MEN COMPETING ON VARSITY,
FRESHMAN AND INTRAMURAL TEAMS**

| Place | Activity | No. Colleges Reporting | Average No. of Men |
|---|---|---|---|
| 1 | Basketball | 189 | 146 |
| 2 | Football | 205 | 124 |
| 3 | Track | 157 | 110 |
| 4 | Baseball | 135 | 108 |
| 5 | Water Polo | 17 | 107 |
| 6 | Crew | 5 | 106 |
| 7 | Swimming | 50 | 93 |
| 8 | Hockey | 22 | 79 |
| 9 | Gymnastics | 38 | 78 |
| 10 | Lacrosse | 21 | 75 |
| 11 | Wrestling | 59 | 67 |
| 12 | Boxing | 56 | 62 |
| 13 | Golf | 52 | 60 |
| 14 | Dramatics | 57 | 60 |
| 15 | Glee Club | 71 | 51 |
| 16 | Univ. Band | 87 | 44 |
| 17 | Student Pub. | 52 | 39 |
| 18 | Debating | 71 | 27 |

**TABLE XVII**
**NUMBER OF CLASS DAYS MISSED DURING THE SEASON**

| Place | Activity | Average No. of Days | No. Colleges Reporting |
|---|---|---|---|
| 1 | Student Pub. | 8.68 | 25 |
| 2 | Glee Club | 7.13 | 6 |
| 3 | Debating | 6.37 | 6 |
| 4 | Crew | 6.00 | 1 |
| 5 | Basketball | 5.87 | 164 |
| 6 | Baseball | 5.33 | 118 |
| 7 | Univ. Band | 4.73 | 56 |
| 8 | Football | 4.52 | 187 |
| 9 | Hockey | 4.20 | 15 |
| 10 | Dramatics | 4.03 | 37 |
| 11 | Water Polo | 4.00 | 8 |
| 12 | Lacrosse | 3.93 | 14 |
| 13 | Gymnastics | 3.73 | 15 |
| 14 | Track | 3.72 | 129 |
| 15 | Golf | 3.66 | 38 |
| 16 | Wrestling | 3.61 | 112 |
| 17 | Boxing | 3.28 | 21 |
| 18 | Swimming | 3.21 | 33 |

In a supplementary questionnaire addressed to college football captains, your Committee asked twelve questions. These questions and the answers to them are as follows: [Questions 2-11 are not included. To summarize: of the 273 football captains, 179 said football was not overemphasized; 237 said a 8 or 9 game season was too few; 201 favored voluntary spring practice; 217 liked the football training table; 269 wanted paid as opposed to volunteer coaches; and 207 wanted the coach on the bench during the game to direct the team.]

1. **As a football player why do you like the game?**

To this question we have 273 replies but several captains give more than one reason. The total number of reasons is therefore larger than the number of replies received.

a. I like it because I like it                                                    44

b. Educational reasons; "game builds up character,"
"football as a man-builder," a preparation for life.              98

c. Develops the body physically and provides contacts        62

d. Emotional reasonings; fighting and competitive spirit,
thrill and excitement, a survival of the fittest, the only game
for men and has a fascination that cannot be explained.        98

e. Friendships made; like the kind of fellow that go into the game     23

f. The game gives an all-around physical and mental development     36

Out of the 273 replies only three did not seem to like the game. They state: "I don't like it!" "I played for a scholarship." "I have ceased to like college football."...

12. **We find that there are several of the collegiate sports and activities that take a great deal more of the players' time than football does. Do you find this to be true? If so name the activity and give details.**

a. Yes.                                                                                      138
b. No (football takes more time than any other activity)                                       87
c. Blank or not to the point                                                                   48

The following activities have been mentioned in the 138 replies that agreed with the question:

|     |                       |      |
|-----|-----------------------|------|
| 1.  | Basketball            | 68   |
| 2.  | Track.                | 36   |
| 3.  | Baseball              | 30   |
| 4.  | Dramatics             | 15   |
| 5.  | Crew                  | 14   |
| 6.  | Debating              | 14   |
| 7.  | Student Publications  | 11   |
| 8.  | Glee Club.            | 0.7  |
| 9.  | Boxing                | 0.5  |
| 10. | University Band       | 0.5  |
| 11. | Golf.                 | 3    |
| 12. | Wrestling.            | 2    |
| 13. | Swimming.             | 2    |
| 14. | Hockey.               | 0.2  |
| 15. | Lacrosse.             | 0.2  |
| 16. | Gymnastics            | 1    |

Chapter 10

## FOOTBALL—THE NFL

College football remained more popular than professional football during the 1930s. Because professional football appealed more to lower income fans than to the well-educated, more affluent college supporters, the National Football League (NFL) was particularly hard-hit by the Depression. As attendance declined, teams folded or moved to more lucrative markets. From twelve teams in 1927, the NFL shrank to ten in 1931 and then to eight franchises the following year. Teams in small towns left for larger cities, usually those which also had professional baseball franchises. The Frankford Yellow Jackets became the Philadelphia Eagles, the Portsmouth Spartans moved to Detroit, and the Duluth Eskimos ultimately became the Washington Redskins. The NFL stabilized in 1934 at ten strong franchises, and the Spaulding Sporting Goods Company commenced publication of its annual football guide the following year—complete with statistics that afforded historical comparisons and greater publicity.

The Literary Digest concluded in October 1936 that if the NFL "never approaches the fabulous popularity of its collegiate cousin, it has, nevertheless, established itself in far shorter time as a big-league sport." Although college football earned an estimated $20,000,000 in business that year, and the NFL only earned $1,000,000, The Literary Digest noted that the pros averaged 15,000 fans per game compared to 5,000 college spectators. The creation of two divisions in 1933 sparked further interest, and by 1940, approximately 120 radio stations broadcast the championship game.

Another sign of the growing popularity of professional football was the emergence of several competing leagues in the mid-1930s. Between 1936 and 1941, three separate leagues claimed the acronym AFL. The 1936-37 American Football League, dubbed "the league with college spirit," had teams in Cleveland, Pittsburgh, Syracuse, Boston, New York, and Brooklyn, but fell victim to poor financial management. Other minor leagues included The Midwest Football League and The South Atlantic Football League.

Professional football appealed to people on several levels. In the first years of the decade the grim nature of the game, which focused on hard-nosed running plays and bruising line play, appealed to fans hardened by the ravages of the Depression. As the decade continued, new rules which promoted spectacular running plays and opened up the passing game provided a brief moment of escape. On a deeper level, football players represented a younger America, a time before factory lines and large, anonymous cities, when people were individualists—self-reliant, rugged, natural men, such as George Musso, who shunned protective pads.

The NFL encouraged "the cult of the hero," which began in the 1920s with the signing of Harold "Red" Grange. In 1930, Bronco Nagurski signed with the Chicago Bears for $5,000. Eight years later, Pittsburgh shocked the football world when it signed Byron "Whizzer" White, the All-American tailback from the University of Colorado, and runner-up for the Heisman trophy, for $15,000 a season. Other stars included John V. McNally (Johnny Blood), a spectacular broken-field runner and pass receiver, Don Hudson, who revolutionized pass receiving by introducing feinting and sharp cuts while running pass routes, and quarterbacks Sammy Baugh and Sid Luckman.

Team owners, such as George Preston Marshall, George Halas, Earl "Curly" Lambeau, Timothy J. Mara, and Art Rooney, were tough and determined business promoters, as well as colorful personalities. In Washington, Marshall dressed his players and cheerleaders in "war paint" for publicity photographs, and introduced marching bands, parades, and other entertainment to attract entire families to see his Redskins play.

As with professional baseball, the owners maintained tight control over the players—see "NFL Player's Contract"—and limited each team to twenty-two players. The clubs paid the players' hospital bills and provided helmets and jerseys, but the players bought most of their own pads and shoes. The average salary ranged from $100 to $125 per game and most players required off-season jobs. At $550 per game, Grange had the highest salary. In 1936, the NFL introduced an annual draft for players whose college eligibility had ended. The teams selected eighty-one college players, but signed less than half of them. Two of first three players chosen, University of Chicago halfback Jay Berwanger—the first Heisman winner—and triple threat Bill Shakespeare of Notre Dame, accepted more lucrative business offers. The draft allowed the NFL to maintain salaries by forcing draftees to negotiate with only one team.

Although NFL owners denied the existence of a gentlemen's agreement against hiring blacks, after Ray Kemp and Joe Lillard were released in 1933, no blacks played in the NFL until 1946. Perhaps improved organization and greater popularity had made a racial ban easier. Certainly it was bad policy to hire minorities when so many whites were unemployed. The owners' contention that there were no qualified black football players was destroyed in 1939 when the NFL failed to draft either Jerome Holland or Kenny Washington. Washington, the UCLA halfback who led the nation in total yards, was the only individual selected unanimously in a 1939 Liberty Magazine poll of varsity players on 110 major college teams as the "toughest opposing player." Yet he was not drafted by the NFL nor selected as All-America by either of the wire services or by Grantland Rice. On NBC radio, sportswriter Sam Balter unsuccessfully challenged NFL owners to justify the league's decision not to draft either player. Blacks seeking to play professional football were confined to minor leagues such as the American Professional Football Association (1936-41) and the Pacific Coast Football League (1940-46).

At the beginning of the decade, the NFL took its cue from college football, which emphasized the single-wing formation and power running between the tackles. The 1932 championship game changed the course of the pro game. The Portsmouth Spartans and the Chicago Bears ended the season in a tie, and the first playoff game in league history was scheduled for Chicago's Wrigley Field in mid-December. Since the weather forecast was for snow and sub-zero temperatures, the teams agreed to play indoors in the home of the Black Hawks hockey team, and to alter the rules to suit the arena, which was only sixty yards between the goal lines and had a solid fence just a few feet from each sideline. The NFL placed the goal posts on the goal line and scrimmaged the ball ten yards in from the sidelines when the play ended near the sideline. The 11,000 spectators witnessed a rough, defensive battle that was decided by a disputed play. Near the end of the game the Bears had a fourth down on the Portsmouth's two-yard line and the Spartans expected another smash into the line by Bronislau "Bronco" Nagurski. The fullback started forward into the line but then stepped back and lobbed the ball to "Red" Grange in the end zone. Despite the Spartans' complaint that Nagurski was not the required five yards behind the line of scrimmage when he threw the ball, the touchdown stood as the winning score.

This playoff game ushered in a new era for pro football. The following year the NFL adopted new rules to make the game more exciting. Now the ball could be thrown from anywhere behind the line of scrimmage, providing for greater deception by allowing the ball carrier to fake as if he was going to plunge into the line before passing. Scrimmaging the ball ten yards from the sideline when a play ended within five yards of it encouraged longer runs, and placing the goal posts on the goal line resulted in more scoring and fewer tie games. In 1932, for example, there were ten tie games and only six field goals, whereas after the rule changes the teams played just five tie games and kicked thirty-six field goals. Finally, the decision to divide the league into east and west divisions enabled the NFL to create two title races and a championship playoff game.

The championship game in 1940 was another watershed. More than 36,000 spectators and 150 sportswriters came to see Clyde "Bulldog" Turner, Sid Luckman and Sammy Baugh compete for the NFL title. Red Barber described the action for the Mutual Network in the first professional football game broadcast on radio. Sid Luckman guided the Chicago Bears to a 73-0 thrashing of the Washington Redskins. Since the Bears were the only pro team using the T-formation, and Clark Shaughnessy's Stanford team was successful with this formation, it became the basic offensive alignment for the postwar years.

Throughout the decade a debate raged as to whether college football was superior to the professional game. Concerned with possible competition, several college conferences dismissed athletic department employees who participated in pro football games. College coaches considered pro football detrimental to the players' well-being and used their influence to discourage the players from joining the NFL. In 1935, Stanford coach Clark Shaughnessy wrote in Esquire—"It is a certainty, however, that this better type did not attend college for the purpose of becoming professional football players. They are marking time until opportunities present themselves to embark on their life's work. Some athletes used the money earned in 'Pro' football to continue their school work. Those players, however, whose interest is solely in football are to be pitied. It is inconceivable that anyone can be so dumb to think that 'Pro' football is a worthwhile life's work."

For the NFL, George Halas replied, "No one is interested in seeing hulking men battering their heads off against one another in mid-field. Working with seasoned players, we are able to develop intricate attacks and employ unorthodox tactics, with maximum deception.... The players enjoy a live colorful game, charged with plenty of visible action and hard, driving, football. So do the crowds." Time magazine weighed in on the NFL side when it commented in December 1932, "Experts are well aware that the best football teams in the U.S. are the eight professional teams in the National Football League." A heavy college line, the paper argued, weighed 190 pounds, whereas the Green Bay line weighed 220. "The first thing that spectators accustomed to college football notice about professional games is an immense, swift precision which makes the game compare to college games as college games compare to the higgledy-piggledy contests of gangling school boys."

In 1930, 55,000 spectators watched the New York Giants pummel a collection of Notre Dame alumni all-stars coached by Knute Rockne in an exhibition game for charity, which showed that the pros were not just a bunch of undisciplined toughs. Four years later, the Chicago Tribune initiated an annual charity match between the previous year's NFL championship team and a collection of all-star collegians chosen by the fans. Approximately 733,000 people wrote in their choices. The contest to select the coaches drew three times more votes. The first game attracted 79,432 fans and 140 sportswriters to Chicago's Soldiers' Field to see the teams play to a scoreless tie. The results demonstrated that a pro team could at least hold its own against college players—a fact which many college coaches had denied on the grounds that professionals lacked the spirit and determination of college players. In 1936, the all-star voting drew almost three and a half million ballots, and the following year more than five million votes. The final document below analyzes the differences between the college and pro games and attributes the growth of the NFL to its rules, its brutality, and to the owners' ability to appeal to the working class.

## NFL PLAYER'S CONTRACT

*[As the following document illustrates, the NFL patterned its methods of player control after professional baseball. The words and numbers in bold type were added to the contract and the underlined words were crossed off in the original contract. "The*

*National Football League Uniform Player's Contract," in Richard M. Cohen, et al.,*
The Scrapbook History of Pro Football *(Indianapolis, 1976), 60.*]

## THE NATIONAL FOOTBALL LEAGUE
## UNIFORM PLAYER'S CONTRACT

The **PRO FOOTBALL, INC**. ...........herein called the Club,
and **A. GLENN EDWARDS** ......., of..........**WASHINGTON, D.C**.
herein called the Player.

The Club is a member of The National Football League. As such, and jointly with
the other members of the League, it is obligated to insure to the public wholesome, and
high-class professional football by defining the relations between Club and Player, and
between Club and Club.

In view of the facts above recited the parties agree as follows:

1. The Club will pay the Player a salary for his skilled service during the playing season of 19**40**, at the rate of **$3,000.00 per season** dollars, for each regularly scheduled
league game played. For all other games the Player shall be paid such salary as shall
be agreed upon between the Player and the Club. As to games scheduled but not
played, the Player shall receive no compensation from the Club other than actual expenses.

**Plus transportation to and from training camp. If team wins championship player
agrees to participate in one exhibition game as per the terms of this contract.
Player is not to receive compensation for exhibition games other than herein stipu-
lated.**

2. The salary above provided for shall be paid by the Club as follows:

Seventy-five per cent (75%) after each game and the remaining twenty-five per cent
(25%) at the close of the season or upon release of the Player by the Club.

3. The Player agreed that during said season he will faithfully serve the Club, and
pledges himself to the American public to conform to high standards of fair play and
good sportsmanship.

4. The Player will not play football during 19**40** otherwise than for the Club, except in case the Club shall have released said Player, and said release has been approved by the officials of The National Football League.

5. The Player will not participate in an exhibition game after the completion of the
schedule of the Club and prior to August 1 of the following season, without the permission of the President of the League.

6. The Player accepts as part of this contract such reasonable regulations as the Club
may announce from time to time.

7. This contract may be terminated at any time by the Club giving notice in writing to the Player within forty-eight (48) hours after the day of the last game in which
he is to participate with his club.

8. The Player submit himself to the discipline of The National Football League and
agrees to accept its decisions pursuant to its Constitution and By-Laws.

9. Any time prior to August 1st, 19**41**, by written notice to the Player, the Club may
renew this contract for the term of that year, except that the salary rate shall be such as
the parties may then agree upon, or in default of agreement, such as the Club may fix.

10. The Player may be fined or suspended for violation of this contract, but in all
cases the Player shall have the right of appeal to the President of The National Football League.

11. In default of agreement, the Player will accept the salary rate thus fixed or else will not play during said year otherwise than for the Club, unless the Club shall release the Player.

12. The reservation of the Club of the valuable right to fix the salary rate for the succeeding year, and the promise of the Player not to play during said year otherwise than with the Club, have been taken into consideration in determining the salary specified herein and the undertaking by the Club to pay said salary is the consideration for both reservation and the promise.

13. In case of dispute between the Player and the Club the same shall be referred to the President of The National Football League, and his decision shall be accepted by all parties as final.

14. Verbal contracts between Club and Player will not be considered by the League in the event of a dispute.

Signed this **6th** day of....**MARCH**......A.D. 19**40**

PRO FOOTBALL, INC....

Witnesses:

(Player)

Original copy to be held by Club Management

## GIANTS VERSUS PACKERS

[*The following document is an excellent example of award-winning sportswriting and illustrates the emphasis placed on the violent, viciousness nature of the game played by "primitive" men. Although this game included several injuries, NFL players generally were injured less frequently than college players. The list of players on both teams and the scoring summary is omitted. Arthur Daley, "New York Giants 23, Green Bay Packers 17," The New York Times (13 December 1938).*]

The Giants and the Packers delved into the realm of fiction for a storybook football game at the Polo Grounds yesterday. In fact, fiction almost seemed too tame a medium for the thriller that the Eastern and Western champions of the National Football League staged for the world title to the delirious delight of a record play-off crowd of 48,120.

Right to the final seconds of a rousing battle of gridiron titans the tension was such that something seemed bound to snap. But when the final gun cracked the New Yorkers had conquered the ponderous Packers from Green Bay, 23 to 17.

Perhaps there have been better football games since Rutgers and Princeton started the autumnal madness sixty-nine years ago, but no one in the huge crowd would admit it. This was a struggle of such magnificent stature that words seem feeble tools for describing it.

The Giants, opportunists to the end, blocked two punts for a 9-0 advantage. Back came Green Bay to make the count 9 to 7. The Maramen surged to a 16-7 advantage only to have the Packers reduce that lead to 16 to 14 at the half. Then the mastodon from Wisconsin flashed ahead in the third quarter, 17 to 16, but back came the Giants for 7 more points and the clincher.

The last quarter was scoreless, but no one dared leave the park. The Packers were applying terrific pressure to the doughty defense of the pupils of Stout Steve Owen. One long pass could win the game for them, and the Green Bay monsters were eternally shooting for that tally.

The clock showed a scant five seconds remaining and the ball spun through the arc-lighted field in a final desperate attempt for a tally. It missed its target and the Giants were the new champions, the first team in the history of the play-offs to win twice.

At the end the spectators were too emotionally exhausted even to try to rip down the goal posts. These stood untouched, silent sentinels of a magnificent football game.

What a frenzied battle this was! The tackling was fierce and the blocking positively vicious. In the last drive every scrimmage pile-up saw a Packer tackler stretched on the ground. Oddly, however, not one of them really was hurt physically, although the battering their spirits took was tremendous. As for the Giants, they really were hammered to a fare-thee-well.

Johnny Dell Isola was taken to St. Elizabeth's Hospital with a spinal concussion. Ward Cuff suffered a possible fracture of the sternum. Mel Hein sustained a concussion of the brain that left him temporarily bereft of his memory. He came to in the final quarter and finished the game. Leland Shaffer suffered a badly sprained ankle.

The play for the sixty vibrant minutes was absolutely ferocious. No such blocking and tackling by two football teams ever had been seen at the Polo Grounds. Stray punches were tossed around all afternoon. This was the gridiron art at its primitive best. In the first quarter the Giants were as perfect a team as ever had been assembled, a smooth, co-ordinated machine that made no mistakes. But in the second session the Packers, fired by a 40-yard touchdown pass, caught that same spark and it was hammer and tongs the rest of the way.

The Giants were ready for this game. When the chips were down they had everything. Quickly they fashioned 9 points in the first quarter in which Jim Poole and Jim Lee Howell gave one of the finest exhibitions of end play ever seen. They smothered Packer rushes at every turn and then, when Clarke Hinkle, an all-league fullback if ever there was—attempted to punt, Howell flashed in, blocked the kick and then caught the ball before it hit the ground.

It was a first down on the Green Bay 7-yard line. The Giants gained a yard in two rushes. Ed Danowski's pass to Cuff was short and the one-time intercollegiate javelin-throwing champion dropped back to the 13 and booted a field goal.

Hardly had the crowd settled back when the harried Packers attempted to kick again. Cecil Isbell was back to punt, but Poole whirled in to block it and Howell made the recovery on the 27. In four plays the Giants were over. A Danowski-Tuffy Leemans pass picked up 5 yards. Leemans went to the 6 and then cut back off the Packer left tackle for a touchdown. Johnny Gildea missed the extra point.

But the thrills were not ended. In the second quarter Tiny Engebretsen intercepted a Giant pass that he carried to the Green Bay 49. In two rushes Andy Uram went to the New York 40 and then Arnold Herber sailed a floater right down the middle. Carl Mulleneaux plucked the ball out of the air on the 1-yard line and stumbled across. When Engebretsen booted the extra point the score was 9 to 7.

Not long afterward Hein recovered a fumble at mid-field and the Giants were off to town again. The critical play was a pass that Leemans spun to Len Barnum. The

Giant freshman caught the ball and fumbled it, but it went out of bounds safely. It was a first down for the Owen men on the 22.

Barnum cracked tackle to the 20 and then Danowski, whose passing touched the heights of perfection at the right time, flicked one to Hap Barnard in the end zone for a touchdown. Cuff converted.

Then sensation piled on sensation as Isbell shot a short spot pass to Wayland Becker. Soar nailed him from behind on the 17 after a mad 66-yard gain. Five times in a row Hinkle slammed inside the tackles until he scored from the 2-foot line on a weak-side plunge. When Engebretsen converted again the Packers were back in the ball game.

Tension mounted during the intermission and when play was resumed a 34-yard off-tackle romp by Bob Monnett was the backbone of a 63-yard drive that finally was stymied by the Giant defense on the 5. So Engebretsen booted an easy 15-yard field goal to give Green Bay the lead for the first time.

Aroused, the Giants stormed back in a relentless advance of 62 yards. The clincher was a beautiful pass from Danowski to Soar to the 6-yard marker, where Soar, Poole and two Packer defenders leaped for it. But Hank came down with the ball. He dragged a Packer defender across for the last big batch of points. Cuff converted.

Still the dizzy pace of this thriller was not ended. The infuriated Packers struck back; reaching the 32 before Danowski intercepted. In the fourth quarter Green Bay reached the 38 and then the 33.

The next play was a Herber-Becker pass that was caught on the 17. But Cuff flattened the Packer end with such a teeth-rattling tackle that the ball popped out of his hands. Kayo Lunday recovering. The break of the game came soon afterward. A Herber-Gantenbein aerial clicked, but Green Bay was using a spread formation and the flanking back had edged up so much that Gantenbein no longer was eligible.

To the violent chagrin of the Packers the play immediately was nullified and it was New York's ball at the point of the foul, the Green Bay 43. So enraged were the ponderous youths from Wisconsin at this ruling that they piled up on the next play, to incur a further 15-yard penalty for unnecessary roughness. Cuff finally missed a 36-yard field goal and the Packers had only two chances left.

They fled 38 yards to the Giant 43 before yielding the ball on downs. Then, as the hands of the clock crawled toward the end, the Packers moved 40 yards to the Giant 40 before the gun cracked for the grand finish of a grand game.

Giant heroes were too numerous to mention. There were Poole and Howell at the ends; Widseth, Parry, Cope and Mellus at the tackles; Dell Isola and the hard-working Orville Tuttle at the guards; and Hein, magnificent as always, at center. Cuff, Soar, Leemans, Danowski and the rest were great backs.

As for the Packers, they had their stars in Bud Svendsen at center, Buckets Goldenberg, Engebretsen and Will Letlow, guards; Gantenbein and Becker, ends; and Hinkle, Herber, Monnett and Joe Laws in the backfield.

## I PREFER COLLEGE FOOTBALL

[*The author wrote this article in response to claims that pro football was better and more exciting than college ball. It did have spectacular plays, Cannon states, but pro football was too similar to professional wrestling which emphasized entertainment over solid play. Unlike in the NFL, college players competed with emotion and loyalty to their schools. College football was better organized, had more strenuous practices, and the coaches studied game films and employed regular scouts. Ralph Cannon, "'I'd Die for Dear Old Dollars!'" Esquire (January 1936), 54, 168, 170.*]

...In order to "sell" their exhibitions, it was necessary for the promoters of professional football to convince the paying public that their game was better and more thrilling than the college contests. Trick rules were introduced, calculated to open up their game and provide long runs and long passes to entertain the spectators: and at the time "the old college try" was given a good sound kidding by players who "knew when to loaf" rather than dissipating their flagging energies in desperate but futile attempts at plays.

But still finding their exhibitions drawing approximately a third of the college turnouts all along the line, another step was made in an effort to establish testimony that their game was stronger and better. An exhibition game was arranged between the professional champions, a team that had been playing together for a number of years, and a pick-up collection of post-graduate college players. Obviously it would have been more fair to pit a collection of former college players against a similar all-star team selected from the pro ranks, but that suggestion did not fit in with the purpose of the contest. Nevertheless, when the game was played under lamplight at Chicago in 1934, the result was a scoreless tie in which the Collegians had all the best of it, and the vaunted Chicago Bear's offensive failed to net even a first down by rushing. It was a sad moment in the build-up of professional football. But they were not through!

In 1935 the game was repeated, with some refinement in the matter of arrangements. In this exhibition the professional Bears scored a field goal and a safety to win, 5 to 0 from an all-star collection liberally sprinkled with unknown wonders from Illinois Wesleyan and San Francisco U., while such famous offensive stars as Duane Purvis and Jim Carter of Purdue, "Cotton" Warburton of Southern California and "Buzz" Borries of Navy were thoughtfully withheld from action by the group of four second-flight coaches in command, one of whom finds it curiously convenient throughout the fall to spend his Sunday afternoons on the bench of the Bears.

Thus, with their supremacy finally established, the pros went out to pack' em in. But just how completely was the pro supremacy established by even this game, which was set-up by the pro promoters? It was a part of their propaganda to speak of the "perfect football" they play. In that respect it is interesting to consider that in their championship season of 1934, the Bears scored 301 points in 14 league games, or an average of 21.5 points per game, practically three touchdowns; and still they could not scrimmage for a first down against a team of college boys who had no motive for playing the game in the first place, and nothing of the team spirit that makes college football supreme. In the second All-star vs. Pro game, the professionals still were unable to make a touchdown. The scoreless tie of 1934 was the only game in 26 exhibitions in which the Bears were unable to tally.

But why shouldn't professional football players put up a better game than amateurs, the same as in any other game, the unwitting bystander asks? The answer is simply that football is a game apart. It is not a game of practiced skill primarily, but instead a game of emotion, enthusiasm, loyalty and drive. It is the "infantry" of sports because of its direct impact, its hand-to-hand struggle of massed groups. Charlie Daley, the old Harvard and West Point All-American quarterback, long ago said it is "a game of war within the limitations of rules and of sportsmanship." It is a game in which ten players sacrifice themselves for the glory of an eleventh player, and while it is reasonable for college players, inspired to idealism by loyalty to their school, to sacrifice themselves in this manner, men earning a livelihood in that hard routine could be rated hardly more than dolts and chumps.

Why is it that professional teams can not simulate this game? The essential difference between professional football and college football is emotion. The most exciting thing in football is the upset, and the upset is always the result of an inferior team's rising to the heights of class and drive on a wave of emotion overwhelming a team superior in form but inferior in emotion. Yale against Princeton last year, and Carnegie against Purdue this year, and a hundred others; these are the great football games; this is great football, football at its best. It is full of emotion, "the old college try," which is so laughable to the pros who do not and can not rise to these peaks of emotion. Yet the man without emotion is a spiritual eunuch, usually a lunatic a half-wit or a criminal.

Football is an inspiring spectacle solely because it happens to be one game in which enthusiasm and emotion has an outlet giving the under-dog a chance against superior skill. The great colleges are supreme because they match teams at the supreme peak of the contestants' physical and emotional lives. All of the great coaches, Rockne, Zuppke, Stagg, have been masters at arousing this white heat of enthusiasm in their players with their "pep" or fire talks. It is the spirit with which the boys play the game that makes football so appealing.

The physical and emotional peak does not last long. A top college team seldom goes at its best more than twice a year, but that best is the best there is in football to see....

There is another factor of the game that the pros have made no effort to put behind their teams. When two college teams come together in a big game, back of both teams stands fifteen weeks of spring practice, a hard summer of conscientious effort by fifty or a hundred hardy young warriors to keep or to get into shape by strenuous labor; heavy double-duty fall sessions of practice including vicious scrimmages, technique drills, signals, strategy and skull session starting on Sept. 10, winding up in a special week or two in intensive work on the opposition's style of offense and defense as outlined by trained and expert observers and scouts whose jobs depend on expertness and success. In addition, on the field both teams are directed by expert coaches who are masters in the art of strategy, "running the game from the bench." Both teams are keyed up by the enthusiasm of student body pep sessions, by flamboyant old grads and by the fire talk of assistant and head coaches. All of this comes out on the field, in the spectacle of the game. It cannot be simulated without exactly equal energy and pressure in every respect. What a team works on in practice shows in the game, and it takes all of this tremendous amount of work and energy to produce a typical big time college football game. It is ridiculous to pretend that the same kind of exhibition can be put on by squads of a couple dozen burnt-out post-graduates who merely go out for their daily practice of running around, kicking or passing the ball without contact scrimmage, without scrimmage against ambitious freshman squads using the rival's plays, without carefully prepared diagrams of offensive and defensive play....

Big college teams now also use moving pictures to study intimately the exact habits of their opponents, individually and collectively, and some schools even make close-up studies of their opponents so that their players can identify their foe-men instantly on the field.

When the pros find it possible to duplicate all of these conditions completely, then they can begin talking about putting on football games in the same class with the big college games. Not before, for it is one of the irrevocable laws of nature that you can't get out any more than you put in. Otherwise perpetual motion would be easy. Just like the college teams, the pros show in their games just what they have been working on in practice. The pros are superior to the good college teams only in things like place-kicking, which the players enjoy practicing throughout their limited drill periods. They profess smoother ball handling, which has never been established by statistics, and even if it were true that they bobbled fewer plays than some college teams it could easily be accounted for in view of the fact that the salaried men are under pressure in their game, as compared with the college boys in their top contests, in about the ratio of a spring exhibition training game between a couple of big league ball clubs and the deciding game of a World Series.

Instead of attempting to duplicate all the energy and work that goes into the big college game, the pros have tried to make the short cut of building up the exhibition end of their game. Their objective is to try to entertain the crowd. The sole objective of the college games is winning.

One sees at the pro games very little good blocking in their plays from scrimmage, although there are efforts at open field blocking to try to put on long runs on passing or kick-catching plays. Passers seldom are rushed, which enables the teams to put on forward passing drills. Linemen stand, instead of charging; runners are stopped with tacklers' hands around their hips, where college ball-players would wrench forward for additional gain. Passes are thrown within the shadow of the goal posts, thrilling the fans; and what is the loss if the other team intercepts? It is still a thrill. That is the aim. Referring to their so-called unorthodox strategy, one leading coach remarked after such an exhibition: "They make enough mistakes in one game to cost a top coach his job!"

Another grizzled veteran of the game points out that the reason the pro games late in the season satisfy the fans is that no football team can go on without scrimmage, and by the end of the campaign the pro play is so ragged that it looks good to the ignorant fans....

The pros themselves make quite an ado over the fact that some of their men are still getting by after ten years of the cautious, self-protective style of game they play. In this respect it is interesting to consider how many college stars are able to stay at the top for even the three years of their competition when they are at their best. In the last fifteen years only two college players have made the All-American three years running—Grange of Illinois and Oosterbaan of Michigan....

This was the first bid of the pros for the paying public—the putting on of a spectacular type of game, irrespective of its soundness as football. The second, and unquestionably the more effective, was the spreading of propaganda in the newspapers that their game was more interesting than college football because of the big scores. A check of the relative scores, however, reveals that the 17-point average of the pros is topped by an average of 25.6 in the Western Conference. This, in spite of the fact that the pros have the goal posts on the goal line to encourage field goals, while the colleges have removed the goal posts to the end zone to prevent unnecessary injuries. The pros also put in a pass rule permitting passes from anywhere behind the line of scrimmage, which was of especial value for a man like Nagurski, who could charge into the line, drawing in the defense, and then toss a pass over them.

The main value of football is in helping develop the characteristics of courage, fortitude, aggressiveness, persistence, the ability to bounce back from stultifying defeat, in the generations as they flow through the colleges. That is the only excuse for the game's brutality. The real All-Americans are the men who are strengthened by this bath of blood and then go on to rise to the top as doctors, lawyers, bankers, publishers, manufacturers, all the useful professions. To make a profession of this exercise is merely a waste. The conventional pay for pro gridders is $100 a week for fifteen weeks with a range up to $4,500 for stars. That is all the crowds will support. But even if pro football could pay the salaries of baseball, it would not be an advisable profession because of the injury hazard. It is practically impossible to get any kind of accident insurance on the players of the non-contact game of baseball, and before pro football can ever bid for crowds large enough to pay a worth-while salary the game will have to approximate the vigor of the college game, which means certain and premature injury to the aging players attempting to keep the pace.

The majority of players who go into pro football do so reluctantly, and because they have been unable to place in business. And they all try to get out of the game as soon as possible. There is always a waiting list of them trying to get jobs as coaches in the minor colleges.

All of the coaches who have aligned themselves with pro football have failed as college coaches. There is no great college coach who has found it worth his while to change his field. Eddie Casey flopped at Harvard. "Lone Star" Dietz failed at Washington State. "Lud" Wray was let out by Pennsylvania. Paul Schissler was let out by Oregon State. "Potsy" Clark will not win at Butler.

The harm of pro football is that it lures a certain percentage of the college products into this blind passage. Knute Rockne indifferently said that pro football was all right when used as Johnny Mohardt used it to pay his way through medical school but too many fall into easy ways and give up their ambitions. They waste the best six years of their lives, and lose step with their fellows. It is curious that the real build-up of pro-football in the press has come since the death of the universally beloved "Rock" who was the one man with the wit, wisdom and influence to put to flight all the arguments for pro football.

Even in the big money and long careers of big league baseball there is a risk. Guy Bush, one of the most successful big leaguers in the filling station business, once remarked to me that "if a young fellow goes into baseball out of school and makes good for ten years without in the meantime building up a business or profession on the side, he is worse off when he gets through than when started in."

The smart college players do not go into professional football. Instead they use their fame and glamour as an entree to their chosen work. At the nadir of the depression several of the players from a certain leading school went into pro football. The next fall they returned to the campus and said to their coach: "Tell the others to stay out of it. They don't do for you all they promise, and those who stay in long become bums. If we don't go along with them, we're sissies."

Such pro stars as Norman Barry of Notre Dame and Benny Friedman of Michigan, after their pro days were over openly stated that football was no game to play for money.

Most coaches warn their players against going into the pro game. The great coaches like to look upon their work as a process of character-development. They point with pride to their "boys" who have gone out into the competition of life and made good.

Pro football has its place. It supplies Sunday afternoon entertainment for the same sporting element that attends wrestling exhibitions, along with a small percentage of the real football fans who are unable to attend the big games on Saturday because of their jobs. It gives the newspapers a little fresh copy for Blue Monday, and it takes care of a few of the more dull-witted grid stars for a few years.

Here pro football has its place, but its place is second place to college football, and always will be because their game is utterly incapable of duplicating either the immense fabric of effort or the deep emotional drive that makes college football so thrilling and magnificent to the millions.

## I PREFER THE NFL

[*The leading NFL teams were the Green Bay Packers, the Chicago Bears, the New York Giants, and the Washington Redskins. Just as the Athletic Journal was a staunch supporter of the college game, The Literary Digest preferred professional football. In this article the author discusses the popularity of the NFL and disputes the notion that the pros did not play with emotion. "Masters of All the Arts of the Gridiron," The Literary Digest (8 December 1934), 32.*]

Three Sundays ago, the New York Giants played the Chicago Bears in the Polo Grounds in New York City. That game clearly demonstrated that professional football is prospering, no longer an "infant industry." Some 50,000 football fans watched that professional football game. On the Saturday before, Fordham played Purdue, on the same field, before 40,000 spectators. Over the whole country that week-end, the Chicago-Bears professional game outdrew all save two college games—Ohio State vs. Michigan, Yale vs. Princeton.

The "gate" is a very sensitive gage in measuring the success of promotional experiments on the playing fields of America. Owner, Tim Mara, of the New York Giants, got a deal of satisfaction out of counting the crowd in the Polo Grounds that Sunday. It was the largest crowd to attend a pro game since the fresh, flaming name and head of "Red" Grange packed the populace into the Polo Grounds back in 1925.

The Chicago Bears were trailing, 9-0, in the fourth period of a game so fast and furious that Grange stayed on the bench, left the dynamiting to younger joints and harder heads. It was a game that was fought on the ground, not in the air. Giants' backs—Ken Strong, Harry Newman, and "Wee Willy" Smith—pounded and squirmed through the 220-pound Chicago line. Other great names filled the air...Hewitt, Lyman, Brumbaugh, Feathers, Ronzani, Nagurski, Molenda—names that had balanced sports budgets for a dozen different colleges a few years ago.

And in that last quarter, Bronko Nagurski, head down, dragging players, plowed twenty-one yards to the Giants' 12-yard line. Beattie Feathers scooted around end, scored in a corner. Manders, dependable Manders—hadn't missed one all year—came in to kick the point after touch-down. He made it! Score: 9-7.

Again Nagurski, 230-pound Nagurski, began hammering away at the battered Giants, blasting deeper into their turf. College coaches, scouts, football players from all over the country watched that drive. The victorious Yale team, a team that had beaten Princeton on sheer "spirit" the day before, looked on as football's "hired hands" bled and sweated for inches of torn turf. Despite an off-side penalty against the Bears, Nagurski carried the ball and half the Giants' team to the 17-yard line in six straight plays.

Manders came in again, sure-footed Manders, who had scored twenty-nine points with his toe last year. The crowd was babbling, limp from the dramatic suspense packed into that curtain scene. Half a million toes curled in 100,000 shoes, half a million finger-nails dug into 100,000 moist palms as Brumbauch kneeled to take the ball from center—placed it. Manders kicked, easily, confidently. The ball went over, neatly between the uprights. Three points; 10-9 was the score. The Bears had won in the last fifty seconds of play.

**THE SPIRIT OF THE PROFESSIONALS**

After the defeat, the Giants, salaried players, professionals all, went back into the locker rooms and mixed bitter, baby's tears with the water from their showers. Talk about spirit—those "hired hands" hated losing to the Bears, just as deeply and tearfully as an undefeated Princeton team had hated to lose to Yale twenty-four hours earlier down in Palmer Stadium.

And the crowd—most of them followers of the college game, and doubting Thomases about the pros—left the game with a community case of delirium tremens, converted into regular town-criers in behalf of professional football. That's how a game grows in America. Slowly, painfully; then all in a grand rush.

The professional game has a corner on most of the dramatic talent. It is a safe prediction that professional football will one day outdraw the college game consistently. Tim Mara points out that the Giants have a better average "gate" now than almost any college team. Without being an alarmist, here is food for thought: As professional baseball grew to be a real industry, college baseball died out.

The college game has met the demands for a better show, and thereby defended itself against the rising competition from the master showmen. Laterals, lateral-for-ward-laterals, and other tricks devised by the college coaches have produced a more spectacular college game. Made to please the crowds, the change should not be criticized. It has given the game back to the players in a large measure....

The professional rule, permitting a pass to be thrown from any point behind the line of scrimmage, deserves much credit for forcing the college game to open up. However, as Steve Owen, coach of the New York Giants, points out: "In the big professional games, the flashy stuff, like the laterals, are conspicuous by their absence."

That is quite true. Power is the word to use in describing professional football.

It's all a part of an excellent show, in which this year's playoff for the National League title will see the professional game moved up among the head-liners, sharing the starring role with the "undergraduate" game—as these salaried masters of all the arts of the gridiron deserve.

## THE ALL-STAR GAME

[*In this document the originator of the all-star game explains the background behind the first game. Although Arch Ward declared the purpose of the all-star game was not to determine which game was the best, a victory by either side was quickly proclaimed as proof of its superiority. Arch Ward, "Chicago Tribune Charity Foot Ball Game. Chicago All-Stars vs. Chicago Bears All-Star Game, 1934," Playbill, Chicago Historical Society Archives.*]

The capacity crowd in attendance at Soldiers' Field tonight is watching a game unique in football history. Never have the greatest players from the college gridiron been pitted against a championship team from the National Professional League. Never until this game was arranged had the fans of the nation chosen the members of a college squad. And never had the public picked its own coaches.

The young men who are representing intercollegiate football tonight were selected for the game by 165,000 persons who participated in the coast to coast poll conducted by the Chicago Tribune, which is sponsoring the contest. Their head coach, Noble Kizer of Purdue, and his assistants, Dick Hanley of Northwestern and Jimmy Crowley of Fordham, earned their positions in a nation wide competition that attracted 617,000 votes.

The Tribune suggested and promoted this game not with the idea that it would serve as a conclusive test of the merits of professional and collegiate football but rather to provide an evening's entertainment for a maximum number of fans at minimum expense. Profits will be divided equally among the United Charities, the Catholic Charities and the Jewish Charities of Chicago.

The Tribune is deeply appreciative of the splendid support it has received from the football public in the promotion of this enterprise. We owe a debt of gratitude to the management and players of the Chicago Bears, to the 35 college stars who came from all parts of the United States to make the game worth while and to the 30 newspapers from coast to coast which cooperated with us in soliciting expressions from the fans on players and coaches.

Arch Ward
Sports Editor, Chicago Tribune

## INCREASED ATTENDANCE AT NFL GAMES

[*Attendance at NFL games increased by 150 percent between 1932 and 1938—attracting more than one million spectators in the latter year. This document summarizes the major rule differences between the colleges and the NFL at the end of the decade and outlines the reasons for the rapid rise in professional football—which now attracted twice as many paying fans per game than did the average college game. Bob Ruark, "Dough for Downs," Liberty (30 September 1939), 34-5.*]

...The steady rise of the professional is based on one specific thing. The professional football bosses have aimed their game at the average man. *They cater to the individual who has had no college football allegiance. They have, in short, built an alma mater, a sentimental attachment, for the non-college man, the gentleman who was forced to forsake education for work at an early age.*

The game's directors estimate that a good three fourths of their mass attendance is compiled of people who never before had been able to work up an acute interest in football because they never had a chance to go to college. To attract this new and fertile customer to their game, the professional owners schedule their matches on Sunday, and charge admission that is not too high for the wage earner.

And the pros give what their followers demand. They play hard rough football and, in the main, play cleanly. Since the start of the professional game, not one player had been killed, and although the same cannot be said for the colleges, where every time a player dies, an immediate cry goes up to abolish the game.

The pros play for keeps, and this attitude is the very bread and meat of the bleacher seats, which is where your true sports fan sits.

The Chicago Bears have the reputation of being the toughest aggregation in the country. No one bothered to collect any statistics on the matter. But the opinion is that the Bears must have averaged one and one half fights last year for every point scored, and they finished the season with a field day against the Redskins. Consequently they are very popular with fans, who are more or less certain that when the Bears play they'll get more than their money's worth.

The prime interest getter in the professional game is the fact that the spectator never knows what to expect. Although the plays are intrinsically simple, the quarterbacks are tops in unorthodoxy. If it wins, it's good. And even a one-sided game is usually interesting, because of the fundamental excellence of both teams. Because each team is well rounded in all phases of the game, there are really no soft touches on the schedule, as is quite often the case among the bigger colleges.

The essential difference in collegiate and professional rules provide a wide latitude which makes the professional game primarily a free-scoring affair, in which no team is immune from several touchdowns per game, This slush scoring is a welcome relief, say, from the Pitt-Fordham epic, which has traveled three years without a score. And it keeps the customers in a perpetual state of frenzy; keeps his tonsils oiled and his blood coursing hot, which is very nice on a cool autumn day.

The college rule makers say a pass may be thrown from a point not less than five yards back of the line of scrimmage. The pros say you can toss a ball from any point back of this somewhat mythical line. This tends to hatch a free-scoring game, with double and triple lateral passes made easy. Gaynell Tinsley of the Chicago Cardinals, who won fame as an end at Louisiana State University, snagged one pass last year that traveled 65 yards from teammate Rock Reed's fingers. Sammy Baugh, who led the league in completions, hung up a new record with 81 completions for a net gain of 1,127 yards!

The goal posts, in the professional pastime, are set flush with the goal line, whereas the collegians have their crossbars ten yards back of the payoff strips. This nearness of the posts gives the pros, who usually boast two or three fanatically perfect kickers, a dangerous offensive weapon in the point after touchdown and the field goal, while the colleges mainly rely on the touchdown itself. The colleges try field goals as a last resort, while the pros will gleefully attempt to sink one from any portion of the field short of the halfway mark. Manders of the Bears and Ralph Kercheval of the Brooklyn Dodgers can drill the eye out of a squirrel, or a spectator, at 40 yards with a place kick. Manders consistently bangs them home at 35 yards between the posts at 50 yards. Riley Smith, who helped make Dixie Howell famous at Alabama, set a new record last year with 22 straight conversions after touchdowns.

But it is in pass defense that the pros really provide the blood and thunder. A pass, particularly a long one is a signal for the stretcher bearers to gird up their loins and ready the arnica.

The college rules say that anything but a clear attempt to catch or break up a pass is interference, and the pass is ruled complete. Last year, with the razzle-dazzle style of play in full swing at the colleges, interference penalties climbed high, to the great disgust of the spectators.

Interference in professional circles runs about the same way, but the interpretation of the rule is apt to be a deal more literal. The man who is receiving a pass, they figure, is a full-grown husky adult with a full realization of what his profession entails. If he is not amply able to take care of himself, if he is not perfectly trained, then he has no one to blame but himself. Of course it is not considered exactly "cricket" to kick out the receivers' teeth, but any honest incidental mayhem is quite all right. It is nothing unusual for three pass defenders to hit the potential receiver at the same time, one high, one low, and one in the middle, but these pros are tough and they manage to come up for more.

And you can run with fumbles in professional football where you can't under collegiate rule. The collegians attempt to prevent excessive pile-ons by claiming that the ball is downed on the spot where the runner's knee touches the ground. In the pro game, however, this ruling fosters the delightful game called hit-him-hard-and-keep-him-down-or-else-he'll-rise-again-to-score.

They pay off on ability in the pro game. There is no comparison between the often slovenly play of the collegians and the sharp precision of the pros. The men are postgraduate artists in their line, and they are not allowed many mistakes. The average pro back must be able to block with the sharpness of a machine-gun burst, run nimbly, tackle viciously, and kick better than so-so. The linesmen must be able to dish it out and take it equally well. And, above all, the pro must be able to think. Few dumb lads last long when they're getting paid to think.

And with an eye ever cocked at the box office, the pro moguls have picked their player for color as well as ability. Baugh was given great publicity at Texas Christian University—he practically put the school on the map—was the year's sensation, not only as a passer but as a kicker. Ace Parker, All-American at Duke, proved to be just what the doctor ordered for the Brooklyn Dodgers. The great Bronko Nagurski was twice an All-American, as both linesman and back. And, of course, a gent named Red Grange did all right. Remember?

Sammy Baugh's prominence has cast a curious light on the professional game, for one thing, it has raised the standards of professional salaries so high that the owners now must pay up or lose their luminaries. Already Keith Molesworth of the Bears and Cliff Battles of the Redskins have deserted to the enemy—the colleges. Molesworth went over as backfield coach at the Naval Academy, and Battles is performing a similar chore at Columbia.

Before Baugh, who made $6,000 his first year in the major, and who didn't sign for a cent less than $12,000 this year, the average amount received by the average pro player for a season was something like $1,500. Battle, a veteran of six years, was making only $2,750 when he was hired by Columbia. That has changed. With the recognition of the sport has come recognition of the players.

This fall may be the best year in the game's history. Owners expect an increase of fully 30 per cent in attendance in every city but Philadelphia, which is still laboring in the shade cast by the University of Pennsylvania and the Army-Navy game. A charter that once could have been bought for coffee-and-cake money, about fifty dollars to be exact, now will sell for no less than $150,000. The West Coast is screaming for representation in the National League. Pro football is climbing.

It takes four years and almost that many thousand dollars to win a diploma and a sentimental college background. The pros will give you, the spectator, an alma mater in thirty seconds for a price ranging from $1.10 to $3.70. As yet the colleges haven't cooked up anything to top that one.

Chapter 11

# GOLF

The decade commenced with the retirement of golfing legend Bobby Jones and ended with the emergence of budding superstar Sam Snead. In between, the Depression had a major impact on the sport, shifting the emphasis from private to public golf courses and from an elite game to a sport for the middle class. The decade also witnessed the growth of the professional golf tour and an increased interest in women's golf.

In 1930, the country's two million golfers spent $15 million on clubs, bought 60 million balls for a total of $36 million, supported 250,000 caddies, and purchased $29 million in golf equipment. These figures all declined precipitously in the first years of the Depression. Membership in the Professional Golf Association (PGA) fell from 2,022 in 1929 to a low of 1,009 in 1933 before rebounding to 1,900 in 1940. Sponsors abandoned some professional tournaments, and prize monies were slashed everywhere. The leading money winner on the 1935 PGA tour earned just $9,543. Two years earlier, 100 club professionals were unemployed, partly due to the switch from hickory to steel shafted-clubs that put many skilled club makers out of work. Although the Depression was the major catalyst for these changes, Bobby Jones' retirement in 1930 also played a part. "Emperor Jones" had lured thousands of spectators to his matches and huge galleries followed him around the course.

The Depression particularly affected private clubs. Most people thought of golf as a gentleman's game and golfing ethics demanded such niceties as complete silence on tees and greens. Damon Runyon wrote, "show us a golf-playing town and the writer will show you a town in which refinement is above the average." The game was particularly popular among businessmen who conducted business as they played golf and socialized in the clubhouse. The Canadian Magazine, for example, wrote in 1931 about the "scores of golfing bums who frankly utilize their golfing ability to further their private ventures in the business world. It is easy to do in golf, practically every corporation president in Christendom belongs to at least one top-notch club and wallows about its links.... Almost all the business executives who do the heavy buying are enthusiastic golfers." When these people felt the pinch of the Depression, their country club memberships, which might include a $500 initiation and a $300 annual fee, were often the first to suffer. Financial problems forced many private clubs to offer low initiation fees, or even pay-for-play days.

The second half of the 1930s was the era of the municipal golf course. Although 179 American cities had pay-as-you-play courses by 1930, the Depression curtailed further development until the WPA poured money into public parks and recreation beginning in 1935. In the next five years the WPA built 207 courses, and by the end of the decade approximately sixty percent of all rounds played were on public courses. In New York alone, public links players increased from 343,000 in 1934 to 600,000 in 1940. The switch from private to public courses reflected not only the hard economic times—public courses charged $1 green fees on weekdays and $2 on weekends—but also better clubhouses and public links.

The United States Golfers Association's failed experiment with a new ball that was lighter and bigger than the existing golf ball indicated the importance of the average golfer to the Association's considerations. Concerned that the success of such long-ball hitters as Bobby Jones and Horton Smith was deemphasizing accuracy for the sake of power, the USGA announced in 1930 that the following year golf balls would be 1.68 inches in diameter and weigh 1.55 ounces. The USGA promised average golfers that, although a 220-yard drive might now travel only 198 yards, it would sit up better and be easier to hit and to putt. Almost immediately there was a groundswell of criticism of the new "balloon" ball. Several newspapers polled their readers and found an almost overwhelming sentiment against it. In a nation-wide poll conducted by the Newspaper Enterprise Association, 6,403 golfers voted against the new ball and 2,163 favored it. Life magazine wrote in May 1931,"If it can be proved to you [USGA] that the majority of players in this country want the golf ball back, will you restore that ball to official standing?" and sent ballots to more than 5,000 golf clubs. Faced with the animosity of many duffers who now faced higher scores, the USGA withdrew its new ball the following year. In a similar vein, the PGA greatly reduced the number of sand traps on its courses because in addition to adding to upkeep costs, they tended to penalize average golfers more than they did professionals.

This period marked the beginning of the modern era in equipment. The USGA legalized steel shafts in 1929 and they quickly replaced hickory clubs and improved scores. Mass production techniques resulted in the replacement of named clubs with numbered irons and the merchandising of matched sets rather than individual clubs that "felt right." When the number of clubs that players carried with them grew to extremes, the USGA limited tournament golfers to fourteen clubs in 1938.

The general public had a choice of dozens of golf instructional books and syndicated newspaper articles written by famous golfers. Golfing magazines included American Golfer, Golf Illustrated, Golfdom, the Business Journal of Golf, Golf News, and Canada's Golf and Sports Illustrated. Surveys indicated that golf was one of the most popular participant sports in the US. In an examination of the recreational activities of college male alumni, golf ranked third behind swimming and tennis, and approximately fifty percent reported that they played golf. Of 355 businessmen and professionals in Iowa, one-half claimed that they were "now doing" golf. A study of the recreational interests of college women found that forty-five percent of the students in twelve women's colleges wished to learn golf (Research Quarterly, October 1935 and October 1939).

Still, golf was an expensive sport—a good set of clubs cost from $35 to $60. As the Depression receded in many urban areas, private club memberships increased, helped by the repeal of Prohibition in 1933 that stimulated dining room business and enabled many clubs to stay open all winter catering to the skiing, skating, tobogganing, and card-playing crowd. As the decade drew to a close, golf regained its popularity. In 1938, for instance, the country's roughly 1,500,000 golfers spent $150 million on clubs, golf fees, balls, and equipment to play on the country's 5,113 courses.

Golf in Canada followed a similar course. The cost of special golf clothing, balls, green fees, bags, clubs, caddie fees, and other paraphernalia, restricted growth in these hard financial times and forced some private clubs to open their facilities on a pay-as-you-play basis to the general public. The number of clubs registered with the Royal Canadian Golf Association (RCGA) declined from 591 in 1931 to 576 clubs five years later. Although golf was fashionable in every province, it was more popular in urban areas where the larger population could support better courses. The prairies were particularly hard hit by the Depression. Per capita income fell by sixty-five percent and more than a quarter of a million people left the region. As a result, despite the Alberta Golf Association's promotion of golf in rural areas by arranging tours of leading golfers, and providing access to urban clubs for members of small town golf clubs, many rural clubs failed. Elsewhere, clubs reduced membership and green fees and fired salaried professionals.

Although golf was popular in British Columbia with its shorter winters, and Winnipeg had a reputation of being one of the "golfiest" cities on the continent, Ontario and Quebec dominated the golfing scene. With 189 golf clubs in Ontario and ninety-four in Quebec, these provinces supported one-half of the country's registered clubs in 1936. The first Canadian Open held outside Central Canada (Saint John, New Brunswick) was not until 1939.

In golf, as with so many sports, Canada's inferiority complex was evident. A common complaint was Canada's inability to defeat the US. Commentators sometimes blamed the colder weather in Canada, complained that Canadians did not work hard enough at their game, or protested that American golfers were subsidized by wealthy clubs and sporting goods firms, which enabled them to concentrate on their games. Some writers believed the problem was psychological, that Canadian golfers were too much in awe of American golfers. Yet, so was the golfing public. The success of the Canadian Open, for example, was measured by the number of American golfers who attended. American golf stars were household names in Canadian newspapers.

When Kenny Black, Marjorie Kirkham, Ada Mackenzie, or C. Ross Somerville won, it was cause for great celebration. After Somerville's victory at the 1932 US Amateur, the London, Ontario, Evening Telegram proclaimed that his "victory over Goodman is possibly the greatest Canadian achievement in the sporting world of the present decade. The United States amateur golf championship is one of the major golf crowns of the world."

Prior to 1935, the Canadian golfing fraternity was under the impression that the Canadian Open was the second most important tournament in North America. That year, thirteen touring American professionals ranked the Canadian Open anywhere from fourth to tenth. Because the traditionalists in the RCGA refused to permit commercial sponsorship, prize money in 1935 was only $1,465. This compared poorly to purses of $10,000 or more in PGA events south of the border and made it difficult to attract the best players. Even when Seagram Ltd. began sponsoring the Canadian Open in 1936, prize money increased to only $3,000, with an additional $600 for the best Canadian golfers.

By mid-decade, golf became a relatively popular sport among educated professional blacks. Golf courses were so expensive that there were few minority-owned 18-hole golf courses. As a result, most blacks played on public courses which, when they were not segregated, often restricted them to particular days and hours. Unlike the wealthier white universities and colleges, few black schools could afford golf courses or golf teachers, and only five schools participated in the first black intercollegiate tournament in 1938.

In 1926, several golf-playing doctors in Washington, D.C., tired of having to travel to New England to play golf, organized the United Golfers Association, which provided events similar to those offered by the USGA. Many of the first black golf professionals, as the article "The Negro Open" reveals, were caddies at segregated white country clubs, where they learned the game well enough to instruct the small emerging black elite which saw golf, and membership in the new black country clubs, as a step up in society. Near the end of the decade, boxer Joe Louis promoted golf among the black community. He hired black pros to instruct him, and sponsored his own tournament. When Joe Louis lost to Max Schmeling in 1936, some people blamed the defeat on Louis' passion for golf.

Golf clubs benefited from the increasing interest by women in golf during the 1930s. They usually played during the week and retired to the club's veranda for tea and bridge on Saturday afternoons when the men dominated. Although there were many excellent female golfers, such as Mildred "Babe" Didrikson, Collette Vare, Patty Berg, Virginia Van Wie, Helen Hicks, Mary K. Browne, and Ada Mackenzie, men generally considered them inferior. The American Golfer, for example, referred to Patty Berg as "abbreviated as to elevation, a bit on the chunky side, and fascinatingly freckled...." Every magazine referred to this "titan tomboy from Minneapolis'" early "tomboy" years. When the women played well, sportswriters such as Paul Gallico referred to them as "muscle molls." As the Document "Ada Mackenzie: Canada's Woman Golfer," illustrates, some of the best women players held similar views.

The 1934 "tiny pants controversy" best illustrates these notions. That summer, three female golfers wore shorts on a golf course near New York and the local golfing association immediately forbade a similar display. Most traditional clubs agreed. The Meadow Brook Club in Long Island, for example, announced, "Certainly women cannot wear shorts here. Neither can men take off their shorts on the course." News-week quoted a New Jersey priest as saying, "any mother who allows her daughter to follow this fashion is guilty of serious sin. We are not living in the Borneo Islands but among civilized people." Although News-week did not necessarily agree, it concluded that fortunately "vanity will prevent women with pool-table legs from revealing them."

In 1935, Gene Sarazen noted that professional golfers could make more money giving golf lectures and demonstrations than by playing tournament golf. In fact, when the USGA declared "Babe" Didrikson ineligible to participate in amateur golf tournaments in 1935 because she was a professional in other sports, "Babe" traveled around the country with Sarazen giving clinics. Country club professionals derived their basic income from lessons and the sale of balls and golf equipment. Although revenue from lessons declined by eighty percent at the onset of the Depression, the increase in female and junior golfers provided the teaching pros with needed money, and forced them to improve their teaching techniques and manners. In the 1920s and earlier, most private clubs recruited their pros from Great Britain, where the best golfers were assumed to live. In 1927, American golfers initiated the biennial Ryder Cup matches between representatives of the British and American PGAs to illustrate the high caliber of US golfers. American victories in four of the first Ryder Cup matches, as well as four of five Walker Cup victories (American vs. British amateur men) in the 1930s, and all four of the Curtis Cup matches (American vs. British amateur women) encouraged American clubs to hire American professionals. Indeed, the 1930s witnessed the emergence of the US as a golfing super power.

In the winter, approximately 300 club pros and tournament golfers played in from 25 to 38 golf tournaments in the "grapefruit circuit," in Florida and California. Here, top golfers such as Lawson Little, Gene Sarazen, Walter Hagen, Harry Cooper, Jimmy Demaret, Horton Smith, Byron Nelson, and Sam Snead played for prize money that ranged from $2,000 to $10,000. Although these tournaments furnished positive publicity in the cities in which they were held, in the first years of the Depression the PGA experienced difficulties finding a sponsoring chamber of commerce. By mid-decade, these events regained their popularity and total prize money gradually increased from $57,300 in 1934 to a high of $174,000 in 1939. Plans for a summer tour in northern cities did not materialize until the 1950s.

As the document "Sarazen on Professional Golf" indicates, few pros could survive on prize money alone, and the star golfers usually had contracts with sporting goods manufacturers which paid them from $5,000 to $10,000 annually. Less well-known golfers could look to the success of Ralph Guldahl for inspiration. In 1937, Guldahl was so poor that he had to borrow clubs to play on the winter golf circuit. He then proceeded to capture the US Open and earn a total of $8,600 in prize money for the year, plus a lucrative winter job at the Miami-Biltmore, endorsements for golf equipment, and offers to play exhibition matches and write magazine articles.

Two events confirmed the success of tournament golf. In 1932 a health resort in Warm Springs, Georgia, successfully held a golf tournament to raise money for charity and to promote the area. This fund-raising campaign, which became known as the "March of Dimes," illustrated how hospitals and charities could benefit from golf. Two years later, Bing Crosby's celebrity golf tournament attracted thousands of spectators and established golf tournaments as money-making events. Still, the PGA avoided autumn tournaments, fearing that collegiate football would dominate the media and commandeer the attention of golf fans. Professional female tournaments did not commence until 1946.

When Bobby Jones retired in 1930 after winning the British and American open and amateur championships, John Tunis called him the "high priest of the religion of golf." Amateur champion Chick Evans wrote in *The Blue Book of Sports* (1931): "[Golf] is an obsession of the spirit, a sportsman's joy and religion. The roof of its great temple is the sky; the trodden fairways are its nave and transept. The trees are like tall candles flaming green upon its altar." Like many other sports, golf was praised for its "carryover" ability to teach self-control, courage, sportsmanship, and endurance, but unlike other games it provided contact with nature and touched men's soul.

Golf was a perfect game for the Depression. It provided a diversion from the injustices of the day, and in the words of Chick Evans, golf "strengthens a man for the trials of the work-a-day world ahead of him." Golf also seemed to confirm the validity of cherished American myths regarding hard work, morality, and national supremacy.

## THE NEGRO OPEN

[*One of few articles in the popular magazines on black golf, this Time article reprinted a picture of the victor, Howard Wheeler, and his young white caddie, from the Chicago* Daily Times. *Note the low paying jobs of the top players and the racist language. Black women, most of whom competed out of Chicago, Washington, and Indianapolis, participated in the United Golf Association's national championship. By 1937, at least two all-black women's golf clubs existed in the United States. Lucy Williams of Indianapolis captured the women's title in 1932, 1936, and 1937 and was runner-up four other years in the decade. Williams' teammate, Ella Able captured the title in 1934 and 1935. "Negro Open," Time (12 September 1938), 35-6.*]

Of the 12,000,000 Negroes in the U.S., about 50,000 play golf—either on public links or on 20-odd private Negro courses. Northern Negroes, settling in large cities, rarely know a brassie from a mashie until they have become prosperous enough to enjoy the game as a pastime. But in the South, where country clubs use Negro caddies in great numbers, many moppets learn the fundamentals of golf along with their ABCs.

Last week, on the Palos Park (public) golf course just outside Chicago, 135 of the country's top-notch colored golfers (including 16 women) met for the 13th annual Negro championships of the U.S. Thirty-four played for money, 101 for fun. Some carried their own clubs, others paid white caddies $1 a round. All were extremely courteous to the lone white competitor, a local enthusiast named Charles Hlavacek who entered the tournament because he disliked to interrupt his habit of playing daily on the Palos Park course.

In the opening round of the Men's Open, most of the gallery followed the favorite, Robert Patrick ("Pat") Ball, Chicago grocer who had won the title three times. Others with a lively following were dapper John Dendy, defending champion who works as a locker boy at North Carolina's fashionable Asheville Country Club; and Hugh Smith, a Thomastown (Ga.) office boy who recently shot a 263 in a southern tournament and was forthwith sent to the national meet by his boss (for whom he caddies weekends).

After the first round, however, the greater part of the gallery of 300 trudged around after lanky, wooly-topped Howard Wheeler of Atlanta—watched him tee up on the edge of a match folder, shuffle along the fairways in a Stepin Fetchit gait, plop down on the greens while waiting his turn to putt. A onetime professional whose occupation has been "just walkin' round" since he lost his job at Atlanta's Lincoln (Negro) Country Club in 1933, 29-year-old Howard Wheeler proved last week that he could still teach folks a few golfing tricks. With a minimum of effort, he got results that would please many a top-flight white golfer: rounds of 68, 73, 72, 71—on a tough, hilly course he had never seen before. His 284 not only won the tournament and first prize of $200 but set a new record for the Negro championship—just three strokes higher than the all-time U.S. Open record set by famed Ralph Guldahl last year.

With this accomplishment, Howard Wheeler took his place alongside Bobby Jones, Charley Yates and others who have made Atlanta a starred spot on the world's golfing map.


### ADA MACKENZIE—CANADA'S WOMAN'S GOLFER

[*The Depression witnessed an increase in the number of female golfers. There were no professional tournaments for women, and few females could afford the time to devote to improving their game unless they were well-off financially. As a result, there were only a handful of women professionals. Wilson Sporting Goods employed Helen Hicks in 1934 to help design and sell women's golf clubs. Termed a "business woman golfer," Hicks was one of the first golfers, male or female, to offer teaching clinics, rather than the traditional exhibition of her skills. Babe Didrikson toured with Gene Sarazen in 1935. That same year, Joyce Wethered played exhibition matches sponsored by John Wanamaker stores in New York and Philadelphia.*

*The career of Canadian golfer Marjorie Kirkham of Montreal was an exception to the rule that reserved club pro jobs for males. Kirkham captured the 1930 Canadian amateur title, and the following year she reached the finals of the Canadian open and the closed—which were held the same week to reduce the players' travel expenses— and in 1932 she won the Canadian Ladies' Open championship.*

*Ada Mackenzie was Canada's premier amateur women's golfer between the wars, having won the Canadian Ladies' Amateur Open in 1919, 1925, 1926, 1933 and 1935. Later, she captured the Canadian Women's Senior Golf Championship eight times. Like other top female golfers, Mackenzie excelled at several sports in school, including ice hockey, tennis, swimming, basketball, and lacrosse, and experienced prejudice against female golfers that made it difficult to get adequate playing time. While in Great Britain in 1920, Mackenzie noticed that British clubs were more accessible to women golfers and returned home determined to start her own club for women. Looking for suitable property, Mackenzie inspected several river valleys near Toronto before settling on land near Thornhill, Ontario. She arranged a bond issue to raise money and sold $100 memberships to 300 women. In 1924, the Ladies' Golf and Tennis Club became the first golf course designed exclusively for women—with restricted hours for men.*

*Ada Mackenzie was also an innovator in women's golf apparel and established Ada Mackenzie Ltd., a successful women's clothing store in Toronto. Playing in the 1927 US Women's Amateur championship, "I was wearing wool, my sleeves were down over my wrists and the skirt was sloughing in the mud. It was just the completely wrong outfit. I lost the match but it was that experience that got me into the ladies' sportswear business."*

*Despite these impressive credentials, as the following article illustrates, Mackenzie shared most of the beliefs of the day. Thirty-one years after she wrote the words below recommending that older women avoid strenuous activity, she won the Ontario Senior's title at age seventy-eight. The section "For the Beginner" was deleted. Ada Mackenzie, "Golf's Your Game. Famous Canadian Amateur Golf Champion Gives These Golfing Tips in an Exclusive Interview with Chatelaine," Chatelaine (July 1937), 18, 26.*]

## FOR THE AVERAGE AND MIDDLE-AGED PLAYER

Don't let yourself get set and feel you can't go any farther. There's no deadline in golf. No matter how advanced you may be there's always something new to learn. New ideas, new theories, new rules, are important. Keep up with them. You're never too old or too good to take a lesson. It brushes you up and gives you a fresh interest. Don't use too many clubs. Fourteen is the limit now for tournament play. Six or seven (as carried by Miss Mackenzie in ordinary play) that will see you through splendidly are driver, spoon, three, five, seven, nine and putter.

Be open-minded about new ideas. Don't be too selfish to play with poor players now and then. Don't take your tournament play too seriously. Some women want to win too much to be able to do it. Golf is a matter chiefly of co-ordination. For tournament play you need to develop a special temperament. You may be a good golfer, but poor in tournaments. You need to be keyed up enough to be on the **qui vive**, yet have everything under control. Poor sportsmanship takes away the glory of any winnings, no matter how great.

If your husband or men friends are good golfers, make them take you along now and then. It's good to play with men—their game is swifter and stronger. But don't be a pest. Let them enjoy their game themselves plenty of times.

And don't hold men up on the course. It's a bad habit women have—often they don't want to let masculine players through. Do it quickly, graciously and decisively, if you're slower. You'll win good will for yourself and spurs for women golfers generally.

Don't be over-anxious to smash last year's record the first time out on the course. Be contented to relax and gradually work your game up smoothly. That feeling that you can hit the ball farther than you ever did before is just spring fever. Chalk it down as such.

## FOR THE OLDER WOMAN

For goodness sake, get all the fun you can out of it. Nine holes or less are enough for you. Don't go too hard it takes too much out of you, and kills any benefit you might get from the grand exercise in the open air. When you get tired—stop. On the average, it's a good idea to play a leisurely game with someone your own age—do plenty of veranda sitting at the clubhouse and be as social as possible about your playing. Don't keep younger members of the family playing with you all the time. Simplify your clubs again now that you're older. Have a caddie whenever possible. And you'll find that fewer clubs cause you less strain. You don't have to think so much. And remember, you're playing now for sheer pleasure. You can even (keep this one in your age group) pick up a ball if you get a bad lie. Make a gentleman's agreement with your opponent when you start out. It's no fun digging out of a hard hole—nobody likes it. With the privilege of greater maturity, you can both kick your ball out of difficult lies. Let the young 'uns scrape the sand pits. Pick people you like to be with, rather than just people you like to **play** with, and enjoy companionship. Stop and admire the setting and the scenery—it's your best way of getting into the country.

And if you really are serious about learning late in life, remember that Mrs. Opal Hill of the United States didn't start to play until she was over 40—and she's a champion. But most of the others (Miss Mackenzie began at eleven, trailing her father around the course with a single club) went at it early. It's more fun if you don't worry anyway.

Why not do most of your playing in early morning or afternoon. It's cooler and pleasanter on the course then.

**AND ABOUT YOUR CLOTHES—AT ANY AGE**

Don't think you can play golf in "any old thing." Not if you want a good game. A modern windbreaker's the thing for cold, windy weather. Don't pile on a lot of woolies—they won't keep out the wind and you'll just be burdened down. Make no mistake about it, you can't play golf if you're cold. For cooler weather play, try a light wool or heavy tweed skirt (a matter of choice) fairly short—just below the knee is comfortable—and a light, wooly sweater. Then your windbreaker. You'll be wiser to get special cleated golf shoes right at the beginning. You can lose a lot of yardage, slipping around on a very wet or very dry day. Socks are probably easier on the feet than just plain stockings. If you're very young, you can wear socks alone, or just shoes and your slim brown legs, bare. But if you're older, wear silk or lisle stockings and socks.

For very warm weather, try a tailored skirt, light and cool, and a thin cotton jersey. Your skirt can be light-weight wool or one of the nice noncrushable linens or sleek synthetic fabrics like sharkskin. Get one with plenty of leg room. It's better not to play in silk—it has a tendency to blow too much, and be bothersome. An all-linen suit in a gay color will be nice for mid-summer. Watch that you have the simplest lines and nothing around your neck or waist that flutters or blows. You can get exciting effect with brilliant colors—and the golf course is your chance to wear the brightest, gayest colors in the world, and look smart. The course is big enough and green enough, and you are small enough by contrast, to make it possible to choose a lot of things you couldn't wear on the street or to the office or a tea party. It's nice to have a neckerchief, provided it's soft and soothing and tied in a neat knot that won't allow any temperamental wind to blow around.

It's better in cotton or linen, and will keep the heat off the back of your neck in summer. Some people can play without any shade, and young girls seem to be able to keep their hair tidy without a hat. But most people find they're happier with a hat of light felt or some gay linen or fabric smartly stitched. Dark glasses have a tendency to let the light in at the side, giving a misleading slant to the ball—so beware. If you can get the kind that just take the glare off, and aren't very dark it's all right.

Gloves are a matter of choice, but you can't just wear any gloves. Definitely not. If ordinary gloves are loose enough to allow hand action they're in the way—if they're too tight they restrict your hold. You must have regular half gloves—Miss Mackenzie plays with a left-hand half glove only of soft leather or chamois. It helps with her grip. For early or late season play there are smart little wool gloves that clip around the little finger and thumb, keeping the back of the hand and wrist warm, like a half mitt. They wear them in England a lot.

And here's an important point about foundation garments. If you're accustomed to wearing a girdle don't go out on the course without one, you'll be uncomfortable and conscious of feeling somehow different—and you won't be able to enjoy your game. Of course you don't want a restricting garment—but you can get a light summer girdle of some cool fabric that gives easily. Shorts are alright on very summery courses—again if you're young. Culottes are favorites of some women, but Miss Mackenzie thinks they have too much fullness. Slacks are alright. But a skirt is usually your best bet if you get just the right kind. Slacks are often good for rainy weather. And there are special rainproof caps, windbreakers and skirts now, that will let you play comfortably, rain or shine.

The main thing is to be dressed so well so comfortably and so attractively that you can forget about yourself completely and enjoy your game to the full.

### SARAZEN ON PROFESSIONAL GOLF

[*As the following article outlines, professional tournament golfers made little money during the Depression and relied upon the sporting goods manufacturers for income. Many professionals earned extra money by "hustling" club members on the golf course. Gene Sarazen, "Pro Golf Is a Sucker's Game," Collier's (10 September 1938), 19, 74.*]

We were sitting around the locker room during a recent tournament and the talk eventually veered around to the remarkable record Ralph Guldahl has compiled during the past two years. Several sports writers were present and a half-dozen professional golfers.

"That's one of the greatest feats ever accomplished in the world of sports," one golfer said, "winning two consecutive Open championships. To win his title last year Ralph had to defeat 170 of the world's best golfers. He had to defend his title this year, not against one man as Joe Louis had to do, but against the whole group at once. Yes, sir, Ralph's feat ranks with what Bobby Jones did a few years ago when he made his grand slam. It's as impressive as Carl Hubbell's twenty-four straight victories a year or so ago. Joe Louis has a cinch compared to Ralph."

"Joe Louis," a sports writer said dryly, "makes about two hundred thousand dollars every time he defends his title. Ralph gets one thousand for defending his. Louis gets his money, win, lose, or draw. The golf champion gets his only when he wins."

"Yeah," another sports writer said, "and when Joe Louis defends his title the gate receipts are divided between him, his opponent and the promoter. When Ralph or any other golf champion defends his title in the Open, the gate receipts are divided between the club that holds the tournament and the United States Golf Association, and a good piece of the money goes toward defraying the expenses of sending the Walker Cup team, a group of amateurs, to England. After all, what do the amateurs ever do for you professionals? Yes, you Pros are suckers. There are about 130 competing in this Open championship. For what? For peanuts, that's what. The total prize money amounts to six thousand dollars."

"Yes, but if you win the Open you make a lot of money playing exhibitions," another sports writer said.

Several of the professional golfers present made rude noises. One of them said, "Last year Guldahl made exactly $7,500 after he won the Open, most of which came from golf manufacturers. All Tony Manero got for winning it was a pretty good job at Boston. Sam Parks made $6,000 out of winning the title in 1935." Then he turned to me. "What did you make out of winning the Open, Gene?"

"I did all right," I told them. "I made exactly $25,000 back in 1932 when I copped the title. Of course I won the British Open that year, too, which helped."

"You guys are crazy," a sports writer said. "Why don't you organize or do something? In any other professional sport the champion has the right to dictate financial terms."

The sports writer gave us all food for considerable thought and after he left, several of us discussed the situation frankly. We came to the conclusion that professional golf is a sucker's game. Only two men have made real money out of professional golf: Bobby Jones and Walter Hagen. Bobby made at least half a million and a steady income of $40,000 per year (I hope he made three times that) out of the by-products of golf: writing, radio, moving pictures, promotion.

**WHAT MAKES TOURNAMENTS?**

Hagen made a million, but today he is cheerfully broke. No one else ever made more than a fair living at golf. I myself have no great complaint. I was lucky to be hot during the golden days of the twenties and when I made it I salted it away. I've got a farm, a cow, and a field of corn up in Connecticut, so if I never hit another ball I wouldn't have to worry too much. I'm making my squawk on behalf of my fellow professionals who haven't been so fortunate and who are being so shamelessly exploited today.

Who makes the National Open? the professional golfers, of course. Since Bobby Jones withdrew from active participation in tournaments, the amateurs have played very little part in the national golfing picture. It is the professional who makes tournaments successful and he gets nothing out of it except the privilege of taking part in a golfing lottery with a very faint chance of winning. And he has to make his living out of this game called golf.

The 130 professionals who competed at Denver spent an approximate aggregate of $50,000 to travel to the tournament. Even during the actual play they paid their own caddies, they paid their own hotel bills and meal bills. I finished tenth in the Open and I felt pretty good about it. My prize money was $150. My expenses were about six hundred dollars.

The gate receipts at a National Open are considerable. To begin with, there is an admission charge of $1.10 to watch the practice rounds. This in raised to $2.20 during the course of the tournament and $3.30 on the final day. It all came to just under $30,000 this year at Denver. Of that the United States Golf Association got about $14,000. The Cherry Hills Country Club got about the same. A proud member of the Denver Chamber of Commerce told me that close to half a million dollars came into the city during the week of the tournament. Everybody made money except the professional golfers.

The pro golfer gets to the course a week or so ahead of time to learn something about it. We pros need practice and every golfer has his own methods of sharpening up his game in practice. But we can't follow our own inclinations in this. The club charges admissions to the practice rounds. We have to put on a show for the spectators who rightly demand a show for their $1.10. Three days before the Open began Guldahl went to the course to get in a couple of practice hours. To his amazement he found a couple of thousand spectators waiting for him and he saw handbills that told of the exhibition he and three others were going to put on that day. It was his first knowledge of it; instead of having an afternoon of practice, he had to go out and shoot golf. Any golfer knows that there is a great difference in the two ways of playing a course.

The next day he and three others had been invited to play an exhibition match at the Denver Country Club. Guldahl and each of the others were to receive a hundred dollars for the exhibition, which was fair enough. That would about square the hotel bill for the week. But they weren't allowed to do it. No, sir, the Cherry Hills Country Club was holding this Open and that was that. The boys had to play on the Cherry Hills course or not at all. If the golfers were broke, let'em eat divots.

**JUST A TOURNAMENT PUPPET**

I'm not finding fault with the people who run the Cherry Hills Club. They treated us all fine. I'm finding fault with the system that makes a professional golfer a mere puppet. He is allowed to express his individuality only in drives and putts. Otherwise he must meekly take orders and we're all about fed up with it.

It is virtually impossible for a golfer to make a decent living out of tournament play. The three big blue-ribbon events are the National Open, the Metropolitan Open and the Western Open. The total prize money offered by these three tournaments is $11,500. A golfer winning all three (a feat comparable to a pitcher hurling three successive no-hit games) would win the magnificent sum of $2,400. Of course he would have to pay his way to all of these tourneys and his expenses would be considerable. Still if he won all three events he would clear about a thousand dollars.

Smart Professionals stick to their home clubs and pass up the tournaments. Right after the Western Open last month the president of the Western Golf Association sent out a blast at the professionals because so few of them had entered the Western. The reason was of course that very few of the players could afford it. This year Johnny Farrell qualified for the National Open but decided to stay home at his Quaker Ridge Golf Club. He frankly admitted that he couldn't afford to take two weeks off from his regular job to chase a rainbow that had no pot of gold at its end.

It is pride that keeps us all bouncing round the tournament circuit. I was mighty proud that year I won both the British and the American Open. This year I had intended to compete in the British classic. I had entered and had steamship reservations. After I came home from Denver I stayed around my farm watching my cows eat. I got to thinking that it would cost me about $2,000 to make the trip to compete in England. And for what? For a possible prize of $500 that the winner gets. So I passed up the British Open.

I might add that not one top-ranking American went to England this year to compete in the event. No one could afford it. When I won my British Open the cash prize was $500 but because of the rate of exchange I got only $318. There was a time when you could cash in after you had won either the British or American open. You could pick up some money playing exhibitions. You can't now. Today Lawson Little, Jimmy Thomson, Harry Cooper and Horton Smith form a team that puts on the greatest golf exhibition ever staged. They have a sound truck and they give talks on how a man can improve his game and then they demonstrate what they've been talking about. A golf manufacturer finances them and no admission is charged....

As a matter of fact most professional golfers are dead too, if they only had sense enough to know it. The manufacturers of golfing equipment are keeping the professionals alive. It wasn't long ago that Ralph Guldahl was selling secondhand cars in California. He didn't have enough money to get to the Open. He tried to borrow it but couldn't. Finally he put the touch on a manufacturer of golf balls, and he was loaned the necessary two hundred dollars. If that golf manufacturer hadn't come through Ralph would still he selling cars.

The smart professionals are men like Jock Hutchinson, Jim Barnes, Henry Picard, Johnny Farrell—they stay at home most of the time plying their trade of teaching. Another reason why the career of a golfing professional is one to be avoided is the fact that country clubs become very fond of the professionals they have. A golf pro seldom is discharged. The club members, having grown fond of them, keep them on. That's great, but it's tough on the young professionals looking for pro jobs. There just aren't any jobs to be had so the youngsters have to depend upon tournament play.

What I am trying to say is that any man is crazy to take up golf as a profession just as he's crazy not to take it up as a pastime. So far all of my criticism has been destructive. Here's a little constructive criticism.

We should have a golfing czar just as baseball does. If a ballplayer has been pushed around he can always get an audience with Judge Landis to state his case. We should have some man in supreme charge of golf whom both players and club officials respect and whose fairness, judgement and honesty would be above question. He should fight the battles for the golfer that the golfer can't fight himself. Such a man as Walter Hagen would be superb for the job.

Prize money in an important tournament should be made to conform with the importance of the event. Our National Open is actually the world's championship of golf. Why isn't the first prize $20,000 instead of $1,000? Why isn't there a substantial prize offered for the Western Open, the Metropolitan Open and the P.G.A. It takes a great champion to win any of these. Where would the money come from?

**A POSSIBLE SOLUTION**

It couldn't all come from gate receipts because no course is big enough to accommodate more than the crowds that now flock to see important tournaments. I have an idea and if it sounds fantastic give it a second thought. I believe that the golfers of America would be glad to subscribe to a fund that could be used as prize money in important open tournaments.

Do you know that there are four million golfers in this country who play regularly? Suppose each of those four million golfers were to be taxed ten cents a year and that money put into a fund for tournament purses. That would amount to $400,000 a year. That fund could be earmarked, put in charge of a golfing czar and his committee, and used as prize money. Even the caddies would be glad to give ten cents a year.

What advantage besides the financial ones for professionals would be derived from this? To begin with, thousands of youngsters now just fooling around with golf clubs would take up the game seriously. Other thousands who don't play would be lured into the game by the promise of rich rewards if they should achieve golfing greatness. Thousands of new courses would have to be built. Golf supply manufacturers (and the thousands of stockholders in their corporations) would enjoy a new and permanent prosperity. The really great professionals could win a couple of tournaments and then, released from financial worries, could concentrate on the real job of the professional— teaching. We are a great country of golfers now. Within two or three years we'd spread-eagle the world in golf.

It's an Idea.

## GOLF—THE UNIVERSAL GAME

*[The following article in the popular health magazine Hygeia refers to psychological studies to support the prevailing view that golf was different from other sports. Golf was therapeutic. It promoted relaxation and better concentration for businessmen and helped to develop wholesome personalities in young people. Golf was ideally suited to the 1930s with its high unemployment, poverty, and insecurities. John Eisele Davis, "Golf. The Game with an Almost Universal Appeal—Soothing, Sociable, and Satisfying, it Affords Both Exercise and Relaxation," Hygeia (April 1938), 305-307.]*

Mrs. Jones was holding one of those cozy afternoon chats with her next door neighbor. "Joe has surely changed. You know he was so tired and irritable when he came from a hard day's work at the office. He seemed to he under a tension, to be so flighty and hurried all the while. I don't know why he decided to play golf, but now although he comes home tired after a round of golf, he is so much more relaxed, seems to be less edgy and fidgety and so much easier to live with."

It was said that John D. Rockefeller, during the latter part of his life, would amble but a few steps around his home but would walk miles following the inviting and intriguing golf ball. Many mentally sick patients who are characterized by instability and lack of concentration will, when properly inducted into the game, play golf for hours. They may show remarkable improvement in the mechanical features of the game, even though they cannot he engaged in other forms of sustained activity. To see some of these distractible types concentrate on golf is quite amazing. Children will play until they are physically exhausted, while persons of all ages and both sexes after once becoming interested in the game will generally keep it up even through old age.

This appeal of golf cannot he explained as a pure, breezy, physical exhilaration of walking and hitting the ball. There is something much more deep seated than that which will account for a different outlook, a freshened orientation which comes to those who are able to play. Only those who look on golf as a mental as well as physical experience will perceive the elements which make up its appeal. Is it possible that this magnetic power of golf, its deeply seated pleasurable elements contain only nature's nerve tonic for the tiredness of the business man and the occupational fatigue and ennui of woman's housework but also the stabilizing factors of a happy attitude so necessary for the child's wholesome development? Play is becoming education. Teachers and parents are realizing today the fertile fields of teaching inherent in the spontaneous play of the child. Psychiatrists are laying stress on play as a balancing element contributing to sane and more happy and effective living. The new approach however is not so much concerned with big muscle building; rather it aims to create wholesome personalities, living and livable human beings, people who can find relaxation and rest from the growing complexities of an increasingly tense milieu, people who really know how to live.

Golf properly played is helpful for the nervous individual because it assists in the formation of habits of quiet concentration. Smith, the successful business man, prides himself on his positive, quick and snappy methods. He is alert and on the job and always tense to spring into the competitive industrial battle. Nervous reactions become set in habit, and he becomes edgy and fidgety. His nerves are off tone. Many such individuals are advised by the doctor who is mentally health-conscious that they need to reeducate and rebuild their habit structure, that they are simply victims of poor habit formation. Mr. Smith tries golf. At first he projects his nervous indecisions into the game. He wiggles his body, wags the club, changes his stance, rails at his club and the course in general.

After playing a few weeks, he is congratulated by the "Pro" because of an improved stability. Mr. Smith informs him that he has landed a business contract which has been uncertain for some time, and he feels more at ease in his game. The discerning person realizes however that while this mental indecision may have had something to do with his spotty playing, the real improvement was due to a gradual reeducation of both mind and body which was slowly replacing habits of nervous tension by habits of improved balance and higher integration.

As a result of observing both the normal and the mentally ill playing golf over a number of years, I firmly believe that golf has a distinct tendency to do this very thing. The nervous golfer is anxious to improve his score. He finds as he plays from day to day that he cannot apply the hurried habits of business to golf. He begins to look over the ball more carefully to survey the contour of the fairway and the greens. He starts his backswing more slowly and is more deliberate about his putting. He begins to slow up his play simply because he becomes convinced that he cannot improve his score by playing in a hurried and careless fashion. All the while, new habits of deliberation are replacing habits of timidity and hesitation, and by a most natural readaptation he gains greater and more satisfactory control of himself.

Then there is a deeply rooted psychic satisfaction which comes to all players as they gradually realize, through improvement in motor skills, an increasing control over the environment and over their own organism.

Psychiatrists are laying stress on the necessity of creating a high sense of self respect in every individual, a sense of personal worthwhileness, if we are to assist them in the organization of a happy and wholesome personality. When we lower a person's sense of self respect, we deal a most serious blow to his mental health. It is not too far-fetched to say that many golfers have added to their mental and physical stability through the psychic readjustment resulting from the game. The player who, as a result of practice and study of the game, is, at the "top of his swing" experiences a delightful exhilaration, a deep-seated and fundamental satisfaction which leaves him with a sense of well being and worthwhileness. There is also the relaxing psychic adjustment from the expanse of shining green grass of well kept fairways. This desirable psychic adjustment, as well as the motor aspects, is becoming increasingly emphasized by progressive educators who are realizing its wide significance in building the socially integrated individual.

In the field of mental rehabilitation, specialists are emphasizing many indirect therapeutic methods as being more effective than frontal attacks; for example, reactivating the negativistic mentally ill patient who does not eat by reawakening the instinctive movements associated with swimming has been an effective procedure. Qualities of confidence and initiative so important in our competitive society are probably best developed by indirect methods. Teachers today are building these psychic qualities through instruction, aiming at the growth and improvement in motor skills. As the child gains in control over himself and his environment he becomes more positive and purposive through understanding and gains in faith and assurance and in ability to adjust satisfactorily to an adult made world. He learns to love the world rather than to fear it.

I remember 12 year old William's first attempts at golf. He was hard to get along with, an irritable youngster. His habit of unduly criticizing others who played with him left him but few friends. On the golf course he would complain about the condition of the green and his faulty clubs and make extensive excuses for his poor shots. Starting in the 120 class, he showed some improvement as a result of steady playing and felt much pleased with himself when, after the first year, he entered the 100 class. With the improvement in his game there came a most noticeable change in his critical attitude. He became definitely more tolerant toward others, less difficult to get along with, and more companionable.

One may naturally say this may all be true, but golf is no different from other games in this respect. One of the main differences between golf and other sports is that golf is a more sustained activity. The average player will put in more hours in golf than does the average player in tennis, handball or badminton. This may be explained in part by the less fatiguing nature of golf and its strong allure. Properly played, golf is a more relaxing and quieting game. The concentration required to play does not allow many distractions, and the wide expanse of fields gives one a sense of freedom from restriction. It is suited to many who cannot play an overstrenuous game such as handball. It is a game forever challenging and intriguing. One may never exhaust its possibilities. The artistic landscaping and wide variety of beauty found make every course a most intriguing challenge to one's cultural as well as practical makeup. Golf is a gentleman's and a lady's game, and the high ethical atmosphere makes it the nice as well as the profitable thing to do. The child may learn many social graces and niceties under most pleasant surroundings while playing with older companions.

There is also the challenge of our newly found pleasure. People need not only a balancing and reactivating hobby but also a constructive means and manner in which to employ their increasing leisure profitably. A sport which they can play in their later years is a hygienic necessity, and golf fills this requirement. It is built for all ages, from 8 to 80.... Golf is the ideal family sport. Brother and Sister playing with Dad and Mother present an ideal picture of mental hygiene in play, the family engaging in a cooperative, social enterprise suffused with deep-seated pleasure as each receive recognition for his unique and individual capacity. They learn to play with rather than against one another, and they try to improve their own score rather than excel the score of some one else.

Burnham has called attention to the fact that the happy personality rewards the integrated individual who has effectively unified his bodily and mental processes. We all give ourselves over to the strongest motivation whether wholesome or unwholesome. All forms of rational play may produce a deep pleasurable motivation to constructive activity and the balance for a hygienic regimen of living so necessary in our hurrying and hurried age.

Chapter 12

# HOCKEY

At the beginning of the decade, ten National Hockey League (NHL) teams and more than thirty minor professional clubs were relatively prosperous and ice hockey recently joined the ranks of major athletics in North America. The NHL, which benefited from a lack of competing attractions in the winter, played before packed arenas in New York, Toronto, Montreal, and Boston until the end of the 1932 season. The best players earned up to $10,000, and the demand for seats was so great that hockey fans in some cities had to purchase season tickets six months in advance. Even when declining attendance forced the New York and Detroit teams to reduce the price of tickets in 1933, hockey fared better than most sports, and the playoffs attracted packed arenas. That year, more than 1,600,000 spectators attended a regular season game. Boston drew 268,000 fans, Montreal's two teams attracted 410,000, and 390,000 watched the New York's two teams, the Rangers and the Americans.

The NHL took advantage of the Depression to dictate salaries and working conditions. As with baseball, a reserve clause in each player's contract bound them to one team in perpetuity, or until they were traded. For the 1932-33 season, the NHL imposed a ceiling of $70,000 on each club's payroll, with no one player to earn more than $7,500, and limited rosters to fourteen players exclusive of goaltenders. The league subsequently lowered the ceiling to $65,000 in 1934 and to $62,500 in 1935. When top players such as Frank Boucher, Hap Emms, Aurel Joliat, and Lorne Chabot refused to report, the owners gave league president Frank Calder discretionary power to suspend any player who held out during contract negotiations, whereupon the players succumbed.

As the Depression worsened, some teams folded, other clubs moved to larger cities, and the NHL fluctuated between seven and ten clubs—divided into two divisions. In 1930, the Canadian Division, sometimes termed the International Division, included the Montreal Maroons, the Montreal Canadiens, the Toronto Maple Leafs, the Ottawa Senators, and the New York Americans. The Boston Bruins, Chicago Black Hawks, New York Rangers, Detroit Falcons, and Pittsburgh Pirates comprised the American Division. In October 1930, Pittsburgh moved to Philadelphia and became the Quakers. After winning only four of forty-four games and continuing to lose money, the team ceased at the end of the 1930-31 season. Ottawa, which also suffered from poor fan support, loaned its players to other teams and suspended operations after the 1931 season. The Senators returned for the 1932-33 season, but soon sold its top players, and moved to St. Louis as the Eagles before disbanding two years later. In 1934, James Norris, who owned the Olympia Arena, purchased the Detroit Falcons and changed the name to Red Wings. In addition to supporting the Red Wings from the profits of his other enterprises, Norris provided funding for the Boston franchise to ensure its existence. When the New York Americans, who were mere tenants in Madison Square

Garden, experienced trouble competing with the Rangers, the NHL assumed control of the team in 1937 and operated it for the remainder of the decade.

After the Montreal Maroons, which captured the Stanley Cup in 1935, collapsed in 1938, the NHL was reduced to seven teams playing in only one division. The Maroons catered to the English Canadians in Montreal and enjoyed a natural rivalry with the Francophone Canadiens. By 1934, generous salaries and extravagant spending jeopardized the team's existence. When the two Montreal teams traded players, the illusion of bitter rivalry became hard to maintain and attendance plummeted. The Montreal Arena Company, which owned both Montreal teams, decided to keep the Canadiens because of its large French-Canadian following. The Maroons pleaded for assistance, but the NHL rejected its suggestion that league receipts be pooled. Even the possibility of transferring to another city was refused because the league stood to make at least $50,000 in franchise fees from a new club.

Other hockey leagues encountered similar problems. The American Hockey League failed in 1932 and the Maritime Senior League collapsed two years later. The Central Hockey Association and the Central Hockey League amalgamated in 1935-36, and the Canadian-American and the International Hockey leagues merged into the International-American Hockey League the following season. In Canada, minor professional teams folded in diverse cities such as Regina, Halifax, Quebec, Windsor, Moncton, and Waterloo. By 1938, only Vancouver hosted a Canadian minor professional team.

During the 1930s, hockey's balance of power between the United States and Canada changed as the commercialization of the game dictated that only professional teams in large market areas could survive. The Bruins played in a 12,000-seat arena. Madison Square Garden accommodated 17,000 spectators. Detroit's arena held 14,000 fans, and the new Chicago arena seated 16,500. By contrast, the largest rink in western Canada was Vancouver's 11,000-seat stadium. Edmonton, with only a 7,000 seating capacity was the next largest building in the west. Prior to the opening of Maple Leaf Gardens in November 1931, the Toronto team played in an 8,000-seat building.

The Depression frightened away many investors, but Conn Smythe convinced some of Canada's leading bankers, insurance companies, retailers, and mining and oil executives to purchase stock. He also persuaded members of the International Brotherhood of Electrical Workers to accept twenty percent of their pay in exchange for Maple Leaf Garden's stock and a pledge to employ only union labor. The prospectus appealed to civic pride by noting that "Montreal, Boston, Detroit and Chicago have all built new arenas in recent years. Toronto dare not lag behind." As the new arenas in New York, Pittsburgh, and Chicago, the cleanliness and comfort of Maple Leaf Gardens attracted women and the more affluent members of society and was an immediate financial success. In 1931, the Leafs set a new attendance record of more than 13,500,000 and receipts jumped from $201,000 to more than $400,000.

In *The Death of Hockey*, Bruce Kidd wrote, "Hockey is the Canadian metaphor, the rink a symbol of this country's vast stretches of water and wilderness, its extremes of climate, the player a symbol of our struggle to civilize such a land." Although few people talked in such poetic terms in the 1930s, most Canadians shared these sentiments. After describing the deep snow and minus 40 degree temperatures in Montreal following the Canadiens' defeat of Toronto in the Stanley Cup, the sportswriter for Collier's reported that hockey was "the national insanity of Canada." "The celebration last year…was in the nature of a public orgy, with bands playing, people parading through the street, speeches from the steps of the City Hall and the conquering heroes being borne aloft on the shoulders of their demented followers." (4 January 1936) City rivalries often blazed to white-hot pitches of hate and frenzied bitterness, but when a Canadian team captured the Stanley Cup the nation celebrated its position as the "greatest hockey country in the world." As T.P. Gorman wrote in Maritimes Sports Illustrated (December 1935), "For the sake of the stamina it builds, the lessons it teaches, the thrills it imparts to players and spectators alike, hockey will always be Canada's greatest sport."

Such feelings were tempered by the flight of Canadian teams to larger urban areas in the US. To many Canadian writers, these changes typified the growing dominance of American commerce and culture. Canadians eagerly bought American mass-market periodicals, listened to American radio stations, and watched American-made movies— at the expense of Canadian or British products. American companies, usually through branch plants, owned eighty-two percent of Canada's auto production, sixty-eight percent of the electronics industry, sixty-four percent of rubber, forty-two percent of machinery, and forty-one percent of chemicals. What had happened in hockey, some nationalists argued, was part of a larger problem—the threat to Canada's national identity.

A common complaint was the growth of commercialism in hockey. As early as November 1931, Leslie Roberts complained in "Americanizing Canadian Sport," (Canadian Magazine) that Canadian sports had fallen prey to invading American ideas. To "make the turnstiles clatter in good old American manner," Canadians were "reconstructing" their games to appeal to American tastes. Now that hockey was "Americanized" from a sport to an industry, he wrote, amateur hockey, whose Allan and Memorial cups were once considered the peak of ambition for Canadians, now existed primarily as a feeder for the NHL. Following the demise of the Montreal Maroons, the sportswriter for the National Home Monthly wrote, "I am concerned as to the future of Canada's representation in a sport which I have been brought up to believe was the Dominion's own.… [I hope] that the National Hockey League will build for the future to assure that Canadian teams will continue in what is the major domain of our great winter pastime."

The Roman Catholic clergy in Quebec was also worried about the spread of American and English-Canadian ideas among French Canadians. Initially, the clergy opposed organized sports, which were usually controlled by the English business elite in Montreal, because of their ties to industrialization and the exposure they gave to Anglo-Protestant values. Despite this opposition, French Canadians packed hockey arenas as fans and as players, and the clergy decided to form its own sporting organizations to better promote Catholic values.

The need to appeal to the less-sophisticated American audience resulted in several rule changes. During the 1920s, the rules ensured that the puck carrier was the focus of the game. Stick-handling and body contact were requisite skills. The off-side rule, derived from rugby, required players to carry the puck over the blue lines. A forward pass to a teammate that crossed the blue line was off-side and the play was stopped for a face-off. It was also illegal to pass the puck forward inside the opponent's blue line. This made for frequent stoppages of play and low-scoring games. In the 1928-29 season, for example, there were 120 shutouts, and Canadiens goaltender George

Hainsworth had twenty-two shutouts in forty-four games. To appeal to American audiences, where the game needed explanation and popularization, the NHL sought to speed the game.

In 1928-29, the NHL allowed forward passing in all three zones, but not across the blue line (the center line did not appear until 1943). The following year, players were permitted to precede the puck across the blue line, although the puck still had to be carried over the line. These changes increased scoring, but were abandoned in mid-season 1929-30 when players waited in front of the goalie for a teammate to cross the blue line and pass them the puck. The following year, the NHL established the present off-side rule in which the puck has to precede the player across the opposing team's blue line. The icing rule was adopted for the 1937-38 season. The result of these rule changes was more passing, team play, and the creation of semi-permanent forward lines such as the Kid Line and the Kraut Line.

To provide spectators with entertainment, the owners sought the best athletes and signed them to long-term contracts. When the Maple Leafs bought Frank "King" Clancy's contract for a league high $50,000 in 1930, spectators around the league turned out in large numbers to see what kind of player was worth that much money. The NHL actively courted the media and encouraged it to publicize the players' antics. Reporters who wrote uncomplimentary stories were banned from the press boxes and denied access to the players. Teams often paid compliant writers, supplied them with interesting stories, and gave them meal money during road trips. Smythe once boasted he could have any story he wanted printed for $50 or less. Thanks to the obliging media, the public avidly followed the careers of such personalities as Lionel Conacher, Syl Apps, Frank Boucher, Joe Primeau, "King" Clancy, Eddie Shore, and Ivan "Ching" Johnson. Howie Morenz was nicknamed "the human projectile" for his habit of throwing up his arms and spinning into a spread-eagle collapse on the ice in an attempt to draw a penalty on an opposing player. His reckless style and headlong rushes up the ice earned him a reputation as the Babe Ruth of hockey. When Morenz died in 1937 from an embolism as a result of crashing into the boards, 200,000 people lined the parade route to the cemetery in Quebec. Aurel Joliat, the idol of French Canada, always wore a black baseball cap when he played. According to Maclean's, "King" Clancy, a 147-pound, hard-hitting defenseman with a fiery temper and an engaging wit, could whip "crowds up to a point where they might at any moment leave their seats and jump the boards to defend the rights of their Galahad."

The best showman was Eddie Shore of the Boston Bruins (1926-1940). Shore's brutal rushes up ice brought fans to their feet. After intercepting a pass at his own blue line, he often retreated, circled his own goal, rushed up the ice, and then passed to an open teammate. Shore, who played with relentless intensity, accumulated almost 1,000 stitches, fourteen broken noses, and five broken jaws during his career. Shore was the most talked-about player in the NHL. In Boston he was a hero, while on the road he was the villain who often led the league in penalty minutes. The New Yorker wrote that Shore had color, meaning "a sort of successful exhibitionism which springs not from conceit but from a justifiable and ingratiating arrogance." Thanks to an adoring press, everyone knew that Shore liked to travel alone and only drank water sent from Canada in two-quart containers. An eight-time all-star and four times the league's most valuable player, Shore knew his value to the team, and his many contract demands made headlines. In 1938, when the Bruins rejected his contract demands, Shore refused to play. Finally, with the fans continually chanting "We want Shore! We want Shore!" the team relented.

The start of a Boston game was pure entertainment. After both teams warmed up, the lights were darkened and the crowd grew silent. Two ushers appeared at the entrance to the rink, one carried a talcum-powdered hockey stick, the other held the gate open for Shore. As Shore stepped on the ice, a spotlight illuminated him, the loudspeakers blasted out "Hail to the Chief," and the crowd broke into a deafening roar. Sporting a black and gold cape, and accompanied by a valet, Shore blew kisses to the fans as he slowly circled the rink.

Hockey's appeal lay in its speed, violent body contact, and non-stop action. The sportswriter for the New York World-Telegram noted in 1933, "To me one of the major thrills is when a swarm of attackers come surging down the ice in a mass drive against the padded little man in the nets. Not once in twenty times will there be a score, but there is always high, primitive drama." Commentators were particularly impressed that the players seemed to compete for the love of the game rather than for the money, and noted the players' Spartan scorn for bruises, cuts and broken bones. American periodicals tended to emphasize hockey's violence and brutality. News-week, for example, noted that "a savage smile constantly reveals [Ivan "Ching"] Johnson's battered teeth, as he trips, butts, and lashes at any opponent who irritates him. Only a few hairs wander on his shiny pate. Though he looks like an old man, he seems to crave a hand-to-hand fight like a bully who feels he can't lose. Yet he has lost often as a count of the number of scars and stitches on his body would reveal. Surgeons have repaired him dozens of times." The Literary Digest proclaimed the opening of the 1936 season "will delight spectators vastly with expert skating and equally perfected rib-jabbing, body-checking and ankle-slashing."

Hockey was violent. Every so often, local policemen skidded gingerly out on the ice to end a free-for-all. Babe Siebert was called the "merry woodsman" for his habit of swinging his stick over opponents' heads like a meat cleaver. When the Boston Bruins attempted to force its players to wear helmets, the idea was met with scorn and declared effeminate. Since no one had died from a fractured skull, the players argued, there was no need to worry.

In 1934 "Ace" Bailey's hockey career, and almost his life, was ended when an Eddie Shore body check cracked his skull. There was always enmity between the Leafs and the Bruins, which probably stemmed from the feud between the Leaf's Conn Smythe and Art Ross, the general manager of the Bruins. The incident took place at the Boston Garden on 12 December 1933. Late in the game, "King" Clancy checked Eddie Shore against the boards in the Boston end. Shore mistakenly thought Bailey checked him. Skating the ice at full speed, Shore spotted Bailey resting on his hockey stick after a hard shift. Approaching Bailey from behind, Shore hit him in the kidneys with his right shoulder. Bailey somersaulted backwards and hit his head on the ice. Leaf assistant manager, Frank Selke, later wrote, "we heard a crack you might compare to the sound of smashing a pumpkin with a baseball bat. Bailey was lying on the blue line with his head turned sideways, as though his neck were broken. His knees were raised, legs twitching." Seeing his teammate injured, Red Horner skated to Shore and punched him in the jaw. According to Selke, Shore's head hit the ice, "splitting open. In an instant, he was circled by a pool of blood about three feet in diameter."

The crowd was in a frenzy, and the police restrained them as the Leafs retired to the dressing room. Smythe punched one particularly obnoxious fan, and was arrested and taken to jail. Both players were carried off the ice. After recovering, Shore entered the dressing room and told Bailey, "I hope you're not badly injured, I assure you it was not intentional." The dazed Leaf apparently replied, "That's all right, Eddie. It's all in the game." Bailey was then rushed to hospital where doctors feared for his life.

American and Canadian papers carried daily bulletins as Bailey fought for his life through two operations for his fractured skull. Toronto fans called Shore a criminal and an animal, and demanded that he be banned from hockey for life. A Toronto Star columnist reported, "Toronto fans are boiling over...most of them who telephone in breathe threats of vengeance...demand[ing] everything from expulsion from the league for Shore to prosecution for assault." Bailey's father bought a gun and took the train for Boston, where he intended to even the score. Other, less passionate observers, noted that "the mishap" was unintentional and that injuries were part of the game. The league suspended Shore for sixteen weeks and Horner for three weeks. Bailey recovered, but his career was over. To raise money for Bailey's expenses, the NHL arranged a benefit game to create a trust fund for Bailey. The game between the Leafs and a team of all-stars at Maple Leaf Gardens (14 February 1934) inaugurated the All-Star game tradition at mid-season.

Ironically, this incident made Shore a celebrity. The New Yorker reported that Shore's name now "attracts crowds that do not know the game." Although the Bruins were at the bottom of the league standings when Shore returned to action, the Bruins drew capacity crowds everywhere they played. The document "Hockey Violence" discusses the emphasis the American press, especially, paid to violence in hockey.

In Canada, radio broadcasts of the Leafs, Canadiens, and Maroons increased interest in the NHL and helped to forge a stronger sense of pan-Canadian identity—an identity in which hockey held a deeply-rooted place. Initially, the Leafs' games in Mutual Street Arena in Toronto were broadcast locally over radio station CFCA. Beginning on 1 January 1933, listeners could hear Foster Hewitt's play-by-play broadcasts of the Leafs' Saturday night games on a 20-station coast-to-coast network. This was one of the first Canadian radio programs to address a national audience. Soon, Hewitt's vivid descriptions attracted larger audiences than did comedians Jack Benny and Frank Parker. By 1934, more than one million fans listened to Hewitt's famous opening line, "Hello Canada and hockey fans in the United States and Newfoundland." That year an estimated seventy-two percent of all Canadian radio sets tuned into his broadcast of the Stanley Cup semi-finals. Following these playoffs, 90,000 listeners wrote to thank Hewitt. By the end of the decade, Hockey Night in Canada's audience increased to more than two million listeners, and Hewitt was receiving letters from hospitals, sanatoria, nursing homes, and from lighthouses in the Bay of Fundy on the east coast, to trawlers off the North Atlantic fishing banks, to Hudson's Bay trading posts.

Hockey Night in Canada broadened the Leafs' following and by the end of the decade, nearly twenty percent of crowds at Maple Leaf Gardens came from outside the city. In Quebec, Phil Lalonde broadcast the Canadiens' games in French, and Charlie Harwood and Elmer Ferguson did the play-by-play of the Montreal Maroons. Each rink had its own unique problems. In Madison Square Garden, broadcasters sat in an iron basket that was hooked to the first balcony and swayed with the crowd's movement.

The broadcast booth in Chicago was located in the organ loft at the end of the rink. In Detroit, the announcers were near the boards. In Montreal, the English and French announcers sat side by side surrounded by the spectators.

Thanks partly to the growth of artificial rinks, more people played hockey during the Depression years than ever before. There were juvenile, junior, midget, senior, rural, industrial, town, regional, university, and district leagues. The International Hockey League began in 1934 with teams in Canada and the US. Minor professional leagues formed and disbanded with regularity. The California Hockey League, The Tropical Hockey League, the Tri-State Hockey League, the Ontario Professional Hockey League, and the Western Canada Hockey League all enjoyed a brief existence. NCAA hockey, which was particularly popular in the north-east, with Harvard-Yale games attracting crowds of 14,000, expanded to the west coast at Loyola, UCLA, and USC. In 1936-37, Harvard, Yale, Princeton, Dartmouth, McGill, Queens, Montreal, and Toronto formed the International Intercollegiate Hockey League, which McGill dominated until the league discontinued play because of the war.

The Allan and Memorial Cup finals, which pitted amateur eastern and western teams against each other, attracted large crowds. Female leagues included teams of factory workers, department store clerks, telephone company operators, and secretaries. Women's teams from every region of Canada challenged for the Lady Bessborough Trophy that was donated in 1935 for the national championship. Outstanding teams included the Red Deer Amazons, the Edmonton Rustlers, and the Summerside (Prince Edward Island) Crystal Sisters. The Preston (now Cambridge, Ontario) Rivulettes won 348 of 350 games during the decade and captured the Lady Bessborough Trophy six times. The team began as a softball team, but turned to hockey in 1931 on a dare and often played before sellout crowds. The outbreak of World War II prevented the Rivulettes from accepting an offer to demonstrate their skills on a European tour. As the headline in the Toronto Star, "Sticks and Fists Fly Freely as Girl Hockeyists Battle," demonstrated, violence was also a part of women's hockey. At this time, the only female sportswriters in Canada were former athletes. In their weekly or daily columns, Bobbie Rosenfeld, Phyllis Griffiths, Alexandrine Gibb, and Myrtle Cook each wrote about the most popular women's sport in Canada—hockey.

Male players not good enough for the NHL often turned to Europe. Although an attempt to form a European hockey league in 1931-32 failed due to the Depression and a lack of good arenas, by the late 1930s Canadians were playing hockey in leagues in England, Scotland, Japan, and in most major European cities.

Community-based senior hockey thrived. In the Maritimes, the larger centers used imported players from Ontario to capture the Allan Cup between 1933 and 1935. When the Canadian Amateur Hockey Association (CAHA) insisted that the league obey the rules of payment and residency, the teams in Moncton and Saint John disbanded and the league folded. According to many Maritimers, the final "outrage" came when the central Canada-dominated CAHA replaced the Halifax team that qualified for the 1936 Olympics with the Port Arthur Bearcats from Ontario.

Canadian amateur rules stated that any player who had a NHL try-out was ineligible for amateur hockey for life, even if not chosen for the final roster. In addition, amateurs lost their status if they played against a professional team in any sport; received money from an employer, other than for traveling and hotel expenses, but not compensation for missed time; or taught or assisted in a sport for pay. With spectators demanding to see skilled players, and the players looking for steady jobs, the CAHA sought to convince the Amateur Athletic Union to liberalize its amateur code. When the AAU refused, the CAHA withdrew in 1936. Hockey players were henceforth permitted compensation for time lost from work while away playing hockey; to use their hockey ability to get a job; to play professionally in one sport and be an amateur in another; to tryout for the NHL and if unsuccessful to return to a CAHA team; to play exhibition games against professionals; and to be reinstated after three years away from professional hockey.

The new rules strengthened senior hockey. Players could remain in their communities, start a business, and still make money playing hockey. Bruce Kidd notes that by the late 1930s, some CAHA players were earning as much as the pros. Maclean's wrote in 1940 that "the CAHA is now, in effect, running a vast professional league, a league that is strongly entrenched, not only in the big cities, but in a score of relatively new fields like the colliery country of Cape Breton, the manufacturing empire at Oshawa, the rich mining belt around Sudbury and Kirkland Lake and farther west at Geraldton and Flin Flon, Saskatchewan wheat towns like Yorkton and Weyburn, bustling coal and oil strongholds in Alberta like Lethbridge, Drumheller, Olds and Turner Valley, and in British Columbia fruit or smelter centres like Nelson, Kimberley and Trail."

The NHL posed a problem for amateur hockey by taking the teams' best players and undercutting fan interest. Finally, in 1936, the CAHA agreed to play by NHL rules in exchange for a promise not to buy more than one player per team per year nor to sign junior-age players. By the end of the decade most NHL teams had agreements with amateur teams to send along their best players. The Maple Leafs dominated in Ontario, and the Canadiens had their pick of the best French-Canadian players. The New York Rangers had the most comprehensive farm system. Every summer, promising youngsters were invited to training camp in Winnipeg. The successful players began their pro career with the New York Rovers of the Eastern "Amateur" League where they learned the Rangers' style of play under experienced coaches. The next stop was the Philadelphia Ramblers in the International-American League before final promotion to the Rangers.

## HOW TO WATCH HOCKEY

*[The following document is an excellent example of Canadian instructional hockey articles written for the American market. Note the many comparisons with baseball and football and the emphasis on scientific play. Contrary to many American hockey commentaries, violence was not emphasized.*

*The author, Lionel Conacher, was Canada's most popular and successful athlete. He helped the Chicago Black Hawks and the Montreal Maroons win the Stanley Cup, was a star halfback in the Canadian Football League, led the professional lacrosse league in goals, played baseball in the International League, wrestled professionally for one year, was the Canadian light-heavyweight boxing champion, and shot golf in the 70s. In 1950, Canadian Press proclaimed Conacher Canada's athlete of the half century. Conacher wrote a daily column on football for the Toronto Telegram under the byline, "Lionel Conacher, Canada's Greatest Athlete." Lionel Conacher (with M.J. Carroll), "Hockey As You Should See It," Liberty (16 February 1935), 44-48.*]

The referee in his white sweater skates out to center ice and blows his whistle. The goalies settle themselves in front of the nets, defense men wheel into position, wings hold themselves poised, centers stand sideways with their sticks in the air, and an expectant hush falls upon the crowd. The referee drops the puck, the centers' sticks clash, and the whole vast auditorium breaks out in a roar. A big league hockey game has begun.

But how many of you spectators know what makes it different from any pick-up game of shinny? You know those men out there on the ice are among the fastest skaters the most expert stick handlers, and the hardest shots to be found playing hockey; that as hockey players they are almost mechanically perfect. But that is not the only difference. Though the rules are exactly the same, the game they are playing is a far different version from the amateur variety. What do you see when you look down from your seat in the rink at one of these professional games? You see twelve men, six to a team, each team trying to outscore the other in sixty minutes of play. That's what the great majority of onlookers see, and they would see exactly the same thing at a game between two junior school teams. But there is a small minority, the "hockey bugs," who see a great deal more, and they are the people who really know how to watch a hockey game.

Until about ten years ago ice hockey was played on the grand scale only in Canada, where it originated. Today five large American cities operate franchises in the two big hockey leagues, and there are at least a dozen more professional teams in the United States. The game is played by thousands of boys in the prep schools and high schools, many of the universities have made it a major sport, and amateur teams galore are sponsored by industrial and social organizations all over the country.

In Europe, too, it has caught on just as rapidly. At the world-famous resorts of St. Moritz and Davos it is played on natural ice. But in London, Birmingham, Glasgow, Paris, Berlin, Stockholm, Oslo, Milan, Vienna, Budapest, Prague, Zurich, Basle, and Berne are artificial rinks comparable to the best we have to offer in the way of Gardens, Forums, and Arenas.

Hockey always did have everything to make it popular with the sport-loving nations of the world. The rules are few and simple enough for every one to understand. The play is never obscured. The puck is always visible. There are few delays and action is almost incessant. And the speed is terrific. Then, too, it has in large chunks that aspect of savage man-to-man combat that draws the customers in such enormous numbers to prize fights and football games. Crowds are thrilled by the sock that can be heard a hundred yards from the ring, or the tackle with the impact that reaches the rim of the bowl. Hockey offers all this in a manner that is most picturesque because the action takes place at such high speed. The element of danger is always obvious, even conspicuous.

Did you know that hockey teams are a well organized as football or baseball teams? Did you suspect that every team in both the big hockey leagues uses a very definite system? The average football fan could tell you after the first five minutes of a game what systems the teams are using. But it would be a pretty safe bet that not more than one person out of every arena at a hockey game could do the same thing. What I aim to do is give you some idea of these systems, as well as a picture of the game as it appears to us on the ice. It may change your whole point of view.

Concentrate now on the goalie. He is as important to his team as a pitcher in baseball. If he lets down for a moment the game may be long gone. And just as the star pitchers are found on the championship ball clubs, the good goal tenders will be found on the winning hockey teams. Last season the late Chuck Gardiner was the stand-out goalie in hockey, and his team, the Chicago Black Hawks, won everything in sight. The year Andy Aikenhead was hot, the New York Rangers won all the ribbons. When Lorne Chabot was unbeatable so were the Toronto Maple Leafs.

A smart pitcher studies the hitters on the other clubs and gets to know their strength and their weaknesses. Clever net minders study opposing forwards in exactly the same manner. It is practically impossible to beat a professional goalie from outside the defense. If a long shot registers, you may take it for granted that it was an accident.

The real test comes when the defense has been pierced. The forward skates right in on top of the goalkeeper. A goal seems certain. Yet time after time the goalie makes what looks like a miraculous save. If the shot had beaten him nobody would have thought of blaming him. It happens too often, though, to be an accident. How, then, does he do it? What he has to do is make the forward aim the puck at a spot where he can take care of it. The best of them—men like Worters, Aikenhead, Cude, and Hainsworth—do it time after time with such ease and aplomb that the technique involved is seldom apparent. But this is how it's done:

Suppose New York Rangers are playing Detroit Red Wings. Bill Cook, wily Ranger forward, gets inside the Red Wing defense. He has only Roach to beat. Roach knows, say, that Cook's favorite shot is into the upper right-hand corner of the net. He leaves the upper righthand corner open just long enough to pull Cook's shot. But before the puck leaves Cook's stick, Roach has closed the gap. It looks as though Roach had all the luck in the world, and that's just what Cook thinks, too, if Roach has done the job properly.

But Roach's job is not over. He knows that about 25 per cent of all goals scored result from rebounds, and before the shot was blocked he was thinking of how he was going to clear it cleanly. If he blocked the shot with his body he was probably careful to angle the puck off to the side. The longer shots he may catch with his hands. Watch the goalies in the next game. See if they are consistently outguessing opposing marksmen and if they make a neat job of clearing.

The real battle in hockey is between forwards and defense men. The forwards are always striving to get in on the goal and the defense men are always fighting to keep them out. Here, too, it is a battle of wits. The soundest defense players in the game—men like King Clancy, Marty Burke, Eddie Shore, and Ching Johnson—are as good as they are because they keep winning the great majority of these battles with forward lines.

Last year I teamed with Roger Jenkins on the Chicago Black Hawks' defense. We knew the systems followed by the other eight teams in the league and, in a general way, how their forward lines would behave. When we were playing a team using a defensive system, like the New York Americans, we knew the pressure would be mostly on our own forward line and we could relieve it occasionally with rushes. But knowing these things isn't really enough. What a defense man should make it his business to find out is what makes an opposing forward dangerous, so that he can maneuver him into a position where he will be harmless. He should also study a forward's little tricks and mannerisms of style, so that the forward will not be able to maneuver him out of position.

Think of the many times you have seen perfect passes wasted and scoring opportunities lost because there was nobody there to take them and you have an idea of the threat Dit Clapper of Boston Bruins presents. With my brother Charlie of Toronto Maple Leafs, who has the most bullet-like shot in the league, we try to hustle his shot so that it won't be on the mark, or force him into a position where the angle is bad. Busher Jackson of the same team is a hard man to handle because he never slackens speed when he hits the defense. So is Nels Stewart of Boston Bruins, because he is big, rough, a good shot, and picks his spots to go; that is, he knows what he wants to do before he reaches the defense.

There are two distinct types of defense men. The first plays a strictly defensive game; the second rushes with the puck and has some offensive strength. Ching Johnson of Rangers and Red Horner of Maple Leafs play the man and let the puck go. They are wonderful body checkers and among the most dependable players in hockey. Notice and you will see that they stop almost as many shots as the goalie. Eddie Shore of Bruins, and King Clancy of Maple Leafs are standouts as rushing defense players. They play the puck first because their main idea is to get started on a rush. If they miss the puck they go for a man.

There is just one danger in this style of play: When a defense man begins a rush, a forward has to fall back in his position. Most forwards are not big enough or trained enough to play defense. The defense is weakened, therefore, anywhere from 50 to 100 per cent. If the rush is stopped and the counterrush reaches the shaky defense, the chances of its being successful are considerably increased. A defense man should never start on a rush unless he can see a clear break and a man with him. If there is nobody with him, he should shoot from a point well out, so that he can be sure of beating the counterrush back. Check on this point and see for yourself how many goals are scored because a defense man goes down on a highly spectacular rush that winds up nowhere and fails to get back into position in time to help stop the return rush.

Look now at the forwards. Their job primarily is to get goals, though this highly important function is apt to be forgotten in this day of systematized play. In the old days forwards roamed all over the ice and their worth was estimated by the number of goals they scored. Today a forward can be valuable to his team without being any great shakes as a goal getter....

Nowadays forwards function as a line and not as individuals. If you want to find out what system a team uses, you must study the movements of the forward line. We'll come to all that in a moment. But in the meantime let me tell you a story to illustrate what I mean by saying that forwards function as a line and not as individuals....

Now let's examine this more or less complicated business of systems. When you look at a team as it takes the ice you realize that, theoretically speaking, it is perfectly balanced in offensive and defensive strength. There are three defensive positions—goal, left defense, and right defense; and three offensive positions—center, left wing, and right wing. Yet all teams are classified as offensive or defensive teams, according to the systems they use.

You have all seen free-hitting baseball teams. The old Yankees were a perfect sample. Their idea was to go out and get runs, runs, and more runs. Offensive hockey teams are like that. They try to overwhelm opponents with the power of their attack. They don't care how many goals the other team scores as long as they score oftener. This makes for wide-open play, but it makes their own goal more or less vulnerable. A team using a defensive system believes in tightening up everywhere and depending upon breaks for its own opportunities to score. As forwards are frequently utilized in these defensive maneuvers, the team's potential scoring power is greatly reduced.

In the history of baseball many clubs have been dubbed the "hitless wonders." They win a great many games by a single run. They haven't much in the way of a scoring push, but they are still formidable because of their pitching and fielding strength. The present-day New York Giants are a fair example of this kind of ball team, and they have their equivalents in hockey in the strictly defensive teams.

That hard-hitting Yankee aggregation of four or five years ago was an old-fashioned ball team. It had so much dynamite in the batting order that it didn't have to bother much about scientific baseball. In the world of hockey Toronto Maple Leafs are something like that old Yankee machine. It has so much scoring punch that it invariably forgets all about defense when it goes into action. But, and this is the point, it's an old-style team playing old-fashioned hockey.... [Deleted history of Frank Neighbour, who Conacher termed the father of modern hockey for developing a defensive system of hockey with the Ottawa Senators.]

Let's take a look now at the various teams in the National Hockey League. You will be able to identify teams using a defensive system by watching their forward lines. Do they stress defense or attack? Look at them closely and you will soon see that, even though they don't all behave exactly alike, their main purpose is to keep the opposing forward line from breaking away. That's simple enough, and right away you spot Chicago Black Hawks, Detroit Red Wings, New York Americans, and Ottawa Senators (now the St. Louis Eagles) as the teams using a defensive system. The offensive teams are Toronto Maple Leafs, New York Rangers, Montreal Canadiens, Montreal Maroons, and Boston Bruins.

I'll take you right out with me on the ice and try to show you how the systems work. Chicago Black Hawks are playing Toronto Maple Leafs and Roger Jenkins and I are again on the Black Hawks' defense. We know we are in for a hard night, for the Leafs have more offensive power than any other team in the league. They have the best forward line in hockey in the famous "Kid Line," consisting of Joe Primeau at center, with Busher Jackson and my brother, Charlie Conacher, on the wings. Here comes the "Kid Line," three abreast, skating like mad, as usual gambling everything on a rush. We know if they don't score they will "die" immediately and loaf back to their positions, leaving it to their own defense to handle the counterrush while they recuperate. Primeau has the puck. He's the pivot man on most of their sorties, a smart playmaker if ever there was one.

"Watch the pass!" I warn Roger.

We spread ever so little, not enough to let Primeau through. Sure enough, there goes the pass to Charlie on the right. Roger skates into him, trying to force him into a corner. I turn and skate toward my own goal to intercept a pass in front of the net. Here's the pass and I take it. I shoot the puck up to Doc Romnes near the blue line. I don't dare leave my position: I know the Leafs will press again in a moment. King Clancy pokes the puck away from Romnes as our own forward line attacks, and starts away on a rush. One of the "Kid Line" goes right on down the ice and takes Clancy's place on the defense, the other two turn and come in with him. That's what it's going to be like all night; they just never let up.

Here's something you may never have noticed about offensive teams: one of their defense men is always a good puck carrier. He's part of the power house, just as on defensive teams forwards become part of the defense. There's Clancy on the Leafs; Eddie Shore with Bruins; Sylvio Mantha with Canadiens; Wentworth with Maroons, and Earl Seibert with Rangers.

New York Rangers is another team with a famous forward line in Frank Boucher and the Cook brothers.... Boston Bruins and Montreal Maroons are teams very similar in type. They feature big aggressive forward lines and play a hard-hitting style of hockey that wears down the opposition. If Roger says anything to me, or if I have any advice to give him on the ice when we meet these teams, it's probably, "Don't get killed!" For, while neither team can show a forward line to compare in scoring punch with the "Kid Line," or in cunning with the Ranger forwards, they are plenty tough because they are always plugging away, and few teams can equal them in endurance. Their plan seems to be to keep on the attack as much as possible and to slow up opponents with stiff body checks, hoping to outlast them.

When we play Canadiens we watch two men in particular—Joliat and Morenz. At least, we used to, though we won't in the future, as Morenz was traded last fall to Chicago. These two brilliant forwards have made the Flying Frenchmen a leading power in the hockey wars for more than a decade....

Now you can leave the ice and go back to your seat. You can see better from there how the defensive teams function.

The St. Louis Eagles, now operating the old Ottawa franchise, still play a defensive brand of hockey. When their forward line carries the puck in on the opposing goal, it is always with the idea that no matter what happens they must be able to get back to center ice in time to face the counterrush. Naturally, and this is true of all teams employing a defensive style, they are holding something in reserve on their rushes, which makes their attacks much easier to handle than the wild highpowered charges of an out-and-out offensive forward line.

The Detroit Red Wings have a slightly different idea. They believe in playing the man. They stick to their checks like leeches and when a goal is scored against them the first question they ask is, "Who scored it?" If it happens to be the opposing left-winger, then the blame falls squarely on their own right forward. That was his check and where was he when the hombre got loose? One thing about this system, it leaves no room for doubt, and a man's crime finds him out instantaneously.

New York Americans have effected a compromise between these two systems. Sometimes they cover their checks, at others they try to get back and check on center ice. Perhaps this is the real reason for their rather spotty performances in the past. One night they look like world beaters, and the next they look as if a church league team might knock them off.

Chicago Black Hawks offer a still different version of defensive hockey. They believe in stemming a rush before it gets fairly started. To this end their Golden Rule is, "Check in the other team's end of the rink!" It proved to be a mighty effective system last year, for Black Hawks flew off with the Stanley Cup. It is a program that calls for a stubborn forward line that can take the bumps and make its own breaks. Last year they had such a forward line, and in Doc Romnes, one of the most underrated center players in hockey. To my mind, there wasn't a better team player anywhere.

That is all there is to know to date on systems. And now it might occur to you to ask, "Which is the better system, offensive or defensive?" To which I can only say truthfully, I don't know. Last year Black Hawks, a team using a defensive system, won the world's championship. But the year before that Maple Leafs, the team using the widest-open system of offensive hockey, copped all the honors. So it would seem that it is not the system so much as the use you make of it....

One last word about the "master minds" of hockey. The best "master minding," contrary to general knowledge, is done off the ice. The job for a leader or a coach is to get the confidence of his men; after that he can get them believing in the system. Switching the players during a game is purely perfunctory. Tommy Gorman, last year with Black Hawks and now with Maroons, Lester Patrick of Rangers, Dick Irvin of Maple Leafs, and Art Ross of Bruins are among the most successful coaches.

Tommy Gorman is a hustler and makes you like him. Lester Patrick, the "Silver Fox of Hockey," has forgotten more hockey than most of us can hope to learn. Dick Irvin is patient, agreeable, and a born teacher. Art Ross was a great player and, though they say he is inclined to be iron-handed, players respect him.

There are long "skull sessions" and "chalk talks" on the trains and in hotels. Tactics change a little, depending on the teams. Hypothetical situations are constructed and the answers figured out in advance. Hockey is getting to be more and more a science. But it is all so much applecray unless there is harmony among the players and between the players and the management. That's the job for the leader, and that's why you only see half the game; the other half is played off the ice and they don't sell tickets.


### HOCKEY VIOLENCE

[*Canadian and American periodicals differed markedly in their coverage of hockey. Although they both glorified individual players, Canadian magazines rarely focused on the game's violent nature or attempted to teach the game's fundamentals. For example, Leslie Roberts, the sportswriter for Canadian Magazine, wrote about hockey's sportsmanship and the lasting friendships the players made. After witnessing a game between the Canadiens and the Black Hawks in 1931, in which neither team made an intentional foul, and the players hugged after the game, Roberts recalled, "as I reached the street there was in my throat that peculiar lumpiness that sometimes comes when one is eye-witness to human fineness at its best. I marched homeward uplifted...."*

*Dink Carroll wrote for American and Canadian magazines. In Maclean's he stated the game became too refined, and that hockey without body contact was like rugby without tackling. In the following American publication, Carroll seems to revel in hockey's violence. Dink Carroll, "The Hard Harrys of Hockey," The Saturday Evening Post (8 January 1938), 18-19, 62, 64.*]

The first time James J. Johnston, ex-matchmaker at Madison Square Garden, ever saw a major league hockey game was at the end of a long day's wrangling, in which he had tried unsuccessfully to match fighters who wanted a first mortgage on the building for their services. It was so late when he emerged from his office that a New York American-Toronto Maple leaf game was in progress, and he stopped a while to watch it.

The player who caught his eye at once was Red Horner, the husky on the Toronto defense, who is known as the league's "bad man." Horner was dishing out the body checks that night, and every time he would throw a flying block into an oncoming forward, Johnston's enthusiasm would move up another notch.

"That Horner's the only guy I've ever seen," he was quoted as saying afterward, "who fights for nothing and doesn't care who he meets or how fast they come."

Boxing Promoter Johnston did not have to know anything about hockey to realize that the game's biggest thrill is in the terrific body clash it provides. His enthusiasm for Horner was the instinctive appreciation of the promoter for the man who stirs the big crowds, and to the hockey mobs Horner personifies.

Every time the Toronto redhead appeared on the ice that night, there was a sudden tightening in the 15,000 fans who jammed the Garden from rail to roof; and the moment he hurled his muscular body in the path of a speeding attacker, Promoter Johnston could see [it] come suddenly and galvanically alive, the vibrant relationship between the crowd and what was happening down there on the ice.

**PAYING PREMIUMS FOR ROUGH STUFF**

This rough bodily contact at high speed is undoubtedly the feature of the game that gives hockey crowds their particular note of hysteria. They are much more excitable than baseball crowds, according to Bill Stewart, newly appointed manager of the Chicago Black Hawks, who is a big-league baseball umpire in the off season. Until this winter, Stewart was also a referee in the National Hockey League, so he is in a position to speak very feelingly as well as authoritatively about it all. He can give you a fearful half hour, telling you about the times he has had to hire police protection to escort him from the hockey forums and gardens around the country, lest he be torn apart by wild-eyed fans.

"It's the body clash," Stewart says philosophically. "It gets them all steamed up. Especially because they're so close to the players and to the action."

To bear out this contention, there was the specific case last year of Detroit fan whose activities were finally brought to the attention of Frank Calder, president of the National Hockey League. The fan, a wealthy businessman, was alleged to be offering premiums to Detroit players for knocking opponents off their skates. This philanthropist was said to pay off in dollars according to the numbers on the backs of visiting players. Thus, for crashing Johnny Gagnon, of the Canadiens, to the ice a Detroit player was supposed to have collected fourteen dollars....

There are other reasons, of course, besides this spectacular bodily contact, for the surprising hold hockey has secured on the American sport public in the past ten years. It is played at such blazing speed that it has been called "the fastest game in the world." It has the color and exhilaration of football and the beauty and rhythm of tennis. It calls for quick thinking and accurate puck handling—particularly in play making, in which it requires the smoothness and delicate precision of baseball. All are pleasing features, which hockey crowds find stimulating to a degree, but it's the body clash alone that stirs them profoundly.

**WHAT IT TAKES TO MAKE A MAJOR-LEAGUE PLAYER**

...Ask big-league managers or coaches what a youngster must have to be a major-league prospect, and they will all give you pretty much the same answer. "First of all," they will tell you, "he must be highly skilled in the fundamentals of hockey—skating, shooting and stick handling. On top of that he must have natural ability—that is, the facility of making the right plays instinctively, without having to stop and think. He must be aggressive and not afraid to muck in. He won't get anywhere unless he's ambitious, and he must be unselfish enough to submerge his own interests for the good of the team. And he must be rugged enough to take the bumps, or he won't last long. But when you see a boy who answers this description you're looking at a potential big-time star."

Now you know why youthful hockey players of major-league promise are almost as rare as snow in June, and why big-league hockey clubs have adopted baseball's scouting and farm systems in their efforts to discover and develop fresh talent. [Deleted long description of Babe Siebert's early career.]

From time to time you hear about, and sometimes think you see, certain flaws in the equipment of major-league players. This one won't pass the puck. Another fights it so hard he can't take a pass. And, in moments of exasperation, you would almost be willing to bet that certain defense players are such poor shots they couldn't hit the end of the rink once in half a dozen attempts. But you never hear, nor does it ever occur to you to think, that any of them fail because they lack courage or a capacity to stand up when the going gets heavy.

Major-league hockey is so strenuous that less than 50 per cent of the players who break in last as long as five years. Less than 20 per cent last ten years, and there have been only isolated instances of players remaining in the league through fifteen seasons. This explains the urgency of the demand and the frenziedness of the scramble for new and promising players. To have such a youngster in your camp and lose him is a major catastrophe in the life of a hockey manager. [Here follows a discussion of Smythe's mistake in selecting Hollett over Bucko McDonald.]

**THE TOUGHEST ICE JOB**

[H]ard-hitting defense men of the type of Bucko McDonald, Red Horner, Babe Siebert, Eddie Shore, Art Coulter, Ching Johnson and Marty Burke, to name only a few, receive plenty of punishment in return for the bumps they hand out. Their job is to play the man rather than the puck, which is one of the toughest assignments in hockey. What makes it so tough is that it requires exact timing to stop a hurtling attacker with a legitimate body check, and if their timing is faulty they are apt to wind up on the deck themselves.

The end of the 1933-34 season could not come too fast for Red Horner, as the Toronto "bad man" was beginning to unravel at the seams. He started the season off by colliding with Russ Blinco, Montreal Maroon forward, and losing three of his teeth. Shortly after that a high stick rapped him sharply in the mouth and one of his new teeth popped out on the ice; the other two went down his throat and nearly choked him. Then he had a bumping contest with big Ching Johnson, from which he emerged with a broken collarbone. Then, just before the play-offs, he broke his thumb and was forced to go through a long overtime struggle with Boston, one of the longest games on record, with his right arm in a cast and his hand incased except for the thumb, which was taped to his stick so that he could hold it.

Maybe this was why Horner went through two of those play-off games with Boston without a penalty. But it was such a rarity that Frank Patrick, who was managing Boston at the time, kidded him about it.

"How come?" Patrick wanted to know. "Two hard games and no penalties."

Horner's smile was just a little forced as he replied: "I guess I must be slipping."

**THE SHORE LEGEND**

Horner has set off more than his share of fireworks, but he has a long way to go yet to match the tempestuous career of Boston's Eddie Shore.

No player ever came up to the major league more marvelously equipped physically than the picturesque battler on the Boston defense, who has been a super-star with the Bruins since 1926. Born on a cattle ranch in far-off Saskatchewan. Shore was on a horse's back from the time he was big enough to hold the reins, which accounts for his bowlegs and his cowboy swagger.

The Shore legend had begun to take shape even before he came East. It was said of him that he was a recruit with such great natural gifts that he was bound to make major-league history, but that he had another side, that of a naive eccentric whose next move was totally unpredictable. There was one story that when he was with Edmonton in the Western Canada League he used to take his own sandwiches along when the team went away on a trip. This impression of naivete was heightened by still another story, ascribed to Goldie Smith, manager of the Melville Millionaires, a crack amateur team on the prairies, of which Shore was once it member.

To Smith, as manager of the Millionaires, fell the task of finding jobs for the players. When Smith first asked Shore if he had any preference in jobs, Shore is supposed to have hesitated only a moment before replying that he thought he'd like to be a barber. To Smith's raised eyebrows, Shore explained: "I've always sort of liked the way they smelled." Smith got him the job, but it wasn't long before he was back asking for another. Smith naturally wanted to know what was wrong with the job he had got him. "Nothing," said Shore, "only the customers complain that I cut them up too much."

Shore lived up to his legend. It has become axiomatic that to stop Boston you must first stop Shore, and from time to time other teams have adopted the harshest methods in an effort to subdue him. More than once Shore has blown sky-high under this kind of pressure, and countered with tactics of his own which were at once so bizarre and unexpected that he has been in the middle of some of the prettiest riots ever staged in major-league rinks....

But Shore, despite his temper, was for a long time the most valuable player in hockey. Other clubs have tried to purchase him from Boston, and when he was at his peak the bids ran as high as $100,000. Lester Patrick, New York Rangers' smart manager, wanted Shore from the moment be first laid eyes on him. [Deleted discussion of Joe Primeau's "delicate temperament," and the Conacher brothers.]

For their strenuous work on the ice, big-league hockey players are fairly well paid. Their schedule runs to forty-eight games, and the maximum salary allowed by the league for the regular season is $7000, though only the superstars rate this figure. Regular salaries may be augmented by bonuses for goals scored, by play-off cuts and by advertising contracts, though owners can prevent them from entering into advertising contracts if they do not approve of them.

The salary limit is fixed, of course, for the protection of owners, but there was something in Charlie Conacher's arguments a few seasons back when he was holding out for more money. "I'll admit $7000 is a lot of money," said Conacher, "but any athlete's playing career is limited. And another thing, a man's income isn't limited in an ordinary business. Nobody ever told John D. Rockefeller that he had to quit taking the money when his income reached a certain figure."

Nearly all the players and most of the fans were inclined to agree that the Leaf's big winger had something there, though it must be admitted that the players of today are a lot better off than their predecessors. Not a man on the old Toronto Arenas, who won the Stanley Cup in 1918, received as much as $1000 for his season's work.

But money isn't everything with them, and some of them have preferred another kind of happiness to the undoubted satisfaction there is to be had from making money. It may have been a weakness in him, but the late Howie Morenz, one of the greatest of them all, signed with the Canadiens for reasons of pure sentiment. Other clubs were after him at the time and were offering him more money. [The article concludes with a discussion of how much Howie Morenz liked playing in Montreal.]


### FOSTER HEWITT—VOICE OF CANADIAN HOCKEY

[*Foster Hewitt was called "the voice of hockey." While he also broadcast football, lacrosse, soccer, tennis, boxing, basketball, and baseball games, Hewitt became famous for his coverage of the Toronto Maple Leaf's Saturday night hockey games. Hewitt, Maple Leafs Gardens' "director of radio," sold advertising, and produced and broadcast Gardens' events. General Motors sponsored Hewitt's hockey broadcast until Imperial Oil assumed sponsorship in 1936. In the following document, Henry Roxborough outlines Hewitt's impact on hockey's popularity. H.H. Roxborough, "'He Shoots! He Scores!' A young Canadian announcer who made for himself a national reputation. His story demonstrates that it is a craft that requires judgement and nerve." Canadian Magazine (December 1933), 13, 35, 41.*]

Every Saturday night from November to April the voice of a young Canadian announcer will be heard over a coast-to-coast network that comprises twenty-four to twenty-eight stations, located in twenty Canadian cities. So numerous are the listeners-in on these professional hockey broadcasts that General Motors, the sponsor, has taken a census that leads to a conclusion that over a million and a half Canadians at one time or another tune in on Foster Hewitt's word picture of the drama of professional hockey.

This young Canadian announcer is one of the real pioneers in sports broadcasting. He was the first announcer in radio history to put the living story of rugby and hockey on the air, challenging the priority of those broadcast stalwarts, Ted Husing and Graham MacNamee.

If some autocratic "Who's Who" commanded us to pick out one of the best known names in Canada's everyday life, the choice would probably fall on this modest young sports announcer, the son of W.A. Hewitt, who was for many years a recognized sports authority, and secretary of the Ontario Hockey Association—the largest and most influential amateur hockey organization in Canada. Young Hewitt's likeness is seldom displayed, yet his name is better known to the multitude than many who are in the headlines as part of everyday routine.

There is reason for this, of course. Few aspirants for national fame have an equal chance with young Mr. Hewitt. He goes into a home only when invited, he enters the most comfortable room, speaks in a tone acceptable to his listeners, never theorizes, never argues, never refers to hard times, often brings cheering news, never overstays his welcome, and returns any other night with a brand new story every time.

Neither does his message appeal only to a special class. Instead, the sports broadcasts find appreciation from the professor and the untutored: the wealthy man in his club and the penniless chap in the hostel: the rugged workers in mines or forests and the bed-ridden patient in the hospital: the dwellers in crowded tenements and the lonely lighthouse keepers on rocky coasts. Regardless of age, location, race or religion, the gospel broadcast by Foster Hewitt is understood and accepted.

Here are just a couple of fragments from letters received by the sports announcer which reveal the age disparity of his listeners.

"We have here a small boys hockey team, all under ten years of age. They call themselves the Maple Leafs and each has taken a Toronto player's name. Some of them nearly cried when they heard of Andy Blair's accident."

And here is a portion of a contrasting letter.

"I just wanted to tell you how greatly my mother, who is over eighty years of age, enjoys your broadcasting of hockey games. She gets as excited as any young person and would not miss the games for anything."

Neither is this listening army localized. On wintry Saturday nights, out on the Pacific Coast—dinner is rushed, dishes hurriedly washed and folks sit down to listen to the hockey broadcast which begins at six o'clock Vancouver time: in rural Ontario at nine o'clock, chores are finished, papers read and thousands await the news from the Maple Leaf Gardens; down on the Atlantic Coast when the clock strikes ten the sport-lovers of Sydney, Halifax, Charlottetown, Moncton, Fredericton and St. John turn their dials to hear the voice of Foster Hewitt broadcasting the same story that reaches Vancouver "four hours earlier".

In Edmonton, last winter the fans were so interested in the hockey broadcasts that the starting of the local professional games was delayed until the radio game was concluded. In Winnipeg, on Saturday nights, the Manitoba sportsmen were viewing the junior games at the Amphitheater Rink, the public address system relayed the Hewitt descriptions of the professionals to the listening onlookers. From the mining camps of Northern Ontario and Quebec; from Fort Simpson and Chesterfield Inlet in the frozen north; from Grand Banks, Newfoundland, expressions of appreciation have been received.

Even beyond the Canadian borders, this native son has his admirers. Down in Pomona, California, thirty miles south of Los Angeles, in the heart of the blossoming orange groves, the hockey broadcasts were anticipated, enjoyed and recalled. And if those distant friends are not sufficiently remote, then be reminded that from Peru in South America, Dr. Ray Bulmer has sent a congratulatory letter to Foster Hewitt.

Through his years of broadcasting, Foster Hewitt has never dodged a tough assignment and some of them have at least involved patience and courage. Three of the toughest jobs were a hockey game, a rugby match and a marathon swimming race. [These have been deleted.]

He has missed only one scheduled broadcast in ten years (and he has "sent out" over 300 hockey games alone). The particular misfortune which spoiled a perfect record of "kept" engagements was the result of toeing-in while ski-ing.

Reliability, versatility and sincerity have undoubtedly contributed to Foster Hewitt's success and yet his simplicity and accuracy have been equally helpful. Unlike many broadcasters, he makes no attempt to paint the lily; he assumes no tricks of oratorical spell-binders; he never considers himself more important than the story he tells. Instead of such artificiality, he speaks the tongue of the common people and honestly endeavors to describe the play in simple language. Here is an illustrative sample of Foster's style of speech when applied to a hockey game—"Leafs are turning it on; Jackson dashes up the far boards, into the corner, passes puck back to Thoms, Thoms to Conacher, Conacher goes around Johnston; he shoots, Aitkenhead stops it, Thoms grabs the rebound, he shoots, HE SCORES". [Section on Hewitt's superstitions has been deleted.]

Although sports are so variable and many reporters will each write from a different viewpoint, Foster Hewitt has been so accurate in his description and so fair in his comment that whenever critics do shoot their inky arrows, the scribes are usually representatives from both teams. That is no mean tribute.


### INTERCOLLEGIATE HOCKEY

[*This article outlines the growth and popularity of men's intercollegiate hockey in North America. Given the games emphasis on violence, it is obvious why the author likes the game. Four action photographs accompanied the article, two of which depicted a fight. The caption read, "Tempers. Flying fists and sticks gave the spectators added thrills." The Canadian Intercollegiate Women's Ice Hockey League collapsed in 1933. "Intercollegiate Hockey. McGill, Minnesota Take Early Leads in Their Leagues," News-week (16 January 1939), 27-28.*]

In the late 1870s, ice hockey was just an informal game of shinny on skates; young men of Montreal, enjoying speed and mayhem, played it under impromptu rules, if any, during the long Canadian winter. But in 1880-81, McGill College took up ice hockey and made a real game of it; three years later, McGill and the newborn Victoria Rink Club of Montreal played the first challenge series, and in 1887 enthusiasts formed the Amateur Hockey Association of Canada, which laid down regulations. From then on, hockey's rapid spread through all Canada was marked by fierce intertown rivalries, fights and riots, showers of bottles and brickbats, and battered referees.

Last week, at Princeton, McGill University showed every sign of maintaining its 58-year supremacy in college hockey by giving the Tigers a 7-0 drubbing in the opening contest of the International Intercollegiate Hockey League race. Scoreless in the first period, the Canadians tallied twice in the second and whipped the puck past Pee-wee Johnson, Princeton goalie, five times in the hectic final period. In the best hockey tradition, a third-period fist fight flared into a brawl that embroiled eight players in a punching, wrestling melee. Referees MacDonnell and Fleet quelled the scrap and ordered one man from each team to the showers immediately—an unusually severe penalty.

Russ McConnell, rangy McGill wing, took high scoring honors with three goals against Princeton. Two nights later, in another league game, he tallied twice as the Canadians beat Yale, 5-2. Ranked as probably the best college player in the world, McConnell scored 44 goals in the ten league games last year and will get his chance in professional hockey next season if he wants it.

While McGill was conquering Yale, the rest of the league also had a busy evening. Princeton beat Montreal 6-3; Queens University (Kingston, Ont.) nosed out Dartmouth 1-0, and Toronto trounced Harvard 11-1.

Despite Toronto's strength, McGill, off to an early lead with two victories, is favored to recapture the title it has held for the two seasons of International League competition. Undefeated in 1937, the red-shirted sextet sustained but one loss last year—at the hands of Queens.

The International Intercollegiate League's geographical layout forms a record of big-time college hockey's spread—from Montreal south through New England and the Atlantic seaboard; from Montreal west through Kingston and Toronto. Continuation of this westerly line leads naturally to the northern universities of the big Ten. During the 1920s, hockey offered Michigan and Minnesota the opportunity of carrying their hot sports rivalry onto the ice. Wisconsin joined them to form a triangular Western Conference league but withdrew a few years ago and was replaced by Illinois.

Last week end, Minnesota beat the Illini 6-0 and 5-2 in the opening conference battles of the year, and this week end Michigan also is expected to get off to a good start against Illinois.

Last season's tie for supremacy between Michigan and Minnesota is a typical result of Western Conference competition. The great disparity in size between the Minneapolis and Ann Arbor rinks gives the home team a great advantage. Then, too, rivalry is so bitter that most referees are forced to favor the local sextet slightly. For these two reasons Michigan usually wins in Ann Arbor, and Minnesota sweeps the Minneapolis games, resulting in a Big Ten draw.

Feeling runs high in nearly all these Wolverine-Gopher contests; one notable fight in Ann Arbor some seven years ago found spectators, coaches, managers, and even the highly partisan gentlemen of the press trading fisticuffs. At the height of this shambles, two rival press services cooperated—the Associated Press representative reached out of the ice-side press box, grabbed a Minnesota player, and held him while the United Press slugged him. During these stirring moments the hockey expert of The Michigan Daily Campus newspaper, danced helplessly about on the second-row seats and shouted: "Kill him! Kill him!" As a result of this affray and others, Fielding H. (Hurry-Up) Yost, Michigan's director of athletics, issued an extremely unpopular edict: no fighting or no hockey. It was grudgingly observed.

Since Big Ten ice teams have stayed out of the east, there is slight basis for comparison of the Western Conference with the International League. However, Toronto beat Michigan 4-2 in 1937 and again 3-2 last year in a comparatively weak season for the Canadians. Thus the standard of play is evidently somewhat higher in the International loop than in the Midwestern one.

A host of less important colleges—hockeywise—in the two regions also turn out teams, many of them good enough in their better seasons to topple the Goliaths. Among these are Clarkson Tech (Potsdam, N.Y.), Boston University, Boston College, Williams, Army, Western Reserve (Cleveland), McMaster (Hamilton, Ont.), Michigan Tech (Houghton), Marquette, Western Ontario (London), Colby, Hamilton, Middlebury, Massachusetts State (Amherst), Colgate, and Cornell. Surprisingly enough, little Clarkson (430 students) averages best in the group and has whipped McGill on occasion.

## AMATEUR HOCKEY

*[Junior hockey flourished during the Depression. The Memorial Cup finals, which were played either in Winnipeg or in Toronto, attracted upwards of 10,000 spectators a game and were broadcast on radio by Foster Hewitt. Departing from NHL rules, there was no limit on how many skaters a team could be deprived of due to penalties, and referees carried handbells rather than whistles. The following article discusses the evolution of amateur hockey in Canada and the changing relationships among the CAHA, the NHL, and international hockey during the decade. Ralph Allen, "Enter The Paid Amateur: Here's the lowdown on the showdown about cash for amateur puck carriers," Maclean's (1 November 1940), 24, 28-30.]*

A Cynic could tell this story in three sentences.

1930— "What is an amateur?"

1935— "Why is an amateur?"

1940— "Where is an amateur?"

In loose but accurate form that tells almost everything there is to be told about the labored genesis of the Brave New World that will send 25,000 amateur hockey players to the post early next December under the most contradictory set of regulations in the history of organized sport.

Those three questions tell the story of a revolution. They tell how it has come about that an undetermined number of Canadian hockey players will play amateur hockey this winter under contracts guaranteeing their weekly salaries; how it has come about that the same athlete who once took the vow of financial chastity can now, legally and honorably, take as much cash money as the traffic will stand; and how this arresting transition has come about not only with the authority of the Canadian Amateur Hockey Association, but with that organization's fervent benediction.

Ten years ago, the Canadian Amateur Hockey Association looked pretty much the same way it looks today. It had something like $50,000 in the bank and something like 20,000 hockey players performing under its paternalistic auspices. Its two big spring roundups—the Allan Cup playdowns for the Dominion senior championship and the Memorial Cup playdowns for the junior equivalent—were the country's two greatest national athletic events, as they are today.

Ten years ago, the restless conscience of the C.A.H.A. was just beginning to give it an occasional twinge. Everybody within the councils of the association, and everybody outside those councils, knew that all the C.A.H.A.'s amateurs weren't all they should be.

But when everything was said and done, what was an amateur? Some coarse hecklers said an amateur was anyone who didn't get caught. This manager gave him his "cut" in a dark corner of the shower room. A few localities, still dazzled by tradition, favored the venerated practice whereby the manager slipped into the dressing room just before the end of the last period and stuffed a wad of bills into the athlete's right shoe, or, if the athlete happened to be left-handed, his left shoe.

Officially, these gaudy subterfuges were frowned upon. An amateur wasn't even supposed to use his hockey ability to get himself a job. When his team went away on trips, he wasn't supposed to be paid by the team in lieu of lost wages. He carried a small card from the Amateur Athletic Union certifying to his freedom from the taint of illicit gain. He paid twenty-five cents for this card, which was called an amateur

card. Without it he couldn't play hockey for any of the teams affiliated with the
C.A.H.A., and they included all the best amateur hockey teams in Canada.

He wasn't supposed to appear on the same rink with a professional hockey player,
either in practice or in competition. Before participating in the more advanced play-
off series, he was required to line up in the middle of the ice beside his team mates and
take the Olympic Oath, a striking ceremony during which the general principles of
amateurism were piously endorsed while the more ingenious endorsees hid their hands
inside their capacious hockey gloves and crossed their fingers.

**AMATEUR ENIGMA**

THAT was the rough perspective in which Homer Jones, who might have been the
average Canadian hockey player, saw amateur hockey in the early 1930's. Homer had
just finished his last year as a junior—out in Saskatoon perhaps, or in Calgary or
Regina or Winnipeg or Montreal. He'd had a pretty good year too. Two National
Hockey League clubs offered him modest contracts for one year, but Homer wasn't
sure he was good enough to play in the National Hockey League.

The rules wouldn't permit him to try out with a National Hockey League team
before making up his mind. The day Homer or any of his pals stepped on the ice at the
fall training camp of a professional team they became professionals—usually for life.

The owner of the rink in Homer's home town took him aside one night and gave
him five crisp new twenty-dollar bills "to keep him at home where people appreciate
a good hockey player." The manager of a senior team arranged for Homer to get a job
in a brokerage office at thirty dollars a week. It was up to Homer whether he worked
at the job or not. The manager also told Homer that at the end of the season the club's
profit would be divided equally among the players. The year before this had come to
$190 a man.

Averaging it out over the year, Homer would be getting pretty close to forty dollars a week for playing hockey. He knew this wasn't strictly according to the rules, but
everybody was doing it. Homer and the other players used to make wry little jokes
about their amateur cards.

It worked, after a fashion. True, nobody was fooled except a few of the more trust-
ing officers of the C.A.H.A. itself. To the layman, amateur hockey became a vast game
of cops and robbers, with the paunchy policemen of the C.A.H.A. striving mightily to
keep any part of the consumer dollar from reaching the athlete who first coaxed it out
of hiding, and the athlete in turn striving just as mightily to invent new ways and means
of getting his fair percentage of the dollar and still retain his amateur card.

If the better part of an entire hockey league moved from Manitoba to the
Maritimes—as one did in the early 1930's when "hockey jobs" and less subtle rewards
were abundant down there by the sounding sea—the C.A.H.A. ruled that any player
who moved from one province to another would have to remain out of the game altogether for a whole season. If hockey players left the country for fertile new fields in
England or the Eastern United States, the C.A.H.A. threatened them with mass suspension. The players gleefully took up the slogan: "The paths of glory lead but to the
gravy."

Even at its peak this running dog-fight between vested authority and the rank and
file did not involve more than ten or fifteen per cent of the C.A.H.A.'s 20,000-25,000
playing members. The others were too young to be worrying about making money out

of hockey—or else not talented enough. Still this upper crust minority represented the C.A.H.A.'s show window and main source of income.

Homer Jones began to ask himself "Why is an amateur?" What was the point of this gratuitous kicking-around he had been taking from his official superiors? Who was more entitled to a share in the amateur hockey profits than the players? The rink owners? The team managers? The C.A.H.A.? Nuts!

Homer went to England and played hockey there for two years at ten pounds a week. In the summertime he worked at a London dog track. Homer kept running into his old hockey pals in the most unlikely places—in Prague and Stockholm and in Paris and Warsaw. London was thick with them. Scores went to New York, Baltimore and Hershey to play in the new Eastern United States Hockey League at from forty to sixty dollars a week. More of them were finding their way to the major and minor professional leagues. The C.A.H.A. had finally legalized "tryouts," which meant that the professional managers could look over their amateur prospects in training with the pros before signing them to pro contracts.

It would not be entirely fair to the progressives of the C.A.H.A. to say that their hand was forced by the resulting decline in revenue. For more years than most of them care to think about, they had been tied to the apron strings of the Amateur Athletic Union. The A.A.U. was Canada's supreme sports body. Practically every important athletic organization in the country was a subsidiary of the A.A.U., a self-governing subsidiary to be sure, but still a subsidiary.

Without the A.A.U.'s blessing, no athlete could compete in the Olympic Games or any other important international event. Without the A.A.U.'s blessing, no hockey player could play baseball or lacrosse in the summer, and the A.A.U. insisted, in the face of growing unrest within the C.A.H.A., that the C.A.H.A. retain the A.A.U. definition of an amateur, as one who derives no financial advantage from playing a game, despite the fact that in actuality the rule was being hypocritically flouted right and left.

**GROPING REFORMERS**

IN SPITE of this formidable hazard, the C.A.H.A.'s growing bloc of reformers kept right on groping toward some compromise between the A.A.U.'s position and the realities of the situation.

The most determined gropers were a University of Alberta professor named Dr. George W. Hardy, and a Midland, Ontario, barrister named George S. Dudley. At first they saw nothing but tall timber. Canadian sports organizations tend to be dynastic. The delegates elect the officers, and the officers go back home and re-elect the delegates. Control becomes both static and despotic. Five years ago the men who were running the C.A.H.A. were pretty much the same men who ran the A.A.U. Asking the C.A.H.A. to rebel against the A.A.U. was like asking a banker to vote Social Credit.

That didn't stop Professor Hardy and Lawyer Dudley from asking. And at a momentous meeting in Halifax in the spring of 1935 the Canadian Amateur Hockey Association, to its own lasting astonishment and gratification, conceived its famous "four points." History, if it's not busy elsewhere, will remember these four points as the Magna Charta [sic] of Canadian sport.

They looked the A.A.U. squarely in the eye and said that henceforth an amateur ought to be permitted:

(1) To use his athletic ability to secure employment.

(2) To compete as an amateur in one sport even though he had competed professionally in others.

(3) To accept lost-time payment from his team when sport took him away from his source of income.

(4) To play with his amateur team against a professional team in specially authorized cases.

The A.A.U. side-stepped successfully for a year, and then at the 1936 annual meeting of the A.A.U. in Regina, Professor Hardy and Lawyer Dudley bobbed up with the four points again.

This time they had fire in all four eyes. Because the lost-time clause hadn't been sanctioned by the A.A.U., Canada's Olympic hockey team had been broken up under sensational and shoddy circumstances just a few months before. The team—a merger of Port Arthur and Halifax players—was on its way East after a barnstorming trip prior to sailing for Germany, when four Halifax players announced they couldn't afford to go away unless some provision was made for their families. Would the C.A.H.A. or the A.A.U., or some other public-spirited institution, kindly arrange to pay their salaries while they were in Europe?

The four Halifax players might far better have asked for the keys to the mint. Didn't they know broken-time was illegal? Didn't they know they were striking at the very foundation of amateur sport? Sure, the players grunted apologetically; but maybe the grocer back in Halifax wouldn't understand.

Amid resounding cries of "Shame!" the four were accordingly banished from the Canadian Olympic team, to be hastily replaced by Toronto and Montreal players whose sense of propriety was stronger and whose children—the cynics remarked—perhaps had smaller appetites.

So it was that Professor Hardy began his final plea to the Amateur Athletic Union by beaming genially around the convention room and then saying clearly and firmly: "Unless we are sunk in decrepitude and senatorial moribundity..."

Some of the boys were pretty slow to get it. By the time they got it, in fact, another year had passed, and the C.A.H.A. had formally withdrawn from the A.A.U. The A.A.U.'s troubles were over—because the other team sports joined the revolt and left the A.A.U. to its own devices.

The C.A.H.A.'s troubles were just beginning.

Pursuing the wraithlike amateur ideal had cost the C.A.H.A. large bales of legal tender. Running its play-offs on the principle that profits are made only by wicked profiteers, and forcing the good amateurs to flee to England or the United States to pick up a living, the organization had seen its bank roll dwindle to an alarming low of less than $7,000. Other complications set in. With the four points as a lever, hockey players began prying the box-office tills with scant regard for the simple rules of balanced economy. Bidding for their services was open and frantic, and with residence restrictions loosened, they developed the migratory habits of a flight of addled mallards.

Even taking these disadvantages into account, hockey flourished under the new arrangement. By last summer the Association was able to show a trust fund of $20,000, liquid assets of $45,000 and a receipt from the Dominion Government for $10,000—a voluntary gift toward the national war effort.

But the C.A.H.A. was still one step behind itself. Far-reaching though it was, the streamlined "four-point" definition of an amateur still evaded the truth. The best amateurs were still being paid off in hard coin—not with jobs or in lost-time allowances, but on straight salary, the same as the professionals of the National Hockey League were being paid. Indeed one National League owner, Ernest Savard of the Montreal Canadiens, went so far as to complain that some of the amateurs around Montreal were being paid more liberally than the professionals. Mr. Savard was not the only National Hockey League figure who professed to contemplate the paradox with acute discomfort and suspicion.

## AMATEURS ON STRIKE

FURTHER and more monstrous embarrassment befell the C.A.H.A. late last winter when a Quebec Senior Hockey League team, the Valleyfield Braves, went on strike during the Allan Cup play-offs. The essence of the matter appears to have been that certain players wanted their club to guarantee that the weekly salaries they had been receiving through the regular season would be continued as long as the team remained in the play-offs. In debating the matter for the benefit of an amused public, neither the officials nor the players had the delicacy to stick to lavender-and-old-lace terms like "expense allowances" and "broken-time remuneration." They spoke bluntly of wages. The episode surprised no one, but it brought the family skeleton right out in the front parlor for one final airing.

Professor Hardy and Lawyer Dudley were right there to greet it. Professor Hardy was completing two epochal years as the president of the C.A.H.A. and surrendering the chair to Lawyer Dudley. So it is that the last of the powerful clique of sincere, able, but oh-so-visionary disciples of Victorian amateurism has either retreated or capitulated. The strangest sentence in the administrative annals of Canadian sport got by the convention with scarcely a ripple of dissent.

"An amateur hockey player," the sentence read, "is one who has not engaged in, or is not engaged in, organized professional hockey."

In short, that definition might even include your old Aunt Minnie; but what it is intended to mean is, that all hockey players are amateur hockey players—saving only the 300-odd active players of the National, International-American and Pacific Coast Hockey Leagues and the American Association, plus retired players of those and other professional leagues since defunct. In its apostolic fervor, the C.A.H.A. followed up by authorizing its member clubs to sign their players to legally binding contracts. There is no limit to the salaries these contracts may provide. From the tentative evidence now available, there is reason to believe that every Senior club, as well as some of the better Junior and Intermediate clubs, will take advantage of this new invitation to mutual protection for club and player.

All right then, we're up to the fiscal year of 1940-41 and "Where is amateur?"

Right there where he's always been—in the lower age and proficiency classifications of the C.A.H.A. He's at least 20,000 strong and he's still playing hockey because it's fun. But what has this kind of an amateur got to do with the kind of amateur "who is not engaged in organized professional hockey?" Why does the C.A.H.A. have to mix its amateur amateurs with non-amateur amateurs? Why doesn't it tie the non-amateur amateurs up in a red ribbon and send them over to the pros with its compliments?

That's easy too. You can't keep 20,000 kids playing hockey, can't help them pay for their referees, and help keep up the rinks that sell them cheap ice, and sponsor the play-offs that make kid hockey an adventure—you can't do these things without revenue. And it is a fact, happy, or unhappy, as you will, that the non-amateur amateurs are the babies that pay the shot. Cuts or no cuts, gravy or no gravy, they're the babies that put that $65,000 in the bank.

But why call them amateurs? Why not, as a simple concession to sanity, drop that first "A" in C.A.H.A. and call it Canadian Hockey Association?

That one's a little tougher. As an individual, Mr. Dudley himself wanted to drop the first or silent "A" last spring. But as president he puts up a businesslike defense of the majority opinion.

"The word 'amateur' has different meanings according to different uses which may be made of it," President Dudley says, with or without his black robe on. "And the C.A.H.A. holds that it can give any definition to this word which suits its purpose. No one nor no organization has a copyright on it. The use of the word has a very definite value in distinguishing the Association from the professional organizations such as the N.H.L. and its minor affiliates. It must be further recognized that the association has registered with it over 25,000 hockey players in all parts of Canada, and that while some may feel that those few players who are accepting remuneration in one form or another should not be classified as amateurs, after all ninety per cent or more of the players competing under the authority of the Association are as much amateurs as those engaged in any other sport in Canada. This, I believe was the determining factor in the decision to retain the use of this word in the name of the Association."

**N.H.L. REACTION**

IT IS an open secret that the practical operators of the N.H.L. are not completely sold on the Hardy-Dudley brand of realism. The C.A.H.A. is now, in effect, running a vast rival professional league—a league that is strongly entrenched, not only in the big cities, but in a score of relatively new fields like the colliery country of Cape Breton, the manufacturing empire at Oshawa, the rich mining belt around Sudbury and Kirkland Lake and farther west at Geraldton and Flin Flon, Saskatchewan wheat towns like Yorkton and Weyburn, bustling coal and oil strongholds in Alberta like Lethbridge, Drumheller, Olds and Turner Valley, and British Columbia fruit or smelter centres like Nelson, Kimberley and Trail.

The first reaction around the N.H.L. was a reaction of studied horror. It was unfair competition, that's what it was. More than one N.H.L. governor hinted darkly that unless the whole sinful project were abandoned, the N.H.L. might call off its various agreements and start a war.

But there won't be a war—not yet anyway. The N.H.L. has the power to work havoc inside the C.A.H.A. by making "player raids" just before or during the late-winter play-offs. But the C.A.H.A. also has the power of sabotaging one of the N.H.L.'s most profitable institutions by withdrawing its sanction of the amateur training schools which most professional clubs now conduct annually as the climax to the previous season's ivory hunting. In brief, if hostilities are ever instituted, the best either organization can hope for is the worst of it.

In the meantime, all is sweetness and light, or a reasonably accurate facsimile thereof. Indeed, at a September meeting of the N.H.L. governors in New York, Dr. Hardy presented such a convincing picture of the C.A.H.A.'s good intentions and/or potential fighting strength that when he departed from the conference room he found his path strewn knee-deep in gold certificates.

These gold certificates are not, of course, for Dr. Hardy's personal use. They are earmarked for the hundreds of struggling little amateur clubs that have been footing the bills for hundreds of struggling little amateur players so that the supply of prosperous big professional players need never dry up at the source.

From now on these little amateur clubs will be reimbursed from N.H.L. funds every time one of their players, past or present, signs an N.H.L. contract. For each player who signs a contract, the N.H.L. will pay $250, plus an additional $250 when the player actually gets into action under the big top. These gratuities will be administered and disbursed on a pro-rata basis by the International Hockey Association, a protective union of the Canadian, British and United States amateur hockey associations of which Dr. Hardy is the charter president.

**WHAT ABOUT THE OLYMPICS?**

BESIDES discharging this beneficent function, the International Hockey Association will safeguard the C.A.H.A.'s revised standards of amateurism against any major assault from outside the boundaries of Canada. The I.H.A. embraces the only three important hockey countries there are, and by a poetic coincidence the I.H.A. ideology is the C.A.H.A. ideology down to the last subsection.

For brutally obvious reasons, world hockey questions are purely academic questions now, but it wasn't always that way. One of the strongest arguments the A.A.U. diehards used, year in and out, against the reformers was that if Canada loosened the amateur barriers the country would risk disqualification from Olympic competition. With the I.H.A. lending support off-stage, the C.A.H.A. today dismisses such pedantic pother in two short sentences.

"If the Olympics are revived after the war, Canada will want to send a team of course," President Dudley says. "But if our rules prove unacceptable to the Olympic officials, I guess. we'll stay at home."

That fervent "Aye!" you just heard came from the lips of a mellowed Homer Jones. Homer is doing all right. He's still an amateur, but he doesn't carry an amateur card any longer. He has just signed a contract to play for one of the best senior teams in the country. He's working on the office staff at one of the big mines for a fairly respectable salary. In addition his contract guarantees him $20 a week for playing hockey, plus a bonus of $200 if his team reaches the Allan Cup final.

Homer isn't rich yet, but he's fairly happy. About once a week he ferrets through his bureau drawer and takes a look at the contract. Looking at it, he remembers all the times he had to sneak into the locker room to collect his "cut;" all the times he signed his name to a lie when he signed his amateur card; all the times he spoke a lie when he spoke the Olympic oath. Homer never felt very guilty about any of these little hypocrisies, because after all he hadn't written the rules; he only played under them, which of necessity meant playing with them.

But he does somehow feel a little better under the new system. "Gosh," he chuckles now and then, "after all these years they've made an honest woman of me.

Chapter 13

## INDOOR SPORTS—BOWLING AND BILLIARDS

Bowling, claimed many popular magazines, was America's national indoor game. Initially, the Depression had an adverse impact on bowling, as the number of teams registered with the American Bowling Congress (ABC) fell from 43,000 in 1930 to 41,000 five years later, and the estimated number of bowlers declined from six to five million. Bowling revived. The ABC, bowling equipment manufacturers, and newspapers such as the Chicago Evening American organized charity bowling tournaments in the larger cities, complete with extensive publicity. These tournaments not only lured thousands of working-class players to the sport but also attracted Hollywood stars and such wealthy entrepreneurs as Charles Schwab and Julius Fleischmann. John D. Rockefeller Jr. had bowling alleys installed at his estate in Pocantico Hills. Bowling was an inexpensive sport—a game cost about 20 cents—and was a good way to socialize and relieve tensions. As a result, by mid-decade, the sport began to revive, and by 1940, the number of bowlers increased to approximately 15 million and there were about 200,000 alleys.

Bowling was a mass participation sport that appealed to all ages, genders, and social classes. Its most important clientele were office and factory workers who played once or twice a week in competitive leagues. A 1940 study found that manual laborers preferred indoor games to outdoor sports. The competition, the fraternization, and the thrill of blasting pins after a long regimented day of work attracted people of all physical abilities.

The new, well-lit bowling establishments, with their neatly-polished lanes, sound proofing, and air conditioning, appealed to housewives and working women alike. Bowling promoters emphasized the game's weight-losing capacities as well as its popularity among Hollywood stars. Membership in the Woman's International Bowling Congress (WIBC) rose steadily during the Depression from 8,985 in 1930 to 81,776 in 1940. The number of cities affiliated with the WIBC increased over the same period from 42 to 382 (in 1938, Vancouver women organized the first Canadian WIBC affiliate), and sanctioned leagues grew from 110 to 2,399. Only the total prize money for the annual tournament reflected the hard times. From approximately $11,000 in 1930, prize money declined to $6,000 three years later, before rebounding to $17,700 at the end of the decade. The publication of The Woman Bowler (Chicago) by John Hemmer and Earle Ward in 1936 indicated the rapid growth of women's bowling, which some experts estimated to be close to one million. Although the previous year, the ABC Bulletin began a "column" on women's bowling, written by a WIBC member, the first edition of The Woman Bowler claimed that as the Bulletin and Bowlers Journal "devote most of their space to the activities of the masculine bowler," the new publication was essential.

William Whyte's study of young Italians in south Boston revealed that bowling alleys were popular winter hangouts for young men on Saturday nights. Bowling provided a public place for young men and women to socialize in a non-threatening environment. Blacks did not share in the bowling boom. Because of the high cost of building facilities, there were few alleys in black neighborhoods, and even twenty cents a line was a lot of money for the unemployed. Just as important, "Caucasian only" clauses in the constitutions of the ABC and the Women's International Bowling Congress excluded blacks from all major competitions. As a result, in August 1939, representatives from Detroit, Chicago, Cleveland, Cincinnati, Columbus, Toledo, Indianapolis, and Racine formed the National Negro Bowling Association to "encourage Negroes to develop their skills in the game of Ten Pins." Later that year the Associaton held its first tournament in Cleveland. The following year women also competed.

Employers encouraged bowling leagues as a way of promoting better industrial relations. More than 150 American companies built bowling alleys on their premises and countless others supported leagues on public lanes. A nationwide poll of 639 companies in 1940 revealed that of the 245 corporations that supported recreational programs, eighty-seven percent sponsored bowling. Enlightened self-interest was at the root of these programs. Earlier studies showed that such games led to improved physical alertness, the assimilation of heterogeneous groups of employees, friendlier relationships between workers and supervisors, and better morale. Dominion Stores, which had the most popular bowling leagues in Canada, reported that bowling "has been promoting a great deal of fellowship among the entire personnel of the whole organization." Canadian National Railway sponsored men's and women's bowling leagues in every major rail center in Canada. Each department entered a team in the league, which concluded with a banquet. The Winnipeg banquet in 1934 closed with a film that documented the building of locomotives in the company's shops.

Unlike most sports, the prize money at bowling tournaments came from the players' entry fees—about $5—rather than from gate receipts. The 1940 ABC national tournament attracted 30,000 entrants from 731 cities, and while the most a bowler could win was just more than $1,000, more than 8,000 individuals won some sort of prize. The best bowlers included veterans Joe Falcaro and Andy Varipapa, and younger experts such as Joe Norris, Ned Day, and Harry Marino.

Chicago led the way with 500,000 bowlers in more than 900 leagues. Next in importance were Detroit, Milwaukee, and Cleveland. As "Ten Million Keglers Can't Be Wrong" explains, there were several variations of the normal ten-pin game. Where people lived generally determined whether they played duck, candle, rubber-necks, or five-pin bowling. Boston was the home of candlepins. Rubber-banded duckpins, which produced higher scores, were popular in western Maryland and Pennsylvania. Duckpins, which originated in Baltimore, spread through the Atlantic seaboard to Miami in the 1930s. Females, in particular, liked the smaller, lighter balls. With a national organization behind it beginning in 1927, and with the help of bowling equipment manufacturers, lane conditions, balls, and scoring were standardized. By 1937, there were approximately 125,000 league duckpin bowlers.

Although five-pin bowling did not publish its first official rule book until 1928, by the mid-1930s about seventy-five percent of Canadian bowlers preferred the five-pin game. Toronto and Ottawa were the hub of five-pin bowling. Montreal and Winnipeg were about equally divided between five and tenpin. Tenpin held a slight majority in Edmonton and Calgary, and dominated in Vancouver. The Maritimes tended to follow

New England's preference for candlepin. In terms of newspaper coverage in Canada, bowling ranked twelfth among all sports and was most popular in Winnipeg, where it ranked eighth in the first half of the decade.

To counteract the negative impact of the Depression, many alleys organized dances and other such events to attract more customers. Five-pin bowlers used a six-inch ball, similar to duckpins, threw a maximum of three balls per frame, and had to knock over the far left-hand pin to record a score. Counting from left to right, the pins were worth 4-2-1-3-5. By mid-decade, the western provinces decided to make the scoring easier for the average bowler. They changed the pin count to 1-4-5-3-2 and made the headpin the scoring pin. Women formed a separate division within the Canadian Bowling Association in 1930, but competed against the men until they established a separate women's tournament in 1935.

## LAWN BOWLING

Lawn bowling, a different but related sport, continued to lag far behind tenpin bowling in popularity. Lawn bowling, which was generally viewed as a sport for people more than 50 years old, benefited from the recreation program of the WPA which equipped many parks with electric lights for evening play. Even so, the American lawn bowling championships in 1937 attracted only 160 participants from twelve clubs, and by the end of the decade the American Lawn Bowling Association had only 70 clubs and approximately 15,000 members.

## BILLIARDS

It is more difficult to estimate how many people played billiards. Some journalists guessed that as many as 10 million Americans played the game. In large urban cities, poolrooms provided young people with a place to socialize. The game's association with liquor, smoking, and gambling ensured that poolrooms remained mostly the preserve of working-class males. The repeal of Prohibition in 1933 had an enormous impact on the game. When taverns reopened, they often contained several billiards tables, which cut into the poolrooms' clientele and profits. For the first time, poolroom attendance declined. Pool and three-cushion billiards shared the spotlight, as balkline declined in popularity due to the boring long runs the top players could produce.

The major manufacturer of billiards tables, Brunswick-Balke-Collender, tightly controlled all aspects of the game. It printed and distributed tips on the art of cue work, changed the name "pool" to "pocket billiards," "pool hall" into "billiard parlor" and, in an attempt to tap the home market, sent out thousands of letters on the benefits of billiards for young married couples between the ages of 21 and 25. To attract larger audiences, the 1935 national championship was held in a large amphitheater and a public address system kept the audience informed of the score and the shot selections. When experiments showed that claret purple surfaces were easier on the eyes than the traditional green, it was adopted for tournament play in 1935. Two years earlier, an intercollegiate billiards tournament was conducted by telegraph. Each team had to execute a series of intricate shots worth a set amount of points. The University of Michigan won the first tournament.

### TEN MILLION KEGLERS CAN'T BE WRONG

[*The following article in Esquire was plagiarized by several authors writing in different popular magazines. Kearney outlines the growth of "our national indoor game" and outlines the reasons for its popularity among all sectors of society. He also discusses the economics of bowling from the proprietor's and the corporation's viewpoints. Bowling was a participant sport that provided exercise, an opportunity to socialize, and a chance to unwind after work. Paul W. Kearney, "Ten Million Keglers Can't Be Wrong. Bowling Is an Outlet for the Inhibited, Who Long to Blow Everything to Helter-Skelter," Esquire (February 1937), 91, 137, 138, 140, 143-144.*]

In these days of high-pressure ballyhoo we have come to measure the importance of athletic pastimes in terms of "the gate." Fifty to seventy thousand spectators at a big baseball or football game is common; championship fights, horse races, varsity crews draw equal crowds and even the polite handicappers of the tennis world have grown accustomed to stadia.

That's why it is surprising to realize that one of the most extensively played games in the country is a sport with little ballyhoo, few spectators, no champion, no professionals in the accepted sense: a sport whose big event of the season collects seven times as much money in contestants' entry fees as it does from spectators' admissions!

That unique pastime is bowling: our national indoor game. It earns the title not only because there are from eight to ten million regular bowlers in the country but from the fact that it is one of our greatest participating sports. The bowling "world's series," for example, is the annual meeting of the American Bowling Congress. Last year this was held in Indianapolis with 15,000 contestants from 387 cities and towns—all paying their own railroad fares, their own hotel bills, their own entrance fees.

When you stop to figure that there aren't half that many participants in the Olympic Games, you begin to realize what a sport this is!

Twenty-five years ago, perhaps, it smelled somewhat too strongly of cigar smoke and beer to he listed among the politer pastimes. But today the lusty art of "kegling" has come into its own. In our more exclusive suburbs, even in the laggard East, you will find chauffeur-driven, 12-cylinder cars waiting for their ladies outside the recreation parlors—you will find over-crowded alleys in girls' schools like Vassar—in hundreds of churches throughout the land from the ultra-modern Riverside Baptist down to some of the smallest—in such top-flight country clubs as Chevy Chase, Wykagyl, L'Hirondele, the Congressional, Sherwood Forest, the Merion Cricket Club, etc. The fact that alleys aren't in the swank clubs just for display is emphasized by the report that Wykagyl paid for the complete installation and subsequent enlargements in one season while the Pelham Country Club wook in $1200 during the first month's operation. That means 4,800 rolled at a quarter a game!

In Hollywood the picture people have become so enthusiastic that alley have been installed on the lots by most of the larger producers while numerous have had private "courts" built in their homes. In short, the whole social complexion of the game has changed in the widespread revival of the past five years, bringing to the recreation parlors a new element bearing the approved stamp of the elite.

That does not alter the basic fact, however, that for 200 years American Ten Pins has been a swell game with an appeal for all ages, an stations, all degrees of general athletic skill. Side by side with thousands of unknown John Doe's and Joe Zilch's you'll find names like Percy and John D. Rockefeller, Jr., E.H. Harriman, Governor McNutt, of Indiana, W.H. Knudson, Arthur Brisbane, and scores of other prominent men who have bowled more or less regularly for years.

But the scope of the game goes far beyond extremes in bank balances or social ratings. You will find in the ranks of regular bowlers such star athletes as Jack Elder, former Notre Dame halfback, Lefty Grove and Jimmy Dykes, of baseball fame. Yet for every bowler of outstanding athletic prowess you will find a hundred others whose physical equipment runs the gamut from spindly-legged high school freshmen to soft-muscled old ladies in the sixties and seventies. Indeed, in Buffalo they boast of a woman who bowls regularly once a week although she'll never see her 80th birthday again!

You get the real tip-off on the popularity of the game from these very contrasts in social and physical ratings. Bowling is inexpensive, averaging from 20c to 25c a game, hence anybody can participate; it is likewise a game in which brawn is unimportant, so the field is wide open for any normal individual who can stand up. Nothing could demonstrate that more dramatically than a match staged last January in which five boys from the New York Guild for the Jewish Blind competed against a team of sighted lads and lost only by the close margin of 16 pins; 654 to 670. The high man for the blind rolled a neat 143.

The only physical assistance accorded the sightless was a special hand rail on the left side of the alley which each bowler used as a guide on the approach. Any pins left remaining after the first ball were called out by number by the pin boy, and the bowler would direct his ball accordingly.... [The section that discusses that strength was not important has been deleted.]

This is obviously the explanation of the universal interest women are now taking in the game, even in the East. The sectional distinction is in order because the Middle West is the center of the bowling world in both masculine and feminine ranks. The last New York State Women's Tournament, for instance, had 90 teams entered for the entire Empire State, whereas a recent women's tournament in St. Louis saw 130 teams competing from that single city!

New York women are catching on, though, as indicated by an attendance of nearly 5,000 at a free course of instruction offered by a local newspaper. Yet in comparison Chicago, capital of the bowling world, had no less than 7,200 competitors in its eighth annual feminine tournament in 1935—and they were experienced performers, not beginners taking lessons. So experienced, indeed, that one of their number—the 14-year old Mary Jane Hubert (who five years ago was completely paralysed!) shot a 209 in her opening game! As a matter of fact, the Telephone Company in Chicago has more women bowlers than men: an unusual situation even for a concern with such an extensive feminine payroll.

Close behind Chicago, which has the largest bowling population and the greatest number of alleys of any city, come Detroit, Milwaukee and Cleveland. And although the pastime is of more recent vogue in the Far West, it has spread so speedily there that in many cities it has become a year-round game. In Texas and southern California especially the air conditioning of recreation halls has brought even the golfers inside on the alleys when the blistering sun is too punishing on the links!

New York, where the 1937 ABC Tourney will he held next April in the 212th Regiment Armory, is an active bowling center with its larger establishments open twenty-four hours a day in true Manhattan style. Not only do the stray nighthawks patronize the all night places, but one established bowling league starts its weekly matches at midnight and rolls far into the early morning hours.

Conservative estimates indicate that there are at least 200,000 regular weekly bowlers on Gotham's 2,300 alleys. And while this is impressive in total, it is not nearly as great a **pro rata** bowling population as exists in scores of Western cities. Indeed, the largest bowling establishment in the East is not in New York, as one might expect, but in Philadelphia where 105 alleys are housed under one roof. Even the distinction of operating the largest one-floor plant goes to Washington, D.C., with an outfit of 50 alleys side by side. Pekin, Illinois, is probably the world's greatest bowling town. With a population of 16,000, it boasts of 120 men's teams and 50 women's teams, or a team for every 95 inhabitants.

Expressive as such figures may be, the most illuminating evidence of Mid-western supremacy in bowling is afforded by the famous Brothers' Tournament which has been conducted annually by Fred Tuerk, Sports Editor of the *Peoria Star*, for the past fourteen years. With only blood brothers eligible—and with a population of only 105,000 on which to draw—this Illinois city last year had no less than 1,700 entries in this meet!

So far, to be sure, we have considered only the big pin game which is usually implied by the term "bowling." On the same alleys, however, there are a dozen small pin games which have sprung from the parent sport: duck pins (Babe Ruth's pet game), candle pins and variations on these known as "cocked hat," "quintet," "the battle game," "nine up and nine down," "four back," etc. These games receive nothing but scorn from regular bowlers. Yet it is interesting to note that Boston, our oldest bowling city which once boasted of more alleys than existed in all the rest of the country, has long since deteriorated into a candle pin town to the utter disgust of the 16-pound ballers. Candle pins are tall, skinny pins for which a 6-inch ball is used: duck pins-a small, squatty variety of the regulation pin—also calls for a small ball without finger holes and is very popular down East outside of Boston and along the Atlantic seaboard from Baltimore south.

The whole Eastern territory, however, is subject to much more variation in taste than prevails to the West. Brockton, Massachusetts, for example, in the heart of the candle and duck pin area, is one of the most rabid Ten Pin cities in the country. And Pittsburgh, flanked on all sides by the regulation game, is quite goofy about rubber-band duck pins.

But out West where men and babies teeth on 15-inch pins, the small ball games are tolerated and bowling means only one thing: American Ten Pins. This is our development of the game of nine pins which Elmer H. Baumgarten had traced back prior to 1200 A.D.: a logical offspring of the older game of "Lawne Bowles" and originally played on a 12-inch alley outdoors but eventually brought inside because keglers would rather play than issue rain checks. [Deleted early history of bowling]

Modern alley, expertly fashioned of edge-grained, virgin white rock maple and Georgia pine, cost around $3,000 a pair. After the finest quality of wood is cut, it takes two years to properly treat the pine and three years before the maple is in condition for laying. And with forty-one one-inch boards for each alley, it takes two experienced men about twenty days to put down a bed.

Pins, too, are considerably more than just bottle-shaped chunks of timber. Good pins, guaranteed to last 1,000 games, are made of the finest grade of maple. With only a half-ounce tolerance allowed among the three-pound pins in any set, unity in quite important. And with a high resistance to wear equally essential, it is obvious that much skill goes into the manufacture of this equipment. The old adage says that "it takes 50 years to make a bowling pin" since only the butt cut can he used. If the stock is not straight grained, it won't last two games—and even if it meets all the rigid require-ments of quality, the wood has to be "cured" for at least eighteen months before it can be turned. In view of all that, $10.50 seems cheap enough for a set of pins that will hold together after being knocked down 20,000 times.

Balls, once wooden but now almost exclusively manufactured of composition materials, cost in the neighborhood of $15 to $17. And since every honest-to-god bowler owns his own ball, one of the most impressive barometers of the sudden rise of bowling is the fact that numerous credit jewelry houses have lately added bowling balls to their merchandise lists. One such concern in Detroit sold no less than $22,000 worth of balls last season!

These shreds of economics are interesting in more ways than one because they add up in a manner quite alien to most athletic pastimes in these high-pressure days. The 32 alleys which were laid expressly for the forty-fourth ABC Tournament in Indianapo-lis represented an investment of approximately $50,000—an investment, however, which was liquidated at the end of the five weeks' play by the ready resale of the al-leys to various recreation establishments.

Quarters large enough to house this tournament (in which only men may compete, by the way) cost around $1,000 a week in rent. Yet the interesting thing about it is that this expansive space is not required for spectators but for participants. Indeed, while paid admissions amounted to some $18,000—a laughable "gate" for any other cham-pionship contest—the entry fees of the bowlers themselves aggregated $150,000.

Something like $95,000 of this sum was posted as prize money, won, naturally, by a relatively small proportion of the entrants. All of which boils down to the fact that bowling has such a grip on its enthusiasts that fifteen thousand of them travel hundreds of miles at their own expense for the privilege of rolling against 60% of their own cash!

Prize money? Yes, bowling has always been a practical sport without any halluci-nations about amateurism. Trophies and medals are awarded for outstanding achieve-ments, but cash awards have always been offered under ABC jurisdiction. Thus, while bowling has never been admitted to the sacred circles of the Olympiad—and can never be considered on the same immaculate scale as tennis, whose "amateurs" travel of the fat of the land—it is still an amateur game in the honest sense of the term because its participants are competing mainly for fun. There are no bowlers who earn a living on the alleys, or, indeed, earn a living in some sporting goods store on the strength of their reputations. So the game is strictly in a class by itself. [Deleted discussion on average bowling scores and scoring 300.]

Interesting as a passing observation, this is by means the sole explanation of bowling's age-old popularity or of its recent sweep into the favor of new circles. Mil-lions of people have frequented the alleys for year for the simple reason that bowling is a swell game, It is good, lusty exercise; it is an ideal vehicle for compete mental relaxation; it is a friendly, neighborly game, skill is involved, to be sure, but not the exacting skill of golf, the lack of which converts a sport into an embarrassing misery for the novice. For the truth is that bowling can be thoroughly enjoyed with less proficiency than almost any other game you can mention. And the best way to prove that is to watch some newly formed club of women, most of whom never had any athletic training before, having the time of their lives on the alleys despite the fact that three balls out of every four rolled land in the gutter long before they reach the pins!

Then, too, there is enough competition in bowling to make it exciting, yet that competition is not acute in the sense that it is directly physical or even greatly dependent on physical strength. Two players of widely different muscular development and athletic education can bowl against each other with complete satisfaction. At the annual tournament the contestants' ages range from 18 to 65 and in many sections of the country father and son tournaments are even more popular on the alleys than on the links, and husband and wife can bowl together with infinitely less risk of divorce than they are exposed to at golf!

Being all-inclusive, bowling is easily the sociable of all games and therein lies its strength. The backbone of the sport in this country are the teams and leagues from offices, factories and mills which have bowled two or three evenings a week for years. Anybody from the boss to the office boy is eligible on equal grounds, and for that simple reason practically every leading concern in the country has fostered bowling as the ideal breeder of improved industrial relations.

The great majority merely stimulate the formation of teams and utilize local public alleys on certain regular evenings. Two nights weekly, for instance, the Bell Laboratories in New York take over 24 alleys in one establishment; in Detroit, employees of the Ternstadt Manufacturing Company take 66 alleys in one establishment for six hours each week. In Newark, New Jersey, the Prudential Insurance Company has 4,000 bowlers among its employees; in various cities the Chrysler Corporation estimates 5,000, and so on.

Something over 150 different corporations have installed alleys in their own properties which run the scale from the U.S. Steel Corporation, to a Wisconsin fox farm with 100 employees. General Electric has 12 alleys in Schenectady alone, 12 more in Fort Wayne, 8 in Cleveland, etc.; in Flint, Michigan, the Industrial Mutual Association, composed chiefly of automotive workers, has 32 alleys in its club house; the Colorado Fuel & Iron Company has at least 18 alleys in five different mines, and so it goes. Starting twenty years ago in a small woolen mill in an isolated city in Michigan, the idea of installing bowling alleys on the plant property has spread until today the largest corporations in the country have joined the ranks.

Already mentioned as an active bowler, John D. Rockefeller, Jr., has had no small part in spreading the acceptance of the game, for its value in better understanding between employer and employee. One of the first things he did in Pueblo after the Colorado Fuel & Iron Company's notorious labor difficulties some years back was to introduce bowling. And in all Rockefeller interests today—including the Riverside Church with its six alleys!—the game rates ace high. [Deleted hints on improving your bowling game.]

Like golf, too, bowling is not physically violent. You'll sleep like a top after three or four games, all right, but there's no danger of overdoing it for one very simple reason; your thumb will get sore from the friction of the finger-grip before you can bowl too long for your own good!

This is one reason why experienced physical directors are placing so much emphasis on bowling in hundreds of high schools throughout the country as well as in an increasing number of girls' schools. It is good exercise—principally because it gives the abdominal muscles a much needed workout—yet it carries its own curb to excess. The famous Bishop Shiell, mainspring of the Chicago C.Y.O., took over no less than 48 bowling alleys for the use of his youngsters. And in Louisville, Kentucky, where a high school league was started last winter with 200 boys, Dr. M.C. Isaac, physical director of the Du Pont Manual Training High School, says, "I think bowling is a wonderful recreational activity, not only for the high school boy but for everyone in general." Now even the faculty members are going out on the alleys with their pupils, and the obvious virtue of it is that they are all enjoying a game which takes the lot of them off the spectators' benches and puts them on the playing floor. Instead of cheering five, nine or eleven selected fortunates, they are participating themselves, thus meeting the criticism some observer once aimed at athletics in general: "the athlete competes and grows stronger; the weakling looks on and grows weaker."

One reason, of course, is that bowling is a participating rather than a spectator sport—and one which the youth can and will pursue beyond middle age. And the reason why he sticks to it, apart from its adaptability to physique, is the fact that it is a sociable game which carries an easy outlet for pent-up emotions in this age of growing inhibitions.

The average man or woman who bowls may not appreciate the psychological value of the game, but intelligent psychiatrists do and recommend it as a mental relaxation. The former Governor Adams, of Colorado, used to explain his frequent trips to the bowling alleys on the grounds that it was the only readily accessible game which tired his body and rested his mind in a short time. And if one attempted to get at the root of the recent popularity of bowling among the "upper crust," he would inevitably arrive at that conclusion as the explanation.

For entirely beyond the appeal of the game as a game, the critical analyst will see in it something which we, who live under increasing pressure, have been mutely crying for. In college we got it easily in gang formation by smashing up the town after the big game—and in adult life many still achieve it by attending conventions, getting marvelously tight and throwing the furniture out of the hotel windows.

In short, the savage in us still rebels at the damnable orderliness of conventional civilization, Individually, we are afraid to flaunt public opinion; in a sympathetic group we are delighted to blow things helter-skelter. Hence the popularity of bowling.

For the essence of bowling is that it permits the most straight-laced citizen to unbend long enough to blast into utter confusion a regimented array of ten neatly arranged objects. A monkey-like pin boy puts them there, row upon row in tantalizing perfection, and for the small price of a quarter you can crash that orderliness into a shambles with a sixteen-pound missile, and win the cheers of your compatriots too!

Verily, bowling is a swell game. And while those who know their business recommend it as a breeder of better industrial relations—and others advocate it as a healthy form of exercise for the immature and the aged—and still others favor it because it is an ideal conditioner for the sedentary—I like it because bowling is the civilized man's last chance to make a hell of a racket without apologizing to a soul!

### WOMEN BOWLERS

[*Few stories about bowling failed to mention Floretta Doty McCutcheon's victory over Jimmy Smith, the leading male bowler. Although she showed that women could compete with men on the bowling lanes, the journalists chose to discuss her hobbies and physical appearance. The Columbus Ohio Citizen, for example, wrote: "One would never expect that fingers nimble and feminine enough to sew attractively could control heavy bowling-balls or direct their faultless course to a perfect score, as she has done on several occasions. Yet she jumped from her kitchen and sewing room obscurity to bowling fame. She acts and looks more like a housewife than a professional record-breaker." Other writers noted that bowling helped McCutcheon lose weight and control her nerves.*

*Bowling equipment manufacturers took advantage of her popularity—she won the 1932 Olympic bowling event—to send her touring the United States giving free lectures and workshops to interested female bowlers. In 1935, McCutcheon traveled 18,000 miles and talked to approximately 25,000 women. William E. Brandt, "The Best Men Bowlers Can Learn From Her," American Magazine (1 April 1932), 73-74.*]

Bowling is one sport-perhaps the only one—in which the leading woman athlete can compete on even terms with the best men playing the game.

When the European teams—men and women—come to New York next winter for the World's International Bowling Tournament, the fair bowlers from across the Atlantic will meet, in the role of the American Bowling Congress' official hostess, a gray-haired woman in her early forties, Mrs. Floretta D. McCutcheon.

They might well expect this placid-looking matron to return to her knitting after she has made them feel at home, but when they toe the line to spin the balls down the shining alleys at the phalanxes of tenpins, they will meet her again, toeing the line now with her sleeves rolled up.

This time she may arouse other than friendly emotions in the visiting frauleins and mamselles and signorinas, for no woman in America can bowl on even terms with Mrs. McCutcheon and like it.

This motherly woman from the West is a combination of champion, exhibition player, and apostle. She calls herself a "bowling missionary." For the past four years she has been making a series of tours of the United States, giving exhibitions of her bowling skill supplemented by lectures to women audiences. She combines her technical bowling advice with discussions of physiological and psychological considerations.

Mrs. McCutcheon has had an athletic career remarkable in many respects. Most champions start young. She had never picked tip a bowling ball until she was 33 years old, an age at which athletes in most of the sports calling for physical exertion are beginning to slide downhill. That was nine years ago.

Her home is in Puebio, Colo. Her husband, a welfare supervisor with a large corporation, needed volunteers for vacancies on teams in the plant's women's bowling league. She was threatened with a nervous breakdown at the time. Her physician urged her to adopt a hobby. So she chose bowling. After one season in the plant's league she had to abandon the game for nearly two years because of her health. When she took it up again she quickly became a sensational pin-smasher.

The high spot of her career was her victory over Jimmie Smith, December 18, 1927, which made the biggest bowling news story that ever coursed the wires of the press. Smith, then our nation's leading bowler, was on an exhibition tour of the West. American Bowling Congress officials asked him to take a look at this phenomenal Colorado woman bowler about whom they were getting reports.

Jimmie's scouting method was to arrange a match with her at Denver. His report to the A.B.C. consisted of the score card. In the three-game match the score stood, "McCutcheon, 704; Smith, 686." To bowling fans this carried the shock golfers would have felt in the defeat of Bobby Jones by a woman golfer in Bobby's best year.

Next to the Smith victory her most renowned performance was at Cleveland in April, 1930, in the "300 Club" tournament. To join this club you must have rolled a "perfect" game, twelve straight strikes across the score board for a total of 300. Only about 700 bowlers in the world are eligible for membership. Mrs. McCutcheon was the only woman competing in the field of 254. She finished fourth.

She started late in life, athletically speaking, but she has gone farther than have the women champions of the sports more widely publicized, such as golf, tennis, and swimming. None of the other women topliners can compete over any long period on even terms with the leading male stars in their sports.

If you came into one of her lectures with your ears plugged you might assume she was discussing some fine point of cookery. She is entirely feminine in appearance, manner, and diction. She is a mother as well as a wife. Her daughter is a student at the University of Colorado.

Her message is that a woman can compete successfully in bowling, at least, without prodigious strength. Compared with men bowlers, she herself rolls a slow ball. She preaches accuracy, coordination, poise. She thinks bowling is exactly the right prescription for a great number of nerve-worn women.

Her message comes straight from the heart, for over and above her phenomenal achievements on a thousand score boards, she prizes the benefits she has derived from taking up the game. At 33 she faced a nervous breakdown. She weighed 211 pounds and her hair was prematurely gray.

Today she weighs less than 170. Her hair is still gray, but she no longer fears any collapse of her nerves. Bowling "made her a new woman."

## THE TREND IN BILLIARDS

*[In this survey of billiards, the author describes the major varieties of the game, their relative popularity, billiard stars, and the future of billiards. To make the game more appealing to women, subtle changes were made in the color of the tables. Lincoln A. Werden, "The Trend in Billiards," The Literary Digest (10 March 1934), 28.]*

There was a time when it was customary for your host, once the cordial was served, to invite you to a game of billiards. But for several reasons, the billiard games have been in the doldrums in recent years and it is a rare discovery to find a billiard room in the home of a friend.

There is, or was, "straight rail" billiards, now practically obsolete, in which points were made when the cue ball caromed off the other two object balls. As the ardent enthusiasts admit, this really wasn't "much of a game."

On the other hand there is "balkline." Balkline requires skill and necessitates from five to ten years before one acquires any sort of proficiency. It is to straight rail billiards something of what contract bridge is to euchre.

**A HARD GAME**

To play balkline on the regulation five by ten foot billiard table, lines of chalk (or the balk lines) are drawn at definite distances from the cushion or edge. In "eighteen-one" balkline, the distance is eighteen inches. The "one" indicates that in order to score a point, one object ball, as least, must be driven out of the chalked areas on each stroke. An adept player controls them so they roll out and then come back into this restricted space. In "eighteen-two" balkline, the same is true except that the "two" signifies the player need only drive one ball out on every two strokes, thus making the game easier.

However, there are two other games that are more in vogue at present. One of them is "pocket billiards," nothing more than what has been generally identified as "pool." Unfortunately, the word "pool," or rather such places known as "pool parlors," became discredited in the American mind. The manufacturers of billiard equipment realized this and while sponsoring other changes also transformed "pool" into "pocket billiards."

Atlho not as old as the other games, three-cushion billiards or "three-cushions," as it is known, has gained tremendously in popularity since it was first introduced some twenty years ago. Three-cushions appeals to those who regard pocket billiards as an elementary game, because it enables the player to profit by good shot-making, allows him an opportunity of establishing a defense in a game against a stronger adversary and also involves the fascinating uncertainty of luck.

Before the second object ball is hit, the player must have previously struck three cushions as well as the other object ball with the cue ball. Calling for the constant use of angles, most of the leading players employ what is known as the "system" to chart their shots with a mathematical exactness that is made possible by the use of the diamond markings installed for that purpose along the border of the table.

"There is also this to remember about three-cushions," said the world's champion Johnny Layton of Sedalia, Missouri, recently, "and that is the player is always thinking of three things while playing. First of all it is the next shot he will attempt, second he is considering how many points he has scored and, third, he will try to leave the balls in such a position that it will be difficult for his opponent on coming to the table to score."

As severe a blow as the economic situation has dealt to the growth of billiards of late years, as well as the fact that many other games, particularly bridge, according to Willie Hoppe (the famous one-time "boy wonder" who started playing billiards at the age of eight), have been a source of great competition, still some sanguine hopes are held for the future. The change in social life, with men gathering at their clubs or fraternal organizations, instead of at the speakeasy, is viewed as a boom to billiards.

Most of the dominating figures in billiards at present have been prominent for years. Hoppe is forty-six, Layton is forty-seven, Welker Cochrane, San Francisco's star, is thirty-seven, Jake Schaefer is thirty-nine, Alfrendo De Oro, the Cuban veteran, is seventy-one.

**A YOUNG PLAYER**

But there is one young player who many yet occupy a conspicuous role in the carom games. Studious-looking, bespectacled Jasper (Jay) Nathan Bozeman, Jr., born in Amarillo,Texas, resides now in Vallejo, California. Winner of the national amateur three-cushion championship at twenty-one, he is now twenty-seven and is considered as one of the most "natural" players the game has seen.

Sharing his love for billiards with that for the outdoors, he spends much of his time along the streams of his native State, likes to pack a gun and stalk for deer. Auburn-haired Bozeman believes, too, that more young players should be attracted to the game and he hopes the sport will enlist their support as golf has.

What the game definitely needs, in Hoppe's opinion, is the key by which every other sport has flourished—youth and personality. Golf had Francis Ouimet and Bobby Jones; tennis, Bill Tilden; polo, Devereux Milburn and Tommy Hitchcock. In each case the imagination of the sport-loving public was aroused as a new hero led the way.

Chapter 14

INTERNATIONAL GAMES—OLYMPICS, EMPIRE GAMES

The Olympics showcased "minor" sports, new heroes, intrigue, and nationalism. Every four years, sports such as bobsledding, speed skating, the shot put, wrestling, and gymnastics captured the headlines, especially when an American or Canadian did well, only to fade into obscurity until the next international games. Following the 1932 Olympics, for example, the president of the American weight lifting association noted that his sport made more progress in the preparations for the Olympics than in all the preceding years. Mildred "Babe" Didrickson displayed her charisma in the 1932 Olympics, and Eddie Tolan and Ralph Metcalfe established black domination in the sprint events. Jessie Owens was the American hero in the 1936 Berlin Olympics.

Each year the Games were declared bigger and better, as the host country sought to surpass the previous Olympics. The 1932 Summer Games in Los Angeles attracted athletes from thirty-seven countries. Fifty-one nations competed in the 1936 Berlin Games. In the 1932 Winter Olympics in Lake Placid, seventeen countries and 252 athletes competed in four sports and fourteen events. Four winters later, in Garmisch-Partenkirchen, Germany, twenty-eight countries and 668 athletes participated in four sports and seventeen events.

There were always numerous stories to cover. At Lake Placid, the European speed skaters were unfamiliar and unhappy with the American group start in which skaters vied for position and the first man to cross the finish line was the winner. Four years later, the Americans were upset as the European-style two-man timed heats were employed and the skaters best able to pace themselves captured gold. In Los Angeles, American weight lifters were bewildered by the European interpretation of the rules. French was the international language of weight lifting and the American team had relied upon a poor translation. In 1932, Finland threatened to pull out of the Games when the International Olympic Council (IOC) declared Paavo Nurmi ineligible because of his inflated expense accounts at an earlier meet. Prior to the Berlin Games the American Olympic Committee (AOC) barred backstroker Eleanor Holm Jarrett for drinking on the ocean liner on the way to the Olympics. Jarrett, an ex-Ziegfeld show girl and night club singer, did not endear herself to the AOC by telling reporters that she trained on champagne and cigarettes. Shortly after her dismissal, the International News Service hired Jarrett to report on the Games. Following these Olympics, the AOC disqualified Jessie Owens for not fulfilling his "moral obligation" to race in Sweden, as he had promised, and for considering turning professional.

The issue of who was and who was not an amateur was also good for headlines (see "Hockey Controversy in the 1936 Games"). When Stanislawa Walasiewiczowna (Stella Walsh) decided to run for Poland rather than for the United States because Poland offered her a job in its New York consulate, many people questioned her amateur status and demanded she be barred from competition. Walsh later defeated Montreal's Hilda Strike to win the 100-meter dash. When Walsh was murdered in 1981, the coroner discovered she was a man. Forced by the IOC to allow Jews to compete for its Olympic team, Germany invited world-class high jumper Gretel Bergmann to try out. Although Bergmann equalled the German record for this event, she was told, shortly after the American team set sail for Europe, that she was unqualified to compete. Germany entered only two women in the high jump, one of whom it was later discovered was a man.

The 1936 American track and field team was not without its own problems. As was customary, prior to the American trials the sprinters were told that the fourth to seventh place finishers in the 100-meter dash would form the four by 100-meter relay team. Two of these qualifiers, Marty Glickman and Sam Stoller, were Jews who resisted considerable pressure to boycott the Berlin Olympics. Just prior to the finals of the relay race, the American track and field officials announced the two Jews and one other qualifier would be replaced by Jessie Owens, Frank Wykoff, and Foy Draper.

As the document "The 1932 Olympic Village" indicates, the Olympics were unaffected by the Depression. Los Angeles wished to showcase both itself and the state. The city floated a $1,500,000 bond issue and a California referendum approved $1 million in state funds. These Games featured the first specially-constructed Olympic village. In addition, the organizers fed, housed, entertained, and transported the 1,408 athletes, including 350 Americans and 127 Canadians, between their events.

For many people, the Olympics were a gauge of the nation's health. Following the 1936 Games, for instance, Sportsman asked, "Did the Games show American youth was superior or inferior physically to that of our neighbors? Are we showing evidence of improved vitality, or are we degenerating and growing weaker and less enduring." The author believed that although Germany won more events, the American win in the decathlon was "unassailable proof that we still grow and train the finest all-around specimens of physical manhood the world has yet produced."

When the Western Home Monthly wrote prior to the Los Angeles Games that Canadians should take pride in their sportsmanship and the fight was more important than the victory, it was a good indication that the 1932 team was inferior to the 1928 team. Indeed, Canadians only captured gold in the high jump and bantamweight boxing. In the intervening years, gate receipts and sponsorships had dwindled and the Canadian AAU was forced to cancel its national training camps and suspend publication of its monthly magazine, the Canadian Athlete. Most athletes and officials paid their own way to the Canadian trials and to Los Angeles. To the chagrin of the Canadian AAU, the only track and field specialists who won medals, including high jump gold winner Duncan McNaughton, trained at American universities.

Canadians were often poorly prepared, coached, and equipped. At Lake Placid, Canada's lone Nordic Combined athlete obtained the latest in ski bindings the day before his event by trading for it. In Berlin, unable to afford to send its shell to Germany, Canada's rowing eight engaged a German company to build a shell. Using this "bloody barge," the team failed to qualify for the finals. But as Henry Roxborough noted, the Olympics "give Canada headline front-page advertising that could not be bought in the international press; by the appearance of our athletes in parade and competition we impress hundreds of correspondents and tens of thousands of spectators that Canadians are decent yet aggressive people; and we tell the world that we are developing an international mind and are anxious to be friendly with the customers whose trade has placed us fifth among the nations of the world."

On the eve of the Los Angeles Games, Roxborough wrote that "Canadian girls are undoubtedly the prettiest and most wholesome looking group of girls who have arrived for the competitions. They constitute a denial of the general idea that a woman athlete must be built like a baby grand piano, and have a face like a hatchet." As befit this patronizing attitude, women competed in only fourteen of 126 events and comprised nine percent of the total competitors. At Lake Placid, twenty-one of the 252 athletes were women. The latter situation suited the Women's Division of the National Amateur Athletic Federation, which earlier failed to exclude women's track and field events from the Olympics.

The politicization of the Olympics reached its height in 1936. Hitler's attempt to employ the Games to illustrate the supremacy of the Aryan race, the subsequent movement to boycott the event, and Jessie Owens' four gold medals combined to make the Nazi Olympics the most extensively studied of all the Games.

The IOC awarded the Winter and Summer Games to Germany before Adolf Hitler came to power. On 1 April 1933, the Nazi party announced a one-day country-wide boycott of all Jewish businesses. Subsequently, Jews were excluded from sports organizations, and lost their jobs as teachers, judges, doctors, lawyers and civil servants. The American Jewish Congress and the Jewish Labor Committee joined with the Non-Sectarian Anti-Nazi League to protest German anti-Semitism and threatened to boycott the Olympics if Hitler continued to defy IOC policy that forbade discrimination on the basis of race or religion. The AAU passed a resolution against attending the Games until Germany complied with IOC policies.

The delegates to the 1933 AOC meeting were divided on the issue. Charles Sherrill, the AOC representative on the IOC, and Avery Brundage, the president of the AOC, declared the Olympics should be free from politics and advocated participation. Others such as Judge Jeremiah Mahoney, the president of the AAU, argued "that participation in the games under the Swastika implies the tacit approval of all that the Swastika symbolizes." Since the AOC was particularly annoyed that Hitler barred all Jewish athletes from competing for the German team, Sherrill and Brundage travelled to Germany several times to investigate the situation and to extract a commitment to the Olympic code. Eventually, Hitler agreed to allow German Jews to compete for the national team, and Sherrill and Brundage promised Hitler would honor this pledge.

The movement to boycott the Olympics intensified in September 1935 when the Nuremberg Laws deprived Jews of their German citizenship. More than 100 Protestant clergymen and educators signed a petition favoring a boycott. Major newspapers and magazines, such as the Nation and The New York Times, joined with senators, congressmen, intellectuals, athletes, and labor and church leaders in denouncing Germany's anti-Semitism. But Avery Brundage, a self-made millionaire and ex-athlete, continued to argue for a strict separation between sports and politics. Earlier, Brundage was an outspoken advocate of Nazi theories, and now he claimed that the boycott was controlled by "alien agitators and their stooges," and that it was a "Jewish-Communist conspiracy." Other opponents of the boycott maintained that Hitler was fulfilling his promises to allow Jews to compete, that sending a strong team would destroy the myth of Aryan supremacy, and that a boycott would provoke anti-Semitism. How can Americans complain, declared Brundage, given our treatment of Negroes in the South? This ferment is described in the documents "The Olympic Boycott" and "Blacks and the Boycott."

The showdown came at the AAU convention on 8 December 1935. Before the meeting, forty-one college presidents asked the AAU to boycott the Olympics. Petitions with 500,000 names, and resolutions from organizations representing 1.5 million individuals demanded a boycott. A Gallup Poll indicated that forty-three percent of Americans favored a boycott. It was the stormiest and most bitter session in history. Despite Mahoney's worries that Nazi propaganda at the Olympics would distort the real situation and give the regime a moral and psychological uplift, the executive voted by a two and a half vote margin to compete, adding the vote should not be "construed to imply endorsement of the Nazi government." Mahoney resigned and Brundage became AAU president. Throughout the controversy, President Roosevelt said nothing.

Many Jewish papers encouraged Jewish athletes to boycott the Games and some Jewish athletes, such as sprinter Herman Neguass, chose not to compete for the American team. So too did the Long Island University basketball team, which won thirty-two consecutive games. Six Jewish athletes were part of the American Olympic team— hoping to win and disabuse Nazi propaganda.

The Olympic controversy was similar, but more muted, in Canada. Canadians knew the situation in Germany but, as their Prime Minister, Mackenzie King, were generally indifferent to the fate of Jews. The Canadian Trades and Labour Congress, Toronto Mayor James Simpson, and prominent church and university leaders supported a boycott, but the Canadian AAU proceeded with the trials. Historian Bruce Kidd suggests Canadian officials simply followed the lead of the British Olympic Association. Most sportswriters opposed the boycott. Ted Reeve suggested that "any good athlete who let the threats of a little trouble in Berlin keep him away....doesn't rate as a champion, no matter how fast he can run or how high he can jump." The document "The Olympic Boycott in Canada" reprints the views of some of the leading Canadian sportswriters.

The Olympics were a propaganda success for the Nazi regime. Germany staged a grander spectacle than did Los Angeles. In addition to a 100,000-seat track and field stadium, there were six large gymnasiums, many smaller arenas, and a closed-circuit television system. Innovations included electronic photo-finish equipment and timing devices. Everywhere there were Nazi swastikas, military bands, search lights, and 100,000 SA and SS troops goose-stepping in parade or acting as policemen. Many non-Germans returned home with a positive view of German organization, hospitality, and order. Reviewing the Games, Sportsman wrote: "The Surprise of the Olympic Games of 1936 actually was the social achievement of the German nation....Yet we have just seen the German people play perfectly the role of a gracious, fair, and generous host literally to millions of guests, and to competitors from fifty-two separate nations, at the same time providing the most elaborate and magnificent architectural setting and comprehensive game facilities and equipment the world has yet seen." Grantland Rice, on the other hand, described the opening ceremonies as looking "more like two world wars than the Olympic games."

## THE 1932 OLYMPIC VILLAGE

[*The 1932 Olympic Games featured several innovations. Electric photo-timing devices provided redundancy for hand timers. Individual teletype printers allowed journalists to relay their stories home in record speed. For the first time, the best three finishers mounted a victory platform shortly after their event and listened to the gold medalist's national anthem as that country's flag was unfurled. These Games also inaugurated the lighting of the Olympic flame at the opening ceremonies. Determined to use the Games to showcase the young city of Los Angeles, the American Olympic Committee began planning in 1928. When the Depression put the Games in doubt, the Committee promised other countries reduced transportation fares to California, and pledged to provide housing, food, and entertainment for only two dollars per day per athlete. The Olympic village, which is discussed in this article, was another innovation. Females were domiciled in a Los Angeles hotel. "Olympic Games as a Depression-Buster," The Literary Digest (18 June 1932), 29-31.*]

A $6,000,000 sock on the jaw is the sport world's answer to the depression.

Two thousand or so athletes from between forty and fifty nations will defy hard times, this summer, and gather in Los Angeles from July 30 to August 14 for the greatest of all international sports spectacles—the Olympic Games that have come down to us from ancient Greece.

When the last race has been run, the last discus thrown, the last hurdle cleared, considerably more than $6,000,000 will have been put into circulation, and many thousands of men (it seems safe to say, altho a definite estimate is impossible) will have been given employment in preparing for and producing the games.

A good-sized contribution from sportdom to the cause of normalcy!

Nine stadiums, auditoriums, and watercourses, whose seating capacities range from 2,000 to 105,000, have been built or remodeled to accommodate a predicted daily attendance of between 300,000 and 400,000. A small city has risen near Los Angeles to house the army of competitors from almost every land under the sun.

The huge expense of it all is being met with almost no public appeal for funds in the country at large.

The State of California and Los Angeles city and county are spending their own money liberally to entertain their anticipated visitors.

Each nation represented finances its own team.

The American Olympic Committee has to raise the relatively small sum of $350,000, to pay the expenses of our own athletes. This canvass, we are told, is not progressing rapidly. As we write, only about one-tenth of the needed sum has been raised, and the drastic cutting down of United States teams is possible....

Says Edwin B. Dooley in the New York Sun: "One gets an idea of the amount of preparation, forethought, and cooperation Los Angeles exerted in behalf of the coming contests by reflecting on the fact that besides arranging all the physical requisites, such as stadiums, auditoriums, and the like, and attending to the details of reduced railroad and steamship rates, medical facilities, hotel reservations, housing-places for women, and the like, it has built an entire village.

Covering no less than 331 acres of what was once an old Spanish rancho, Olympic Village consists of 550 specially designed two-room houses, comfortably furnished and containing all modern conveniences.

It has five miles of streets, eight miles of water-pipes, forty private kitchens, a hospital, fire-houses, and refrigerator building; also an amphitheater for the entertainment of the athletes."

This village has excited the wonder and admiration of all who have seen it. Charles W. Paddock, himself a celebrated Olympic athlete, adds further details in an article copyrighted by the Sper Syndicate and quoted from the Los Angeles Evening Herald and Express:

"There is room enough in each little house for four athletes, however husky they may happen to be, and the finest beds obtainable have been provided for their rest. Each house is provided with ample closet space and a shower-room.

Each group of national representatives will be housed as a unit, and altho there are rows on rows of bungalows, some extending almost a half-mile in length, no athlete will have to walk more than 200 feet to reach a steam-room or bath-house, or more than 400 feet to find a recreation-hall or dining-room."

The picturesque and historic parade of nations, one of the main features of the opening of the games, will take place in the presence of President Hoover, and other dignitaries, in Olympic Stadium on the afternoon of July 30, announces the Los Angeles Times:

"Thereafter will follow in Olympic Stadium, eight days of track and field athletics, two final field hockey games, three days of demonstration lacrosse, five days of gymnastics, two days of finals of the equestrian sports, a night game of American football, and the closing ceremony, which will be held on Sunday, August 14.

During these sixteen days and nights, there will be two days of weight-lifting, seven mornings and evenings of wrestling, and five days of boxing in Olympic Auditorium; thirteen days of fencing in the State Armory; three nights of track cycling in Rose Bowl Stadium at Pasadena; one day of road cycling; eight days of yachting in Los Angeles Harbor; eight days of swimming, diving, and water polo in the Los Angeles Swimming Stadium; five days of rowing in Long Beach Marine Stadium, three days of equestrian sports at Riviera Country Club; preliminary field hockey games at the University of California at Los Angeles, and two days of shooting at the police pistol-range in Elysian Park.

Events of the modern pentathlon will take place in five different stadiums.

During the entire period of the games, the Olympic fine-arts competitions will be held in the Los Angeles County Museum in Olympic (Exposition) Park.

The demonstration American football game, played in Olympic Stadium on the night of August 8, will be between a team of graduating seniors of Harvard, Princeton, and Yale, and a similar team from California, Stanford, and Southern California universities."

In preparation for these gala games, California and the city and county of Los Angeles have already spent a fortune.

To insure financial success of the games, "the people of the State three years ago voted a $1,000,000 bond issue, the money being used by the organizing committee for construction work with the understanding that it would be returned to the coffers of the State from profits of the games," writes Erskine Johnson in a review syndicated by Newspaper Enterprise Association in its Every Week Magazine.

"Approximately $1,000,000 will be expended by the United States and forty-nine other countries to send their athletes to Los Angeles for the games, and to house and feed them during their stay in the 1932 Olympic city....

According to figures produced by the organizing committee of the games, approximately $480 per athlete will be spent by each country entered for transportation and housing. Los Angeles officials of the games have informed the various nations that the athletes can be housed and fed during their sixteen-day stay in Los Angeles at a cost of $2 per day for each athlete....

### HOCKEY CONTROVERSY IN THE 1936 GAMES

[*At the Lake Placid Winter Games, which suffered from warm weather, the US captured twelve medals, including six gold. The Games had an enormous impact on the growth of winter sports in the US, particularly figure skating and skiing. Canada won seven medals and one gold. Canadian women did extremely well in speed skating, which was a demonstration sport. The hockey contests especially concerned Canadians. In 1932, Canada worried that the strong American team would take advantage of the fact that most good Canadian players were professionals and thus ineligible for the Games. In the 1936 Winter Olympics, the English team won hockey gold. When both teams played in the finals, Olympic officials awarded gold to the English team because it had defeated the Port Arthur Bearcats in what the Canadians thought was a preliminary game. The ethics of using Canadian hockey players to play for the English team is the subject of the following article. "Hockey Blast and 'Caesar's Wife.' Gustavus Kirby's Charge that England's Winning Hockey Team was Unfairly Recruited Evokes Rejoinders," The Literary Digest (29 February 1936), 38.*]

The 1936 Winter Olympic Games backfired in New York with the arrival from Germany of Gustavus Town Kirby, Treasurer of the American Olympic Committee, and former President of the Amateur Athletic Union.

Returning from a trip to Garmisch-Partenkirchen, where the English team won the hockey championship, Mr. Kirby clutched a microphone in his hands and blasted a condition he called "outrageous."

"Amateur hockey," Mr. Kirby shouted at reporters who came to meet him, "seems to be becoming a stench in the nostrils of honest sportsmen. While I am not criticizing American hockey, it is like Caesar's wife. But the English played Canadians on their team on the theory they were born in England and "once an Englishman, always an Englishman," altho actually they were Canadian nationals.

"There are more than sixty Canadian players in Europe," Mr. Kirby continued. "All of them are supposed to be amateurs, but I'd like to ask how they make their living. But that does not trouble me as the way the British used Canadian players on their team."

**ANNOYING OPEN DOOR**

"I will admit that they were English-born, but they lived in Canada all their lives. What annoys me is that it leaves a door wide open for similar practises in track and field. Having been successful in using these players in the Winter Olympics, Great Britain would be able to use South Africans, Australians, and athletes from all her Dominions this summer."

Mr. Kirby's attack on the make-up of the English hockey team, which caused one of the several international flare-ups before the Winter Games began in Germany early this month, evoked little sympathy from sports-writers. Instead, they lifted the "Caesar's wife" phrase out of the statement and fired blasts of their own at an old target.

Typical comment by Dan Parker, New York Daily Mirror columnist:

"Gustavus Kirby's bleat about the questionable amateurism of English hockey players recruited from Canada for the Olympic Games would carry much more weight were it not that the same situation exists right under his own nose in the so-called Eastern Amateur Hockey League, with the connivance of Mr. Kirby's Amateur Athletic Union." (The A.A.U. is the governing body of amateur hockey in the East.)

**U.S. NOT ABSOLVED**

"America is guilty of the same thing of which Mr. Kirby accuses England—that of using star Canadian hockey-players who happened to be born in the country they represented in the Olympics. Frank Shaughnessy, Jr., of the U.S. sextet, was born here but is really a Canadian, since he has lived in Montreal most of his life and learned his hockey at McGill. Back in 1924, Ray Bonney, Larry and Joe McCormick and Herb Drury, who were on the U.S. Hockey team, took the oath of American citizenship the night before the boat sailed for Europe."

Turning to hockey, in a discussion of commercialism in amateur athletics, Joe Williams of the New York World-Telegram wrote: "Amateur hockey, particularly as it is interpreted in the East, is about as amateur as Jim Londos, the wrestler.

America was forced to send a mediocre hockey team to the Winter Olympics because the selection committee didn't dare nominate the more expert and better known 'amateurs.' This would have been akin to sending Ching Johnson and the two Cook brothers (of New York Rangers Professional team) over as Simon pures."

## THE OLYMPIC BOYCOTT

[*The following article outlines America's knowledge of Hitler's anti-Semitic activities and discusses the movement to boycott the Berlin Games. James Broughton, "America and the Olympics," The New Republic (6 November 1935), 357-358.*]

American participation in the eleventh Olympic Games to be held next year in Berlin has become a bitterly controversial matter. The champions of non-participation have been increasingly active during the past months. The Anti-Nazi Federation has collected 30,000 protest signatures. A widely representative group has formed the

Committee on Fair Play in Sports. Influential individuals such as Governor Earle of Pennsylvania, New York Supreme Court Justice Pecora, Samuel Untermeyer, Heywood Broun, New York Representative Emanuel Cellar and organizations like the National Council of Methodist Youth, the American Youth Congress, the Catholic War Veterans have warmed up for the battle. Nevertheless authority for final action rests entirely with the sports-minded American Olympic Committee, whose answer is that three teams for the Winter Olympics of February have already been chosen and are booked to sail on the S.S. "Manhattan" on January 3.

Aside from the question of American approval of the Hitler regime, the fact remains that the only legitimate excuse the American Olympic Committee can make for withdrawal is a proved violation by Germany of its Olympic pledge to give equal opportunity for participation in the Games to all athletes, no matter of what country, race, color or creed. Because of censorship, news from Germany is difficult to confirm, but the following items have been authentically proved and illuminate the position of Germany in regard to the spirit and practice of the Olympic Games.

In the first place it is obvious that Germany's team will be a political one. German sports are controlled by the government under the Sport Commissar, Hans von Tschammer-Osten, an appointee of Hitler responsible for all Olympic arrangements. Without issuing a direct edict against Jewish athletes, von Tschammer-Osten first ordered all Nazi athletic groups to bar Jews, and then coordinated every branch of sport into the Reich Association for Physical Culture by requiring every Aryan organization to belong. Unless affiliated with Nazi clubs, Catholics and Protestants are not allowed to engage in sport. Through these Aryan groups under the direction of von Tschammer-Osten the training of athletes for the Olympic Games is being conducted as a direct function of the German government, an unprecedented violation of the democratic and independent status of world sports and one that makes Jewish training or qualification impossible.

Last year Bruno Malitz, sports leader of the Berlin Storm Troopers, published a book entitled "The Spirit of Sports in the Third Reich," distributed gratis to every athletic organization. Malitz writes: "We must never forget that our sports are built upon hatred...Jewish leaders of sports, Jewish athletes, and their Talmud-infested friends the pacifists, political Catholics, pan-Europeans and the like, have no place in our German land. They are worse than cholera and syphilis, and much worse than famine, drought and poison gas." Furthermore, he remarks that Nazis "can see no positive value in permitting dirty Jews and Negroes to travel through our country and compete in athletics with our best."

On August 9, 1935, when asked why there were no Jews among the 230 German athletes in the sixth international university games at Budapest, George Fischer, manager of the German team, explained that "non-Aryans in Germany do not possess the Aryan competitive spirit."

On August 6, 1935, all sports clubs in Germany were ordered to set aside the month of September for discussion of anti-Semitism. On September 25, Dr. Goebbels' paper, Der Angriff, stated in connection with preparations for the Olympic Games that "no arrangements for the housing of visitors and Olympic teams will be made in the homes of Jews." Over the entrance to Garmisch-Partenkirchen, site of the Winter Olympics, a sign was placed proclaiming: "Jews not admitted." A photograph exists to prove this.

The psychological difficulties of competing under conditions of hatred are well represented in the case of May Friewald, Polish champion hurdler, who was shouted at and spit at by a Dresden mob when it was revealed that she was a Jewess.

No Protestant or Catholic can train or compete for the Olympic Games unless he or she is a member of a Nazi-controlled athletic organization. Repeatedly Catholic youth groups have been prohibited from engaging in any sports of their own sponsoring; this is now held an offense against the state. Last July the Catholic sports organization, Deutsche Jugendkraft, was officially dissolved although it had been assured sanction by the Vatican Concordat of 1933. Its property was confiscated for the alleged reason of hostility toward the state. Exactly a year before, Adelbert Probst, head of the Deutsche Jugendkraft, was killed by Storm Troopers.

As for discrimination against the Negro, Julius Streicher prevented a scheduled match in Nuremberg last March between the Negro wrestler Wango and a German. "It degrades our race," he said, "to permit a Negro wrestler to fight a white man. He who applauds when a black man throws a white is not worthy of Nuremberg or German citizenship."

Despite the natural apprehension that such facts must arouse in the minds of Jewish, Catholic and Negro athletes, some of whom will surely represent the United States, the American Olympic Committee reiterates its stand that participation in the Games does not mean endorsement of the Nazis and that American athletes will not be sacrificed for the promotion of a "misguided" boycott of Germany.

Of the forty-nine nations, including the United States, that have accepted the invitation to participate, Holland is the only country so far to withdraw, ostensibly for lack of financial support of the teams, although the Haagsche Post of The Hague editorialized against holding an Olympiad in a country "filled with the Streicher spirit." Although Mr. Avery Brundage, president of the American Olympic Committee, says that the United States is the only country that has raised any issue about participation, it is definitely known that organizations in Spain, Belgium, Norway, Denmark and Sweden have promoted movements for withdrawal.

In the Winter Olympics, held from February 6 to 16 at Garmisch-Partenkirchen, the United States will be represented by sixty-six competitors in speed skating, figure skating, hockey, bobsled and skiing, three teams of which are already elected. For the summer Olympics, present plans provide for a team of 411 men and women. Money for the winter sports has already been raised. The fund campaign for the summer events never begins until March before the August competition. "It should be remembered," Mr. Brundage says, that "no tryouts anywhere in the world, including Germany, have been or will be held for the main events of August until early next summer." Despite anti-Nazi propaganda it will be a simple matter to make up a full team from those anxious to compete in Berlin. The majority of American athletes want to compete, although many of them are likely to be Catholics, and Jews and Negroes are certain to be included.

Despite the vigorous pleas of Judge Jeremiah Mahoney, president of the Amateur Athletic Union, the Olympic Committee contends that he won't get to first base with his boycotting at the December 5 convention of the Union. Of the thirty-four associations in the A.A.U. only four are officially known to be opposed, although a poll conducted by The New York Daily Mirror claimed that nine favored withdrawal. The sentiment remains divided and the controversial sparring goes on. But the American Olympic Committee happens to be referee as well as protagonist. Its judgment stands firm: America will go to the Olympics in Berlin. Even so they have found it wise to prepare a counter-propaganda campaign, soon to be launched, which will involve addresses by Lowell Thomas and other influential public-address artists.

## BLACKS AND THE BOYCOTT

[*In 1935 and 1936, twenty-six blacks were lynched in the United States. Although the Black press reminded its readers of the hypocrisy in the US that kept American Blacks from playing in the NFL or in major league baseball, it generally opposed a boycott. The Philadelphia Tribune and the Chicago Defender emphasized that performing well would undermine Nazi racial views of Aryan supremacy and foster a new sense of black pride. The German press contemptuously referred to the American blacks as the country's "black auxiliary."*

*Eighteen blacks qualified for the team, twelve more than in 1932. Even so, blacks comprised only 4.4 percent of the American team, concentrated in track and field, boxing, and weight lifting events. The fact that these athletes attended white universities, indicated the inferiority of training facilities at black colleges. Oswald Garrison Villard, "Issues and Men," The Nation (15 August 1936), 185.*]

There is something extremely humorous, as well as entirely satisfactory, in the way that Negro Americans are carrying off all the honors in Berlin—up to the time this is written. Already it is clear that if the United States triumphs at the end of the games it will be because of the representatives of those Americans who in many states of the Union are disfranchised; who are segregated and discriminated against in many parts, and in all cities, of the Union. Their triumph is highly amusing because it has taken place in the presence of Adolf Hitler, the leader of spurious Aryanism, so that that noble champion of sports and of humanity was compelled to congratulate the German winners in his private room at the stadium in order not to have to shake hands with any of the dark victors from the United States. There are so many of these that a European wit is quoted as saying that he hopes there will be a couple of white men and girls on the American team in 1940.

Well, even at home these triumphs of the colored men ought to have their good effect. Nearly all of them are or have been university students; they have shown stamina, courage, good manners, self-control, loyalty to the team, and in the reports of the drinking that took place on the Manhattan on the voyage over there has been no intimation that any of the colored men were among the offenders, of whom Mrs. Jarrett was singled out for such exemplary punishment. As for their not being received by Adolf Hitler, I agree with Richards Vidmer of the Herald Tribune that it isn't at all likely they will be "either perturbed or petulant." I should think they would be rather relieved not to have to take the blood-stained paw of that monster to whose everlasting discredit is to be set down the killing of over 1,250 people in that single night of the blood-purge of June 30, 1934. But if he were the most estimable character, these colored gentlemen would still be above and beyond feeling hurt. We Americans have trained them too well for that with our own discrimination, our own slights, our own insults, which do not even spare their women, which often poison their childhood and youth, precisely as the Jewish Children in Germany are tortured to their very souls by being told in their schools that they are inferior beasts, mere contact with whom is leprous. No; the colored gentlemen who represent the United States in Berlin will not come back with any heartaches or swelled heads, but with the solid satisfaction of having contributed to the national victory, if victory it should turn out to be. And if it should appear that that victory alone prevented the Germans from walking off with all the honors, the gods on the heavenly Olympus would certainly shake with Homeric laughter.

Perhaps the news of the victory may shame our Congress into passing that anti-lynching bill which it is allowing the Southerners to defeat year in and year out. Perhaps it will enable the President to receive and honor the colored victors in the White House where Mrs. Roosevelt recently did an extremely generous and fine thing in receiving the inmates of a Negro girl reformatory. Perhaps the government itself might undertake to abandon some of those discriminations against Negro civil servants for which the special dishonor belonged to William G. McAdoo and Woodrow Wilson. Perhaps the army might feel as if it could let down its caste bars and give a really square deal to the colored Americans. Perhaps West Point with its 1,800 cadets might find room for more than one Negro student and not subject those admitted to the brutal ostracism which had made life at West Point for Negroes who endured the ordeal call for greater strength, moral and physical, than was ever displayed at an Olympic.

One thing I must record with great satisfaction. In the South the reaction to these Negro successes will be far more generous and friendly than would have been the case a few years ago. I have seen some superb editorials from Southern editors' pens ridiculing or denouncing that Senator from South Carolina who walked out of the Philadelphia convention of the Democratic Party because a Negro clergyman pronounced the blessing. The foremost of these commentators was a Richmond editor, and a reader of The Nation has written in to urge that The Nation ascertain his name and put him on its Honor Roll for 1936. I think it should be done, but there will be a number of the newer generation of Southern journalists who will be ready to welcome these Negroes and publicly honor them, as, for example, that admirable son of Josephus Daniels, Jonathan Daniels, who now conducts the Raleigh (North Carolina) News and Observer. I do not wish to be unduly optimistic, especially as long as lynching continues, but I think we have gone a long distance from the days when the whole South roared in outrage because Theodore Roosevelt invited the most distinguished Negro of his time, Booker T. Washington, to luncheon at the White House. Indeed, we have gone far from the spirit which led some Southerners of the basest type to kill Negro soldiers returning from France in order to "teach them their place" because they had been associating so freely with Frenchmen—and women.

There is nothing more wonderful in all the United States than the patient endurance of wrong, injustice, and oppression by the Negroes—too patient by far. But in spite of it they are steadily coming to the front with their great singers, great actors, writers, and poets. And now they win the greatest honors at the Olympics—to share then with us white Americans!

## THE OLYMPIC BOYCOTT IN CANADA

[*In Berlin, when the Canadian delegation marched past Hitler's box during the opening ceremonies, the athletes gave the Nazi salute. Although team officials stated it was done "as a gesture of friendship," Canada was the only Commonwealth team to do so. Because the Communist party and its tri-weekly newspaper, The Worker, initiated the Olympic boycott in Canada, the supporters of the Games sought to label their opponents Communists. In October 1935, the Maritime Sports Illustrated reprinted the opinions of various Canadian and American sportswriters regarding the boycott. The following document includes the former views as well as the letters to the editor in subsequent issues. Colin A. Gravenor, "Canada Should Withdraw from the Olympic Games. A Message to the Canadian Olympic Committee," Maritime Sports Illustrated (September-October 1935), 9-11.*]

Within a few weeks the Canadian Olympic Games committee will sit in solemn conclave. The plans for the thirteenth Olympiad will be before them. When the date for this meeting was set there was only one problem "How can we send our strongest team?" Now the problem is changed. The officials will have to ask "How can we honestly send a team at all?"

It will take money and organization to send any group of athletes and the accompanying officials to Europe. If appeals are made to our Dominion, provincial, or municipal governments for funds must not also the question come up "Does not our aid in sending the Canadian team to Berlin mean that this government is endorsing a policy of religious intolerance and racial persecution." Any government that gives as much as a five cent piece to sending the team is certainly putting the stamp of approval on the atrocities of the Nazi regime!

Should an appeal for funds for the Olympiad meet with your approval you can well make your donation—but to some future Olympiad—by making out your check to those deserving causes the Y.M.C.A. the Y.M.H.A. or the Columbus Club. They will produce future Canadian Olympians. Yet does not any person who donates directly to sending a team to Berlin say in as many "Here young Canadian athletes, here is money to go and accept the hospitality of a government that hates Jews, Catholics and Protestants."

We firmly believe that our Canadian Olympic committee is not composed of a group of men who hate Jews, Catholics and Protestants. Yet if those men were to aid Canadian athletes in attending the Games would they not also be echoing the words of the man who donates the money?

We would not presume to tell our Olympic officers what should be done. That is their duty to decide. But in this country—which still happens to allow free thought, belief and speech—we can at least bring to the attention of the body, the opinions of a number of persons who may be well classed as authorities on the subject.

In this issue we present the comment of a well known Canadian sportsman, Henry W. Sylvester, and along with it we give you the opinion of the leading sport writers and sport officials of the United States including the president of the A.A.U. of the United States. In our next issue we hope to express the opinion of Canada's own sport writers and sport officials. We will endeavour to ask all of the outstanding men in these fields and present a similar expression of opinion—either pro or con—in the next issue.

In the meantime the issue is squarely before Canada's Olympic body. We cannot promise our readers anything further than every member of the body will read these and the following words. We will make sure that they do!

Then we can watch their decision with interest.

For it will be interesting. "Can we honestly send a team at all?"

## IS CANADA READY TO ENDORSE NAZISM?

By HENRY W. SYLVESTER.

Should Canada withdraw from the Olympic Games?

Has the forthcoming Olympiad lost its true function as the great festival of international sport and goodwill? Should the Olympiad be transferred from Berlin?

The time for wondering is past! Let us face facts!

While the forces back of the new outrages against Catholics, Protestants and Jews are not clear, the facts are clear enough. So deeply has the rest of the civilized world been stirred by recent German outrages that there is a general spreading feeling that the Nazi's "must be told."

The proposal to move the Olympic Games from Berlin, or the withdrawal of our country from the games offers the most effective way to show world opinion of persecution.

Nazi Germany wants the Olympic Games.

It wants it enough to give promises that it will break as easily as it renounces the international treaties and obligations to foreign powers. It wants the approval of the world for its recent behaviour. Attendance at the Games means that the nations that attend and accept Hitler's hospitality, agree with his ideas. The Olympiad means a big profit for its tourist trade. And isn't money needed badly by Germany for her additional armies and armaments? Hitler has promised his Nazi's [sic] that the nations of the world do not dare refuse his invitation.

But Hitler domination does not extend into Canada. Free thinking Canadians can see no sense in accepting promises that can be broken as easy as the famous scrap of paper." Nor will Canada endorse persecution and intoleration. Nor is Canada anxious to donate heavily to the German war chest by aiding the success of the Games. As to whether Canada dare not refuse Hitler's invitation...we shall see!

The proposal to remove the Olympic Games from Germany offers the most dramatic, and therefore the most effective opportunity to "tell Germany." Nazi papers have the temerity to assert that statements regarding outrages are not true.

The Berlin correspondent of the London "Times" is the authority for the statement that no reliance whatever can he put on Nazi promises of good conduct, of which there is no intention of keeping.

## ONLY NAZI'S REALLY ELIGIBLE

The "Commonweal," the famous Catholic weekly says: "The German government which does not respect a covenant solemnly arrived at with the Holy See, can hardly bother a great deal about "pledges to athletes."

Furthermore no Jews, no Protestant, no Catholic can train or compete or prepare for the Olympic Games unless he or she is a member of a Nazi official athletic association. In an official calendar issued by the German Olympic body, Adolf Hitler is pictured with the slogan "I summon the youth of the world!" This, by way of effrontery, should constitute a new world record. Of course every Nazi participant would have to "heil Hitler" who will formally open the Games...if they are held?

The Games are supposed to promote international friendship and by exhibitions of sportsmanship and fair play. Fair play in Germany! Can anyone who reads the press dispatches believe this possible? Just a minor case flashed into the paper recently with Gretel Bergmann, girl high jumper of Wuerrtemberg, who was barred from the field trails because as a Jewess she was ineligible in an official Nazi athletic body.

Not only with the object to impress Germany, but to preserve the very nature of the Games, the Games should be moved from Germany....

Canadian Olympic officials are individually hopeful that some simple solution may be found. There is no doubt that the nation itself feels much as the United States in the matter.... With the tide of opinion mounting high against Canada being represented at the Berlin Olympiad, Canadians will view the decision of the Olympic body with great interest.

**Maritime Sports Illustrated (October-November 1935), 17.**
**BETTER COLLAPSE OF THE OLYMPICS THAN ENDORSEMENT**

Says Elmer Ferguson of the Montreal "Herald"

The drive in the United States against participation in the Berlin Olympics reached the staid portals of the Senate this week. Washington was told that such participation would undoubtedly create ill-feeling towards amateur athletics by Roman Catholics, Hebrews and others whose peoples are being "purged" by Hitler Czarism in Germany. A resolution offered sets forth that "American sportsmen should not defile themselves by association with adherents of a government so intolerant and so un-sportsmanlike."

It is a point well taken, in theory, one that has already been expounded in this column, but a point which thus far has carried no weight with an Olympic Committee which, giving consideration only to cold facts as affecting its own affairs, contends that since Germany is not restricting the personnel of the American team or that of any other nation as to race or creed, there doesn't seem to be any sound reason for boycotting and thereby spoiling the Olympic Games of 1936. The makeup of its own Olympic squad is a purely internal matter for Germany alone to decide, say these amateur leaders in a fashion that may be eminently practical, but in view of the circumstances might better be termed coldbloodedly practical. They express fear that American withdrawal would not only wreck the 1936 Olympics, but would cause the collapse of the Olympic idea. What of it? Better the collapse of the Olympic idea than the endorsation, through association, of a nation which supports a government perpetrating the present atrocities, an association utterly foreign to the real olympic traditions.

**Maritime Sports Illustrated (December 1935), 14.**
**"READERS OF 'SPORTS' EXPRESS THEMSELVES ON THE OLYMPIC GAMES QUESTION IN LETTERS TO THE EDITOR"**

This is an example of the numerous letters we have received on the Olympic question. Further letters, both pro and con, will be published in the future.—The Editor.

Dear Editor:

I have before me a news item which expresses the attitude of the AAU of Canada convention held recently in Halifax, regarding participation in the Berlin Olympics. This was done in spite of resolutions and letters of protest from leading sportsmen and liberal minded people throughout Canada.

Can it be that these delegated sportsmen to the Convention are desirous of the trip to Germany, and would sacrifice the most beautiful tradition of amateur sport to achieve this end?

Adolphe [sic] Hitler and his fascist government has carried on extreme persecutions against Jewish, Catholic, Masons and sportsmen who refused to accept his policies. This persecution has been developed to such a frenzy that it borders on insanity, as the news item dealing with the death of the Jewish football player proves. Hitler's intentions are now to utilize OUR Olympics to glorify militarism and fascism.

Should the Olympic Games be held in Germany they will cease to be what they have been in the past. If we permit the games to be held in Germany they will become a mockery after 1936.

It is no longer a question of pro or con, it is an issue whether we shall have the Olympics with us hereafter. All sportsmen must give an emphatic "NO" demanding the removal of the Games from Germany!

Maurice Rush,
Vancouver, B.C.

Dear Editor:

Why don't you change the attitude of your magazine toward the Olympics? You should get right behind to make a success of the Games from a Canadian viewpoint!

Frank Harley Jnr.,
Ottawa, Ontario.

Dear Editor:

What has politics to do with sport? Leave that to the politicians and leave sport to the athletes.

Allan J. Walters,
Regina, Sask.

Dear Editor:

Congratulations! I am a Roman Catholic who is glad to see your magazine take a real stand against the Olympic Games! Outside of the fact that there isn't a chance for Canada to achieve anything, if I put down what I think about Hitler and his methods this paper would burst into flame. Hoping he does too.

Charlie O'Brien,
Mount Pleasant, Ont.

## THE 1934 BRITISH EMPIRE GAMES

[*Following the 1928 Olympics, several English-speaking countries were unhappy with American dominance of the medals and the lack of sportsmanship shown by some nations. Several Olympic officials of British Empire teams discussed the viability of hosting another meet half-way between Olympics that would take place in a more friendly, family-type atmosphere, and better prepare these countries for the Olympics.*

*Without the efforts of M.M. "Bobby" Robinson, the Empire Games would have foundered. Robinson, manager of the Canadian track team and sportswriter for the Hamilton Spectator, convinced the city of Hamilton, Ontario, to build new sporting facilities, provide travel subsidies for poorer countries, and supply visiting athletes and officials with meals and accommodation. When the English team threatened to withdraw at the last minute, Robinson persuaded Hamilton to provide a travel subsidy and threatened to replace the English team with an American squad.*

*Three-hundred athletes from Australia, New Zealand, Bermuda, British Guiana, England, Scotland, North Ireland, Newfoundland, and South Africa arrived in Hamilton in 1930. They competed in six sports in fifty-nine events. Women were limited to swimming and diving events. In 1934, women's track and field events were added.*

*The Games unleashed an outpouring of imperialist sentiment. At the opening ceremonies the athletes sang "God Save the King" and "Rule Britannia." Canadian sportswriter H.H. Roxborough wrote that "today the British Empire is held together by sentiment rather than force; and whatever develops friendships will stimulate that understanding and good will." Four years earlier, Canada convinced Great Britain to declare that it, New Zealand, Australia, and South Africa were "autonomous communities within the British Empire, equal in status, in no way subordinate one to another in any aspect or their domestic or external affairs...." The Games were a chance to keep the new Commonwealth united.*

*The British Empire Games were a success. Every event was sold out. According to the final count, the Games cost Hamilton $4,000, but the city emerged with $8,000 in new facilities. As a result, the British Empire Games Federation originated and new Games were scheduled. The next Games were awarded to South Africa, but when that country refused to allow Blacks and Asians to compete, Canada and several other countries succeeded in having the 1934 games transferred to London, England. Sydney, Australia, hosted the 1938 Games. This document describes the 1934 Games—which now included women and athletes from India, Rhodesia, Jamaica, Trinidad and Hong Kong. H.H. Roxborough, "Empire Field Day," Maclean's Magazine (15 July 1934), 9, 46.]*

If time and space were illusions and it were possible immediately to project ourselves into all parts of the British Empire, we would at this moment be astonished at the prevailing concentration upon things athletic. For this is the year when the senior sports champions will compete at London, England, in the second Imperial Games; and the stars of the Empire will run, jump and throw in the City of Melbourne, Australia.

Are these sport events so momentous that they can temporarily overshadow tariffs, treaties, budgets and other national problems? No; but to the masses they are more interesting. The name of South Africa's Prime Minister may not be generally known, but if the son of a former Boer should outsprint the fleetest runners of the Empire, that athlete's name would be known and respected throughout the English-speaking sporting world.

Indeed, so significant have the Empire Games become that not only will England, Ireland, Scotland and Wales be strongly represented, but New Zealand, Australia, India,

South Africa, Rhodesia, Jamaica and Canada will also send their leading track and field athletes, swimmers, boxers, wrestlers, bicycle riders and bowlers.

Canada is so thoroughly aroused that the current plan is to spend $35,000 to dispatch a contingent of 100 men and women athletes.

But numbers alone will not ensure the success of the British Empire Games. The quality of the competition will be more important. Will the rivalries be keen and the performers capable? They certainly will.

In early August, in the heart of the Empire, Canadian stars will meet hundreds of battling competitors fully charged with the will to win honors for themselves and their nation. Included in the list of track and field stalwarts will be J.P. Metcalfe, an Australian athlete who has high-jumped six feet six and one-half inches and has exceeded fifty feet in the running hop, step and jump. New Zealand's representation may include W.J. Savidan, who placed fourth in both the 5,000 and 10,000 metres races at the last Olympiad, and Jack Lovelock, the world's record holder for one mile, now a student in England but born in the island Dominion. If the Irish Free State chooses to compete—and she probably will—then Dr. Patrick O'Callaghan, twice Olympic champion hammer thrower, or R.M.N. Tisdall, current 400 metre Olympic title holder, if in training, would almost certainly necessitate the raising of the green flag to the top of the centre staff. India has a good hurdler and sprinter; South Africa won three titles in the first Empire Games and is certain to be athletically prominent; and you can't overestimate the strength of England and Scotland which won ten first and ten second places in the 1930 meet held in Hamilton, Ontario. Indeed, the rest of the Empire is so athletically capable that only the strongest Canadian team can maintain our position of second only to England.

## CANADA'S PROSPECTS

UNFORTUNATELY, most of the experienced campaigners whose speed and power have given Canada an enviable international reputation in recent years are now out of competition. Percy Williams, Olympic hero of 1928 and Empire champion of 1930, will manage the current Imperial team but will not compete; Alex Wilson, quarter-mile Empire titleholder and the fastest quarter and half-miler ever raised in Canada, will coach the team and is ineligible for competition; Phil Fdwards, whose masterly strides have earned international points for his adopted land may prefer study to racing, and even if he should run he must represent British Guiana. Duncan McNaughton, native of Cornwall, Ontario, and later resident of Vancouver, the reigning Olympic champion high jumper would he a welcome addition to the team but at time of writing is a doubtful entrant; while Eddie King, who advanced to the final in the Los Angeles 1,500 metres race, is also an uncertain starter.

In some of the jumps and most of the weight events, Canada's recent performances have not reached the standard required in international competition. This year, unless some budding athletes suddenly blossom into championship flower, the Dominion's performances will he ordinary. [The long list of Canadian male athletes and their chances of success has been deleted.]

## OUR GIRLS SHOULD WIN

But regardless of the failures or successes of mere men, you can depend upon it that Canadian girls, unless official differences interfere, will lead the Empire. The English lassies are particularly good in weights events, while Miss Clark from South Africa is a former holder of the world's hurdling record; but feminine Canucks have always displayed international strength. In April three United States indoor titles were won by Toronto runners and even though our weight-throwers are comparatively weak, it does not require an astonishing gift of prophecy to foretell that Canadian girl athletes will win the Empire track and field title.

It is also hopeful to recall that in every internationally important athletic programme, some Canadian—Sherring, Kerr, Goulding, Thompson, Williams, Mc-Naughton, Wilson, Grosse, Cook, Catherwood or Strike—has been inspired to amaze the world. [Predictions of how Canadians will do in each event have been deleted.]

**THE SCHOOLBOY GAMES**

The culmination of the second Empire Games in mid-August will not conclude Canada's 1934 bid for sport recognition. For our schoolboy stars, the curtain will just be rising.

Throughout the early summer each province will hold provincial schoolboy championships, after which the outstanding sectional athletes will move to Hamilton for the national trials. Following the latter tests, twelve of the best athletes, providing their scholarship is also commendable, will be taken to Vancouver, outfitted in national togs and subjected to a week's training.

On October the tenth, these twelve sporting Galahads will sail to Australia in quest of the schoolboy championships of the Empire. They may even perform in New Zealand, and if they do a period of four months will be saturated with athletic adventures that will shame the story books.

Naturally, these expeditions to Australia and England require labor and money. Is the expenditure of $35,000 by Canadians likely to pay worth-while dividends?

Among the Empire Games liabilities would be listed the objection raised by South Africa to the inclusion of colored athletes in the Imperial contests, and the resulting change of venue from the Republic to the Motherland.

Equally dangerous with the incitement of racial differences, is the threat of a flag problem. Owing to the fact that so many of the Commonwealths and Dominions which make up the Empire now have their own national flags, the suggestion has been made that each unit should have a distinctive flag and that the Union Jack itself should be flown only for Empire purposes. Canada, of course, has no separate national flag and probably will continue to carry the Empire ensign.

Disputes over the number and qualifications of officials are always associated with international jaunts, and this year's games are keeping up with the tradition.

Even though flags, races and personalities tend to spoil the ideals of sportsmanship, still there are reasons why Canada should continue to play with the rest of the world.

No individuals or nations like to be remembered as "spongers," yet the Dominion has received more favors than she has bestowed. When the first Empire Games were held in Hamilton in 1930, England generously sent a team of more than 100 and thus assured the success of the games; while the cost of providing a trip to Australia for a dozen Canadian boys is almost entirely contributed by Australian sportsmen. Surely when our share is comparatively small, we would be ungracious if we declined to pay something toward our own fun.

Furthermore, international sport is helpful because it creates favorable publicity and fosters better understandings. Finland and Japan are quite conscious of these influences, and the successes of the Nipponese at Los Angeles and the lusty encouragement given them by the enthusiastic Yankees created a friendly atmosphere that has done much to discourage war propaganda.

The nations of the British Empire need that same binding tie. After all, the cost of the trips to England and Melbourne will not equal the salaries paid to ten Members of Parliament—and the influence for good will perhaps be more evident.

Chapter 15

## MARKSMANSHIP—ARCHERY, SHOOTING

According to the December 1934 issue of Harper's Monthly Magazine, in terms of sporting goods sales, archery was the fifth-fastest growing sport in the US and trapshooting was eighth. Municipal playground and recreation departments, as well as private amusement parks, established archery ranges and arranged tournaments. By 1933, there were some 300 private archery clubs and more than 10,000 college students participated regularly in archery. The game was played by the Boy Scouts and in private camps. Gunnery was even more popular. By 1934, trapshooting had five million followers. Skeet shooting, which was invented in the mid-1920s, grew to 2,500 clubs with more than 100,000 members one decade later. At the end of the decade, Time reported that there were more civilian rifle clubs than private golf clubs.

The popular magazines attributed the increased popularity of marksmanship sports to the unsettled conditions of the 1930s. The March 1939 editorial in The American Rifleman, "Archery for Women," attributed the popularity of guns to its ancient link with primitive man, and glowingly described the benefits of outdoors and nature, compared to creeping urbanization.

Archery grew at a more moderate rate than gunnery. Lacking spectator appeal, archery championships were often held in relative obscurity from reporters. Even multiple national champions Russ Hoogerhyde (1930-32, 1934, 1937, and 1940) and Jean A. Tenney (1937 and 1938) were rarely mentioned in the national press. Several novelty events in the 1933 national championship illustrated the state of the sport, when national records were established for the longest standing shot (478 yards) and the farthest prone shot. Here, the participants lay on their backs with bows strapped to their feet. Two years earlier, the introduction of international rules for target shooting made possible the comparison of scores throughout the world, and in 1933, the United States joined the International Archery Association.

The National Archery Association actively encouraged women competitors and allowed women to compete in male tournaments as well as in their own events. In the latter, women were to enforce the rules and conduct the shooting. Since the average force expended to shoot an arrow was forty-five pounds for men and thirty pounds for a woman's bow, women rarely did well in the longer distances. To many people, archery was a perfect sport for women. "There is no form of exercise better suited to women," wrote Dr. Robert Palmer, physician and former American archery champion, in 1933. "It strengthens every muscle of the body without danger of any of the injuries which are only too often accidental to other sports." In 1930, the NAA allowed colleges to save on travel funds by sponsoring "telegraphic matches" between women colleges, and two years later, its Annual Intercollegiate Archery Tournament attracted 560 women from sixty colleges. "Archery for Women" reveals some of the reasons why school and college administrators considered archery a "girl's sport."

## SHOOTING

Participation in gun sports developed quickly in the 1930s due largely to the efforts of the National Rifle Association (NRA) and to the publicity the NRA received from sportswriters. Most shooting contests originated from military-oriented programs. In rapid-fire pistol competitions, for example, competitors shot at man-sized targets—the full-sized man was changed to a side-facing silhouette in 1935, and to a more rectangular body and head target in 1939. National rifle and pistol matches were controlled largely by the US War Department, which spent $500,000 in 1940 alone in sponsoring the national championships at Camp Perry on the shores of Lake Erie.

The National Rifle Association, which received funding from the War Department, devoted itself throughout the 1930s to promoting rifle and pistol sportsmen's clubs, and between 1928 and 1938 it increased paid membership from 25,500 to 49,300. "The National Rifle Association," and "Rifle Competitions" detail the role of the NRA in promoting shooting as a sport. In 1930, rifle and pistol competitions were highly localized and the rules varied widely from area to area. Most sportswriters and the general public took little interest in them. By the late 1930s, the NRA's public relations committee secured the active cooperation of several nationally-syndicated sports columnists, providing the NRA with greater media coverage. "Rifle Competitions" details the NRA's attempt to go beyond telegraphic matches to establish a system of regional and national competitions using standardized rules.

Under the motto, "Every American boy and girl is happy with a rifle," the NRA offered support and membership to YMCA's, summer camps, and colleges. Although the Junior Rifle Corps was discontinued in 1933 due to economic hardships, affiliated junior clubs increased from 524 in 1928 to 1,151 ten years later, due to the NRA's portrayal of junior rifle training as a matter of safety, similar to swimming instruction.

On the intercollegiate level, shooting as a sport was hindered by the women's anticompetitive movement, apathy to Reserve Officer's Training Corps that saw military instruction in schools downgraded from mandatory to voluntary, and to students' criticism of militarization. Intercollegiate competitions often relied on mail contests in which the NRA scored target sheets mailed in to its headquarters rather than on shoulder to shoulder tournaments. Because the ROTC supplied coaches and ammunition, riflery survived the depression better than most intercollegiate sports and by 1940 riflery replaced horseback riding as the favorite all-season sport for collegiate women. Elsewhere, as the document "Why Men Won't Let Women Shoot" illustrates, most men frowned on women's shooting.

Rifle and pistol shooting in Canada also had its roots in the military. Canada's equivalent to the NRA was the Dominion Marksmen. Although the Canadian Small Bore Rifle Association began in 1932, with the decline in prestige of the military between the two World Wars, shooting sports in Canada received little attention in the popular press. Canadians did well in international meets, especially at Bisley, which remained the mecca for Canadian riflemen. Each year the Canadian Pacific and the Canadian National Railway companies held a small bore rifle shoot to determine the twenty members to represent Canada in the International Railway Rifle Competition among the United States, Great Britain, and Canada. The selection, "He Won All the Trophies," illustrates the connection between shooting, military experience and police training, as well as the physical and mental attributes considered necessary for success.

Trapshooting, inspired by the desire for shooting practice when game birds were out of season, was molded into a popular sport by the Amateur Trapshooting Association. Amateurs could compete for cash prizes, but could not receive money for teaching shooting, or be employed by gun, ammunition, or trap and target companies. In flight, the clay saucers approximated the swift, steady flight of quails. By 1934, trapshooting had five million followers and attracted hundreds of male and female participants to the Champion of Champions Shoot at Vandalia, Ohio, where individual state titlehold-ers shattered more than eleven carloads of sand and plaster of paris targets in their quest for national titles. Until skeet shooting was invented in the mid-twenties, many people felt trapshooting might be detrimental to field shooting. Although both sports used identical clay birds and spring-catapult traps, the mechanical monotony of trapshooting, which employed only one trap with competitors remaining in the same location with their shotguns raised to their shoulders, allowed skeet shooting to make tremendous strides in the Depression years.

William Hernden Foster, outdoorsman and editor of the National Sportsman and Hunting and Fishing magazines, is usually credited with inventing skeet. During the World War I, Foster sought to improve his small game shooting skills in the off sea-son and experimented with two traps at opposite sides to double the number of shoot-ing directions and angles. To advance his new sport, and, according to Time magazine, because Foster wanted to promote the arms and ammunition business and attract ad-ditional advertising to his magazines, he launched a country-wide campaign in 1926 to name the new sport, then termed "Round the Clock Shooting." More than 10,000 people submitted names to the National Sportsman, and Gertrude Hurlbutt won the $100 prize for suggesting the Norse word for shooting—skeet. Foster established the National Skeet Shooting Association the next year.

In 1935, the first National Skeet Shooting Championship attracted 124 contestants. The following year, 225 shooters from thirty-one states competed in the national tour-nament in St. Louis, attracting more than 6,000 spectators. Skeet shooting had arrived as a national sport. It now had more than 2,500 clubs, published the monthly Skeet Shooting News, and many sporting magazines, including Country Life, began publish-ing skeet news regularly. "Skeet Shooting" details the growth of skeet in these early years.

Skeet grew quickly because it was easy to learn and achieve good scores. Hunters could use their own field shotguns to fire a succession of shots from various angles at targets that simulated the flight patterns of game birds, and since the sport catered to small groups it possessed a social aspect akin to golf and tennis. A skeet field could be laid out for as little as $250, and a hour of shooting cost only $4.50—$1.50 for clay pigeons, and $3 for shells. On the other end of the financial spectrum, wealthy coun-try estate owners built their own fields and invited guests each week to compete in intimate friendly rivalries. The enthusiasm of Bobby Jones and Hollywood stars such as Clark Gable and John Barrymore, who had a private skeet clubhouse on his Beverley Hill estate, further promoted the sport.

As with most other sports, skeet benefited from technology. Initially pulled manually, by the end of the decade, traps were controlled by remote control and an electric variable timer threw the targets with unbiased irregularity. Coaches also emerged to instruct the large numbers of new converts. One of the oldest country clubs in the United States, the Brookline Country Club of Massachusetts, hired skeet champion Ollie Mitchell to manage its portable two-unit skeet field. To help clubs recruit additional members, Country Life sponsored a novice skeet tournament in 1939 that attracted 500 two-man teams from Canada and twenty-five American states and immediately became the largest skeet shooting tournament to that date.

As with archery, skeet shooting attracted women and young people. In 1938, for example, twenty percent of all registered skeet shooters were women and children. Not allowed on golf courses on Sundays, perhaps many of these competitors were initially golf widows and orphans. Of the seven amateur skeet champions in 1938, only one was more than twenty-one years of age, and the youngest was twelve. The female winner was a seventeen-year-old Akron schoolgirl, Patricia Laursen, with only two years' of shooting experience.

## ARCHERY FOR THE FUN OF IT

*[The following account of archery details the reasons for the sport's popularity. The philosophy behind John Tunis' ninth book,* Sport for the Fun of It, *was that sports should be played by young and old for enjoyment, for moderate exercise, and for relaxation from the worries of the world. John Tunis,* Sport for the Fun of It. A Handbook of Informaticn on 20 Sports Including the Official Rules *(New York, 1940), 4-8.]*

Archery is sometimes regarded as a pastime for cranks. Nothing could be further from the truth. Archery is not a fad. On the contrary, it is an ancient sport enjoying a slow yet steady growth in modern times, and attracting devotees of both sexes and all ages. (In fact Miss Dorothy Smith, now Mrs. Cummings, who was woman's champion from 1919 to 1926, won her first title at the age of 15). The advantages of archery are that it appeals to everyone from the Boy Scout to the retired professional man or woman. The college girl who dislikes contact games such as basketball, the former athlete now in business who needs exercise combined with relaxation and the housewife who wants to play a game and hasn't room for a tennis court in her backyard, all find archery does exactly what they require. Moreover it has one advantage almost no other sport possesses. It's one of the few kinds of sports in which women—up to the distance of 60 yards can compete on even terms with men.

Archery is excellent for posture. It develops the chest, straightens the back, and is especially useful in crippled and post-operative cases, while with light weight bows under a doctor's direction, sufferers from cardiac trouble who can enjoy no other game find they can shoot a bow and arrow. Archery is decidedly not a spectator sport. It's a playing game, one for everybody, and not confined to a single season of the year. In fact archers shoot outdoors in Summer and compete indoors on ranges in Winter, and it is therefore a year-round sport. Today a wounded war veteran shoots from his cripple-chair and is well up with the leaders. Recently a big game hunter tossed away his rifle and took up archery instead. Many rifle hunters are doing this. Thus, archery often becomes the hobby of a whole family.

There are no gangs of paying fans in the bleachers at the National Championships. There are no bleachers. Instead one finds eighty targets in line with a double shift of archers of both sexes going steadily from early in the morning until late in the afternoon. Almost the only spectators are popper and mommer who have come to see their twelve year old win his first place medal (worth $.75) in the Junior American, and the four ladies in a huddle who are the wives of that crack team which won a state title earlier in the summer. Archery is for the sportsman; the eight year old Girl Scout or the seventy year old president of a big bank in Cleveland who never misses a championship each Summer....

One factor in the more rapid growth of archery in recent years has been the construction of public ranges all over the country by the W.P.A. Today there are seventy-two municipal ranges in various cities and towns throughout the country in Arizona, California, Connecticut, Colorado Delaware, Illinois, Indiana, Iowa, Kansas, Louisiana, Massachusetts, Michigan, Minnesota, Missouri, New Jersey, New York, Ohio, Oklahoma, Oregon, Pennsylvania, Tennessee, Texas, Washington, Wisconsin, the District of Columbia and even in Hawaii. Here is proof that archery today is a national sport.

At present there are about three hundred clubs affiliated with the N.A.A. of which the majority are located on municipal courses. They average thirty-seven members as compared with twenty-five members per club for those having a private range. There are in addition many thousands shooting each year in schools, colleges and summer camps, as well as home-made ranges on many lawns where one can easily set up a target. Archery is not an expensive sport. Bows are made of lemonwood, osage orange, and yew, and a good lemonwood bow costs $5 or $6. For a beginner arrows can be bought as cheaply as three dollars a dozen, while matched footed pine arrows come to $9 a dozen, or less than a dollar apiece and a target at which to shoot costs $5. Most matched tournament arrows today are made of Port Orford cedar and footed with beefwood. The best grade cost about $18.00 a dozen, but good ones may be secured for around $12.00 per dozen. About ten dollars will purchase equipment for a boy, girl or a beginner to learn upon. Equipment for experts costs more, and one can pay $35 to $50 for a first class yew bow. Many learn how to make their own equipment—a phase of the hobby that few sports can match. But even with an ordinary bow, such advances have been made in manufacturing in recent years, that Robin Hood's feat has no longer become unusual even for archers who do not win titles. Incidentally, you will have plenty of choice for equipment, as there are some 400 manufacturers of archery equipment, and today a summer camp for the training of competent instructors exists in Roxbury, Vermont.

Organizing an archery club is not difficult. It costs two dollars a year for an individual to join the N.A.A. which is always ready to assist in formation of a club, arrange matches with teams in the neighborhood and otherwise help promote the sport in your vicinity. The N.A.A. also encourages club championships, state tournaments and interclub contests, as well as camp and school matches, by mail and telegraph. For eleven years it has conducted an Intercollegiate match by telegraph. This contest has grown so fast that last year 150 teams with 1,184 archers competed, and 83 different colleges were represented. A tournament consists of a certain number of what are called rounds. A "Round" in archery is a number of arrows shot at fixed distances. The customary rounds in the United States are [the American, the Metropolitan, and the York]. Besides these rounds there are other standard rounds for women, for team play and for juniors.

Nearly all women's colleges today make archery a regular sport, while it is popular at the state universities of Alabama, California, Iowa, Illinois, Kansas, Minnesota, Ohio, Wisconsin and others, as well as at Northwestern, Purdue, Drake, Pittsburgh, Southern California, Toledo, Wichita and dozens of other coeducational institutions. This reminds me of a striking contrast in sport which presented itself during a trip among the eastern colleges last Spring. At an old and noble university for men I was taken to watch Spring football practice. Before that instrument of torture called a tackling dummy, stood a hard-chinned man in baseball uniform with a baseball cap pulled well down over his eyes. A long line of dejected-looking youngsters stood waiting their turn to chastise the dummy. Beside the gibbet stood the coach, clapping his hands and snarling at each candidate....

We inspected the playing fields, we looked in at various sports, we returned in an hour, and the torture, both physical and verbal, was still under way. Next day I visited another ancient institution of learning, devoted, this one, entirely to women. A trip of half an hour by car round the campus was revealing. It was a warm Spring afternoon and on every side were girls playing. They were playing tennis, they were playing lacrosse, they were playing golf, they were playing badminton, they were shooting at archery targets in great numbers. There they were, all playing, all enjoying themselves in the open air. Nothing but happy faces of young women playing games. A contrast to the masculine educational scene.

## ARCHERY FOR WOMEN

[*Caroline Coleman was the assistant supervisor of physical education for women at the University of California at Berkeley. In this article, intended for teachers of physical education in secondary schools and universities, she notes the gender differences in archery between school clubs and adult clubs and explains why teachers thought archery was a good sport for women. Caroline W. Coleman, "Archery as a Physical Education Activity," The Journal of Health and Physical Education, (May, 1933), 32-33.*]

HOW CAN we account for the greatly increased number of school and college archers in the last few years? How can we explain their new contagious enthusiasm? Is it because they have caught that enthusiasm from the teacher and from archers in the world at large, or is it due to the teacher's conviction that archery has unusual corrective values and that it is an ideal activity for students who are below par physically?...

Archery is a fascinating, beautiful sport to watch. The casual observer longs to be standing on the shooting line as beautifully poised and to be sending arrows as cleverly to the mark as he sees the archers doing. The scientist finds a challenge in the precision which the sport demands and in the interesting problems which are still unsolved, concerning the mechanics of the arrow's flight. Many whose professions make it difficult for them to time their recreation with others find in archery a stimulating, invigorating exercise.

Archery is not a sport for weaklings, primarily. We can understand the reasons for so classifying it, because of the almost universal custom in schools and colleges of relegating archery to the physical education classes for girls and women. The opposite situation prevails in clubs and tournaments, however. The following instance may be typical: a young unmarried woman became interested in archery several years ago and started coming to the regular Sunday shoots of a local archery club. When the writer joined the club a year or two later, she was welcomed especially by this young woman. "I do hope you come regularly. Sunday after Sunday. I have been the only woman present. The other women come only occasionally, to please their husbands." Originally, club members had been open to women without payment of dues. The men's dues were designed to include wives and children, and other women felt most welcome to attend without charge. The women are a minor element in the large tournaments, also, and usually comprise from 25 to 35 per cent of the total number of participants.

Unquestionably, the interest in archery is increasing and I know of no other sport for which the stage is more opportunely set for continued growth. Improved methods of construction have made it possible for makers of archery equipment to sell bows and arrows for less money that ever before. An increasing number of city officials are finding areas that can be set apart as archery ranges. The archers have increased their understanding of the science of shooting. They teach more efficiently than they did formerly, and more people are learning to enjoy the sport. For instance, we have learned that the average woman is more successful at archery if she uses a comparatively weak bow, although accuracy demands thereby that she exert unusual care to eliminate minor errors of shooting form....

And then there are the benefits from the point of view physical education. The teaching of archery provides a splendid opportunity for developing the conscious control of a well-balanced standing position which should be maintained throughout the activity. The unusual type body leverage required for the draw quite often results in body-twisting, head-tilting, shoulder-hunching, and in making one hip very prominent by the concentration of body weight on one foot. The change to even balance invariably improves the shooting. Girls are especially interested to recognize faulty standing habits and improve them, when these can be presented from such an objective point of view. Further, archery demands the use of the upper back and shoulder muscles in a way which is valuable for posture control and which is unequaled in other sports....

Accordingly, the reasons for developing archery in schools and colleges are unlimited. Departments of physical education for women in colleges and universities have already made great progress in this development, but the men have scarcely made a beginning. Further, I have been told by archery teachers in other parts of the United States that very few physical education departments in secondary schools have organized archery for either boys or girls.

Apparently, the number of secondary schools in California which are equipped to teach archery is larger than elsewhere. This number has been increasing rapidly in the last few years. Again, it has been largely a girls' sport to the present time. Just this year, however, one of the schools decided to offer archery to girls and boys on one day as part of an experiment in co-educational physical education. The response of the boys was overwhelming....

It is gratifying to realize, too, that makers of archery equipment have set unusually fine standards in the way of helping schools and colleges organize for the teaching of archery. Many firms have representatives who not only go out and teach the teachers, but outline ways of equipping the range and the archers at a minimum of expense. Further, they are prepared to sell either finished equipment or raw materials; and some of them give instruction in the making of finished equipment from raw materials.

Therefore, let us do the popular thing, and give our students the opportunity to enjoy archery!

### GUNS AND THE AMERICAN CHARACTER

[*The American Rifleman was published by the National Rifle Association of America. This editorial is an excellent example of the importance the Association placed on guns and the attributes it believed that nature and the outdoors bestowed on Americans. "Editorial. Pendulum," The American Rifleman (March 1939), 4.*]

...We become one of the world's greatest military powers to save the world for democracy by force—and within a few years destroy our military machine in order to save the world for democracy by a pacific example.

We worry no end about the spread of Communism, and then make heroes of the Communist-Anarchist forces of "Loyalist" Spain because we dislike that Fascism which had its inception in the effort to abolish the Communism we had earlier ranted against.

We appropriate money to teach our citizens how to shoot—and pass laws to prevent their learning.

What had all this to do with us as sportsmen? Just this: the swings of the pendulum have become wider—and wilder—as the average American has seen more of city streets and less of the fresh-turned plow furrows and virgin forest; and his eyes have turned more to traffic lights and less to misty marsh sunrises and irradiant mountain sunsets; as his ears have been attuned more to swing music on the radio and less to the organ in the tall pines, the fairy cymbals in the mountain stream, the drum beat in a horse's hoofs; as he has learned more from cloistered professors and less from Mother Nature.

The steady, dependable, clear-headed, fair-minded men; the men who have combined a true modesty with indomitable courage; the men who have established themselves as leaders and have been able to carry through without cracking mentally or physically in every great crisis of American history, have been men who were essentially out-of-doors men and sportsmen. In their moments of greatest stress they have turned to some flat rock on the bank of a tumbling stream, or a log in a wooded glade; to a creaking saddle and an open trail; and there, with out books, without experts, alone with the clean, clear-cut verities of Nature around, about, and within them they have made their decisions, healed their hurts, and regained their strength to carry on as leaders of men.

The Pendulum swings, but so long as it is weighted by men whose delight is in the field and the forests; men who love dogs and guns; men who can thrill to the rush of a buck or the rise of a covey, that Pendulum must persistently seek a resting-place in the sane middle ground between both extremes.

This Spring, a troubled one for the world, may Americans turn from their streets and highways to the woods and trails; from sitting and paying athletes to entertain them, to rising and doing for themselves; from aping others' thoughts and theories, to thinking for themselves—**out by themselves** except for the sun and wind and trees and the good earth. That way lies saneness—and an honorable Peace.

## THE NATIONAL RIFLE ASSOCIATION

*[The following two articles from The American Rifleman outline the role that the NRA played in promoting shooting sports. The Competitions Division of the NRA sought to duplicate baseball's system of local and regional playoffs leading to a national championship. It also attempted to establish and publicize national records for pistol and rifle shooting to allow sportswriters to draw comparisons across the country. "Editorial," The American Rifleman (January 1931).]*

### A NEW YEAR—A NEW START

The year 1931 represents the sixtieth milestone in the history of the National Rifle Association of America. That in itself is cause for confidence in the future. In the past sixty years the sportsmen of this country have passed through many periods of depression, and through many whirlwinds set up by reform movements running the entire gamut of human emotions in the direction of theoretical control of shooting, forest preservation, game propagation and crime prevention. The fact that the Association is not only still doing business, but is today in the strongest position that it has ever occupied, is ample cause for New Year's congratulations.

The membership of the N.R.A. has increased approximately tenfold in less than a decade. The carefully weighed conclusions of the Association in regard to legislation affecting shooters is not only listened to with respect, but is actually sought by legislators in all parts of the country. The opinions of the N.R.M.A. in regard to small-arms and ammunition design and construction are no longer considered as the ravings of a bunch of lunatics, but are listened to and given due consideration by the commercial and the governmental arms and ammunition experts. The National Rifle and Pistol Matches, with their invaluable School of Instruction, are now at last permanently provided for in basic law, and the number of men who will receive instruction and participate in the matches will be the largest in 1931 of any preceding year. The programs conducted by the Association for the benefit of more than 2,000 civilian rifle clubs and approximately 40,000 individual members take in a wider scope than at any previous time in the history of organized rifle and pistol shooting in this country. There will be more police officers actively undergoing training in the proper use of firearms during 1931 than has been the case in any previous year in the nation's history. Rifle instruction will be a featured part of the program in more boys' and girls' summer camps and in more high and preparatory schools in 1931 than ever before. There will be more ranges operating in public parks and buildings under the supervision of public officials in 1931 than at any time in our history.

These are not the visionary assumptions of some secluded reader of horoscopes, but well-considered, substantial statements of fact based upon past records and present reports received from all sections of the United States. Of course, we are far from the realization of our ideals in the matter of the education of the American public to the value of rifle and pistol shooting as a sport. We must go far along the road before the majority of police officials and police officers in the country are made to realize the importance of proper instruction in small-arms and marksmanship. We have a tremendous job of education on our hands before municipalities are persuaded of the advisability of appropriating money or setting aside land or buildings for the installation of municipal ranges and the payment of qualification pay to peace officers; but, like a snowball rolling down hill, each step forward in our program increases the size and momentum of the movement of which the National Rifle Association has for three score years been at the same time the standard-bearer and the motivating power.

It will be of interest to many people to know that the N.R.A. expended during 1930 approximately $20,000 over and above its expenditure for 1929, exclusively for such purposes as the increase of police marksmanship, increased awards of medals and trophies to State shoots, regional shoots and similar interest-promoting activities; for assistance to municipal leagues in the installation of ranges, the securing of equipment and the award of medals and trophies, for improved personal service to hunters in solving their problems of equipment, and last but not least, for the education of the American public through magazine and newspaper articles to the value of the shooting game as a man-building sport rather than a man-killing, gangland enterprise.

The widespread industrial depression had prevented many men from renewing their affiliation with the Association, and prevented many others from taking out their initial membership. It has done nothing to kill their enthusiasm and interest. With improved conditions in 1931, all of these men will be adding their weight to the advancement of the shooting game.

The conclusion of this, your Association's sixtieth year of service to the American shooter and the American nation, will give cause for gratification to every man who has conscientiously done his bit for the good of the game.

Happy New Year.

## RIFLE COMPETITIONS

*[As a result of the experiment discussed below, shooters were classified as either experts, sharpshooters, marksmen, or unclassified, based upon their performance in recognized tournaments. Similarly, tournaments were divided into four divisions based upon their importance: Class AA (the National Championship at Camp Perry); Class A (Regional and the National Midwinter Tournaments); Class B (State tournaments); Class C (local clubs or league tournaments). "Classification to Feature 1939 Tournaments," The American Rifleman (April 1939), 18-20.]*

A far-reaching change in the nation-wide competitions program of the National Rifle Association is now undergoing final study by the Special Competitions Committee appointed by the Executive Committee at its February Meeting.... The general principle will apply equally to the small bore rifle and to pistol and revolver shooting. No effort will be made to incorporate .30 caliber rifle shooting in the program at this time because of the fact that the selection of National Match Rifle Teams in state competitions and the payment of the expenses of each team to the National Matches out of War Department funds has already solved many of the problems which the new program attempts to solve in the case of small bore rifle and pistol shooters.

The new program is much broader than anything heretofore attempted by the National Association. It represents another step along the road which has seen small bore rifle and pistol shooting develop in a few short years from a state of highly localized competition with a diversity of regulations, target and programs into reasonably well standardized sports more and more accepted by the public as important activities in the national sports picture. The very fact that rifle and pistol shooting have developed so rapidly has resulted in growing pains of one kind or another.

The 1939 program is aimed at the correction of weaknesses or the improvement of the existing situation in four important directions:

First, the object is to encourage newcomers and shooters of only average ability by providing a nationally recognized classification system, by requiring the more important tournaments to adopt this classification system and to award class prizes, and by encouraging the sponsors of all tournaments, regardless of their size, to similarly adopt a classification system based on nationally recognized averages.

Second, it is the hope that the new program will protect the interests of the more expert shots by providing ample incentive in the way of adequate awards and also by providing for the determination of the important national championships entirely on a shoulder-to-shoulder basis so as to eliminate any question of the relative ability of the men who are publicized as the outstanding national ranking shooters.

Third, and one of the most important features, is the improved publicity which will result from the operation of the entire plan. There have been two major factors hindering wider publicity for rifle and pistol matches. One has been the multitude of matches and "championships" which have confused sportswriters and have led to the belief that the sport was not organized on a truly national basis. The second factor interfering with better newspaper publicity has been that local club shoots were purely local affairs and were not in any way tied in with either the Registered Shoots in the same area or with the National Championships at Camp Perry. It is believed that the program now under consideration will to a great extent remedy both of these difficulties. It will provide for officially recognized tournaments of various grades, in much the same way that baseball provides for leagues of various degrees of importance, so that sport writers will find it easier to understand what they are writing about and consequently will be more inclined to cooperate and give space to shooting activities. Furthermore, inasmuch as the scores made even in local tournaments will be official scores registered by the National Rifle Association and included in the computation of shooting average which will fix a man's national classification for competitive purposes, it is believed that sportswriters will come to understand that their local clubs are actually a definite part of the national shooting program rather than being merely a small group of local sportsmen shooting at targets for the fun of it.

While it is obviously not feasible in this first year of the plan's operation, it is nevertheless hoped that eventually the program can be so integrated that each local club will select its outstanding marksmen in each of three classes, sending them to the State Championship Tournament. The State Tournament will in turn determine the leading marksmen in the state in each of three classes and they will be sent to the regional Championships. The Regional Tournaments will determine the Regional champions in each class and they will be sent to the National Matches where the National Champion will be determined shoulder-to-shoulder on a common firing line under identical shooting conditions. The number of Regional Tournaments to be eventually established will of course depend on the growth of the game, on the density of shooting population in various areas, and on the availability of adequate range facilities and properly trained range and statistical personnel.

## WHY WON'T MEN LET WOMEN SHOOT

[*In the following article, the author, an avid hunter, argued men were unfairly prejudiced against female hunters. Although Mackay acknowledged some women fitted the prevailing negative stereotypes, she asserted times were changing and women not only made good hunters, but they were also unwilling to stay home and knit all day. Col. H.P. Sheldon rebutted Mackay's statements the following April. He conceded some women could be excellent hunters, if they were serious, but contended their psychological and physical handicaps made this difficult. Gwendolyn R. Mackay, "Why Won't Men Let Women Shoot?" Country Life and the Sportsman (December, 1937), 88, 122.*]

There has always been a terrific amount of feeling on the part of men about women shooting. No one seems to know why or how this feeling originated but like most things of that sort with men, it has become a habit and one that I think is very unfair to a great many sportswomen.

There seem to be two main grounds on which the male bases this feeling: A, "Women can't take it," and B, "Women are careless and therefore unsafe to have as shooting companions."

To be absolutely fair to both sides of this argument, let me say at the beginning that there are two distinct groups of women shots. The first answers perfectly to the above description: scatterbrained, chattering women, who are not sportswomen in any sense of the word, who think that shooting is fast becoming the "smart" thing to do, who have never taken the time to learn intelligently about guns, and who are too conceited to realize the tremendous danger not only to themselves but to their fellow shots every time they go out in the field.

Then there are the sportswomen in whose defense I am writing this article: the ones who have patiently and diligently learned the careful use of firearms and who have been made to realize, beyond the shadow of a doubt, by constant example and personal experience, the terrific responsibility of owning and operating a gun. Those women who can sit in a duck blind for nine or ten hours with their hands and feet half frozen and never once suggest quitting; those who can walk in line all day during upland bird shooting, keep in line, and never cross a fence or a stream without breaking their guns; and those who can ride for hours in red Carolina mud and, seeing the dog on point, can dismount quietly and, without visible excitement, carefully flush the covey of quail, picking their birds to shoot without becoming confused. Then last, but by no means least, women who can shoot in any drive both here and abroad, never pull across the line, and never shoot low in front, who will let a bird go entirely rather than "hog" someone else's shot, and who will never lose their heads no matter how hot the corner is—these are the women who have earned the right to shoot anytime, anywhere, beside any man, without being a nuisance or a menace. Fortunately, there are more and more such women joining these ranks every year.

No one would dream in this day and age of suggesting that women can't hold their own in tennis, golf, flying, sailing, or in the hunting field. Why then this age-old phobia about our shooting?

I do not hold that women are better shots than men or even just as good. I think the average man is better at all forms of sport than the average woman, but I do say that we can be just as careful as men in handling our guns, and that we must be even **more** careful than they, if we are to overcome their deep-rooted prejudice. Safety is the basic and fundamental rock on which to build up our reputation, and those women who realize this and follow it through should be made welcome at any shoot, just as they are in the aforementioned fields of sport.

I also think that if women would shoot twelve-gauge guns, especially in drives and also for duck, men would have more respect for them. Almost every man I know, tells me it is impossible for us to handle a twelve—"It kicks too much and it is too heavy." That is a fallacy. There is no reason, if your gun fits you properly and you get it up right, why it should ever kick you and as for its being too heavy, I can only say that I am of average size and strength and I have carried one all day long, walking up pheasants and have not passed away yet!...

Then there is another angle to my viewpoint. Certainly the days of sitting home with your knitting while the big, virile husband goes out to do sports are over. I don't think that most men crave any longer the fragile, delicate type of wife who can only be shown off to good advantage in flowing tea gowns in the drawing room! Not at all!

I think wives, like everything else, have had to change with the times and I believe men prefer this new type. I know lots of them who have motored all night with their husbands through driving snow so that they could be sure of being in their blinds with their decoys all rigged out before the morning flight and then after a bitter, freezing day have come home with only one or two duck, and sometimes none at all. Then too, I know women who have gone down South on shooting trips with their husbands where they have had to sleep in little cabins with all their heavy clothes on, in unbelievable heat, so as not to be eaten alive by mosquitoes. I have seen women walk ten miles a day over those endless Scotch moors, carrying their shells in one pocket and their lunch in the other, always going, either up or down hill through heather, fighting those detestable little biting "midges" with one hand and carrying their own with the other, until they were purple in the face and their tongues were hanging out!

These are the kind of women I mean who should be welcomed to shoot with men— the ones who really love the sport enough to overcome any discomfort—and these are the wives who should be encouraged and helped with their shooting instead of being, grumbled at and left at home—to knit!

## SHOOTING IN CANADA

[*J.L. Brown, who reported regularly on sports for this popular Canadian publication, discussed the major role the Dominion Marksmen played in promoting shooting sports in Canada, and Canada's success in international competitions. The article also revealed the growing urbanization of Canada. J. Lewis Brown, "Anyone Can Shoot," National Home Monthly (October 1939), 20, 68-69.*]

Canadians should, and do, take naturally to shooting. Descendants of pioneers who lived by the rifle, they have made rifle shooting a great national sport. They live in one of the few civilized countries in the world where opportunities for hunting abound. From coast to coast, in every province, they are surrounded by invitations to participate in one of the grandest of all outdoor sports. By well-planned game conservation Canada may hope to remain a sportsman's paradise for many years to come, But one thing she cannot do. She cannot permanently retain vast wildernesses at the very doorsteps of her cities. Constantly frontiers are being pushed backward. Where yesterday's buffalo herds roamed, cities stand today. Where moose and deer wandered undisturbed a few short years ago, are small booming towns, sprawling factories, mills and mines and cultivated farms. With this changing picture comes a change in a sport that is older than Canada. For the marksman, man or woman, boy or girl, who loves the thrill of a shot well and truly aimed needs no living target. He finds pleasure in matching his skill with rifle or shotgun against the skill of others or in shooting "solo" for the pure pleasure of testing the keenness of his eye, the steadiness of his muscles and the perfect co-ordination of a body that is physically fit.

More than twenty years ago the shooting enthusiasts of Canada were bound together in a nationwide organization designed to increase national interest in a great and growing sport and promote the feeling of fellowship among the legion of sportsmen who take pride in their aim. The organization was founded in 1916 and was known as Dominion Marksmen. The enthusiasm with which it was greeted everywhere gave early indications that its name was well chosen and that it soon would be thoroughly representative of sportsmen from coast to coast.

Dominion Marksmen in its two decade of existence has accomplished even more that it set out to do. Today its activities surpass the fondest dreams of it founders. Its members include men, and women, of all ages and of all classes. It has developed a sense of brotherhood among marksmen and provided opportunities for clean sport to thousands who might never have enjoyed them. It has placed Canadians in a high place amongst the marksmen of the world, with shooters from Canada capturing empire and international awards in a number far out of proportion to Canada's population.

In twenty years thousands of Canadians have enrolled in this Dominion-wide body. Among them have been leaders in business and finance and the professions. Many have commenced their association at the age of twelve or thirteen years. Many of them are far past middle-age. Today it would be difficult to find a city or town in Canada which does not boast at least one group of sportsmen in this fraternity of marksmen.

Many of the leading photographers started out with the most inexpensive cameras. In target shooting many of the finest scores today are made by a man or boy who started out with a five dollar rifle. For its the determination to succeed that counts. Realizing that many Canadians are enthusiastic about shooting as a sport but do not possess expensive equipment, Dominion Marksmen in 1936 organized a new series of competitions for anyone old enough to use a .22 calibre sporting rifle. Based on the same plans as other competitions, this new series attracted immediate, nation-wide interest and enthusiasm. In a little over two years, more than 1,850 clubs were formed with a total of some 17,000 members. Sporting Rifle Competitions already held give evidence of a keenness and skill equal to that shown in other Dominion Marksmen competitions and the enthusiasm of this new group of shooters is unexcelled. Just how many Canadians are actually engaged in this sport is difficult to estimate but the current membership is over 35,000 all particularly active in target shooting of one sort or another, and this figure does not include the thousands of shooters unregistered nor those engaged in hunting activities....

As the popularity of target rifle shooting increased, and more clubs were formed, it was only natural that clubs should wish to compare their ability to the ability of others; and so, in 1931, Dominion Marksmen announced its Senior Small Bore Rifle League. It is open to teams of seven men (with five high scores to count), from any registered club. Each team shoots three matches, and at their conclusion district champions are announced who then shoot off for the Dominion Championship....

For training purposes, the Canadian Militia and the R.C.M.P. are equipped with rifles known as .22 S.M.L.E., and which are not quite so accurate as modern high grade target rifles. Because of this, they did not consider it worth while to enter the Dominion Marksmen Small Bore Rifle League, as they would be handicapped because of their equipment. Therefore, in 1935 a .22 S.M.L.E. Rifle League was introduced, open only to teams which are authorized to use these rifles. Competition has been exceedingly keen each year, and as in the case of the Senior Small Bore Rifle League, the scores show improved shooting ability.

One might reasonably ask the question, "Where does all this shooting lead?" Well, while most shots are content to enjoy the thrill of competition and the many benefits that the sport brings with it, there are two competitions that the .22 rifle marksmen train for each year. Every summer on the famous Connaught Rifle Ranges at Ottawa a small army of Canada's finest shots, from Halifax to Vancouver, gather for the Lord Dewar International Rifle Competition, the Bisley of all small bore shooters. To the Dewar matches come the Dominion's leading marksmen, drawn from all types of shooters across the country. All compete in matches over fifty and one-hundred yard ranges, and it is from this group that the Canadian Lord Dewar Team is selected. The team then competes against units from the Mother Country, the United States, Australia, New Zealand, India and South Africa, and a place on the team marks the holder as one of the best marksmen in the game. In selecting the final team, the Dewar committee takes into consideration the shooter's year-round ability, as revealed in the records of Dominion Marksmen which are made available to the committee.

Then in the fall comes the nationwide .22 Sporting Rifle Championship which will attract over five thousand entries this year. Last year entries came from as far afield as the Yellowknife Mining Camp, from which dog teams brought the targets down to civilization. To this shoot and other competitions sponsored by Dominion Marksmen, many of Canada's famous marksmen can trace their early training....

Although specializing in .22 sporting rifle and .22 target rifle shooting competitions, Dominion Marksmen also organizes revolver competitions for police units as well as skeet and trapshooting tournaments all the year round throughout the Dominion. This organization has also improved the standard of shooting in most of the police forces of Canada, to say nothing of the many competitions provided each year for the air force units, Royal Canadian Naval Volunteer Reserve and other defence forces of the Dominion.

## HE WON ALL THE TROPHIES

[*As part of the North American experiment to inculcate company loyalty and proper work habits among its employees, the Canadian National Railways (CNR) organized industrial recreational programs in the late 1920s. Unlike many company athletic organizations, the CNR's recreational association belonged to the employees, who organized, conducted and financed their own sporting activities. In towns from the Atlantic to the Pacific coast, railway employees competed in a wide variety of sporting activities. The Canadian National Railways Magazine regularly reported on local rifle and pistol matches. "He Won All the Tropies," Canadian National Railways Magazine (March 1935), 18, 29.*]

A CANADIAN National Railways policeman has held: Every Canadian revolver and pistol championship since 1927; Every United States revolver and pistol championship at some time or another; Has taken practically every Canadian trophy for revolver and pistol shooting out of existence, by virtue of consecutive victories—but has given them all back for further competition!

Such is the proud record of Constable R.G Pickrell, member of the Investigation Department of the Canadian National Railways, Winnipeg.

And until the Armistice was signed at the conclusion of the Great War, he had never fired either a revolver or a pistol!

Without question the outstanding revolver and pistol shot on the North American Continent, and with few better in the world, he carries his honors modestly and fulfills his duties as railway constable at the C.N.R. depot in Winnipeg quietly and efficiently.

Never in the history of revolver or pistol shooting on this Continent has any one person held such a galaxy of trophies, medals, honors and records. For not only does he hold to his credit many Canadian and United States records, but also holds a world's record, made at Springfield, Mass., in 1933, when he scored 246 out of a possible 250 shots...

As a young lad in 1914, he enlisted with the 12th Battalion of the London Rifle Brigade, and saw active service in France. Young Pickrell took a great fancy to the machine gun and soon attained a high degree of proficiency, not only in shooting, but knowledge of its construction and uses. Some time after his arrival in France he was commissioned Battalion Machine Gun officer, a position which could only be held properly by officers with skill, daring, initiative and a complete supply of what is popularly known as "intestinal fortitude."

In 1916 Lieutenant Pickrell transferred to what was then known as the Royal Flying Corps, which gave him an enlarged field for machine gun work. He spent two years with the air force and flew on the Ypres, Douai and Somme fronts. Lieut. Pickrell modestly admits having had "something to do with disabling a few enemy planes", and in air fighting was wounded four times. He was also twice wounded with the infantry....

During the war he had met many Canadians, especially in the Air Force, and believed "these Colonials" were splendid chaps. Thus he decided that Canada might be a good place to live, so he sailed for this Dominion.

On arrival at the eastern seaboard, nothing looked particularly interesting to Lieut. Pickrell, so he decided to strike out for the "wild and woolly" west, and arrived in Winnipeg in the fall of 1922. His profession was flying, so, trough the old Canadian Air Board, Pickrell entered flying service in Northern Manitoba....

After three years of this work, Pickrell's boyhood ambition to get into police work returned. In 1925 he signed on as a constable with the Canadian National Railways Investigation Department, Winnipeg, and has been happily engaged at these duties ever since.

For many years in Winnipeg there has been much interest and activity in competitive revolver and pistol shooting, especially in police circles. Contests were held at various places each month, and when one of these was mentioned around C.N.R. Police headquarters, Pickrell went along with the Railway Police team to see what it was all about.

He was immediately smitten by the revolver shooting bug. He practiced diligently and with such perseverance and success that today he is the champion revolver and pistol shot on the Continent.

In 1926 he was a member of the Railway Police team, which won the MacMillan Trophy. He displayed such proficiency and skill that he was appointed instructor and took charge of training the Canadian National team. For the next two years his team cleaned up police team matches in Canada. In 1928 he took a revolver team to Camp Perry, Ohio. Pickrell's team lost, but he captured the individual International Pistol championship.

During the latter part of the same year Constable Pickrell, entitled to the rank of captain in the militia by virtue of his rank with the Royal Air Force, joined the Winnipeg Grenadiers Regiment. He soon created much interest in revolver, pistol and machine gun shooting, and in 1930 was placed in full charge of weapon training, including revolver, pistol, Lewis gun, Vickers gun and rifle shooting for the regiment.

Since this time Captain Pickrell has attended all the Canadian and United States revolver and pistol championship shoots and has carried home cups, medals, championships and records.

Pickrell carries his honors very modestly, and the thousands who pass him each day on their way to and from the trains little realize that the smart looking young fellow in the blue uniform of a Canadian National Railways' constable, is one of the world's greatest marksmen with revolver or pistol. "To what do you attribute your success with the revolver and pistol?" he was asked recently.

"Physical fitness is one of the most important items" was his quick reply. "No man in the world can shoot well if he is not physically fit. Championship shooting calls for practically as much physical training as the average athlete gets for any other championship meet. That may seem a peculiar statement, but it is true nevertheless.

"In other words, it is mostly a question of nerves. Your nerves simply must be perfect to do good championship shooting. I was never a heavy smoker, but when I am training for the championship shooting season, I quit altogether. The old adage 'to be moderate in all things' is most important to successful championship shooting and must be applied here.

"My advice to the younger generation who are interested in revolver, pistol or rifle shooting, is to prepare themselves physically. It is most important of course that they live properly and eat plain but good food, and get plenty of sound sleep. Clean living means a clear eye and steady nerves and staying up late at night does not mix with either."

## SKEET SHOOTING

[*The rapid growth of skeet is an excellent example of the importance of sport journalism in the promotion of athletics. William Foster wrote a monthly column called "Skeet" in Outdoor Life, and national journals such as Time, Esquire, News-week, and Collier's published regular reports on the fundamentals of skeet and its growing popularity. By the end of the decade, the sport's promoters were becoming worried that youngsters, both male and female, tended to dominate tournament play. The following excerpt was one of the early explanatory pieces on skeet shooting. "Wild Game, Those Clay Birds, When Skeet Is the Sport," The Literary Digest (4 July 1931), 31-32.*]

WATCH THE PRETTY BIRDIE!

Here it comes, soaring right at you! But don't duck!

Take careful aim with your gun.

Bang!

And another pigeon bites the dust, rather, turns to dust.

But don't call out the S.P.C.A.

These pigeons are made of clay, and are thus cousins of your own insensitive dinner-plates.

Clay-pigeon—or trap-shooting, in a word, but with a new name—skeet—and under a much more difficult technique.

A skeet-shooter fires from every conceivable angle, as he does in actual hunting. C. William Duncan explains in the Philadelphia Public Ledger magazine. In trap-shooting, "he gets mainly straightaway birds and slight quartering angles. The equipment in skeet is the same as used in trap-shooting, but there are two traps instead of one.

"Clay targets, by their swift flights from every possible angle, both singly and in pairs, provide a thrill equated only by the speedy travel of winged game.

Owing to the use of a high trap at one side of the field and a low trap at the other, shooters are offered targets which rise as from the ground, or that come sailing down.

They get incoming and outgoing targets, high and low targets, singles, and pairs flying in opposite directions."

The skeet bug, infecting its "victims" with skeetitis, has attacked thousands, we are assured. And now those who have this malady "suffer" as violently as those who have "the golf bug, the race-track fever, the baseball germ, and other deadly maladies." So far, however, Mr. Duncan admits as he proceeds:

"Skeetitis has not attacked as many persons as have the others, but it is growing rapidly, and we know not to what extent it will spread.

Wilmington, Delaware, is one of the cities where skeet-shooting is most popular. One Saturday morning there, I listened in vain for the chatter of the golf, tennis, or baseball fan, but heard instead the perpetual question:

"Are you going to the skeet-field this afternoon?"

Wilmington is, without a doubt, skeet-minded, and proponents of the game there say there already are more than 600 recorded skeet-shooting organizations in this country, and probably as many more unrecorded.

So wide a choice of angles and elevations not only prevents any possibility that the sport may become monotonous, but also gives the shooter practice that will develop him into an expert field shot.

In rural communities, and even near large cities, there are usually tracts of waste land suitable for this sport. The skeetfield should measure about 250 by 500 yards....

The program is divided into units of twenty-five shots, to be fired from the eight shooting-stations. Two single shots are fired from each station, and in addition there are four sets of doubles.

To round out the twenty-five, each contestant has an optional shot that may be taken from any station he chooses, while he also selects the trap from which the target is to be thrown.

To start the program, both traps are loaded, and the first shooter steps to station Number 1. Placing one shell in his gun, he calls "Mark," and Number 1 trap is released.

This gives him a straightaway shot, so-called. The result—"dead" or "lost"—is announced by the referee, who should stand somewhere behind shooting position Number 4.

The scorer marks the record on the tally-sheet the heading 1-R, indicating that the target flew to the right.

Reloading his gun, "the shooter again calls 'Mark,' and the next clay 'bird' is released from number 7 trap." Then, it is an "incomer," flying from the left, and the result is scored in the column marked 1-L.

The shooter then moves to station number 2 and shoots at a target from number 1 trap as it flies out at quarter. And his next chance is to break one from number 7 trap, a "quartering incomer." The same procedure follows at each station in sequence until the singles program of sixteen shots is completed at number 8.

Next comes the doubles program, eight shots being taken in order from stations 1, 2, 6, and 7. With two shells loaded in his gun, the shooter gives the signal, and both traps are sprung simultaneously, releasing two targets. One files away from the gunner, the other comes toward him. He shoots first at the outgoing "bird" and then at the incomer, and it isn't easy to bring them both down.

Finally, to round out the twenty-five-target program, the shooter is given one optional shot. He may take it from any station he selects, and also choose the trap from which the target is thrown.

"The skeet-shooter uses his favorite shotgun rather than one of special type, because the ordinary gun is best adapted to breaking targets thrown as they are in skeet, and also because the gunner wants to improve his skill in the field or on the marsh," says J.H. Otterson, an authority on the sport. As we read on, Mr. Otterson is quoted thus by Mr. Duncan:

"One rule of the game prohibits raising the gun to the shoulder until the 'bird' has left the trap and is actually in the air. This is to develop the 'quick-on-the-trigger' technique one must have when shooting game-birds.

The chief advantages of this sport are, first, that it offers a series of shots similar to those encountered in actual hunting; and, secondly, that the shooter may use the same gun to which he is accustomed in the field.

If the gun meets his requirements for hunting, it will serve equally well in bringing down skeet targets. Any gun bored so open that a clay target at twenty or twenty-five yards can get through the pattern is too open for ordinary use.

If a gun is too heavy and cumbersome to swing fast at skeet, it will show the same disadvantages in the field....

Now, coming to the subject of shots from various angles, Mr. Duncan returns to his interview with Mr. Otterson, whom he quotes thus directly in The Public Ledger:

"Frequently we all miss the first target at the number 1 position by overshooting. This target starts directly overhead and descends rapidly in its entire flight. It should be seen well above the barrels before pulling the trigger, in order to place the shot load below the head of it.

Incoming targets from the high and low trap-houses at station number 8 seem most difficult for the novice who has not acquired the correct technique."

Chapter 16

# RACING ON LAND—AUTOMOBILES, CYCLING

Americans loved automobiles. In the 1930s, there were approximately twenty-five million cars on the road and the American Automobile Association estimated that one-quarter of them were used almost entirely for pleasure. One form of enjoyment was determining the top speed of an automobile or motorcycle. In 1934, Sir Malcolm Campbell increased his land-speed record of 253 mph to 301 mph. Most cities and towns in North America had their own clubs which staged periodic races. An indication of the sport's growth was the debut of two weekly publications, National Auto Racing News (1934), and Illustrated Speedway News (1938).

At the beginning of the decade, about three-quarters of the approximately 350 race-tracks in the United States were located in county or state fairgrounds, and were from one-quarter to one-half miles long. The International Motor Contest Association used the yearly state fairs in the mid-west to operate a circuit for open wheeled "Big Cars." Daytona Beach, Florida, and Bonneville Salt Flats, Utah, hosted most land-speed record trials. In 1931, the last major board track, Altoona Speedway, closed. This left only Indianapolis and the Atlanta Raceway as non-dirt racing tracks. The emergence of midget auto racing in the second-half of the decade expanded the number of racing tracks to approximately one thousand by decade's end. Midget cars were easily adaptable to football stadiums, baseball diamonds, and large indoor halls.

Although auto racing maintained that the sport was the "great outdoor laboratory of the automotive industry," in reality most automotive companies maintained their own testing grounds. Drivers and spectators were fascinated by the thrill and danger of ever-increasing speeds. The Indianapolis 500 attracted the highest paid attendance of any single sporting event. In 1930, more than 170,000 onlookers were present when one mechanic and four spectators were killed when a racing car left the track. During the decade, the fastest qualifying speed for the Indianapolis 500 increased from 113 in 1930 to 130 m.p.h. at the end of the decade. The average speed of the winning driver increased from 100 to 117 m.p.h. In 1929, Henry Segrave set the land-speed record of 231 m.p.h. A decade later, John Cobb's vehicle reached 369 m.p.h.

In 1930, the American Automobile Association (AAA) adopted a new formula for Indy cars which limited engines to a maximum of 366 cubic-inches piston displacement and two valves per cylinder, forbade superchargers, required two seats and a riding mechanic (as existed prior to 1923), and mandated that cars weigh at least 1,750 pounds and have two independently-operated braking systems. The AAA sought to encourage domestic automobile companies to participate in the racing business by limiting competition to stock car-type engines, variations of which the public could buy from automotive dealers. The chairman of the AAA racing committee declared that if manufacturers "would enter cars purchasable at dealers it would be sure to arouse interest, as the spectator cares a great deal more if a car with the same name, engine, and chassis as the one he owns and drives is the winner rather than a special creation costing from $5,000 to $12,000 of which not more than three are built." Although these changes bankrupted specialty-type car makers such as Harry Miller, whose cars demonstrated matchless power and speed in the 1929 Indy 500, they encouraged Chrysler, Buick, and Studebaker to design new engines. In 1930, Studebaker entered a team of five racing cars based on its luxury touring car, the "President."

In 1936, Indy speedway turns were widened and the outside wall was angled inward to prevent cars jumping over the walls. The same year, the AAA limited total fuel consumption to 37.5 gallons to further reduce speeds and save lives, but seven cars ran out of fuel before reaching the finish line. Even worse, speeds were not reduced—the top five cars all went faster than the winners of the previous Indy. The following year, the fuel limitation was removed. Because of wear and tear on the paving stones, asphalt was laid over the track's turns in 1937. At that time, Indy was one of only two such tracks still operating in the country. The other was at Syracuse.

The end of most fuel restrictions in 1937—cocktails of alcohol, benzol, and acetone remained banned—and the freedom to use superchargers, returned Indy 500 to pure racing cars. For the 1937 Indy, Fred Offenhauser, Harry Miller's foreman before purchasing the company, designed a supercharged engine which produced 450 b.h.p. and placed it in a streamlined chassis. This dual overhead-cam Offenhauser engine, which powered a single-seat roadster that kept most of its weight concentrated on the left side to help the car through the turns, became the model for the famous "Indy car."

Other types of automobile racing also were affected by the Depression. As the document "Midget Auto Racing" indicates, one method of countering economic problems was to reduce engine size to allow more people to compete. The first modern midget car race was held in Sacramento, California, in 1933. The next year, Gilmore Stadium opened in Los Angeles as the first speedway built especially for midget cars. Inexpensive, and adaptable to almost any surface, midget racing spread quickly throughout the country.

## SIX-DAY BICYCLE RACES

Bicycling made a comeback in the 1930s. Precipitated partly by the cycling events in the 1932 Olympic Games, bicycle sales increased each year. The cost of CCM's bikes, which sold for between $35 and $55, remained unchanged throughout the decade. Bicycling also benefited from the Depression that forced many families to give up their cars, and from the motion picture industry that initiated an advertising campaign that displayed movie stars riding bicycles. In 1935, American factories produced 750,000 machines. The next year, experts estimated that about four million Americans owned bikes. Consumers could choose among 3-speed gear shifts, tandem bikes, three-seaters, six-seaters, and racing bicycles made of aluminum alloy that weighed only 13 pounds. Some railroad companies provided special trains to carry cycling enthusiasts and their wheels to scenic spots for one-day outings.

Cyclists pushed for cycle paths in parks and urged local governments to construct special trails beside city roads. In Chicago, a petition signed by 165,000 people resulted in the creation of 100 miles of bicycle paths. Detroit created "handlebar paths" in its parks, as did cities from Washington to Oklahoma City. The League of American Wheelmen, which largely comprised bicycle manufacturers, re-emerged in 1933 and cooperated with the Amateur Bicycle League of America in lobbying for bike trails in public parks and resorts. Amateur cycle races grew with the burgeoning interest in bicycles. The League of American Wheelmen sponsored races, and the Century Road Club of America held its first annual national championship in 1935.

The 1930s created an ideal set of circumstances for professional six-day bike races. The new hockey arenas in north-eastern United States and in Canada sought to fill their buildings with paying customers by temporarily converting them into velodromes. For 50 cents or so—women often admitted free—individuals could watch cycling races for as long as they wanted. Reporters and athletes relished the mounds of free food—many riders actually gained weight over the six-day event. The velodrome had a circus or an amusement park atmosphere. Jazz bands played in the infield as cyclists whirred around the track, and their partners ate and slept in full view of the audience. The cheers from the crowd, the array of colors worn by the riders, the smell of hot dogs and cigarettes, the gambling, the frenzied jams, and the real possibility of a thrilling crash attracted large crowds to arenas in cities such as New York, Newark, Chicago, St. Louis, Portland, Montreal, and Toronto.

Teammates took turns riding around steeply-angled (45 to 60 degrees), pine board tracks, called "saucers." At six to ten laps a mile, bikers reached speeds in excess of 40 m.p.h. and covered about 2,700 total miles in six days of racing. The team that recorded the most laps in six days was the winner. In case of a tie, points were awarded for timed sprints. These sprints were held about six or seven times a day in the early evening and points were awarded depending on each team's finish. For the last hour or so of the race, there were constant sprints. It was at these times that riders suffered broken collarbones, gnarled fingers, fractured ribs, and concussions.

Since more than one-half of the racers were from Europe, native-born bikers made good copy. Canadians did well at cycling. Doug Peace, for instance, won four national championships and competed in the Berlin Olympics. William "Torchy" Peden, from Victoria, British Columbia, was one of the most popular and successful riders of the decade, winning 38 six-day events in his career. Peden played to the gallery by jumping his bike up and down like a bucking bronco, snatching ladies' hats or scarves from their heads and wearing them for several laps, and steering his bike with his left leg while pedaling with his right.

Between races, Peden attacked the world's cycling record for a paced mile on his CCM $800 gold-plated bike with its 151-geared wheel. In November 1931, near Minneapolis, Peden pedaled one mile behind a motorcar fitted with a steel windscreen at a world record speed of 74 m.p.h. In addition to earning publicity for CCM, such exhibitions promoted the upcoming six-day bike races.

The promoters controlled almost every aspect of the race, which sometimes cast doubt on the sport's propriety. Riders were paid under contract according to their skills and popularity. "Six-day Bicycle Races," reproduced in this chapter, details the financial aspects of these races. A top team might share $25,000 to $50,000 from prizes and commercial endorsements for the five-month bicycling season. To ensure a competitive race, promoters refused to pay riders who lagged more than five laps behind the field, and prevented the strongest riders from pairing together. Teams of the same nationality, wearing jerseys with their national colors, made good rivalries and therefore excellent publicity. The riders colluded with each other. When the spectators went home for the night, riders agreed to coast slowly around the track to save energy until late morning. The presence of underworld gangsters, such as Al Capone, the difficulty of telling who was leading a sprint and who was being lapped, and the problem of determining how many laps each team had completed led to charges of fixed races. This, and because almost every race was decided in the last hour or so, led to the decline of the sport near the end of the decade.

### DEATH TAKES THE WHEEL AT INDIANAPOLIS

[*One of the many annual racing events was the Pikes Peak, or Race to the Clouds, competition on Labor Day. During the early 1930s, this event, as many other races, suffered when automobile manufacturers reduced their sponsorships. When local merchants recognized the positive economic impact of the Pikes Peak race on the area, the road was improved and the race grew from fourteen to nineteen entries. The most successful driver was Louis Unser.*

*For risking their lives, Indy drivers shared a purse of $81,800 in 1931. Two years later, the total purse fell to $54,450, before rebounding to $87,050 at the end of the decade. Louis Meyer and Wilbur Shaw each won Indy twice during the decade. This article examines America's fascination with speed. Arthur J. Daley, "Death Takes the Wheel at Indianapolis," Liberty (6 June 1936).*]

...Death rides as a passenger in every car that whizzes past the green flag at the start of each race. Frequently he reaches over and takes the wheel. Then there is just one more tragedy added to a long, long list.

The 500-mile classic at Indianapolis every Memorial Day draws 100,000 to 160,000 spectators. How so? They certainly are not there just to see some thirty-odd cars spin madly around the huge saucer. Their interest is far more sanguinary than that. They jam their way into the stands and crowd the infield waiting and almost hoping for a crash.

When thirty cars are flashing by at a speed of more than two miles a minute something is bound to happen. Human nerves can last just so long. Machine perfection must have some vulnerable spot.

Around and around the racers whirl. The crowd is tense and silent. Suddenly, as one car tries to pass another, the margin of safety is cut too fine. They touch momentarily and one caroms crazily up toward the top of the bank.

The driver might right his car in time. A tire might blow out as a result of the extra tension. The car might slam into the retaining wall, burst into flame, collapse like a paper box, shoot right over the top, or come sliding down and be hit by other machines.

At the famous Brooklands track in England a car skidded halfway around and, still going backward, went hurtling up to the top of the speedway. The tail missed the wall by inches, and then the machine swooped down the incline. Four cars avoided a crash by a hairbreadth, and then the original racer came to a momentary pause at the bottom. The driver regained control and started out after the others again. For the crowd it was a thrill—for him it was just part of the game.

At Salem, New Hampshire, Death took the wheel as Fred Comer was riding a curve rather high. A tire burst. His car went rolling down the track, spiting fire and strewing wreckage. Attempting to avoid him, Jimmy Gleason overturned and was tossed out of his machine.

Gleason landed directly in front of Ray Keech, who spun his wheel over frantically but did not quite make it. Striking Gleason a glancing blow, and then losing control, he went smashing into the wreckage, with Bob McDonough and Lou Moore piling on right after him. It was a terrific crash, and yet Comer was the only one killed.

In most hazardous sports the spectator is safe. But not in auto racing. In Italy a few years ago a car ran into the crowd, killing nineteen, injuring twenty-six. When Sir Malcolm Campbell was making one of his world-record attempts at Daytona Beach, his car hit a bump. His feet left the pedals, and only by clinging desperately to the steering wheel was he able to stay in. But his goggles were jolted down a bit, momentarily blinding him. He managed to brush them back into position, but remarked after he had come to a safe stop that had his auto skidded at all or deviated the slightest bit from its true course, he would have ripped into the crowd a quarter of a mile away in four seconds.

When Frank Lockhart was killed on that same beach, his car sailed through the air 1,000 feet. A few months prior to his death Lockhart skidded and bolted into the ocean, where he was found pinned to his machine and still conscious as the waves washed over him.

There is probably not one driver who has not been in a smashup. Few retire to live to old age. Yet the fascination of the game is so keen that they cannot give it up. One would suppose them the most fearless of all men. Barney Oldfield, perhaps the greatest of them all in his day, said, "You can bet your life we fear in those races. If a man doesn't fear, then he has no brains."

And yet this is the same man who drove to New York from Chicago with his nephew at the wheel of a stock automobile at an average speed of over sixty miles an hour, and on unbanked roads with plenty of turns certainly as dangerous a trip as any Barney ever had on a speedway—and remarked, "I dozed most of the way."

:

Perhaps that dozing was not so extraordinary, after all. A group of Englishmen were engaged in the monotonous and sleep-inducing pastime of circling a track in a nonstop-record attempt. One of the drivers finally fell asleep at the wheel, and the car shot off the track and was wrecked. No one was hurt.

That is one of the strangest things about this game. There are two accidents, let us say, in one race. They are practically identical. Yet in one the driver escapes uninjured and in the other he is killed.

These automobile racers are daredevils. There can be no denying that. Yet their cautious preparations for each test are painstaking to an extreme. They take their motors completely apart before a race. Everything must be perfect to the millimeter or to the thousandth of a second. The front axle and the steering mechanism are studied with high-powered microscopes, and when the car is reassembled each adjustment is made by itself, after a special run around the track.

They couldn't improve on that for preparedness. And yet this macabre game claims one victim after another, star and novice alike. Think of Louis Chevrolet, Frank Lockhart, Ray Keech, Jimmy Murphy, Dario Resta, Joe Boyer, Parry Thomas, Jimmy Gleason, and Bob Carey. All were killed, young men most of them.

Perhaps the most gruesome death of them all befell Parry Thomas. This English driver was the immediate predecessor of Segrave and Campbell as Britain's champion speedster. He was seeking a new world record on the Continent back in 1927. Like a bullet he drove his car, faster and faster until he had hit 180 m.p.h. Then Death took the wheel. A driving chain snapped. It ripped through its protective covering, tore the windshield off, and decapitated the unfortunate Thomas.

That was an accident at terrific speed that ended fatally. Here is one that didn't. An Italian, after that same record, had got up to 150 m.p.h. when his car hit a bump and turned a complete somersault. His wife, on the side lines, fainted. Horror-stricken friends found him totally undamaged except for an old-fashioned black eye.

Not a few automobile racers have endured injury and even death to save spectators. When a tire burst on Joe Boyer's car, he deliberately drove into the fence in order to keep from running into the crowd. His dying words were, "I'm glad I saved them."

An even more striking example of this same trait was furnished by Norman Batten in the Indianapolis classic a few years back. His courageous effort required long minutes of agonizing torture. Scooting along the back-stretch, and more than two miles away from the pits, his car suddenly burst into flame. He could either "bail out" and let his blazing machine run wild or he could stay in it. Bailing out would have meant a wholesale smashup, so he stuck to his guns. First one hand was so badly burned that he could not drive with it. He switched to the other until he could no longer hold the wheel. Did he give up? He did not. He stood on the seat and steered with one foot until he reached the pits. They had to take his seared and scorched body to the hospital, but he had saved the lives of spectators and fellow drivers.

Most of the accidents on a speedway are attributable to skidding, the main worry of any automobile driver. The all-time record for skidding undoubtedly belongs to Lou White, who went sideslipping a full half-mile.

It happened almost ten years ago. White was standing on the bank of the Hudson one winter's day, and he noticed an inviting expanse of clear ice. He had his racing machine pushed out and a course cleared.

Faster and faster he drove around, always taking the precaution to slow up a bit at the curves. Then, when he had attained a speed of 114 m.p.h., he thoughtlessly tried to take a turn on the fly. The next thing he knew, he was skating sideways toward open water. He had gone half a mile and had just reached the dangerous thin ice when he managed to straighten out.

It could be only a deep-seated love of the game that would impel a man to take chances like that. Even on the speedways the rewards are slight in comparison to the risks. The highest total prize money for a year was $380,000, and the most any driver ever got in a season was the exceptionally high sum of $105,000. Jimmy Murphy won that a few years before he crashed and was killed. There are mighty few pilots, however, who ever got what might be termed "big money."

Racing drivers are perfect gluttons for punishment. Billy Arnold won at Indianapolis in 1930. He tried to repeat in 1931, but his car caught fire and he just escaped with his life. A year later his machine hit the retaining wall and was wrecked. The total damage to Arnold was a broken collarbone. He was back again a year later and undoubtedly will be around this May.

The rewards are slim, the risks great, and the thrills many. And Death is always ready to take the wheel.


## RACE WITHOUT DEATH AT INDIANAPOLIS

[*Death was almost an annual occurrence at Indianapolis. In the accident-marred 1931 race, two people were killed in practice and three cars went "over the wall" in the race. The following two years witnessed the death of seven individuals. Despite these fatalities, engine power steadily increased from 1934 to 1937. Following a spate of accidents in 1938, officials restricted engine displacement to 274 c.i. and eliminated riding mechanics. Still, speeds increased. "Race Without Death," Time (11 June 1934), 55-57.*]

The noteworthy thing about Indianapolis' 22nd annual 500-mile auto race last week was not the closest finish on record, not the new track record (104.863 m.p.h.) set by Bill Cummings, but the failure of Death to make its appearance.

What Mardi Gras is to New Orleans and the Derby to Louisville, the 500-mile classic is to a city which once rivaled Detroit as an automobile manufacturing center. Last week a crowd of 135,000 was sitting in the unroofed stands when the 33 cars, after gathering speed for a lap, rolled past the starter in groups of three. Around the 2 1/2-mile brick oval with an unsteady, insistent roar, sidling awkwardly at the turns, straightening out for speed on the straightaways, whirled the bright-hued machines hardly bigger than toy-store cars. After 30 miles George Bailey of Detroit ran his Scott Special into the outer retaining wall, bounced over to the ground. A broken wrist was his only injury. That was the worst wreck of the race. Fifty miles farther on two more cars skidded with only minor hurts and the rest of the field was warned to slow down while the wreckage was cleared away.

That lull in the race became important at the finish. Cummings, driving a four-cylinder Miller Special, with No. 7 painted on its yellow hood, streaked across first, barely ahead of a black Duray. To make sure he had finished the race Cummings kept on around the track twice before he slowed down at his pit. Mauri Rose, driver of the Duray, who had led the race from the 250-mile post to the place where Cummings passed him 200 miles farther on, learned that he had lost by 27 seconds. On the ground that Cummings had illegally gained three quarters of a lap while the cars were supposed to have slowed down, Rose's backers lodged a protest which held up payment of the prize money pending a decision by the American Automobile Association contest board.

**The Men**. In almost every sport there is someone whose nickname is "Wild Bill." "Wild Bill" Cummings got his from his father who was a racetrack driver from 1907 to 1921. Young Cummings was born within earshot of the Indianapolis Speedway, learned to distinguish Barney Oldfield's car by its sound, promised his mother that some day he would win the 500-mile race. He gathered speed slowly, first as a Western Union messenger boy, later as a taxi driver. When he was 16, he began driving in motorcycle races, graduated to automobiles two years later. He finished fifth in the 500-mile race of 1930, entered unsuccessfully for the next three years. Meanwhile he made a good living out of a shop called Ned's Brake Service and a night club in the suburbs. When the night club failed last winter Cummings bought a beer tavern. Two nights before last week's race, he spent the evening there with taxi driver friends, went home and stayed in bed until nearly time for the start.

If the A.A.A. decides in favor of Cummings, he will get $35,000 in cash prizes and 600 points toward the U.S. auto-racing championship which is awarded each year by the American Automobile Association to the driver who compiles the best record in official races. Race drivers who compete in short dirt track races not sanctioned by the A.A.A. may earn as much as $4,000 a year. Drivers good enough to get regular backing in such important races as those at Indianapolis, Oakland, Detroit and Syracuse, may earn up to $15,000 a year in prizes. Winning the Indianapolis Classic often means a job with a manufacturer. Tommy Milton, who won in 1921 and 1923, is on Packard's engineering staff. Billy Arnold, who won in 1930, is with Chrysler. Famed Ralph De Palma is doing sales promotion for Ford.

**The Cars**. A good racing car costs anything up to $20,000. The purpose of auto-racing at Indianapolis is mechanical improvement and economy. This year, a new rule required cars to use not more than 45 gallons of gasoline. In Cummings' tank was a new type of gasoline developed by Standard Oil of New Jersey which may be ready for the market in two years. With it he got 20% more than normal mileage, had 8 1/2 gallons left at the finish. Tire-makers consider the 500 miles at Indianapolis equal to 40,000 of ordinary wear. Only nine tires were changed in the race last week.

In the last ten years, motors made by Harry A. Miller, 59-year-old Los Angeles designer, have won eight times. Last week, nine different makes qualified for the race. Miller fours won first, second, third, fourth and seventh places. Harry Miller makes his cars and motors in a 40,000-sq.-ft. factory in Los Angeles....

**Tracks**. The Indianapolis Speedway, built in 1909 by Carl Fisher and associates, cost $1,000,000. It was originally made of macadam, later topped with 3,200,000 paving blocks. As bumpy as a cobblestone road, it is now the only hard-surface speedway left in the U.S. The old brick tracks at Tacoma and Minneapolis, the wooden tracks at Sheepshead Bay, Cincinnati and Beverly Hills, are no longer used. Syracuse, Oakland and Detroit, big-league tracks sanctioned by the A.A.A., are of dirt.

Current technology in auto-racing is toward road-racing, which used to be popular in the U.S. 25 years ago. In Europe road-racing remains profitable and popular. Last week in Rome, Carlo Pintagudea and Mario Nardilli, driving a Lancia at an average speed of 56 and one-quarter m.p.h. won the Lictor's Gold Cup—a 3,500-mile race for touring cars over a course that includes four mountain ranges and 97 cities round Italy and Sicily—in which two drivers were killed, a score injured.

## MIDGET AUTO RACING

[*As the following article illustrates, midget auto racing, which featured many spills but few casualties, owed its existence to the Depression. So too did Class C motorcycle racing. When Harley-Davidson and Indian companies withdrew their sponsorship from Class A factory motorcycle teams, many riders were unable to afford the specialized 350 cc and 500 cc machines used in Class A events. To involve more people, the American Motorcycle Association created Class C competitions for 45 c.i. side-valve and 500 cc overhead-valve engines, and restricted fuel to pumped gas. In the first national Class C championships held in 1934 at Jacksonville, Florida, the winner completed the 200-mile race in 3 hours and 39 minutes. The American Motorcycle Association helped rejuvenate the sport by initiating contests between clubs based upon membership and members' mileage. "Midget Auto Racing," The Digest (4 September 1937), 28.*]

### MIDGET AUTO RACING

A half dozen years ago midget racing was unlisted on the sports calendar. Today it competes with big car racing. Statistics tell the story. Upwards of 125,000 people attend midget auto races from coast to coast each week. The national weekly "gate" is about $50,000 and the purses paid average $20,000.

This sport of racing midget cars began in 1932, when a few mechanics and drivers thought of cutting down stock automobiles as a pastime. They shortened the wheel base and narrowed the tread. The next step naturally was to race your car against the other fellow's.

At first the midgets used motorcycle motors. Then a boy of 18, Bill Betteridge, fresh from high school, thought he would build a midget. His dad, who operated a garage, had traded a paint job for several pieces of metal which once had been a miniature car built for road use. From his outboard motorboat Betteridge recruited a motor, being the first person to install an outboard motor in a midget car. He staged the first exhibit of small cars in May, 1933, at Denver.

In August of the same year Dominick Distarce got together eight midgets and put on the first midget auto race, in the Loyola Stadium at Los Angeles. Today there are perhaps twenty-five tracks operating on a weekly basis. Best known are those at Sioux City, Ia., Detroit, Mich., Latonia, Ky., New Haven, Conn., Freeport, N.Y., Camden, N.J., and Frankford, Pa. Eastern tracks have become the center of midget auto racing.

Most of the drivers have come from the big car professional ranks. The possibility of making $300 a night is attractive. To them midget racing is no longer a pastime but bread and butter with a little champagne and caviar on the side.

Practically all the cars are built by their owners and their drivers, who then share the purse. If a car has a commendable record, the owner will get 60 per cent and the driver 40. Otherwise an added inducement for the driver is necessary and the purse may be divided evenly. Few ace drivers own their own cars; they are the counterpart of jockeys, hired by a sponsor to race his car.

The best cars can attain 100 miles per hour on a straightaway track, with an average of 50 for a track that is never more than one-quarter of a mile around. Short-track racing gives the spectator a bird's-eye view of the whole race—and adds to the thrills.

Most popular type of motor is the English 2-cylinder J.A.P., a motorcycle motor. Another favorite is the Offenhauser midget motor, whose designer has built many cars for the Indianapolis races. He sells the motor for $1,475 and the complete car for $3,000, the finest thing in midgets today. Most cars, of course, are still built by the mechanics of the sponsor. Floyd Dreyer is the one man who will sell a custom-built midget.

Drivers usually are big-car men who have turned to the new and lucrative field. A few had their start in the midgets, an instance being Duke Nalon, of Chicago, who races on the eastern seaboard.

Other outstanding drivers are George Souders, who won the Indianapolis 500-mile race in 1927; Frank Busco, 300-mile champion in 1934; Johnny Sawyer and Jimmy Snyder, both of whom made their marks with big cars; Ernie Gesell, a college boy who stepped straight into racing and has never done anything else; and Bill Schindler. Schindler usually is to be found in the big money on eastern tracks despite the fact that he has only one leg. Driving a big car at the Mineola Fairgrounds last October, he went through a fence, lost his right leg by amputation, but came back to establish himself as a leading contender in eastern midget racing. Since a hand brake is used, and there is no clutch, a man can get along with only one leg.

Leading promoter on the east coast is Bill Heiserman, a former motorcycle champion, with seven tracks in his circuit. He introduced midget racing in the east in December, 1933, at the New York Coliseum. Audiences were not interested. But Bill knew that he had something, and next year took his midgets to the Municipal Stadium at Freeport, a Long Island suburb of the metropolis. Only $266 was taken in the opening night. It was eighteen weeks before the thing really clicked. He is now playing to 7,500 people at Freeport twice a week. Recently he paid $1,927 in purses on a single night.

### SIX-DAY BICYCLE RACES

*[For part of the decade, bicyclists could choose between two circuits—John Chapman's National Cycling Association controlled the New York and Chicago races, and Willie Spencer owned two tracks in Canada and six in the US. As the two colorful promoters feuded, they sought to sign as many as possible of the top riders to exclusive contracts. In 1934, Spencer forbade his riders from competing in Chapman's events. Two years later, the growing cost of staging the events, and a decline in spectator interest, forced Spencer into bankruptcy. In the last race he sponsored, the riders, fearful that they would not be paid, staged a short "strike." Chapman, the czar of the sport, retired at the end of 1937. The next year, for the first time in nineteen years, Madison Square Garden promoted only one six-day race.*

*Racing bicycles weighed 19 pounds and cost $100 each. A team used about six bikes a race. At $5 a tire, teams went through four pairs in six days. This article documents the financial aspects of six-day bike races. "For Six Days and Six Nights Thirty Men Pedal, Catnap, Eat Ten Meals a Day, Take Strychnine. They Work on a Salary or Percentage and the Best Make $20,000 a Year," Fortune (March 1935), 88-93, 121-122, 124.]*

Of all the shows presented in Manhattan's Madison Square Garden, six-day bike racing is one of the most consistent profit makers. The December, 1934, gate topped $100,000, and that figure will probably be duplicated when the riders return to the track early this month. While these are no sums to compare with the intake of a World Series, a Notre Dame-Stanford football game, or a world-championship heavyweight fight, it is interesting to know that the "six-days" have in years past frequently grossed a quarter of a million a week. Indeed the bicycles did gallant work in holding the deficits of boxing and other sports down to $59,000 for 1934. And for several years now the sport has been experiencing a mild revival of several earlier heydays.

The six-days are a metropolitan phenomenon largely unknown to the hinterlander who can see little sense in the endless spinning of fifteen teams of cyclers in a pine bowl, ten laps to the mile, for 147 consecutive hours. Indeed they spawn a peculiar fan, entirely distinct. Whereas excitement is the magnet that draws the ennuied gentleman to a football game, hypnosis is the source of satisfaction at a bike race. The rhythm, the ceaseless repetition, the whir of the cotton and rubber tires, the relentless monotony of even the brightest of silken comets, all contribute to a pleasant mental anesthesia.

To the rest of the audience, the great bulk of the 100,000 (annual average per race) who trudge up the ramps in Madison Square Garden, bike racing is either an exciting, legitimate contest—or a stupid nightmare. In the former class are patrons of European descent, mostly Italian, German, or French, who knew cycling in their homelands as a national glory. Abroad bicycles are as much a part of the landscape as mustaches. The highways of France, Belgium, Germany are still alive with cyclists, bicycle manufacture is an important industry, and annual road races such as the Tour de France are among the most popular sporting events of the year. So expatriates represent about 50 per cent of the American promoter's audience.

Bicycle racing is, above everything, a spectacle. To the customer who drops in for an hour during the first 146 hours it is a pageant, a circus.

In its 147th hour it achieves its greatest excitement. Then the house is packed at any track because the real strategy and speed and skill of the riders leap to a brilliant crescendo, taut with recklessness and surprise. Every rider is on the track, one teammate pumping for dear life, the other waiting his turn to join the pace. Then it is that tailenders put on power, perhaps drug-induced (many riders dose themselves with strychnine) and steal a lap from the week-long leaders. On one occasion a team that had been feigning sickness all week came from far behind. The leaders permitted them to go to the fore thinking they couldn't hold the pace, but they did. Around the track whips a flaming pennant of riders, the standings flash from the press box every few minutes, pandemonium bursts from the brasses in the band, hot-dog vendors lay aside their baskets, the man who starts the sprints cracks his pistol steadily, and the customers rise to cheer a blinding kaleidoscope that very few of them can understand. This is the climax toward which the whole show is built.

But for the initial 146 hours the audience pays from forty cents to $3.85 to watch a staged performance in which clowning is as important as fast pedaling. Torchy Peden and Gerard Debaets are cycling's No.1 funnymen. Jules Audy, platinum blond and pretty, is a great box-office attraction too. Torchy specializes in snatching hats from railbirds, steering with his feet, wearing pink corsets and other paraphernalia from a large and droll collection. Because he makes people laugh, he is a valuable asset. His boss will see to it that he is well paired.

The pairing of riders is the **modus operandi** by which the bike-race impresario keeps interest alive from year to year. The cast of his production numbers thirty stars, joined into fifteen teams. The typical **mariage de convenance** is that of a fast rider to one of unusual or amusing personality. As in handicapping horses, the racing objective is a dead heat. Individual colors are given to each team, always nationalistic in order to draw patriotic customers from the foreign population represented—though the green, white, and red of Italy as likely as not will be carried by an Australian and a Canadian....

On the track the riders circle at the habitual speed of about twenty-five miles an hour. They will be strung out single file and you will observe the leaders, one after another, pull out from the lead and drop back from first place to last. It may puzzle you at first that these alterations of lead evoke no enthusiasm from the audience. But that is because, until the final moment, it doesn't matter who is at the head of the pack and the gentleman who rides there is merely doing his fellows a courtesy. The field rides in close single file behind him to take advantage of the partial vacuum he draws in his wake. Not a material factor at low speeds, it is nevertheless easier to follow than to lead, and in six days of riding every ounce of energy counts. Students of streamline advertising will understand this slip-stream phenomenon—riding in the lee of a motorcycle (motor-paced races, they call them) a rider can pedal at eighty miles an hour. By common consent each man takes his turn playing bowsprit to this sea-serpentlike craft for perhaps a couple of laps—unless a jam starts.

A jam is the real fun. The speed rises to forty miles an hour, the audience to its feet. Technically, a jam is the confusion that results from the attempt of one team to gain a lap on the entire field. Then there will be no rest for either partner, pedaling furiously out into the open, racing madly for the lee of the tail end of the procession. But the tail end, a tenth of a mile away around the track, is eternally vanishing. It is a stern chase and a long one. The perfect order of the field is gone, men tangle and go down, the crowd roars, pandemonium is loose. Then, as suddenly as it began, it is over. The field has either held or been overtaken by the ambitious team that began it all, the relieved partners cycle wearily back to rest, the fifteen on the track fall again into line.

The ultimate winner of the race, of course, is the team that has stolen the most laps. In case of a tie, the race is decided on "sprint points," a special mystery presently to be divulged. Ordinarily at the finish the winning team is seldom more than one lap ahead of the second-place team, and close behind is bunched the field. During the course of a long race half a dozen teams are forced out, being distanced, disqualified (for roughriding or loafing), broken up by injuries, or just plain withdrawing. [Deleted early history of six-day racing.]

Those are the prime facts that every bike fan knows. As he watches the race he is likely to select some team as his favorite, and may offer (through the track officials, via an usher) $5 or $100 or a live duck as a prize to the winner of a special sprint of, say, half a dozen times around. On the sounding of a gun the riders speed up for the sprint and the winner collects the reward. Screen and stage stars and merchants (to advertise their wares) have posted as much as $500 for the full mile of ten laps. It is a prime opportunity for an exhibitionist and these little special sprint races are an essential part of the entertainment. Their brief excitement draws many a patron through the turnstiles at no expense to the management. Meanwhile there is a regularly scheduled series of sprints—artificial climaxes—at 3:30 P.M., 8:30 P.M., 10:30 P.M., 12:30 A.M., and 2:30 A.M., ten in each group, two miles apiece. At many tracks these sprints bring no financial reward for the riders, though it is frequently announced through the loudspeaker that a five-or ten-dollar "preme" has been posted for each. The only actual reward is on the score sheet—six points for first place, four for second, etc. During the final hour points jump to seventy-two for first, but second is still four.

The public's demand for jams has proved too much of a temptation for bike showmen, and to satisfy the demand they have devised the staged jam. Attempts to steal laps, in recent races, infallibly occur during the late evening sprints, when the largest crowds are present. They are started on a secret signal from some track official. This is a fact that few bike fans know and the trick is made possible by the also generally unknown fact that riders are paid a straight salary of $50 to $300 a day ($1,000 a day in boom times) or a percentage. There is therefore no immediate inducement to try to win the race. Victory, however, brings prestige, which in turn leads to a larger daily salary in the next race.

There are rarely any laps stolen during the weary hours between 4:00 A.M. and noon. Riders have a gentleman's agreement not to try lap stealing during this period, and pedal just fast enough to keep erect—about five miles per hour—reading their mail or their newspapers as they circle the track in an interlocked chain. All spectators are barred from the house from 6:00 A.M. to 7:30 A.M. One comic incident—part of the bike legend—occurred when a rider got drunk and started a furious jam at seven in the morning, lapping the field fifty times. But the judge had gone out to breakfast.

One more item has the promoter for sale: the accident. Though it is not true that a spill, bringing perhaps permanent injury to one or more riders, is deliberately instigated by a promoter, it is nevertheless true that a spill does not vex him. The more wrecks, the more customers. The ever present possibility of bloodshed keeps audience suspense keyed high—and so sets a commercial value on a spill. Unashamedly the promoter turns it to good use, as evidenced by the universal bike-race advertising slogan, "Spills and Thrills!" Nor is the health of the performers of great concern to the promoter; his contract with the rider stipulates that pay stops the day the latter is forced out of the race and also that the promoter is not liable for damages in case of suits, or hospital bills beyond superficial first-aid treatment.

In the U.S. the partnership between gruff, bespectacled Promoter John Chapman and the Madison Square Garden, now headed by colonel John Kilpatrick, has dominated the market since 1920. New York is, of course, the big-money city of any professional sport; it is the particular bonanza of the six-days because of its large population. The other cities in the Chapman circuit are Chicago, now run by his man of all work—once his press agent—Harry Mendel; Buffalo, where the arena has an inadequate seating capacity (4,500); Philadelphia, Detroit, and Boston, where his bike races have not been financial triumphs. Chapman's chief profits come from the biannual New York shows.

A rival circuit covering more territory is operated by the pink-cheeked, blond Willie Spencer, onetime champion rider from Toronto. It takes in two good racing cities, Montreal and Toronto, and several others from which an uncertain gate may be counted upon: Pittsburgh, Kansas City, St. Louis, Minneapolis, Milwaukee, Cleveland. Two other figures of relative obscurity are George Harvey and Richard Wahrburg of New York, who occasionally stage a race; this year they promoted one in Louisville.

Having inspected the simple structure of bike racing's hegemony, consider what it would cost you to stage a race in a representative U.S. city—**not** New York or Chicago—and what your chances of making a profit would be. Your gross intake might average $20,000. You must remember you would first have to get the consent of either Mr. Chapman or Mr. Spencer since these two hold all the desirable riders under contract. With this consent, you pay:

**For Riders** .................................................................................................. $7,000

Riders in your race would work on a percentage basis or on a flat salary—with topnotchers getting a guarantee of around $300 a day, the rest scaling down to $50 a day. Our figure $7,000 represents 35 per cent of an average gross of $20,000. Riders will pay you for their food at $7 a day apiece.

**For Rent** ...................................................................................................... $4,000

**For publicity**................................................................................................ $2,000

Banquets for the press, free meals for reporters all through the race and preliminaries lasting a fortnight, liquor by the case, tubs of iced beer, and perhaps occasional "gifts" for the sports editor's favor—these will consume most of the 10 per cent set aside for advertising. Part will go for legitimate advertising: newspaper space, car cards, billboards.

**To build the track** ...................................................................................... $5,000

It must be built of high-grade, white-pine strips, by experienced carpenters, who will probably be required by the landlord to erect it in ten hours. This necessitates a huge crew. You will also have to tear it down after the race, the salvage being practically worthless.

**For Officials** ................................................................................................. $700

These figures add up to $18,700 and make your profit only too easy to arrive at:

|  |  |
|---|---|
| Estimated gross | $20,000 |
| Total expenses | $18,700 |
| **Net profit** | **$1,300** |

If $1,300 seems small reward for months of careful planning, weeks of ballyhoo, and six days' feverish excitement, FORTUNE has at least left you a dream. For your costs remain relatively fixed however great your success, and if you have staged your show so well that the public pays not $20,000 but $30,000, the extra ten is all net.

But life and the weather being what they are, the margin of net is very small considering the risk. A blizzard may ruin your house (races are always held in winter) and other unpredictable factors may not only lop off your small profit but put you heavily in the red. The experienced Mr. Spencer is rumored to have lost $5,000 this

January in Kansas City. Though bike racing is not new in the U.S., its revival outside New York and Chicago has come only during the past four years: as yet the great mass of Americans are uneducated to its charms. In Chicago the gross of the last race was about $61,000. A rough estimate of the last race at Madison Square Garden runs as follows:

**Income**

| | |
|---|---|
| Gate (97,808) | $100,000 |

**Expenses**

| | |
|---|---|
| Building and dismantling | |
| Track, cleaning, etc. | $10,000 |
| Riders | $25,000 |
| N.C.A. percentage | $1,000 |
| Other expenses | $8,000 |
| Chapman, 25 per cent of profit | $6,000 |
| | $50,000 |

**Net revenue to Madison Square Garden      $50,000**

(Which normally gets $25,000 for the rent of its facilities for a week.)

At the Garden, as elsewhere, no single set of figures may be called typical, as the gate receipts vary over a much wider range than the costs. Consequently the relation of the profits to the gross is likely to shift several hundred per cent.

The national gross earnings of the six-days for a season are now estimated in the neighborhood of $400,000, of which some $175,000 is collected at the Garden turnstiles. Prohibition gave attendance a boost when 11,000 New York City saloons were closed.... But depression brought a fast decline—at the rate of $100,000 a year—the bottom being reached in 1932-33, with tickets cut to half price and sales away down. Attendance this season has crept up to about 75 per cent of the banner year.

The bike riders who bring in these sums range in stature from jockey to giant, in age from eighteen to fifty. There is no definite type. These only must the rider have: courage, a desperate endurance, and—for the galleries—a personality that will distinguish him from his whirling competitors. He is, on the average, more intelligent than most athletes—and age is not such a handicap to him. Women fascinate him, and he them. And like his promoters he **can** make a good deal of money.

Pete van Kempen, Belgian world champion with twenty-seven firsts in major races, in the past earned $1,000 a day but now gets only some $300. Van Kempen is a somber, middle-aged man—the sports writers call him "colorless." He commands his salary on sheer ability. At one time he could ride any other cyclist in the world into the ground, but Debaets is probably fastest today. Torchy Peden, already referred to as a humorist, is a 200-pound Canadian, with twenty-six victories to his credit. He also gets about $300 a day. But Torchy is paid as much for his clowning as his riding. These two men are the top-notchers. Ranging right along with them come such stars as Georgetti Letourneur, and McNamara. Georgetti has a tremendous Italian following in New York, Letourneur is popular because he is dapper and winning in personality. McNamara because of his reputation built up in twenty years of sport. He is "the grand old man." "The iron man," a bike-racing generation's idol. He has sustained twenty-one major bone fractures. All are crackerjack riders.

These are the high-salaried stars. The remainder of the world's supply of 175 riders, 60 per cent of whom are Europeans, earn anywhere from $200 a day to $50. If they work on percentage, they may get nothing, as was the sad case in Detroit last fall. Chapman has a tendency to match two ace riders together making the contest unbalanced (the team of Letourneur & Debaets won five in a row this winter), but Chapman gets more "names" than Spencer. Spencer keeps quality better distributed. Recently he has experimented with three-man teams, which does not give more employment to riders, for the number of teams is cut from fifteen to nine. With Spencer usually staging ten races a year (two in each city) and Chapman about eight, steady work is available for all riders during the six-month season. In summer a few earn additional money at the outdoor velodrome at Nutley, New Jersey, where one-day sprint racing is being introduced. Peden will get $200 for two nights a week.

Taking Mr. Peden as a typical topnotcher, we find he rides sixteen races at $1,000 each which means $16,000 to him. Outdoors he will add another $4,000 or so, making an annual income of about $20,000. At the other end of the scale is the rider whoworks approximately eight races a year for $300 a week, with another $200 picked up at Nutley, or a total of about $2,600 a year. But he must also consider the probability of being distanced and forced to withdraw, or hurt, which is a hazard good and poor must face, but which is much more apt to happen to an inferior rider. Expenses will be as modest as he cares to make them. Though Mr. Peden is in great demand and may fly from race to race, the second-rater does not need to. He will travel six to an automobile with bikes strapped on behind. Equipment will cost all $200 a year—for new bikes, tires, etc.

Thus if the six-day bike rider were frugal (which he usually is) he could do quite well by himself. The promoter may make more—and his health will last longer—but the six-days have made no millionaires. Messrs. Chapman and Spencer continue to have an effective monopoly on success and even their profits are hardly the envy of the sporting world. Yet the grind goes on, still a unique, a colorful—and even a gradually expanding—phenomenon of American life. There is nothing else under the sun quite like it. Until you have sat through the long drone of an evening's riding, risen tothe madness of a never to be forgotten final hour, you can hardly call yourself a student of contemporary folkways. But whether you will ever go again will depend upon a variety of factors in your psychology. Only one thing is certain: you never can tell till you've tried.

## Chapter 17

# RACING ON WATER—YACHTING, MOTOR BOATING, ROWING

As with automobile and airplane racing, speed attracted spectators and skippers alike to boat racing. As the decade began, American Gar Wood broke the 100 mph world water speed barrier. For several years, Wood and Kaye Don of Great Britain took turns setting new records. As the decade ended, Malcolm Campbell established a new standard of 141.7 mph. British and American manufacturers vied with each other to produce the most efficiently designed hulls and the most powerful motors with the best weight to power ratios. Not surprisingly, the industry adopted recent aircraft and automobile technology, including wind-tunnel testing. When interest in Gold Cup motorboat races began to decline about mid-decade, organizers sought greater speeds by designing supercharged engines and removing all hull restrictions. The three most important motorboat races were the Harmsworth Trophy, the Gold Cup, and the President's Cup. Near decade's end, the President's Cup displaced the Gold Cup in popularity.

Depending on the season, sailors raced in the waters off California, New York, and Florida. The prize trophy for freshwater sailing was the Canada's Cup—which the US monopolized. Canadians dominated the International Trophy for working fishing schooners. But it was the America's Cup that most symbolized supremacy under sail. The Scientific American noted in 1934 that, "perhaps the most important sporting trophy in the world open to international competition," was the America's Cup. In the 1930s, the best minds and engineering skills of Great Britain and the United States, including a half a million dollars per challenge, went into Cup races.

The Depression had a major impact on yachting. The average length of yachts declined over the decade as did the number of active boats. In 1932 and 1933, no schooners competed for the Astor Cup. Membership in the New York Yacht Club (NYYC) fell precipitously from a high of 2,237 in 1930 to 1,515 in 1937. Despite lower membership fees for younger members, resignations continued to outnumber new members and the Club went into debt. The declaration of war in Europe further reduced membership. In that year, the NYYC reported 33 active yachts compared to 43 the previous year.

Between 1870 and 1929 there were only 13 attempts to wrest America's Cup from the United States. In the latter year, the NYYC altered the course to give foreign yachts a better opportunity to win. Racing off Newport, Rhode Island, rather than in the congested in-shore waters off New York, made for an off-shore race with strong winds. Previously, the NYYC refused to race if the wind exceeded 25 mph. As British challengers needed to have a stout boat to cross the Atlantic Ocean, the change of venue promised a fairer race. In addition, for the first time, the NYYC placed restrictions on competing yachts. All yachts were to be Bermudian-rigged Class J boats. The first yacht to cross the finish line four times was the winner. Of course, the American defenders were still favored because of their knowledge of local waters and the opportunity to test race their yachts against other American competitors. In 1930, for example, the yachts of four NYYC syndicates competed to defend the Cup.

That year, Sir Thomas Lipton, who challenged for the Cup on behalf of the Royal Belfast Yacht Club of Northern Ireland, returned for a fifth and final attempt. The 80-year old grocery magnate, now best known for his tea company, lost in four consecutive races to Harold S. Vanderbilt's Enterprise. Lipton's Shamrock V was not raced much, whereas the American yacht competed against three other J-Class yachts in the American trials. Losing with good humor five times, Lipton became popular in New York as "the world's best loser," and Mayor Jimmy Walker presented him with a silver loving cup on behalf of the American people. The next challenge was marked by acrimony and international distrust.

In 1934, T.O.M. Sopwith, an innovative English designer of boats and airplanes, challenged Vanderbilt's *Rainbow*. Shortly before *Endeavour* left for America, its crew struck for better wages, and Sopwith replaced them with amateurs, including his wife. *Rainbow's* crew were skilled professionals. The *Endeavour* was probably the faster of the two yachts, but Vanderbilt sailed brilliantly, winning the series four races to two. *Endeavour* won the first two races. In the next race, Vanderbilt outmaneuvered Sopwith on the last leg. When Sopwith entered the harbor, he raised the protest flag as was the British custom. Because the NYYC rules required flying the flag immediately after the protested incident, Sopwith's protest was disallowed—which almost created an international incident. One British writer commented, "Britannia rules the waves, but America waives the rules." This fourth race is the subject of "America's Cup Races: A Critical Narrative of the 15th Defense." *Rainbow* won the fifth and six races, although the final match was also marred by protests from both yachts.

Three years later, Harold Vanderbilt handily defeated Sopwith, as *Ranger* captured four consecutive races from *Endeavour II*. This time, the American yacht won with superior tactics, sails, and design. It was a victory for American engineering, as *Ranger* was the first America's Cup boat tank-tested. *Ranger*, the last J-Boat built, entered thirty-seven races in 1937. Of the thirty-four completed races, *Ranger* won thirty-two, in the process setting three speed records, winning by an average margin of more than seven minutes.

During the decade, women increased their participation in international yachting competitions. Elizabeth Hovey sailed aboard *Yankee* in the 1934 Trials. Three years later, five women competed in the Trials, and Gertrude Vanderbilt and Phyllis Sopwith served as timekeepers for their husbands. As with other sports, the journalists concentrated on the women's clothes rather than on their yachting prowess, and several yachtsmen objected to women sailing in international yachting races.

The Depression and yachting's reputation as a sport for the wealthy caused Canadian participation in sailing races to decline in the 1930s. On the East coast, the success of the *Bluenose* fishing schooner in defeating American boats helped to boost regional pride in trying times. Skipped by Angus Walters of Lunenburg, Nova Scotia, *Bluenose* lost only one series between 1921 and 1938, when the International Trophy was discontinued.

### MOTOR BOATING

Motor boating was deemed more democratic than yachting. In terms of popularity, motor boat racing overtook sailing during the Depression. Boats were now less expensive than cars. A midget-class motor boat sold for about $125. At the 1936 Motor Boat Show in New York City, more than 200 manufacturers displayed their wares and The Literary Digest reported there was an increased optimism in the industry. The Canadian Power Boat Association grew from two clubs in 1927 to more than 100 in 1939, and crowds of 50,000 watched the annual motor boat races at the Canadian National Exhibition in Toronto. Boating in the United States benefited from government money that built huge irrigation lakes in the western States. Informed estimates placed the number of motor boats in the US in 1938 at 1,600,000—with the most boats on the Eastern seaboard, followed by the Great Lakes and the Pacific coast.

The most cherished motor boat race was the Harmsworth, which was emblematic of the world's championship. Next in importance was the Gold Cup Championship, the

President's Cup, and the National Sweepstakes. There were races for all sizes, classes, and horsepowers—from Midget to Unlimited. More than 40 colleges and preparatory schools took part in the National Intercollegiate Outboard Regatta. On the East coast, in 1933, fifteen colleges and twenty-five high schools and preparatory schools in Canada and the United States competed in the Eastern Intercollegiate Outboard Motor Championship. To prevent the wealthy from dominating every class, the One-Twenty-Five Class was limited to boats costing less than $750.

## ROWING

Rowing maintained its faithful supporters, but rarely made headlines outside of rowing hotbeds. Since intercollegiate rowing was an expensive sport—an eight-oared shell cost from $800 to $1,600—only about fifteen universities could afford a rowing team. Perhaps the biggest name in rowing was George Pocock, who built and designed approximately ninety-five percent of the shells used by American colleges and Olympic teams.

Rowing regattas remained an annual event in many Canadian towns, especially the Royal Henley near St. Catharines, but interest in rowing also declined in Canada. While Ontario remained the center of rowing, it was a team from Saskatchewan that captured the public's attention near the end of the decade. The team practiced in Wascana Lake, a small man-made body of water in the riverless town of Regina. In four of the first eight years of the Depression, drought almost completely dried up Wascana. Even in normal weather, the Regina Boat Club rowers had to make a right-angled turn part way through the course. Despite these problems, beginning in 1934 the Regina four-man team began to win rowing regattas in Canada and the United States.

### AMERICA'S CUP RACES. A CRITICAL NARRATIVE OF THE 15TH DEFENSE

[*The controversy between Thomas Sopwith and Harold Vanderbilt in the fourth race of the 1934 America's Cup reminded many experts of the 1895 America's Cup when British challenger Lord Dunraven became so upset over a ruling that he sailed home without finishing the series. Sopwith's challenge was the first by the British Royal Yacht Squadron since that date. In the following article, Alfred F. Loomis discusses the fourth race of the 1934 America's Cup series. Loomis was editor of* The Yachtsman's Yearbook, 1934, *and author of several books on sailing. Partly as a result of this controversy, Vanderbilt began campaigning for a change in the right-of-way rules. In 1936, he published a pamphlet, "A Suggested Revision of the International Yacht Racing Right of Way Rules," and three years later he wrote* On the Wind's Highway. Ranger, Rainbow and Racing, *in which he analyzed several of his races, including the controversial fourth race discussed below. Alfred F. Loomis, "The America's Cup Races. A Critical Narrative of the Fifteenth Defense," in Loomis, ed.,* The Yachtsman's Yearbook, 1934 (New York, 1934), 16-21.]

### Fourth Race, September 22nd

Course, triangular: beat, close reach, broad reach. Wind east, moderate.

It was remarked to me by a veteran Canadian yachtsman at the conclusion of the second race, when **Rainbow** was two down and two to go, that if this had been a fisherman's series the loser would have asked a layday "to effect necessary repairs." My friend saw in Vanderbilt's willingness to continue racing when he was losing great hope for the betterment of international sport. Be that as it may, Sopwith asked for a delayed start at the conclusion of the third race and was granted a layday for the purpose of adding to his equipment a Genoa to replace the one torn at the start of the second race.

To those who are at all superstitions it seemed at the time that he would swap luck for his new Genoa. Subsequent events deepened their superstition. The layday wasted a breeze of the strength that **Endeavour** seemed to like best. The day following saw nerves at the snapping point and evoked from Sopwith allegations of two fouls committed by the defender of the Cup. Also he lost the race.

From the moment the red flag was lashed "hand-high," as someone picturesquely phrased it, in **Endeavour's** rigging, interest in the performance of the yachts was dwarfed by curiosity as to the outcome of the protest. But the race itself was interesting. Before the start **Endeavour** bore away from the line on the starboard tack, jibed, and began to reach back on the port tack, **Rainbow** followed the challenger away from the line, also on the starboard tack, and after **Endeavour** had jibed, altered course to port as if she too were about to wear, but hung for an appreciable interval, with her boom to port. She then completed the jibe, came on the wind on top of **Endeavour**, and reached for the line. This is as I saw the maneuver from the Coast Guard cutter **Modoc**, which was directly astern of **Rainbow** at the moment when her boom crossed from port to starboard. At the time it occurred to none of us on the **Modoc** that a foul had been committed by either competitor. From our vantage point it appeared that Vanderbilt, the master tactician, had at last executed one of his perfect starts, and that while he had put Sopwith at a disadvantage by jibing on his wind, the maneuver was legal and eminently proper. Sopwith thought otherwise and based the first part of his protest on this situation. It is pertinent to add that a friend of mine, far better versed in such matters, who saw the incident from a different angle, expressed the opinion that Vanderbilt had fouled Sopwith. This same man, having had time to think the situation over, decided that Sopwith fouled Vanderbilt. Which proves, if further proof were needed, that yacht racing is a matter of opinion rather than of fact.

The start having been effected, the two yachts with quadrilaterals and staysails filling their fore triangles held the port tack for a little more than half an hour. The easterly wind was at 12 knots. **Endeavour** tacked to starboard in an effort to work clear, was covered, and returned to the port tack, with **Rainbow** covering again. The defender initiated the next move, when, five minutes later, she came to the starboard tack in an attempt to lay the weather mark. **Endeavour** carried on a minute longer when she too tacked, her wind entirely clear. This was one of the occasions, it soon became apparent, when Sopwith sailed his boat well, and let her worth be known. She rapidly overhauled **Rainbow**, whose Genoa, hastily substituted for working headsails, failed to speed her up, and arrived at the mark to weather of **Rainbow** and in a position to tack first-and round ahead. This **Endeavour** did, 23 seconds in the lead.

It was an advantage thrown away, for in shifting from double headsails to Genoa, **Endeavour** bore off so far that she appeared to be heading back for the starting line instead of for the second turn of the triangle. **Rainbow**, whose reaching headsail was already set, kept a little high of the new course and quickly hauled up on **Endeavour's** weather quarter. At this point occurred the incident that gave rise to the second part of the challenger's protest. Sopwith luffed sharply and field his luff until he had come within perhaps fifty feet of **Rainbow's** starboard side. Vanderbilt did not respond, as the windward boat is required to do when under the rule the leeward boat has the right to luff (or when there is doubt as to the right of the leeward boat to luff) and Sopwith bore away again. This was the maneuver as I saw it front a point less than half a mile astern. I was not so placed that I am able to offer an opinion as to where **Endeavour** would have struck **Rainbow** if the luff had been continued. Nearly two hours after the incident occurred, when **Endeavour** was reaching up to the finish line in **Rainbow's** wake, Sopwith flew the protest flag. It was answered by the committee boat and hauled down before the line was crossed.

This, then, was the contretemps that set the yachting fraternity by the ears. That Saturday night and Sunday in Newport harbor and town no one interested in "sticks and strings" talked of anything but the protest. Nobody outside of official circles knew just how the written protest had been phrased, but nearly all interested bystanders with whom I talked guessed that it would deal primarily with the incident at the turn and that a violation might also be claimed against **Rainbow** at the start.

I knew then (Sopwith has since proclaimed the fact) that the challenger had objected to **Rainbow's** "skinned-out interior" before the racing began, and I knew from observation that in an attempt to put **Endeavour** on what he considered a parity with the defending yacht, Sopwith had stripped his boat of a bathtub and other plumbing fixtures. This had seemed to me like pretty small potatoes, but I could appreciate how a man who felt that he had been imposed upon would be on the lookout for what he considered further infractions of the rules.

If my personal opinions are of any moment (always remembering that in racing, opinion transcends circumstance) I may say further that I feel that from the receipt of the challenge from the Royal Yacht Squadron down to the publication of the New York Yacht Club's finding on the protest the holding club had acted from the broadest interpretation of the generosity of true sportsmanship. The rules for the construction of the competing yachts and for the sailing of the match were absolutely fair. When, in midsummer, there was a question as to the fitness of **Rainbow's** interior equipment, she was made to conform with the spirit of the rules as well as with their letter. Upon his arrival in America Sopwith was offered the use of a trial horse by a member of the yacht club, and in an initial spirit of friendliness tuned up his boat against her. On Vanderbilt's invitation he had sailed in **Rainbow** on the New York Yacht Club cruise. When, egged on, as it appeared, by the allegations of a British newspaper correspondent, Sopwith lodged an eleventh-hour ultimatum regarding **Rainbow's** constructional compliance with the rules he had been told in effect that he could strip **Endeavor** to the bare hull if it would make him feel better. Finally, the defending club had postponed the start of the first day's race to save Sopwith from hopeless defeat.

Knowing and feeling these things and having so high a regard for the sportsmanship already exhibited by the New York Yacht Club, I listened to many of the discussions of the situation and delivered myself of one forcefully optimistic opinion. "Whatever the committee does," I said, "it will not throw out the protest on a technicality. It may strain a point as it has already done and give the challenger the race, even though the foul is not clearly established. But, animated by a spirit of sportsmanship, it will not deny Sopwith his hearing and set aside the protest on the score that the flag was not promptly flown."

But that is what the club did, employing these words over the signatures of the race committee: "The requirement of the rule that the code flag "B" must be promptly displayed where a yacht has cause to protest another yacht for infringement of the rules occurring during a race was obviously not complied with by **Endeavour**, even under the most liberal interpretation of the rule in question. Under these circumstances, the protest not having been properly made, this committee has no power to entertain."

In the findings of the committee there is also legalistic explanation, some of which appears fallacious to a lay mind like mine which can absorb only the written text of a set of rules and has not the agility to go behind the words and ascertain what they are meant to mean. But the gist of the matter is that Sopwith did not fly his flag promptly. His protest was not disallowed. It merely was not entertained. I am told by persons in a position to know that I am foolish to be excited about the New York Yacht Club's handling of this delicate occasion. I am told that if I, as one of the public, knew all the facts leading up to and concerning the protest I would concede that the committee had acted in a way best calculated to soothe ruffled feelings and smooth troubled waters.

But it is because I am one of the public and because I think that racing can be indulged in by sportsmen without recourse to the protest flag that I feel bitter. We Americans are accused with and without reason of conducting our sports on a business-like basis. Whether or not Sopwith was the beau ideal of sport has nothing to do with the case. When he flew his protest flag the American public was put on the spot. "Up to their old Yankee tricks," thought the English. "At it again," said yachtsmen who have heard of earlier protests and how they were treated. And all eyes of the sporting world were focused on the race committee into whose hands the vexing question had been unceremoniously thrust. For the moment the committee was not a subdivision of an organization unimportant in American national affairs. It was the Committee of the Nation. Its findings would be the public's findings. Its sportsmanship, or the lack of it, would epitomize American sportsmanship.

And the Committee of the Nation, acting according to its lights, and fearful, it is said, of reopening the Dunraven chapter in the history of the America's Cup, allowed it to be said once again that American sportsmanship suffers from anaesthesia.

## THE BLUENOSE

[*It was not unusual for 30,000 Nova Scotians to watch the Bluenose race. As the following article illustrates, the Bluenose's dominance of the North Atlantic Fisherman's Trophy was partly due to the times. With the fishing industry in decline, large schooners, such as the Bluenose, were no longer being built as motor-powered boats began to predominate. The reference to Captain Pine as "unlucky Lipton" refers to Thomas Lipton's five unsuccessful attempts to win the America's Cup. "Hailing the 'Bluenose' and the Unlucky Lipton of the Fishing Fleet," The Literary Digest (31 October 1931), 40-41.*]

Her Majesty, Queen **Bluenose**, still reigns supreme on the North Atlantic, and, perhaps, she will reign there forever. The possibility is in the offing that she will not be challenged again, that that picturesque sports institution, the fishermen's race off Halifax, may not be sailed again.

Altho the **Bluenose** won handily in two straight races this year, there were moments when the determined Gloucestermen seriously threatened her throne and crown. Sailing the **Gertrude L. Thebaud**, captained first by Ben Pine and then by John Matheson, they made two gallant, worthy races.

The American entry against the sturdy salt banker, **Bluenose**, had plenty of sympathy, because of her many sporting attempts to carry off the North Atlantic Fishermen's Trophy. Captain Pine's decade-long, persistent quest of this trophy makes him worthy to be called the Lipton of the fishing fleet.

The men of Halifax honored a stout opponent, and gave the Gloucestermen a burst of applause, according to a Halifax dispatch from James Robbins to the New York Times.

Many of the Canadians, we read, "exprest their regret that the **Thebaud** had not won the race. It was about agreed that the wood for the spars of a vessel that could beat the **Bluenose** is still in a tree." Continuing:

"Right at the start of the second race, of which the **Thebaud** got the better, there were thrills enough to excite the backwoods people who came down from the hills just to see the ships.

The **Bluenose** had her bow half a length ahead, but the **Thebaud** nosed up to weather of her by a little more than inches and, taking the wind from her, went by her. It was a clever start on Captain Matheson's part.

Instead of engaging in a rocky shore luffing match, as they did yesterday under the same conditions, both skippers went about the business of getting out to sea.

In this the **Bluenose** blew along faster for a time, and went ahead. Then the **Thebaud** moved up. It was first one and then the other in front."

Later in the race, Mr. Robbins tells us:

"It was their mainsails, winged-out foresails and scandalized staysails that were drawing. Their jumbos were lifeless forward, and their headsails, covered as they were, lay like a so-much-a-pound wet-wash out for an airing.

Each time the **Bluenose** moved into a lead which it appeared she would keep, the **Thebaud** spurted along. Just before the lightship was reached, the **Thebaud** poked her jib and bobstay ahead. Quickly, however, the Canadian boat nosed out again. They jibed around the lightship, with a burst of sunlight in their sails, twenty-five seconds apart, the **Bluenose**'s canvas and rigging first taking the lunging-over strain.

It was a close haul of seven miles from there to the outer automatic buoy. The **Bluenose** pointed higher, and heeled more with less ballast in proportion to her larger size. That was where she won the race. They had to tack to reach the buoy, which the **Bluenose** rounded fifteen minutes before the **Thebaud**."

The North Atlantic Fishermen's Trophy, "which has been kicking around dusty attics in Halifax for eleven years, is here to stay a while longer, and it may be here for good," hazards William H. Taylor in a Halifax dispatch to the New York Herald Tribune:

"Capt. Ben Pine, who didn't go out in his vessel to-day, was on the fence as to whether he would make another try for the prize. First he said he wouldn't, and then he said he might.

It will mean building a new vessel, if they do come after the trophy again. **Thebaud**, even if she were at her very best, isn't fast enough to beat **Bluenose** if **Bluenose** is also right, as she is now. A good big vessel can beat a good little vessel, and she did.

**Bluenose** will beat any vessel they send up that is as much smaller, in length, tonnage, and sail area as the **Thebaud**, unless somebody invents an entirely new type of fishing schooner. If they want to beat the Lunenburger, they will have to send up a vessel of **Bluenose's** size, and a fast one at that. There are so such vessels fishing out of Gloucester now, and, the fishing business being what it is, it is doubtful if such a vessel could be made to pay in Gloucester.

The Lunenburgers are mostly salt fishermen, and can use such schooners to advantage on their long trips, but Gloucester is mainly interested in fresh fish, and vessels as big as **Bluenose** don't pay dividends fresh fishing. Furthermore the Gloucester fleet, except for a few old vessels, is strictly a power fishing fleet, and the old sailing schooners are gone, as a commercial proposition.

They are still fishing under sail in Lunenburg, but even here power is creeping in, and in a few years, most of the fishermen predict, the schooners will be carrying big engines and short sail. So, if another racing fishing schooner is built to follow the many that have tried to beat **Bluenose**, it will be purely a sporting proposition, with little chance of a return from fishing on the money invested."

And when Captain Walter received his trophy as victor in the race, Captain Pine was presented with one, too, "in recognition of the sportsmanship which has made him a leading figure in racing in the fishing fleet," according to Mr. Taylor.

And there's a final Lipton touch!

### THE NATIONAL MOTORBOAT SHOW

[*George Reis was one of the best motorboat racers of the decade. He won both the Gold Cup and the President's Cup three times, and the National Sweepstakes twice. To keep the large crowds that lined the waterways informed, race organizers mounted huge loudspeakers on launches along the main course. As this article illustrates, motor boating benefitted by the emphasis on leisure, power, and practicality. "Power Boating Has Entered a New Era. The Annual National Show of Motor-Craft Accents Yachtsmen's Swing Away From Sail To Engine Propulsion," The Literary Digest (27 January 1934), 32.*]

Hard on the heels of the Automobile Show comes the Motor Boat Show, presenting more sleek, shining surfaces and again the dull, dignified gleam of more powerful motors and more pretentious gadgets to the eyes of power boat enthusiasts. The Motor Boat Show is no violent "swing to the left"; it presents no radical, swirling stream-lines nor any revolutionary departure into the field of "aero-dynamics" as did the Automobile Show. But then one must remember that stream-lining is not news to power boats—Robert Fulton incorporated the principles of stream-lining in the first power boat at a time when the Conestoga wagons were still lumbering over the continent, stopping every breath of a land breeze that blew against their barge-like sides.

Water-craft derived their lines from their companions, the fish, while land traffic still labored along, ignoring the fact that even the creeping mud turtle is stream-lined.

For obvious reasons, the Motor Boat Show, which closes this Saturday after a week's run in New York, does not yet rival the Automobile Show as an American institution. The significant comparison suggested by the popularity of the Motor Boat Show arises from the fact that there is no similar fashion pre-view for the sail craft. "Practical...Power"—there is the answer. It is not the American manner to wait for a wind when gasoline will get you where you are going far more quickly. The old, ever alive controversy of "Sail vs. Power" will not be settled by any such slim margin as the Motor Boat Show, but the fact remains that power boating has grown to take its place along with ready-made suits and baseball in mass production and mass-pleasure, while the sail is going over the hill with the horse as a luxury, a tradition, and a matter of sentiment.

Leisure lovers will always dot the horizon with the white splash of a sail against blue sky or gray—their deep enduring affection for the gentle lift of deck and the gleam of the bright work and canvas, will make sure of that. But the younger men and the inlanders and the grizzled oldtimers like Gar Wood who still thrill to the toe-curling roar of a motor and the rifle-cracks of the water slapping against the belly of a rocketing boat—those are the men and that is the lure that makes the power boat a part of to-morrow's America.

Very few laymen or very few inlanders could tell you the time that was clocked to win the **America's Cup**, that aristocratic "Old Mug" of yachting. The time is unimportant; the fact to remember is that America won, or more in keeping with sentiment and tradition, that Lipton lost again. But in power boating, in the Harmsworth, **time** is the all important factor. Wood breaks 120 miles per hour! That is speed on land at Indianapolis or Daytona Beach or in the air or anywhere. Or when the saucy little outboards skip from wave to wave, the mongrel's bark of their exhaust rattling over the water as they zoom along at a mile a minute, that too is speed.

The year 1934 for power boats will be dedicated in more than ever determined assaults on old speed records, assaults that begin next month with the international Miami-Palm Beach-New Smyrna regatta in Florida waters, and wind up with the Harmsworth at Detroit and the President's Cup at Washington, D.C., next September. In description of the Florida regatta, George H. Townsend, president of the American Power Boat Association, says: "The regatta, in which seven countries—England, France, Italy, Hungary, Spain, Canada and the United States—probably will compete, will afford the first international outboard team racing, inaugurate extensive international racing for boats of the Gold Cup type, and will be of championship caliber, as the same boats must race on three successive week-ends to determine the winners. This Florida regatta will be to the Harmsworth what the six-meter team racing is to the **America's Cup** in yachting. But the Harmsworth, like the **America's Cup**, is restricted to the very wealthy. This new regatta will enable the foreigners to come here without spending a quarter of a million dollars."

## GAR WOOD AND SPEEDBOAT MANIA

[*Gar Wood, the subject of the following article, was the premier speedboat racer in the US. His disputed victory in the 1930 Harmsworth Trophy match in the Detroit River illustrated national attitudes toward competition. Kaye Don's English boat,* Miss England II, *won the first heat in the best of three final. In the second race, Gar Wood was determined to get a fast start, but he beat the starting gun by 10 seconds (five more than allowed). Don, following close behind, also false started and both boats were disqualified from the competition. This enabled Wood's second boat, driven by his brother, to win easily. Then the controversy began.*

*Did Wood deliberately lure the British boat across the line? If so, was this within the ethics of good sportsmanship. British and Canadian papers were outraged, especially when Wood was reported to have said that he won by "a smart Yankee trick." Although some American newspapers deplored Wood's method of victory, many praised him. It was "the old hidden ball trick," reported one sportswriter. Another journalist declared that while England might have faster boats, the US had smarter captains. As in other sports, he continued, the object was to win, either by superior ability or by superior strategy. In 1932, Gar Wood and his* Miss America *set the speed record for unlimited hydroplanes at 124.86 m.p.h. Frank C. True, "Speedboat Mania. Many Regattas this Year Will Attract Larger Crowds than a World Series Baseball Game,"* Esquire *(September 1937), 79, 116.*]

You are driving along a secluded shore road with the family some weekend afternoon when, suddenly, a thundering report of a cannon echoes in the hills: there is an ear-splitting roar of unmuffled motors as a score of speedboats streaks past the judges' stand: a lawyer pursues a banker, followed by a doctor, and an undertaker trails in the wake of the trio. An allegory? No. Another motorboat regatta is under way. The cannon you heard was the starting gun.

A gallery of thousands on shore trains, binoculars, on a screen of foaming spray as phantom-like drivers, crouching low, disappear toward the first turning buoy. What manner of lure is this! What has caused motorboat racing to become the most rapidly growing sport in America? And why have hundreds of college students foregone summer vacations in Europe to spend the season in greasy racing clothes, jolting, hammering, over rough water at a high rate of speed?

Picture a comely young society girl inviting her spotless beau out to the garage to watch her dressed in overalls, overhaul an outboard motor for the next regatta. Yes, a large slice of America has succumbed to the attractions of speedboat racing. More than four hundred regattas will be held throughout the country this year, many of which will attract crowds larger than a baseball world series.

Gaily decorated yachts are anchored about a two and one-half mile race course: loud speakers blare forth the most minute details of the race as an official in charge of the broadcasting follows every move of the drivers from his lofty perch atop the committee boat: six or seven speedy patrol boats, manned by experts, wait patiently with motors idling, ready to dash out and rescue some overturned driver from the path of onrushing boats.

Speedboat racing, make no mistake, is a rough sport, but sum up all its tragic possibilities, then consider the fact that during its entire history in America only one man has lost his life—and it still is held that he, William Freitag of Philadelphia, died of heart disease. Quite obviously, the goddess of fortune rides with those who take death in their teeth on choppy waters. And what an ideal way to banish the monotony of business worries!

A powerful speedboat, traveling at seventy miles an hour, accidently hits a buoy at a turn; flames flare up as the boat lunges into the air like a swordfish on a line; screams of distress rise from the multitude on shore. Surely death has claimed a victim! But no! Floundering about in the water, kept afloat by his life jacket, the driver has suffered nothing more than a ducking. Being thrown clear of his boat—as practically all drivers are—and landing twenty feet away in the water is far more convenient than plowing a furrow with one's nose in a concrete highway, as most automobilists are forced to do. And it makes a great difference in fatality statistics at the end of the year. With mushroom rapidity, regatta associations and boating clubs have multiplied, spreading to the most remote sections of the country. Few are the college campuses in the East which do not boast of representation in regattas. More than forty colleges and preparatory schools will be represented in the National Intercollegiate Outboard Regatta at Saratoga Springs, New York, this year.

You cannot find a more democratic sport than motorboat racing. In the outboard classes, millionaire and clerk compete side by side, lend each other spark plugs, borrow money until street clothes are donned and go arm in arm to the yacht club's regatta ball that night. Of course, it you should aspire to win a national championship, based upon point scores throughout the season, you'll need a minimum of $15,000. But if it's pleasure only you're after, a few hundred dollars will suffice—and you'll probably have more fun than the chap who has to worry about paid mechanics and a large fleet of racing boats.

From a few scattered outboards in the country ten years ago, plugging along at less than 20 miles an hour, this phase of motorboat racing has increased to a point where the record now is 74.34 miles an hour, held by Jean Dupuy, young French newspaper publisher. From crude two-cylinder affairs, motors have developed into highly perfected four-cylinder power plants of more than sixty horsepower. Back of each driver who has distinguished himself to any degree in outboard racing is a colorful story. Take Fred Jacoby Jr., of North Bergen, New Jersey, for instance. He shattered all rules of financial requirements in winning the American Outboard High Point Championship Trophy for the second successive time last summer. But that was not all he shattered. He won more victories in a single season during 1936 than any driver in the history of racing. For first place in a race, 400 points are awarded: 300 for second, 225 for third, etc.

Jacoby, a 36-year-old scenic artist, has broken record after record during the last two years. He had two things other drivers didn't have—exceedingly fast boats and a clever mechanic for a brother. Together they toured the regatta circuits of the East, South and Middle West, spending long and weary hours on highways at night, their boats and motors being carried in a trailer attached to their car. One has to watch the roads ultra closely under such circumstances. A collision with thousands of dollars worth of boat racing equipment aft means more than a bent fender. But they reached their goal. Spectators have never heard of Emile Jacoby, the brother. No medals or prizes were awarded to him. But Fred knows what made those boats go fast.

Each sport, of course, has its towering personality; the pinnacle around which other names revolve. On the water the gray-haired Gar Wood, the "Silver Fox" of Detroit, is supreme. He was supreme when speedboat racing virtually was unheard of by the general public. Since 1920 he has successfully defended the Harmsworth Trophy, symbolical of the world's unlimited speedboat championship. His Miss America X, or Hell's Calliope, as she appears to spectators, with her forty-eight powerful cylinders belching flames skyward, has traveled 124.915 miles an hour—faster than anything else has ever been propelled on water.

Racing boats may come and go, but when this queen of the water comes forth with her four 12-cylinder motors, possessing 7,600 horsepower, everything else stands aside. Safely over the 50-year mark, Gar is comparatively slight of build, looks older than he really is, talks little and thinks much—especially when a race is in the offing.

What wealth is to most persons, boats are to Wood. It was on one gloomy, miserable day, years ago, that Gar, wondering what he was going to do for a living, stood watching some men unload a truckload of coal in Minneapolis, Minnesota. Then and there he conceived the idea of a hydraulic hoist to lift the bed of the truck and dump the coal out. Fortune followed, but Wood followed boats. He has been following them since.

High speeds have come only through unrelenting competition. During the nine years when Gar was playing the lone hand in establishing new one-mile records, the mark was increased from 74.87 miles an hour with Miss America I, in 1920 to 93.12 miles an hour with Miss America VII in 1929. Then began the international drama of machinery. England chafed at the bit. Lord Wakefield sought to surpass this bloomin' Yankee—and did it temporarily.

The battle started in the Summer of 1930, when the late Sir Henry Seagrave driving Lord Wakefield's Miss England II, shot over the surface of a Scotch lake at 98.76 miles an hour. That British challenge was all Wood needed to "get going." Gar took Miss America X to Indian Creek, a placid body of water in Miami Beach, Florida, and regained the record early in 1931 at 102.25 miles an hour. It was the first time man had ever gone more than 100 miles an hour on water.

But the fight had just begun. Think what he would of the British, Wood had to admit they were stubborn. With the American record only too weeks old, Kaye Don of London took Miss England II to Argentina and made 103.49 miles an hour. Not satisfied with that, the British driver took the boat to Italy several weeks later and clipped off a mark of 110.22 miles an hour. The situation looked dark for Gar. How fast could man go without committing suicide? Already the record had exceeded the wildest of dreams.

But Gar was not to be outdone. Early in 1932, throwing caution to the winds, he increased the record to 111.72 miles an hour, then settled back and smiled with assurance at the little island across the Atlantic. Imagine his amazement when Lord Wakefield built a new boat, Miss England II, which Don drove at 119.81 miles an hour that summer. Was there to be no end to such a struggle? More brute horsepower was added to Miss America X. Her engines were supercharged. Wood would bust a record or a boat, he resolved. He succeeded in the former. On the St.Clair River near his summer home in Algonac, Michigan, that fall the gray thatched veteran blazed over the water at 124.915 miles an hour. That stopped the British.

Following in the footsteps of his father is young Gar Wood Jr., a high school youth of Algonac who won the interscholastic individual outboard championship last year and will defend that crown this year. It was an eventful day when young Wood had his first racing experience in Florida in 1934. His debut was far from resembling the ability of his shrewd father. If he didn't fail to get his motor started in time, he failed to get anywhere after he did get it started. Gar stood on he bank, a classic picture of meditation, shaking his head in philosophical disappointment.

Something had to be done. No son of Gar Wood could make such an exhibition of himself before thousands of spectators. The "something" was left to Orlin Johnson, the unsung hero of many a thrilling race; the mechanic who rides with Gar Sr.; the man who has had his skull battered in crackups and come back for more. Under the coaching of Johnson, who knew Gar Sr's technique as well as the latter, young Wood shot to the fore and some day, undoubtedly, will step into the shoes that have made international speedboat racing famous.

But what about the colleges? How and when did outboard racing gain a foothold on the campus? No playwright ever wrote a funnier comedy than the birth of intercollegiate racing in 1930. When the Colgate University Outing Club announced it would sponsor the first intercollegiate regatta there were derisive smiles. The college boys, it seemed, were about to get their hands dirty and their kidneys jarred on rough water.

But, like most guesses born of condescension, the prophecies of the seasoned onlookers were wrong. What football had meant to stadiums, the college boys transferred to the regatta course. Their initial regatta at Lake Skaneateles, New York, breathed the air of the campus and made the ordinary regatta seem as colorless as a bookkeeper's conversation. With oil-besmeared faces the youngsters proceeded to invade the confines of the top notch drivers of the country. In 1933 a high school youth, Lewis G. Carlisle of East Islip, New York, won the American high point championship. The following year he was succeeded by Joel Thorne, racing under the colors of Rutgers University. Today the attitude toward the school boys is one of profound respect.

With most youths who go in for racing the initial obstacle always is the same-parental objection. But that barrier usually is removed. At first anxious mothers wring their hands on shore as grim-faced sons streak past them. After the race, proud fathers claim the credit and the worries of the mother are relegated to the background as another embryo champion spirals his way to fame and glory. The same holds true of daughters, although there are only a limited number of the "weaker" sex participating nationally. Cylinder oil and rouge make a nasty blend.

But injustice must not be done to the women of speedboat racing. When man, disgruntled at the loss of his domain of golf courses, deserted dry land and fled to the open water for sport, he felt secure in his belief that he had gone where woman could not follow. But not only has he been followed, but passed—passed in several of the important racing events of the country.

Only the sympathetic mind of a mother is capable of accurately perceiving the chagrin which gnaws at the masculine heart as some "frail" woman catapults over the finish line ahead of the field at a regatta. Time was when man was prone to converse in solemn tones of alleged profoundness on single-step hydroplanes, four-cycle motors and piston displacements, considering the mere presence of a woman as insulting to the intellectual depth of the brotherhood, but, like other masculine shams, this one has been gaily revealed to public derision by feminine hands. There are at present only about thirty women actively engaged in racing, but they are doing a masterful job of it.

Imagine a member of some varsity football squad being forced to look at the back of some sorority sister's head as her boat whizzes past him. Or, even more humiliating, to finish second to a high school girl, not to mention the fact that many a "man's man" has been beaten by the mother of several children.

So, you conclude, motorboat racing cannot, after all, be a very rough sport? Climb into a dry-goods box, strapped to the "hurricane deck" of a bucking bronco, and go for a ride—on your knees—and let your reeling brain and bruised body answer the question. But let us have a look at some of these women. Are they of the Amazon type? Most of them are comely college or high school students, the remainder being sports-loving women who refuse to be relegated to the bridge tables.

Not only are most of these women superior on the water, but they are equally capable in the arts and similar activities. Take Mrs. Ruth Herring of Fort Worth, Texas, for instance. She, the mother of a 12 year-old son, was the peer of American women outboard drivers in 1935, holding two world's records. Those records, it should he emphasized, were not limited to feminine competition, but were open to any one who could surpass them. Her one-mile time trial record in Class A, Division 2, was established at Lake Spavinaw, Oklahoma, the speed being 48.25 miles an hour. The record which she surpassed also had been held by her. Her five-mile competitive mark in the same class was made at St. Louis, the speed being 43.43 miles an hour.

And there is Mrs. Maude Rutherfurd of Sands Point, New York, and Palm Beach, who established a lap record in the National Sweepstakes at Red Bank, New Jersey, and boosted the record of Class E inboard runabouts to 45.045 miles an hour in Palm Beach, competing against many of the best men drivers in the country. She is small, slender, blonde and extremely tanned; always ready to take a chance in a close race.

Besides being an expert horse woman, Mrs. Elizabeth Sharp of Tulsa, Oklahoma established an outboard record, since surpassed, of 50.070 miles an hour. Twenty year-old Ruth Do Roo of Flint, Michigan, a junior in Michigan State College, persuaded her father to buy her an outboard racing boat in 1932 and, at the age of 16, won the national championship in Class A, Division 1. Since that time her trophy room has presented a problem of space. In 1935 she won the Michigan state championship in her class for the third time. To her, racing, swimming, skating and trapshooting are "great fun," but her real hobby embraces good literature and cooking, she says.

Pretty little 16 year-old Marion Rowe of Vinton, Iowa, who requests that she always be referred to as "Miss" for fear some one will think "Marion" is a boy, never had seen a racing boat prior to 1935. What she did after stepping into one, however, comprises a story far too long for this space. Imbued with the tense eagerness that could he expected of a high school dramatic student, she readily accepted the invitation of Commodore Hamilton Tobin of the Mid-West Power Boat Association to take a ride. The next day she bought a racing boat—and won her first race. Speedboat racing claimed another "incurable."

When Mrs. Veryl Pantages married into the theatrical family she confronted the prospect of either becoming an "outboard widow" or buying a racing boat of her own. She chose the latter course and proceeded to set a fast pace that was stopped only by motherhood. Her husband, Rodney Pantages of Los Angeles, gladly would exchange trophies with her. Today their small daughter, Nanette, "pilots" a specially built toy racing boat, **Little Shot, Jr.**, around in the Pantages bathtub.

Whether speedboat racing is an ephemeral or permanent addition to major sports remains to be seen, but just now there are no earmarks of decay.

## ROWING TECHNOLOGY

*[Technology was just as important to rowing as it was to power boats and yachts. The following article discusses the evolution of the rowing shell during the 1930s. William Inglis, "Revolution in Rowing," Esquire (May 1939), 87, 185-186, 188.]*

Tom Bolles, head coach of Harvard crews was looking at the new varsity shell of Massachusetts Institute of Technology. Robert Herrick, dean of those Harvard veterans to whom rowing is a sacred cult, stood at his side. Bolles studied the shell's fine body, noted her broad beam and deep draught well forward, fullness that made for easy entrance into the water and prevented the tendency to dip at the beginning of the stroke. He observed that the hull gradually tapered away aft almost to a vanishing point; so that the long, slim form of the boat resembled that of a streamlined railroad train.

With the utmost care he scrutinized the outriggers and braces of the shell, all formed of aluminum alloys, which made the boat fifty pounds lighter than any other eight he had ever seen; for in all other shells these parts are made of steel. If the rig would stand the strain, the saving in weight should add to the boat's speed.

"She ought to get off the line fast," was Tom Bolles' only comment. Mr. Herrick nodded. Experts don't become enthusiastic over novelties: they've seen so many fade.

She did get off the line fast, and her crew—the M.I.T. varsity 150-pounders—were smart and strong enough to hold their advantage, reaching their climax by winning the American Henley at Princeton over a big field, which included Yale, Harvard, Columbia, Cornell, Pennsylvania and Princeton. The Tech lads modestly ascribed their victory to *It*, which is the nickname they have given to their wonderful light boat. As a matter of fact, Harvard had beaten them in two earlier races, when they caught a couple of "crabs" and had other mishaps; but this time they turned in a truly rowed race and showed themselves a good crew in a very good boat.

The 150-pound freshman crew of Manhattan College, New York, a newcomer in the American Henley, were barely nosed out by Pennsylvania in the junior event, and led Princeton, Columbia and Cornell over the line. Their coach, Allen Walz, was so impressed by the speed of *It* that he ordered one like it from the Cambridge Boat Company, a group of M.I.T. scientists, who designed and built the novel racing machine. Also Tech has a new shell for its regular varsity crew, a little bigger and heavier than *It*. Experts, always skeptical about new methods, have not yet made up their minds as to just how good the three light shells are.

Thus has begun the most radical revolution in boatbuilding since Thomas Doggett bequeathed a perpetual yearly Coat and Badge for the swiftest Thames wherryman, and old Clasper began to build best-and-best racing boats for English universities, more than a century ago. Like many other revolutions, it may fizzle out into nothing—or it may mark the beginning of a new era in the fiercest of all athletic sports. Neither the invention of the sliding seat, to take the place of slithering with greased leather-seated breeches on thwarts with the grain of the wood set fore and aft, nor the substitution of the swivel rowlock for the thole-pin and clumsy box rowlock, promised more in adding speed to racing shells. At this moment the new boat's prospects seem bright.

For an art that has been practiced through so many generations, boatbuilding has advanced but slowly, its many errors corrected by trial and no sooner set right than others spring up in their place. Yet you get a vivid picture of progress when you compare the delicate but staunch racing shells of today with the heavy, clinker-built arks in which the coxswains of the Oxford and Cambridge crews of the 1830's ran along the gunwale and shoved off from a pier for a racing start. Note that the ancient coxswains and oarsmen raced in fuzzy, bell-crowned beaver toppers, and you see how heavily they were handicapped compared with the bareheaded, barebacked racers of today. Modern oarsmen work as hard as the old boys, but they get a much faster run for their money.

Their boats are things of beauty, smooth-skinned, designed to slip through the water with the least possible resistance. The hulls, of thin, polished cedar, seem fragile as eggshells, yet they are so strongly framed and stoutly braced that they last for years under strains and stresses that would rack an ordinary boat to pieces. The West Side Rowing Club of Buffalo have a shell they got ten years ago from Columbia College, and it was twenty years old when they got it. They still train crews in it. Manhattan College has a shell that John Johnson built at Travers Island thirty-five years ago. Their crews raced in it for two years, and they still train in it.

The average eight-oared shell is sixty feet long, twenty-four inches wide and of six inches draught, perhaps a trifle larger for extra heavy crews. From the bowman's seat to the cutwater, she is decked over with heavy silk, oiled to make it waterproof, and there is a similar deck from coxy's perch to the rudder post. For the rest of her length she is open as a viking's ship—which, by the way, was built along similar lines and could be rowed at high speed when there was no sailing breeze. A racing eight costs fourteen hundred dollars, old style or new.

To laymen and even to most rowing men, all racing shells look alike; yet the expert eye will detect differences, minute in size but with important effect on speed. Sometimes these are so slight that they can be proved only by actual measurement, but, slight as they are, they are of vital effect. The ratios of length to breadth, breadth to draught and length to draught, are often varied, though for years every designer has been constantly looking for the perfect combination that will yield the greatest speed. As for the sections—that is, dimensions of the boat at right angles to her length—they vary almost to infinity. Should the bilges be hard or slack, the deadrise be great or small, the sides vertical, flaring out, or with tumblehome?—that is, sloping inward like the side of a burgundy glass. On all these questions specialists get into hot arguments which probably won't be settled this side of the millennium. [Deleted description of an earlier MIT boat race.]

Seattle has been the capital of the rowing world since the crews of the University of Washington made a clean sweep of all three events in the Intercollegiate regatta at Poughkeepsie in 1936, then went to Berlin and won the championship of the world at the Olympics, and swept the Hudson again last year. Seattle is quite as famous for its Pocock racing shells as for its Boeing airplanes. All the crews at Poughkeepsie last year raced in Pocock shells, and so did most of the others in America.

Pocock does not depend on tank tests for his theories of design. He carries in his mind the outlines of what a perfect shell should be. As a schoolboy in Middlesex, England, he helped his father and grandfather build racing shells for Eton and Oxford. At seventeen he won the *Sportsman's* prize for single sculling, and used the money to take him and his older brother, Dick, to Vancouver, B.C. They worked as lumbermen until Hiram Conibear, the first famous coach of the University of Washington crews, invited them to Seattle, where they set up a modest shop back of the University boathouse. William E. Boeing was so impressed by the strength and fineness of their work

that he engaged George to run his airplane factory, but after seven years of success
George returned to his beloved boat shop. Dick went to Yale with Ed Leader, in 1922,
and has built Yale's boats ever since.

The program in the Seattle shop is very like what goes on wherever racing boats
are built. The first part of an eight to take shape is a row of upright posts, upon which
the keel, upside down, is solidly mortised. Next the gunwale is laid down and connected up with the keel by ribs, giving the structure an appearance not unlike the skeleton of a snake. Now the skeleton is turned right side up, and the frames are put in
place. All these parts are made of Alaska cedar, a white wood that combines lightness,
strength and a rigidity like that of steel.

The frames support the sides of the boat against all pressures. The whole interior
is so intricately joined together that the labyrinth of little timbers makes you think of
a nest of jackstraws, yet each strut and stringer has its special work to do in resisting
strains. The last item in knitting the boat into a rigid body is a set of metal braces running diagonally from side to side and riveted into the gunwales at the ends. Pocock
uses tubular steel for these, as well as for the outriggers....

Looking at the newly designed Massachusetts Tech shells alongside the Pocock
fleet that will race at Poughkeepsie, the ordinary observer would say that they are alike.
Set the boats on racks side by side, and they still seem to be of identical size and shape,
though essentially they differ as much as race horses differ from trotters.

Before laying down the M.I.T. keel, in the shop of the Cambridge Boat Works,
naval architect Robert C. Allyn drafted a design based on tests that established the most
efficient lines. In these tests, small models of racing shells were towed through tanks
with uniform power to determine which form offered least resistance to the water.
While the figures recording the experiments cannot be quoted here, the result may be
stated—the form of hull that goes through the water with least friction resembles in a
general way the form of a raindrop falling through the air.

Besides the advantage Mr. Allyn believes he has in this scientific model, the Cambridge Boat people have made a radical departure in the construction of their outriggers
and braces. Pocock tried outriggers of duraluminum on his shells five years ago, but
went back to steel tubing. Otto E. Wolff of Cambridge Boat experimented with various alloys of aluminum, in combination with copper, silicon, magnesium and chro-
mium, until he found a light, stiff metal that keeps its shape and rigidity under all
working conditions and resists salt water erosion. He has not published the formula for
it, since he is still experimenting, but the builders have rigged the M.I.T. boats with it,
and thus far have won most of their races. The reason is not hard to discover:

A Massachusetts Tech shell, aluminum rigged, weighs 225 to 240 pounds.

Other modern shells, rigged with steel, weigh 280 to 290 pounds.

As the rowing game consists of the most economical application of man power plus
the elimination of everything that hinders speed, it can be imagined how much faster
a crew can row a boat fifty pounds lighter than the boats of their competitors.

Coach Cedric Valentine will not start a Tech crew in the Poughkeepsie regatta this
year, so the new boats will not undergo the supreme test of the four-mile race; but they
will meet all the best crews in the East in the American Henley and in many mile and
three-quarter events. Decisive victories, even at the shorter distances, will prove the

excellence of the new model and rig. Their performance will be watched with keenest interest not only by all the rowing colleges and schools from coast to coast but by the seventy clubs and ten thousand rowing men who are members of the National Association of Amateur Oarsmen, besides some forty or fifty clubs, with four thousand members, not in the Association. These clubs have at least 1500 boats used in training and racing, and the schools and colleges have 1000 more. Valued as low as $1000 each, this fleet cost $2,500,000. Add to this the value of boathouses and equipment, and we have a total investment of $5,000,000 or $6,000,000 in the sport of rowing.

There is a possibility that racing shells may be built of the new aluminum alloy, though it is certain that aluminum alone will not stand the wear and tear of rowing. Walter Hoover of Detroit, who won the Diamond Sculls at Henley—the amateur championship of the world—a few years ago, had a single scull shell made of aluminum, which he tried out at Philadelphia. It did not survive hard usage. The new alloys have not yet been tried in hulls.

Oars have been improved in recent years, though not to the same degree as the shells. They are still twelve feet long, with gently curved blades thirty inches long and six to seven inches wide. They used to be made of solid spruce, but now they are tubular, made of strips of spruce molded and fastened together with casein glue, under pressure. They weigh eight pounds and cost eighteen dollars apiece, a little more than the old type. They are one pound lighter than the solid oar, and they insure crews against the danger of knots or flaws hidden in the thickest part of the loom, where the most strain comes. The faulty oars used to break when they were most needed. If the break came within the first twelve strokes of a short race or the first half-minute of a long one, the referee called all boats back for a fresh start; but beyond that starting margin each boat had to abide by its own accidents. [Deleted story of most famous broken oar.]

Donoghue of Newburgh-on-Hudson, who made most of the racing oars in those days, found that by gouging deep grooves down both sides of the shaft of the oar, he could discover flaws that did not appear on the surface. Also, he saved a few ounces of weight without diminishing the strength of the oar—on the same principle as the I-beam used in building skyscrapers. Grooved oars were safer than solid ones, but there was still a margin of danger in the heart of the oar.

This was finally eliminated when several geniuses hit upon the idea of making tubular oars of laminated spruce. Ted Shea of Springfield, Massachusetts, was one of the first if not the very first to make the hollow oars. He sold his business to the Montague Oar and Paddle Corporation, of Foxboro, who made the Ted Shea oar and are the largest manufacturers of racing oars in this country. The layers are less than a quarter of an inch thick, and if the least sign of a knot is found, that strip is thrown out.

George Pocock makes his tubular oars of Engelmann spruce, a West Coast growth, backed with ironwood. The lighter oar is easier to handle on the recover, and it can be whipped out of the water with a sharper release. But its greatest virtue is that you can rely on it to pull through the hardest race without any liability of crashing at a crucial moment.

Chapter 18

# RACKET SPORTS—TENNIS, BADMINTON, TABLE TENNIS, SQUASH

In 1935, Americans strung their rackets with enough gut to stretch from New York to St. Louis. Among the ten fastest growing sports on the basis of sporting goods sales were badminton, squash, table tennis, and tennis. The most popular racket games gave the middle classes what they wanted. The game must be easy to learn, inexpensive, and provide strenuous exercise in a brief time. As the document "Sports for the Fun of It" illustrates, the successful sports emphasized these qualities.

American tennis star Donald Budge wrote in 1939 that "tennis yields to no other game...in the premium it puts upon seasoned judgment, quick mental reaction, alert reflexes, and painstaking patience and perseverance in coordinating the hand and eye to take a moving ball upon the face of a racket. Tennis demands, too, the physical attributes of speed afoot, excellent condition, and staying power." By the 1930s, tennis discarded many of its aristocratic trappings and emerged as a popular sport for men and women. Colorful personalities such as William (Big Bill) Tilden and Helen Jacobs, and star players such as Helen (Little Poker Face) Wills Moody and Donald Budge attracted tens of thousands of spectators to major tournaments and induced magazines and newspapers to hire these personalities to write about their sport for their thousands of followers. Davis Cup matches were broadcast on radio.

Studies of sports preferences in the 1930s revealed the popularity of tennis. With quick-drying courts, slower surfaces, and easier to control balls, the average tennis player could now have longer rallies and more fun. Tennis also benefited from technological advances in lighting technology. The 1936 report of the Tennis Committee of the Toronto Cricket Club remarked that the recent innovation of night tennis had proven especially beneficial for those members who worked in offices during the day.

American women's colleges offered tennis as part of their physical education program more than any other sport, although in terms of time allotted, tennis ranked sixth. Eight of ten high school girls in Des Moines, Iowa, reported that they liked tennis "very much" (swimming and basketball came second at seventy four percent), and one-half wanted tennis instruction. W.C. Fuller, who coached Helen Jacobs and Helen Wills, noted that girls were better tennis students than boys because the "average girl feels that tennis is one of the few outdoor sports in which she can excel, and is willing and eager to focus her mind and heart on it." (American Magazine, August, 1935) In terms of numbers of high schools involved, interscholastic boy's tennis ranked only behind basketball, track, and football. And for men over age twenty, one survey noted that in order of frequency of play, tennis, table tennis, and swimming were the three most popular sports (Research Quarterly, October 1933; December 1934; March 1939).

In the early 1930s, exclusive tennis and country clubs felt the pinch of the depression and some made their facilities available for a fee. Membership at the Toronto

Cricket Club, for example, declined in 1931 from 701 to 609 and the finance committee reported "the most important matter confronting the club and each and every member [was] obtaining new members." The growing popularity of tennis averted the crisis and the number of clubs affiliated with the United States Lawn Tennis Association (USLTA) expanded from 600 to 800. The number of participants in 1940 was 500,000.

At least a million and a half people played on courts not affiliated with the USLTA. With rackets costing from $5 to $17, and a dozen balls at $4, tennis was no longer prohibitively expensive. Local, state and federal relief funds assisted in the construction of tennis courts in urban playgrounds and recreation centers. The Works Progress Administration (WPA) provided additional money for municipal recreation programs, and by the end of 1937, 3,500 tennis courts owed their construction to the WPA. Improvements in lighting further expanded the availability of tennis courts. Although Time reported in 1936 that cosmopolitan young men and women in white clothes played tennis, municipal courts opened the game to a new sector of American society and diminished the dominance of elite private clubs. Never before was tennis so popular.

Black America, or at least the professional classes, also joined in the craze for tennis. The American Tennis Association (ATA) for Black Americans, for example, sported 28,000 members in 145 clubs in 1940. Black players participated in a summer circuit that included thirty-five sectional and state tournaments culminating in the annual ATA championship. The 1940 championship at Wilberforce University in Ohio attracted 1,500 spectators.

Tennis was still racist and top players as Jimmie McDaniel, termed the "greatest colored player ever," and Ora Washington, the "Black Helen Wills," who won the ATA from 1929 to 1935 and again in 1937, were rarely mentioned by the white press nor permitted to play against the best white players. In December 1929, the NAACP charged the USLTA with discrimination when it refused entry into National Junior Indoor Tennis Championships in New York to two young black men. The USLTA initially replied that it had no by-laws preventing blacks from playing in its tournaments and the players merely need be members of an affiliated club, but later stated that its policy was to discourage blacks as "we believe that as a practical matter, the present method of separate associations for the administration of the affairs and the championships of colored and white players should be continued."

Most tennis commentators, including Grantland Rice, Paul Gallico, Al Laney, and W.O. McGeehan, were also biased in their coverage of women's tennis. Articles on women's tennis usually concentrated on personalities rather than on tactics and skills. When two top women played, the match was often termed a "cat fight," whereas a similar match between men would be a "clash of the gods," or a "classic confrontation." A Canadian tennis critic wrote of two women players that the "masculine-like severity of their stroking belied their feminine grace of figure."

In the 1933 US Open, Helen Jacobs wore pleated shorts for the first time, and the tournament soon became publicized as a "battle of skirts versus shorts." When Jacobs beat the skirted Wills in the finals, women's tennis shorts boomed. Earlier, Helen Wills' decision to play in short skirts and bare legs led thousands of young women to follow her example.

Between 1927 and 1933 Wills lost no sets in singles competition anywhere in the world. During that remarkable stretch she won 180 consecutive matches. Playing well past the age which most male authorities considered dangerous to women's health, Wills Moody captured eight Wimbledon, seven US, and four French national titles, and expanded the definition of female beauty beyond that of frail and pale.

As "Wills on Tennis" demonstrates, many of the best women players spoke out against gender discrimination. Helen Jacobs wrote in 1934 (Liberty, August) that married women could still play tournament tennis and sustain a good marriage. Look at May Sutton Bundy, Hazel Hotchkiss Wightman, Marjorie Van Ryn, Helen Wills Moody, and Molla Bjurstedt Mallory, she said. "I should think that a woman whose interests, through tennis, became diversified, whose experience with people and life were amplified by reason of her contacts, would be more attractive to her husband than one whose interests were narrowed down to a small sphere of household cares." Certainly the public enjoyed women's tennis, and in 1931 the American men's and women's national singles championships were held simultaneously at the same venue.

Tennis was less popular in Canada, where private clubs dominated the field. Canada's Davis Cup players came almost exclusively from Toronto and Montreal, with an occasional entry from the West Coast. In the Maritimes, tennis made great gains among businessmen and office and store clerks, but was not popular with blue collar workers. When Canada hosted a Davis Cup match against the US in Montreal in 1931, temporary stands were constructed as Canada lacked a permanent tennis stadium. According to the Western Home Monthly (April 1932), tennis was "not so hot as an entertainment for the spectators, because in ninety out of every hundred tennis matches between ranking players the result is a foregone conclusion before the first service shot has crossed the net, the paying guests do not like that.... Fewer surprises are sprung in tennis than in any other sport offered to the public today."

Normally, interest in tournament tennis increased through May and June before climaxing in late July with the finals of the Davis Cup. Although the American team competed in the finals seven times in the 1930s, it only won in 1937 and 1938, thanks to the play of Donald Budge, Frank Parker, Gene Mako, and Robert Riggs. In the former year, Budge employed an explosive serve and a devastating topspin backhand to capture the Grand Slam. Budge, Moody, Jacobs, and Alice Marble were all Californians.

Like the USLTA, the Canadian Lawn Tennis Association sent its best players abroad for experience, but unlike the US, Canada was less competitive internationally. Marjorie Leeming was one of the few Canadians to perform well outside the country. In 1931, Marcel Rainville beat an American (Sidney Wood) for the first time in a Davis Cup match. Although this victory prompted optimistic talk about the future, Canada never achieved Davis Cup success. Most observers alluded to the Canadian climate, the lack of indoor facilities, and the dearth of good coaching to explain Canada's tennis failures. In 1935, for example, Canada withdrew from the Davis Cup, citing the early May starting time for the American Zone contests that did not give its players enough time to prepare. Most top players held full-time jobs and, according to Maclean's Magazine, didn't work diligently at their tennis for fear that it would distract from their work. The document "What's Wrong with Canadian Tennis" reflects the attitudes of the traditional elite clubs that sports should not consume a person's life.

Amateur tennis came under considerable attack. In 1940, John Lardner reported in News-week that ninety-five percent of the amateur players were "frankly on the make." John Tunis wrote in Esquire (August 1939) "to be a champion at Wimbledon means, among other things, a $25,000 lecture contract.... It means contracts with newspaper syndicates at flattering terms, opportunities to sing at the Waldorf with Coleman's Band, articles in the big magazines, chance to place the 'Eleanor Tennant Tennis frock,' the 'Eleanor Tennant sports shoe,' the 'Eleanor Tennant pantie' and the 'Eleanor Tennant girdle' in Fifth Avenue department stores." Professional tennis player Vincent Richards estimated that in 1933, Helen Wills Moody earned $15,000 a year from her writing, drawings, radio broadcasting, and costume designing for dressmakers. Most amateurs were less fortunate.

Professional tennis began in 1926, but as Scribner's Magazine noted seven years later, there was less money in tennis than in almost any other professional sport. Times were changing. The proliferation of public courts opened the game to a wider variety of players, some of whom wanted to benefit financially from their talents. In 1930, Tilden's decision to sign a motion picture contract with Metro-Goldwyn-Mayer and to form Tilden Tennis Tour Inc. accelerated the movement of players into the professional ranks. Tilden, who won Wimbledon in 1930 at age 38, had captured America's imagination in the 1920s with his theatrics and athletic strokes. Vincent Richards, a fellow playing pro, wrote that Tilden turned the derision of linesmen into an art. "He transfixed the blundering official; he craned his neck at him, and sometimes he would merely smile and that hurt most of all. The whole gallery loved it.... Even when playing a dub in the first round he gave the audience something for its money and, incidentally, made the dub feel good. If it were possible to do so, he usually permitted his early-round opponent to take a long lead in each set and then he would put on the pressure and come from behind. The gallery loved that, too." When Ellsworth Vines, Donald Budge, Fred Perry and Helen Jacobs turned pro in the late 1930s, professional tennis was firmly established.

As the document "Tilden and Professional Tennis" reveals, the professional tour was arduous. The Cleveland Press reported in 1936: "In the midst of the doubles match Tilden was informed that the net receipts were less than $500 and that the promoter, Tom McKee, had disappeared. Whereupon Tilden halted the match, stalked into the box office and remained there to thrash matters out for 45 minutes, while the crowd— what there was of it—waited.... In the end, Tilden and his manager, Bill O'Brien agreed to accept $200 and the tennis program was resumed." That year, Tilden divided the players into separate eastern and western traveling troupes. They met only at the annual US Professional Tennis Association Championship.

A persistent issue during the decade was open tennis. American Lawn Tennis surveyed the leading amateurs in 1930 and found that all but one favored playing against professionals. Four years later, The Literary Digest supported such an event and reported eighteen of the best twenty-two American amateurs did as well. Many tennis clubs wished to host such events for the revenues they would generate, but the USLTA refused sanction unless it was promised fifty percent of the profits. When the Greenbrier Golf and Tennis Club hosted an unauthorized open tournament in 1937, the USLTA suspended the six amateurs who participated and canceled the club's association membership.

## BADMINTON

Whereas Americans dominated tennis in North America, Canadians were supreme in badminton. The 1935 edition of the *Canadian Official Badminton Guide* crowed,

"There can be no denying the fact that Canada has risen as a mighty power in world-wide badminton, able to stand on her feet with any nation, and considerably better than most...it seems no exaggeration to say that Canada rates with the best." Although Canadians routinely won American badminton tournaments, instead of complaining, as Canadians tended to do in tennis when the reverse was true, Americans embraced competition—which they hoped would eventually make them better players. Esquire reported in 1939 that the competitors were "inspired by the superior play of the Canadian amateurs, who journeyed to some of our open tournaments, showed us more than a thing or two about what could be done with a bat and shuttle, and, incidentally, returned home laden with...[the] symbolic spoils of victory."

Badminton's growth in Canada was sparked by the adoption of a faster shuttlecock that made the game more strenuous, and by visiting British badminton teams in 1930 and 1933 that demonstrated their superior skills. In addition, British professionals, such as J.F. Devlin at the Winnipeg Winter Club, accepted jobs in Canada and sparked interest in these clubs. Quickly it seemed every city, town, and village in Canada offered badminton tournaments, and, unlike many sports, every region of the country produced top players. Doug Grant was from Halifax, Nova Scotia, and Dorothy McKenzie, the Canadian women's champion, 1936-1940, and the first Canadian to win the All-England championship, was from Swift Current, Saskatchewan. By the late 1930s, badminton benefited from excellent newspaper coverage. The 1939 Toronto city championships were so popular the club turned away paying spectators. A year earlier, the Maritime Intercollegiate Athletic Union included badminton as an intercollegiate sport. Private companies joined the craze and constructed courts on their premises. When Jack Purcell inquired about this practice, one company executive replied, "simple enough, we've got a big office staff here. There are over a hundred of them. This brings 'em together in the right recreational atmosphere. It's the best investment we've ever made. It pays off heavily in improved morale."

In the 1930s, the Associated Screen News initiated a series of short ten-minute films designed to depict different aspects of Canadian life to audiences in the United States, Great Britain, Australia, and Asia, as well as to Canadians. Significantly, one film was entitled "This Badminton Racquet." "Badminton in Canada" outlines the growth of badminton in Canada and reflects the country's growing sense of self-importance.

The Literary Digest noted in 1933 that "badminton is crossing the Canadian border as certainly as the migrating birds fly over in the fall." One of these players was Jack Purcell, the world's greatest badminton player. Purcell played a series of exhibition games across the United States to promote badminton. In Los Angles, he played the American champion, George Williard, in front of 4,000 spectators at the Ambassador Hotel, and later the two players toured with Tilden's professional tennis troupe. Williard played exhibitions in movie houses across country and amazed audiences with his showmanship. British professionals, some of whom came to American clubs through Canada, also contributed to the growth of badminton.

Badminton grew rapidly in the US in the 1930s. The September 1936 issue of the Sporting Goods Journal reported that "indoor and outdoor courts are being installed everywhere, while schools, colleges, and clubs are installing the game as a physical education activity." Articles in The Saturday Evening Post, Collier's, The Literary Digest, News-week, and the Christian Science Monitor reflected badminton's widespread public appeal. When Hollywood stars such as Bette Davis, Douglas Fairbanks, and Joan Blondell took up badminton, the game garnered further attention and News-week reported at the end of the decade that badminton was the fastest growing game played with a racket.

As with most racket sports, part of badminton's appeal was that it was an easy game to learn and play. Young and old, rich and poor, men and women, and athletes and sedentary office workers could participate, whether at an exclusive country club, a YMCA, a church hall, an armory, a school gym, or just in the back yard. To counter-act earlier beliefs that badminton was a "sissy" game, its supporters emphasized that it was a game of stamina, speed, coordination and agility. Two games were comparable to three sets of tennis, and they could be played in half the time. Indeed, the game's supporters noted, tennis players such as Sidney Wood played badminton as a condi-tioner. Badminton was appropriate for contemporary life. "It is a game peculiarly suited to our temperament, our habits, and the chronic time shortage from which we all suf-fer when it comes to fitting recreation hours into our daily schedule of living," ex-plained Country Life in 1932.

## TABLE TENNIS

Table tennis also contended with notions that it was an effeminate game, and its pro-ponents frequently mentioned noted athletes in other sports who played this "he-man" sport for a "real workout." Babe Ruth used it to sharpen his eye. College football coach Alonzo Stagg praised table tennis for its cleverness and speed, and Esquire wrote that tournament players "train for this grind as religiously as Jesse Owens prepares himself for some major track meets."

Unlike other racket games, this was a period of controversy for table tennis. Rule changes set the game to 21 points in 1929, lowered the net to allow for more attack-ing shots, and in 1936 prohibited stalling—one match in the world championship lasted eight hours and was finally settled by a coin toss. In 1937, the US withdrew from the International Table Tennis Federation over the issue of amateurism. But the most con-tentious issue in the US was the struggle for control of the game between the Ameri-can Ping-Pong Association that represented Parker Brothers, which held a trademark on the name "ping-pong," and the United States Table Tennis Association which rep-resented competing manufacturers. "The Table Tennis Wars" details this struggle. Eventually the table tennis supporters emerged victorious.

## SQUASH AND OTHER RACKET GAMES

Squash was promoted as an ideal game for urban businessmen who were confined to the office and wanted to keep fit in the winter, but had few leisure hours to spare. Thirty minutes of squash, claimed The Literary Digest, was perfect for "anyone seeking to drive away the mental and physical cobwebs that come at the end of a hard day's work."

At the beginning of the decade, participants could choose between squash tennis and squash racquets. As the few magazines that covered the game mentioned, squash tennis was the only racket game of American origin. The rapid speed of the ball made it difficult to play and led to short rallies. Squash racquets flourished in large eastern colleges, where athletic directors taught it as a conditioning game for post-college life, and in private clubs as far west as St. Louis. Recent college graduates flooded to New

York and demanded to play squash. Whereas squash racquets' popularity grew, squash tennis declined so much that by the end of the decade it was principally a New York game, with small followings in Cincinnati, St. Louis, Chicago, Omaha, and Havana. News-week, one of the few magazines to cover the sport, lamented "the sad but undeniable growth of squash rackets at the expense of squash tennis."

Although squash racquets was a British game, sportswriters such as those in The Literary Digest noted that it "was typically American in its demand for speed," and "as in most of the games of foreign birth, the Americans have introduced a blistering speed and a hard, smashing type of play into Squash Racquets." In addition, the American game employed a harder rubber ball and a slightly smaller court. Unlike badminton, table tennis and tennis, squash racquets appealed to people's aggressive tendencies and their desire to vent the day's frustrations. This made it an ideal game for contemporary urban society. Businessmen in New York, Philadelphia, and Boston, declared The Literary Digest in 1934, "discovered that it was a real man's work to chase that little black ball around the four gleaming white walls of a squash court, these tired business men and bankers were the life of the game."

Racquets and court tennis were the racket games of the wealthy. In a typical game of racquets, which might best be described as handball with a bat, a player used from 12 to 20 bats at $7.50 each and two dozen balls at eight cents apiece. There were only thirteen racquet courts in the United States.

Court tennis, termed "the king of games and the game of kings," was even more exclusive. Played in only the most exclusive clubs, no more than 500 Americans ever played on one of the country's twelve courts and fewer than 10,000 people ever watched the game. "With yachting and polo no longer monopolized by the monied folk," declared The Literary Digest in 1931, "it remains as the most exclusive of all athletic pastimes."

Platform or paddle tennis, by contrast, was ideal for everyone. Portable, inexpensive, easy to play, designed to be played in a small space, either indoors or outdoors, on any surface and in any weather, platform tennis grew quickly, especially in the northeast. The Paddle Tennis Association was founded in 1934, and the first national championship was played the following year. Four years later the first court outside the United States was built in Nova Scotia.

Like other racket sports, handball, especially four-wall, did not accommodate many spectators. Although numerous universities taught handball, the single-wall game owed its popularity to the eastern beaches near New York. Four-wall was a popular YMCA game.

Women were encouraged to play most racket games, and in the 1930s they did well in badminton, table tennis, tennis, and squash. Country Life noted in 1932 that badminton "is the only sport on record at which the women play is actually on a par with the man," since they excel in anticipation and coordination, and have "quick eyes." Most commentaries were not as complimentary. The New Yorker, for example, commented on the women's squash racquets championship in 1934 that "Miss Page made the mistake of playing the ball up and down the walls instead of into the corners, so that her opponent had to cover the court only from side to side instead of from end to end. This fault is characteristic of all the women squash-racquet players we have seen. Like lady golfers whose universal weakness is not driving but putting, lady squash-players are weak at the department of the game that calls for finesse rather than strength...they play with an appalling expenditure of energy and no show of intelligence whatever."

Since society still viewed females as relatively frail creatures with limited stamina, most racket sports required females to play briefer matches than their male counterparts. The Amateur Athletic Union required female handball competitors to "submit to a physical examination before the start of the championship, or furnish a doctor's certificate issued not more than thirty days prior to said championship, certifying to her fitness for competition."

## WHAT'S WRONG WITH CANADIAN TENNIS?

[*In 1931, 290 tennis clubs were affiliated with the Canadian Lawn Tennis Association. Of these clubs, Ontario had 67, Quebec 56, Alberta 48, British Columbia 40, Manitoba 26, Saskatchewan 24, Nova Scotia 18, and New Brunswick 11. The following article reflects upper-class, British elitist perspectives toward the role of sport in society and their attitudes towards the materialism of the US. John Holden, "What's Wrong with Our Tennis?" Maclean's Magazine (15 September 1930), 13, 78-79.*]

What is the matter with Canadian tennis?

Something evidently is. Each year we take a more or less graceful trimming in the Davis Cup contest. Queen Mary scarcely ever has a chance to watch one of our representatives from the royal box at Wimbledon. At Forest Hills we either do not enter at all or else make quick tracks toward the nearest exit; bowing to applause for our sportsmanship, it is true, but licked for all that. Even our national championship is carried away whenever Uncle Sam sees fit to pay carfare to Canada for a few of his ranking players.

This is not as it should be. If tournament tennis is really the wholesome sport for amateur players that it is claimed to be, we ought to be in there at the finish, fighting in the final for possession of the world's premier prize, as we do in several other sports, and, once in a while at least we should carry it home in triumph and a heavily insured box.

The common or vacant lot variety of tennis, as distinguished from the more highly cultured tournament game, is certainly a worth-while sport. It is claimed by many to be the world's most popular game, and when one considers that it is played with gusto by every civilized nation on earth and by some that have not advanced from beyond the breech-cloth and tin-can-necklace stage, there is ample basis for the claim. It is thoroughly British, the modern game having originated in England; it requires both physical and mental agility and Canadians possess plenty of both; it promotes friendships, elevates teacup gossip, is fine for reducing and the uplift of fallen arches [sic]; it affords the girls a chance to display nut-brown arms and dimpled knees, and to a great extent it supports the white-flannel-trousers industry.

But is tournament tennis a worth-while sport? Let's look into the matter.

A few years ago the writer sat in the gallery at Forest Hills and watched a prominent Canadian player battling in one of the advance rounds with an up-and-coming American. Each contestant had won two sets. The fifth and deciding one was a desperate struggle, each man putting everything he had into strokes that sent the ball streaking back and forth like a white comet.

Breathlessly the gallery hung upon each stroke. Long since, it had burst the bounds of polite hand-clapping; it voiced its approval of each point-winning shot with reverberating roars of encouragement.

Even in those tense moments of stress and strain, however, it was obvious that the Canadian was playing for fun. He grinned like a schoolboy when he won a hard-fought rally; he gasped "good shot" when he lost. He never even frowned when a questionable decision was called against him. His attitude was that of a gentleman and a sportsman to whom, after all, tennis was merely a game.

His opponent's attitude was different. He wasted no breath in calling "good shot;" he glared at the linesmen; he gritted his teeth and muttered to himself. He was enjoying himself about as much as does a hooked fish that battles with a fisherman.

It happened that I knew the history and antecedents of that American youth, and thus I realized why he was in there to do or die.

His father was an unlettered immigrant who was then engaged in the highly utilitarian but somewhat undistinguished business of collecting garbage. By stinting himself, and also by hinting to householders that in United States cities an occasional tip has been known to speed the family ashes dumpward, he had sent his boy to high school. There Young Hopeful had gazed with shrewd eyes upon the different avenues to fame, fortune, and peachy girl friends, and had decided that proficiency in sport is an excellent means of acquiring all three.

**A PASSPORT TO FAME**

After school hour Junior sought employment as an assistant groundsman at tennis courts which were rented by the hour. He asked for no pecuniary remuneration; all he desired was an opportunity to play and learn.

He secured it. The courts manager was no mean player himself and he adopted the boy as his protege. By devoting all his after-school hours and all of his Saturdays and Sundays to the game, Junior was able in two or three years to defeat his mentor. Tennis was his vocation; the securing of an education his avocation. He won a minor tournament or two, sought one of those university scholarships which are not too difficult for an athlete to obtain at certain institutions, captained his university tennis team, and now, in America's premier tournament, he was battling his Canadian opponent with an intensity of purpose which few Canadian amateurs ever show in any sport.

Why shouldn't he? A good showing would carry with it social recognition, an opportunity to secure free trips to other tournaments, to earn money perhaps by writing about the game, to acquire a position in the business world which college boys who are personally unacquainted with the captains of industry achieve only by years of plugging and a large measure of good luck.

No such material considerations animated the Canadian. He was no poor immigrant's son. Already he possessed professional and social standing. A tennis court was to him a playground, not a battlefield upon which from childhood he had waged war against poverty and social obscurity and lack of opportunity. He played tennis as a sportsman—and was beaten by the youth who could not afford to lose.

The difference between those two players indicates, to the writer's mind, the difference between wholesome amateur tennis and another variety of the same game, that is neither very wholesome nor strictly amateur. We cling to the first variety, as sportsmen should, but others do not, and thus they are able to trim us with the neatness and celerity of a fruit grower going over a peach tree.

Here the game is played for pleasure only, by men and women who can afford to pay for their pleasure. When they step out on a court they do so in order to engage in friendly competition, not to spend. hours in the dull practice of a single stroke. They do not curtly refuse to play with their inferiors in skill because said inferiors cannot give them good practice. They do not regard proficiency in tennis as passport to social or business success. In winter, most of them drop the game altogether and take up badminton, sliding down hill, or cross-word puzzles. They are real amateurs and splendid sportsmen, genial winners and good losers. And it is fortunate that they are good losers because often they are called upon to meet players of the more intense variety, and they usually have plenty of opportunity to exercise the accomplishment.

The best United States players do not play for immediate pleasure. They play with an eye to ultimate and indirect prizes. The case of the garbage-man's boy is by no means an isolated one. Today, on scores of courts, particularly in the tennis centres of New York and California, a multitude of youthful aspirants, most of them poor as a homesteader but ambitious as a new politician, are working at the game as earnestly as another multitude of golf caddies work at golf with the hope of some day becoming famous professionals.

Fathers encourage their sons to take the game seriously, with an eye to the cultural and material benefits to be derived from travel at the tennis association's expense and handshaking with the successful men who manage tennis affairs. Mothers are not averse to basking in the reflection of whatever fame their daughters may be able to acquire.

**THE MAKING OF A CHAMPION**

For years the system worked well and the Americans were the world's champions. Then the French adopted their methods and went them one better, and became in turn the world's best.

Take, for instance, the case of Rene Lacoste, that once bright star of the tennis firmament. Rene's wealthy father wished him to learn the automobile business, but Rene had more ambitious ideas.

"Thanks for the overalls," he replied in effect, "but I'm afraid they give me spiritual indigestion. Please pass the white flannels."

Finally dad consented to a tennis career with the proviso that his boy should become a world's champion, and Rene set to work to master the game with a degree of intensity that outdid the ordinary American effort. He came to Forest Hills, which was then the world's tennis capital, and throughout a hot summer he spent an incredible number of hours every day on the courts. Not only did he take unlimited lessons and practise every stroke with infinite patience, but he compiled a reference book in which the weakness of every opponent whom he met was carefully noted. He lived tennis, slept tennis, and dreamed tennis. Nothing else mattered at all. As a result he became the world's champion. Now he divides his time between business and tennis, with result that he has dropped from the dizzy height which he then occupied—proof that championships are won only by those who are willing to devote every atom of their physical and mental energy to the game.

Consider Henri Cochet, who next climbed to the tennis pinnacle. Did that serious-faced young man ever play for fun? Not so one could notice it with the naked eye. His father was a grounds-keeper; and at an age when other youngsters were shooting marbles young Henri was collecting francs for chasing refractory balls at French tournaments. He adopted tennis as a profession as deliberately as a Canadian adopts law or medicine, and he gave as much time and attention to it as any one ever gave to any profession. He now owns a string of sporting-goods stores in France, and thus, every time he annexes another cup, he can capitalize the feat, just as Bill Tilden makes golden hay as a journalist when his tennis sun is shining.

Do American girls take the game as seriously as the boys? I'll say they do! This spring I asked a States champion if she still retained the office job which she held last winter.

"No," she replied, "I'm devoting my summer to tennis."

Every day when the weather permits, Sundays included, that ambitious young lady spends two hours or more on the courts. She never plays with other girls even her sister cannot coax her into a friendly match because girls cannot give her the high-class practice which she desires. She plays only with men—singles, never the more sociable game of doubles—and good ones at that. Usually they beat her, but that is precisely what she wants. By playing against superior players she improves her game, by meeting inferior ones she not only would fail to improve it, she might even get careless and let this or that stroke deteriorate.

I remarked that she seemed to be taking the game pretty seriously, and she candidly admitted that it was her principal interest in life.

With the example of Helen Wills Moody and other women stars before her eyes, why shouldn't it be? She has her eye on the national championship and if she ever wins it she knows that she will be amply rewarded for her years of painstaking effort.

Contrast the attitude of this would-be Lenglen with that of a Canadian school teacher whom I saw recently in an Ontario town. Miss Canadian possesses a natural forehand drive that is one of the most graceful and forceful that I ever saw. She possesses no other good stroke, but she could acquire all of them, and with her speed of foot and high intelligence, she could become a better player than the Miss American mentioned above if she would devote herself to the game with equal intensity. She has the old-fashioned ideas, however, that tennis is merely a pastime; therefore she will never appear on the centre court at Wimbledon or collect five hundred dollar for writing a single tennis article.

Thus, in a pageful, we have the reason why Canadians do not shine in world tournaments. We look upon tennis as a sport, when, in the higher competitive sense, it is not. It comes very close to being a profession. Its leading exponents are amateurs in a technical sense, yes, but in a practical sense, since most of them can and do capitalize their fame they are no such thing.

In order, therefore, to capture the Davis Cup or the world's championship Canadian players must change their mental attitude. They must cease to regard tennis as a game that is played for fun; they must look upon it as a business so exorbitant in its demands, for six months of the year at least, that it leaves no time whatsoever for any conflicting pursuit, least of all continuance at the old job, to interfere with training.

All of which leads us to a pertinent question: Is tennis leadership worth the price which must be paid in neglected business, abandoned pleasure, physical and nervous strain, financial hazard, and what not?

## WILLS ON TENNIS

[*Helen Wills overshadowed all other women tennis players of her day with her accuracy, determination, consistency and pace. Her default to Helen Jacobs in the US Singles Championship in 1933 generated more arguments than probably any other women's match. She married Fred Moody in 1930 and they divorced seven years later. In 1939, she married Adrian Roark. In this second of two articles, Wills discusses the reasons for the growing popularity of tennis in the US and takes a feminist stance on some of the major tennis issues of the day. Her answers to the following questions were omitted: is it difficult to change from one surface to another? Which matches do you remember most clearly? What is the value of thinking during a match? What do you do with your trophies? Helen Wills, "Tennis," The Saturday Evening Post (28 May 1932), 29, 33, 46.*]

Several innovations in dress were seen in tennis last season. New was the trouser skirt of Lili de Alvarez. Another was the appearance of bare legs upon the Center Court at Wimbledon. The stockinglessees, whom I know, but shall not betray, should be complimented.

Briefly, the decline of the stocking is as follows: In 1929 the bare-leg fashion for tennis appeared definitely. It was approved by both player and onlooker at the championship in Paris. The French are quick to adopt innovation in dress for sport. But not so the English at Wimbledon. The few players who dared appear without stockings on the outside courts brought forth comment from onlookers and the press. The following year flesh-colored hose was seen daily on the Center Court. Last year bare legs reached the inner sanctum of Wimbledon—the Center Court—but as the effect was the same at a distance as that of flesh-colored stockings, no one in the audience was aware of the innovation. In such a way is change affected. Nowadays, white stockings on the court—clumsy things, such as used to be worn—actually offend the eye.

### SHORTS OR SKIRTS

The trouser skirt, in its present development, is far from beautiful. It may improve. Lili de Alvarez's model cannot compare in its effect with the pretty dresses she used to wear for tennis. It looks something like a peculiar Chinese suit with the trousers cut off just below the knees. On the other hand, divided skirts, with pleats cleverly arranged so as to hide the fact that the skirt is divided, were being worn regularly by several of our own players during the summer. A skirt arranged in this fashion is comfortable, is less likely to blow about on a windy day, or when a player is reaching for a difficult ball.

Shorts are so generally unbecoming to women that it is unlikely that they will be seen anywhere in tennis where there is an audience. However, on private courts shorts and bathing suits as apparel for tennis are often seen.

Skirts were shorter than ever last summer on the court, although the long skirt is the fashion elsewhere. Both Eileen Whittingstall and Betty Nuthall wore shorter skirts than in 1930, as did our players. An ideal dress, not yet introduced, would be a model adopted from the Greeks—a pleated tunic dress, ending well above the knees, such as is seen in Greek sculpture. The pleats at the waist could be caught in by a narrow band and the upper portion of the dress would meet in points at the shoulders, leaving a low neck line front and back, and perfect freedom for the arms. If kept classic in line, a tunic dress of this sort should be quite charming.

The freedom in dress of the modern woman tennis player has doubtlessly enabled her to play a faster and better game. We marvel that Mrs. May Sutton Bundy and Mrs. Lambert Chambers ever got about the court in their long skirts. How uncomfortable we would be, trying to play with our waists squeezed in and our arms hampered by shirt waists with long sleeves and high collars. We can hardly believe that champions of other days used to wear straw sailor hats perched on the tops of their heads.

An amusing item from a newspaper article came to my attention the other day. It was dated 1876. It bears on the subject of women's dress in tennis. The correspondent wrote, "I do not think any lady can, or will ever be able to play the game [tennis] as it is very hard work for a man, and dress is such a drag."

Women players have conquered dress and the game as well. They have learned to last through long matches, to run full speed over the court, and to meet hard opposition with energy and determination. It has not made them less feminine nor has it detracted from their good looks. Of this there is ample proof.

It appeared last summer that the standard of play for women's tennis in this country had greatly improved. It seemed that there were more young players playing well. They were closely matched, so that there was scarcely an outstanding favorite. It was always hard to tell who the winners of the various matches would be. Close competition like this is excellent practice, and there will he evidence of further improvement this year.

In the infancy of tennis someone suggested that in mixed doubles the male should send only easy balls to the lady player on the other side of the net. It was thought not quite gentlemanly to hit the ball hard. Someone said a rule ought to be drawn up so that "a lady could refuse as many serves as she likes."

We feel rather offended, now, if the man on the other side in mixed doubles sends us an easy serve. We would rather he bowled over by a cannon ball from William Tilden's or Johnny Doeg's racket than receive a gentler service.

The feminine mind in sport reflects the general trend of feminine thinking of the day. The ideas and, along with them, inhibitions imposed upon us by previous generations are being dispelled. It was gradually discovered that it was possible for women to derive pleasure from active participation in sport. Strange, indeed, that this was scarcely more than fifty years ago. Woman's mind was supposed to be protected from too strong doses of anything intellectual for fear it might become more interesting, and her body was protected from any strenuous exercise, for fear it might become more healthy. Muscles were a horror and sun-burned complexions a tragedy in a young girl's life.

**WHERE WOMAN IS AT HOME**

Public sentiment towards sport for women has correspondingly undergone a change. Our grandmothers didn't dream of the interest that we take in sport. Not many years ago it was believed that no lady would take part in a tennis game where the public was admitted as audience. An amusing little story fits in here about someone from Virginia who plays tennis. She took up the game, and because of her unusual natural ability, she began to play quite well on her court at home. But there were few people for her to play with and no tournaments. So she entered several of the tournaments about New York and Boston, and at the climax of the season took part in the Nationals. Here she did very well, and as she was a newcomer, attracted no little attention. She returned to Virginia thrilled by the fun she had had in the tournaments. She went to call at once upon her grandmother. After welcoming her, her grandmother said sadly, "To think that I have a granddaughter who plays tennis in public—and with her picture in the newspaper."

From what I have seen in England I am led to believe that our English sisters are a little ahead of us in their interest in sport. Almost every English girl knows how to play tennis—not a championship game, of course, but one with a certain degree of direction, and usually a fairly good drive. The reason for this is that almost every English garden with the space for a tennis court has one.

The grass grows easily, lines are marked out, a net and backstops are set up, and there is a court which will do very nicely for a game before or after tea. The tennis court in England is brought into the scheme of family life. It is not surprising that everyone knows how to play. Large country places will have sometimes five or six grass courts—as many as some clubs—and several hard courts. A racket is always part of week-end equipment. There, literally, hundreds of small tournaments are going on all summer all over England in out-of-the-way places that we, if we were travelling, would never hear of. These offer remarkable opportunities for practice for young players. A remarkably good young girl player will appear at Wimbledon, as if out of nowhere. She has never been heard of before. She will have been playing for a number of seasons and gaining her experience in these out-of-the-way tournaments.

On the street in the summer, in London, you see young men and girls hurrying away from work with their rackets in their hands. Because of the long evenings, tennis can be played until almost eight o'clock. It is easy for the working girl to arrange to play two or three times a week, if she wishes.

Many of the large department stores and factories have sports grounds which are conveniently located, so that their employees can enjoy the pleasures and benefits of exercise in the open. Here they have tennis, cricket, croquet, badminton and other games, as well as a center for social gatherings—a clubhouse for entertainments, dances, and so on. Perhaps such an arrangement would not be so feasible in connection with our factories and large concerns where great numbers are employed. The mixture of nationalities, each seeking its pleasures in its own way, might defeat the plan. However, there would be many who would enjoy the sports grounds. Undoubtedly, others who had never before played games would become interested. Everyone should have the right to the pleasure that comes from sport, and it seems a great pity that many should be deprived of it because of not being able to belong to a club or because there are no available playgrounds.

Public parks and playgrounds are helping, but there are not, as yet, enough of them. Tennis is being furthered by the Public Parks Playground Association, which is encouraged by the U.S. Lawn Tennis Association. I was interested to hear the other day, from the president of the Playground Commission of San Francisco, that there is more tennis being played in San Francisco in the public parks and playgrounds than in any other city in the United States.

Tennis, perhaps more than any other game, can be fitted in with the busy American life. In a short time—even in an hour—two sets of tennis can be played. Two sets are enough in one day for anyone. I always limit my own practice to two sets in an afternoon. Tennis is, as well, an economical sport. Equipment is not costly, and when

well cared for, lasts for a long time. Balls are better than they used to be because of
the new way in which they are made, with heavier felt and cemented seams. If the
racket is strung with a heavy grade of gut, and not too tightly, so that strain on the
frame is avoided, it should last for six months.

Of course this is not for tournament play. Rackets for match play should be strung
with special fine gut, and with the tightness of a violin string. Often the strings breaks
before they are used. I find that I need about twenty-five frames for a summer's tennis tour. These I carry unstrung, so that the frames will not be under tension until I need
them and have them strung. Eastern tennis, with its grass court—often damp—and
sudden thundershowers play havoc with rackets in tournament trim. Sometimes the
frames warp from the dampness in the air. They will almost always do this on ship-
board, too, unless wrapped in water proof packages.

In the past year there has been a widespread growth in the popularity of tennis. It
may be that the economy of the game has made its appeal. Another reason for its increased popularity is that it is inevitable. The wonderful exercise that it offers, its speed,
its amusing moments, are attracting more and more players.

**THE IDEAL COURT**

"What kind of court would you choose if you were going to build one?" If I had
my choice, it would be asphalt. Asphalt courts are not the most beautiful to look at,
because they are gray in color. Their virtues, however, are many. They are absolutely
smooth. The ball always bounds in the way it should. There are never any surprise
bounces such as you have on grass frequently, and sometimes on clay. The footing is
absolutely safe. There is no danger from slipping as there is on grass, nor from sliding as on clay. There are probably fewer ankles turned and leg muscles strained upon
asphalt than upon any other surface. Too, asphalt is the most economical in upkeep. It
fosters a true, fast, accurate type of tennis, speedier than any other except that played
on wood. For a beginner, asphalt is the ideal surface because it encourages a rapid
game.

The superiority of the asphalt court for learning purposes is proven by the number
of California players who have done well in the large Eastern tournaments. California
has been a veritable cradle of tennis. There have been many champions from this state.
Mrs. May Sutton Bundy, a National champion of former days, went to Wimbledon,
where she was the first American woman to win the English singles title. Mrs. George
W. Wightman—Hazel Hotchkiss—learned her game on the asphalt court, as did
Maurice McLoughlin and William Johnston. So did Johnny Doeg—champion in
1930—and Sidney Wood. Ellsworth Vines, present champion, is the latest offering of
the Western hard courts. Among women players are Miss Helen Jacobs, Mrs. Lawrence
Harper, Mrs. Van Ryn and Miss Dorothy Weisel. There were so many Californians in
the Eastern tournaments last summer that, for the sake of convenience, the tournament
should have been held in California.

**BALDNESS STRIKES THE BASE LINES**

The last point in favor of the very hard court is that the grass courts have become
so poor. With each passing year they are worse. With the exception of the grass courts
at Wimbledon and a few other courts in England and the United States, the turf upon
which tournaments are being played can hardly be called good. It is not the fault of the
clubs where they are situated, because no expense or labor is spared in caring for them.

Either the climate of the Eastern States is unsuited to the growing of proper grass for tennis courts, or else the best methods and grasses have not yet been found. The latter is unlikely, because no end of experiment has been carried on. Last summer most grass courts were suffering from heat, rust, dry rot and depredations of insects, and, in many cases, old-fashioned baldness along the base line. Even the fiercest defenders of tradition and the grass court admitted that something would have to be done.

## THE DAVIS CUP

*[In this document, John Tunis, tennis player turned sportswriter, describes Davis Cup action in five different eras. In 1903, termed "The Age of Innocence," the twelve-year old Tunis and his brother paid 25 cents to watch the British team defeat the Americans at the Longwood Cricket Club in Boston. In 1914 ("Tennis Comes of Age") there were now six countries challenging for the Cup and Tunis watched Australia defeat the US before a huge crowd (paying $2.00 a seat) at New York's West Side Tennis Club. By 1927, ("the Dollar Decade") there were twenty-five countries chasing the Cup. In that year, Tunis watched the "Three Musketeers" from France defeat the Americans at the German Cricket Club in Philadelphia. The following selection describes the nationalistic fervor and intensity of Cup play in 1932 and 1937. John R. Tunis, "The Story of the Davis Cup," Harper's (December 1938), 374-381.]*

### TENNIS ACROSS AN OCEAN

1932: the twenty-second year. There was a cordon of gendarmes thrown wide round the gates of the Stade Roland Garros on the last afternoon of the Challenge Round, and you had to show your tickets to get through that line. Once inside, I climbed to the top of the stadium with Cesar Saerchinger, the European Director of Columbia Broadcasting System. Short-wave transmission had been perfected and for the first time an oral, play-by-play account was going across an ocean. Millions were following each move on the red court in Paris during the afternoon.

By this time France had gone tennis-mad. Every little cafe had its loudspeaker on the sidewalk and a knot of listeners standing about. "La Coupe" was a household word. Interest was intense, single tickets for the matches cost four hundred francs or sixteen dollars—if you could find a speculator who had one to sell....

We climbed the rickety ladder to the broadcasting perch eighty feet in the air behind the court. At Longwood [site of the Davis Cup matches in 1903] the press had been represented by one man from the Boston Transcript and by Fred Mansfield, the umpire, who for the love of the game used to telephone an account of the matches to the Herald. At Roland Garros a special section of the stands was devoted to the press, with reporters by the dozen from every capital of Europe, sob sisters, special writers, columnists, and sports authorities from half a dozen nations. There was even a man from Egypt. Meanwhile across the court, our platform—which ran the length of the stands but was only six feet wide without any railings—swayed under its burden of reporters in a new medium. A dozen camera men with their guns trained on the court and twice that number of radio commentators and mechanics filled our narrow perch. Beside me a French youth rippled phrases into his mike, on the other side a German gutturaled the story to Berlin, and farther down the line an Italian was talking. It was a lovely scene....

I had guessed three-thirty as the moment to take the air. We were in luck, for Borotra and Allison, a man from Bayonne and a boy from Austin, Texas, appeared just at the moment following the intermission after the third set. But this time the famous Four Musketeers who had won the Cup at Philadelphia were losing ground, Lacoste was through. Cochet was weakening and Borotra was a veteran too old to withstand the challenge of a generation of young Americans. He dropped the first two sets to the fine volleying of Wilmer Allison. But tennis matches of a Musketeer never went by default. In the third set he became suddenly the Borotra of his prime. In the fourth he went from strength to strength, drawing reserves of courage from his fanatical supporters in the stand. The crowd was almost beyond control as he began to stab his volleys past the tiring American.

"Un peu de silence s'il vous plait," pleaded the umpire vainly. From the swaying platform—so flimsy it might topple any moment—I tried to describe this amazing scene to dispassionate Americans three thousand miles away, to explain what it meant to the French to have their champion come from behind, to portray the emotional crowd in the stand, waving the little red-white-and-blue paper parasols which colored the stadium as Borotra won game after game. So we came into the fifth set. Allison, volleying with a firm hand, at last reached matchpoint. Borotra exerted an extra bit of pressure and drew an error. Another matchpoint. Again the Basque saved himself and France, this time with a netcord shot. You could hear his groan of relief from the platform. Now the gallery was beyond control.

"Borocco, Borocco, Borocco," they yelled, their nickname for their favorite. The umpire appealed for quiet but no one paid any attention and it took a gesture of agony from Borotra himself to
still them. Then the third matchpoint came up.

Borotra served. A fault. The second service. Over the line. A doublefault and the match was won. Allison tossed his bat high in the air.

No...wait a minute. That ball was called good. I was speechless. I forgot I was broadcasting. That ball **good**...? Pandemonium. For some minutes everybody was shouting. Finally order was restored and the match resumed. But the punch was gone from the American's game. Exhausted, he let Borotra storm through to victory. The Coupe Davis was saved for France. Ten thousand cushions rained upon the court as the Basque, still wet, came to the box below us, where he was embraced by the President of the Republic.

Our time on the air was up. In fact we had gone half an hour over, but so exciting was the struggle that New York had kept the wires open. Had I described the match correctly? Had I mentioned that decision? Yes, but it was not till six weeks later—when a friend who had listened with a portable set on a Jersey beach told me that he had heard my exclamation as a linesman saved the Cup for France—that I found out. I had described the first sporting event across an ocean and the last victory of France in the Davis Cup.

## LIFE AND DEATH

1937: the thirty-second year. Possibly the French had been the first to perceive the national prestige attaching to a victory in this world sport. They were by no means the last. By 1937 every nation in Europe laid plans during mid-winter for the next summer's campaign. Likely candidates were excused for months on end from their military service. Governments stood ready to furnish unlimited sums for expenses. For by this time money was a necessity if you hoped to capture possession of the Davis Cup.

On what was money spent? First you must have a professional trainer, a Tilden, a Kozeluh, or a Nusslein. These men come high. Then you must find a captain, some older player willing to spend all his time developing champions, and a masseur to keep the team in shape. **En voyage** you must live well. The Dohertys in 1903 stayed at private houses; now Davis Cup stars stop only at Grand Palace Hotels—our team always puts up at Grosvenor House in London. Last year the Germans started their campaign early in May, playing in Milan, Prague, Brussels, and Paris before reaching Wimbledon early in July to take part in the Interzone Final against the United States. You must either transship your side across an ocean or send them jaunting around the capitals of Europe for three or four months. Sometimes gate receipts help out, sometimes not. What does it matter? The Davis Cup is important. Government chiefs realize this— none better than the dictators.

1937 was not a record year for entries because only 24 nations challenged to try to take the cup from England, the holder; but it was significant as showing the strength of countries hitherto little known as sporting nations. France, holder of the Cup only a few years previously, was badly beaten by Czechoslovakia. The summer before they had lost in the first round to the Yugoslavs. Nor have we heard the last of that country in the matches for the Davis Cup.

In July, 1937, it was the Germans—conquerors of the Czechs—who stepped upon the Center court at Wimbledon, headed by their blond champion, Gottfried von Cramm, to meet the Americans led by another redheaded Californian named Donald Budge. Three weeks earlier in the English championships Budge had beaten the German rather easily in three straight sets, and he seemed likely enough to repeat when, with the teams even at two matches apiece, the champions of Germany and the United States faced each other in the deciding contest.

By this time we were in an era of shorts, but they were not worn by either Budge or Cramm. Curiously enough, champions seem able to handicap themselves in this way and still conquer all comers in abbreviated garments. Notice also another change since the early days. Instead of the one extra racket which Larned and Doherty each carried on court, Budge and Cramm appeared with seven or eight bats in their arms. So great is the speed of the modern game, so tensely strung are the champion's bats, that three or four may snap a string in the course of a match. Observe that the balls are taken from a frigidaire back of the umpire's chair, where they have been kept at a fixed temperature all night. Originally they were just tennis balls, of any weight, size, bound, or temperature. Now all balls are standardized, conforming to mechanized tests which limit the bounce to 53 inches when dropped on concrete from a height of 100 inches, the weight to 2-21/16 ounces, and the compression to between .265 and .290 inches. This shows the point to which the American talent for systematization and organization has taken what was once a friendly match for a Challenge bowl.

The struggle began. Old-timers have said it was the greatest match ever played at Wimbledon. Great is a large word, but probably never had the standard of play on both

sides of the net been so high. For points were not lost; they were won. There is a difference. Moreover, they were won several times in each rally. You were watching su-
per-tennis by super-players. Tilden afterward declared it the finest match he had ever
seen.

Cramm won the first set. Budge waited for the avalanche to pass. But the second
set came and the avalanche persisted. Two sets up for Cramm. Not until the third did
a reaction start in the German's game, and Budge working to the net managed to make
some winning volleys. Slowly the tide turned. The American won the third set after a
fight, and the fourth. Only a player armed at every point, with no physical or moral
weakness, could have evened the score against a champion playing like Cramm.

It was seven o'clock when the fifth set began. The German showed he had a kick
left by serving and driving faultlessly. He was soon 4-1. Then Budge became the grand
champion. His service in pace and accuracy was hardly inferior to Tilden's at its best.
Slowly he fought back and evened the score. In the fourteenth game he had five match-
points before he finally won the set and the match. Both players were completely exhausted and so was every single spectator.

One must admit that Budge's tennis that afternoon was a step forward in the game.
The technic of sport does not stand still. Nor yet does the power and influence of the
Davis Cup. Looking back, some things about that magnificent struggle are clearer.
Most champions play better for their country in team matches than in tournaments
when they are on their own. But Cramm had never played like that before. Nor ever
did again. How to explain this?

Possibly because the German was playing for his country and something more. It
was common knowledge that Cramm had never been a member of the Nazi party.
Despite his efforts in sport for the Fatherland, he had never been in Hitler's good
graces. Those who are not for a dictator are against him. What a chance Cramm had
at Wimbledon. Imagine his triumphal return to Berlin, that emblem of world supremacy
in sport by his side. Germany on top. First the Olympic Games, then the Davis Cup.
Would the Fuhrer not forgive anything of the man who was the artisan of the first
German victory in this international event?

But he failed. Cramm failed by a few inches which separated the ball from the
baseline in several critical rallies in the critical games of the last set. By a shot or two
in the alley, and not just inside the court, by a few inches on the wrong side, once when
he was leading 4-2 and again at 4-3. By the merest fraction of a second in the timing
of his racket.

Accordingly this summer he is in disgrace, a prisoner in his native land. Do you
suppose that if those few balls had been inside the court in the last set, if Cramm had
captured the Davis Cup, he would now be in a concentration camp? If so you misun-
derstand the mentality of dictators.

This is 1938. Tennis has changed and so has the world in which we live. Thanks
to the press, to radio, to easy means of communication, and to widespread interest in
athletics, the Davis Cup has been "sold" to the entire world. Today it is a matter of
growing national importance. President Lebrun, Foreign Secretary Sir Samuel Hoare,
and Secretary of State Cordell Hull have all presided in recent years at the drawings
for the Davis Cup and set the governmental kiss of approval upon the contest. It has
become a test of national superiority.

Longwood is no longer prominent in the sport. One hears little about it now; can
that be because Longwood is still a club primarily for people who want to play and do

not care overmuch for the prominence attaching to Davis Cup matches? And what will the Davis Cup be in 1960? Will there be a national holiday, will the President and his Cabinet attend the Challenge Round, will the Stock Exchange close as the matches between the United States and Japan are played and televised to hundreds of millions of fans in a waiting world? Will they be played in a double-decked Rose Bowl seating half a million spectators, and will the star of the Japanese team commit hara-kiri on the center court rather than return defeated to be killed in Japan by an angry populace?

Impossible? Absurd? Perhaps. But who in 1903 would have visualized the changes which the machine age has wrought in what was once a pastime and nothing more?

## TILDEN AND PROFESSIONAL TENNIS

[*From January 9 to 15 in 1935, Tilden's professional troupe played in six cities. Although the American Lawn Tennis preferred the amateur game, it was sympathetic to Tilden and provided considerable coverage of the professional game. The following article describes the type of tennis played by the professionals and illustrates the market for such exhibitions and the problems of barnstorming in North America. "Travels of the Tilden Troupe," American Lawn Tennis (20 January 1935), 12-14, 34.*]

Reenforced by George Lott and Lester Stoefen, William Tilden and Ellsworth Vines opened the 1935 campaign of professional matches at Madison Square Garden, New York, on Wednesday, January 9, the first of more than seventy similar exhibitions that are to be staged during the next two or three months. They will cover the United States and extend into Canada, where at Vancouver professional tennis will be seen. It was almost exactly a year after Vines had made his debut as a pro, and the ranks of the latter were tremendously strengthened by Lott and Stoefen, double champions of the United States....

Scenes that have become familiar were witnessed at the Garden, although with some differences. The program was a lengthy one on paper. Tilden and Lott were to lead off with a best of three set match; then would follow a keenly awaited battle between two outstanding doubles pairs, Tilden and Vines and Lott and Stoefen, all of whom have shared in the possession of the national doubles title; and finally there was to be an encounter between Vines and Stoefen. The first match was fairly short, Tilden beating Lott in straight sets. Then after an interval of ten minutes or so, the four men went on the court—canvas stretched over a cement floor—for a contest that was to run to five sets and 87 games and continue until 12:25, with Tilden and Vines coming through after losing the first two sets. The Vines-Stoefen match was then called off, owing to the lateness of the hour and the desperate exertions of the four men.

It had been asserted that the Garden was sold out, but there were probably 2,000 to 2,500 unoccupied seats at 8:45, when the peak was probably reached. No need existed for seating people on the floor near the court, as had been the case a year earlier. The less expensive seats were fully occupied, but there were vacant blocks lower down, particularly at the ends of the court. One New York newspaper gave the attendance at 16,000 and another at 15,000: it was probably about 14,000. The receipts are given as $424,682.... The singles match passed off quietly, but the doubles was so full of excitement that it roused the gallery to a pitch rarely seen at a lawn tennis match, the applause being deafening and almost continuous during the good play. It may be added that the play was like the proverbial flitch of bacon with its fat and lean streaks—nearly evenly mixed between good and bad, there being little of the medium variety on display.

Lott opened against Tilden by winning the first game, ending it with an ace. Tilden went into a lead however and ran out the set at 6-4, in spite of the fact that he was slow of foot and making many errors off the easiest kind of shots. Lott found that he was no match for Bill at the back of the court and so he came to the net consistently. In the second set Lott had his opportunity at 4-3 and game point on Tilden's service—only to miss the point narrowly. The play was still nothing to rave over, although there were brilliant flashes and plenty of heady play. Tilden was always ready before Lott, who towelled and drank water freely. Lott pulled up to 5-all and then Tilden came with a rush and ran it out by much better play.

There were fireworks at the start of the doubles. A lob was put up to Vines and before he could hit it Lott ran back, lifted the Stop netting at the end of the court, ran farther back and tried to get to the ball, but failed. Lott and Stoefen won the first set at 6-3, having it all over their opponents. They got the second also, but only at 16-14. Tilden and Vines were both improving but Lott and Stoefen still appeared to be their masters. Lott was broken through for an 11-10 lead, but Vines lost his service and the battle was still on. There was a great deal of lobbing, the ball being hit very high as there were no girders for them to touch. The end of the set came in the thirtieth game when Vines erred badly and lost his service for a 16-14 set. Lott was very fast in getting to the ball and was also the best of the four. It was then 10:53, with little chance of the Vines-Stoefen battle being put on.... [Tilden-Vines won the next three games 13-11, 8-6, 6-4.]

**AT PHILADELPHIA**

Within twenty-four hours from the time he played 109 games in seven sets of singles and doubles against George Lott and Lester Stoefen at Madison Square Garden, New York, William Tilden gave another superman demonstration at Convention Hall in Philadelphia. On January 10 he stayed on the green canvas covered court for 100 games in eight sets from 9:30 pm. until 50 minutes past midnight. Before a crowd of 6,283—slightly surpassing the record attendance at the indoor meeting between Tilden and Ellsworth Vines in this city in 1934—Tilden put on this iron man flourish, so remarkable for a man about to turn 42.

To all appearances the evening was to be a short one. Vines and Stoefen came on the court first and the former speedily defended his position against the first challenge of this recruit in the professional ranks, scoring at 7-5 6-3. Then Tilden and Vines beat Lott and Stoefen for the second time in successive days. Similar to the New York victory, this one was gained in five sets, but in one hour and 45 minutes instead of three hours. The score was 12-10 2-6 6-2 0-6 6-2. It was 11:15 when Tilden and Lott came on for their single encounter, without benefit of rest. The doubles had commanded attention enough, Vines having been particularly resplendent, but the singles was the real thriller, waged long into the morning with the verdict finally swinging to Lott at 7-5 9-11 9-7.

Not only were there dramatic changes in the tide of fortune, with Lott coming from far behind to win both the first and third sets and Tilden doing the same in the second, but also there were shows of temperament and demonstrations by the crowd that added to the excitement. At one time Tilden really provoked trouble by asking Lott in an exasperated tone, "Won't you please let me get set before you serve?" Two points from match for Lott in the second set Tilden waited for the noise to subside before serving but he was finally forced to continue in spite of the clamor. Again, in the fifteenth game of that set play was stopped while there was an argument over a "let," with both men reversing their attitudes after each had seemed to gain his point. On all these occasions the crowd was unruly, interspersing whistling and heckling with prolonged applause. As for the play itself, both men brought off marvelous shots. Tilden was particularly fine in the early part of the third set, but Lott came to life at 1-3 and 15-40 on his own service chopping heavily from the base line and going in regularly to volley. Both men were tired as the score went to 6-all, Tilden not even attempting to reach some of Lott's serves. Tilden saved two match points at 6-7 but finally went down before Lott's aggressiveness in the sixteenth game....

## LITTLE RUNWAY AT WASHINGTON

Handicapped by a boisterous gallery that overflowed the inadequate seating facilities at Catholic University's gymnasium, the Tilden professional tennis troupe failed to produce for Washington, DC fans on the evening of January 11th the exciting and high grade of play which marked the two previous exhibitions in Philadelphia and New York. The over-capacity crowd of 3,000 so hampered the players that they decided to limit the feature doubles event between Tilden and Vines and Lott and Stoefen to the best of three sets. Once again Tilden and Vines denied the amateur champions of the pleasure of their first professional win in doubles. The score was 9-7 7-5.

Two single matches, also the best of three sets also were played during the 3-hour exhibition. In the first match, when the gallery disturbance was at its height, Lott scored his second professional win against Tilden. This time it was in straight sets, 6-3 6-4, but the outrageous conditions prevented a real tennis match. Some semblance of order was effected by the time Vines and Stoefen went on for the other singles. With the disturbers in the gallery probably worn out by their earlier activities the two tall Californians produced the best match of the meeting. For a while in the first set it would seem that Stoefen would get his revenge for the treatment Vines gave him the night before in Philadelphia. But after going into a 4-1 lead, Lester saw his advantage slip away as Ellsworth gradually found his best game and evened at 4-all. Here Stoefen again threatened, but Vines' accurate drives finally forced Lester to bow at 7-5. Then, after coming back to take his opening service game in the second set, Stoefen ran up against a Vines who was at or near his best. In a few minutes he reeled off six games in a row for the set and match.

Half an hour before the opening match was scheduled to begin some 2,000 eager spectators comfortably filled the circus seats at the north end of the gym and the balcony seats at the opposite end. Many of the chairs which lined both sides of the court and some at the south end also were filled early. Spectators sat about four feet from the white painted sidelines on the green canvas stretched for the court surface over the board floor. Several yards beyond the baseline black cord nets served as backstops. Overhead the regular gymnasium lights illuminated the entire hall, while several high powered projectors, installed along either sidewall focused their rays directly on the court. Equipment for supporting horizontal bars, ropes and rings, and other gymnasium paraphernalia stretched across the hall low enough to make lobbing a more skillful stroke than usual, and only a few were attempted by Lott and Stoefen. Those that

Tilden and Vines didn't kill were knocked out of play by striking the overhead obstructions.

Although the entire setup left much to be desired, the chief fault was the encroachment of the gallery upon that part of the floor which should have been left free for the players. Latecomers holding $2.20 tickets naturally raised a rumpus when they found their seats filled by the overflow of the $1.10 spectators.

The umpiring was fair, but the officials seldom attempted to quiet the gallery, and in one instance A.O. White, who umpired the first match, added to the confusion when he almost fell through the chair as the seat gave way. The veteran Ton Mangan handled the doubles and Herbert Shepard was in the repaired chair for the final match. Linesmen seemed to be of more bother than they were worth; time and time again players were forced to check their stroke and their stride for fear of crashing into linesmen as well as spectators.

Tilden and Lott walked on the court for the opening match while an amplified phonograph record provided music for the occasion! After some delay play began with George drawing first blood on his service as a drop shot trickled over the net and left Big Bill standing at the back of his court while the crowd yelled.

At that moment a mob of humanity packed around the main entrance to the gym, surged into the front row $2.20 reserved seats which evidently had not been sold or else their purchasers were unfortunately among the last arrivals. Play was stopped for five minutes until the general commotion subsided. It appeared to be the beginning of the end for Tilden before the match had more than started. And so it was—Tilden gave the impression of simply going through the motions and seemed only concerned with getting through with it. When Lott put stuff on his serve making it bound toward the sideline gallery, Tilden simply did not try for a return, telling George (and the general assembly) that he refused to take a chance of injuring a spectator. Consequently George varied his serve somewhat to meet the conditions but occasionally slipped one too far to the side and Bill resigned himself to his fate. On several occasions Bill appealed to the common sense of the disturbers when calls of "Sit down in front" and "What's the matter, Tilly?" interrupted the match. At one point in the proceedings Lott showed his disgust by whacking a ball in the general direction of one particularly obnoxious disturber. And so it went—an exhibition of something, but not lawn tennis!...

## LOTT-STOEFEN WIN AT PITTSBURGH

The Tilden troupe arrived in Pittsburgh Saturday, January 12th, very tired after three nights of play in New York, Philadelphia and Washington. Nevertheless they gave an exhibition which pleased a gallery of about 2500 enthusiasts in the Duquesne Garden, Pittsburgh's mid-city ice skating rink which had been hurriedly prepared for the matches. The playing space was ample, the only drawback being the overhead supports which interfered with high balls and made lobbing rather uncertain.

Vines had his hands full with Stoefen in the opening match and only his steadiness enabled him to win after nearly two hours of play. The score: 1-6 6-8 6-3.

In the doubles the first set was a walkover for Vines and Tilden, but the second was more closely contested and went to Lott and Stoefen. Lott's apparent indifference was a mystery to the crowd, many of whom could not understand his tricky cross court shot and odd spin, so different from the driving, smashing shot of the others. As the first singles match had taken up so much time, it was decided that but three sets would be played, much to the regret of the crowd. Lott and Stoefen finally won at 1-6 7-5 6-3.

The singles match between Tilden and Lott was an anti-climax, as there was never any doubt about Tilden winning, despite a twisted ankle. No animosity, as press agented, was in evidence and Lott even went so far as to double fault intentionally to give Tilden the first set at 6-4 after the latter disagreed with the linesman's decision. Tilden maintained his pressure throughout and took the second set at 6-3, justifying the crowd's interest in him as the leading personality of the troupe and always a favorite in the city where he lived during the war....

**DOLLAR A HEAD AT BOSTON**

Although the professional troupe played a set of record length in their doubles match at the Boston Garden on January 14, this set will go down in history as great only in the matter of length; it held none of the excitement that one hour and forty-five minutes of hard fought play should. Rather it was a monotonous, drawn-out affair, with service monopolizing the spotlight, and as things turned out it meant nothing in the ultimate outcome, since Lott and Stoefen won the set while Vines and Tilden took the next two for the match, 29-31 6-3 6-4. Some 5,592 spectators paid $5,958 to see the play, which represents about half the "gate" at the Tilden-Vines match of last year....

**PROVIDENCE TOTALS 1,200**

Further signs of the strain of play and travel upon the four members of the Tilden troupe were evident on the night of January 15 in Providence, R.I. According to F.C. Matlek, writing in the Providence Journal, "Approximately 1200 fans saw the matches, all of which lacked the dash and fire that usually are connected with exhibitions by stars of the net world." The doubles was cut down to the best of three sets and Vines was the only one of the four to maintain a championship pace, his placements carrying himself and Tilden to an 8-6 6-3 victory, service again counting almost everything.

## BADMINTON BOOM IN CANADA

[*Jack Purcell, the world's professional badminton champion in 1933, was, claimed Collier's in 1935, "perhaps the greatest champion we have today in any sport.... As champion, he is so far above the rest of the field that he has virtually run out of competition. As an example, not so long ago he defeated D.C. Hume, the then English champion, by a 15-3, 15-10 count, and he followed this up with a smashing win over Jess Williard, the American Champion, 15-10, 15-2." Purcell, who introduced deception to the game, was also an excellent tennis player and golfer. Here, Purcell details the growth of badminton in Canada and the reasons for its popularity. The long list of famous Canadian hockey players, golfers, tennis players, and sailors who played badminton was deleted. Jack Purcell (with Ken W. MacTaggart), "Badminton Boom," Maclean's Magazine (1 March 1935), 21, 49-50.*]

I had missed winning the All-England, but from the moment of my elimination in the semifinal round of that great tournament in March, 1931, I had planned a second invasion of the British Isles. A decision, however, made by the Canadian Badminton Association in the fall of that same year, declared me ineligible to compete further as an amateur and caused an abandonment of my plans to again cross the Atlantic. Suddenly to find myself barred from amateur competition just as my enthusiasm for the game had reached its height and I had visioned myself as carrying Canada's colors to victory in the classic event of the badminton world, was a stunning blow, but I am glad to say that my interest in badminton has steadily increased since that eventful day in 1931, and as a professional, I have had an unusual opportunity to witness badminton's conquest of Canada, during which the game has rapidly become one of our most played pastimes from coast to coast.

**CANADIAN TRIUMPHS**

Glance over the three seasons since that trip to England shows an amazing record by Canadians in the old English game. They have consistently invaded the United States and defeated the best players, both amateur and professional, that the republic could offer. And they have kept intact this record against the stars of the British Isles who have come to the Dominion as professionals, after unblemished records as top amateurs.

There are approximately 50,000 members of badminton clubs in Canada, and a very large number of players who belong to no clubs but find their badminton wherever they happen to be. Most of them have taken up the game within the past four of five years; very few have been playing over ten years. But even the most optimistic of this old guard would not have ventured to predict in 1925 that Canada would be sitting soon on top of the badminton heap.

Canada's definite triumphs have been in the United States, where Canadians have won literally every match in which they have played.

In March, 1934, Miss Elizabeth Kennedy and Mrs. Harold Wilton, of Montreal; Douglas Grant, the Canadian Champion; and Dr. Raymond Cramer, of Guelph, teamed up to invade the New England annual tournament. This Boston event is considered the classic of the United States badminton meets, because Boston is the hotbed of United States badminton and here the best players of the republic always gather.

The little Canadian band, which had entered the matches in a spirit of adventure and with no particular plan of winning swept the tournament, brought back to Canada all five New England titles, and proved a superiority over the United States players in every department of the game. Grant defeated Walter Kramer, leading United States amateur in straight sets, 15-7, 15-2....

**EVERYBODY PLAYS**

Up in Schumacher, Ontario, the members of the McIntyre mine staff are playing badminton every night in a specially built clubhouse which contains splendid equipment. In Windsor the Frontier Club was recently inaugurated, and a disused market building was transformed into a fine badminton club. In Toronto, the Badminton and Racquet Club has utilized a former street-car barn and is developing players of international calibre. The Carlton Club has turned an old curling rink into a fine court building, while the Flurlingham Club plays nightly in a building that once housed the Paylowa dance hall.

At Chapleau, Sudbury, Kapuskasing, Cochrane and similar but more remote towns and cities, fine clubs are flourishing. At Port Elgin, a spirited club is attracting attention. In little Clarksburg, Ontario, a recently formed club meets nightly. Residents of Arnprior removed pews from a deserted church and laid out two good courts. Appleby

School at Oakville has one of the finest playing courts in a former barn. And a private club in the town purchased an unused airplane hangar and brought it to Oakville, where it was reassembled to provide the most practical facilities for badminton. In the larger Western Canadian cities fine clubs have been erected, while dozens of small places all through the West have taken to the game enthusiastically.

As an evidence of the importance of the game today, plans for new school gymnasiums and church recreational quarters throughout Canada invariably include accommodation for badminton. These buildings are usually designed to be of such dimensions that at least one good badminton court can be laid out.

All this has been the result of the game itself. Until recently the newspapers, engrossed with older sports, paid little attention to badminton. Only within the past two years did it break into radio, when play-by-play accounts of important championship matches were broadcast direct from the courts. But with over 60,000 people playing badminton in clubs scattered from coast to coast, the game has merited attention and news reports of its progress and performances. The very fact that Canada's national titles are at present held by persons in such widely separate points as Halifax, Ottawa, Quebec and Vancouver, indicates the breadth of its hold on Canadians and the extent to which it has captured Canadian fancy.

The reason for this Canadian capture of the game is because of its strenuousness, for badminton is a strenuous game despite the fact that parents find it an ideal sport in which to meet their youngsters. Badminton can be as exhausting as any game played on foot today, and is even more tiring than tennis in the opinion of some players who are prominent in both games. Most players prefer a doubles match in badminton because few are equal to a hard singles match.

Canadians like strenuous sports. They have triumphed in both sprint and marathon running, and they produce the best hockey players for many nations. Their national sport, lacrosse, is renowned for its testing of endurance and stamina. So, when they discovered that badminton was not a "la-de-da" sort of game in which tea-drinking and polite chatter were more important than the game itself, they took it to their bosoms and adopted it.

**A WORLD SPORT**

For about twenty-five years badminton had been played in certain sections of the country, but it had been restricted to a few favorably situated persons. Very little attention was paid to it by the general public, and even with the formation of the Canadian Badminton Association in 1922, there was little evidence that it would develop suddenly into one of the most played games in the country. Even until 1925, the game was confined to a few clubs formed in the garrisons across Canada. Members of these clubs had at their disposal the spacious and entirely suitable drill halls of the militia's armories, which provided space for courts. But these clubs had small memberships and the public gained little knowledge of the game, the "la-de-da" opinion being the usual response to mention of it.

But, during this period, golf and tennis were becoming more and more prominent in the lives of grown-ups. All children play hockey and baseball and football, but long before they become adults these games usually have been relegated to the position of occupations of a few gladiators who entertain the masses. When golf and tennis began to enroll new recruits every summer, the public became game-conscious.

Then these players stowed away their rackets and clubs at the end of each summer. Some hardy spirits would stick it out until the first snow drove them inside, filled with vim, vigor and vitality. With the arrival of winter, they found themselves filled with muscular energy and a consuming desire to vent it on something, and, fulfilling the Canadian desire, the more strenuous this something, the better.

In 1925, several badminton clubs outside the armories came into being. Large buildings, especially constructed for badminton, were erected in several cities. Almost overnight the general public, the people who play golf on public courses and tennis on public and modest courts, sensed that this game was the answer to their needs, a winter pastime which provided recreational exercise. Swiftly on the heels of the big clubs came the smaller clubs. Membership fees were low. Cost of equipment, it was gladly discovered was small. The demand for buildings created the supply, it seemed; and barns, dance halls, lodge halls, former skating rinks and every other adaptable type of building became the home of a badminton club.

Whole families enrolled as members, parents recognizing that badminton offered the competitive inducement which made the sport more attractive to children. Clubs were formed in offices. One bank office in Toronto launched a small association which overnight enrolled a membership of over 200 players. A trust company office staff pooled resource to rent space, and ninety persons signed up and became active players. The thud of shuttlecocks on tightly stretched gut began to echo across Canada, until today it resounds boldly from the walls of foreign clubs as Canadians sweep down any opposition to their conquering march.

And it isn't a case of Canadians being the top nation merely because nobody else play the game. They don't occupy the unenviable position of the little boy with all the marbles. Last summer saw the formation of the International Badminton Federation, evolved because of the necessity of a world-governing body of greater international authority than the British Association, which had hitherto formulated rules and policies…. And Canada was rewarded for her capture of the game by being given two seats on the council of the federation, equal to England, Ireland, Scotland and Wales. France, the Netherlands, New Zealand and others hold one seat on the council.

## THE TABLE TENNIS WARS

*[In this article, John Tunis uses the struggle for control over the game of table tennis to portray the machinations behind American sport in the Depression, which he claims was now more big business than it was athletics. John R. Tunis, "Sport in Miniature," The American Mercury (February 1934), 211-6.]*

The interesting thing about Ping-Pong (Reg. by Parker Bros. in U.S. Patent Office) is not its infernal ubiquity, but the fact that today the game is nothing more or less than American sport in miniature. A typical and delightful example of our genius for seizing an amusing pastime, popularizing it, selling it to the sporting millions, organizing it, over-organizing it, and finally turning it from a game which a few ordinary people enjoy playing, into a first class racket.

A racket? Yes, certainly, like football, baseball, golf, tennis, and other high grade American sports. Ping-Pong (Reg. in U.S. Patent Office by Parker Bros.) is a racket today. With absolutely everything that a really modern up-to-date sporting racket should have, including an Association (the American Ping-Pong Association), a national championship with a broadcast of the final rounds, champions male and female, an authoritative ranking list, a magazine—as usual, "the official organ of the Association"—a Rules Committee which will doubtless soon succeed in making the game as unintelligible as intercollegiate football, and all the impedimenta which seem to attach themselves to athletics in this land. Including, of course, our old friend the amateur-professional question, for it is hinted that more than one of the celebrities of the game is "assisted" in his efforts to promote good clean sport.

Originated by a London sporting goods dealer named Hamley in the late nineties, it was a quiet pastime, a sort of fad for parlors like mah jong or backgammon during many years. Following the war came a revival of the sport abroad. The thing grew rapidly; probably because of the poisonous climate it was a good game for winter both in England and on the continent.... But the thing did not catch hold here for some years, and it was not until 1925 or 1926 that it began to be played much in this country, due possibly to the fact that Parker Brothers of Salem, Mass., games manufacturers, had bought the American copyright to the name. Controlling the sole right to make and sell equipment, they had managed to keep prices at such a level that it was an expensive proposition for the individual.

Sport in miniature. Watch it grow. Already, you observe, Big Business is creeping in. Over a long period of years the Parker Brothers spent considerable sums in promoting the game, and when the turn came and the sport grew out of the fad class, they naturally enough felt they were entitled to some of the rewards. But in order to get the rewards they could hardly afford to sell tables at a price that would put them within reach of the homeowner in the suburb, and this so irked some of our younger citizens along the lower East Side of Manhattan, who lacked means to purchase official tables at over $40 apiece, that they began to manufacture their own equipment and went ahead as best they could. Before long these youngsters from the Y's and Boys Clubs along the East Side were so good that they were trimming everyone. When the first national championship was held back in 1930 it attracted 360 entries, and an outsider from the East Side Boys Club, Marcus Schussheim by name, was the winner.

By this time the game had become a real American sporting racket. If there are shamateur athletes in golf, tennis, and the bigger sports, so they are to be found in Ping-Pong. (Reg. in U.S. Parent Office by Parker Bros.) Yes, it is sport in miniature. Charges and countercharges flew back and forth. On one side you are told that the champions tried to hold the manufacturers up for cash; on the other hand you are informed that they demanded he use their equipment. Who is right is hard to say, nor does it make any particular difference. Whatever the reason, or wherever the right lay, the actual result was that the East Side Boys Clubs and the various Y's throughout Manhattan began turning our champions in mass production. Before long an entirely new association was formed, called the New York Table Tennis Association, using outlaw equipment made by other firms. Today there is a bitter war on between the two bodies, families are divided and the best of friends won't speak to each other.

Yes, it's all pretty funny. Each gang plays precisely the same game, in exactly the same way, under what are really the identical rules, with everything alike except the name. Let me explain. If you play Ping-Pong (Reg. by Parker Bros. in U.S. Patent

Office) you must use a Parker table, serve with a Parker paddle, and play with an official—which means a Parker—ball. If you don't, you play table tennis. Or maybe it's Table Tennis. Now, is that clear? No? Very well, then, put it another way: if you use Parker Brothers equipment you are playing, whether you meant to or not, Ping-Pong. (Reg. by Parker Bros. in U.S. Patent Office) So that in a contest in which both opponents used Parker Brothers paddles, they would be playing Ping-Pong. (And I'll ask you to take the rest of it for granted from now on.) Whereas if neither players used Parker Brothers paddles they would be playing Table Tennis. If one did and the other didn't, they would be playing...well, I don't know exactly, figure this one out for yourself.

Imagine this. It was the Parker Brothers who donated the Parker Cup for Intercity competition between New York and Chicago, and also the Parker Brothers who generously gave another trophy named curiously enough the Parker Cup, mere coincidence that, for the national championship.... [There follows a long list of famous athletes and movie stars who play the game.]

The Table Tennis crowd lack neither playing ability nor energy, and at present the United States Table Tennis Association is in process of gestation, with branches in New York, Chicago, and Philadelphia. The Ping-Pong (etc.) crowd, being older and possibly more experienced, are already well organized and consolidating their position. The rivalry between the two camps is intense, and if authority, prestige, and financial support are in the Ping-Pong (etc.) camp, the Table Tennis gang can hardly he said to miss many opportunities.

Last winter the bright minds of the crowd went to Gimbels and sold them on the idea of staging a National Tennis Championship, with admission charged, prizes, and all the rest of it. The tournament actually turned out to be a success, with a large gallery present every evening of the week, although they were competing with a big stamp show under the same roof. Naturally it was not long before the other bunch got to work, and the Metropolitan Ping-Pong (etc.) championships were held in the grand manner in the ballroom of the hotel New Yorker. All would have been well had not a ringer crept in. This person, in the shape of Sol Schiff, a red-haired lad of fourteen from the East Side Boys Club, practically stole the show.

However, he had his troubles. Observe how far we are getting from anything resembling sport, and how the thing degenerates more and more into a racket. Before many rounds the sponsors of the tournament discovered that an enemy was in their midst, and decided to make quick work of the invader. One of their experts was drawn against him, and this gentlemen in serving managed to dent the ball so that it fell flat without bouncing. For most of the first game, to the intense amusement of the audience, Sol was swiping the air.

At last, however, he realized what was up, proceeded to emulate his adversary's methods, and catching up on a 4-14 lead went on to win the game and match to the cheers of his enthusiastic partisans. His later victory in the finals did not cause those who had sponsored the tournament to jump up and down with joy.

Today Ping-Pong (etc.) is a real American game. Sport in miniature. All the usual sporting cliches are used by its devotees, all the current banalities regarding its beneficent effect upon the health, manners and morals of mankind are dragged forth, all the inanities which our athletics seem inevitably to attract are poured out upon it. Ping-Pong (etc.) is "character building," it is "scientific," it is a "fine, vigorous form of exercise." Now its sponsors are frantically engaged in proving that it is no prissy sport; but strenuous athletics requiring the physique of Tunney and the stamina of Tilden.

Your crack player carries around as many paddles as a tennis champion does racquets, and although paddles are still made of sand paper pasted on wood as in the good old days, the kind most favored are those of pebbly rubber which enables cut and spin to be administered to the ball. In Ping-Pong there is no regulation about the size of the paddle, nor about the ball except that it must be the "Official Association Ping-Pong Ball, so branded."

Estimates—not from the commercial sponsors, needless to say—are that five millions play the two games in this country alone. There are millions playing abroad, and the Japanese Ping-Pong Association has over 200,000 registered members. In this country there are tournaments all winter in every big city. Recently the Chicago American started a novice competition that attracted over a thousand entries.

As a game it is displacing pool and billiards, and in some parlors they have removed the rim from billiard tables to adapt them for table tennis....

What is the main difference between us and the cracks? Well, the cracks as a rule stand well back of the table, whereas the dub stands close up and scoops every shot on the half volley. Placed well to the rear of the rear of the table the champion returns the hardest hit drives with a chop, or a topspin stroke in which he hits over the ball, thus causing it to rise and drop in the opposing court. The dub has one service, seldom effective; the crack has three or four all made with spin, a twist or a bounce which leaves the average player fanning the air.

Nowadays a national championship is an affair which demands work and preparation months in advance. Tournament committees, publicity committees and other committees function weeks before the great moment arrives. The 1932 championships in the Waldorf attracted several thousand spectators every night of the week, all space about the tables was jammed, and the boxes crowded with on-lookers in evening clothes. On the floor were fourteen tables in two parallel rows of seven, a high net separating the two lines, a number over each table, and a number on the back of every contestant in order that they might be identified.

As in the Davis Cup matches, every contest was properly umpired, while the Parker Cup, perpetual symbol and so forth, was high on a raised platform at one end of the room where the referee and his assistants sat in state. And in their newly pressed evening clothes. Round about the corridors was exactly the same feverish atmosphere that is to be found surrounding an international golf or tennis championship, except that the location was a grand palace hotel instead of a stadium at Forest Hills or a green plain outside Garden City.

Nowadays a big tournament will not only clear expenses, but leave a nice little balance over for the treasury of the Association. In fact, says Mr. Clark, on the opening of the 1933 championships held at the Palmer House, Chicago, they actually had more paid admissions than on the first afternoon of one of the major tennis championships at West Side. This notwithstanding the fact that the ping-pong tournament began on the day of the bank holiday last March. Like its older brothers, Ping-Pong (etc.) is now Big Business, and likely to become more so. Look for news of it this winter in the press. Step by step you can trace its development from the unpretentious thing our fathers knew forty years ago; from a pastime to a craze, an athletic contest, a business, and finally a racket. American sport in miniature.

## SQUASH VERSUS SQUASH TENNIS

*[Since the British squash ball was too slow for the cold temperatures of most North American courts, Canada and the US adopted a harder rubber ball and played in a court that was two and a half feet narrower. This article outlines the reasons for the success of squash rackets compared to rackets and squash tennis. H.R. Knoll, "Keep Moving Your Feet," Esquire (February 1935), 50, 154, 156.]*

Squash rackets is a game that many players would die for, and that they will die for if they play it long enough. It is a whirling, exhausting, bitter game that can be played for fun but that more often is played in the spirit of root hog or die. Two contestants with no fear of heart failure isolate themselves in a
windowless, high-ceilinged room and then proceed to go mad. The play is forcing and, in a way, dirty, for it is calculated to make the opposition run, leap, twist, and at last come close to collapse. The tempo rises as the game progress. The rackets speak with a sharper tone, and the ball as it hits the front wall snaps like the breaking of timber. The strategy of attack and defense become intricate and must be executed with split-second precision. Power, speed, endurance, and craftiness must be available in large measure, and they must be synchronized so that on point after point the wearing destructiveness of the pace can be maintained. Between points the players may lean against the wall for support, their faces empty of color and sweat dribbling onto the floor; but when the ball is served again, so fanatical is the bugginess that the game breeds, they are after it tirelessly, relentlessly—all they know or feel is that they must meet the competition and, if possible, overpower, it.

Squash rackets flourishes because it is a fighting game. It is the pat answer for the man who dislikes the airy gracefulness of badminton, the galloping boredom of volley ball, the twitching of ping-pong, and the inconsequentialities of such indoor activities as deck tennis, box ball, and tiddlywinks. In squash rackets you can get hold of the meat. You can use your physical and mental capacities right up to the limit. You never have the frustrated feeling of not being able to let yourself go. When the ball rebounds off the front wall and you move into position for the shot, you have an awareness of freedom that no other game can give. You can make a soft shot, loop the ball high into the air, send the ball through any crazy angles that you choose—or you can lay into it as if you wanted to knock the walls down. Laying one away, smacking the ball so hard that it becomes a squirting black streak—that is the kind of catastrophic, complete satisfaction that is somewhere on the other side of Paradise. And the competition is no remote, cobwebby thing: it is right beside you, alive, tangible, fighting. You don't need a telescope to see that you are concerned with a battle.

In the United States squash rackets has boomed within the last fifteen years. Starting with the Ivy League and the clubs around Boston, New York, and Philadelphia, it has moved westward until it is now pretty much national in scope. Graduates of Eastern colleges, moving out to the hinterland in order to make a living, brought the game with them and, when they could not find courts everywhere, established courts in athletic clubs, old barns, old dance halls, and Y.M.C.A.'s. In the Middle West there are courts in most cities of any account and in many of the universities....

Squash rackets is an importation from England, and is descended from the ferocious game of rackets, which is believed to have originated in a seventeenth-century debtor's prison. Rackets has to a large extent been superseded: it is too expensive for anyone but a debtor or a well-heeled capitalist, and, beside, since it is the "fastest game on foot," it demands near-perfect conditioning. The rackets court is almost twice as long as the squash rackets court and is surfaced with a special imported material applied by English workmen. Four officials are needed to conduct a formal match, one of them being occupied mostly with handing out new equipment. Bats may he broken at the rate of two hundred dollars' worth an afternoon; the ball has to be replaced about every ninety seconds. This rackets ball is interesting if only because it may be older than the players using it. Its core is of tightly wound cloth, its cover of white leather. When the cover is nicked, the core is returned to England (or was until September 1) and new leather sewed over it. Aging and the hammering of play improve its resiliency.

Originally intended as a training game for rackets, squash rackets has become the game to play. It is strenuous but does not keep a contestant doing the hundred-yard dash for an hour on end. It is less dangerous than rackets, for not all rackets players go through life keeping both their eyes. Officials are not needed in informal play, and only one is required in matches between clubs. The racket, though it is never guaranteed and will break easily enough if slapped against a wall, can be made to last a full season....

Women, as might be expected, have invaded the game and ordinarily play a pat-the-ball, catch-the-butterfly style which some people find perfectly charming. A few years ago a team invaded England and was trounced. The report when the players returned home was that they had had no large reservoir of players to draw from, most American girls in an economic position to play being more interested in languid comfort, cigarettes, and cocktails than in sports. Moreover, the English girls, had had the advantage of playing with men, while American men for unexplained reasons would rather compete among themselves than against their womenfolk. This is not to say, however, that all American girls fail to reach a proficiency which is terrible to behold in the female of the species. When the English girls came to this country and played on American courts, they took a beating....

Squash rackets will never be popular in the sense that it will draw big gates and make the headlines. The construction of the courts makes large crowds of spectators impossible. A court with a seating capacity of three hundred is exceptional, and the usual capacity is about fifty. There has been some talk of building glass courts at least for the championship matches, but, by and large, most players feel that the game belongs to them, and that commercializing it would only take the sport out of it and breed a new race of tramps. For their own playing they are satisfied to go off by themselves and have it out without benefit of officials or spectators. That they love the game is indisputable. In the fall of the year when the smoky haze settles over the horizon, they regret the finish of outdoor sports but have the satisfaction of knowing that for the next six or seven months they can engage in an indoor sport for which they do not have to apologize to anybody.

**RACKET SPORTS FOR THE FUN OF IT—HANDBALL AND PLATFORM TENNIS**

[*In the following excerpts from his book, noted sportswriter John Tunis outlines the reasons for the growth of handball and platform tennis. A constant theme for each racket sport was the exercise it provided in a short period of time, the famous people who played the game, the ease of learning the game, and New York's domination. John R. Tunis,* Sport for the Fun of It *(New York, 1940), 139-45, 183-9.]*

### HANDBALL. A CITY SPORT

But the game we discuss in this chapter is a city game. And if you want proof of its popularity as a playing sport, take a ride around an American city like New York and notice on every solid wall the same sign: "NO HANDBALL PLAYING"

...The spread of handball, like the growth of many other playing games in the United States, has been much assisted in the last five years by relief programs. Since 1935 the WPA in various parts of the country has constructed 1,365 new courts, almost all for the single-wall game. The reason why this variety of handball has been favored is obvious. A regulation indoor four-wall court costs money [from $5,000 to $6,000]. A one-wall court...can be put up for a third of the above sum. The growth of the one-wall game is therefore understandable.

Yet the four-wall sport is still the national favorite and even played extensively in French Canada where it is extremely popular. At present four-wall handball has a wider scope than the one-wall game, being played in every state in the Union, whereas the latter sport is confined to the coast. Arthur Wehrmann, Chairman of the Metropolitan Committee of the A.A.U. states: "it should be noticed that practically all one-walled champions have been developed in the east, where the west has monopolized the four-wall championships." The one-wall titleholders in 1939 were from the Manhattan area. Harry Michitsch, singles champion, and Harry Goldstein and George Baskin all came from the Trinity Club in Brooklyn, N.Y. Miss Lucy Caruso who won the Metropolitan woman's title and has been champion several years running, comes from Brooklyn.

Both games, but the one-wall kind especially, are city games. This explains to some extent the fact that its champions have consistently been Jewish boys. Stanley Frank in his book, "The Jew in Sports," has this to say about the prominence of Jewish athletes in one-wall handball.

"Handball thrives in congested cities, due to the very nature of the game and its requirements when played informally. A brick wall, the pavement, and a soft rubber ball are easy to find, whereas the country cousin never misses level sidewalks with open fields so abundant for baseball and football.... This is particularly true of Jewish kids who live in the more crowded districts. The blank wall of the corner grocery is not very exciting, but it is far better than nothing and a lot safer than the middle of the street. So Jewish boys play handball in self-defence and in time, excitement does come in major tournaments as they grow up with the game."

The general growth of handball can best be shown by the interest in the A.A.U. championships every season. Several years ago in Los Angeles, front row seats for the finals were sold at $22 apiece, and were all gone before the match began.... Charles J. O'Connell of New York, himself a player, long an official, and the historian of handball in the United States says: "The present popularity of single-wall handball is due to many factors—to the standardization of the ball, the revision of the rules and the construction of standard courts. But the most important factor has been the keen interest and pleasure by galleries witnessing championship or club matches.... At present it has adherents of all ages and both sexes. Around New York it is a growing sport among women at beach resorts, and a recent tournament at Manhattan Beach had almost a hundred entrants. In agility, speed and strength the top-notch ladies can give a fair male player a really good game...."

As a method of obtaining a workout in a short time, handball has no superior. It is one of the easiest of all games with a ball for the beginner. There is no racquet, club, or expensive equipment necessary. It is excellent training, develops footwork in other sports, besides being a top-class conditioning game. [Tunis noted that a ball cost $.40 and gloves $1.00-$3.60]

## PLATFORM-PADDLE TENNIS

Paddle tennis was first played on a P.& 0. liner Bombay-bound some fifty years ago by that inventive (athletically speaking) race, the Britons. In 1922, Frank P. Beal, then secretary of the Community Council of New York, introduced a similar game to the city playgrounds. Instead of a tennis racquet he used for cheapness sake a paddle of laminated wood with a short handle, a slow bouncing ball of sponge rubber, and a net 2 feet 6 inches. His court was an area of concrete 39 feet by 18 feet. This game he called Paddle Tennis.

The sport took hold. It was fascinating to play and had tremendous appeal for the youngsters. It was lots of fun, too. Boys and girls in city blocks which were shut off as play areas found it an ideal form of exercise. Here was a game which could be played on concrete pavement or on dirt, on the streets of the metropolis or at nearby beaches. When the youngsters went out to Long Island for the day they found their favorite sport at hand. Jones Beach built 24 paddle tennis courts, and they were full in hot weather. In 1931, the National Recreation Association reported that 216 cities were using the game as part of their health program. By 1939, there were 92 courts at Manhattan Beach, with some 64,000 players competing. Paddle Tennis was here for keeps.

In the meantime older age groups discovered the pastime. In 1928, two suburban commuters, James K. Cogswell and F. S. Blanchard of Scarsdale, New York, began looking around for some form of outdoor exercise during the cold days of spring and fall when tennis courts and golf links were unusable. They attempted badminton on a concrete driveway, but too often play was spoiled by the wind. Deck tennis proved satisfactory, so they built a small platform on which either game could he enjoyed. Then they stumbled on the playground game, enlarged their platform and constructed the first court for what is now called to distinguish it, Platform Paddle Tennis....

This sport has something. Its growth was not due to any high pressure selling. No sales campaign is responsible for its popularity today, but simply the fact that everyone who sees it played wants to have a try, and everyone who tries goes away convinced that he must build a court of his own. As a means of quick outdoor exercise during the winter months when other games are impossible, Platform Paddle Tennis is certainly in a class by itself.

Several country clubs in the New York Metropolitan area realized this. They began gingerly experimenting with the game, and by November 1934 three of them joined together to form the American Paddle Tennis Association, an amateur, non-commercial organization devoted entirely to the interests of the game. In 1940 those three charter member clubs had grown to seventeen, and the Association was holding official championships every winter near New York. At this time the sport was listed by athletic goods dealers as one of the ten fastest-growing games in the country. It had spread all over the United States, and at present the Association estimates there are some 500 platforms in existence with about 20,000 active participants as far west as California and Hawaii.

The court dimensions are 44 feet by 20 feet. Consequently you can put four paddle tennis platforms in the area of your regulation lawn tennis court. The size is the chief difference between platform paddle tennis and the older game. With two exceptions, rules are the same as those of lawn tennis. First, in the platform game, only one service is permitted. This was necessary to speed up play, and due to the small surface, to prevent domination of the game by the server. Second, balls may be taken off the back and side wiring of the court in a rally as in squash. This fact enables the use of a smaller court than would otherwise be possible, and also tends to lengthen and add excitement to the rallies. When first attempted the carom shot seems odd, but the average player soon becomes adept at what from the sidelines appears to be a most difficult stroke.

That's one of the great advantages of Platform Paddle Tennis. Anyone can pick it up in a short time, and with slight practice play a really good game....

Country and beach clubs have found their memberships growing and their usefulness to the community doubled by installing a paddle tennis platform during the months of winter. In fact at least one tennis club near New York which was obliged every fall to let its courts and property lie idle until the next spring, got on its feet through paddle tennis. With only 75 members, they found themselves losing ground soon after the depression, so they built two platforms for paddle tennis over their dirt courts. Immediately new life came into the club with people who wish to keep outdoors in winter. Their membership was doubled, and today this organization has six paddle tennis platforms and a lively group of players who keep going the whole year round.

Costs of the game are not high, once your platform is built. Balls of sponge rubber can be bought for $.25 and both the balls and the short-handled, oval-shaped racquets which are really glorified ping-pong bats can be used a long while.... As a rule the complete court with wire backstops costs about $500 to construct. Platforms ready to put into place are purchasable now from certain lumber firms at a price of $595. These platforms have the advantage of being built so they can be put in place over alawn tennis court directly the frost comes. With the arrival of spring they can be moved out of the way and stored until desired the following fall....

Moreover this is a sport which is especially valuable for the American college athlete after graduation. Charley O'Hearn, crack Yale quarterback in the early twenties was a paddle tennis champion not long ago. Arthur Huguley and Bell Ticknor, former Harvard football aces enjoy the sport; and Rowland B. Haines, for many years squash tennis champion, is also an adept [sic]. Sidney B. Wood, 1931 Wimbledon singles champion and ranking star at lawn tennis, won a doubles title in the platform game the first time he ever handled a bat.

On the other hand, you don't need to have been an All American athlete to enjoy this pastime. Arthur Murray the dance teacher keeps fit with a paddle tennis court.... It's the sport of sports for the business man who wants to combine fun and exercise in a short space and in a short time.

In this miniature tennis you serve, smash, lob and drive as in the older game. Strategy and tactics are identical. There is the lob, the stop volley, the drive, the smash and all the features that make lawn tennis such an engrossing pastime, **plus** the carom shot off the wire netting that adds variety to the sport. Boys and girls take to it and pick it up quite as rapidly as their elders. When those two Manhattan commuters developed this from the game kids on city playgrounds had enjoyed for years, they brought into existence a new and vital playing game. Platform Paddle Tennis today is the year-round, all-weather, all-age sport.

Chapter 19

## RECREATIONAL SPORTS—VOLLEYBALL, SOFTBALL

P.R. Brammel's national survey of secondary education in 1934 advocated encouraging students to engage in sports with a "carry-over" value into adult life. Female athletic organizations shared his belief that schools should foster "lifetime" recreational sports that emphasized participation and enjoyment over winning, and promoted the students' health and feelings of well-being. Factories, banks, and offices also sponsored a variety of recreational sports for their employees. Two of the more popular such sports were volleyball and softball.

### VOLLEYBALL

Many people received their first exposure to volleyball in intramural play in elementary and high schools, where, along with basketball, it occupied the foremost position in terms of enjoyment and numbers. This interest continued in university. In women's colleges, for example, volleyball ranked second behind field hockey. At mid-decade, a national study of 5,000 adults' leisure hours reported that among sporting pastimes, volleyball ranked ninth, and that it was popular among industrial, settlement, parks and playground, church, and YMCA leagues. The Works Progress Administration noted that volleyball was one of its most popular sports, and the Board of Park Commissioners for Minneapolis reported that volleyball had the third largest number of participants in 1937, behind only baseball and football.

Robert Laveaga, whose *Volley Ball—A Man's Game* (1933) was the first volleyball book, also contributed to the sports' growth. Volleyball has several advantages. It is suitable for every age, may be played year round, in or outdoors, and by all. Volleyball equipment was simple and inexpensive and the game could be played in school or church gymnasiums, on beaches, in the backyard, or in industrial plants. In addition to teaching quickness, footwork, and body control, the game helped to straighten the spine by bringing the shoulders up and back and the head back to see over the net. It was a better game than basketball, its supporters argued, because there was no body contact and in the course of a game everyone played each position. It was a team game that anyone could play without fear of injury.

For many women instructors who disliked competition, strenuous activity, and physical contact, and who wished to foster carry-over pastimes, volleyball was ideal. To improve the game, the Volley Ball Committee of the Women's Athletic Section of the American Physical Education Association lowered the net, reduced the court from 60 by 30 to 50 by 25 feet, and substituted a specific time limit rather than play to 15 points.

More competitive play was offered by the YMCA, which sponsored national tournaments, including an over-35 veteran's event; by the United States National Volleyball Association (1929); and by the Amateur Athletic Union, which initiated a national championship in 1928. The overhead serve first appeared in the national tournament in 1929. The growth of volleyball in Canada paralleled that in the United States. Schools fostered activity-oriented volleyball, while the YMCA promoted competitive games. The first national volleyball organization meeting in Canada was held in 1939.

## SOFTBALL

"Softball is the Shirley Temple of the sports world. Almost overnight," claimed Popular Mechanics (June 1936), "it has skyrocketed to national popularity. More than one million Americans are playing it while several millions more shout approval from the grandstands of lighted fields and specially constructed softball parks. It has national, section and state governing bodies, a standard set of rules, and even umpire associations." By the end of the decade, more than five million players and seventy-five million spectators attended softball games.

Softball was also popular in Canada, where almost every city, town, and village had a league. By 1937, Ontario offered provincial championships in seven different categories based on population size—from Senior A for populations more than 50,000 to Junior B for districts less than 3,500. When a reader wrote to the local newspaper in Vancouver, British Columbia, complaining of the lack of newspaper coverage of softball in the city, the editor replied, "It would take the entire editorial staff—the circulation department, most of the accounting staff and both telephone operators to cover softball as you suggest."

Softball was a mass-participation sport. Churches, YMCAs, Rotary clubs, municipalities, community centers, banks, and industrial and commercial firms all sponsored leagues. Minority communities supported their own teams. Although the game had working-class roots, and was most popular on the West Coast and in the Midwest, few regions were excluded.

Softball originated in the late nineteenth century, when a pudgy, slow-moving ball was batted around in large armories. Sometimes called mushball, indoor ball, playground ball, kitten ball, or twilight ball, softball did not become popular until the Depression. It was cheaper than baseball, took less space, and, with the adoption of Daylight Savings Time, could be played in the evening. Minimal admission fees allowed the legion of unemployed to attend. For many small communities, the local softball team provided needed entertainment and a morale boost. Star players, both men and women, became local heroes. For similar reasons, many companies hired players to compete for their team and provided equipment and travel expenses, including uniforms emblazoned with the company's name. The better players frequently switched jobs for better "salaries." Later in the decade, barnstorming pitchers sold their services to sponsors for about $35 a game. Famed pitcher "King Kong" Kelly reportedly earned $45,000 this way in his best year.

The WPA assisted in the growth of softball by building more than 3,000 athletic fields between 1936 and 1940, many of which included lights. In Canada, softball was a popular sport in the government-controlled work camps for single, unemployed males.

At the beginning of the decade, each region used different-sized balls and bats, played under different rules, and employed varying distances between the bases and from the pitcher's mound to home plate. The momentum to standardize the rules grew out of the 1933 World's Fair in Chicago. On short notice, two Chicago newspaper reporters arranged for eighteen teams from twelve states to play in a tournament at the Fair. The fact that each team played by a different set of rules led to the creation of the Amateur Softball Association, a standardized set of rules, and an annual national championship. The 1939 World's Amateur Softball Championship in Chicago attracted teams from forty-three states, two Canadian provinces, and Puerto Rico.

Softball's popularity also attracted several promoters. George Sisler, former manager of the St. Louis Browns baseball team, and the American League's career batting leader, formed the American Softball League and reportedly made a fortune out of the game. Sisler controlled a chain of lighted baseball diamonds in St. Louis and regularly attracted more spectators than the local baseball teams. Phil Rosier, another former professional baseball player and later a sportswriter, organized the National Softball Association. The two organizations differed in the size of the ball, the distance between bases and between home plate and the pitcher's mound, and the number of players— most teams added a tenth player, the short fielder. On the West coast, businessmen created softball leagues and sold team franchises for $600 to $1,500. In southern California, movie stars, labor leaders, and businessmen all bought franchises. Team names, Slapsie Maxie's Curvaceous Cuties, Balioan Ice Cream Beauties, Bank of America Bankerettes, and Columbia Pictures Starlettes, indicated the intended spectator appeal of the women's teams.

Unlike most other female sports, softball was not controlled by college educators— although they approved of the game—nor were the rules modified for the players. The working-class origins of many of the best women players contributed to the game's image as a rough sport and thus maintained softball's male following. The document "Women's Softball" provides a typical account of female softball players and discusses the popularity of the game among women.

## THE GROWTH OF VOLLEYBALL

[*The following extract from the author's account of volleyball for the 1939-40 edition of the* Volleyball Guide Book *was reprinted in* Recreation. *Rogers, Director of the National Physical Education Service, discusses the growth of volleyball in the US. James E. Rogers, "Volleyball—Popular American Sport," Recreation (December 1939), 502, 532.*]

Volleyball is rapidly becoming America's great recreational sport for both young and old. It is essentially a game for recreation and participation. It is a players' game, not an onlookers' athletic spectacle. If reliable statistics could be gathered as to the number of people playing volleyball in schools, on playgrounds, at colleges and universities, in Y.M.C.A.'s and Y.W.C.A.'s, in boys' clubs, settlements, churches, and athletic clubs, it would undoubtedly rank among the first ten national major sports from the point of view of participation.

Volleyball takes its place with bowling, tennis, golf, baseball, and basketball as a popular American sport, finding favor with millions. Softball and volleyball are the two new games showing remarkable growth in recent years. There are many reasons for this. Both are primarily recreational sports that are inexpensive and easily played without the need for the long training and specialization that goes with high powered competitive athletics. Football, baseball, and basketball have become highly skilled and specialized. They are good games but have lost their recreational character for the mass of people.

Municipal recreation departments and authorities, in their reports, show the phenomenal increase of interest in volleyball as one of the major games throughout the country, on playgrounds and in recreation centers. With hundreds of leagues for all ages and groups with many tournaments and with thousands of players, volleyball has become popular both as an outdoor and as an indoor game. A recreation executive recently states that he felt figures would reveal that more volleyball was played on playgrounds than anywhere else. This may be true, but similar recent statements from other groups and organizations prove that the same growth and trend are true in Y.M.C.A.'s, boy's clubs, churches, colleges, and schools.

For years volleyball has been the popular game in Y.M.C.A.'s and Y.W.C.A.'s. It is a favorite among industrial leagues. With business men it has taken the place of basketball, which has become too strenuous and skilled for older men.

A report issued for the Boys' Clubs of America is most encouraging, showing that throughout the country volleyball has increased rapidly and is practically one of the major items in the physical education athletic program. Of 114 clubs recently reporting on their athletic program, 95 per cent stated that volleyball was a part of the program.

Today volleyball is one of the outstanding sports in the intramural program of our colleges and universities. Observation of the game in recent visits to more than fifty institutions of higher education in various parts of the country has confirmed the belief that volleyball ranks among the first ten, if not the first three games, in popularity and number of players. Dr. May, of the University of Michigan, has stated that it is one of the best liked games in the elective service program required of all freshman students.

Reports from boys' and girls' physical education programs in junior and senior high schools show that in this area there has been a phenomenal growth. Some cities and states report wide participation. In Maryland, volleyball is one of the favorite games among school children. It ranks high in the program.

There are still, however, sections in which more can be done in the public schools to promote the game. The new modified rules for juniors or beginners, as formulated by the national committee, will help tremendously in the public schools. One can fairly say that there is a definite trend forward and that volleyball has become an integral part of the physical education programs in all schools, especially in our large cities.

...It is a game that is used on different occasions. It is played at picnics and social gatherings. It is used as a social mixer. It is one of the most popular of co-educational and co-recreational sports.

When one considers the hundreds of leagues, the thousands of tournaments, and the many organizations and groups interested, the many indoor and outdoor places and occasions where volleyball is played, one feels confident in saying that with bowling, tennis, golf, softball, basketball, and baseball, volleyball ranks in the ten great American games that people play for recreation and enjoyment.

## THE GROWTH OF SOFTBALL

*[The American Softball Association was the largest amateur athletic organization in the Western world. Initially, major league baseball supported softball's growth, but as the new game began to attract more spectators than baseball, the owners said less and less about softball. The following account is a summary of the National Recreation Committee discussion group on the growth of softball. The author was secretary of the Department of Physical Education for the National Council of the YMCA, New York. Recreation, the successor to Playground (1908-1929) and Playground and Recreation (1929-1931), was produced by the National Recreation Association and was "devoted to leisure-time enrichment." John Brown, Jr., "Softball Problems—Hearing on Present Situation," Recreation (28 December 1934), 445-446.]*

The eighty delegates who attended this session reported an amazing increase in the game of softball during the past year. There were more participants and more teams. Formal and informal leagues and tournaments were organized in all parts of the country. This increase was beyond the fondest dreams of any advocate of this particular game a few years ago. It was present in all sorts of institutions, affecting all ages and both sexes. Inter-city, district, state and national tournaments were held.

In the national tournament held in Chicago, promoted under the auspices of the Amateur Softball Association of America, forty-six qualifying teams participated, representing over thirty different states and Canada. You can get some idea of the local interest in that game when I tell you that one hundred and twenty-one policemen were assigned to handle the crowd attending it....

The national association which promoted this particular tournament was the outgrowth of a meeting held in Chicago two years ago, convened by the National Softball Association. At this meeting thirty-six different states and Canada were represented and a committee was organized which attempted to codify the existing rules.

I have referred to two different national bodies—the National Softball Association and the Amateur Softball Association of America. The former is sponsored primarily by manufacturers interested in promoting the game because of their desire to sell equipment. It is interested in promoting inter-city games between professional teams with one team in each city. The Amateur Softball Association of America, on the other hand, is a different organization with a different set of officers. It is interested in all-star amateur sports in cities on the part of all sorts of teams representing local communities.

The Playground Baseball Committee of the National Recreation Association has functioned since 1923 in the promotion of the game, particularly along the lines of rules standardization. It was recently enlarged to include representatives of other national agencies interested in this sport and is now known as the Joint Rules Committee of Softball. It is continuing its efforts towards acceptance of one standardized set of rules. This committee is primarily interested in stimulating interest in keeping the game recreational, amateur, as a neighborhood event, contributing to wholesome community play for all. It is representative of the national organizations interested in the sport and has formulated the rules from this point of view.

Now, attempting to summarize some of the things that developed in our conference, I would say that softball is not now for softies. It has shifted from being a game of many names, some of which were bad names, like "kitten" ball, implying that it had nine deaths. In passing, you may be interested in that the official rules now call for seven rather than nine innings. It is no longer going to be known as indoor baseball or diamond ball or night ball, but softball. We hope instead of many there will be but one set of rules, which, of course, may be adapted to suit local equipment conditions.

This game has not had any parent. It has been on the doorstep of many organizations, clamoring for admittance but no one has taken it in. It is now being taken in and it is going to be fostered and we hope that it will grow up as a member of the family of real play and recreative activities in all communities.

Heretofore, this game has been going nowhere. We believe now that it is really starting to go places, with one name, one game, one set of rules, sponsored by one joint committee representing all of the national organizations interested in this sport, with one guide which will be the official handbook.

From this I think that we as recreational workers can get the following suggestive points of view. The game will no longer be classified as a minor game; from our standpoint, it will be a major game. It will not be confined to the playground but have its place really in the neighborhood. We will not think of it as a kid's game but for all age ranges, not only for boys but also for men and for girls and women. Not only will it be a daytime and twilight game, but also a night game. It is coming from obscurity into prominence, from being unorganized to being organized—not for the few but for the many. Continuing to be informal it will also be formal.

The Joint Committee will be enlarged to represent more of the organizations, all of which will be united in the revision of the rules which is now in process. It is hoped the rules will be universally accepted with a view to keeping softball a community game of the people, for the people, by the people, as a means of adding to their more abundant living.

## WOMEN'S SOFTBALL

[*In 1939, Ted Shane's article about softball in* The American Magazine *praised the calibre of women's play, but added, "Naturally, girls worry a lot more about how they look than men do, take time out to powder their noses, and say 'Gosh darn!' when they break a beet-red fingernail fielding a fast one." The following article from* Esquire *illustrates the growth of women's softball and the prevailing attitude toward athletic women at the time. Herb Graffis, "Belles of the Ball. Women's Softball Has Come a Long Way Since the Bloomer Girls of Chicago Spit Their First Tobacco,"* Esquire *(June 1940), 70-71, 173-175.*]

...It was fifteen years ago that the Bloomer Girls of Chicago presented the debut of girls' softball outdoors. In that period the game has grown to the extent that now there are more than 600,000 young women playing softball, and the game has its bob-haired Ruths, Deans, Gehrigs and DiMaggios. Girls have graduated from softball teams into quite substantial salaries as minor executives of companies that employed them primarily as athletic advertisements. Girls have paid college tuition with the money they've earned playing softball—not, of course, out-and-out as softball players, for it is an amateur game and under conscientious control as strict as widespread amateur sport can be. The softball girls have gone into wedlock and traded their bats for skillets, their diamonds for didies. One of them, at least, has entered a convent. She is Miss Ann Harnett, a high school teacher who starred with the Rival Dog Food team which is one of the game's major clubs.

So, while the supreme male may regard the lady softballers as freaks of nature who don't throw as though they were trying to escape from a strait-jacket, the ladies themselves have been building a new sports attraction by glorifying feminine inconsistency in a muscular manner. It's guessed by those who ought to be able to call the shots fairly accurately, that about 90,000,000 Americans watched softball in 1939. Girls' teams were the major attractions of this pastime that night lighting has helped to boom into popularity as neighborhood entertainment.

The crowd appeal of the softballing males is merely that of baseballers scaled down to neighborhood dimensions, plus playing time that fits conveniently into the evening schedule of the citizen who enjoys having his dinner digest while seeing a living picture that has a plot subject to change without notice. Softball by the ladies has the assets of game time that meets the citizens' requirements of evening relaxation and the sudden shifting of scripts by home runs or fumbles, but with a lot more....

Women's softball has grown tremendously despite the comparatively small amount of newspaper and radio plugging it has received. Its large city newspaper publicity has been received mainly as the result of promotions conducted by certain newspapers. When a paper plugs its own sports promotions the other papers in town ease up, and give affairs promoted by the competition only minimum mention.

A young lady who works for a neighborhood plow plant or dairy outdraws Hedy Lamarr or Ann Sheridan in many a community where these females are competitively billed as entertainment. When the local young lady known as Spike or Mickey can do that, you may be sure that she appeals to fundamental instincts. Maybe the instincts are upside down and the cave girl is delighting her male by giving birth to a timely triple which the male considers he has sired by his loud cheers and advice. If that's the case, softball's remarkable growth may be regarded by the deep thinkers as evidence supporting the belief of some pathologists and psychologists that the females are getting more and more masculine, and vice versa, each succeeding day.

Cases of cryptorchism pop out every so often in the annals of female athletics. The Olympic games have included contestants whose performances have been notable when classified in the ladies' department, but who later have been subjected to surgical attention with the result of disqualification on the grounds of being biologically suited for shaving brushes instead of powder puffs. It is the jealous nature of some males to suspect that lady softballers who are males' superiors in throwing, catching, running and batting, enjoy such superiority because they possess the fundamental male attributes not as much in evidence as skill on the tabloid diamond.

That cheering delusion of the male is blasted by such female softball stars as Catherine Fellmeth. Catherine is a high-browed, attractive young matron of about 28 years. As Mrs. Rutherford, she has Mr. Rutherford's meals cooked on time, gets their 5-year-old youngster fed and put to bed, gets the dishes washed, then goes out to sparkle as a performer on a Chicago team that figures prominently each year in the national softball championships. To keep her biceps in condition for sweeping, dusting, wielding the skillet, washing the dishes and the baby's things, Kitty adds to her softball exercise that of winning the Chicago women's bowling championship, heaving the discus 113 feet 7 and a half inches, and putting the shot 41 feet 1 3/4 inches; the latter two feats being performed at the 1939 national A.A.U. track and field championships, at which Kitty shared with Stella Walsh the glory of being the only double victor among the contestants.

These are young ladies who work in machine shops, bakeries and laundries—fields of endeavor not explored by Junior Leaguers—and at least one young lady horse-shoer, on the roster of leading softball teams. In labor in machine shops and during the employment of applying a bootee to a Percheron, a young lady must he excused if she chooses to tuck a wad of niggerhair into her mouth and munch away vigorously. The chances are the money she's making is pretty badly needed at home. So long as she helps the folk, it is not exactly chivalrous of the male to cast aspersions on her character because she plays softball the hard way. That exercise may work off energy left over after a day's toil at the lathe or with the beer wagon horses.

A very bright young man who has had the assignment of being host to girl's softball teams sponsored by out-of-town customers of his company, ventures the suggestion that a great deal of the apparent toughness of girl softballers is strictly an act to impress the male. He says that he has taken the girls around to see the sights, and in response to their requests, has begun tours of night clubs. He says that the girls always act like ladies on these jaunts. He does not recall having finished any of these tours, although his thirst and resistance have been developed to a high degree by experience with visiting buyers. The young ladies, without straining themselves, get the hardy young man in a stage of inebriation known as flying blind and the last thing he ever remembers is hearing gentle voices saying, "we'll ship the poor thing home by cab and really go out and have some fun." What they consider fun he does not know because he comes out of a turkish bath just in time to see them full of shrieks and animal spirits at the next evening's game. After a light supper of five aspirin tablets on thin toast he again tries to outdrink any one of the girls, only to suffer again the most ignominious fate that can befall a customer's man.

The mystery of the way of the maids with the men is further deepened upon examination of the case of Miss Dorothy Klupping, who emerges from women's national softball championships as the Dizzy Dean of that pastime. Miss Klupping, a pitcher for the Down Drafts of Chicago, is known to the softball opera lovers as Boots. She is a legitimate blonde, of a shade of hair that even her foes in the crucial struggles call "honey blonde." She is a bit over 5 feet high and when seen away from her strenuous employment would not be recognized as a muscle moll....

Boots will walk into her team's dressing room before a game and still the nervous chatter of her compatriots by remarking, "them tramps ain't got a chance. They can't hit me." That, of course, is hearsay from her teammates, as this investigator has not been in the dressing room of a ladies' softball team. But what she does do before the naked eyes of the multitude is plenty to reveal performing color.

She will receive the ball from an umpire. She will appraise it carefully, stitch by stitch; read the printing on the cover; toss the ball gently up as though testing its weight. Then, with an expression of disdain so queenly all the crowd winches [sic], Boots will toss the ball over the park fence.

Another ball will be tossed out. She will repeat her act. The manger of the opposing team will run onto the field yelling that Boots be tossed out of the game for contempt of court, lese majesty, spitting on the sidewalk, homicide and other charges managers make in women's softball games.

Boots will look coy at the umpire and pout. "The very idea!" she'll protest. "Here I am just warming up and he wants to have me benched because I'm a bit wild. Make him get back minding his own business, Mr. Umpire, or maybe one of my wild ones will tear his fat head offen [sic] his lazy shoulders." [Similar discussions of Eleanora Duse, Freda Savona, Dot Underwood, and Mary Skorich have been deleted.]

When the National Screw champions were disbanded by the lure of more lucrative jobs in the southland, Alameda (Calif.) girls hammered down opposition in winning the 1938 and 1939 national titles. These brawny and sunkist cities have it over their sisters of the cinema sector to the south of them as players, but in oomph, impartial critics give the Los Angeles maidens the decision.

Marty Fiedler, former minor and major league baseballer, and his brother Irving, organized a women's softball league around Los Angeles. They got eight sponsors to invest $1,000 apiece in backing the teams.... It's been a very profitable entertainment venture for the astute Fiedler brothers have seen that the teams are quite closely matched in proficiency and have ballyhooed their shows with such sparkling lines as the slogan of their Sunset Park "where the stars come out each night." The yokels and the locals used to come to get ganders of the movie stars. Now the girl softballers themselves are the attraction. Two teams of the Fiedler league's girls toured Japan and drew big crowds. Girls' softball hasn't scored to any appreciable extent in Japan, although in western Canada and in a few spots in Mexico it is an established sport.

Although southern California's girl softballers haven't the performing class (according to competent national judges) that the standout teams in other sections show, the calibre of their work is improving so speedily that it is expected southern California soon will be represented by brilliant teams at the national championships. Then, so apprehensive males fear, there may be a brisk battle as an added attraction. Florida has the reigning beauty queen of softball, Miss Paulette Nolan, outfielder for the Dr. Pepper Girls of Miami Beach. One look at the radiantly lovely Miss Nolan is said to do more for the world-weary male than a series of treatments by old Doc Pepper, her sponsor, in person.

With Miami Beach and Hollywood in a battle of curve tossing for the world's title, there should be the bitterest, most beautiful competition ever beheld by the eyes of mortal man.

To tell the truth about it, the softball girls weather fairly well. There is a lady named Lorraine Gehrke, who has completed her tenth year with the original Bloomer Girls' softball team, and never missed an inning of shortstopping during that stretch. You might be disposed to think that a lady Gehrig, in contour and solidity, would resemble a wholesale butcher's block. However, in verity, the rollicking and durable Lorraine has a considerable edge in pulchritude and streamlining over many another nice lady whose sliding has been done from one chair to another in changing bridge partners, instead of over skinned diamonds that abrade the hide like a nutmeg grater.

Though all but Lorraine have fled from the line-up of the pioneer Bloomer Girls, Ed Baumgardner, who still manages the team he founded in 1924, says that he will parade members of his old line-ups in competition with any other group of Floradora veterans and bet that his old team shows minimum of wear from matrimony, maternity and chronology.

It might be so. Naturally the girls' softball talent is selected from a physically superior group. In this connection, it is interesting to note that most of the star girl softballers are of established American stock. In the lineups at the national championships there are far fewer names of obviously recent foreign origin than will be found in major league baseball rosters. Only during the past three years have the softball expert observers seen many youngsters of foreign-born parents or grandparents come into the game.

The American parent seems to encourage his female progeny in the sprightly pastime of softball. Fathers whose names once were on scorecards of major and minor league, and scholastic ball games have their names kept luminous by their maiden children whose diamond feats are thrilling the neighborhoods. One of this corps of lassies, Shirley Jameson, is the daughter of the once-renowned Tubby Jameson. Miss Shirley is of such proficiency that when one tells her daddy that if he were as good at baseball as his daughter is at softball, he would have outglammoured Babe Ruth, all that Jameson here can do is to nod agreement.

There still is abundant opportunity for better staged management in women's softball. Some teams persist in swathing themselves in the superdrooper bloomers which are, beyond all question, the most godawful creation an aesthetically illiterate modiste ever hung on the human form divine. The color combinations of many of the suits are reasons for playing many games at night, for it is a certainty that man, woman or child of normal vision must suffer unpleasant disturbances at the pit of the belly upon viewing the bilious colors that clash on softball uniforms.

Considering the physical requirements of softball, it is amazing how many a neat set of gams is revealed by the tastefully attired maidens who perform in shorts instead of in the superdrooper pants. The girls do get their knees, legs, and hams skinned by slides, and as the result of being sent bounding on their beautiful bottoms by contact with other sturdy maidens. But it is just such mishaps that stir the mothering instincts of the crowds—65% of which are males—and add another appeal to the game.

As a matter of fact, somewhat unpleasant to organized baseball, girls' softball is showing the swiftest rate of increase in sports draw. Around Chicago, for instance, girls' softball at five parks, over an 18 weeks season, drew about twice the season's crowd Chicago's American League White Sox drew. The New York Rangers and Roverettes, playing at Madison Square Garden last summer, averaged more than 9,000 customers per game. The Rangers and the Roverettes, so it is said by authorities who are well acquainted with girls' softball all over the country, are by no means among the nation's most expert performers. However, their brand of softball is amply adequate to give the trade its money's worth.

This pastime is drawing its own group of fans, many of whom have switched from other sports, and some of whom are entirely new as sports entertainment enthusiasts. There is a lively grade of violence toward the umpire exhibited at close contests between the girls, and ingenuity shown by the players in inciting the crowd against the arbiters. All of that adds to the gaiety of the show. Perhaps one of the umpires' problems accounts for the hideous superdrooper pants previously mentioned. Mr. Harry

Wilson, who has worked many of the big games in ladies' softball, tells of a case of an umpire being rebuked by a lady catcher, thus:

"Listen, big boy, if you would take your lamps off the batter's knees long enough to look around maybe you would see more of these pitches coming over as strikes."

You can't send a doll to the bench for a remark like that. You have to listen and like it. That's what the country is doing about the girls' softball games.

Chapter 20

**TRACK AND FIELD**

In March 1935, Maple Leaf Gardens in Toronto agreed to sponsor an indoor track and field meet on the condition that Glenn Cunningham and Chuck Hornbostel competed. This was typical of track and field during the decade. Personalities and rivalries sold tickets. For outdoor meets, sprinting events were the most popular, and if Jesse Owens, Thomas "Eddie" Tolan, or Ralph Metcalfe were entered, spectator interest was usually high. Indoor, the mile was usually the feature event. In the early 1930s the quest for the 4-minute mile, featuring the magic names of Glenn Cunningham, Bill Bonthron, Gene Venzke, and Jack Lovelock, ensured large crowds. The 1934 Milrose Games in New York, for example, attracted 16,500 fans to watch an assault on the "four-flat."

The Olympics provided the biggest boost for track and field. The publicity surrounding these games catapulted the most successful athletes into immediate fame, if only fleetingly, and the sport benefited as a result. During non-Olympic years, track and field suffered financially as it struggled to compete with football and baseball. In a typical example, the University of Michigan track and field team earned $980 for the school in 1938, but cost $12,765.

Although some companies sponsored track teams and such ethnic groups as Germans and Scots formed their own clubs, high schools, universities and colleges dominated men's track and field. A 1938 study of interscholastic boys' programs discovered that 130 of 170 urban schools provided interscholastic competition in track for the 12th grade. Only basketball and football, with 133 schools each, were more popular. Stanford and the University of Southern California dominated track and field.

Ontario, especially Hamilton, was the center of track and field in Canada and the supplier of the largest number of Olympic athletes. Similar to the US, interest in track in Canada declined in the last half of the decade and the athletes had few meets in which to compete. Unlike colleges in the US, Canadian universities produced almost no nationally-ranked track and field athletes. The best Canadians often went to American colleges with their better facilities and more specialized coaching. Athletes that remained in Canada, trained with organizations such as the Toronto Achilles Club or the Monarch Athletic Club in Toronto, the Montreal Mercury Athletic Club, police athletic associations, and Scottish track and field societies. In 1933, more than 12,000 spectators attended the annual track and field games of the Manitoba Scottish Athletic Association. At the beginning of the decade, Percy Williams set a world record in the

100-meters at 10.3 seconds. Phil Edwards, a Canadian via British Guiana, represented Canada in three Olympics. In 1932 and 1936, he finished third in the 800 meters, and third and fifth, respectively, in the 1500-meter race.

Encouraged by two Olympic games, North American athletes set new standards in almost every event. Of the twenty-four metric and non-metric world records set in the previous decade, all but four were broken by 1936. To some writers, these new world records provided evidence that the "race" was advancing rather than deteriorating. Improved technology, better coaching, and more competition were the main factors. Beginning in 1935, hurdlers jumped over an L-shaped hurdle with weights at the base—rather than over an inverted T. Since runners who knocked over three or more hurdles in a race were disqualified, the L-shaped hurdle lowered times. Pole vaulters used lighter and more flexible bamboo poles, runners benefited from starting blocks and better tracks, high jumpers now twisted their bodies and rolled over the bar. The physics department at Haverford College designed a new system for timing races in 1930 "that eliminated the human element" and was accurate to 0.01 seconds. Unlike earlier versions, the light beam at the finish line could be activated only by the runner's chest. In another advance, cameras took 100 exposures a second and every one-hundredth picture was stamped with the time to a fraction of a second.

When a discussion of records arose, few sportswriters failed to note that black athletes ruled the sprinting and jumping events. The domination of short races began in the 1932 Olympics with Thomas "Eddie" Tolan and Ralph Metcalfe. Tolan's 10.3 for the 100-meter sprint set a world record. He followed this with an Olympic best in the 200-meter. The later successes of Jesse Owens, Ed Gordon, Eulace Peacock, and Ben Johnson promulgated the notion that blacks were biologically suited to these sports. Educational and social science journals published the results of anthropometric studies that equated racial origin with muscle length, arm size, tendons, joints, head shape, and neurological responses—anything that might explain why blacks jumped higher and ran faster than whites. The general conclusion was that blacks' success was due to either a longer heel bone or stronger achilles tendons. Race rather than skill became the explanatory factor.

At the intercollegiate championship in May 1935, Jesse Owens exploded into public prominence by setting world records in the 220-yard race, the 220 low hurdles and the long jump, and tying the record for the 100-yard dash. Several days later, after reporting on Owen's record-breaking victories, the New York Times noted "A theory has been advanced that through some physical characteristic of the race involving the bone and muscle construction of the foot and leg the Negro is ideally adapted to the sprints and jumping events." The Times presented no alternate theory. A lengthy article in Harper's Monthly Magazine the following year hypothesized that "Possibly Negroes are especially well fitted emotionally for the sort of brief, terrific effort which sprints and jumps require." At decade's end, Eleanor Metheny, noted physical educator at State University of Iowa, took anthropometric measurements of 102 black and white students. She concluded that there was a statistically significant difference in bodily proportions and hypothesized that blacks' longer legs, forearms and hands, and narrower hips would make them better sprinters and jumpers; but that their smaller breathing capacity would prevent them from doing well at longer distances.

Not everyone accepted such findings. Sportswriter Westbrook Pegler wrote in 1935 "It is a doubtful compliment to a Negro athlete...to attempt to account for his proficiency on the field by suggesting that he is still so close to the primitive that whenever he runs a foot-race...his civilization vanishes and he becomes again for the moment an African savage in breechcloth and nosering legging it through the jungle to keep ahead of a charging rhino." In the document "Why Blacks Run Fast," black physical anthropologist from Howard University, W. Montague Cobb, provides a reasoned argument on behalf of environment over race.

Native Americans faced similar prejudices. Ellison Myers Brown, a Narragansett Native of Rhode Island, was a marathon runner. The press invariably referred to him as "mahogany-hued," "dark-skinned warrior," or "Redskin," and depicted Brown as being a typically undisciplined, uneducated, child of nature. He would "much rather learn to keep a good line of traps than explore the alphabet," declared the Boston Daily Globe. Whether Brown won or lost, the press attributed it to his heritage. Sportswriters expected a Native to run, and as a result, Brown received no credit for his hard work and courage. These stereotypes were reinforced by Brown's family and supporters who beat tom-toms and wore headdresses at the Boston Marathon.

The best black male athletes attended white colleges in the north and west, which had much better programs than the black colleges in the South. Jesse Owens, for example, enrolled at Ohio State University where he participated in dual, conference, NCAA, AAU, and Intercollegiate Amateur Athletic Association meets. As other blacks, Owens was barred from on-campus housing, could attend only one theater in town, and could not eat at a university restaurant.

Black females, by contrast, mostly raced out of clubs and segregated high schools and colleges. Tuskegee Institute in Alabama led the way. Under athletic director Cleveland Abbott, Tuskegee formed a women's track team in 1929 and added women's events to its famous Tuskegee Relays—the first major track meet sponsored by a black college. Soon, several other black colleges added women's track and field. In 1936, the Tuskegee team finished second at the National Amateur Athletic Union Track and Field Championships. When Tuskegee won the title the next year, it was the first time a black team of either gender captured a national championship. Since the AAU sponsored white-only meets where Southern laws permitted, most black colleges had only three major meets a year.

Unlike black sportswomen who generally received encouragement from their communities, white females were driven from track and field by media criticisms and female physical educators. The 1928 Olympics provided ammunition for those opposed to women participating in highly competitive athletics. In the women's 800-meter event, five contestants did not finish, five collapsed upon completing the race, and the remaining runner fainted in the dressing room. Sportswriter John Tunis called them the "eleven wretched women." The Women's Division of the National Amateur Athletic Federation seized this opportunity to petition for the removal of all women's events from subsequent Olympics. In a compromise, the IOC eliminated the 800-meters and added the women's javelin and 80-meter hurdles.

In 1931, the Women's Division of the National Amateur Athletic Federation declared one of its aims was to "Promote competition that stresses enjoyment of sport and the development of good sportsmanship and character rather than those types that emphasize the making and breaking of records and the winning of championships for the enjoyment of spectators or for the athletic reputation or commercial advantage of institutions and organizations." For them, track and field symbolized the evils of athletics in which only a few gained prominence. It subjected women to debilitating physical and emotional stress, which led to serious injuries and difficult pregnancies.

Track and field presented a masculine image of power, strength and speed, and women educators feared such sports would develop masculine physiques and behavior traits. Many male sportswriters wanted female athletes to exude beauty and femininity, rather than strength and power. Sportswriter Paul Gallico wrote in The Reader's Digest (15 June 1936) "Females who don track shorts and jerseys and run and jump in track meets are just wasting their time...they carry too much weight from the waist up unless they are built like boys (in which case this doesn't count, because they aren't ladies); and finally they ought to get a look at their faces as they break the tape at the finish of the 100-yard dash, twisted and contorted and pitted with the gray lines of exhaustion." Canadians agreed. Writer Elmer Ferguson wrote in Maclean's (1 August 1938) "I can't go for those violent, face-straining, face-dirtying, body-bouncing, sweaty, graceless, stumbling, struggling, wrenching, racking, jarring and floundering events that some girls see fit to indulge in. Sorry again, but I like grace, sweetness, rhythm, freedom from sweat and freedom from grime among the girls."

The exploits of Mildred "Babe" Didrikson briefly revived enthusiasm in women's track. Between 1930 and 1932, Didrikson broke American, Olympic, or world records in five different track and field events and led her basketball team to the AAU national championship. She swam close to world record times in short distances, bowled 170, and later was the best female golfer. After winning two gold and one silver medal in the 1932 Olympics, a reporter asked Didrikson, "I'm told you also swim, shoot, ride, row, and box, and play tennis, golf, basketball, football, polo and billiards. Is there anything at all you don't play?" "Yeah," she replied, "dolls."

Unfortunately, the Babe's arrogant and blunt manner, and her rejection of conventional femininity such as dresses and dolls, made her an easy target of those who wanted to abolish women's competitive sports. Paul Gallico described her as a "muscle moll," and people questioned her estrogen level. This is what track did to women, it made them mannish. The final document in this chapter provides a typical illustration of early public reaction to Didrikson's successes.

Interest in women's track declined during the 1930s, especially after the 1932 Olympics. Of the twenty-nine AAU districts in 1934, only eleven held track championships, and the following year the national championships attracted a mere several hundred spectators. The 1937 indoor national meet was cancelled for lack of sponsors. A survey of seventy-nine female high school and college physical educators in 1938 concluded that schools around the country placed track and field at the bottom of their priorities and generally included them only as electives. Major Canadian newspapers devoted only fifteen percent of their coverage of track and field to female athletes.

North Americans generally did poorly in long-distance events. In fact, at mid-decade, undergraduates at Yale, Harvard, Princeton, Cornell and several other universities successfully petitioned for shorter races. Some squads refused to practice until the coach agreed to limit the distance they ran in practice. The premier distance event was the Boston Marathon. Each year as many as half a million spectators lined the route to cheer their favorites. Many came to gamble on the number of the winning runner. The number of marathoners generally was about 200. These were people who ignored

popular belief that marathoners died young. Many of them were also unemployed or
worked during the day and trained in the dark. Dave Komonen, a recent immigrant
from Finland to Canada, was named Canadian male athlete of the year in 1933 but was
unable to find work. The next year, Komonen moved to Sudbury and worked as a
carpenter in the mines until 8 P.M. each night. He captured the 1934 Boston Marathon.
Paul deBruyn, a German immigrant to the United States who spent his evenings shov-
elling coal into furnaces, won the 1932 marathon. Walter Young of Verdun, Quebec,
was living on welfare when he captured the 1937 Boston Marathon. Verdun rewarded
Young's efforts by making him a city policeman. Canadians from Ontario, Quebec, and
Nova Scotia did well at Boston. On average, about five Canadians finished among the
fastest twenty marathoners.

Better shoes made long distance running easier. In the previous decade, runners
wore stiff, heavy, leather-soled shoes. Canvas sneakers with dense rubber soles and
heavy stitching were also popular. This footwear chafed the skin and caused blisters,
bunions, and bruises. Some runners toughened their feet by walking barefoot on
beaches. Samuel T.A. Ritchins of Boston aided runners by designing a custom-made
shoe that included a metatarsal pad, side perforations for ventilation, outside laces to
avoid chafing, tanned calfskin, and crepe rubber soles. Ritchins' shoes weighed only
five and a half ounces and were colored white to reflect the heat.

## JESSE OWENS

[*The Literary Digest reported extensively on track and field. The following article is
representative of the emphasis on track personalities in American magazines. "Two
Men and a Track-Meet. Whatever the Outcome of the Big Ten Championships, Jesse
Owens of Ohio State and Willis Ward of Michigan—Both Negroes—Are Expected to
Monopolize Attention of Spectators," The Literary Digest (25 May 1935).*]

Most important of Mid-Western outdoor college track-meets, this year's Big Ten
Championships (Ann Arbor, Michigan, May 24-25) are narrowed by experts to two
teams: Ohio State and Michigan. Chief reasons for the prophecy are two Negroes: Jesse
Owens of Ohio State, and Willis Ward of Michigan.

Born on his father's farm in Danville, Alabama, on September 12, 1914, Owens—
one of seven children—went to Cleveland with his family when he was four. Playing
tag in front of Fairmount Junior High School, Owens impressed an onlooker with his
speed in eluding "it." The onlooker was Charles Riley, track-coach of the school.

Riley asked young Jesse why he didn't go out for track. After a long argument, the
Negro, with legs developed beyond his years, agreed to report. His sensational track
and field career started soon after the game of tag, and Owens never has forgotten
Riley, to whom he sent his first watch won in intercollegiate competition this year.

### CERAMICS AND TRACK

Owens still holds three national scholastic and three State records set as a schoolboy. After he did the century in 9.4, alumni of twenty-eight colleges and universities
tried to convince him that his future career lay with their alma maters. He entered Ohio
State, and, as a sophomore—his first year as an intercollegiate competitor—he has

taken part in nine intercollegiate meets, scored 115 individual points, twenty-one firsts, two seconds, and two thirds.

A thorough gentleman, Owens is a good student. His chief academic interest is ceramics, and he plans to teach in a negro college after taking his degree.

Owens worked his way through college his freshman year by pumping gas at a filling-station. Last fall, a negro representative in the Ohio House got Jesse a job as a page-boy. His most embarrassing moment came when he was called to the Speaker's rostrum while a resolution was read praising his achievements. Jesse blushed, fumbled with his tie; representatives and fellow-pages roared and applauded.

Like Joe Louis, the negro boxer from Detroit who fights Primo Carnera next month in New York, Owens helps support his family: each week he sends part of his salary to his folks in Cleveland.

Negroes have monopolized the sprint-events on American tracks in recent years. Anthropologists forward the theory that their superior feet and legs are the reason. In any event, Owens is superior.

Larry Snyder, his coach, thinks he can do twenty-seven feet in the broad-jump. He was seven inches back of the take-off board when he cleared 26-1 3/4 at the recent Drake Relays.

Entered in the 100, 220, and broad-jump events at Ann Arbor, Owens attracted most attention this year at two meets: the National A.A.U. indoor championships in New York, when he lowered the world sixty-meter record of 6.6 then leaped to a new world indoor broad-jump record of twenty-five feet nine inches at the same meet; at the Drake Relays he set a new American broad-jump record of twenty-six feet one and three-quarter inches. The world record, held by Chuhei Nambu of Japan, is twenty-six feet two and one eighth inches.

**FASTEST HUMAN**

Other noteworthy performances: tied the world record for the sixty-yard dash at the Big Ten indoor meet at Chicago this year in 6.1; tied his own world record for sixty yards at the Butler Relays in Indianapolis; did the hundred-yard dash from a flying start in an unofficial trial in 8.4 on April 23, 1935, at Columbus, Ohio, the fastest time ever recorded for that distance by a human traveling under his own power.

Star of the Michigan-Ohio dual meet held at Ann Arbor earlier this month, Owens took four of Ohio's seven first places, winning both dashes and the low hurdles and broad-jump. Ward did not compete for Michigan in that meet.

Willis Ward, Michigan's 196-pound all-round athlete, is entered in the century, the high-jump, the broad-jump, and the high-hurdles in the Big Ten meet. A one-man team in himself, he is a crack sprinter and hurdler, and a good field-event man in addition to playing end on the football-team.

Before the Big Ten outdoor meet of this week-end, the best performances scored by these two Negroes in the events they are scheduled for were: 100 yards: Owens, 9.4, Ward, 9.6; broad-jump: Owens, 25 feet, 9 inches; Ward, 24 feet, 2 inches.

No loafer on the track, Ward isn't too prompt in social engagements. Some time ago his fellow-townsmen of Saginaw, Michigan, invited him to a huge banquet in his honor. Ward showed up twenty-four hours late.

**DRAWING THE COLOR-LINE**

The color-line is drawn more sharply in football than in track. Last fall, 1,500 students and faculty members at Michigan signed a petition urging that Michigan's crack end be put into the game against Georgia Tech. Authorities ignored the petition, and substitutes for both teams were sent in. A substitute made the error that contributed to a Michigan victory.

Ward was breathing over the shoulder of George Anderson of California at the finish of the century in the Coast last month. But he tied for first in the high-jump (his record is six feet seven inches) at Berkeley, and won the 120-yard high hurdles, and, also the broad-jump, in the same meet.

Enjoying the services of Owens for the first time this year, Ohio State never has won the Big Ten Championships in track, won by Illinois last year. The Big Ten meet, held without interruption since 1901, has been won thirteen times by Michigan, twelve by Illinois, three times by Chicago, and three times by Wisconsin.

Non-members of the Conference, California has won once, Stanford once (with Notre Dame) and Missouri once. From 1907 to 1917, Michigan altho a leader in the records of winning teams, was not a member.

Indiana finished second last year, largely through the efforts of Chuck Hornbostel, now at Harvard, and Ivan Fuqua.

## WHY BLACKS RUN FAST

[*Dean Cromwell, the head coach of the 1936 American Olympic team, wrote in 1941 that "the Negro excels in the events he does because he is closer to the primitive than the white man. It was not so long ago that his ability to sprint and jump was a life-and-death matter to him in the jungle. His muscles are pliable, and his easy-going disposition is a valuable aid to the mental and physical relaxation that a runner and jumper must have." At this time, "scientific" studies sought to identify racial anatomical features that brought athletic success. In 1926, the Anthropology and Psychology section of the National Research Council organized a "Committee on the Negro" to promote anthropological and psychological studies on the American Negro.*

*Cobb, an associate professor of anatomy at Howard University, examined Black athletes' accomplishments in the sprints, long jump, middle distance and field events and refuted claims that these victories were due to anatomical advantages due to race. W. Montague Cobb, "Race and Runners," The Journal of Health and Physical Education (January 1936), 3-7, 52-56.*]

As the physical anthropologist scans the fascinating panorama of contests in simultaneous progress at a great track meet like the Penn Relay Carnival, he becomes aware of an association between certain types of bodily build and special events. Conspicuous contrasts are the large, heavily muscled, occasionally paunchy athletes who put the shot and throw the hammer farthest, and the tall, lean young men who jump the highest. The leading high hurdlers are tall and the stellar distance men of medium to slender build. In the other running and field events distinctive types of bodily build are less apparent. Almost every variety of human form and style of performance competes successfully in the relay races which endlessly circle the track.

Since athletic accomplishment is jointly dependent upon physical constitution, technique, and the will to achieve, it is obvious that in a few specialized events a particular bodily build may confer advantages which cannot be overbalanced by any amount of training and determination on the part of the less gifted. In the shot put, great bodily weight is an advantage, increasing the impetus imparted to the shot; in the high jump it is a handicap, adding to the load which the muscles must lift from the ground. Similarity, it can be shown that tallness is of advantage to both weight man and high jumper.

Among the sprinters and broad jumpers a diversity of physical types is seen. It is apparent that here determination of the influence of bodily build on performance will be more difficult.

As the anthropologist surveys the striving field in the stadium, he sees nothing to suggest an association between race and competition in any particular event. He notices Negro youths in nearly every phase of competition. Their bodily build varies like that of other athletes. The weight men are big fellows, while those topping the bar are more sparely built. However, a number of recent comments in the press upon the current success of American Negro sprinters and broad jumpers have either directly ascribed this success to a longer heel bone or stronger tendon of Achilles than those of their white competitors, or implied that in some way it has been due to racial characteristics. The wide circulation which these suggestions have received warrants a careful appraisal of the facts.

**SPRINTERS AND BROAD JUMPERS**

In the 1932 Olympics two American Negroes, Eddie Tolan and Ralph Metcalfe, carried off top places in both the 100- and 200-meter dashes, Tolan setting new Olympic records in each event; and another Negro, Ed Gordon won the broad jump. Since the tenth Olympiad Negroes have continued to dominate the national field in the sprints and broad jump in the persons of Metcalfe, Jesse Owens, Eulace Peacock, and Ben Johnson.

[Deleted long list of the accomplishments of Metcalfe, Owens, Peacock, and Johnson in the sprints; and the successes of African-Americans in the broad jump, middle distance, and field events.] There is thus no running event and few field events to which Negroes have not contributed some outstanding performer and there is no indication of ineptitude in any event in which no champion has yet appeared. It is to be noted, however, that the sprint and broad jump champions have appeared in a rapid succession, culminating in the present group of contemporaneous performers. For this reason they have been especially conspicuous in the public eye. It is this prominence which has probably stimulated the notion that these stars might owe their success to some physical attributes peculiar to their race....

But let us look in other fields. There have been those who felt that continued European victories over Americans in the weight-lifting contests, despite the intensive advertising campaigns of American vendors of bar-bells and other muscle-building and allegedly masculinizing agents, indicated superior inherent European capacity in this line of endeavor. There are people who ask if the fact that professional boxing, once the Irishman's pride, now affords prominence to so many Hebrews, Italians, and Negroes, might not be due to changes in racial physique. Recently the authorities who elucidate the reasons for the meanderings of the Davis Cup have been quite busy....

**CHARACTERISTICS OF A SPRINTER**

Most sprinters can broad jump well. If they learn to leave the ground properly after a good run, their inertia will carry them a respectable distance. It used to be thought that participation in one event detracted from ability in the other, but Hubbard, Owens, and Peacock have helped usher this idea into discard. For convenience here, sprinters and broad jumpers are considered together.

It is obvious that superior sprinting and broad-jumping performances require a certain combination of physical proportions, physiological efficiency, and personality which are recognized by the track coach as natural capacity. By methods ably explained in a few manuals on the subject, the coach is able to impart training and technique which convert this potential capacity into the actual ability to perform.

The personal histories and constitutions of our sprinters have not yet been sufficiently analyzed for the formula for the perfect sprinter or jumper to be given. We are not able to say what measure of natural capacity is due to physical proportions, or to physiological efficiency or to forceful personality. Nor can we weight capacity and training scientifically. This does not mean that strongly biased opinions on the subject are non-existent. For instance, it has been said that superior sprinting and jumping ability must be a matter of nine-tenths capacity and one-tenth training because the Negro is not disposed to subject himself to rigorous training.

Despite the fact that adequate data are not available for scientific analysis of sprinting and jumping ability, many useful conclusions may be drawn from a common-sense approach to the problem. We know first of all that the physique, style of performance, and character of our champions have been highly variable.

**PHYSIQUE, STYLE OF PERFORMANCE, AND CHARACTER**

When the track coach arrays before his mind's eye the galaxy of stars who have done the hundred in 9.6 seconds or better, he notes no uniformity of physique, style of running, or temperament. This group includes the Negro constellation just discussed and Arthur Duffey, Jackson Sholz, Loren Murchison, Charles Paddock, Chester Bowman, Frank Hussey, Charles Borah, Claude Bracey, Emmett Toppino, George Simpson, James Owen, Robert Grieves, Frank Wykoff, Foy Draper, and George Anderson.

Some were tall (Anderson, Metcalfe, Peacock); more were short (Paddock, Tolan, Hubbard, Draper, Grieves, Toppino). Some were slender (Simpson, Anderson); others stocky (Drew, Metcalfe, Paddock, Bracey). Some were well proportioned like Owens, Grieves, and Anderson, but there were a few who could hardly have served as models for the Greeks.

For finer distinctions, data of desirable precision are not available but we can say from general inspection that there have been long-legged champions and short-legged ones; some with large calves and some with small. Record-breaking legs have had long Caucasoid calves like those of Paddock and short Negroid ones such as Tolan has.

In the matter of style, there have been fast starters like Hubbard and Simpson and slow ones like Paddock and Metcalfe. We have had "powerhouse" sprinters such as Metcalfe and smooth graceful flashes like Owens whose performances seem without effort. Most of the runners have been mouth breathers; Metcalfe is a nose breather. Owens follows no rule in breathing. The first fifty yards is the faster for some men, the last half the better for others. Paddock started fast, "died" in the middle, and swept to the finish with a final burst, using the orthodox "jump" finish very effectively. Some men use a long stride, others a short one, and so on.

In respect to temperament, again we find no homogeneity. Some maintained calm well before a big meet others tended to become extremely nervous and required careful handling to he sent off their marks in peak form. Some could ignore efforts by competitors or their sympathizers to gain psychologic advantage; others have been licked before starting a race. Some of rugged constitution could partake of a wide range of edibles and stand a long season, others had to diet carefully and could not long remain at peak. There have been champions of great courage who were undaunted by defeat or misfortune and others who reacted very severely to "bad breaks." [The section on training and incentive has been deleted.]

### ANTHROPOLOGICAL CHARACTERISTICS

We have seen that the variability of the physical, physiological, and personality traits of great sprinters and jumpers, and inadequate scientific data prevent a satisfactory statement as to just what traits are responsible for their success. We have seen also, the importance of training and incentive. Let us now go to the anthropologist. He has to deal with men categorically designated as American Negroes, but they do not look alike. Genetically we know they are not constituted alike. There is not one single physical feature, including skin color, which all of our Negro champions have in common which would identify them as Negroes.

From his photographs Howard Drew is usually taken for a white man by those not in the "know." Gourdin had dark straight hair, no distinctly Negroid features, and a light brown complexion. In a great metropolis he would undoubtedly be often considered a foreigner. Owens and Metcalfe are of rather intermediate physiognomy. Owens is light brown, lighter than Metcalfe. But Owens has somewhat frizzled hair while Metcalfe's is dark, smooth, and wavy. Hubbard, Tolan, Johnson, and Peacock are darker and more definitely Negroid than the others, but not one of them even could be considered a pure Negro according to Herskovits' recent definition.

Extending his view, the anthropologist fails to find racial homogeneity even among the white sprinters. We find blond Nordic and swarthy Mediterranean types and various mixtures. In fact if all our Negro and white champions were lined up indiscriminately for inspection, no one except those conditioned to American attitudes would suspect that race had anything whatever to do with the athletes' ability.

Our situation thus appears hopelessly complicated. Variability is so great in the pertinent characters of both sprinters and Negroes as special groups, that to ferret out and evaluate what the two have in common will be difficult if not impossible.

### TEST CHARACTERS

Another approach to the determination of the influence of race in the making of our Negro sprint champions is the comparison of selected Negroid characteristics which conceivably may affect running capacity, with the conditions found in our Negro stars.

The Negro is long of limb, that is, he has long legs and arms relative to the length of his trunk as compared with the white. In addition, the leg of the Negro is said to be long in proportion to his thigh. Possibly this might be of significance in broad jumping, as leaping animals such as the kangaroo have extremely long shins, and very short thighs. The belly of the calf muscle of the Negro is short and the tendon long, whereas in the white, the belly, which produces the prominence of the calf, is long and the tendon short. The size of the pelvis, which is small in the Negro, would also appear of little importance to the runner or jumper.

In one study it was found that the nerve fibers of the Negro are larger in cross section than those of the white. As with electric conductors, the larger the nerve the easier and quicker the passage of the impulse, so this finding would imply better muscular coordination in the Negro.

It would be desirable, of course, to have for comparison the dimensions of all our stellar athletes, Negro and white, but as such data are not available it will be of value to compare the results of an examination of one of the Negro stars with recognized standards. Accordingly, the following data on Jesse Owens are presented and discussed. [This has been deleted.]

## SUMMARY AND CONCLUSIONS

Since man has begun to measure the quality of high athletic performances with stop-watch and tape he has constantly improved. This has been due not to a betterment of human stock but to experience and better nurture.

No particular racial or national group has ever exercised a monopoly or supremacy in a particular kind of event. The popularity of different events with different groups of people has, and probably always will vary, though not necessarily in the same direction.

Negroes have been co-holders but until Owens not single holders of the world's records for the standard sprints. The split-second differences in the performances of the great Negro and white sprinters of past and present are insignificant from an anthropological standpoint. So are the differences in the achievements of the two races in the broad jump.

The physiques of champion Negro and white sprinters in general and of Jesse Owens in particular reveal nothing to indicate that Negroid physical characters are anatomically concerned with the present dominance of Negro athletes in national competition in the short dashes and the broad jump.

There is not a single physical characteristic which all the Negro stars in question have in common which would definitely identify them as Negroes.

Jesse Owens who has run faster and leaped farther than a human being has ever done before does not have what is considered the Negroid type of calf, foot, and heel bone.

Although the world mark for the broad jump has remained the property of Negro athletes for a surprisingly long period, it would seem that the technique of the jump is the only feature involved in the matter of supremacy, for Negro and white sprinters have demonstrated equal speed for the preliminary run.

Chuhei Nambu, the retiring world's champion broad jumper, belongs to a people with an anatomical build the opposite of the Negroid in pertinent features. The Japanese are short of stature, short of limb, long thighed, and short legged. If the view that racial anatomy was important in the Negroes' success were correct, these are just the specifications a jumper should not have. Hence we see no reason why the first man to jump twenty-seven feet should not be a white athlete or the first man to run the mile in four minutes a Negro.

## BABE DIDRIKSON

*[In 1930, the Dallas Employers' Casualty Company hired Mildred "Babe" Didrikson as a secretary so that she could play for its basketball team. When the company*

*organized a track team, Babe won two events at the 1930 AAU National Champion-*
*ships. Two years later, Didrikson entered the same competition, which also served as*
*the trials for the Olympics. In a space of three hours she won six gold medals and set*
*four world records. At the 1932 Olympics, in which she was permitted to enter only*
*three events, Didrikson won two gold and one silver medal. Following the Games, the*
*AAU disqualified her from future competitions because her picture had appeared in a*
*testimonial for Dodge cars which said, "One look at its trim beauty and you know it*
*has class." Although Didrikson claimed that she neither received money for the testi-*
*monial nor authorized it, the AAU responded that Babe would be reinstated only if she*
*proved her case by suing the advertisers for loss of her amateur standing.*

*The following article, which appeared under the category "Personal Glimpses,"*
*illustrates the early post-Olympics attitudes towards Didrikson and details her Olympic*
*experiences. "The World-Beating Girl Viking of Texas," The Literary Digest (27 Au-*
*gust 1932), 26-28.]*

T'was a lucky day for American athletics when Ole Didrikson and his better half
came over the Atlantic from rugged Norway.

Under the Texas sun they prospered and raised seven children. The sixth of these
was a slim, wiry lass with the blue fire of sea-king ancestors in her eyes and the ac-
tinic alchemy of American sunshine in her system.

The Viking capacity for berserk rage in battle filtered down to the Texas maid as
a disposition to attack the most prodigious feats with hot resolve and a soaring confidence in her own power of achievement.

Her name was Mildred, but she had another name—her mother vows it is not a
nickname—that made her a rival of one of the most famous and popular Americans of
history—Babe Ruth.

Yes, and Babe Didrikson, heroine of the Olympic Games, breaker of records, and
winner of championships in an amazing variety of strenuous athletic sports, threatens
to outdistance the home-run king as a figure of captivating interest to all the nations
of the world.

"Perhaps," suggests one of her home-town papers, the Dallas News, "she supplies
the proof that the comparatively recent turn of women to strenuous field sports is developing a new super-physique in womanhood, an unexpected outcome of suffragism
which goes in for sports as well as politics and threatens the old male supremacy even
in the mere routine of making a living."

Grantland Rice, after playing golf with her, a novice, and seeing her beat his own
score, proclaims her "without any question the athletic phenomenon of all time man
or woman."

The Dallas Journal, enumerating her home-town's reasons for honoring her, includes these items:

"Unofficially has equaled every Olympic record for women.

Winner single-handed of the National A.A.U. women's track and field meet in
Chicago July 16.

Twice given all-American honors as forward on Golden Cyclone Girl's basket-ball
team.

Holder of world's record for baseball throw.

Has approximately 100 medals won in individual competition.

Miss Didrikson herself is quoted: "I brought back eight first-place medals of gold and two second-place medals of silver, and a bronze medal for fourth place. I made eight world's records in the last month and I am terribly, terribly happy."

Babe Didrikson broke four world's records in Olympic track and field events. First, the javelin throw. Then two in the 80-meter hurdles—first she smashed the previous world's record and then in the finals she smashed her own. And her fourth was in the high jump, which, as we shall see, did not end as happily as most of her contests.

Sports authorities hail her as Marvelous Mildred, and "the one-girl track team."

One of the most recent bits of news about her is that she will compete in the women's national golf tourney this fall. During the Olympics she played her eleventh match. She was credited with 82 for eighteen holes, and with drives of 250 yards.

Run with us over the tale of her Olympian feats in the Olympics, where she was, as Westbrook Pegler wrote for Chicago Tribune Press Service, "of all the remarkable characters, the one of whom you undoubtedly will be hearing the most in time to come."

It was the first full day of competition, but already the thousands upon thousands who jammed Los Angeles's great Olympic stadium were groggy with the record-breaking spree. The spectators fall silent for a moment.

A leather-lunged announcer broke the hush. The name of Mildred Didrikson reverberated through the bowl.

A tall, powerful, graceful girl stept [sic] into the center of things, with a confident toss of her bobbed head. She held a javelin in her powerful hand. Babe, of Dallas, was ready for her first Olympic trial.

She took a running start to hurl the long, wooden, steel-tipped spear.

Then something happened she hadn't counted on. The javelin "slee-upped," to use the pronunciation with which Mr. Pegler credits her. It "slee-upped" out of her hand, and what a mighty "slee-upp" it was. That javelin just kept "slee-uppin" right along, and it didn't come down until it had traveled 143 feet and 4 inches.

The fans broke into a roar, writes Mr. Rice in one of his North American Newspaper Alliance accounts, the moment the javelin "struck and quivered in the green turf. The crowd knew a world record had been shattered without waiting for any announcer." The old record was 132 feet 7 7/8 inches.

The amazing feature of Babe's toss was that it was practically devoid of trajectory. According to Braven Dyer in the Los Angeles Times, "It might just as well have traveled ten feet more, but for the fact that she threw the wand much after the manner of a catcher pegging to second base. The heave had absolutely no elevation, and sailed practically in a straight line from the time it left Miss Didrikson's mighty right arm until it dug its way into the green turf on the Olympic Stadium."

Then, look at what Babe did in the eighty-meter hurdle trials.

"I'll smash this one, you see," Babe told her pals, continues Mr. Dyer.

"Bang! They were off. Miss Clark of South Africa led. Babe began to run a little faster. When they got to the fifth hurdle the Texas girl pulled up even with her rival. This wasn't enough for Babe. Not by a long shot. She didn't want to win—she wanted a world record. On she went, clipping the barriers with all the technique of an expert male. She hit the tape with all the fury of a Texas tornado. Her teammate, Miss Schaller, beat Miss Clark for second. And the time, of course, a new world record, 11.8 seconds. The old record was 12.2 seconds.

"Babe may lower the mark again in the finals. She'll probably be disappointed if she doesn't."

And as a matter of fact, that's just what she did, bringing it down to 11.7 seconds. Mr. Rice describes the whirlwind finish in a copyrighted North American Newspaper Alliance dispatch thus:

"She and Miss Hall came over the last hurdle side by side. Miss Hall had come along like a runaway kangaroo at the finish, and as the two struck the clay path together the startled Texan saw she was closer to defeat than she had ever been before. She had to call upon everything she had in those last ten yards to slip in front by less than the span of her hand. But the answer is that she was winner.

Not even the great Nurmi broke four world records in one Olympics. The Babe came here to run amuck and she is running two amucks."

It is sad to have to record that bad luck now overtook her. Entered in three events, she had set three championships as her goal. She had two of them. And now came the high jump as the final test. Damon Runyon in a copyrighted Universal Service dispatch tells how Babe fought it out with Jean Shiley.

"The bar is put at 5 feet 4 inches, and both Jean Shiley and Babe (Whattagal) Didrikson clear it at that height, while the mob yells. Miss Gisolf, of Holland, who set the old world's record at 5 feet 3 1/8 inches, goes out when the bar is at 5 feet 3 inches.

About this time, Jean Shiley hangs up a new world record in the women's high jump with the bar at 5 feet 5 1/2 inches. Miss Didrikson tries it at the same height, but knocks the bar down. She tackles it again, and this time clears the bar to fall in a heap in the sand patch on the other side.

The bar is raised to 5 feet 5 3/4 inches. Jean Shiley and "the redoubtable Babe" both miss their first attempt. Miss Shiley stands erect, stretches herself with her hands high above her head, starts a little run from a crouch, but fails again. So does the Texas wonder.

Jean Shiley misses her third and last attempt at the bar at 5 feet 5 3/4 inches, and the crowd groans as Miss Didrikson also knocks the bar off just as it looks as if she may get over successfully. The crowd likes the Texas girl and glories in her athletic feats. Now the pair, tied for first place, are to jump it off, each having one trial at 5 feet 5 3/4 inches.

Miss Shiley makes one of her poorest efforts of the day. Now comes the Texas girl. She clears the bar and is well over when the end of the horizontal drops from its support. It seems she hit it with one foot after she is over. The crowd groans in sympathy.

Now the horizontal bar is lowered half an inch and Miss Shiley goes over nicely, landing standing up. Miss Didrikson also clears it, to land in her usual sprawl.

The officials go into a huddle. It seems some one raises the point that Miss Didrikson does what they call "diving" in going over. The athlete's head is supposed to follow the other sections of the body over the bar.

The official argument is quite lengthy, and finally the decision goes against the Texas wildflower, altho she appears to be having her say to the judges. Miss Shiley is the winner. (But, according to the New York Times, Miss Didrikson will share in the record recognition.)

Is there anything in the athletic line that Miss Didrikson can't do? Enraptured sportswriters tell of her prowess in running, jumping, hurdling, shot-putting, discus, javelin, baseball, tennis, golf, hockey, boxing, wrestling, riding, polo, billiards, pool, skating, football, fencing, basket-ball, swimming, diving, shooting.

But Westbrook Pegler detected her in one failure—"at a ping-pong table on the veranda of the Brentwood Country Club after eighteen holes of golf. She was too enthusiastic for ping-pong, and couldn't keep the ball on the table." Reading on in this Chicago Tribune Press Service account, we find her playing a golf game. Mr. Pegler writes: "She showed up at the course looking much more feminine than she had seemed in her flannel track overalls at the Olympic Stadium, and as the round loafed along, the Babe belting long drives from most of the tees, but dubbing some of her iron shots, her personality became clearer. She hit a long one at the eighteenth, and turned around to say, 'Gee, I sure would like to learn to play this game.'

Before that, on one of the tees, a dozen players, caddies, including several girls, gathered around to watch the Babe hit. This was only the eleventh time she had played golf, but, as she says, she plays best at any game when she is under pressure. She whaled one. It flew straight from the club more than 200 yards, and they began comparing her with Helen Hicks."

Two years ago, Babe had "never competed in any athletic event." But one day, "in a sporting-goods store, shopping for a pair of gym shoes, she picked up a fifty-pound weight and did tricks with it. This caused talk, and was, she says, the first feat of her athletic career, as it brought her to the attention of one Melvin J. McCombs, the man who employs her. He had been an athlete himself, and now became her coach. Nobody else had anything to do with her athletic development. Several coaches have been admitting responsibility for this, lately, but the Babe disowns them all.

'Melvin J. McCombs was my only coach,' she said (according to Mr. Pegler). 'If there is any credit in that, he is entitled to it.'

"Can you sew?"

"You think you're foolin'?" the Babe said. "Yes, I can sew. I sewed me a dress with seven box pleats at the front and some more in back—a sport dress it was—that won the first prize in the Texas State Fair at Austin, last year."

"Cook?"

"Cook some," she said. "Like gettin' dinner if I have to, and such cookin'. But I'm better at washin' dishes."

"Did you ever have any doubt of yourself in anything you try?"

"No, I generally know what I can do. I don't seem ever to get tired. Sleepy, but not dog-tired. I sleep more than most people."

It is my purpose to suggest that Babe Didrikson is not the boastful party that she may have seemed to be from some of her isolated remarks about herself which have found their way into print during the Olympic Games. In Chicago, as a single-handed team, she won the women's A.A.U. championship, but when she alludes to that she is not a feminine Joie Ray bragging. You ask to know something about her. Instead of sucking her finger and simpering, she tells you how it is. That's fair.

As for instance, "Do you think you can dive?"

"I know I can dive. I can dive off that high tower. I am going to fancy-dive. I sure love to hit that water."

"Have you a lot of medals?"

"Yes, a lot, but the collection is spoiled now. That silver medal for the high jump spoiled it. All the rest were gold—firsts."

The Babe weighs about 120 pounds, and her athletic style generally resembles that of the good male athletes in all the sports which she had tried. She is lean and flat, with big arms and leg muscles, large hands, and the rather angular jaw which the magazine illustrators have established as the standard for cowboys.

This chin of the Babe's, the thin, set lips, the straight, sharp profile, the sallow suntan, undisguised by rouge, regarded in connection with her amazing athletic prowess, at first acquaintance are likely to do her no justice. But, the mouth can relax and the eyes smile, and the greatest girl athlete in the world just now, with a special liking for men's games, is as feminine as hairpins. She is a great competitor, come all of a sudden to prominence, who may yet add to her Olympic championships of the track and field and her sewing championship won in the Texas State Fair a title in the fancy dives and a national golf championship.

It's a mistake to think, however, that Mildred's talents are purely muscular, a mistake against which Muriel Babcock warns us in the Los Angeles Times. Take a tip from me, says Miss Babcock, continuing: "The Babe can sew, and cook a mean meal. In the wardrobe that she brought with her from Dallas is a blue crepe party dress which she made herself.

The week-end before she left Dallas for Chicago tryouts, "Mama" (Mrs. Ole Didrikson of Beaumont) came to town to help Babe get ready.As Babe told her sister, Mrs. C.F. Cole, Santa Monica:

"Ma thought I'd have to be sewed up and all my clothes mended. But I fooled her. Everything was all ready. We just visited."

Chapter 21

## TURF, HORSE RACING, EQUESTRIAN SPORTS

### THOROUGHBRED RACING

R.L. Speers, Canada's most successful horse breeder in the 1930s, liked to say that every man who had a bit of money should have a hobby and a worry—and he can have both if he owns a race horse. This was particularly true in the early years of the Depression, when purses declined precipitously (even stake races such as the Preakness fell by as much as fifty percent) and attendance plummeted. In the long run, the Depression helped horse racing, as many states legalized racing and pari-mutuel betting to pay for their growing tax burdens. By 1937, *Racing Manual* estimated that more than $450 million was invested in racetracks, the country's 11,000 thoroughbred horses were worth approximately $20 million, and its 400 breeding farms were valued at $100 million. With new tracks and races in Florida and California, the industry was able to rotate events so there was a horse race somewhere in the country virtually every weekday of the year. The total number of racing days increased from 1,599 in 1929 to 2,199 ten years later. During the same period, individual races grew from 11,133 to 16,967.

Thoroughbred racing survived the lean years of the early 1930s and by 1937 total purses surpassed previous highs. Purses and stakes declined from a total of $13,674,000 in 1930 to a low of $8,516,000 in 1933, before steadily increasing to $15,312,000 at the end of the decade. Thanks to the demands of tourism, the Florida land boom, and the interest of Hollywood celebrities such as Bing Crosby and Harry Warner, and wealthy scions of society such as the Widners and the Whitneys, new tracks emerged in Hialeah, Gulf Stream, Santa Anita, and elsewhere. For a $1.10 entrance fee, spectators benefited from new technology such as the totalizator, automatic starting gates, electric timers, and saliva and urine tests.

Kentucky was the breeding home of thoroughbreds, followed by Virginia, Maryland, New York, and California. The most important racing states were New York, Illinois, Kentucky, Maryland, and Florida. Here, a thriving circuit, which included Toronto and Montreal, rotated among spring, summer, and fall meetings. Perhaps the most exciting racing events were the triple crown wins by Gallant Fox (1930), Omaha (1935) and War Admiral (1937), and the 1938 match race between Seabiscuit and War Admiral that attracted a crowd of 40,000. Each year, the total number of horses raced increased—from 8,232 in 1929 to 12,804 ten years later.

The King's Plate, the oldest continuous horse race in North America, was the most important race in Canada. In 1938, the Plate was restricted to three- and four-year olds. The following year, it became a race for three-year-olds. In 1933, thoroughbred racing in Canada represented an investment of $40 million and employed approximately 1,000 full, and 2,000 part-time workers. Racing was popular in every province. Based on the frequency of newspaper coverage, horse racing ranked seventh in Vancouver, sixth in Halifax and Winnipeg, fifth in Montreal, and fourth in Toronto—where crowds of 10,000 to 25,000 regularly attended Saturday meetings.

Horse racing in Canada hit its nadir during the Depression. Several of the bigger stables folded, and betting and attendance figures dropped precipitously to pre-First World War numbers. As the document "Racing Needs a Surgeon" explains, stimulants, ringers, and other illegal practices dismayed the paying public, encouraged the larger Canadian stables to race their horses in the United States rather than in Canada, and discouraged Americans from sending their best horses to Canadian meets. In the West, R.L. Speers took advantage of this situation to create a racing empire. He gained control of the meets in Winnipeg, Regina, Saskatoon, Calgary, and Edmonton and supplied the tracks with horses from his own breeding farm in Manitoba. By mid-decade, Speers had replaced R.S. McLaughlin as Canada's largest breeder. An innovator, Speers initiated the *Red Book of Canadian Racing* in 1930 to keep an accurate and comprehensive record of the sport, introduced the daily double to North America in 1931, and installed the first closed automatic starting gate on the continent in 1939.

Horse racing was inextricably tied to gambling. At the beginning of the decade, pari-mutuel betting was legal only in Kentucky and Maryland, but the need for additional revenues to pay for mounting relief costs encouraged state legislatures to legalize on-track betting as an additional source of revenue. This issue provoked heated debates. Journals such as Good Housekeeping, Country Life, The Rotarian, The Nation, Esquire, and Time debated the merits of legalized gambling. Individuals who favored on-track betting argued it would provide needed tax revenues, perhaps $100 million a year, attract money into communities near racetracks, create jobs, and take gambling out of the back alleys and poolrooms and into the sunshine. Since people were going to gamble anyway, the state should benefit. Reflecting the anti-Puritan spirit that brought an end to prohibition, urban voters tended to favor on-track betting. Southern states argued that legalized gambling would promote tourism. Texas claimed that it would encourage county and state fairs. New Jersey said it would improve horse breeding, and

California maintained that gambling would encourage agriculture. Sometimes, underworld gamblers colluded with politicians. Santa Anita, Hialeah, and Belmont Park, for example, had friends in the state legislatures. Rockingham Park track, New Hampshire, employed thirty-two state legislators as well as the governor's brother.

Their opponents argued that legalized gambling would partner the state with the sordid sub-culture of touts, bookmakers, dope peddlers, and gangsters in their search for profits. Gambling hurt those who could least afford it, as well as their families, friends, and employers. According to Good Housekeeping, the manager of a department store claimed that, "A number of my employees have to be dismissed every racing season. They're forever running to the telephone, spending their time poring over form sheets, and worrying about their bets instead of keeping their minds on their jobs." "The very foundation of morality and the character of our people is being undermined by legalized, commercialized, and advertised gambling," claimed the Governor of Texas, James Allred, when he repealed racetrack gambling. "Within its shadow stalks every kind of racketeering.... Embezzlements, suicides, swindling and social disasters have followed in a dire chain of events." Other opponents drew pictures of shoeless children, starving families, bankrupt companies, and increased narcotic traffic.

Gradually, legalized betting spread. By 1936, twenty-six states permitted parimutuel betting and New York allowed bookmakers at the tracks. Total bets soared from $174 million in 1934 to an estimated $400 million in 1937. And this was only the legal betting. Illegal gambling on horse racing was estimated at $4 million daily. Bookmakers, protected by the local police, provided lower odds than did the tracks' parimutuel systems, but offered 40 to 70 races on which to wager, and sometimes granted credit to regular clients. These illegal "poolrooms," often run by professional gamblers and ex-bootleggers, relied heavily on the telephone for betting lines, wagers, and off-setting bets. Moe Annenberg, who held a virtual monopoly of the wire services, is the subject of the document, "The Annenberg Race Tip Empire."

**HARNESS RACING**

The Depression was particularly hard on harness racing. With only an eleven-week season, and small purses—in 1933, the top pacers won less than $5,000—only wealthy horse owners could afford to participate. An influx of young horsemen and women who were attracted by the opportunity harness racing afforded of driving their own sulkies kept the sport alive. Society scions such as Elbridge Gerry, Dunbar Bostwick, and E. Ronald Harriman also liked to drive. Because, among other factors, the victorious horse had to win two heats, harness racing did not benefit as much from legalized gambling as did thoroughbred racing. It was not until extended evening meetings under lights were adopted in 1940 that the sport began to prosper. The creation of the US Trotting Association in 1938 to regulate the sport also helped promote trotting.

Trotting tracks were located from New England to California. The former was the cradle of the sport. The best breeding regions were in Kentucky and southern Ohio. Races varied from small county fairs to the Grand Circuit with its premier event for three-year olds, the Hambletonian in Goshen, New York. Greyhound was the premier trotter of the era. He set world records at one, one and a half, and two miles, and won 32 of the 36 races he entered between 1934 and 1940.

## EQUESTRIAN SPORTS

In 1936, The Literary Digest wrote that, "officially marking the opening of the New York social season, and the ending of the horse show year, the riding and jumping events during the 7-day stand brought a capacity of starched shirt fronts and ermine wraps and over 450 horses from the United States, Canada, Chile, France, the Irish Free State, Great Britain, and Sweden." For the participants, horse shows were mostly non-commercial as prize money was extremely small. While there were horse shows in every state, the thirty-one events in New York made it the center of the sport. Dressage events in the US commenced with the 1932 Olympics. Horse jumping contests, especially the international military jumping contest, were the most popular events.

## RODEO

In 1935 a contemporary magazine wrote that Col. William Thomas Johnson was to the rodeo, what Ned King was to the National Horse Show, George Foly was to the Westminster Dog Show, and what Jack Curley was to professional wrestling. Thanks largely to William Johnson's promotional skills, rodeo prospered during the Depression. Although some marginal organizations failed, prize money continued to increase at most major rodeos. In 1935, the average cowboy earned approximately $2,000 a year, but by 1937, Time estimated that the thirty or so best cowboys made between $8,000 and $15,000 annually. As was the case elsewhere in society, cowgirls had less opportunity and earned less money. Some cowgirls, such as Tad Lucas and Vera McGinnis, enhanced their incomes through endorsements and movie roles. The 1936 rodeo in Madison Square Garden lasted nineteen days and attracted nearly a quarter of a million spectators. Crowds of 100,000 viewed rodeos in Cheyenne, Denver and elsewhere.

The formation of the Rodeo Association of America (RAA) in 1928 furnished the basis for the sport by providing a central organization, accurate record keeping, and comparable events across the country. To acquire the association's approval, a rodeo had to include bronco riding, steer bulldogging, and calf and steer roping. The RAA issued points to each winner, and at the end of the year it named the champion of each event. The cowboy with the most total points was declared the World's Champion Cowboy.

In 1931, W.T. Johnson assumed control of the prestigious Madison Square Garden rodeo and brought in record crowds. That same year, his rodeos in Boston and Chicago attracted larger crowds than any other sporting amusement and Johnson created a successful eastern rodeo circuit with additional stops in Detroit, Philadelphia, and Indianapolis. Each rodeo was stocked from his own ranch. In addition to Johnson's rodeos, and the RAA circuit in the west, there were numerous smaller rodeos in the southwest that were not affiliated with any organization. By the end of the decade, more than one hundred rodeos were held in the US.

The largest rodeo in Canada was the Calgary Stampede. When attendance declined each year from 258,500 in 1929 to 174,700 three years later, the directors of the Calgary Exhibition and Stampede took drastic measures. Admission prices were cut from 50 cents to 25 cents. First place prizes fell from approximately $175 to $125. Although some directors believed that this measure would discourage American cowboys from coming to Calgary, thirty-one of the 300 cowboys were Americans in 1933.

Some cowboys were so poor they accepted extra jobs tending to the livestock at the Stampede to pay their entry fees. Attendance began to rise in 1933. In that year, chuck wagon races became a regular feature. By the end of the decade, the Stampede attracted 240,000 spectators—in a city of but 85,000 citizens.

Following a successful strike by the cowboys for larger purses prior to the 1936 Boston Garden rodeo, Johnson sold his company, including 600 cattle and horses, and a staff of 150, to Everett Colburn and M.T. and W.J. Clemens for $150,000. The cowboys formed their own Cowboys Turtle Association.

As with Hollywood movies, rodeos afforded the audience a chance to escape from the real world for a few hours. Spectators were entertained by cowboy bands, basketball games on horseback, horseshoe pitching, fancy roping tricks, and beauty contests among the cowgirls. The press also noticed. Newsweek featured the rodeo in a 1933 edition, and Time followed two years later. The monthly cattleman's magazine Hoof and Horns (established in 1931) gradually progressed from listing upcoming rodeos to including RAA standings (1934) to becoming rodeo's official organ (1937). The bimonthly Western Horseman publicized California rodeos.

### POLO

Judging from the claims of some popular magazines, polo was positioned to become America's most popular sport. The Literary Digest compared polo to hockey on horseback and predicted that it would become the greatest spectacle in sport. Esquire stated that polo "will be the next great college sport." Accompanying this fanfare was the belief that polo had progressed from being a social function of the wealthy on Long Island to a sporting event of the masses. Polo, a few sportswriters claimed, "had gone democratic." In 1935, in what was termed "dollar democracy," the United States Polo Associations lowered gate fees for the U.S. Open from $11 to $1 and permitted anyone to attend.

At the international level, Mike Phipps, Thomas Hitchcock, Steward Iglehart, Winston Guest, and Eric Pedley helped the United States regularly defeat the less democratic British for the International Polo Challenge Cup.

Indoor polo also grew in popularity during these years. In 1934, sixty-three clubs in New York, New Jersey, Pennsylvania, Maryland, Ohio, Illinois, Connecticut, Massachusetts, Rhode Island and Canada competed against each other. Indoor polo teams played with three riders a side and used a small soccer-like ball. Indoor polo was also a college sport. From the initial group of Yale, Princeton, Harvard, West Point, and Pennsylvania Military College, which had their own riding rings, the number of college polo teams grew to twenty-seven by mid-decade, and the handicapping system for the national championship was discontinued in 1935. In many of these institutions offduty R.O.T.C. officers volunteered their services as polo coaches.

### RACING NEEDS A SURGEON

*[By 1930, the pari-mutuel system was already in use in France, England, Australia, Canada, South America, and Cuba. Under this method, all money bet on a specific race was pooled and after deducting a percentage for the state and the racetrack, the*

*remainder was divided among the winning bettors. Gamblers considered pari-mutuel betting the fairest and most honest system. The totalizator instantaneously transmitted every bet to a central office, added the bets on each horse, and then displayed the odds. Unlike in the US, racing was never prohibited in Canada and illegal betting did not reach the same proportions as it did south of the border. The first completely electrical totalizator was built in the US in 1927, but it was not until 1933 that it was used in America—at Arlington Park, Chicago. In this article, the author details the impact of the Depression on thoroughbred racing in Canada. Douglas Eppes, "Racing Needs a Surgeon," Maclean's Magazine (15 February 1937), 24, 36-37.]*

Wanted! A doctor, a surgeon preferably, to operate on the corpus of Canadian horse racing. He'd have to be exceptionally skillful with the knife; fearless, too, for the patient is in a bad way and all the reassuring bulletins broadcast by interested publicists will not soften the hard truth that his life cannot be prolonged without a major operation—perhaps several. Which may sound a bit sad to lovers of the Sport of Kings, but, alas, like many doleful things, is undeniably true.

How did the patient get into this distressing condition? Was it a sudden seizure, or was it caused by one of those insidious maladies that begin with a minor ailment and develop gradually into a highly critical, perhaps fatal, illness?

The latter diagnosis is nearer the mark, for, to exchange metaphors, Canadian racing has been steadily going downhill for several years and during the past year reached a new low level.

What other deduction can be drawn from the following facts?

That Canada's leading owner and thoroughbred breeder is offering his farm for sale, and intends to establish a new one in California, where he plans to race most of his stock in the future.

That several of our prominent owners are confining their turf interests to the United State during the summer months, when our own season should be at its height.

That the wholesale slashing of prize moneys or purses has caused keen dissatisfaction among horsemen, has virtually put an end to the old-time invasion of American owners, and made daily programs a carnival for the cheapest type of thoroughbreds.

That, day after day, the same low-grade horses gallop around the tracks, so that John Public no longer enquires about the form of a racer but now demands, "Whose turn is it?"

**CANADIAN OWNERS DRIVEN AWAY**

When it was announced that Harry C. Hatch, Toronto turfman, had decided to transfer his pretentious stable to California and race there, the announcement created quite a flutter in turf circles. For the Hatch name is a big one in Canadian racing. Some say the biggest. His Oxford-Cambridge hooped silks are known on every course in Canada and on many in the United States as well, but after this season they seldom will be seen in Canada, for Mr. Hatch has publicly stated that he cannot find races in this country suitable for his horses. In addition, there are other matters in connection with our racing which are said to have dissatisfied him.

Other outstanding turfmen who now race extensively across the border during the Canadian season are Edward Seagram and R.S. McLaughlin. Mr. Seagram's stable is small compared with those he campaigned with in recent memory, but it contains some first-class performers which very rarely have been afforded an opportunity to stretch their legs over their native tracks. Unless it be a two-year-old, one seldom sees a top notch McLaughlin racer from the close of the Woodbine spring meeting until it reopens in the fall, and here again the lack of opportunity for good horses is the reason.

The slender purses offered at most meetings have frightened away the best horses. Outside of the Ontario Jockey Club, an owner has to be satisfied to compete for offerings ranging from a low of $400 to a high of $800. The value of the purses at one meeting this summer averaged $500. Remember that second, third and sometimes fourth money is included in this sum, and it will readily be seen that the owner of the winning horse reaps no El Dorado. There are occasional handicaps in which purse values may run from $1,000 to $2,500, but such handicaps are rare.

Contrasting these pitiful offerings with the bountifully endowed purses distributed by tracks across the international boundary, it is no wonder that owners prefer to compete there. Still less wonder that good American horses remain in their own country. The inevitable result is that Canadian racing devotees must be satisfied with sport provided by inferior types, many of which never win from one season's end to another. And yet they are welcomed and catered to at the average Canadian meeting.

Who is to blame for introducing this amazing cavalcade of low-grade horses into the sport? Unquestionably, the track managements cannot escape their share of it, which is the major share. Racing with them is strictly a business though one may well except the Ontario jockey Club, which has tried its, utmost to keep it a sport and one doesn't operate a business for the purpose of losing money. Falling off in speculation and in attendance, as measured by the good old days when "the goose hung high," has caused a shrinkage in receipts, and though frantic efforts have been made by most track operators to entice the public into their grounds by newfangled forms of speculation, and the lowering of entrance fees and betting units, they haven't proved entirely successful.

**THE DOPING EVIL**

And so the horse breeders and owners, the backbone of the turf, have been made the goats. Purses have been cut here and there, and former rich stakes cancelled. These economical measures have helped out the track owners, but most decidedly not the horse owners, nor the public, which has learned the bitter lesson that cheap racing is dear racing, because it so often means entire absence of form standards.

George Hardy, prominent Toronto business executive, is president of the Canadian Thoroughbred Breeders' Association, a representative turf organization whose interests are easily identified by its name. He is a practical turfman, for he has owned, bred and raced horses over a lengthy period. Anything he has to say about turf matters is worth listening to, and to him this writer addressed the question: "What is wrong with our racing?"

"The public is not getting the protection to which it is entitled," was the ready response.

What did he mean by that? Mr. Hardy was asked. Whereupon he mentioned the doping of horses—a pernicious practice which, he stressed, is decidedly harmful to the breeding industry and equally hurtful to the pocketbooks of the racing public.

Why should it hurt the public? he was requested to explain. Because, he pointed out, it establishes a false and unreliable standard of form. Take, for example, a track where the management is zealous in enforcing the rule against the employment of noxious drugs to increase the speed of horses, and where, to use a turf phrase, "they have to run cold." Horse A beats horse B by perhaps five lengths at this course. That establishes horse A's superiority in the minds of the public. The scene shifts to another track, at which doping regulations are not so strictly enforced, and to the bewilderment of the fans, horse B now beats horse A. In the majority of cases, the answer is that horse B has been doped; that, unless he gets his "shot" he will not show his best efforts.

Mr. Hardy believed that the Government could quickly put an end to the doping evil on tracks if it adopted the same methods as it does when a drug addict is arrested and baled to court. In such cases, the source of supply is run down by the authorities. Why not, he asked, follow the same procedure in racing? Find out who is supplying noxious drugs to those offenders who have been banned by track officials for administering them to horses in their charge. The United States Federal Government had done that, he pointed out, and one well-known turfman had received a severe penitentiary term.

A word of explanation might here be interjected. At three tracks—those of the Ontario Jockey Club, the Hamilton Jockey Club and the Niagara Racing Association a saliva box is in service, and a member of the R.C.M.P. and a Government veterinarian are on hand to test the saliva of any racer which the stewards direct to undergo examination. Naturally this has reduced the doping evil on these tracks to a minimum. On other tracks there is no such test, although the stewards, if they so wish, can order the track Veterinarian to examine any horse suspected of having been stimulated. It may only be a coincidence, but records reveal that at those tracks where the saliva test is rigidly enforced, racing is decidedly more formful.

Mr. Hardy believed that the conduct of racing could he improved if more attention was paid to the selection of stewards and other important officials. That opinion seemed to be generally held by many owners whom this writer interviewed.

"Practical men are badly needed in the stewards stands," asserted one well-known horseman: "men who know and understand horses, who are able to handicap them, and who are thoroughly conversant with racing rules. We have too many dummy stewards in Canada and too many officials who shrink from responsibility. And the public knows it and comments on their weak handling of flagrant offenders against the racing code. How can any major sport flourish when its officials lack the confidence of its patrons?"

**CANADIAN SECRETARIES NEEDED**

There is another cause for grievance—the employment of foreign-born secretaries at many Canadian meetings. A racing secretary holds the key position. It is his duty to prepare what is known as the condition book—sometimes irreverently termed "the horseman's bible"—in which are listed the particulars for every contest to be decided at the meeting. Naturally the task requires a thorough knowledge of Canadian horses. Such knowledge is scarcely possessed by a nonresident of this country, who comes here for a brief period, and who by reason of his duties at American tracks often is compelled to frame his racing programs when not on the actual scene of operations. In other words, he has not the requisite information at hand regarding the equine material on which he must work. The result follows in the cancellation of races in the condition book.

Here indeed is a source of irritation to horse owners and public alike. Let us suppose that a track management has announced in its condition book that a $2,500 handicap will be decided on a certain day. On the eve of the race, however it learns that only four entries have been received, these representing the best horses at the meeting. In nine cases out of ten, the management will cancel the handicap race and substitute a cheaper contest. Which means that the good horses will remain in their stables while their more lowly brethren cavort around on the running strip.

Why was this handicap race cancelled? Because it would not evoke speculative interest, and track management are mainly dependent on their betting rake-off—five per cent on each dollar wagered—for their revenue. Small entry lists do not attract as much money into the pari-mutuels as larger ones. Hence, rather than incur a loss, the management calls off the race and substitutes a cheaper one. Naturally it benefits too by ways by purse reduction and increased wagering. Not so the horse owner or the public. The first loses a golden chance to compete for a well-filled purse—all too rare these days—while the public misses an opportunity of seeing good racers in spirited competition.

Then there's the vexatious "claiming" problem. Claiming races, it should be explained, are turf events in which a horse may be claimed from an owner for a sum specified in the conditions of the race. In principle, such races are excellent because they prevent a horseman from entering a racer worth, say, $3,000, in a contest in which $1,000 horses compete. But the trouble in Canada is that there are all too few events for the higher rated horse, with the result that the owner perforce has to enter the animal at a lower value, and generally loses him to some astute horseman. Incidentally, there are some owners who have built up their stables in this manner—a practice hotly resented by those horsemen who have been correspondingly despoiled. Here, the solution seems to be in the return to the old-time selling races which permitted an owner to buy his horse at an open track auction.

**THE REMEDY**

Racing in Ontario suffers from the fact that it is divided into two camps. Tracks under the jurisdiction of the Incorporated Canadian Racing Association are in one; those loosely termed "Independents" are in the other. It is unfortunate that the former body, generally known as the I.C.R.A., should be the weaker organization numerically, but as it licenses all trainers and jockeys, and has taken a leading part in stamping the pernicious practice of doping on its tracks, it can be regarded as the bulwark of the sport. At any rate, it is so regarded by racing patrons. But for reasons best known to themselves, the independent tracks resolutely remain outside its fold. Which is just one more reason why horsemen and lovers of racing are at one in their advocacy of a controlling body for the sport—not necessarily a commission—which is capable of blending all jockey clubs and turf associations in one harmonious whole.

With the creation of a controlling board, committee, or anything you like to term it, racing may creep out of its present slough of despond and regain its former proud place in the affections of its patrons. Certainly it could lose nothing by the appointment of a governing body composed of representatives of the tracks, prominent owner-breeders and a nominee of the Government, which, to revert to my early simile, could play the role of surgeon and remove the evils now inexorably strangling it.

And chief among the evils that require the skillful use of the surgeon's knife I number: The cluttering of our tracks with cheap, unsound horses; the practice of appointing "safe" but spineless racing officials; the purse-slashing methods now universally in vogue; the selection of foreign-born racing secretaries when competent Canadians are available; and the wishy-washy methods adopted by some managements in dealing with the greatest menace of all to clean racing—the administration of noxious drugs to thoroughbred horses.

### GAMBLING CZAR MOSES ANNENBERG

*[In the first segment of this expose (30 July 1938) the author noted that while the average bettor gambled only about $4 a day, close to $400 million was bet at American racetracks, and an additional $4 million a day changed hands illegally. Following the legalization of on-track betting, many tracks fell under the influence of criminal syndicates that viewed horse racing as an opportunity to earn profits, skim money, and launder ill-gotten earnings. M.L. Annenberg, the subject of the following article, created a communication empire of two major racing papers, the Daily Racing Form and the Morning Telegraph, along with various tip and scratch sheets. F.B. Warren, "The Annenberg Race Tip Empire," The Nation (6 August 1938), 123-126.]*

In my preceding article I described the workings of the poolroom betting game, a billion-dollar industry with more than a million steady participants and with roots sunk in hundreds of communities in every part of the United States. What integrates and makes possible this far-flung empire of profits? The answer lies for the most part in the services of one agency—an agency which, whatever the uses to which it is put, breaks no laws, is in itself completely legal. At its head is Moses L. Annenberg. He is the man who was far-sighted enough to make an arrangement with all the major tracks in the country whereby all their information service became the exclusive property of his racing-news distribution service. He is also the man who developed that mass of minutiae which is known as the "racing journal" and which is indispensable to poolroom betting.

Annenberg is both a man and a series of companies or corporations. His companies operate directly or by relays in all states of the Union. He is a quiet, soft-spoken man in his middle fifties, owner of the powerful Philadelphia Inquirer, a daily and Sunday newspaper, for which on August 1, 1936, he paid $15,000,000 in cash. It is the unit of his holdings in which Annenberg has made his largest single investment. Until November, 1937, he was owner of the Miami, Florida, daily and Sunday Tribune, for which he had but recently completed a new $300,000 plant equipped with more than $500,000 worth of new machinery and color presses. It had been reported for some time that he was interested in buying out his rival daily, the Miami Herald, for purposes of consolidation. Frustrated in this, he disposed of his Miami Tribune overnight to publishers from Akron, Ohio, for an undisclosed amount, apparently taking as partial consideration one of the Akron buyer's chain, the daily Independent, in Massillon, Ohio. Philadelphia and Massillon, therefore, are now the only two cities in which he operates the conventional type of daily newspaper. His magazines are the multi-colored Radio Guide, Screen Guide, Official Detective Stories, and Click—all produced in a Chicago plant. They have large circulations, and, as all but the last title indicate, are designed for specific reader-groups.

None of them, however, are an index of the Annenberg importance. None of them as yet have made any real contribution to the vast Annenberg fortune. That fortune stems largely from the publication of racing journals and the maintenance of a national leased wire service which furnishes information as to betting odds and pay-off prices, widely used by operators of poolrooms. Annenberg neither owns nor operates pool-rooms, but his publications and other services having to do with racing and betting are sold, licensed, and otherwise offered to poolrooms, making it possible for such places to operate more effectively; and for gathering, collating, and distributing such service the Annenberg ventures have reaped and continue to reap a fabulous income. This racing-publishing network has a multiplicity of remarkable functions and objectives.

First, there is the New York Morning Telegraph, a seven-day morning publication. Counting its various incarnations, it is more than 100 years old. The Annenberg-owned Telegraph of today, selling at a quarter a copy, prints twelve or more pages of complex, copyrighted racing charts, tipster and handicapper selections, and a scant two pages of news. Since all racing and gambling addicts may not be able to afford a 25-cent daily there is a skimpier 10-cent daily called the Racing Guide, which is issued from the Telegraph's plant. It contains an abridged type of chart, betting odds, and tipster selec-tions, but lacks the voluminous data on the "past performances" of the horses sched-uled to run. The player or bettor has to turn to other publications for that.

Racing Form is the major Annenberg track publication. It is not one newspaper; it is <u>seven</u>. In identical format, and without the aid of matrices or electrotypes supplied from any central source, it is produced in its entirety six days each week in six cities of the United States and one in Canada. New York, Chicago, Miami, Houston, Los Angeles, Seattle, and Toronto each has its own building, plant, mechanical and edito-rial equipment and personnel. At each point of publication the advertised price per copy is 25 cents, but at more distant points it sells often for as high as 50 cents per copy. So carefully is its distribution guarded and controlled that its retail outlets usually could sell a few more copies than are supplied. This has the effect of making the hydra-headed publication virtually a sell-out, which means immunity from the huge waste and loss which other publishers incur by the acceptance and crediting of returned unsold copies. The income of the seven-edition, seven-city Racing Form is such as to stir the dreams and whet the envy of the publishers of conventional newspapers. But their dreams are futile. They could not compete with the Annenberg chain singly or in coa-lition. It would cost millions, and they could not duplicate Annenberg's copyrighted charts. Usage over more than two decades has established the eye-acceptance as well as the content of Annenberg's charts, so that no other type of record could or would serve the racing addicts' requirements.

Paralleling the 25-cent Form in Chicago is the Annenberg-owned, pink-paper daily Chicago Telegraph at 10 cents a copy, similar to his Guide in Manhattan. In Los An-geles his local Telegraph at 10 cents a copy is the running mate of his 25-cent Form. Thus in three centers of mass population, Annenberg has discouraged competition by serving each grade or class of reader-addict.

Supplementing all of the dailies so far mentioned there is a large format six-day daily published in Cincinnati under the name Daily Racing Record. It is published by the Cecelia Company. This is the same company that on August 1, 1936, was revealed as the corporate structure through which Annenberg purchased the Philadelphia In-quirer. Included in this property are twelve daily publications advantageously spotted over the map to solve the problem of swift, effective, and timely distribution. These papers, or at least one unit thereof, reach every town or area where there are bettors patronizing local poolrooms in ample time to enrich the prospective player's track knowledge for the day and to give him tips, advice, handicaps, weights, and riders.

A substantial percentage of the poolrooms' habitual patrons are too poor to pay, or are simply averse to paying, for the Annenberg publications. This element expects the poolrooms to maintain a supply of these dailies for them just as saloons in the old days supplied free lunch to their "regulars." Therefore the poolroom operator must put in a supply of "house copies." Without them the volume of play in his poolroom might be reduced by as much as a third. The players who read these papers have several hours to study and absorb all the "dope" and reach decisions as to which tips to take.

There are millions of American men and women who have never seen a professional racing paper and to whom the textual and tabular content of such journals would be as unfathomable as are Babylonian or Chaldean hieroglyphs. The Racing Form, most representative of the Annenberg daily journals, is five columns wide, a bit larger than the conventional two-cent news tabloid. It averages from 28 to 40 pages, depending on the number of race tracks in operation on a given day. Its major front-page dispatches concern races that are being held on the date of issue, with less space devoted to those races that were run the preceding day. In a 28-page paper of 140 total columns such news content may occupy an aggregate of 12 to 16 columns, leaving the remaining 124 columns for tipster selections and charts.

These give the results of the previous day's races at all tracks, and then list for each race the entrants that will go to the post that day at every track throughout the nation. "Past performances" for all the horses in their last six to ten races follow, providing the bettors with a picture that is almost photographic as to the qualifications and achievements of every entrant. The addict learns from this for what distances his personally fancied contestant seems to run best, how well or how badly he performs under varying weights, what horses he has run in front of or behind in preceding races, what jockeys, good or bad, have ridden him, and whether they finished first, second, third, or eleventh. He reads what the track conditions were in past races—fast, dull, muddy, or heavy. He can determine thereby whether the animal is a good or indifferent runner on a muddy or dry track. He can see whether he is a quick or a slow starter, whether he is a good stretch runner and finisher, or tires and drops out of the running.

From the charts the bettor can tell where his horse was at every stage of the running in previous races. These positions are noted at the track, called and recorded by a crew of trained observers, and worked into the charts. Chief of the crew is the expert with field glasses who watches every phase of the running. As the barrier is sprung he calls to his sheet-writing clerk or aide which horses got away first, second, third, etc. He repeats this "call" at the various stages or fractional mile posts. From his post he cannot possibly identify all the horses running at the far side of the track by any physical characteristics or markings of the animals. He distinguishes each horse by the colors of the owning stable, which are worn by the jockey, and with lightning rapidity and uncanny memory converts a color into a name for his clerk. Of the current crop of such "Calling" experts, men like C.J. ("Chuck") Connors and Lincoln Plaut, to name but two of the Annenberg employees, and David Leighton, who performs a similar service at certain tracks for the Associated Press, rate among the miracle men of their craft. All important tracks today utilize one type or another of high-speed cameras with which the result at the finish line is photographed. This has not supplanted and will not supplant the professional "Caller." Racing patrons do not concede after several years of the use of cameras in recording finishes that they equal or excel the work of these living observers.

Thousands upon thousands of races run in America have been observed under field glass and "called" only by Annenberg experts. For twenty years his men have been making this highly technical and completely individualistic tabular record of races. Each chart is individually copyrighted, and violation of these copyrights is dangerous. If any rival printed a chart of a race showing horses exactly the same distance apart and running the same distances from each other at various stages of the race as an Annenberg chart, it could only be because the newcomer or his employees had filched the chart called and made by an Annenberg employee. No two pairs of human eyes could ever see a horse race with precisely the same distances between contenders.

Even this statistical material is not all there is to the racing paper. At every track trainers and owners hold early morning workouts of their horses. An effort is made always to cloak these workouts with as much secrecy as possible. An owner or trainer does not want the public to know that he has a particularly swift horse that has not yet proved itself in public tests; he may not want anyone to know that one of his proved horses that went stale is again rounding to top form. A surprise or unexpected win means a long price. An important person in the racing field is the "clocker," whose job it is to be present at any and all hours after daybreak, to sit at a point of vantage, split-second stopwatch in hand, and clock and record all workouts. His reports are dispatched by telegraph to the Annenberg base points and rewired over the leased network to all the chain's publications.

All of this informative material is compiled, grouped, and transmitted by telephonic and telegraphic circuits with amazing speed and accuracy between noon (Eastern Standard Time) and five or five-thirty (Pacific Coast Time) each afternoon so that the next day's racing journals may go to press by seven in the evening, be on the streets locally by eight, and rushed by motor trucks to railway stations and post offices for zonal distribution. Failure of these bundles to arrive in a major city such as Cleveland, Pittsburgh, or Kansas City is a calamitous event. Fortified with "the dope," the bettor possesses confidence; denied it, he is pitting ignorance against the minutely informed bookmaking brotherhood.

In no Annenberg-owned publication is any reference ever made to the leased-wire news and poolroom news transmission system embracing in different areas the General News Bureau in Chicago, Nationwide News Service, operated also from Chicago, but with important base and news-disseminating facilities in New York, and the Ohio Nationwide News Service, which supplies service to poolrooms and other outlets within that state and adjacent areas. Their activities are never the subject of publicity. The youngest member of the Annenberg wire-service family is a wired-radio organization known as Teleflash, and it is something of an exception on this score. It is liberally advertised in his New York Telegraph as a disseminator and distributor of sporting news and bulletins for restaurants, cafes, saloons, and even for private offices, homes, clubs, etc. The records of the New York Police Department show dozens of seizures of Teleflash machines and of their ultimate return to the telephone company from which the Annenberg interests lease or rent them. No records exist outside the

Teleflash organization to indicate how many of these instruments are in service in Greater New York. Apparently there are hundreds of them, but energetic police measures are now driving them out of barrooms.

The weekly rentals paid by bookmakers to Nationwide and Ohio Nationwide News Services reach an aggregate that would not be looked upon disdainfully by the Maharajahs of the richer native states of India. My own extended inquiries in all parts of the nation indicate service being supplied from these sources to more than 2,000 poolrooms at weekly fees running from $300 or $400 each to as high as $800. An average of $500 weekly per station for 2,000 such outlets would point to an annual income of more than $50,000,000. As I have indicated in my first article there are probably many more than 2,000 such outlets.

The Federal Communications Commission at a hearing on March 18, 1936, reached the point where it was ready to delve into the national dissemination of racing news by wire. It had before it a large number of informed persons, including officers, counsel, and the president of the American Telephone and Telegraph Company, Mr. Walter S. Gifford. Mr. T.G. Miller, a vice president of A.T.& T., testified that the company as of that date was serving two such horse-race services, "the Nationwide News Service and the Interstate News Service, the latter a subsidiary of the former." His evidence indicated that Interstate operated in twenty-three cities in six states, while Nationwide was then functioning in 200 cities in thirty-five states and three provinces of Canada. Mr. Miller testified that between April 1, 1931, and December 1, 1935, these and other sporting news services paid $2,841,071 for wire rentals and that "total revenues of the phone company from horse-racing services now run about $43,000 a month." Mr. Samuel Becker, counsel to the commission, produced records showing that Nationwide then had under lease "11 private long-distance lines, 13 telegraph sending machines, 151 receiving machines, 105 Morse terminals, and 58 telephones." He said, "Nationwide paid the A.T. & T. more than $555,000 for 1935." At no time in the course of the investigation was the telephone company held responsible for the use to which its equipment was put.

Statistics brought out in the investigation showed poolroom service supplied to more than 200 cities, but that means much more than merely 200 customers. A wire service to Fort Wayne, or Nashville, or New Orleans, or any city of more than 15,000 population is directed to a "terminal" where a local employee ties it in through local telephone connections to every account or customer in the community and possibly to outlying suburbs. Andrew W. Kavanaugh, Director of Public Safety for Miami, Florida, testified that his city had 200 poolrooms. This figure for a community of 150,000 normal population substantiates the professional estimates of 800 such places in Chicago, 350 in Kansas City, an equal number in New Orleans, and 1,200 in New York. Each point of "reception" means a weekly toll to the empire that gives to Moses Annenberg an income that would satisfy any captain of American industry.

## HARNESS RACING

*[In standardbred racing, "the only truly American sport," the average driver was more than 50 years old. In addition to the Grand Circuit and country fairs, standardbred*

*racing took place at several important chains of half-mile tracks in New England and Ohio. The Hambletonian was one of the few harness racing events to attract much newspaper coverage. In the mid-1930s, the 30,000 spectators who came to watch this meet included a mixture of millionaires, farmers, gamblers, society people and actors. The following article discusses the Grand Circuit, Hambletonian, and the differences between pacers and trotters. "Greyhound at Goshen. Harness Veterans Polish Up for Hambletonian," News-week (25 July 1938), 20.]*

The drowsy town of Goshen, N.Y., awakens twice a year—for each of its two trotting and pacing meets. The first was held last week at E. Roland Harriman's 1/2-mile Historic Track—oldest trotting layout in the United States. The second, featuring the classic Hambletonian, Aug. 10, will take place at William Cane's 1-mile Good Time Park from Aug. 8-13.

Goshen's opening meet drew society folk and harness-racing followers from all over the country. For in addition to the regular races, Greyhound, the world's foremost trotting horse, was an added attraction.

Driven by Sep Palin and paced by two galloping horses who also pulled sulkies, the sleek 6-year-old made a heroic effort to improve on his own mile record for a two-lap course, 1:59 3/4. A gusty wind and the hard sun-baked clay track slowed Greyhound to 2:01. But he ran his customary stylish race, with a strong finish, and unquestionably proved himself still the "King of Trotters."

A year ago, in Lexington, Ky., he romped around a 1-mile track in 1:56—fastest time ever achieved by a trotter. A fortnight ago in Cleveland, Greyhound sprinted the final quarter in 0:26 4/5—a new record. Besides these marks he holds a dozen others at various distances.

Practically everyone who has visited the silvery-coated horse in his stall roots for him. His personal appeal is magnetic—a face radiating intelligence, quiet friendly manners. The only time he forgets his good horse sense is when he sees a cigarette. Given an opportunity, he'll snatch one right out of your hand; he prefers them to carrots. Always around to see that he doesn't is the 60-year-old Palin who has nursed Greyhound from colthood.

Greyhound is owned by E.J. Baker who seldom sees the champion trot; he stays home in St. Charles, Ill., and gets satisfaction out of reading the horse's press notices. Unlike many pampered champions, Greyhound has no private van in which to tour the country. He goes along just like one of the mob—fourteen horses to a freight car.

The freak of the Goshen meet was 70-year-old Pat O'Connell, a bricklayer who works all winter to feed Kelly, his only horse. Since 1925 Pat has been driving in hard luck and he swore not to shave until he won a race. Twice last week Kelly stepped home in front, but the Irish veteran hesitated to part with his bushy growth; it gained him more publicity than he'd ever received before.

**Coming Events.** Last week's meeting at Goshen was the third stop of the touring tribe of harness devotees who move annually over an itinerary called the Grand Circuit. First it was Toledo, then Cleveland. After Goshen comes Old Orchard, Maine; Agawam Park, Mass.; a return trip to Goshen for the classic Hambletonian; Springfield, Ill.; Syracuse, N.Y.; Indianapolis, Ind.; Reading, Pa.; and then finally the windup at Lexington, Ky., Sept. 24-Oct.1.

## BREEDING

By nature all horses are gallopers. The trotting and pacing gaits are generally believed to have originated in England. In the eighteenth century, methodical British farmers wearied of bumping over rough winter roads. In place of the gallop, they experimented with a quick walk. But it wasn't fast enough. Out of this grew the new gaits; but only a few horses were willing pupils.

The ancestor of all harness horses was Imported Messenger, a high-ranking English flat-racing stallion of the late 1700s. In one of his descendants, an American-born horse named Hambletonian 10, breeders discovered a sire whose colts could readily be coaxed to trot or pace. After siring 1,288 foals, he died in 1876 and now lies buried in Chester, N.Y.—a 4-mile trot from Goshen's race tracks.

Hambletonian's blood runs in the veins of every harness racer on American turf. Most of the present-day champions are bred on one of the three leading farms: Dr. Ogden M. Edward's Walnut Hall in Donerail, Ky.; Lawrence B. Sheppard's Hanover Shoe Farms in Hanover, Pa.; and Gage B. Ellis' Village Farm, Langhorne, Pa.

The layman often confuses trotting and pacing—and with good reason. Both are carelessly referred to by harness racing men as trotting. A true trotter steps with his right front foot and his left rear foot simultaneously, then with his left front foot and right rear foot. A pacer's right front leg and right rear leg are hobbled with a stiff brace so that he steps with both together. Likewise his two left legs, fore and aft, move as a unit.

About 60 per cent of the events held in this country are trotting races; and 40 per cent are for pacers. Since a hobbled pacer has less chance of recovering if he stumbles, this dangerous type of racing is losing favor with the drivers.

On the whole, the pacing gait is believed to be slightly faster. Dan Patch, champion pacer around the turn of the century, ran a mile in 1:55 1/4—a mark still beyond Greyhound's reach.

No harness horse can compare in speed with a running horse. In setting his record of 1:34 2/5, Equipoise would have led Greyhound by approximately a furlong. But the speed of harness racers is constantly improving, whereas runners seem to find progress more difficult.

In the last 50 years the galloping horse has clipped only 5 1/2 seconds off the mile record, while trotters have reduced their best speed over twelve seconds. The introduction of the bike wheel in place of the sulky's old-fashioned high wheel in 1892 accounted for only two seconds of the improvement.

Once the stepchild of the turf, harness racing is growing steadily. In the United States last year, events took place on 800 tracks and purses were increased $100,000 to $3,000,000. But it's far from a get-rich quick pastime. Operation of a trotting stable is estimated to cost 50 per cent more than flat racing because the expenses are greater and the individual prizes are small.

Perhaps that's why the gangster element shows little interest in the sulky game. No chance for big profits and no jockeys to fix. The favorite usually wins. Trotting and pacing appeal more to people with an excess supply of money and a genuine fondness for untainted sport. Owners, some of them are society women, frequently train their horses and race them as well. The charge of a prearranged trotting or pacing match is unheard of.

## THE NATIONAL HORSE SHOW

[*Box office receipts for the 1931 horse show in Manhattan totaled more than $70,000. Major horse shows also took place in Boston and Toronto. California, New Jersey, Maryland, Pennsylvania, Virginia and Connecticut were additional popular sites. The following article discusses the sport's finances and its attempts to attract crowds based on exciting events rather than on viewing members of high society. "The National Horse Show," Fortune (November 1932), 26-30.*]

For the seven days commencing November 9, the National Horse Show Association will pay the Madison Square Garden Corporation in New York between $25,000 and $30,000 for rent. The exact amount is a family secret, a matter of individual bargaining that varies from year to year. Additional expenses, totaling some $100,000, will include such major items as $40,000 in cash prizes, a $12,600 payroll, $8,000 for installation work, $7,000 for advertising, and $9,000 for bringing over and putting up the Canadian, Irish, etc. teams—which, of course, also comes under the head of promotion. Foreign team expenses totaling $27,000 are divided three ways among the three great indoor shows—New York, Boston, and Toronto. Also to be spent are such minor sums as $300 here and $800 there for rosettes, flags, cedar trees, disinfectants, peat moss, and announcement board; $60 handouts to the more influential of the Garden police; and a tidy little sum—say $1,000—available to the Entertainment Committee for lunches. The Horse Show ball, and the promotion of general gayety among the exhibitors.

Particularly important is the Entertainment Committee's role. For upon its measure of success in making him feel at home depends the goodwill of the exhibitor, and upon the exhibitors' collective goodwill depends not only the $15,000 or $20,000 which the National Show may get in entrance fees but the far larger sum which comes in through the box-office window. [The early history of the horse show and the list of current directors has been deleted.]

All of which means that in this year's Show no dead classes will be kept out of sentiment. No trotters, no four-and six-horse commercial teams, no polo ponies. Instead, plenty of foreign teams—this year, the Canadian, the Irish, etc. On Sunday night a gala performance, with no reserved seats and at lower prices, which will include a couple of chukkers of polo, a mounted basketball game, a bareback triple-bar jumping exhibition in fancy dress, a hunt team with a pack of hounds—all to the accompaniment of strains from the Sixteenth Infantry Band. Exhibitions on alternate nights by either the Canadian Northwestern Mounted or the New York State Police and Commissioner Mulrooney's finest—something that will interest the man in the street as well as the horse owner, that will bring out every policeman in New York and his brothers and his sisters and his cousins and his aunts. In short, Mr. Tweed and his fellow directors hope to make the Horse Show safe for democracy. And in so doing to resurrect some of its former social traditions, since in the eyes of the U.S. public even the Canadian Northwestern Mounted Police are no more potent drawing card than serried boxes of resplendent dowagers.

## OTHER HORSE SHOWS

The National Show, which has caused all this bother and in behalf of which these gentlemen have labored so diligently, is at best but the grand climax to an eastern circuit which goes merrily on irrespective of whether the National or the Boston is to be its No. 1 show. And the $120,000 which the National's committeemen have assessed themselves a mere drop in the bucket. Depression tales about oatless owners turning their horses loose on the town or no, there are today between 30,000 and 40,000 show horses in the stables of some 6,000 U.S. exhibitors. Or over $50,000,000 worth of show horseflesh, presentable horses being worth from $1,000 to $10,000.

Consider the statistics: 40,000 horses exhibit their charms annually at 200 different shows from California to the New Jersey coast; win a total of $600,000 in cash prizes (next to the National's $40,000 come Boston's $30,000, while shows like Ohio State Fair etc. offer $20,000); cost their owners a total of more than $1,000,000 in operating expenses every year; with their trainers and grooms run up board, lodging, and transportation bills coming to perhaps $5,000,000 or $6,000,000. And are, in the financial analysis, chief *raison d'etre* for the 1918-founded Association of American Horse Shows, an arbitrary organization that meets in Manhattan each January to co-ordinate dates, draw up the next schedule with a minimum of conflicts (since exhibitors ship from one show to another), and which is to horse showing what the jockey Club is to horse racing.

Not all horse shows belong to the Association. Beyond the pale of its 116 members is a small, proud clannish group of Virginia shows that has its own Circuit, and a number of Army post shows and shows that take place at state fairs. Important among the later are the great Michigan and Illinois fairs, and the famous Kentucky State Fair, with its $10,000 stake for saddle horses. But they are exceptions, and at the average non-Association member's fair (members include the St. Louis, Springfield, Rochester, Ohio State, Toronto, and Chicago fairs) the horse is lost in the welter of pigs and cattle. As to whether such shows do better financially than the ordinary ones, opinion differs....

One thing they agree on—the impossibility of classifying shows. Each one is a law unto itself—Springfield indoor, Rochester outdoor, Devon big, Pipping Rock small, Kentucky State Fair for saddle horses, Bryn Mawr for hunters, and so on. In spite of which, herewith three rough divisions:

1. Small, one- or two-day country club shows, small or informal according to their respective communities, where prizes are too small to attract the big exhibitors and where Junior takes his jumper (jumpers, hunters, and children's classes predominate at these shows) over the hurdles and comes home with a ribbon.

**Examples**: Lenox, North Shore, Southampton, Greenwich, Boulder Brook, Bronxville, Montclair. No slight, as the outsider might suppose, but a courtesy is the refusal of the Paul Moores of Morristown, who own the country's greatest hackneys, to show them at the Morristown shows—since any one of six of their horses would stop the show, send junior home ribbonless and in tears.

2. Eastern and western circuit shows, mostly outdoor where, to the accompaniment of a Colosseum atmosphere, some with night sessions under blazing calcium, and the tension of $1,000 stakes, all classes are exhibited. Big eastern circuit names: Devon, South Shore, Rochester, Syracuse, Springfield, Brockton, Cohasset, Bryn Mawr, West Point, Fairfield, Rumson, Danbury. Western: Coronado, Santa Barbara, Stockton, San Mateo—the latter an eight—day affair with a $25,000 prize list.

3. The great fall shows, which include the Big Four (Boston, New York, Toronto, and Chicago's International) and such shows as the American Royal at Kansas City and

the Los Angeles County Fair at Pomona. Where all classes are exhibited, special features introduced, military classes emphasized, and only the best amateurs survive.

To envision the horse show purely in terms of this third group is to overlook the forest for the trees, even if for the tallest trees. The small, social shows are much more fun. And even your average serious (in contradistinction to social) exhibitor, who has four horses and ships to eight or ten shows a year, will think twice before graduating his hunters or hackneys from Group Two to Group Three. (The long list of exhibitors and their pedigrees has been deleted.)

## THE HORSE

The show horse itself, object of all this enthusiasm, solicitude,and expense, can look forward to some six or seven more years of life than the race horse. The latter has usually lost its prime at six, but the happy show horse may prance about rings until it is twice as old (Flowing Gold is twelve, Seaton Pippin eleven) and then be kept for breeding another six or eight years. Stud fees for show horses are less than for racers, ranging from $50 to $250 as against $100 to $3,000 for the great track stallions.

Now although the matter of judging a horse is an intricate and complicated affair often involving hours of profound meditation, a show horse's good points are in general less a matter of tape measure than of spirit, and can be appreciated by any layman. First thing to look for is intelligence—in the shape of the head and ears, the width between the eyes. Other desirable features: a long front, short back, large quarters. Again, a horse should not wing and should have good and true hock action—so that when you stand in front of him he is traveling evenly. And, most important, it should be well-mannered—a bad-mannered horse rarely covers itself with glory in the ring.

Here are some of the horses that do cover themselves with glory pretty consistently, conforming not only to the above requirements but to a host of more technical ones (such as being well ribbed up) upon which judges' decisions are also based. [These 13 horses and their owners have been deleted.]

## THE JUDGES

Horses are judged on conformation, quality, action, and way of going, the comparative emphasis of these criterions varying with different shows and different types of horses. In spite of a great deal of back-stage gossip, few judges are venal. Their errors or frequently due to insufficient knowledge or to in attention. At great shows they are usually above reproach, but at smaller shows often exhibit sheep-like tendencies, being much affected by previous records of the entries, and often overanxious to give wealthy exhibitors (on whom the business depends) a ribbon....


## EASTERN RODEOS

*[W.T. Johnson's control ended in 1936 when the cowboys refused to perform at the Boston rodeo until they were promised more prize money. Johnson acceded to their wishes before terminating his association with the rodeo the next year. As elsewhere in society, cowgirls earned about sixty-five percent of the men's purses and had fewer events in which to participate.*

*To determine the champion in each event, the Rodeo Association of America established a system of points based on the amount of prize money offered by each show.*

*In Class A shows, for example, each event was worth a total of 1,000 points, whereas Class D events were worth 250 points. Frank Menke's Encyclopedia of Sport for 1939 summarized the eight events that were used to designate an all-around champion. Bronco Riding: with saddle and one rein, time limit 8 to 10 seconds, rider must spur horse. Bulldogging: dogger leaps off horse, grasps steer by horns and twists him to the ground. Calf roping: roper must rope calf, throw him by hand and tie three feet together. Steer Decorating: similar to bulldogging, except cowboy places rubber band on animal's nose instead of twisting down. Steer Riding: cowboy rides steer for 8 to 10 seconds with nothing but a loose rope around steer's body that is held with one hand. Single Roping: steer roped by hand and brought to a halt facing horse without throwing steer. Team roping: one cowboy ropes steer by the head, other by the feet. Bareback riding: same as steer riding, except horses are used instead of steers. "Rodeo," The Digest (30 October 1937), 35.]*

As their city's annual rodeo began this week, staid Bostonians peered down their noses at bucking broncos, whose sole aim in life was to throw their riders to Kingdom Come; at "wild" cows, which stamped and pawed defiantly, daring anyone to try to milk them; and at Brahma steers, which bucked and kicked and tried every way possible to prod their riders loose.

Blase New Yorkers gaped and gawked at a similar spectacle last week and drawling Louisianians will stare at the same novelty two weeks hence in Baton Rouge.

To the people of these three cities, their rodeos are single annual events. To the cowboys and cowgirls competing in the shows, the three are mere stop-overs in a nation-wide circuit which starts in Denver in January, hops, skips and jumps across Phoenix, Tucson, Fort Worth and the rest of the country, and winds up in Baton Rouge in November.

Rodeos are big business today, rate second among professional sports in paid attendance. They even boast a trade association: The Rodeo Association of America. Although many amateur rodeos operate on their own, professional rodeos must belong to the rodeo association if they want to put on an authorized show. And to association rules governing kind and quality of livestock, prizes and guaranties, these shows must conform.

Skeptical Easterners deride the rodeos coming to their towns as mere carbon copies of western shows. But rodeo men reply that eastern shows are far more expensive to produce (because of heavy transportation costs) and compare with western shows as the American League with a sand-lot ball team. As a matter of fact, the rodeo recently held in New York's Madison Square Garden, which distributed prizes totaling $43,190, is the biggest in the country, even bigger than the Pendleton and Cheyenne roundups.

Rodeos attract the cream of the crop among cowboys, who first learn of then through the magazine, Hoofs and Horns, official spokesman for forthcoming shows. Listed in Hoofs and Horns are the time and place of all shows and the prizes offered. Cowboys pick out the most attractive shows, prepare their horses and outfit and come out after the prize money.

Contestants competing in rodeos do not draw salaries. Instead they must shoulder their own traveling and living expenses (usually a minimum of $300), and hospitalization costs, when, as and if. Before they can enter an event, they must plump down an entrance fee ranging all the way from as low as $5 in the West to as high as $100 in the East.

Curiously enough, entry fees for the less hazardous events are the more costly. Rodeo men reason that if a contestant gets thrown off a bronc, no one can tell whether or not he is a good rider. But let him miss a couple of tries at rope throwing and his amateurishness will soon give him away.

Jaded rodeo audiences like best to see a cowboy ride a bronc. In saddle bronc riding, the horse has a committee saddle strapped about him, which has no bridle, merely a halter and rein. The cowboy, when astride his mount, must hold the rein in one hand, keep the other aloft. If he should touch the horse with his hat or free hand during the ride, he is penalized. While astride the horse during the required ten seconds, he must "scratch" the flanks with his spurs. Smart cowboys know they can keep their feet loose and "scratch like hell" while the horse is rearing. But once the bronc starts down, the rider's feet had better be stretched earthward and braced for the shock, or else.

To cowboys, probably the toughest contest to enter is steer riding. Brahma steers used in the event come from the salt grass marshes of Texas and the Gulf coast of Florida. They are descendants of the sacred cattle of India. Cowboys call these steers the toughest, fastest and meanest animals on their size afoot.

In steer riding, the Brahma is chosen by lot and corralled into a chute. A loose rope is drawn around his withers. The cowboy climbs aboard, forms a loop with the slack (which he holds in his upturned palms), and the panic is on. The steer rushes out of the pen, bucks, rears, sways, tries every way to throw his rider, tries even to gore him. The rider must stay on top for eight seconds and must scratch the steer as well. His performance is judged by his skill in staying on top and by the meanness of the animal.

For their efforts—and pains and aches and bruises—cowboys, on the average clear about $1,500 yearly above expenses. Some thirty of them make between $8,000 and $15,000 a year. To the cowboy who earns the greatest number of points in rodeos throughout the year go a trophy and a title from the Rodeo Association of America. To the greatest scorers in individual events go similar awards.

Most cowboy contestants prefer the hazards of rodeo to a job on a ranch at $45 a month. Which is all very well—that is, if they live.

## THE CHALLENGE OF COLLEGE POLO

[*Despite claims that polo was becoming more democratic, it was an expensive sport. Membership in exclusive polo clubs ranged from $2,000 to $10,000, with an additional charge of from $125 to $500 a year. Room and board for one polo pony cost about a dollar a day, and most club players liked to have a string of eight horses or more. The price of a good mount was approximately $700; then there were the shipping expenses involved in competing around the country. Even riding academy players paid $8 to $20 a game. Mallets were $4.50 each, polo outfits cost $100, and helmets sold for $15. Robert O. Foote, "The Challenge of College Polo. Predicting that the Galloping Gladiators Will Ride Football off the Campus in Coming Years," Esquire (June 1935), 67, 123.*]

Polo will be the next great college sport in America. A strong statement, but one supported by trends which cannot be denied. Many polo enthusiasts look for a transition of popularity from college football to college polo within five or ten years. The more conservative say twenty to twenty-five years and look back upon the way in which football eased baseball out of the campus picture as a basis for their estimates.

In the first place, there is the manner in which the horse is intruding into the sports of America. We are going as horse-crazy as the English; racing is flourishing everywhere; everyone is riding and polo as the acme of horsemanship is coming in for increasing attention. This interest, of course, must grow immensely for polo ever to challenge football, but supporters of the galloping game contend it needs only to be seen to make converts. The colleges of the land, aided and abetted by army influence, already are becoming show places for polo in localities where it has been but faintly heard of in the past.

Secondly, there is the encroachment of professional football upon the exclusiveness of the gridiron sport as a college game. Professional football has had a hard struggle but it has definitely arrived. It was when professional baseball became strongly entrenched, around the turn of the century, that interest in college baseball evaporated and the more pronouncedly university sport of American football usurped first position.

With football being taken over by a commercialized faction in a way that threatens soon to rival the amateur game in public esteem, there is a feeling, slight in some schools, more noticeable in others, that the colleges should turn again to something that will be more characteristically their own sport. Polo is the logical answer.

Here is a game that fits in with both trends; it probably will never be played professionally and it uses horses in the most thrilling manner imaginable. Polo and football have many points in common. Both are played by teams and both are human contact sports; both have the same object, to get a ball through a goal at one end or the other of a large field. Polo takes about as long for a game as football; it is much easier to understand than football, yet has its fine points to hold the attention of the expert; it has even more of the element of real danger that makes the hair stand up on the head; it can be witnessed by a larger number of people because the field is longer. The mounted sport calls for exceptional skill and aptitude, high courage and genuine sportsmanship. It has football beaten two ways from the Jack for the character-building about which gridiron coaches love to preach to luncheon clubs. And, developed by a college student, it becomes a life long sport if he can afford it; no four years and quit—or turn pro.

Moreover, polo already is a college sport to an extent which is seldom realized. It has had its own Intercollegiate Polo Association for more than ten years, with seven school members, and it is also played wherever the Reserve Officers Training Corps maintains mounts, at a score of schools scattered all over the country. It is made a special study at eight or ten preparatory schools. It is not confined to the wealthy—many a lad is playing polo, and fairly good polo, in agricultural schools from Michigan to Alabama, who never saw a game before he went to college and who perhaps waits on table [sic] for his living, between classes and games.

This summer there will be held, unless postponement becomes necessary in plans of the United States Polo Association, which sponsors the Intercollegiate Polo Association, a national college polo tournament which will be truly deserving of the name.

So-called national tournaments have been held in the past, chiefly for Eastern schools, with occasional visitors, Arizona or Oklahoma. But 1935 is set to mark the starting of college polo on a nation-wide basis, with various circuit contests, the winners from which will meet at some central point to play for a genuine championship. The lines upon which this tournament will be conducted and its probable contestants will be:

Eastern: Princeton, Yale, Harvard, Pennsylvania Military College, Cornell and Norwich.

Central: Michigan State, Chicago, Illinois, Iowa State, Missouri and Ohio State.

Southwestern: Oklahoma and Texas.

Western: Arizona, Stanford, Oregon State and Utah.

Southern: Alabama Poly, Georgia and Florida.

The Intercollegiate Polo Association was formed in 1925 and a beautiful trophy put up by General Robert Lee Bullard. Yale finally obtaining permanent possession by its third victory in 1928. Then Gouverneur M. Carnochan, now president of the Association, offered another handsome trophy, which is still being competed for. However, intercollegiate polo proves it has broken away from sectional bias by decreeing that the former event shall hereafter be the Eastern Championship and that the more truly representative competition outlined above shall become known as the National Championship.

Because they have turned out so many fine polo players, the tendency in thinking of college polo is to call to mind Princeton and Yale and, perhaps to a lesser extent of recent years, Harvard, where it has been played since the 1880s.

Attention to what these schools mean in the polo world was strikingly attracted when a "kid team" out of college only for a few years, represented the East in defeating the more highly ranking Western team in the intersectional matches at Meadow Brook club on Long Island in the autumn of 1934.

That Eastern outfit consisted of James P. Mills and Michael Phipps, but lately out of Yale, and Billy Post, 2nd, and Winston Guest, polo prides of recent Princeton teams. They showed the college influence in being able to subordinate individual brilliancy to team endeavor and thereby put over the big sports surprise of the year.

In years past Yale gave to the polo world Louis E. Stoddard, now president of the United States Polo Association, and J. Watson Webb, to mention but a pair. Harvard is always remembered for its R.L. Agassiz and Devereux Millburn, top notch players of the past; for the noted Dillingham family and such recent recruits as Elbridge T. Gerry.

In these schools and others such as Penn Military, the game is partly played by men with their own ponies, probably from polo families or polo-mad prep schools. They are the chief feeding grounds for club polo and from them will come the internationalists and intersectionalists of the future.

However, it is the United States Military Academy that is the real cradle of college polo. Enthusiastic young poloists go out from it to the regular army service; eventually, when they have had their first jump or two in rank, find themselves assigned as military instructors at some freshwater college where a mention of polo is greeted only with a snicker, and proceed to turn the R.O.T.C. horses into polo ponies with amazing response from student body and public. There are plenty of universities and agricultural schools around the country where the polo turnout is fifty or sixty candidates, just about as big as the football squads. In fact, nearly every polo schools reports more aspirants than can be mounted.

In view of this it is interesting to examine a little more closely the polo setup at the Point, where it has been an official sport since 1906. Ten carefully chosen men make up the varsity squad for Army, with ten on the plebe squad and eighty turning out for intramural polo. All mounts, of course, are supplied by the government; the athletic association bears the entire cost of equipment, even to personal garments of the contestants. Of course, that means football is supporting polo. That the day will come when this is reversed is an optimistic suggestion around the polo barns.

West Point can make a year-round sport of polo; the horses only get two months of rest. The season starts September 1 and ends June 12. That is because polo is both an indoor and an outdoor game (under slightly different rules). For Army it is not necessary to alter the rules, as the Academy has the finest riding hall in the country, 555 feet long and well surfaced, with the goals offset from the ends thirty feet, thus allowing the regular outdoor penalty shots and outside play. The game is in high favor, and places on the squad are much cherished.

Incidentally, the same rule of all cadets being eligible that is so much disputed in football, applies to Army polo. You will find famous polo names from other schools bobbing up again on the Point's squad. Such as Harry Wilson, who was on the fine Arizona University polo team of 1929 and who is a son of Colonel "Jingles" Wilson, who, like Colonels Lewis Brown and J.K.Herr and Majors "Red" Erwin, Charlie Gerhardt and C.C. Smith, was an ornament to West Point polo of earlier days.

Now turn to Oklahoma University and see an example of how the Army influence spreads the game. Oklahoma and Missouri are the newest members of the Intercollegiate Polo Association, which includes the charter members Yale, Princeton, Harvard, West Point and Penn Military. These seven are equalled in big league college polo by many non-members—Stanford, Arizona, etc.

Oklahoma is polo wild because army officers brought the game there, men like Captain J.J. Waters, Jr., and Captain George R. Hayman. Perhaps the fact that Will Rogers is a native Oklahoman and a patron saint of polo has something to do with it, but at any rate Oklahoma put itself on the map by sending a team East in 1931 that lost in the Intercollegiate finals to Army. The game has been played there since 1920, and enthusiasm, always keen among the students, has spread to the townfolks of Norman and to the big cities of the region. Most of the players come not from the wealthy but from the boys off the ranches. Any inclination they might have to become snooty because they are polo players is taken out of them by having to groom their mounts.

That is a variation from Penn Military, which gets along without government aid and where the polo players pay about $225 a year for the playing privilege on college horses, with about one-quarter of the boys having their own strings. Such is not the general rule; even Harvard and Cornell profit by the R.O.T.C. horses which are practically the only mounts at places like Ohio State, Utah, Iowa State, Chicago, Norwich.

The latter is one of the most poloish spots in the land and is pointed out as an example of what may be accomplished in developing college consciousness of the game. Norwich is located at Northfield, Va. Out of a student body of 215 it has a polo squad of twenty-five and its R.O.T.C. cavalry unit of sixty horses is available to any boy who qualifies, at no cost to him. More turn out for the sport than can be handled. The game has been played there since 1910.

Many things, it is granted, must be accomplished before polo can become widely successful as a college sport, but they are being brought about perhaps as rapidly as were the developments of college baseball from 1850 to 1885 or of college football from 1876 to 1920.

There must be, as one immediate necessity, some means of handicapping players as is done in club polo. That will be hard to work out satisfactorily. No harder than to equalize mounting. The team on R.O.T.C. horses is no match for the privately mounted squad from Yale or Princeton, even if they be equal, player for player. Perhaps the "nationalization" of all mounts sent to a tournament might be the answer. It will take terrific argument to persuade a boy proud of his own polo horses to let someone else ride them—yet that very thing is constantly done in international and intersectional polo.

Polo, of course, is an expensive sport. Since the squads may be much smaller, however, it is doubtful if it would cost much more than the running of university football. Football pays its way now and that of many another sport. When polo reaches the point where it is self-supporting in the colleges, when public attendance will pay for it, the greatest advance will have been made; from then on it is likely to challenge the place of football. That day is nearing for the big universities and will follow in due course in the smaller colleges. Just give it ten or fifteen years, plead the polo advocates.

Chapter 22

## WATER SPORTS—SWIMMING, DIVING, WATER POLO, SYCHRONIZED SWIMMING

At the beginning of the decade, about forty percent of Americans knew how to swim. Since approximately ten percent could swim at the beginning of the century, swimming had progressed rapidly. A study of the alumni from six colleges who graduated between 1927 and 1938 discovered that seventy-six percent of them swam. A 1935 analysis of business and professional men in Iowa reported that fifty-five percent of them "enjoyed" swimming. Similarly, in a study of high school girls, seventy-four percent claimed to like swimming "very much." Part of the reason for this popularity was the availability of swimming areas. To make their cities more attractive, many city councils sought to preserve their lake fronts by constructing attractive parks and beaches. Waterfront parks provided lifeguards and changing areas. In addition, between 1936 and 1941, the WPA built 770 swimming pools. Since public pools were rarely built in working-class neighborhoods, and as swimming pools usually charged a small admission, swimming as a sport remained a middle-class endeavor. "Swimming: The Great American Sport" discusses the importance of more appropriate swimming attire and better sanitation and swimming techniques in the growth of swimming.

In 1935, when Lenore Kight was America's best female freestyle swimmer, Time wrote "Brunette, 22, she is a shade less effective than her rivals photographically, a shade faster than any of them in the water." Eleanor Holm Jarrett, the world's premier backstroker, the same magazine noted, "is the handsomest girl athlete in the world."

Unlike track and field and basketball, journalists considered swimming an ideal exercise for women. It rounded the body and made muscles long and supple. Female swimmers, termed "nymphs," "queens" or "beauties," were often photographed emerging from the pool, showing some cleavage and a full smile. Many of the top female swimmers and divers took advantage of the sport's sex appeal to turn professional following successful Olympic debuts. Time, for example, noted with surprise in 1933 that "unlike most girl swimmers—who soon acquire exaggerated bonhomie and so much sophistication about posing for pictures that screen tests are almost superfluous if and when they get to Hollywood—Lenore Kight is almost timid in demeanor." These women joined exhibitions rather than compete against one another. The first women's professional swimming championship took place in Cleveland in 1937. The winner of this half-mile race won $1,000 and the second-place finisher won $500.

In men's intercollegiate competitions, Michigan and Yale dominated swimming and Ohio State produced the best divers. As an illustration of the general lack of interest in collegiate swimming, in 1935, only thirty-six colleges competed. The 142 swimmers represented the largest turnout until that time. As the document "Fancy Diving" notes, private swimming clubs were responsible for the development of America's best swimmers.

America's swimmers and divers dominated the world in this decade and the United States produced a plethora of famous athletes. Adolph Kiefer of Chicago was the premier backstroker. He won his first U.S. championship in 1935 at age 16, and for the next eight years he went unbeaten in more than 250 races from 50 to 1,500 yards. Kiefer revolutionized the backstroke. Rather than copying the other swimmers who used their arms to push water directly under the body, Kiefer swept the water away to the side just below the surface. Katherine Rawls captured the AAU low-board diving championship as well as the 100 yard free-style and medley events. Helene Madison dominated the free-style. Eleanor Holm Jarrett won twelve AAU backstroke titles, captured a gold medal in the 1932 Olympics and was the leading contender in the 1936 Olympics until she was removed from the team on board ship to Germany.

Canadians also liked to swim, especially in the many freshwater lakes and rivers. The Canadian National Exhibition in Toronto sponsored amateur and professional races. The Canadian Amateur Swimming Association attempted to streamline competition, but the Maritime provinces were not members and the drought conditions in the Prairie provinces limited meets in the West, where many lakes and rivers evaporated in the summer. In some areas, government relief projects constructed swimming pools.

The confining nature of swimming attire at the University of Toronto indicated the quality of swimming in Canada. In 1937, Toronto newspapers blasted the university's women swim team's new skirtless suits and forced the women to wear inside aprons.

The major swimming news story in the first half of the decade was Japan's phenomenal showing in the 1932 Olympics. Comprised of young male swimmers still in their teens, who appeared as "midgets" compared to the "husky American boys," the Japanese team captured every men's race but the 400-meter freestyle that Buster Crabbe won. Although Japan did not adopt swimming as a recreational sport until 1900, hundreds of pools were constructed and the national swimming association used the latest technology to film and dissect proper stroke techniques. After taking some of the best American swimmers to Japan for exhibition meets, the American coach stated the Japanese were serious threats, but no one listened.

Following the 1932 Olympics, the experts tried to explain why the Japanese were so successful. Some people attributed the Japanese victory to either their diet, a better use of oxygen, or to their team spirit. As a homogeneous people, the latter group claimed, the Japanese were willing to make greater sacrifices for "cause and country." According to an article in Fortune (1934), "When a Japanese swims, he does nothing else. He doesn't drink or smoke or go out with geisha girls of an evening. He just swims." More astute observers noted that the Japanese Swimming Federation emphasized hard work and closely monitored their swimmers, unlike the Americans who used a laissez-faire approach. Initially, many people believed the Japanese had developed a new crawl stroke. One swimming coach recalled that he constantly explained that the Japanese did not invent a new stroke, rather they sped it up. In addition to encouraging smaller swimmers, the Japanese victories in 1932 provided evidence for swimming coaches' efforts to improve swimming instruction in the nation's schools and universities.

Prior to 1932, few divers turned professional, but the exposure given to "fancy" diving in the Los Angeles Olympics encouraged the best divers to become professionals and put on exhibitions around the world. The United States dominated this sport; it captured every gold medal in the springboard event and nine of twelve in the high-platform.

**WATER POLO**

The decade ushered in major changes in water polo. At the beginning of the 1930s intercollegiate water polo was in disarray. The American game used a half-inflated ball which was easily dragged under water and thus much of the game was played underwater where neither spectators nor referees could see the action. As a result, the game was violent and injury-filled. By 1938, American universities switched to the international game which forbade violence and used a fully inflated hard leather ball which was difficult to drag under water. Not everyone favored the change. Arthur Daley, for example, lamented in Collier's (1938) the end of this "distinctly American sport...built around rousing American lines," in favor of the "sissy" international game in which it was even a foul to splash water in the face of an opponent.

**SYNCHRONIZED SWIMMING**

Synchronized swimming, usually termed ornamental or fancy swimming, was in its infancy in the 1930s. The first recorded use of the word "synchronized" was at the 1934 Chicago World's Fair, where Katharine Curtis's "rhythmic" swimmers performed in the Century of Progress Exposition. Five years later, Curtis devised rules for a dual meet between her swimmers at Wright College in Chicago and Chicago Teachers College as part of the annual teachers' day program. This exhibition aroused considerable interest in Chicago swimming circles and led to a movement to get synchronized swimming included in AAU competitions. The first world's synchronized swimming championship took place in 1940 at the Shawnee County Club, Illinois. In Canada, beginning in 1926, synchronized teams competed for the Gale Trophy. Clubs performed figures and strokes, and music moved from background sound to be part of the program. Swimmers wore long black gym stockings sewn to bathing suits. The following documents illustrate the major themes in water sports during the decade.

## SWIMMING. THE NEW GREAT AMERICAN SPORT

[*Swimming strokes changed constantly. Although film was first used to study strokes in 1928, it was not until the Japanese victories in the 1932 Olympics that Americans began serious research into stroke mechanics. Other than the breaststroke, no strokes had a prescribed style. In mid-decade, the butterfly developed out of experiments to make the breaststroke more efficient. The following article examines the growth of swimming in the US and analyzes the economics of the sport. In a side-bar on bathing budgets for 1934, the author noted that membership in a beach club cost $250, a two-piece, tie-silk bathing suit sold for $25, beach sandals were $7.50, and "smoked glasses" were $1. "Swimming. The New Great American Sport," Fortune (June 1934), 81-89.*]

If the statisticians are right, the American nation will go for a swim about one billion times this year. If the social agencies who count noses have counted well, these billion swims will be indulged in by some 30,000,000 people. Swimming makes its appearance more and more constantly as the first sport to which Americans turn in the leisure the New Deal (or unemployment) has brought them. And as, year by year, the National Recreation Association reports an increased patronage of "facilities offering water sports," it becomes evident that we have a new Great American Sport.

The 30,000,000 people who go swimming every year are a number incomparably larger than any other sport can claim. This is both commonplace and curious. It is commonplace because, after all, "Throngs jam Beaches as City Swelters in Torrid Grip" is not an unfamiliar journalistic trope. But it is curious because swimming as a sport of any popularity is barely as old as the century—and only after 1920 did its participants begin to grow at their present astronomical rate. In the public mind today, swimming is somehow compounded out of the one-piece bathing suit, chlorinated water, state park commissions, the six-beat crawl, rubber giraffes, the ultra-violet end of the solar spectrum, and Gertrude Ederle. And as was once said of the automobile, it is apparently Here to Stay.

In our modern industrial world, swimming presents an immediate anomaly. Despite the 30,000,000 people who practice it, few entrepreneurs have been able to commercialize it. It is true that a commercial bathhouse at a big beach is a nice investment: Mr. Joseph P. Day, New York's famous real-estate auctioneer and speculator, makes a profit of about $1,000,000 a year from his 25,000 cubicles and his three beaches—Manhattan, Oriental, and Brighton. It is true that the Jantzen Co., maker, in its own words, of "the suit that changed bathing to swimming," had net sales of $4,700,000 in 1930, its peak year. It is true that the B.V.D. Co., by entering into competition with Jantzen, has added a pleasant increment to its underwear business, has increased its sales sixfold in four years. It none the less remains that the 30,000,000 customers of swimming have enriched very few people. Swimming remains essentially a noncommercial, non-professional occupation—the one sport-for-sport's-sake in which everyone can indulge.

The rich and the poor can swim. So—better still—can the male and the female: the bisexuality of swimming is one of its qualities of uniqueness as a sport. Men don't like mixed doubles at tennis; the male golfer regards the mixed foursome as a stench and a hissing. But segregate the sexes on a bathing beach and they will make kindling of your barricades, for swimming tones not only the muscles but the emotions of its participants.

Why then, is the rise of swimming a twentieth-century phenomenon, and more specifically a phenomenon of the last decade? There is a threefold answer—anatomical, physiological, and technical—and the first, the anatomical, reverts again to this question of sex.

The bathing costume of the female used to weigh, when water-soaked, from ten to fifteen pounds. Part of this was contributed by that lovely object, the swimming corset, which ladies were by modesty forced to bend on before getting within 100 yards of mean high water.... But today, when a woman's suit may be a costume of tie silk, weighing as little as an ounce and covering an area perhaps no more than half a square yard, swimming is not only possible—the full voltage of the cosmic urge is now behind it. Therein lies Reason Number 1 for swimming's recent growth.

Reason Number 2, the physiological, has an equal and even more startling validity. Bathing, the antecedent of swimming, survived the fall of Rome. For a number of centuries it even survived the discouragements of medieval Christendom, which frowned upon it as decadent. But then, in the sixteenth century, with a dramatic suddenness, bathing vanished from the Western World. It was killed by Christopher Columbus whose men brought back from Haiti something that Europe had never known before; the *Spirochaerta pallida*, the germ of syphilis. This new disease swept all Europe like a forest fire—and although the doctors of the century knew very little about it, they drew the excellent conclusion that mixed and multiple bathing probably had something to do with its spread.

They were quite right. And since they had no means of sanitation against it, and the science of bacteriology was unknown, it was not only proper but wise to let bathing sink to the state of a lost art—which the sixteenth-century world in its panic promptly did. Unfortunately, for centuries after the first emergency had passed, the cult of the hydrophobe continued. People kept on hating water without knowing why; their aversion to it continued throughout the eighteenth-century and a good part of the nineteenth. It was not, for example, until 1850 during the presidency of Millard Fillmore, that the first bathtub was installed in the White House. Water, people had come to think, leached away the essential salts of the body; a person immersing himself in it was likely to suffer the fate of a lump of sugar in a cup of tea. Even as late as 1875 Mary Baker Eddy laid down the doctrine: "The daily ablution of an infant is no more natural or necessary than to take a fish out of water and cover it with dirt." Suffering under pronouncements like these, it is small wonder that the public remained skittish about taking to the water.

But the third reason, the technical, for swimming's twentieth-century rise, strikes right at the heart of the business. The plain truth is this: not **until the turn of the century did anybody really know how to swim.**

Some savant has pointed out the curious fact that the only animals who have mastered upright locomotion—man and the apes—are the only ones who cannot swim by instinct; man must be taught or he will drown, and the apes cannot even be taught. Until the twentieth century, swimming was badly taught. The breast stroke, a highly intermittent, tiring, and inefficient movement of the arms, plus a frog kick of the legs, was the standard stroke for the beginner. The English Mr. J. Trudgen had, in the middle of the nineteenth century, either invented or rediscovered a double over-arm stroke accompanied by the so-called scissors kick, which was sometimes known as "Spanish swimming." It was pretty good but not good enough. [The short history of the development of swimming strokes has been deleted.]

Now that the basic discovery had been made, refinements followed fast. As the crawl developed, woman was likewise in the process of casting away her garments, and it soon became evident that not only could she swim, but that she could swim very well; that in some ways she had the potentiality of swimming better than man. Her lighter muscles were almost an asset, her smaller skeleton gave her less weight to propel, and her subcutaneous layer of fat gave her a greater buoyancy. She was, in fact, better streamlined. By 1917 the Amateur Athletic Union gave in; it recognized that women were a factor in competitive water sports for them.

One woman, Gertrude Ederle, responded beating men's swimming records—something that had never before happened in any other field of sport. Moreover, women showed men some highly important improvements in technique. [The early history of women swimmers has been deleted.] Gertrude Ederle earned $150,000 (of which she herself got only $50,000) as a byproduct of her exploit. Until 1931 she taught in a swimming pool at Rye, New York, at present she is doing nothing.

Since Gertrude Ederle's day (and including her) seven women have swum the channel, but only six men. Only one other of these women was an American—Mrs. Mille Gade Corson ("first mother of two to swim the channel") of New York. The other five were English. But no other woman has equaled the Ederle record. Ederle was, for a time, the No. 1 popular idol of her country; then the other sex, in another element, took her accolade away. That was when, a little less than a year later, Charles Angustus Lindbergh flew the Atlantic.

EDERLE had much the same effect on swimming that Lindbergh had on aviation. She boomed it. She made it a tremendous vogue. Parents began having their children taught to swim at the ages of five and six, specified by coaches as the ideal time to begin. Older people took lessons. The mills of the Jantzens began to grind; they ground exceeding small as to suit area, but swiftly and more swiftly, and the red Jantzen diving girl shortly burst forth on the windshield of every motorcar in America—until the short-tempered state of Massachusetts suddenly rose up and made this innocent decoration a cause for driving-license cancellation.

But vastly more important: by this time governments were concerning themselves with swimming; even in parched prairie cities hydraulic and sanitary engineers and boards of health and architects banded their talents together for the construction of municipal swimming pools; states with a littoral began to conceive it their duty to give their citizens the means to indulge in what was now so unmistakably their favorite sport. Swimming thereupon took on one more quality of uniqueness; it became the only sport to which, in any degree, governments applied the principle of socialism and, out of taxes, constructed or the benefit of all the means to group health and recreation.

In the U.S. there are today some 8,000 swimming pools. Approximately half are indoor, half outdoor. This figure states and cities have achieved from a standing start in 1901—for it was not until that year (we were three-quarters of a century behind England, here) that the first municipal swimming pool in the country was opened in New York City.

Of these 8,000 pools, 80 per cent have been built since 1920 and 50 per cent have been built since 1925. Average attendance per pool is 46,000 a season; average fee twenty-five cents for children, fifty cents for adults (average cost of operation per swim—for municipal pools—is nine and one-half cents). There has grown up largely in the last decade, an elaborate technology of construction. Once a pool was just a pool; water was changed every so often, on the old fill and draw system (keep the water running in, let the overflow spill out), but there was no bacteriological control of its purity), no city or state officer had jurisdiction over it, there were no rules or regulations for its safety or the skill of its operators. The rules governing the cleanliness of its bathers were sketchy. In other words, the general run of early swimming pools was decidedly not kosher.... Today, however, some thirty-two states subscribe to the swimming-pool code drawn up by the joint Bathing Place Committee of State Sanitary Engineers, and the Public Health Engineering Section of the American Public Health Association. This is a formidable document of twenty-eight major sections, and almost 150 pronouncements of proper standards for the design, construction, and operation.... Each potential swimmer must be provided with twenty-seven square feet of pool space, says the code, which like-wise specifies a rigid control over the sanitation and safety of the individual swimmer.

All this means money.... Pool swimming is now, on an average, just as hygienic as ocean swimming—much more so than ocean swimming in the vicinity of a large city, none too particular about its sewage disposal; fastidious swimmers can-not always forget the dispiriting cartoon of Jewish ladies, up to their waists in the water of one ocean beach, which the New Yorker published a few years ago with the caption, "Look, Mrs, Klopp, pineapples."

To the West Coast go honors for the largest indoor and outdoor pools in the country. [The list of the largest pools has been deleted.] A municipal pool of reasonable cost and proper maintenance can, on the average, break even if it charges ten cents a swim—not too much of a drain even on a juvenile purse. Yet out of the billion swims a year that this country takes, only, some 350,000,000 are accounted for by pools. The balance is made up by the swimming that America does at its 16,000 supervised beaches—private, commercial, state, and city.

Topping the list of ambitious state developments for recreation comes Jones Beach in New York—a triumph of Al Smith and State Park Commissioner Robert Moses, who got it built. It cost the state $14,000,000 and took two years in the building, but it stands today as a monument to governmental enlightenment. Out of seven miles of mosquito-infested barrenness the state created seven miles of clean bathing beach, policed by 700 men who daily rake the sand clean of twenty tons of rubbish. It built two bathhouses—one of 10,000 capacity, another of 5,400. To the smaller bathhouse is attached a salt-water swimming pool (100 by 150 feet), a smaller wading pool for children. If you don't want the pools you can souse yourself in the breakers of the Atlantic. If you don't want the breakers either, you can walk inland for three minutes, enjoy the still-water swimming of Zach's Bay—for Jones Beach is essentially a reconditioned sand bar, with the Atlantic on one side and Great South Bay, of which Zach's is a minor indentation, on the other.

Here is the great swimming sanctuary for the middle class; designed for people who can neither stomach Coney Island nor afford the cabanas of the Atlantic Beach Club. And last year some 3,200,000 of them patronized Jones Beach; on hot Sundays attendance sometimes ran as high as 100,000. The defect of Jones Beach is likewise its virtue; it is thirty-three miles from Manhattan, and not a subway in sight. Your own car, a bus, or a train are the only means of reaching it.

If you want to go farther up the Atlantic seacoast from Jones Beach you'll first bump into society—although of varying strata. You will find the Beach Club at Southampton; a simple structure but saturated with Elegance. Farther eastward is the Maidstone Club at Easthampton where first flourished that bathing adornment of the twenties, the cabana: a sort of cross between the old English bathing machine (without the wheels) and a speakeasy. Here, in the days before repeal, you played backgammon, drank your illicit cocktail, and went out to swim.

From Long Island you would make a long jump to the mainland and find yourself at the Spouting Rock Beach Association which would be more familiar to most people as Bailey's Beach, at Newport. Here, in theory any rate, you stand at the absolute center of the country's bathing aristocracy; the very waves begin to take on a faint and distant chill, as if they suspected you of being Not Quite.

But thereafter you are in New England; at Provincetown gone utterly phony as the aftermath of its artistic invasion some fifteen years ago; then along the Massachusetts south shore with the beaches becoming simpler, more rudimentary, more in the spirit of an earlier day except that the swimming is better, and the bathing load runs higher....

South and east of New York, you will first come to the Atlantic Beach Club on Long Island, which is gilded and glittering and ostentatious although not very socially snooty in its admission requirements. Then, going back to the mainland, you reach New Jersey where the country's bathing load probably reaches its absolute maximum. Most of the Jersey coast, from Asbury Park to Atlantic City, is a jam of commercial bathhouses and boardwalks until it finally peters out in the fine white sand of Cape May.

Florida, despite the disadvantage of the collapse of its land boom some eight years ago and the occasional devastation of a hurricane or a tidal wave, does very well with its beaches....

There is no space here to dwell upon the pros and cons of Florida and the Gulf Coast versus California and the Pacific Ocean, no space to juggle with hurricane, earthquake, climate, and local pride. There are good beaches on the Gulf, good beaches on the Pacific—the best at Santa Barbara and La Jolla, although many a Coronado, San Diego, Santa Monica, Long Beach, or Catalina enthusiast would dispute that statement. [The description of locations to swim inland has been deleted.]

The mores of the beach are in a queer state just now. Private beaches make their own decency laws; on public beaches the U.S. still frequently exhibits a puritanism that would not be understood in Sweden, for example, where men and women are likely to swim nude to together, not just at nudist beaches, but where they please. Nudism continues to gain in the U.S., but it remains segregated. Half of the 300,000 practicing nudists practice in the East, but even in the New York area, where there are six camps, they are well concealed from public view. Only sixteen other states have nudist camps (usually one each); the South is backward about nudism and so is the West. Not all nudists swim, but most nudist colonies have pool or pond or river.

The more conventional swimmer is up against it to be certain when he may be committing some sort of breach of the peace. Curiously, more rules now bind men than women. Men started taking their tops off a few years ago, and Societies for the Prevention of Things Like That immediately got busy. Thus in Atlantic City a man may be put in the hoosegow for toplessness whereas women are subject to no rules at all. Women, on the other hand, have not yet tried taking off their tops in Atlantic City. They have tried, however, to wear a combination brassiere and pants, with a hiatus between; Mayor Bacharach and his council are now in prayer over that one.... Freest U.S. swimming is in California; particularly at Malibu Beach where the movie stars bathe, and no policemen are allowed. California has few restrictions, Malibu has none. At the other end of the spectrum come a few places in northern New Jersey. North Haledon, New Jersey, is apparently the headquarters for what can best be labeled a prudist colony; here, according to statute, women must wear two-piece suits—not only with knee-length trunks but with long sleeves. Ocean Grove, Asbury Park's most immediate neighbor, is another stickler for the proprieties; there was even a time when it was illegal to use the ocean on Sundays, even if incased in linoleum, and small boys of four whose mothers were godless enough to let them go wading on Sunday were chased to dry land by vigilantes.

Elsewhere in the country, however, rules are more or less uniform. Coney Island and Jones Beach and many others agree that men must keep their tops on, that women must not even slip down their shoulder straps. Almost everywhere it is illegal to undress in an automobile, or behind that distant sand dune, or anywhere other than a bathhouse.

To the generality that no entrepreneur makes much money from America's love of the water only a few exceptions need be made. As we said before, Mr. Joseph P. Day owns Manhattan, Oriental, and Brighton beaches alongside Coney. His 25,000 bathhouses cost $29 apiece to build, and from each he receives an average annual income of $50. In addition to bathhouses, he owns bungalows, pools, handball courts, and restaurants. His net profit from all, after deducting $600,000 in expenses, is around $1,000,000 each year.

Jantzen, whose diving-girl automobile sticker appeared on four million cars in 1924, sold 26,832 suits in 1920 and 1,587,338 suits in 1930. In that peak year its market sales were $4,700,000. Last year sales dropped to 567,216 units for which it was paid $1,800,000. But still it's a good business—the best bathing-suit business in the world; and the thirty styles of suits (retail price from $4.50 to $9.95) are carried by department stores, sporting-goods houses, and specialty shops in sixty-eight countries, and orders for the first seven months of the 1934 fiscal year show a 45 per cent increase in dollar volume over 1933. [Discussion of B.V.D. has been deleted.]

It is interesting to note that bathing suit styles originate in this country, not in France, and B.V.D. sells more suits at $8.50 than at $4.50.

No one makes much money. Professional swimmers make money from exhibitions and once in a blue moon somebody like Johnny Weissmuller crashes the movies in a modest way—but the pickings for professional swimmers are pretty slim; not at all to be compared to the pickings from other professional sports. A commercial pool owner, in a good year, might make $5,000 over his expenses.

And so swimming obstinately remains the refuge of the amateur, the comfort of the mass. Moreover it is lessening its only disadvantage; the disadvantage that in profiting from its pleasures you might inconveniently drown. Beaches are patrolled today with a new thoroughness and new technique. Of the billion swims the nation takes, only 7,712 drownings resulted in 1932—the latest available year of record. Automobiles annually kill more than three times as many people; falls take toll of more than twice this number. It remains however a startling fact that of these 7,712 drownings, 6,610 were of men and boys. Yet even so, a record of less than eight deaths per million swims is a pretty good record.

Certainly, in present-day America, swimming is not only a source of health; it provides a prophylaxis against ennui, a safety-valve against the evils of boredom. A bored people is likely to be dangerous people. The Romans knew that; they entertained their populace by throwing Christians to the lions. Today, encouraged by the state, we throw ourselves into lakes and pools and ponds and rivers and oceans—beyond question America, amphibious America, has thus been enabled to wash away some of its many sins with the cool water on its lean bodies.

## SWIMMING AS A COMPETITIVE SPORT FOR FEMALES

*[Of sixty women's colleges surveyed in 1933, fifty provided swimming instruction, forty-two had life-saving classes, twenty-six offered diving lessons, and twenty-eight required its graduates to be able to swim. The following year, half of the high school girls surveyed desired coaching instruction in swimming. This placed swimming behind only tennis in popularity.*

*American and Canadian Olympic-caliber swimmers were almost exclusively white, middle-class individuals who could afford to join private swim clubs and train under salaried coaches. Although the rule was not enforced, as late as 1938, the AAU required that women's bathing suits "be of dark color with skirt attached. The leg was to reach within three inches of the crotch and cut in a strait line around the circumference of the leg. The suit should be cut not more than 4-1/2 inches from the pit of the neck in front and not more than 10 inches from the pit of the neck in back, and not more than 2 inches from the crease of the arm in front and 3 inches in back."*

*The author of the following article was a member of two American Olympic swimming teams and was now assistant director of the Life Saving Service of the American Red Cross in New York. Here, she defends competitive swimming for females and calls for better training and longer distance events. Note that one of her arguments in favor of competitive swimming is that many Olympic swimmers later married or became successful in business. The Sportswoman, established in 1924, was the official organ of the United States Field Hockey Association and the United States Women's Lacrosse Association. Ethel McGary, "Ethel McGary Favors Competitive Sports for Women If Wisely Supervised," The Sportswoman (November 1931), 11-12.]*

With the approach of the 1932 Olympic Games in Los Angeles, the question of women's participation in them will again be raised. Ever since the award of the 1932 games some four years ago, much opinion has been voiced, pro and con, regarding competition for women. Some of the criticism has been of a sensational nature and not strictly to the point. Those in favor of the possibility of competition for those interested in it, believe all adverse criticism can be met on grounds that do not mean great compromise.

It is more or less an accepted fact, I believe, that practically everything in life involves competition of one sort or another from the fundamental "survival of the fittest" on. Then why not sanction competition through "the promotion of sports and games wisely supervised"? This is the key to the situation, namely, competition safely and sanely handled. Since there always exists a certain amount of competition, it really seems more logical to work for improved conditions in this through education rather than gain the opposition of this group, a rapidly growing one at that, banning the activity altogether.

The record of the women who participated in this so-called "highly intense specialized competition," especially open meets, is not nearly as bad as one might be led to believe by their opponents. In all approximately sixty women have been members of Olympic Swimming teams in the last three Olympiads. Investigation shows that about 20 are married, some 25 or 30 are busily engaged in business or professional pursuits, and from 10 to 12 of the 1928 team are still in colleges. Practically all, with one exception, are actively interested in swimming today and report no harm resulting from their activities, but on the contrary retain a pleasant memory of an experience which taught them the best possible health habits.

The most outstanding reason for this is that one can't do one's best consistently and feel right unless one has trained and is in good condition. The possibility of achieving this state through moderate and sane training is often completely overlooked by most people who put forth arguments on the subject.

One can't be a swimmer of any calibre at all without practice, and it follows logically that the more regular and more often the practice, the more accustomed the muscles become to the activity and the easier the performance, the result is increase in speed with the same effort expended. This is none other than the law of exercise and response through quicker reaction giving subsequently greater speed. By regular practice, I mean between 300 and 400 yards of swimming, twice or three times a week, done at a moderate pace and followed by two or three short sprints after a reasonable rest period. With this amount of work, the so-called drudgery of swimming is over and the individual is free to do as she pleases about more work in the water. Figured from the time basis, this amount of work will not take more than 15 minutes in all. Ten minutes being more than adequate for the distance work, and three minutes for the sprints with an extra allowance of two minutes for either event. Contrary to the current belief, this practice will be as beneficial to the sprinter as to her sister who enjoys longer events. However, too much cannot he said on the subject of working gradually up to the distance starting with perhaps, a hundred yards and adding 25 or 50 yards as the case may be, being careful to keep the pace even throughout, and concentrating on stroke perfection rather than speed at all practice sessions.

Coupled with saner training comes the selection of better events,—events which will be interesting and at the same time worth while. I believe if the races were lengthened the girls themselves would recognize the fact that they were no longer up against events where a little fight was all that was necessary, and would take a greater interest in technique. In general, the recommended events for school and college women's swimming meets are 20-,40-, and 60-yard races in the three standard strokes, crawl, back stroke, and breast stroke. On the other hand, amateur competition for approximately the same age group involves events from 100 yards to 500 indoors and up to one mile out doors. The 50-yard event was abolished some 5 years ago, as not being an adequate event, since so little depended on the ability of the swimmer, and so much on luck in taking off the right second. In the first place, a swimmer has to be very highly keyed up for a dash event, because she knows the second she strikes the water she has to work arms and legs to the limit till the end, or else she hasn't a chance. It means fight is all, and form little, as one does not get a chance to get started in 30-, 40-, and 60-yard dashes. An event of 100 yards means, a girl has to know a lot more about swimming, and to have practiced regularly with a smooth stroke, or else she will be lost in the shuffle, and hopelessly outclassed. In swimming distances of 100 yards or over, whether in competition or not, one is bound to get the feel of the stroke never gotten in short dashes. From the standpoint of strain, we find there is no apparent strain shown after distances between 100 and 3,000 yards, because the muscles are accustomed to that amount of work, and have become strong through practice. When called upon to react even more quickly than usual, they are up to their job, which is the secret of training. Outside a normal amount of sleep and wholesome food with a moderation of sweets, that is all there is to training.

Then, too, there is the danger of girls who now participate in nothing but short dashes in their college pools making the most dangerous type of swimmer. Because of the fact, that they are not used to going more than 60 yards and then grasping something, they are apt to get in trouble when they begin exhibiting their speed in places where there may not be a convenient tank edge to grasp. Likewise, swimmers who are used to going 300 yards or more are fairer judges of their own ability and endurance.

I recommend a revising of the program of events for women in swimming meets at schools and colleges, making way for longer distance events which would necessitate real swimming and operate toward general safety. Longer events will not slow up your swimming meets. If the swimmers are very far apart in ability the use of a handicapping system will make the race interesting to all concerned and will tend to raise the standard of competition. The girl will not be out to beat her opponent but rather will be put to it to beat her best time. So far as heats are concerned, it should be left to the judgment of the instructor as to whether her competitors are in condition to swim heats and finals, a fact which should be determined by training conditions.

I have little sympathy with the statement, that "it takes too much out of a girl to swim a long race twice." In the first place, the idea of heat is to give a large number a chance. In general, there will he two or three who are faster than the others, and an attempt will be made to keep them apart until the final, as is done with ceded players in tennis. A suggested program of events would include 100-yard events in crawl, back stroke, and breast stroke, a 200-yard crawl event, and a 400-yard relay, a diving event, and one novelty, such as a tandem event, or a pigeon race.

I am not trying to prove that competition must be a part of everyone's life, but that girls can compete in swimming races without injury to themselves, and enjoy them, and gain, at the same time, in swimming and watermanship through moderate, safely, and sanely conducted practice and competition. Granted, there are some who do not care for such things yet enjoy swimming. To these water plays and pageants offer a large and interesting field.

## FANCY DIVING

[*The author of this article was a nationally-recognized authority on diving and was the swim coach of the Downtown Athletic Club of New York City. Beach and Pool, established in 1926, was a monthly publication "devoted to the development and operation of the nation's beaches and pools." Here, Spongberg outlines America's chances in the 1936 Olympic diving events. The description of how to dive was deleted. Frederick A. Spongberg, "Rhythm and Precision of Fancy Diving," Beach and Pool (July 1935), 181-182, 197-198.*]

I have been asked to write a few lines on the subject of "Fancy Diving." Of course, we all know that diving is a gymnastic feat, therefore it should be performed like a gymnast; by that I mean, that each dive should be executed with rhythm and precision. [The description of how to dive has been deleted.]

We all know that the Olympic Games are to be held in Berlin, Germany, in 1936, and believe it or not, Europe is after our scalp as far as diving goes, and is doing her utmost to bring out talent that can take the measure of the American divers.

Of course, it is well understood that our strongest competition will come from Japan, as far as swimming is concerned, but, from the way it looks now, we have some excellent swimmers, boys as well as girls, who will, without a doubt be right up to world's championship caliber by 1936, so we are sure to see some pretty stiff competition in aquatics.

We don't have to worry very much about our men divers, they are the cream of the world right now and have been so for many years, so have our girl divers, but, will our girl divers be as successful at the coming Olympic Games as they have been heretofore? Well, that is a question very hard to answer.

It seems to me as though the International Federation on Swimming and Diving, in making their rules for women divers at the 1936 Olympic Games has decided to give the European girl divers an excellent chance to take the measure of the American girl divers.

The diving rules for girls at the 1936 Olympic Games are rather severe on our girls; first of all there will be only six dives. Three compulsory and three optional dives. Well, to decide a World's Championship in Fancy Diving, on only six dives, seems to me ridiculous, and I cannot see how such ruling came about, without some stiff objection from America at the meeting of the International Federation, at which meetings the rules for the Olympic Games are made.

Bear in mind, our girls are accustomed to making ten dives, and have worked hard to perfect some of the more difficult dives, just because they had a higher scoring value in the diving table on degree of difficulty, only to find out that the dives they have been practicing so diligently have been removed from the table of degree of difficulty, and will not be permitted for women at the 1936 Olympic Games.

The competition in women's diving at the 1936 Games will be so keen, that to be a diving judge will require the services of an expert, and I don't mean maybe. Of course the rules cannot be changed now, so the next best thing to do, is for the coaches to get their prospective divers together and start training hard and seriously, bearing in mind that the girl divers of Uncle Sam will have the hardest competition ever faced, because of the few dives required and because of the part Lady-Luck will play in the outcome of the contest.

The reason I say luck will have a great deal to do with the final outcome of the tryouts is this—because of the few dives involved. There are going to be, perhaps, fifty divers or more, trying out for a place on Uncle Sam's Team, where we used to have only fifteen to twenty-five at the most.

With some of the more difficult dives prohibited, the girls more or less, will have to use the same dives for their optional selection of dives, therefore we will have a great number of contestants executing their dives so much alike, that it will be a mighty difficult task for a diving judge to give his just award.

Remember, that out of all these dives, only three or perhaps four will have to be selected. Now, aren't you glad that you are not one of the judges?

The slogan for the next year should be—Dive-Dive-Dive and then some more diving! If you heed this slogan, there is no question but that America's girl divers will again be victorious at the Olympic Games in 1936.

What about the men divers? I don't think we will have to worry about them! With Dick Degener of the Detroit A.C. and Marshall Wayne of Florida diving for Uncle Sam, I am quite safe in saying—"It's in the bag." As far as the men divers, go, who the third man will be, remains to be seen, so there will be no prediction from me at this early date. Consult your horoscope or go to a crystal gazer, they know just as much as I do as to who that third man will be—but don't take as authentic what they tell you.

## JAPAN'S SWIMMING SUCCESSES

*[As this article illustrates, Japan's success in the 1932 Olympics brought forth demands for better swimming instruction in the schools and for the formation of a national swimming committee to conduct research and coordinate training methods. Although many American high schools and universities had pools, they were used for recreational purposes rather than for instruction, and swimming was rarely part of the curriculum. Swimming instruction, its supporters argued, would develop healthy individuals and would greatly reduce the high annual deaths by drowning. "Where, we wonder," wrote Beach and Pool, "do Lebanon's [Indiana] pool opponents think that the 8,000 yearly drownings occur? Certainly not in swimming pools." Robert W. Brenner, "Keep Our Swimmers in the Swim," The Athletic Journal (December 1934), 32-34.]*

Will there be no end to the mark smashing in swimming competition? For a decade now, every aquatic meet of national importance has produced a new swimming star splashing through the waves to the headlines. It seems that every time Weissmuller, Kojac, Crabbe, Al Schwartz and, lately, Jack Medica took their lightning starts at the report of the gun, they were off to swim their particular distance faster than it had ever been negotiated before.

But great as the improvement in records has been, it is not entirely satisfactory. It is not what it could be if we judge by the results of international competition.

Americans have always been confident of their success in Olympic Games, especially in swimming where there were no Nurmis or other outstanding foreign stars to fear. Perhaps this is what made the results of the last Olympiad hurt all the more. We had a team composed of our top-notchers. They had beaten many existing marks. But along came a small group of diminutive Japanese who were literally to swim away with head honors!

The Japanese representatives were young; some only fourteen and fifteen years old. They were slight physical specimens compared with our champions. Torao Takemura is now but twenty years old, 5 feet 4 1/4 inches in height and weighs 139 pounds. But the Japanese were trained! Not only were they in condition but they were fortified by an exceedingly intelligent reconstruction of our own crawl stroke and a knowledge of conserving their energy for the longer gruelling races. As Mr. Ralph Summeril, an official at the Olympic Games, has said:

"The Japanese have something the Americans lack. It is a stroke that conserves their muscle power to the best advantage. The application of this stroke, difficult to explain without illustration, brings into use more and stronger muscles than does the American stroke. It can also be shortened by a tiring swimmer in a way that does not affect his form. So many of the exhausted American swimmers lose their form badly."

This explains one advantage held by the Japanese two years ago. Still another is explained by Mr. John Wray of the St. Louis Post-Dispatch, who has tabulated the Japanese timing of a distance race. Of this he says:

"When Kitamura won the 1500-meter race, he swam the first 100 meters in 1:16, the next twelve centuries in approximately 1:17 each, the fourteenth hundred in 1:14 and the last century in 1:11. He broke the record.

In this country our swimmers set no thought about the managed pace, but are intent on beating their man. As a result, they frequently are exhausted by high speed spurts which react unfavorably at the finish."

Thus, the demonstrated superiority of the Japanese in the last Olympiad would seem to be a result of better training of their athletes—better coaching in stroke and in the analysis of the race. Apparently, that is where we fell down. Our material is of sufficiently high caliber. The constant succession of national record breakers indicates that our swimmers are better than ever before; in fact, some have recently lowered even world marks.

The great majority of high schools, equipped with no tank or having none immediately available, do not sponsor swimming. Teams from most of the others are poorly coached—usually by some instructor having no technical knowledge of or training in swimming.

A case of swimming conditions, humorous if it were not so pathetic, is told by Earl Jansen of the University of Illinois, a well known Western Conference diver. This past summer Jansen was asked to be a judge of diving at a swimming meet held just outside of St. Louis. The contestants were thoroughly unorthodox, but the regulation swimming events were run off as speedily as a 1:14 100-yard and a 7:48 440-yard event would permit. Then came the usual *piece de resistance* of the meet—the diving events. Jansen was given the individual lists of dives selected by the divers. We can imagine his amazement when he saw such dives listed as the "Victory Dive," "Statue of Liberty," and the "Ham and Egg." Jansen confessed that, in spite of his years of competition which included the Intercollegiate Meets, he had never heard of those. They turned out to be of the "standing-sitting-standing" dive variety.

This is of course an extreme case. But it is a fact that there are few satisfactory training grounds for future champion swimming material. Outside of a few athletic clubs and Y.M.C.A. organizations, there is no opportunity for an ambitious swimmer to gain the finer technique in the water until he reaches a university.

Japan and Italy have seen the value of swimming. They and a few other nations have found it an ideal mass exercise—one that is self-sufficient and not harmful to the heart and other vital organs. They have made a knowledge of swimming as universal as the elementary subjects of education. This is not a program designed to produce international champions, but that result must follow. The more people who take up swimming, the greater will be the number from whom record breakers may be chosen. And this is not the only factor. Where so many individuals of the population are given instruction, there is great emphasis placed upon the competency of that instruction and the constant training of coaches to keep them abreast of new developments in swimming.

Competency of instruction is something sadly needed even among our university coaches. We have some excellent coaches who really know their swimming. We see them producing winners year after year. But, considering the colleges of the country as a whole, they are in the minority. Think of the variety of training methods now in use. One coach had his dash swimmers working on 880's; another restricts them to 100 yards at a stretch. One coach prescribes a meal of boiled egg and toast before a swim; another allows, or demands, beefsteak, baked potatoes, vegetables and coffee. There is no excuse for such a variance in training ideas. Some one must be right! The coach who is wrong is perhaps doing his best according to his own conception of swimming training, but he is doing wrong to the swimmers subjected to his charge. More than that, he is possibly depriving the United States if a competitor who could reclaim for her the prestige that once was hers.

Olympic swimming championships, in themselves, mean little. It matters little that a Japanese can swim a certain distance a few seconds faster than our swimmers. But superiority in international competition indicates a great deal. It shows the winner is on the right track—using available material to the best advantage. If we are going to have competition in swimming, let us make an earnest effort to win.

This means taking advantage of all new developments in swimming technique and training methods, and disseminating this knowledge so that all may benefit by it.

The annual Intercollegiate Swimming Meet always offers an opportunity to study swimming methods in practice in other parts of the country. But some more complete and speedy system of comparing notes is necessary. The number of people privileged to witness one of these meets is limited, and too frequently they are so busy with their own interests and possibilities that they do not see much else.

The writer remembers when Moles of Princeton startled the assemblage at the 1929 Intercollegiates with a record smashing 2:35 in the 200-yard breast stroke. The former record had hovered around 2:40 for years until Moles, employing the then new underwater swimming to some extent, an innovation in the breaststroke, led a fast field by five or six seconds. Now—five years later—we are first seeing this record breaking aid come into general practice. The use of the under-water stroke should have been explained to all swimmers everywhere long before this. New developments in stroke and style, at present, can only be picked up by individuals through the exercise of the utmost effort and observation.

We need what we might call an Olympic Swimming Committee which will be active all through the four year interval between games, rather than for four months;

an alliance of coaches who are in a position to learn of all advances in the sport and who will conscientiously and intelligently pass this knowledge on to others.

In international swimming competition, we are up against a united front in Japan. Swimmers of that country are from the first taught the most efficient stroke and all are given the same opportunity to benefit by the latest developments. We should do the same. Most of our coaches would gladly scrap their own obsolete training methods in favor of a system recommended by a prominent body of experts who had given the matter careful study. Many university conference organizations form the nucleus around which a national board of swimming research might be built.

The material gathered could be spread throughout the country by several means to insure a clear understanding of new developments in swimming by every interested coach and swimmer. Exhibitions by our more advanced swimmers, accompanied by illuminating lectures explaining stroke and racing technique, would be of great value in spreading the gospel of modern speed swimming. These would give an opportunity for all to see how to do it and to hear why to do it. Books, pamphlets and motion pictures could supplement the personal crusade. Some plan of this sort, thoroughly worked out, would without a doubt do much to keep all coaches informed up to the latest minute.

The only reason Japan beat our swimmers in the last Olympiad was that her swimmers were better trained, both as to swimming stroke and as to timing of races. That margin of good coaching resulted in a clear cut superiority over our physically larger representatives. We have the potential swimming champions, but, as Gray has written, "Full many a flower is born to blush unseen." Let us treat all the seeds the same—give them all the benefit of the latest and most efficient treatment. Then we shall grow more winners!

## WATER POLO

[*When the Federation Internationale de Natation Amateur adopted a fully-inflated ball in 1937, the more rugged American game was doomed. This article portends the demise of the "Old American" game of water polo. The caption of the accompanying photograph indicated the problem. It read, "Yale and Princeton deplore the gouging, strangling, kneeing, belly-thumping; the sinus; the mastoid." "Water Polo," Time (16 March 1931), 25.*]

Seldom does water polo attract attention except when it is wetting the spectators who sit too close to the tank at swimming meets. But last week water polo loomed in the news. All winter the eastern colleges had been bickering about it. Last week the Intercollegiate Swimming Association announced that, in spite of complaints, it would not alter the rule making competition in water polo compulsory for member colleges. Immediately appeared editorials in the Yale *Daily News* and the *Daily Princetonian*. The *Princetonian* urged Princeton to resign from the Association. The *News* accused the Association of side-tracking a resolution to drop the game. Both spoke ominously of injuries, of unhealthfulness.

There are two kinds of water polo: the soccer game and the Old American Game. The soccer game is played with a hard leather ball fully inflated. Since it is difficult to drag the ball under water, spectators can see what is going on. This kind of water polo is comparatively harmless, though tiring. It is sanctioned by the Amateur Athletic Union, by western colleges and universities, and is played in the Olympics. The Old American is sanctioned by the Intercollegiate Swimming Association and played by Pennsylvania, Columbia, C.C.N.Y., Yale, Syracuse, Rutgers, Navy, Princeton. Recently Dartmouth resigned from the Intercollegiate Swimming Association to get out of playing it. The Old American is played with a half-inflated white rubber ball which is dragged under water as soon as it is tossed in and usually kept there until a goal is scored. Bubbles, choked cries, limbs eccentrically twisted rise to the surface. Faces reappearing after long confinement under water are sometimes empurpled, sometimes tombstone-pallid. Spectators find little science in it but enjoy the agonized grimaces of the players and the thought of what gouging, strangling, kneeing, biting, mauling and belly-thumping goes on subaqueously.

Claim defenders of the Old American Game: 1) No one has ever been killed at water polo. 2) There have never been serious injuries. 3) The players do not think it is too rough; complaints come from faculty members, medical advisors. 4) There is no harm in it if played strictly according to the rules. 5) "Accidental" blows lose much of their force under water.

Claim objectors: 1) No referee can see what happens under water; strange and harmful ways are used to make a man let go of the ball. 2) Referees have not enforced the rule that no player may be ducked until he is within four feet of the ball; general and immediate ducking for everyone in the game is a tradition. 3) Many players sustain injuries every year.

In a game 20 years ago between New York and Chicago for the U.S. water polo championship, the star of the Chicago team did not get out of the pool. His body was found at the bottom. He was revived with difficulty.

There was an epidemic of sinus trouble at Princeton last year. Almost all veteran water poloists have had their eardrums punctured at some time. Occasionally the eardrum fails to heal quickly and pus runs out of it. Mastoid may result. Suggested objectors: the Intercollegiate Swimming Association refused to alter its rule about the Old American Game because oldtime officials of the Association like to play it themselves in the New York Athletic Club, would hate to see it become outmoded.

Wrote Defender H.A. Gosnell, recently secretary of the Intercollegiate Swimming Association: "Objectors know nothing about the game...they shrink from putting their heads under water.... The hullaballoo [sic] in the student papers...is that of ignorant kids looking for a good news story...."

## WATER PAGEANTRY

[*In Canada, Montreal dominated synchronized swimming in the 1930s. When the national championships were held in Winnipeg in 1933, it was the first time most people in the area viewed the sport. With no manual to follow, the few clubs on the prairies improvised their own figures. To promote her sport in the United States, Katharine Curtis, the "first-woman of synchronized swimming," provided detailed outlines of different combinations, stunts, and progressions that formed the basis of water pageantry routines. Katharine Curtis,* A Source Book of Water Pageantry *(Chicago, 1936), Preface and Introduction.*]

## PREFACE

This book has been written for use by those who are interested in the grace and rhythm of swimming. All of the material in it has been tried out and developed during twenty years of experience with girls in summer camps, high schools, normal colleges and universities, in a wide variety of programs which ranged from informal meets, splash parties, swimming club performances and elaborate pageants to the Modern Mermaids who performed at the Century of Progress in 1934....

## INTRODUCTION

In the past, much stress has been laid on developing and coaching the speed swimmer and little or no attention has been paid to the problem of developing the abilities and interests of the average and mediocre swimmer. It is possible to provide the average as well as the excellent swimmer with a means of enjoyment in the water which will offer as much personal gratification in performance as the competitive speed swimmer. Ease and relaxation accompanied with a feeling of pleasure which is a part of the joy that comes from performance well done, can be made available to every swimmer. Stunt swimming broadens the scope of achievements for the average swimmer and increases his confidence in his ability in the water. It offers infinite possibilities for the development of poetry of motion with accent on ease, line, rhythm, and harmony of bodily motion rather than speed. For the purposes of this book, stunt swimming has been defined as including all swimming activities other than standard swimming strokes.

The water pageant is well adapted for providing a means of display or exhibition of the end products of the motor learning involved in stunt swimming. It provides a means of expression for a group interested in stunt swimming. Through the unit of the water pageant, the teacher is able to stimulate interest in swimming, foster stunt swimming and provide training in rhythm. It offers an opportunity for the students to participate in group activities adapted to individual abilities as well as learning to work in a group as a responsible part of the whole. The water pageant offers an opportunity for self-directed creative efforts by the student. It is a device through which the work of the Art, Music, Dramatic, Household Arts, English, History, Business and Physical Education Departments may be coordinated in the formation of the completed pageant.

In the water pageant, all grades of swimmers from the beginner who does not venture out of the shallow water, to the finished swimmer may be used. Before considering a water pageant, it is well to take an inventory of the abilities of the swimmers on hand and the numbers available for work. This inventory will be a determining factor in the degree of difficulty of the routines to be presented. The completed water pageant in Part I, Professor Bullfrog's School, has been used in a university pool with university students of excellent ability, in a Normal School pool with three times as many younger and less experienced students, and at a summer camp on an open lake shore with children from seven to sixteen years of age with a wide range of ability, all with uniform success and popularity in spite of the varience [sic] of swimming ability and ages of the three groups...

The entire action of a water pageant is held together by a plot or a story. Almost any story with a "Watery" element and popular appeal may be used. The story suggests characters and continuity of action. Part I, Completed Water Pageants, demonstrates the way in which poetry and prose may suggest characters and determine the continuity of the action throughout the pageant. The routines to be presented in the pageant may be suggested by actual wording of the story or merely be inferred in the synopsis of the story contained in the program given to the audience. In a good many cases, the story indicates the basic figures to be used in creating the numbers or routines which make up the pageant. Part II contains water pageant plots, in a good many cases with the author's suggestion for numbers for presentation and pageants given at universities and clubs not under the direction of the author. Part III, a compilation of Sea Mythology, offers endless opportunity for the development of water pageants.

Music is an important part of the water pageant. It sets the rhythm of the swimming and aids in creating the mood indicated by the story. After the stunts have been chosen, and progression determined, the music must be selected. The most popular tempos are the march and waltz to both of which all standard strokes and stunts may be performed. A kind of hybrid stroke may be done to the rhumba rhythm. When the music is selected, the stunts and figures are adapted to the measures of the music in much the same manner that one might adapt dance steps to form a dance routine. This book will be found to be most useful if the basic stunts are treated as simple steps which may be combined to form a complete number or routine. Parts I, II, and V, all have routines with suggestions for music. An analysis of the basic steps or stunts were combined and set to measures of music in the complete number.

It is possible to use many types of music. The piano, a small orchestra, an accordian, victrolas ranging from the portable to the machine with orthophonic attachments, and ukeleles have been used with uniform success. This, of course, is entirely dependent upon the individual situation. It has been found to be expedient to use a tom tom during practice periods, keeping in mind the number of measures for each basic step and the duration of the entire routine. Experience has proven that the length of the average victrola record, two and one half to three minutes, is as long as even excellent swimmers can do constant swimming and maneuvers. A whistle has been used to great advantage to indicate changes in the routine for students inexperienced in swimming to music, since they often have difficulty hearing the music.

Costuming is one feater [sic] not discussed at length. Suggestions, however, will be found in Parts I and II. Experience has proven that the costume to be most desired is the simplest one. The author has had experience with costumes ranging from realistic wired lobsters claws and headdress, to simple colored swimming suits which merely suggested the character portrayed. The latter was as effective as the former and did not tax the endurance of the swimmer. Details that have been used effectively will be found in the parts previously mentioned.

An additional feature which must be considered seriously when creating routines and patterns is the line of vision of the audience. An elaborate figure floating number may be lost entirely if the audience is seated on a level with the swimmers. The ideal situation of course is one in which the audience is seated above the pool so that they look down on the field of activity. To a certain extent, decoration and properties must also be considered from the audience viewpoint. Simplicity in decorations and properties, as well as in costuming is extremely effective. Line, color and design should suggest the desired setting for the plot rather than attempt to realistically portray it. If a pageant is to be presented at night and colored lights are available, they may be used very effectively in creating the mood of the story. Suggestions for decoration will be found in Parts I and II. Individual situations, however, call for individual treatment.

Suggested races, games and camp specialties in Part VI will be found useful in planning the informal meet and splash party as well as a source of humor in the pageant. The appendix contains graded stunts both in the water and off the board with points for difficulty awarded. These offer great possibilities for the development of a type of competition in which form, beauty of motion and rhythm would be considered.

Aside from the idea of the water pageant, the material in this book many be used to present an individual number at a splash party, informal swimming meet, as the basis for a Swimming Recital which contains a fair balance of serious figure swimming and floating, stunts and humorous events which are suggested, and also as numbers during events in a competitive swimming meet. The audience seems to derive more pleasure from watching the synchronized swimming than they do from the speed events because they can visualize themselves doing the former with the realization that they could never attain the world champion speed class.

It is sincerely hoped that this book will prove to be an inspiration to the teacher and that through the material found herein, she will be able to broaden the scope of activity thereby increasing the possible achievements of her students. Enjoyment in swimming is available to all, it knows no age limit or season. It is the one sport to which one may turn for relief from everyday cares and emerge refreshed in mind and body.

## Chapter 23

## WINTER SPORTS—SKIING, FIGURE SKATING, CURLING

In December 1936 the tiny town of Ketchum, Idaho, readied to duel with St. Moritz, Switzerland, as the home of the top winter-sports resort in the Western Hemisphere. Several years earlier, W. Averell Harriman, chairman of the Union Pacific Railroad, hired expert Austrian skier Count Felix Schaffgotsch to find the best skiing terrain served by the railroad, and to design ski trails, toboggan slides, and ski-jumps for this area. Schaffgotsch selected Sun Valley, which received its name from the semi-circle of mountains that sheltered it from the high winds. The slopes were free of trees, the peaks rose to 12,000 feet, and snow was plentiful. Actress Claudette Colbert helped launch this one million dollar investment.

The construction of the Sun Valley resort area, with the continent's first chair tow, illustrated the phenomenal growth of skiing. In 1934, manufacturers of ski-equipment reported a twenty percent increase in sales over the previous year. This was followed by a thirty-three percent growth in 1935. Based on sporting goods sales, skiing was America's most popular sport by the end of the decade. In 1940, Americans spent $20 million on ski-related items—sales of ski clothes topped $6 million, skis and bindings sold for $3 million, skiing instructional classes earned $500,000, and lodging and transportation each cost $3 million. Of course, some people purchased ski clothing only for its style and ease of movement. By the end of the decade, the number of skiers in the US was estimated at two million by the Red Cross and at one million by Time magazine.

As the first document illustrates, railroad companies were essential to the growth of skiing. The Appalachian Mountain Club of Boston organized the first ski train, called a "snow train", in 1931 when the Boston and Maine Railroad carried 200 club members to the White Mountains. The weekend was so successful it was repeated, and by the middle of the season the railroad added three sections to accommodate the increased traffic. The following year, several railroads offered transportation from New York City to the Catskill and the Adirondack mountains. Soon, the central concourse in Grand Central Station, New York, prominently displayed daily temperatures and snow conditions in skiing centers in New York and New England, and several railroad companies initiated ski clubs along their lines.

In Canada, the Canadian Pacific Railway scheduled regular excursion trains to ski centers. Ski racks attached to each train were color-coded and when the passengers disembarked, their equipment was waiting on the platform. In Ontario, special weekend ski trains transported skiers to resorts in the Laurentians and the Gatineau Hills. In the first Dominion Slalom race in 1929, Canadians were completely outclassed by an Austrian skier. Two years later, a team representing Oxford and Cambridge also proved Europeans far superior in slalom racing. In fact, this was the first time that steel edges were used in Canada. Canadians were still far behind the best European skiers in training and techniques at the 1936 Olympics in Germany—especially in utilizing an extreme forward position of the body and knees, employing the inside edge of the outer ski, tucking the knees into the hill, and using poles for pivoting. The first professional teaching school opened in 1932 at St. Sauveur, Quebec. Here, Austrian and German skiers taught the Arlberg crouch. Demand exceeded supply. Four years later, the Canadian Amateur Ski Association opened the Canadian Ski School to train ski instructors and to enforce professional standards.

Skiing also benefited by exposure in the 1932 Winter Olympics in Lake Placid (this was the last Olympics to feature solely Nordic events and male-only ski competitions), and from the many newsreels shown prior to feature movies that portrayed attractive men and women dashing swiftly and gracefully down white hillsides at high speeds. Rope tows, chair lifts, aerial tramways, T-bars, J-bars, and (as at Mount Tremblant) tractor-pulled sleds made downhill skiing practical for the weekend skier, and soon downhill skiing became more popular than cross-country. As the number of skiers neared two million by the end of the decade, national and state parks cleared ski trails. The Civilian Conservation Corps built more than thirty miles of ski trails, and private enterprise poured millions of dollars into improving ski resorts.

In 1938, Utah's national forests hosted 88,000 skiers, Oregon's parks entertained 140,000, Colorado 110,000, Washington 106,000, and California attracted 639,000 skiers. In Canada, the mountainous province of British Columbia provided a natural home for skiing, and Revelstoke was termed "the Capital of Canada's Alps." Skiing was a popular winter sport in Ontario and Quebec. An estimated 53,000 Ontarians, from the Governor General to the common worker, skied in 1938, especially in the Ottawa region. In Quebec, farmers discarded their snowshoes for skis and hockey people began to worry that skiing was affecting attendance at Canadien hockey games. Quebec's climate was especially conducive to skiing and as early as 1930 an estimated

20,000 to 25,000 skiers left Montreal each winter weekend for the foothills of the Laurentians. By the end of the decade, ski-related purchases in the Laurentian mountains exceeded $1 million. Elsewhere in Canada, except for New Brunswick, geography limited skiing.

Skiing provided thrills and excitement for the entire family and substituted hard muscles for "flabby fat." For urbanites, as one magazine noted, "the crisp winter air blew the cobwebs out of your brain and the foul city air out of your lungs." Roaring fires in log cabins, wide-open spaces, rolling snow-covered hills, and invigorating fresh air attracted young and old to the ski slopes. The supposed connection between health and morality was a common feature in popular articles written about skiing. Boys' Clubs and YM\YWCAs sought skiing instructors. The Boy Scouts debated the merits of a ski badge.

By the end of the decade, approximately one-quarter of all ski equipment sales were made by students going on their first ski trip. Skiing books flooded the stores. In 1936, skiers could choose from among the following recently published instructional books: *Improve Your Skiing*, *The Complete Book of Ski-ing*, *Ski Tracks*, *Skiing*, and *Ski-ing Exercises*. Between 1929 and 1939, more than 215 articles on skiing appeared in popular magazines. Eight editions of *Modern Ski Technique* appeared from its inception in 1932 to 1937. Newspapers printed weather information at local ski resorts as well as snow train schedules. Ski publications included The Skisport, Ski Bulletin, Skiing, Ski Illustrated, Ski West, Ski-Week, and California Ski News.

Skiing was also popular in colleges and universities. By the late 1930s, twenty-three New England schools offered skiing as an extra-curricular program. Dartmouth College, New Hampshire, which played a leading role in the development of winter sport in America through its winter carnival and its Outing Club, annually admitted some 200 students into its winter recreational skills class. In 1935, eastern schools formed the Intercollegiate Ski Union and the following year the Pacific Coast Intercollegiate Ski Union commenced.

Despite the lack of qualified instructors, skiing benefited from the emphasis on coeducational sporting activities that could be continued after graduation. The Women's Section of the American Physical Education Association, for example, encouraged schools to include skiing and skating in their physical education programs, and skiing became one of the more popular outdoor activities in women's colleges. Although skiing could be a competitive sport, educators liked the fact that it was primarily a participatory activity. The crisp winter air and sunshine invigorated body and mind.

Influenced by the Norwegian tradition, North Americans confined their skiing to ski-jumping and cross-country prior to the 1930s. But with the addition of ski tows, resorts, downhill trails, and artificial snow, slalom and downhill skiing soon dominated. Walter Brown, coach of the 1936 US Olympic hockey team, and son of George Brown who controlled Boston Gardens, was credited with developing the snow machine. In the early 1930s, Walter Brown was searching for a way to fill Boston Gardens with snow to hold an indoor winter show. According to News-week, one day he noticed that a Boston fish store packed its cod in finely-chopped ice. When the fish dealer showed him how the ice-grinding machine worked, Brown merely ordered a much bigger machine.

**FIGURE SKATING**

Prior to the 1930s, figure skating attracted few spectators. The US Figure Skating Association's decision to host the 1930 World Figure Skating Championships in New York City, and the figure skating competition at the Olympic Winter Games in Lake Placid in 1932, attracted attention to the sport. Prior to the Olympics, the European competitors practiced in New York in front of interested reporters and magazine writers who further promoted figure skating. The indoor icerink at Lake Placid lured large crowds, especially when Beatrice Loughran and Sherwin Badger finished second in pairs and Maribel Vinson took bronze in women's figure skating.

Most contemporaries attributed the growing popularity of figure skating to Sonja Henie, the "Fair Maid of Norway." Henie captured three Olympic gold medals and held the world's amateur figure skating title from 1927 to 1937. In the latter year, Henie became a professional and traveled to the US to perform in New York, Chicago, Pittsburgh, St. Louis, Minneapolis, and Boston for $20,000 per show. Prior to her arrival, sportswriters and the general public were apathetic. What would Henie do that other skaters had not done? Previous professional ice shows were sparsely attended, and some journalists forecast the tour would be "a calamity show." But this blond, blue-eyed "queen of the ice" entranced the opening-night audience with her ballerina-like skating, her theatrical air, her charm and poise, and her beauty. The tour was a huge success. The next year, 20th Century Fox signed Henie to a five-year contract for two movies per year. Her first movie, "One in a Million," was a big hit and by 1939, Henie's Hollywood's popularity trailed only that of Shirley Temple's and Clark Gable's.

Henie's "healthy and wholesome beauty" was touted as the model for young women. Liberty magazine wrote in 1937, "But there are no muscles that you can see. She hasn't one touch of the 'muscle moll' that the sportswriters write about and laugh over. The strength seems to radiate through the prettiness and the feminine charm of hers, but in those skating costumes she is—literally—like a Dresden china doll."

Henie's financial success set the pattern for other ice carnivals and convinced other amateur champions to turn professional. Henie's popularity was particularly evident in the growth of the number of young women, ages 10 to 18, who began figure skating lessons. A 1933 study of high school girls in Des Moines, Iowa, revealed that three-quarters of them liked skating, and that twenty-three percent desired coaching. Males were less inclined to take part in figure skating, which was sometimes termed "fancy skating" and had a reputation as a "sissy" sport. Nevertheless, by 1938, the WPA had constructed 2,400 ice-skating rinks—which served thirteen million skaters that year. By the end of the decade, sporting goods figures indicated that skating ranked sixth in terms of sales.

The best figure skaters joined private clubs. Here, better instruction based on standardized tests, consistent judging, and such interesting activities as ice shows, attracted youngsters to the sport. Clubs in Toronto and Ottawa pioneered the marriage of theatrical devices, costumes, lighting, choreography, and comedic routines throughout North America.

**CURLING**

"At first sight, probably no sport seems more ridiculous than curling." This initial sentence in a News-week commentary on curling was typical of North American

444SKIING BECOMES BIG BUSINESS

coverage of the sport. The author compared curling stones to enormous muffins, poked
fun at the use of household brooms, and snickered at such curling terms as bonspiels,
buttons and hacks. He then noted, "But there is more to curling than this."

In 1938, there were but 4,000 curlers in the US, most of whom lived in areas con-
tiguous to Canada. When the best American team played Canada in 1938 for the Gordon International Medal, which was symbolic of the North American championship,
few people in the host town of Utica, New York, apparently knew about the event—
so little publicity did curling receive in the US.

Prior to the formation of the Dominion Curling Association in 1935, a questionnaire
sent to each province discovered that of 22,604 registered curlers in Canada,
Saskatchewan led with 5,000, followed by Manitoba with 4,050 members. With no
professional hockey teams, few downhill slopes, and plenty of leisure time in the winter, prairie farmers took to curling. In some clubs, day-time hours were reserved for
farmers, who sometimes paid for their membership with produce. The townsfolk
played in the evenings. Winnipeg, whose 1935 annual bonspiel attracted 232 rinks, was
curling's headquarters. The West dominated interprovincial curling and usually captured the Macdonald Brier Tankard. Elsewhere, curling was particularly popular in
Scottish areas in Ontario and the Maritimes. In Quebec, the sport remained almost
exclusively English.

The highlight of the curling season was the Brier, which was emblematic of the
Canadian curling championship. In 1927, the first year of competition, eight rinks from
various urban centers, only one of which was from the West, vied for the Brier trophy.
In 1932, the competition was limited to provincial representatives, plus Northern
Ontario, and four years later British Columbia and Prince Edward Island sent teams.
Winnipeg teams dominated the Brier, which was held each year on the artificial ice of
the Toronto Granite Club. Finally, in 1940, after poor coverage of the Brier by Toronto
newspapers and constant agitation by western members, the Brier traveled to Winnipeg.

### SKIING BECOMES BIG BUSINESS

*[Skiing was expensive. Boots cost from $7 to $12, bindings sold for $4 to $9, poles
ranged from $3 to $8, and hickory skis cost $10 to $18—with an additional $6 for steel
edges. Then there were clothes, lodging, transportation, and food to purchase. As this
article indicates, skiing was big business. In the 1920s, only a handful of American
companies made skis. As the demand for skis increased, more companies entered the
market. By the end of the 1930s, at least twenty different North American companies
competed for the skiing market.*

*In 1935, Saks Fifth Avenue installed Manhattan's first indoor department-store ski
slides. The following year, Madison Square Garden ground 500 tons of ice into flaky
snow and created a 152-foot skiing trail on a 45 degree angle, a ski-jump, and two
miniature skating rinks. More than 12,000 New Yorkers came each day to the city's first
indoor winter sports show to watch the skiers and fancy skaters, to inspect the latest
in skies and ski-wear, and to talk to representatives from various ski resorts. At the end
of the ski season, the New York Times reported that New York department stores had
increased their ski business by 250 percent over the previous year. Hazel K. Wharton,*

*"Skiing. A Healthful Outdoor Sport Grows in Popularity and Becomes Big Business for Hotel Keepers, Railroads, Apparel and Sporting-Goods Makers," Review of Reviews (December 1936), 46-48, 78-79.*]

Rising from a background of snow, trails, Christianas [sic], wax, and good-fellowship, a fast-growing new business has come into existence. Empowered by enthusiasm and freighted with happiness and health, the sport of skiing forced the trend with business following as swift as the skier himself coasting down the hills.

Strange as it may seem, the whole thing is based on altruism...and on shrewd business men. Railroad officials, for example, wondered why so many people had apparently gone wild over a sport which required low temperatures and deep snow, ordinarily staid passengers became frolicking children. So the officials put on skis, to find the "why" themselves. They enjoyed it, took lessons, and became enthusiasts.

The same thing happened in other lines of business. To observe conditions at first hand buyers visited skiing-centers. They, too, leaned to ski in order to find the requirements of the sport. They experienced the thrills and spills, felt the surge of joy brought about by vigorous exercise in exhilarating air. They went abroad to study European winter resorts and costumes.

Designers of clothing found a new outlet for their talent. The continental influence in winter-sport togs melted into an American composite combining the best European points with American ideas and domestic workmanship. American mills were found adaptable in developing new cloth. Facilities were extended to weave hard-finished gabardines, twills, and wind-proof parka cloth. Factories turned to the making of ski suits, caps, mittens, socks, sweaters, boots, skis, poles, and bindings in large quantities. A few years ago a gabardine ski suit cost $50. Now one just as good but more practical can be bought for $20, simply because American mills and factories are producing more. Good hickory skis can be had at $7, whereas imports of the same grade were double that price.

Manufacturing, retailing and other branches of merchandising are all feeling the benefit of the sport. Books on skiing technique have been published. Insurance has found another field for accident policies. Buses, automobiles and trailers, too, are used to convey skiers thus necessitating the buying of gasoline. Small communities without industries are profiting. Hotels and guest house in snow regions now stay open throughout the year. And the railroads in the north have added another season to their transportation calendar.

Until a few years ago skiers found winter-sports facilities at only a few places—near Dartmouth College in New Hampshire, at Montreal, at Lake Placid in New York, and in the Pocono mountains of Pennsylvania. Equipment was difficult to obtain. In fact there were only a few thousand people in the entire nation who found pleasure in skimming the snow-covered trails and slopes on skis.

Scandinavians brought the sport to this country. They built a few jumps and maintained a few trails for competition where large numbers had congregated. In 1908 the Lake Placid Club, in the Adirondacks of New York, pioneered in skiing through their Sno Birds. They also built jumps and laid out trails. And because it was the only place in the country with sufficient winter-sports experience, Lake Placid was awarded the 1932 Winter Olympics. The games added impetus to skiing, for many spectators found a new diversion when they tried it themselves.

In 1930 the Canadian railroads dispatched a few trains especially for skiers. That same year the Boston & Maine Railroad sent snow trains from Boston to New Hampshire, and for five years successfully operated the only such trains in the United States.

In the latter part of 1934 representatives of ski clubs called on railroad companies in New York City to arrange special transportation for the purpose of skiing. In January 1935 the New York, New Haven & Hartford Railroad sent out New York's first snow train, to Norfolk Conn. It, too, was successful. The New Haven Line sent out several other snow trains at special rates in 1935, and last year the New York Central and Lackawanna railroad, followed suit. New York skiers had a choice of excursions to the Berkshires, the Catskills, the Adirondacks, and the White and Green Mountains.

When the railroad companies agreed to run these special trains they realized that they needed the cooperation of other businesses in order to make the transportation pay. Baggage-car concessions were granted to stores, so that equipment could be rented or sold enroute. Arrangements were made for skiing instruction. Small towns in snow regions agreed to reduce rates and provide trails and slopes; it was worth that effort to get guests in an otherwise dull season.

Last winter department and sporting-goods stores in New York stocked heavily with winter-sports equipment. They hired the services of noted instructors and installed booths for the dissemination of information regarding winter resorts, accommodations, weather, and transportation. Two stores built indoor practice slides. Newspapers published columns about the sport as well and weekly reports of conditions in various sections of the northeast. At Grand Central Station huge charts were erected showing temperatures and depth of snow at skiing centers.

Leading up to the season now about to open, pep meetings were held in New York City, at which motion pictures of skiing were shown and informal talks were given. New clubs were formed. Many individuals gave both their time and money freely to develop the sport. Among these were Mr. W.A. Gluesing and Mrs. Florence Fuller, who worked unerringly to arrange meetings and promote skiing in older to get more transportation. Through their efforts a new resort developed.

During the summer of 1935 a few enthusiasts had gone to North Creek, N.Y., in the Adirondacks, arranging accommodations at low rates at the two hotels and in practically every private home, laying out trails and establishing a ski school. When the first snow train pulled in on January 11, 1936, the town was filled to capacity. Through popular demand six other New York trains were sent there, carrying over five hundred passengers. After the skiing season the town purchased the whole of Gore Mountain, where the trails and slopes are located, and enlarged all facilities in preparation for this year.

That is a fair example of what skiing has done for small communities in the snow belt. In all the state parks of the northeast new trails have been laid out and open hills have been cleared of rocks and stumps. Camps and shelters used by bikers are drawn into use and many new ones were built. The trails were marked and designated as to grade and length, and whether for novice, intermediate, or expert skiers. Maps were issued giving, locations and descriptions of trails.

Even new parks have been acquired. Officials of the New Haven Railroad worked with the state of Massachusetts to develop sites close to existing rails. Last year Beartown State Forest was opened near South Lee, Mass., a little over three hours' ride from New York. C.C.C. workers cleared trails and slopes for all classes of skiers. This winter another Massachusetts park, East Mountain State Park in the Berkshires, near Great Barrington, will be ready. Recently the new Gilford Recreation Project in New Hampshire was constructed at a cost of $350,000.

On Friday nights and Sunday mornings the railroad terminals are jammed with a gay, laughing crowd in winter-sports togs holding long ungainly-looking skis and poles. Several sections of snow trains pull out. Enroute the skiers industriously wax their runners while they discuss the latest relevant news and the eternal questions of wax and weather. Spirits soar. Friendships spring up. When the trains return the beginners join the others in promising themselves more such trips.

In the northeast the season extends from the beginning of the year until spring. About fifty miles up the Hudson, at Bear Mountain, New Yorkers find their closest skiing grounds. Inland and a little farther north there is a slightly longer season in the Catskill Mountains. In the Adirondacks there is a wide choice of terrain ranging from easy grades to steep, over-the-mountain rails. There are camps and shelters for those who, with a pack on their backs, make trips of several days' duration.

In New England, beginning with the Litchfield Hills of Connecticut, the region extends north through the Berkshires of western Massachusetts, where there are a number of state parks. The Green Mountains of Vermont offer a longer season, particularly in the vicinity of Mt. Mansfield.

Perhaps the most noted skiing section is in the White Mountains of New Hampshire. More than a score of small towns enjoy a winter season developed through seven years of snow-train service from Boston. The Appalachian Mountain Club, which maintains a number of large huts, has done a great deal to build up this region, as well as has Dartmouth College.

The daredevils gather for late spring skiing at Tuckerman's Ravine above the timberline on Mt. Washington, highest peak in the northeast. Heavy winter storms usually pile fifty feet of snow in a natural bowl. Frequently naked above the waist, skiers plunge over the Head Wall at breakneck speed, zig-zagging their course to keep control down the steep incline.

Farther north the Laurentians of Canada provide deep snow for about four months. Some Sunday trains take skiers from cities to a given destination and pick them up at different points on the return trip. For many years the French Canadians in the Province of Quebec have had large clubs, each with a band, ceremonies, and a distinctive costume, devoted to snow-shoeing; but this slower sport is now giving way to skiing, especially among the younger generation.

Not only in the cast has the sport of skiing rapidly developed. It has spread across the northern rim of the nation, through the Rockies of Canada and the United States and into the high mountains of the Pacific coast. Already Mt. Baker and Mt. Rainier in Washington, Mt. Hood in Oregon, and Mt. Whitney in California are well-known in this recreation and a network of trails extends through all the parks.

For 1937 extensive plans have been made for a successful season. Promoters have been scouting new places and exacting certain conditions before transportation arrangements are made. Accommodation rates must be kept at a reasonable point. Practice slopes and trails for novice, intermediate, and expert skiers must be maintained. Entertainment, instruction, bus and ski-towing service must be supplied. Accurate weather conditions must be reported. The towns have awakened to a new source of revenue and are eager to comply with such demands.

Another venture in the west is attracting a great deal of attention. In a wide basin, 6,000 feet above sea level and hemmed in by mountains rising up to 12,000 feet, the Union Pacific Railroad has developed a skiers' paradise at Sun Valley, Idaho. Electrically-operated chair-lifts run 2,000 to 6,500 feet up the mountainsides, thus saving an arduous climb. Trained guides and a graded school for instruction are available. After a day of exercise on varied terrain these sportsmen return to a luxurious lodge and may dive into an outdoor hot-springs pool for a swim in mid-winter.

During the five years in which the Boston & Maine Railroad pioneered in the snow-train business it carried over 59,000 skiers. Last year, almost 40,000 entrained from New York City (beside the uncounted number who traveled by automobile) and approximately 37,000 paid almost $100,000 in fares to four New England railroads.

It has been estimated that 30,000 pairs of skis were sold in New York City last year. Since the stores were sold out last year they are doubling their stock this year. If these 60,000 who are expected to buy skiing equipment spend $40 each for skis, poles, boots, and clothing, a moderately low price at which fair furnishings can be bought, it will represent a turn-over of $2,400,000 for New York City alone.

At some stores complete furnishing cost as high as $300. Besides, many of last years' skiers will add to and replace their present equipment and some will invest in the more expensive types. There are many new gadgets on the market and there are skiers want, such as parkas, ruck-sacks, creepers and goggles.

Last year some of the skiing centers entertained more than 500 guests in a single week-end. Food and lodging for the two days could be obtained for as low as $4.50 per person. Many paid more than that, and spent money for entertainment, instruction, and other things as well. If $8 were accepted as the average spent by every skier at the resorts, villages would be richer by $4,000 for one weekend; and the season usually lasts nine of ten weeks. Small wonder that these small towns in the snow regions are eager to supply adequate facilities. Their dull season has suddenly become bright and shining....

There is a reason for the mounting enthusiasm. The spirit of good-fellowship is more pronounced in skiing than in any other sport. It is found on the hills and trails, in hotels and resorts, and particularly on returning trains when whole carloads join in singing. The vigorous exercise in the keen air relaxes nerves and muscles, engenders a feeling of well-being and stimulates health.

So, throughout the world where the snow lies deep, there are winter playgrounds for sportsmen. Recreation is moving into a new field, draws no line of distinction in either age or class. The baby born only two years ago growing into a husky youngster. Who knows what his stature will be when he eventually reaches maturity?

## FIGURE SKATING IN THE UNITED STATES

[*John D. Rockefeller Jr.'s decision to turn the sunken plaza in front of Radio City into a skating rink symbolized the popularity of skating in the 1930s. In 1938, a survey of the alumni of six American colleges revealed that in terms of participation, skating was their fifth-most popular recreational sporting activity. In the following article, sports-writer John Tunis outlines the major reasons for the growth of figure skating. The introductory paragraphs on the early history of skating were deleted. John Tunis, "Skating (Figure)," Sport for the Fun of It (New York, 1940), 224-229.*]

Today there are ice rinks in the most unexpected places: in Richmond, Virginia, as far south as Miami in Florida, in Westwood, Los Angeles, in Fort Worth, Texas, and even in a clime as tropical as Hollywood. Every winter ice shows in Manhattan turn away thousands of paying guests in their weekly runs; in 1939, there were unfulfilled telephone calls for 22,000 seats, making sporting history in the metropolis. The reasons for this increased interest in skating are many. The first, and not least important is the publicity given to figure skating in recent years by these ice shows, and specially by Sonja Henie both in person and in the movies.

Up to 1930 about all the general public knew of the art of figure skating was through photographs of a girl poised on one leg, with obscure references to spins, eagles, leaps and so forth. That year the United States Figure Skating Association was given permission by the International Skating Union in Europe to hold the Figure Skating Championships in this country for the first time. The former organization approached the executives of Madison Square Garden in New York. They had never heard of people actually paying cash to watch skaters. However, the Garden being at the time in none too prosperous a condition, they decided to take a chance and staged a show. To their surprise, it was a success. The crowds came in large numbers to watch a young 18-year-old Norwegian make her first appearance in the United States. This was the debut here of Sonja Henie

Well known in Europe where she had already been twice Olympic champion and was later to defend her title for the third time, she was merely a name in the United States. But her fame drew the gallery; everyone who saw her went away enchanted, and the free skating on the last night of the competition attracted 10,000 clients who paid $20,000 in cash to watch her. The American sporting public was impressed; and so were the executives of Madison Square Garden.

Within the next few years there followed the development of native skating stars; Maribel Vinson, Robin Lee (both of whom competed in the 1936 Winter Olympics at Garmisch), Oscar Johnson and the Shipsteads. This was just what the doctor ordered. The beauty and the thrill of skating helped, and the good looks of many feminine contestants didn't hurt either. A year or so later, a widely publicized interview with Everett McGowan, a top-flight lacrosse and professional hockey star who had gone into skating, dispelled the idea that this was a sport for sissies. He reported that five minutes of the pastime took more out of him than anything he had ever tried.

The second big factor in the growth of skating has been the development of artificial ice. Formerly hockey and skating were dependent on the weather just as skiers are today. Synthetic ice-making did away with all this. It assured the success of hockey leagues and ice troupes. Several years ago a new invention helped the sport. It was called Iceolite. Invented by a lady chemist, this substance freezes at 120 or 130 degrees F. It is impervious to weather or moisture and can be pressed off with a hot iron the way you press your pants. Currently, Iceolite cost about $2.50 a square foot, so to freeze a small rink, 100 feet by 50 wide, would set you back around $12,500.

Thanks to synthetic ice, the skating troupes flourished. The first great ice show was held at the Chicago Exposition in 1934 when the Black Forest Ice Village provided one of the leading attractions. This gave the boys an idea. Edward H. Mahlke of Chicago produced an ice show with Oscar Johnson and the two Shipsteads which ran sixteen months at the Hotel Sherman in Chicago. In 1936 the Ice Follies staged their first show in New York and the public was becoming skate-conscious. It was being impressed upon them by the feats of Oscar Richards, the Manhattan skating octogenarian and others, that you didn't have to be young and pretty to have lots of fun on skates, and that even at the age of 80 you could do many figures on the ice.

The third factor in the spread of the sport in the United States recently, has been the development and improvement of the shoe skates.... Today, authorities say that thanks to the modern skate-shoe, no one's ankles are too weak for skating. Tiny tots of eight and nine are now doing jumps and turns which their elders would have considered daring twenty years ago. Helped by the modern rocker with its broad blade and crenulated toe, everybody's [sic] on a skate today.

One sporting good manufacturer reports that up to 1933 mostly hockey skates were sold. This used to be called the "all-round" skate: it had narrow tubes with no heel on the shoe and was high and flat off the ground. This skate was bought both by boys and girls. Since the increase in figure skating began, all this has changed. Now 85% of skates sold girls are figure skates with a broader edge, closer to the ice, and rockered.

All this, the streamlining of skates which made figure skating easier, the invention of artificial ice, the entrance of showmanship into exhibitions, helped build up the increased interest in this participating sport in recent years. But probably if one single person more than another is responsible, it is Sonja Henie, the 30-year-old Norwegian who held the World's Amateur Figure Skating title from 1927 until she turned professional in 1937.

Sonja with crowd-lure in her eyes, a pair of high-priced skates and two sturdy legs, grossed $700,000 for 29 shows in five cities on her first cross-country tour in 1938. Subsequent trips have not been unprofitable. Her entrance into motion pictures—she leapt into the big ten of the movie world in one year with a single picture—helped sell the nation on skating. Sporting goods stores all report that the sale of rocker skates doubled after the release of the blonde Norse maiden's films.

Other ice troupes have had a hand in popularizing skating, too. The Ice Follies started it back in 1936 with a capital of $6,000. They used to travel in busses. Before long they had three special cars attached to limited trains, and in 1938 played to nearly a million customers. Incidentally, Madison Square Garden in New York, originally built for prize fights, had 20,000 at its indoor bouts in the winter of 1939, while ice skating and hockey drew over 1,000,000.

At least 50 new rinks have been constructed in the recent years in various parts of the United States and Canada; in big cities and small ones. Calgary, Edmonton and Saskatoon north of the border, Hollywood with its Pan Pacific arena all had new rinks. Saskatoon spent $40,000 on an ice plant following seven lean financial years. Vernon and Nelson, two towns of 5,000 people in British Columbia have enclosed rinks. Crookston, Minnesota, population 6,000, erected the finest structure of its kind in any city of the same size in the country. Their new Winter Sports Arena cost $72,000; the town put up $29,000 and the rest was furnished by the WPA. This arena, 233 feet long by 110 wide, is expected to pay for itself in ten years. But to January 1, 1940, the WPA had built 691 ice skating rinks and repaired or improved 155 more, with a total skating area of 43,000,000 square feet. [How to flood a rink has been deleted.]

Figure skating is much easier indoors on artificial ice than outdoors. Prescribed figures are difficult with the grit of a city on the ice. But the main thing is to skate. To get out some where and enjoy the sport. Sonja started when she was eight. Maribel Vinson began at four. On the other hand, lots of former inter-collegiate athletes between 40 and 50 have recently taken up figure skating as ideal exercise and fun. Here's one sport for which you are never too young, never too old to make your athletic hobby.

## ICE SHOWS IN CANADA

[*The oldest continuous winter ice show in Canada was the Quebec winter carnival. It usually included dogsledding, snowshoeing, skating, skiing, tobogganing, and hockey. The Toronto Skating Club, which hired many European instructors, trained some of North America's best figure skaters. By the end of the decade, competition from commercial ice shows began to diminish interest in club ice extravaganzas. The following article examines Canada's role in the growth of ice carnivals. Frederick Edwards, "The Biggest Show On Ice," Maclean's Magazine (1 March 1938), 8-9, 40, 42.*]

Just eight evenings from the date of this issue of Maclean's Magazine there will be on exhibition in the city of Toronto one of the most astonishing and, in some respects, bewildering phenomena the field of modern sports entertainment has to offer.

At Maple Leaf Gardens in the goodly metropolis, crowds will pack the auditorium to its capacity for four successive nights. The rink seats 12,450 people. Standing room to the legal limit will be sold as well; say an average of 13,000 on each of the four evenings. The estimate is quite conservative. That is, 52,000 people; and 52,000 is a lot of people to draw to an indoor sports entertainment anywhere. Ask your nearest professional promoter.

Those folks will come from all over. Most of them, naturally, will be Torontonians, but there will be crowds pouring in by train and car and bus from numerous Ontario towns and villages. Others will arrive from far distant communities in provinces east and west, and from the United States, the latter probably including a sprinkling of wistful-eyed talent scouts from Hollywood. There will be spectators whose homes are in Europe, and, following the precedent of former years, at least one or two from the West Indies and South America.

There is more to it than that. This sports entertainment has nothing to do with the Stanley Cup, the National Hockey League, tennis, the six-day bike race, championship boxing, wrestling, football, or any sort of a championship whatsoever. It is not a professional show, although there will be a handful of pros, among the entertainers; perhaps one per cent. It is not promoted by the astute and effervescent Mr. Conny Smythe, who on this occasion is just the landlord, with the rent money in the top drawer. Its direction and control are in the hands of amateurs who employ professional talent sparsely where there is a positive need for professional assistance, but not otherwise.

No commercial organization makes a nickel from those 52,000 admission fees. The money taken at the gate goes for the promotion of figure skating as a sport, after the overhead is paid. In the overhead, though, are included wages for musicians, stage hands, dress designers and dress-makers, electricians and scores of other workers whose behind-the-scenes efforts are necessary to the success of the enterprise.

The show will not be ballyhooed. There will be no extensive advance publicity or advertising campaign to build up a demand for tickets. All the tickets were sold five weeks ahead of the opening night. The spectacle will present around 400 performers, whose ages range from under six to over sixty years. It will cost between $40,000 and $50,000 to produce—$10,000 a night at the lowest possible figure. It represents the professional promoter's dream of bliss—and it is run entirely by amateurs.

**FIGURE SKATING IS NEWEST CRAZE**

This particular show, the Thirty-first Annual Carnival of the Toronto Skating Club, produced this year in partnership with the Granite Club of Toronto, is just one of many. In Montreal, Ottawa, Winnipeg, Regina, Vancouver, Calgary, Edmonton, there are skating clubs which produce ice carnivals. New York, Boston, Chicago, Cleveland, and a dozen other United States cities, as well as London, England, have suddenly gone completely gaga over similar spectacular doings on skates. But, because it has been going on for so long, has built up so large and enthusiastic a permanent public support, has so great and diversified a group of skilled performers to draw from, and is planned and directed by men and women with so many years of practical experience behind them, the Toronto Carnival tops them all. After you have been fussing around with any project, however ambitious, for thirty years, you begin to get the hang of how to do it.

Figure skating is the newest craze, and it promises to break all records in popular acclaim since Irene Castle first bobbed her hair. Swing music isn't in it compared with this business of doing didoes on the short steel blades with the serrated toes. For generations regarded as an exotic and slightly sissy pastime, numbering among its devotees only a handful of Society (with a big S), people who had time and money to spend on such foolishness, figure skating, sometimes called fancy skating, has at long last come into its own.

Today the butcher, the baker, and the candlestick maker, as well as their wives and offspring, their sisters and their cousins and their aunts, are keenly aware of the sport. Things have developed to the point where both the sub-deb and the shop girl are exhibiting a passionate interest in such intricate convolutions as the outside-inside, the inside-outside, the double three-change-double three, the loop-change-loop, and the bracket-change-bracket.

The sudden—and it is sudden, comparatively speaking—popularity of figure skating and its related ice carnivals is traceable to a number of contributing influences, among them the final triumph of truth over error visible in the general acceptance of the fact that snow and ice and cold weather need not necessarily compel a complete hibernation of the human race. The scientific discoveries which made practical the production of artificial ice at low cost have been an important factor, as they have been in the world sweep of that fastest of all competitive sports, Canada's own national game of ice hockey. The circumstance that Sonja Henie, former world's champion figure skater, has advanced to stardom in the cinema is important, too, for the motion-picture influence is international and overwhelming when it comes to guiding popular opinion.

Long before Hollywood heard of skating, however, the ice carnival itself was slowly carrying figure skating toward the sudden public acclaim of the past couple of years. And Canada has had a great deal to do with the development of the modern ice carnival. Thus far most of the world's greatest individual skaters have come from Europe; but the ice spectacle, whose appeal depends primarily on mass dancing rather than on the skill of individual performers, was Canadian in origin, with the Toronto club the pioneer in the field. For years traditional ballet numbers have been a feature of the Toronto show. And now the "ice ballet" is broadening out to include all kinds of mass dance interpretations, some of them extremely modern in feeling.

Figure skating, itself, of course, has its own special fascinations. It develops muscular control and coordination to a notable degree, and it is graceful, exhilarating, and not too demanding of the human physique. Most skating clubs today have among their members a few enthusiasts who may be seen daily practicing the simple preliminaries at the age of five, with a solemn concentration far beyond their tender years. At the other end of the parade, there are gallant oldsters of seventy out on the club rink two or three evenings a week, enjoying a waltz, or inscribing intricate patterns on the white ice with skill and eclat.

Figure skating is not too expensive for the moderate income; less costly than skiing, or, in the long run, than hockey. You can pay as high as $22.50 for a fine pair of figure skates, and $35 for specially constructed boots; but you can buy them, too, for $5 and $12 respectively. Strike an average between these extremes and you will have a good idea of the outlay involved for equipment in the case of a run-of-mine skater. Elaborate costumes, such as you see in the rotogravure pictures, are expensive, of course, but they are not essential to the happiness of the ordinary skater who goes out for the exercise.

Club membership fees are not high in most cases, because the surplus revenue from club-sponsored carnivals is ear-marked for the purpose of advancing the sport, and that keeps the dues down. Some Canadian clubs admit junior members practically without charge, and in all cases the price of a membership for a small boy or girl is purely nominal. They like to catch their future champions young. In fact they have to if they are to develop champions at all, for it takes years of practice to perfect a really top-notch skater in international competition.

The sport is intensively organized, with basic rules and regulations accepted in every skating country. The international body is The International Skating Union in English, Union Internationale de Patinage in French, and International Eislauf-Vereiningung in German. Over in England the National Skating Association of Great Britain controls things, and in Canada the ruling organization is the Figure Skating Department of the Amateur Skating Association of Canada. The figures which must be learned before a club member can qualify for competition are the same the world over—the eights, loops, brackets, counters, and the rest of them—and these, of course, plus an equal skill in the free skating division, form the foundations upon which Olympic competition is organized.

**A GORGEOUS SPECTACLE**

So much for the sport, as a sport. Recent developments have brought the spectacular features of figure skating so largely into the foreground of the picture that already some of the older sportsmen are beginning to shake their heads and ask whether this is figure skating or the show business they are mixed up in.

The professional theatre has taken to figure skating in a big way. Carnivals held in New York, Chicago, and other American cities this winter had more the look of a

"George White's Scandals" than a figure-skating convention, and in London three all-ice revues were shown on the stages of leading theatres, including a Covent Garden—of all places—ballet presentation. There exists a definite trend, deplored by some, applauded by others, toward stressing the interpretive side of skating through the elaboration of ballets, pantomimes and dance numbers; and this has led to a distinct change in figure-skating technique, which is now regarded by the "interpretive" school as being a means to an end rather than an end in itself. The end, of course, is the interpretation of music on ice through the dance. Zealous and stern devotees of figure skating as a sport are grumbling more than a little about this newfangled tendency; but the general public eats it up, which is why 52,000 people will see the Ice Carnival in Maple Leaf Gardens this March.

Any ice carnival promoted by any skating club demands a tremendous amount of enthusiastic and self-sacrificing effort on the part of its membership, whether participating in the spectacle, serving on committees, or just fetching and carrying on behalf of the good cause. This figure-skating business must have something. The Winter Club of Montreal, the Minto Club of Ottawa, whose members for years have specialized in pair and four skating, as well as the clubs in Winnipeg, Regina, Edmonton, Calgary, run their own shows successfully year after year, and it is worth noting that every club helps out every other club, sending featured skaters from its own membership to add a touch of outside glamor to the show. In Vancouver, where the climate is less wintry than in the easterly provinces, the local ice fiestas are almost altogether in the hands of visiting skaters, but the clubs back them, and their members are planning now to take them over in another winter or two. [The description of how to prepare for an ice carnival has been deleted.]

**ALWAYS A SELL-OUT**

...When the Ice Carnival was first organized in Toronto thirty years ago, it was a free-for-all charivari in fancy dress of one night only. Later, as public interest increased, it developed into an ordered and disciplined entertainment for two nights each winter, and the two-night rule was in force for many years. In 1935 the demand for admissions so far exceeded the supply that the carnival Committee made it a three-night show, feeling that loss of interest might result if the public felt there was no chance of seeing the show.

That was only three years ago, yet after having sold out the house for the 1937 show, actually a month before the opening date, and still having disappointed and clamorous applicants for tickets camped on the front porch with blood in their eyes, the schedule was hoisted to four performances this year; and again the thing was a sell-out five weeks before the opening.

Perhaps more important even than the remarkable success of the ice carnival is the fact that Canadian skating clubs are making a definite contribution to international good will by missionary work, south of the border. Skaters from Montreal, Ottawa, Winnipeg and Toronto are featured performers in a score of similar spectacles in New York, Boston, Chicago, Cleveland, and a score of other United States cities and towns every winter. Our champions have carried the Canadian idea of what ice is for [sic] across the American Republic from ocean to ocean, have been acclaimed everywhere. The Toronto show directly inspired the creation of the recently established Cleveland Club. After putting on shows for the Ohioans for three or four seasons, the Canadians advised and assisted the Cleveland enthusiasts in the organization of their own home enterprise, which now has a membership of more than a thousand. That is Toronto's baby, and its parents are proud of it.

Make no mistake about the success of the ice carnival as an amusement enterprise. There are a dozen or more shows touring the United States right now, and in many of them Canadian skaters are starring. Sonja Henie has her own troupe, which grossed $140,000 for seven performances in Detroit. Her gross for six days at Madison Square Garden in New York was $156,000. Said the New York Times: "It is safe to say that New York has now been awakened to a form of entertainment that had partly escaped its notice heretofore."

Figure skating has reached the heights. And Canada has had a great deal to do with putting it there.

### CURLING—THE ROARING GAME

[*The Scottish influence and the construction of artificial rinks during the decade assisted the growth of curling in the Maritimes. Based on newspaper coverage in the first half of the decade, curling ranked sixth in Halifax and Winnipeg, ninth in Montreal, twelfth in Toronto, and fifteenth in Vancouver. In Brier play, Manitoba captured the national curling championship six times during the decade, and Ontario and Alberta each won the title twice. In general, curling attracted older men. The average age of the 1935 Brier competitors was over 50. The creation of the Dominion Curling Association in 1935 helped to promote the sport by standardizing rules for hacks, stones and sweeping. J. Lewis Brown, "Aye! The Roarin' Game," National Home Monthly (March 1936), 27, 52.*]

Almost synonymous with recollections of Scotland are golf, curling and whisky and many there are that contend the last named is a definite affinity of the other two.... However, the question of the moment is a pastime, democratic and ancient; a recreation which is embracing the world, or at least wherever Jack Frost can hold forth; the venerable game of curling which was born or at least reared in bonnie Scotland, and which heritage from the land of heather has been given to both the male and female of the species....

Curling has invaded the far reaches of the country. Thousands depend upon it for their winter recreation, and from the modern artificial plants to the hamlets where single sheets of outdoor ice are maintained there is but one law, the Royal Caledonian. Even in the prairie provinces curling is almost akin to a fetish. Farmers bring produce to town to pay their curling fees, and it is the rule that the farmers have the ice in the daytime and townsfolk at night. Men and women, boys and girls are banded together in clubs and leagues in this grand old Scottish pastime, and how they can curl! Their record of victories in the Macdonald Brier tankard, a competition emblematic of the curling championship of Canada, by far excels any other part of the Dominion. Curling to them is what baseball is to the United States, and when the Winnipeg bonspiel is in session, to which rinks from Alberta, Saskatchewan and Manitoba throng, the daily papers even get out extra addition recording the scores of the important games.

But to the Canadian curling world, the ultimate is to be a member of the rink which wins the Macdonald Brier tankard. This competition was first played in 1927 as an annual playdown for the Dominion title. It is held each year on the artificial ice lane of the Granite Club, Toronto, provincial winners and one sectional winner, northern Ontario, competing in the round robin final, each rink meeting all of the rest during the championship and the team with the best percentage of wins and losses being declared the champions. As this is written it is possible that when this year's championship begins on March 2, the tenth annual series, every province in the Dominion will be represented, for British Columbia will be making her first appearance and Prince Edward Island has asked for recognition. Unfortunately there was some question as to whether or not the Island province's entry was received in time, but the final decision was in favor of the island. The important fact is that Canada is now wholeheartedly and nationally curling conscious; ably represented in what will unquestionably be another battle "Wi' Besom and Stane."

Eight championship rinks competed in the first championship and Halifax proved the winner with six victories and one loss.... In 1935 the Thistle Curling Club, of Hamilton, Ont., as Ontario champions, wrested the title from the west. They will defend it this year. This rink, composed of Gordon Coates and the three Campbell brothers, Duncan, Donald and Gordon, the last named as skip, gained their reward after three attempts as Ontario champions.

I only mention them individually from the host of marvelous curlers who have played in the various championships because their success was the result of a rather unique effort on the part of Dr. Bertram, of Dundas, Ont. Several years ago, when this quartette were about sixteen and seventeen years of age, the curling doctor took them in hand and taught them the game with one purpose in mind, the winning of the Macdonald Brier. That they achieved their ultimate goal emphasized the fact that even in curling correct teaching is an important factor—and they are never too young to learn. The publicity surrounding the "kid" rink's triumph will unquestionably cause many other young men to turn to curling.

If the many interesting developments of future Dominion championships could be foretold, particularly in the winning of the Macdonald Brier tankard, for after all that is the zenith of Canadian curling, no hesitation is necessary in declaring that with all parts of the country united in purpose and sport, curling will achieve new heights of excellence and gain thousands of new adherents.

# SELECTED BIBLIOGRAPHY

## PRIMARY SOURCES

### MANUSCRIPT COLLECTIONS
Acadia University, Wolfville, Nova Scotia
African-American Historical Society Library and Archives, SF
Archives of Ontario, Toronto
Baldwin Room Toronto Reference Library
California Historical Society, SF
CFL Hall of Fame Archives, Hamilton
Chicago Historical Society
City Public Library of San Francisco
Dalhousie University, Halifax, NS
Free Library of Philadelphia
North York Public Library, Ontario
San Diego Historical Society Research Archives
Swarthmore College, PA
University of California, SF
University of California, Berkeley
University of Prince Edward Island
University of Toronto

### NEWSPAPERS
*New York Times*, miscellaneous
*Chronicle Herald* (Halifax), miscellaneous
*Toronto Globe*, miscellaneous

### SPORTING AND POPULAR MAGAZINES
*American Lawn Tennis*, 1931-1936
*American Legion Magazine*, miscellaneous
*The American Magazine*, 1930-40
*American Mercury*, miscellaneous
*The American Rifleman*, 1930-40
*American School and University*, miscellaneous
*American Ski Annual*, miscellaneous

*The Athletic Journal,* 1931-36, 1938-40

*Atlantic Monthly,* miscellaneous

*Baseball Bulletin,* miscellaneous

*The Baseball Magazine,* 1930-40

*Beach and Pool,* miscellaneous

*Boxing News Record,* miscellaneous

*Bulletin of the Canadian Journal of Health, Physical Education and Recreation,*
    1930-40

*Canada Life,* miscellaneous

*Canadian Aviation,* miscellaneous

*Canadian Forum,* 1930-40

*Canadian Magazine,* 1930-40

*Canadian Monthly,* 1930-40

*Canadian National Railways Magazine,* 1930-40

*Canadian Sports and Outdoor Life,* vol. 1, no. 1, 1932

*Chatelaine,* miscellaneous

*The College Physical Education Association, Proceedings of the
    Annual Meetings,* 1930-40

*Collier's,* 1930-40

*Country Life & the Sportsman,* 1930-40

*Digest,* vol. 1, 1937

*Esquire,* 1930-40

*The Football News,* 1939

*Fortune,* 1930-40

*Good Housekeeping* 1930-40

*Harper's Monthly Magazine,* 1930-40

*Hygeia,* 1930-40

*The Journal of Negro Education,* miscellaneous

*Journal of Health and Physical Education,* 1930-40

*Liberty,* 1933-40

*The Literary Digest,* 1930-37

*Maclean's Magazine,* 1930-40

*Mind and Body,* 1931-38

*The Nation,* 1930-40

*National Home Monthly,* 1932-40

*The NCAA News Bulletin,* miscellaneous

*Negro Historical Bulletin,* 1937-40

*News-week,* 1933-40

*The New Yorker,* 1933-40

*The North American Review,* 1930-31

*Outdoor Life,* 1936-40

*Outlook and Independent,* miscellaneous

*The Physical Educator,* 1940

*Playground,* miscellaneous

*Research Quarterly,* 1930-40

*Recreation,* 1931-40

*Rotarian,* 1931, 1934-40

*Saturday Evening Post,* 1930-40

*School and Society,* 1930-40

*The School Review. A Journal of Secondary Education,* 1930-40

*Scientific American,* 1930-40

*Scribner's Magazine,* 1930-40

*Soaring,* miscellaneous

*Sportsman,* miscellaneous

*The Sportswoman,* miscellaneous

*Time,* 1930-40

*The Western Home Monthly,* 1930-32

*The Writer's Monthly,* 1930-40

*Yachting,* miscellaneous


**GENERAL—SPORTS, CHARACTER, AND MORALITY**

Paul Bender, "Opportunities for Character Education in Athletics," *The Athletic Journal* (October 1939), 30-6.

Karl W. Bookwalter, "The Co-educational and Co-Recreational Use of Physical Education Activities," *College Physical Education Association Proceedings* (December 1940), 62-9.

George Carens, "A Sports Editor Views Intramural Athletics," *The College Physical Education Association, Proceedings* (1936), 61-4.

Ruth H. Colby, "Juvenilia and the Sporting Page," *The Writer's Monthly* (September 1938), 80-2.

Parke H. Davis, "College Sports Decline," *The North American Review* (November 1930), 449-54.

"Does Radio Cut the Football Gate?" *The Literary Digest* (16 July 1932), 32-3.

Leo Fischer, "Inside the Press Box," *Esquire* (November 1938), 89, 181-3.

Paul Gallico, "Women in Sports Should Look Beautiful," *Reader's Digest* (August 1936), 12-4.

John L. Griffith, "Do Athletics Contribute to Education?" *The Athletic Journal* (January 1932), 26-34.

John L. Griffith, "Superiority vs. Inferiority," *The Athletic Journal* (April 1935), 20-1.

Foster Hewitt, *Down the Ice. Hockey Contacts and Reflections* (Toronto, 1935).

"Intramural and Interscholastic Athletics," *Mind and Body* (March 1934), 330-6.

William M. Lewis, "The Outlook for College Athletics," *The Journal of Health and Physical Education* (December 1931), 8, 9, 43.

Mark MacIntosh, "Are Sports Worth Their Salt?" *School and Society* (4 March 1939), 277-9.

Jack McCaffrey, "The Sport Story," *The Writer's Monthly* (November 1936), 146-8.

Bernice Miller, "Growing Need of Physical Recreation Among Employed Women," *The Journal of Health and Physical Education* (November 1930), 3-8, 43.

Janet Owen, "Publicity–Your Right Hand Man," *The Journal of Health and Physical Education* (October 1936), 481-4, 520-2.

Julia H. Post, Mabel J. Shirley, *Selected Recreational Sports for Girls and Women* (New York, 1933).

James Edward Rogers, "The New Challenge to Physical Education," *The Physical Educator* (October 1940), 11-3.

H.H. Roxborough, "Money Talks," *Maclean's Magazine* (15 March 1930), 17, 73, 75.

Henry Roxborough, "The Illusion of Masculine Supremacy," *The Canadian Magazine* (May 1935), 15, 55.

Howard J. Savage, "Athletics for Women from a National Point of View," *The Journal of Health and Physical Education* (June 1930), 12-6, 42.

Bill Stern, "I've Got Those Broadcasting Booth Blues," *Liberty* (28 December 1940), 44-6.

John Tunis, "Changing Trends in Sport," *Harpers' Monthly Magazine* (December 1934), 76-86.

Left Wing, "Public Enemy No. 64B. The Football Broadcaster," *The Nation* (9 October 1935), 405-6.

Left Wing, "Men Who Make America's Gods," *The Nation* (27 February 1935), 245-7.

Fred Wittner, "Shall the Ladies Join Us?" *The Literary Digest* (19 May 1934), 42-3.

"World at Ringside by Proxy," *The Literary Digest* (5 October 1935), 32-3.

**AERONAUTICS**

Kim Beattie, "Canada Flies Again," *Liberty* (6 July 1935), 38-40.

Reed Landis, "Air Races Promise New Thrills," *The Chicago Visitor* (July 1930), 10-12.

Ray McPhie, "Gliding—Sport of the Air," *Canadian Aviation* (February 1931), 13, 14, 30-1.

Howard Mingos, "New Things in the Air," *The North American Review* (July 1930), 53-9.

**BASEBALL**

"Baseball. Major Leagues Go in for Night Life in Big Way," *The Literary Digest* (1 June 1935), 20.

Dink Carroll, "Big League Stuff," *Maclean's Magazine* (1 July 1935), 21, 32-3.

H.L. Chaillaux, "Winner Take All," *The American Legion Magazine* (November 1937), 38-9, 57-8.

Robert Considine, "Ambassadors of Baseball," *Liberty* (12 March 1938), 16-7.

Mrs. Joe Cronin, "The Private Life of a Baseball Wife," *Liberty* (2 May 1936), 10-1.

Daniel M. Daniel, "Bright Prospects of Sunday Baseball," *The Baseball Magazine* (January 1934), 343-4, 354, 381.

James M. Gould, "The Ladies Adopt Baseball," *The Baseball Magazine* (December 1934), 289, 296, 330-1.

Joe DiMaggio, "How Much Is a Ballplayer Worth?" *Liberty* (18 June 1938), 15-6.

Ford Frick, "Centennial," *Baseball Magazine* (June 1939), 290.

"Hard Times Hit the Minors," *The Literary Digest* (30 July 1932), 37.

W. R. Hoefer, "It Isn't Cricket," *Baseball Magazine* (August 1939), 416, 425-6.

"How Tony Gives Latin Tone to Our National Game," *The Literary Digest* (2 July 1932), 37.

"Is the American Boy Quitting Baseball?" *The Literary Digest* (12 July 1930), 35-6.

Jerry D. Lewis, "Basehits Incorporated. By a Major-League Club Owner as Told to Jerry Lewis," *Liberty* (20 February 1936), 23-5.

Rev. C.M. McConnell, "Passing the Preacher," *Baseball Magazine* (July 1934), 354-5, 380-1.

"More Light on Night Baseball," *The Literary Digest* (27 September 1930), 36-7.

"The Baseball Centennial. A Suggested Address to Your Committee," The National Baseball Centennial Commission, 1939.

Rud Rennie, "Changing the Tune from Gloom to Cheer," *The Literary Digest* (16 June 1934), 25-6.

Ken Smith, "Ballpark Hazards," *Baseball Magazine* (July 1938), 339-40, 377.

Eliot B. Spalding, "I Like Baseball, But–," *The American Mercury* (June 1938), 181-6.

"War Versus World Series," *The Literary Digest* (12 October 1935), 36.

"Will Baseball Bugs Become Night-Hawks," *The Literary Digest* (31 May 1930), 35-6.


**BASKETBALL**

"Basketball. Midseason," *Time* (19 February 1934), 40-1.

"Basketball. Winter Sport Attracting 80,000,000 Spectators Each Season," *The Literary Digest* (12 December 1936), 37-9.

David Brace, "Why Women Should Supervise Girls' Athletics," *Spalding's Athletic Activities for Women and Girls. Official Basketball Guide for 1930-31* (New York, 1931), 66-7.

Ruby L. Brock, "The Effect of the New Guarding Rule on Women's Basketball," *The Journal of Health and Physical Education* (February 1933), 38-40, 52-3.

J. Lewis Brown, "Basket Madness," *The National Home Monthly* (February 1940), 39-41.

John Bunn, "Should the Center Jump Be Banned?" *The Athletic Journal* (December 1935), 6-7.

Kyle Crichton, "Hooping it up," *Collier's* (8 February 1936), 29-30.

"The First National Intercollegiate Basketball Tournament," *The Athletic Journal* (February 1938), 26.

Leo Fischer, "Thar's Gold in Them Hoops," *Esquire* (April 1938), 67, 202-5.

Melvin Goldsmith, "Controversial Basketball in the Far West," *The Literary Digest*, (26 January 1935), 38

Frances Kidd, "Is Basketball a Girls' Game?" *Hygeia* (September 1935), 834-5.

"Point a Minute," *Time* (24 January 1938), 49.

Quentin Reynolds, "Court Marshal," *Collier's* (14 January 1939), 19, 35.

*Spalding's Official Basketball Guide, 1930-9.*

"Western Women Begin Athletics," *The Western Home Monthly,* 88 (Winnipeg) (September 1931), 26-8.

"What They're Saying about Basketball with the Center Jump," *The Athletic Journal* (February 1938), 5-7, 42-5, 47.

Left Wing, "The Build-up of Basketball," *The Nation* (27 March 1935), 357-9.

**BRITISH BALL GAMES**

J. Lewis Brown, "Canada's Place in Cricket," *National Home Monthly* (July 1937), 22, 39, 43, 60.

"Cricket, the Englishman's Baseball Game," *The Literary Digest* (27 January 1934), 30.

"The Greater Game. In Which the Author Champions Canadian Rugby and Maintains that the Thousands of Cheering Fans Cannnot All Be Wrong," *The Canadian Magazine* (1930), 18, 43.

"Is Rugby the Remedy for Gridiron Roughness?" *The Literary Digest* (14 November 1931), 36-8.

Stephen Leacock, "Cricket for Americans," *Atlantic Monthly* (June 1940), 766-9.

"Rugby. Cambridge Gives Us a Few Lessons in British Game," *The Literary Digest* (14 April 1934), 24.

"Rugby Pays Its Own Way Through College," *The Literary Digest* (January 1934), 30.

"Rugby Rebuilds on Old Foundations," *The Literary Digest* (31 March 1934), 24.

J.S. Smith, "English Rugby Revived in Canada," *The Literary Digest* (5 January 1935), 35.

**COMBAT SPORTS**

Ben M. Becker, "Amateur Boxing on the Upswing," *Boxing News Record* (1939), 114-7.

Jack "Kid" Berg, "English Vs. American Styles," *The Ring* (January 1931), 20-1.

"Boxing. Schmeling Commutes Across Atlantic—For What?" *News-week* (29 May 1937), 19-20.

"'Brown Bomber' Gets the Notices," *The Literary Digest* (6 July 1935), 32-3.

Kyle Crichton, "Sock, Brothers. No Wrist Is Left Unslapped in the Effort to Keep College Boxing Mild and Gentlemanly," *Collier's* (30 January 1937), 41, 43.

Edward Doherty, Noll Gurney, "Struggles to the Death in the Prize Ring. A Vivid Chronicle of Tragedies that 'Couldn't Have Happened'—But Did," *Liberty* (1 July 1933), 5-8.

"Dusky Meteor. Joe Louis of the Dead Pan, Marvel of the Prize-Ring," *The Literary Digest* (13 June 1936), 36

Joel P. Glass, "Intercollegiate Boxing Booming," *The Literary Digest* (19 January 1935), 35.

Steve Hannagan, "Black Gold," *The Saturday Evening Post* (20 June 1936), 14, 74, 76.

Archie McKinnon, "White Dynamite, Muzz Patrick," *Maritime Sport Illustrated* (Oct./ Nov. 1933), 12-3.

Bernard F. Mooney, *Wrestling for Beginners* (Columbus, Ohio, 1935).

Hugo Otopalik, "Amateur Wrestling—Builder of Boys and Men," *The Athletic Journal* (January 1935), 16-17.

"Report of the N.C.A.A. Wrestling Championships, *NCAA News Bulletin,* 6 (May 1938).

George Shaw, "The Boy Who Beat Six Champions. A Quick Sketch of Jimmy McLarnin, Probably the Greatest Little Human Fighting Machine Ever Produced in Canada," *Maclean's Magazine* (1 December 1932), 18, 48-9.

John Tunis, "Fencing," *Sport for the Fun of It* (New York, 1940), 69-108.

Wakefield Speare, "Forty-Seven Fights Up. Scenes from the Chicago Boyhood of Barney Ross, Leading up to the World's Lightweight Championship, *Esquire* (January 1934), 119, 148.

Jim Tully, "Today's Greatest Prizefighter," *Liberty* (13 August 1938), 47-8.

"Where Are the Irish Fighters?" *The Literary Digest* (29 March 1930), 42-3.


**FIELD SPORTS—LACROSSE, FIELD HOCKEY, SPEEDBALL**

Helen M. Barton, "Speedball—The New Game in Physical Education for Women," *School and Society* (24 August 1935), 262-3.

"Field Hockey. 10,000 Women Devoted to Organized Shinny," *News-week* (31 October 1936), 21-2.

Lewis B. Funke, "America Takes Her Place in the Hall of Fame," *The Literary Digest* (17 February 1934), 32.

Martha Gable, "The Increasing Popularity of Lacrosse for Girls," *The Journal of Health and Physical Education* (November 1935), 31, 60.

Fred I. Lorenson, "What's Wrong With Our Lacrosse?" *Maclean's Magazine* (1 August 1931), 12, 41.

Barbara Strebeigh, "The National Field Hockey Tournament," *The Sportswoman* (January 1932), 8-9.

4

SELECTED BIBLIOGRAPHY

## FOOTBALL—CANADIAN

J. Lewis Brown, "Kicking the Ball Around," *National Home Monthly* (September 1935), 20, 57.

J. Lewis Brown, "Murderers in the Football Stands," *National Home Monthly* (October 1938), 22, 38.

J. Lewis Brown, "Senior Football and Sham Amateurs," *National Home Monthly* (September 1937), 22-3.

Dink Carroll, "Just an Old-Fashioned Coach," *Liberty* (31 October 1936), 39-41.

Dink Carroll, "Startling Football to Come. Can the East Come Back?" *Liberty* (24 September 1936), 41-4.

Dink Carroll, "Should Canadian Football Go American?" *Liberty* (3 December 1938), 13.

Harold F. Cruickshank, "Can the West Win the Rugby Championship? A Revealing Authoritative Review of the Handicaps that Prevent Our Western Teams from Clinching Titles," *Liberty* (9 November 1935), 15-7.

John DeGruchy, "Maclean's All-Star Football Teams for 1939," *Maclean's Magazine* (1 December 1939), 14-5, 50-1.

J. Norvil Marks, "Prairie Kick-off. Western Squads Prepare for the Annual Grid Wars while a Rules Showdown Approaches in the Canadian Rugby Setup," *Maclean's Magazine* (1 October 1939), 17, 27-8.

J. Norvil Marks, Dink Carroll, "Football Forecast," *Maclean's Magazine* (1 October 1938), 10, 41-3.

Phil Pryor, G.C. Alexander, "Football Fever Grips Western Rugby World," *Maritime Sports Illustrated* (September-October 1935), 16-8.

Harry Randall, "Will the West Kick Through?" *Maclean's Magazine* (15 September 1935), 14, 38-9.

Leslie Roberts, "'Americanizing' Canadian Sport," *The Canadian Magazine* (November 1931), 8, 41.

Michael J. Rodden, "It's a Scandal. A Slashing Attack by one of the Dominion's Outstanding Football Coaches on Sham Amateurism and the Americanization of the Canadian Game," *Maclean's Magazine* (1 November 1936), 21, 39-40.

J.S. Smith, "The Greater Game. In Which the Author Champions Canadian Rugby and Maintains that the Thousands of Cheering Fans Cannot All Be Wrong," *The Canadian Magazine* (November 1930), 18, 43.

"Winnipeg Rugby Football Club, 1930-1938," Winnipeg Rugby Football Club 1938 Souvenir Program (Canadian Football Hall of Fame and Museum).

Scott Young, "Joe Ryan. He Licked the East and Put Winnipeg's Rugby Football Club on a Playing Basis," *Liberty* (7 October 1939), 11-2.

## FOOTBALL—US COLLEGE

Forrest C. Allen, "Should College Athletes Be Paid? Yes!" *The Rotarian* (October 1938), 21-2, 60.

W.J. Barnett, "Night Football in High Schools, Yes!" *The Journal of Health and Physical Education* (October 1932), 30, 56-7.

Dana X. Bible, "The Educational Value of Football," *The Athletic Journal* (January 1935), 24-5.

Byron F. Boyd, "Youth Swings into Action. American Young Men in Training to Fight Traditional Rivals on Gridiron Instead of Battlefield," *The Football News* (14 September 1939), 1.

Ralph Cannon, "The Mashed Potato League," *Esquire* (October 1937), 79, 178 180-1.

"College Gold-Mine," *The Literary Digest* (10 October 1936), 41-3.

Edwin B. Dooley, "Where Does Football Go From Here?" *The American Magazine* (October 1933), 55, 137-9.

Edwin B. Dooley, "Watch that Pass!" *The American Magazine* (October 1935, 46-7, 88-92.

Floyd R. Eastwood, "Causes of College Sport Accidents; Preliminary Findings from a Study of Safety in College Physical Education," *Research Quarterly* (October 1934), 63-9.

"Football," *New Yorker* (30 September 1933), 63.

"Football," *Hygeia* (October 1934), 876-7.

"Football Deaths. What Shall We Do to End Them?" *The Literary Digest* (26 December 1931), 24-5.

"Foot Ball in Colored Colleges," annual reports in *Spalding's Official Foot Ball Guide* (New York, 1930-40).

"Football Injuries," *Hygeia* (September 1933), 776.

"Football's Perennial Controversy," *The Literary Digest* (9 January 1937), 32-4.

"Football Talks Back," *The Literary Digest* (19 January 1932), 35-7.

Benny Friedman, "6-Man Football. How Far Will it Go?" *Liberty* (29 January 1938), 27.

James M. Gould, "King Football Begins His Short Reign," *The Baseball Magazine* (November 1934), 546-7, 569-70.

Christian Gauss, "Our Professional Football Amateurs, *Scribner's Magazine* (December 1931), 587-93.

Herb Graffis, "The Alumni Discover Education," *Esquire* (January 1938), 51, 139-40, 142.

John L. Griffith, "Should College Athletes Be Paid? No!" *Rotarian* (October 1938), 23-4, 59.

John L. Griffith, "Are College Athletics Commercial and Is It Necessary to Subsidize Athletes to Produce a Winning Team?" *The Athletic Journal* (November 1938), 14, 42-44; March 1939, 26-31.

Paul F. Hagen, "Night Football in High Schools, No!," *The Journal of Health and Physical Education* (October 1932), 31, 57.

Dick Hyland, "Football. The Killer?" *Liberty* (4 February 1933), 16-9.

"N.C.A.A Rewrites Rule Book to Draw Bigger Gates," *News-week* (28 September 1935), 19.

"Letting the Air Out of College Football, *The Literary Digest* (27 June 1931), 40-1.

J.H. Nichols, "The Football Problem in the Liberal Arts College," *The College Physical Education Association, Proceedings of the Fortieth Annual Meeting, 1936* (1937).

Alfred E. Parker, "Training for Athletics and Health," *Hygeia* (November 1933), 983-6, 1040, 1042.

Ike Petersen, "One for the Money," *Esquire* (November 1935), 34B, 192-4.

Lawrence Perry, "The Football Brahmins Make Peace,"*Scribner's Magazine* (November 1934), 289-93.

Ralph Piper, "Night Football Is Here to Stay," *The Athletic Journal* (April 1939), 36-8.

Marvin S. Pittman, "Football—Sport or Spoils," *School and Society* (13 August 1938), 213-7.

"Report of Rules Committee," *The Athletic Journal* (March 1932), 19-26.

Grantland Rice, "For Students Only," *Collier's* (14 February 1931), 10.

Frank Scully, "Stumble-Backs. Does Football Make Players Stupid?" *Liberty* (9 October 1937), 53-5.

Clark Shaughnessy, "Two for the Show," *Esquire* (November 1935), 35, 190-2.

Clark Shaughnessy, "The Era of Pitch and Catch," *Esquire* (September 1935), 23, 146, 149.

"Stanford Editor vs. Football Fans," *The Literary Digest* (28 November 1936), 37-8.

"The Status of Intramural and Interscholastic Athletics," *School and Society* (3 March 1934), 266-7.

"A Student's Survey of the Football Situation, *The Athletic Journal* (April 1933), 43-5.

George Trevor, "Strategic Trends in 1933 Football," *The Literary Digest* (14 October 1933), 20.

John R. Tunis, "American Sports and American Life," *The Nation* (25 June 1930), 729-30.

"Varsity Football," *School and Society* (21 November 1931), 699-700.

Ed Weir, "The Technique of Filming Football to Aid the Coach," *The Athletic Journal* (November 1934), 17.

Ernest H. Wilkins, "College Football Costs," *School and Society* (19 March 1938), 381-4.

"Will the Lively Football Start Another War?" *The Literary Digest* (12 September 1931), 35.

Left Wing, "Football. Hope of American Education, *The Nation* (27 November 1935), 615-6.

Stanley Woodward, "The Game Is Geared for Touch-Downs," *The Literary Digest* (22 September 1934), 36.

**FOOTBALL—NFL**

"Football—a School and College Game," *The Athletic Journal* (October 1938), 18-9.

George Halas, "We Play Football for Keeps," *Esquire* (October 1934), 106, 308.

"Let's Look at the Facts," *The Athletic Journal* (March 1934), 18-9.

Steve Owen, "We Play for Pay. But We Want to Win," *Liberty* (30 October 1937), 45.

Ike Petersen, "One for the Money..." *Esquire* (November 1935), 34b, 192-4.

"Pro Football Versus Collegiate," *The Literary Digest* (31 October 1936), 40-1.

"The Professional-Amateur Game," *The Athletic Journal* (September 1935), 21.

Clark Shaughnessy, "...Two for the Show," *Esquire* (November 1935), 190-2.

**GOLF**

"Ball Crusade," *Time* (1 June 1931), 48-9.

"Bawling Out the New Golf-Ball," *The Literary Digest* (13 June 1931), 38-9.

J. Lewis Brown, "War-Time Golf," *National Home Monthly* (June 1940), 18, 38, 40, 42.

"Canada Cheers 'Silent Sandy,' Her Golf Hero," *The Literary Digest* (1 October 1932), 31-2.

Dink Carroll, "Let Go of Those Clubs!" *Maclean's Magazine* (15 May 1938), 18, 34.

Miles Coen, "Is the Golf Snob on the Way Out?" *Liberty* (16 May 1936), 17.

"The Coronation of the Emperor Jones," *The Literary Digest* (2 August 1930), 33-5.

Chick Evans, "The Religion of Golf," in *The Blue Book of Sports* (Los Angeles, 1931), 267-8.

Herb Graffis, "Storms in Already. There's a Cloud for Every Silver Lining, Even When Your're Paid to Play Golf," *Esquire* (March 1937), 94, 122.

Walter Hagen, "Fairway Queens and Rough Cats," *Esquire* (August 1934), 81, 89.

"Hard-Hitting Helen of Hewlett," *The Literary Digest* (17 October 1931), 32-3.

W.O. McGeehan, "The Man Who Will Fill Bobby Jones's Shoes," *The American Magazine* (June 1930), 32-3, 98-9.

"More News of the Great Golf-Ball War," *The Literary Digest* (11 July 1931), 34-5.

"The New Ball and Your Golf Game," *The Literary Digest* (31 May 1930), 38-9.

"Pat for Patty Jane," *The Literary Digest* (7 March 1936), 40.

Gerry Purcell, "Can a Canuck Win It?" *MacLean's Magazine* (15 August 1939), 12, 14.

Dudley B. Reed, "Exercise. To Golf, a Grand Servant of Man But a Poor Master," *Hygeia* (October 1938), 911-4, 951, 952.

Quentin Reynolds, "So She Took Up Golf," *Collier's*, (9 May 1936), 26, 86.

Quentin Reynolds, "Sam Snead—Golfer," *Collier's* (29 May 1937), 13, 56.

Gene Sarazen, "The Gates Go Down. How Golf Professionals Learned There Is More Money in Pleasing Than in Puzzling Their Public," *Esquire* (July 1935), 40, 174-5.

John R. Tunis, "Golf," in *Sport for the Fun of It* (New York 1940), 109-138.

John R. Tunis, "Why Be a Badger. Analyzing those Slightly Infantile Business Men Who Become High Priests of Tennis and Golf and the A.A.U.," *Esquire* (September 1939), 36, 99.

"Winter Troupe," *Time* (17 January 1938), 33-4.

**HOCKEY**

Clifford Bloodgood, "Hockey Fans in Big League Baseball," *The Baseball Magazine* (January 1934), 367, 376.

J. Lewis Brown, "Tragedy and Glamour in Hockey," *National Home Monthly* (January 1939), 4, 18.

Dink Carroll, "Hockey Needs Its Hard Harrys," *Maclean's Magazine* (1 March 1937), 18, 44-5.

Kyle Crichton, "Hockey Jockey," *Collier's* (4 January 1936), 21, 37.

Frederick Edwards, "Magnates Under the Microscope. Managing a Professional Hockey Club Is One of the Most Nerve-wracking and Fascinating Jobs in Existence," *Maclean's Magazine* (1 January 1932), 17, 28, 32.

Elmer W. Ferguson, "Red-Ink Hockey," *Maclean's Magazine* (15 November 1938), 14, 33-4.

James C. Hendy, "Sport's Royal Family," *The Canadian Magazine* (December 1936), 20, 24-5.

Foster Hewitt, H.H. Roxborough, "He Shoots. He Scores!" *Maclean's Magazine* (15 December 1937), 14, 43-4.

Foster Hewitt, *Down the Ice. Hockey Contacts and Reflections* (Toronto, 1934).

"Hockey. The Return of Eddie Shore," *The New Yorker* (10 February 1934), 73.

"Hockey. Trio of Puck-Chasing Pugilists Lure Arena Crowds," *News-week* (27 January 1934), 20.

"Puck-Chasers Open Bruising Season," *The Literary Digest* (14 November 1936), 53-4.

Ted Reeve, "Hockey Hopes. Highlights on the Season's Outlook for the Big League Exponents of the Fastest Game in the World," *Maclean's Magazine* (1 December 1930), 8, 50, 58.

Ted Reeve, "Hockey's Frozen Assets," *National Home Monthly* (February 1933), 16, 45.

Leslie Roberts, "It's Always Open Season. Some Reflections on the Gentle Art of Sportsmanship," *Canadian Magazine*, May 1931, 8, 30

Leslie Roberts, "'Americanizing' Canadian Sport," *Canadian Magazine* (November 1931), 8, 41.

H.H. Roxborough, "Eight-Star Conacher. He Has a Continent-wide Reputation in Five Major Sports and is Expert in Others," *The Canadian Magazine* (November 1934), 8, 30.

H.H. Roxborough, "Hockey Export. It's Still a Million-Dollar-a-Year Business, but Foreign Countries Are Beginning to Develop Their Own Players," *Maclean's Magazine* (1 January 1939), 6.

H.H. Roxborough, "Hockey Grows Up. Rinks, Rules and Equipment Have Been Improved but It's Still the Same Old Game," *Maclean's Magazine* (15 December 1939), 17, 26.

H.H. Roxborough, "Is Hockey Losing Color?" *Maclean's Magazine* (1 November 1939), 8, 47, 49.

Alexander Sayles, Gerard Halleck, *Ice Hockey. How to Play and Understand the Game* (New York, 1931).

Roger Treat, "How to Watch Ice Hockey," *Esquire* (February 1940), 88-9.

### INDOOR SPORTS—BOWLING, BILLIARDS

"Billiards Comes of Age," *The Literary Digest* (2 November 1933), 32-3.

"Congress Bowls," *Time* (22 March 1937), 60, 62.

Quentin Reynolds, "Cue Tips," *Collier's* (5 April 1935), 26, 51.

"Cushions, Concentration, and Luck," *The Literary Digest* (18 April 1936), 42-3.

"Lady Bowler," *The Literary Digest* (1 February 1936), 38-9.

"Lawn Bowlers," *Time* (23 August 1937), 32-3.

Lewis Brown, "Kissing Them in the 1-3 Pocket," *National Home Monthly* (April 1937), 22, 40, 42.

"Pin Congress Draws Alley Champs. Bowling Feature Outdraws Olympics in Its Entries," *The Literary Digest* (27 March 1937), 32-3.

"System Sports Activities," *Canadian National Railways Magazine* (1931-8).

John Tunis, "Bowling," "Lawn Bowls," *Sport for the Fun of It. A Handbook of Information on 20 Sports Including the Official Rules* (New York, 1940), 32-60, 170-82.

**INTERNATIONAL GAMES—OLYMPICS, EMPIRE GAMES**

Fred Beck, "The Tenth Olympiad. And What We Can Expect of Canada," *Western Home Monthly* (July 1932), 11-2, 46-7.

Foster Hewitt, "On to the Olympics," *Canadian Comment* (February 1932), 23-4.

John T. McGovern, "A Review of the 1936 Olympic Games," *Sportsman* (September 1936), 20-5, 68-9.

"Non-Aryan Victors in Nazi Olympics," *The Literary Digest* (29 August 1936), 33-4.

"Olympics. Nations Eye Each Other," *News-week* (1 August 1936), 20-1.

"Olympic Wrath," *Time* (4 November 1935), 61-2.

"Our Friends the Enemy in the Olympic Games," *The Literary Digest* (30 July 1932), 30-3.

*Report of the American Olympic Committee* (New York, 1932).

*Report of the American Olympic Committee* (New York, 1936).

J.S. Smith, "Canada at the Olympiad," *Canadian Magazine* (July 1932), 26-7.

Paul Washke, "The Eleventh Olympiad," *The Journal of Health and Physical Education* (November 1936), 539-42, 587-8.

Mel Wharton, "Olympic Village. The Answer to an Athlete's Prayer," *Hygeia* (August 1932), 722-4.

"The XI Olmpiad, Berlin," *Beach and Pool* (February 1936), 5-6.

**MARKSMANSHIP**

Dave Craft, *The Teaching of Archery* (New York, 1936).

"The Revival of the Bow and Arrow," *The Literary Digest* (29 July 1933), 26.

John R. Tunis, *Sport for the Fun of It. A Handbook of Information on 20 Sports Including the Official Rules* (New York, 1940), 3-17.

"Again—Forward!" *The American Rifleman* (17 May 1939), 8.

"At Vandalia," *Time* (5 September 1932).

Bill Cunningham, "Aiming to Please," *Collier's* (7 August 1937), 18, 47.

William Harnden Foster, "Skeet. Champion—In Name Only?" *Outdoor Life* (December 1939), 72-3.

William Harnden Foster, "Skeet. Our Novet Tournament Set a Record," *Outdoor Life* (March 1939), 100-2.

G.M. Garlington, "Hail the Riflewoman," *The American Rifleman* (January 1931), 16-7, 24, 26.

"Gunbugs," *Time* (30 September 1940).

"International Rifle Shoot," *Canadian National Railways Magazine* (October 1935), 17, 30.

R.M. Nichols, "A New Form of Skeet," *Country Life* (September 1933), 49-50, 76.

"Skeet. Shotgun Golf Holds Its First National Tournament," *News-week* (7 September 1935), 25.

Lawrence B. Smith, "In Praise of Trapshooting," *Country Life* (February 1934), 70-1, 80.

Lawrence B. Smith, "Trapshooting as Practice for Field Shooting," *Country Life* (May 1933), 50-1, 84.

Hart Stilwell, "The Watermelon Kid," *Esquire* (June 1940), 47, 122, 124-5.


### RACING ON LAND—AUTOMOBILES, BICYCLES

"Bike Grind. Six-Day Racers," *The Literary Digest* (28 November 1936), 38-9.

"Boom in Bikes," *The Literary Digest* (28 September 1935), 33.

Lee Davidson, "The Race to Nowhere," *The Rotarian* (December 1937), 28-31.

John E. Lodge, "The Bicycle Comes Back," *Reader's Digest* (August 1936), 88 (reprinted from *Popular Science Monthly*).

Arthur Shumway, "One Way to Die," *Esquire* (February 1934), 32, 142.


### RACING ON WATER—YACHTING, MOTOR BOATING, ROWING

Colville Colton, "Sculling Ace," *Maclean's Magazine* (1 September 1935), 18-9.

"Cornell Reigns Again on the Hudson," *The Literary Digest* (12 July 1930), 38-40.

"The Cup Races," *The Nation* (18 June 1930), 693-4.

"Fighting the Battle of the Harmsworth Trophy Over Again," *The Literary Digest* (26 September 1931), 30, 32-3.

Harry Foster, "The Poor Man's Harmsworth Trophy," *Liberty* (7 September 1935), 26-7.

Alfred F. Loomis, ed., *The Yachtsman's Yearbook, 1934* (New York, 1934).

Andrew D. MacLean, "Motor Boating—The Sport That Has Come Back," *The Canadian Magazine* (May 1931), 45-6.

Everett B. Morris, "Rutgers Is Intercollegiate Champion," *Yachting* (August 1933), 57, 88, 90.

Herbert L. Stone, "In Defense of the America's Cup," *Scientific American* (September 1934), 117-9.

Harold S. Vanderbilt, *On the Wind's Highway. Ranger, Rainbow and Racing* (New York, 1939).

"Yachting. An Adverse Wind of Controversy in the Cup Races," *News-week* (29 September 1934), 18.


## RACKET SPORTS

"Amateur Players Ask for Open Tennis, " *The Literary Digest* (17 February 1934), 34-5.

Eddie Bauer, "Badminton Grows in Popularity," *The Journal of Health and Physical Education* (November 1936), 579, 590-1.

Mercer Beasley, "Competition for Cup Players," *Esquire* (May 1934), 47, 158, 163-4.

Fessenden S. Blanchard, "Paddle Tennis as a Year Round Sport," *Sportswoman* (March 1931), 65.

"Bouncing Game. Table-Tennis Speeds Up, Crowds Out Old-Fashioned Playing Styles," *The Literary Digest* (29 May 1937), 33-4.

Mrs. William E. Bramwell, "Badminton and the Oldest Badminton Club in the World," *The Sportswoman* (May 1931).

J. Lewis Brown, "Court Rackets," *National Home Monthly* (January 1937), 18, 35, 38.

Coleman Clark, "The Revival of Ping-Pong," *Country Life* (January 1933), 55-6, 78.

Coleman Clark, "Table Tennis Comes of Age," *Esquire* (December 1936), 80, 177-9.

R.L. Condy, "Lawn Tennis, *Saturday Night* (12 September 1931), 9-10.

"Court Sports. Six Games with a Common Factor. It's a Racquet," *News-week* (14 March 1936), 30-2.

Kyle Crichton, "Stand Back and Swing," *Collier's* (16 November 1935), 31, 36.

Parke Cummings, "This is a Players' Game," *Esquire* (March 1938), 69, 174, 176.

Allison Danzig, "Court Tennis," *Esquire* (August 1934), 92, 130-1.

Allison Danzig, "A Pell-Mell Iron Man," *Esquire* (November 1936), 77, 132, 134.

Frederick Edwards, "Can Canada Win the Davis Cup?" *The Western Home Monthly* (April 1932), 26, 50-1.

John E. Fitzgerald, "Why We Lose at Tennis," *Maclean's* (1 September 1939), 12, 37.

Robert D. Forster, "Progress Is the Keynote," *Spalding's Official Badminton Guide* (Brantford, Ontario, 1935).

Corinne Reid Frazier, "The Revival of Badminton. An Old Favorite Comes Back," *Country Life* (August-September, 1932), 41-2.

W.C. Fuller, "Girls Are Made of Star Dust," *American Magazine* (August 1935), 28-9, 118-20.

Robert E. Hart, "Table Tennis Leaves the Parlor," *Esquire* (January 1935), 76, 120.

Milton Holmes, "A Feud for Two," *Esquire* (December 1934), 81, 160, 162.

Helen Jacobs, "The Psychology of Tennis Clothes," *Good Housekeeping* (June 1934), 31.

Helen H. Jacobs, "Shall I Turn Professional," *Country Life* (July 1933), 64-5.

Helen Hull Jacobs, "Do Marriage and Tennis Mix?" *Liberty* (18 August 1934), 32-3.

Helen Hull Jacobs, "Man Against Women in Tennis," *Liberty* (1 June 1935), 20-2.

"New Laurels for the Much-Crowned Tilden," *The Literary Digest* (25 July 1931), 38-9.

"Old Sport, New Rage," *The Literary Digest* (25 January 1936), 37-8.

Arthur E. Patterson, "The Parent of the Racquet Games," *Literary Digest* (21 April 1931), 32-3.

Coleridge Petersen, "He Played His Own Game," *The Canadian Magazine* (July 1931), 13, 48.

Bernath E. Phillips, *Fundamental Handball* (New York, 1937).

Jack Purcell, "The Boom in Badminton," *The Saturday Evening Post* (29 February 1936), 24-5, 76-7.

Marcel Rainville, "Tennis Look Up," *Maclean's Magazine* (1 June 1937), 19, 40.

Herbert Reed, "The Davis Cup," *Scribner's Magazine* (July 1933), 27-9.

Quentin Reynolds, "Quick Work," *Collier's* (2 October 1937), 18, 58.

Quentin Reynolds, "Watch the Birdie," *Collier's* (23 March 1935), 17, 34.

Vincent Richards, "The Astonishing Mr. Tilden," *Esquire* (August 1937), 51, 176.

Vincent Richards, "Ex-Amateur," *Liberty* (8 July 1933), 20-3.

"Robert Grant 3rd, King of Racquets," *News-week* (7 March 1938), 27.

"Squash Racquets Gaining New Popularity," *The Literary Digest* (20 January 1934), 26.

John Tunis, "Maker of Champions," *Esquire* (September 1934), 71, 126.

John Tunis, "That Open Tournament," *Esquire* (September 1937), 67, 153-4.

Donald C. Vaughan, "Shuttlecock Shots on the Rise," *Esquire* (December 1939), 88, 127.

Lincoln A. Werden, "Squash in the American Winter Diet," *The Literary Digest* (5 January 1935), 34.

Victor Weybright, "So We Walked Off With Badminton," *Esquire* (May 1935), 58, 113.

Jack Wright, "Talking About Tennis..." *Maclean's Magazine* (1 July 1931), 11, 63.

**RECREATIONAL SPORTS—VOLLEYBALL AND SOFTBALL**

"America's Fastest Growing Game," *Popular Mechanics* (June 1936), 834-7.

John Brown, "Developments in Volley Ball," *Recreation* (November 1932), 378-81.

Kyle Crichton, "Not So Soft," *Collier's* (10 August 1935), 24, 38.

Leo Fischer, "Not So Softball," *Esquire* (June 1937), 73, 140, 143-4.

Leo Fischer, "Softball Steps Up," *Reader's Digest* (June 1939), 134-5.

Ted Shane, "Baseball's Precocious Baby," *The American Magazine* (June 1939), 36-7, 150-1.

Frank Taylor, "Fast and Pretty," *Collier's* (20 Agust 1938), 22, 23, 38.

John Tunis, "Volleyball," *Sport for the Fun of It* (New York, 1940), 315-28.

Dick Williams, "Softball Isn't Sissy. How Baseball's Stepchild Has Outgrown Its Parents," *Liberty* (23 September 1939), 51.

## TRACK AND FIELD

Frederick Lewis Allen, "Breaking World's Records," *Harper's Monthly Magazine* (August 1936), 302-10.

Karl Diem, "Machines as Field Judges," *The Journal of Health and Physical Education* (May 1936), 314-5.

Eleanor Methney, "Some Differences in Bodily Proportions Between American Negro and White Male College Students as Related to Athletic Performance, *Research Quarterly* (December 1939), 41-53.

"New Mile Record—Civilization's All Right," *The Literary Digest* (29 July 1933), 26.

Herbert Reed, "Weather Clear, Track Fast for Four-Flat Mile," *The Literary Digest* (2 June 1934), 38.

Larry Snyder, "My Boy Jesse," *The Saturday Evening Post* (7 November 1936), 14-5, 97.

"Track. Colored Mercuries Wear Spiked Instead of Winged Shoes," *News-week* (20 July 1935), 26-7.

"Track Ends a Boom Run on the Boards," *The Literary Digest* (17 March 1934), 24.

Harry Vinock, "Five-Six-Seven-Hurdle!" *Esquire* (July 1936), 72, 147-8.

"Western Athletes' Rough Way with Records," *The Literary Digest* (13 June 1931), 36-8

## TURF, HORSE RACING, EQUESTRIAN EVENTS

"American Kings of the Sport of Kings," *The Literary Digest* (27 September 1930), 32-3.

Dink Carroll, "The King's Plate," *Liberty* (28 May 1938), 9-10, 24.

Lester H. Clee, "Should We Legalize Horse-Race Betting? No!" *The Rotarian* (August 1936), 12-3, 58-9.

Maxine Davis, "They're Off. An Article on Race-Track Gambling," *Good Housekeeping* (June 1939), 26-7, 199-204.

"Dollar Democracy at Meadow Brook," *The Literary Digest* (14 September 1935), 36-7.

Robert Saunders Dowst, "This Betting Business," *Esquire* (February 1939), 74-5.

Robert Ordway Foote, "Polo Goes Democratic," *Esquire* (July 1934), 50, 113.

Robert V. Hoffman, "Polo on the Campus," *Country Life* (June 1933), 37-40.

"Horse Show," *Time* (16 November 1936), 72-3.

"Horse Show. Precision Riding by Canadian 'Mounties' Is Feature of Glittering Show," *The Literary Digest* (14 November 1936), 55.

"Horse Shows and Hunts," *The New Yorker* (18 November 1933), 79.

Robert F. Kelley, "The Galloping Game Moves Indoors," *The Literary Digest* (10 February 1934), 24-5.

Robert F. Kelley, "The Galloping Game Goes to College," *The Literary Digest* (9 June 1934), 54-5.

John Kieran, "Horse and Buggy Days," *The American Magazine* (August 1938), 32-3, 149-50.

"Layers and Players," *Time* (30 April 1934), 5, 21-2.

"Pari-Mutuel Tonic Puts New Life in Race Season," *The Literary Digest* (29 July 1933), 27.

"A Primer for Polo Players and Watchers," *The Literary Digest* (2 September 1933), 28.

Quentin Reynolds, "Racers in Harness," *Collier's* (15 August 1936), 15, 40.

"Scions of Hambletonian 10," *Time* (28 August 1933), 35-6.

Evan Shipman, "Life in the United States. Trotting Races Today," *Scribner's Magazine* (October 1933), 231-5.

Frank Steele, "From Range to Rodeo," *The Country Guide* (February 1934), 5, 55.

Dayton Stoddart, "Race Tracks. A Billion-Dollar Racket with Murder on the Side," *Liberty* (15 February 1936), 22-6.

"The Thoroughbred Industry and 'The Sport of Kings,'" *The National Home Monthly* (July 1933), 12-3, 36, 51.

"Trotters and Pacers in a Come-Back," *The Literary Digest* (1 August 1936), 35-6.

B.F. Warren, "The Billion-Dollar Poolroom Racket," *The Nation* (30 July 1938), 106-9.

Lupton Allemong Wilkinson, "The Sport of Kings," *The North American Review* (September 1930), 33-9.

Stanley Woodward, "The Horse Before the Cart," *The Literary Digest* (11 August 1934), 32-3.

## WATER SPORTS—SWIMMING, DIVING, WATER POLO, SYNCHRONIZED SWIMMING

K. Abe, "Swimming Japan. What Can it Do in the Coming Olympiad?" *The Journal of Health and Physical Education* (June 1932), 20-2.

Fred A. Cady, "America's Diving Monopoly," *Liberty* (13 July 1940), 50-3.

Arthur J. Daley, "Don't Splash, Please!" *Collier's* (19 February 1938), 22, 51.

"Females in Water," *Time* (22 April 1935), 44.

Ben Grady, "Americans, Japanese, and Swimming," *The Journal of Health and Physical Education* (April 1934), 35, 58.

James S. Kearns, "Record Turn-Over," *Esquire* (June 1936), 97, 128.

R.J.H. Kiphuth, "Japan Challenges America in the Water," *The Literary Digest* (12 May 1934), 24.

Howard T. Ploessel, "Give Swimming Its Rightful Place," *The Athletic Journal* (September 1935), 46-7.

Frederick A. Spongberg, "Suggestions for Judging Fancy Diving," *Beach and Pool* (May 1937), 17, 24, 33.

"Sportswomen. Athletic Queens Remain Lovely Ladies," *News-week* (29 July 1933).

## WINTER SPORTS—SKIING, FIGURE SKATING, CURLING

"America Cradles Scandinavia's Sport," *The Literary Digest* (10 February 1934), 22.

Parke Cummings, "If They Toil Not, Neither Do They Spin," *Esquire* (December 1938), 63, 166.

"Curling," *News-Week* (15 February 1936), 24-5.

William T. Eldred, "The Growth of Skiing," *The Athletic Journal* (December 1939), 32, 34.

Robert D. Forster, "Engineering a Ski-Jump Tower," *Scientific American* (February 1932), 86-8.

Harold Gore, "A Well-Balanced Physical Education Program Should Provide for Winter Sports Trends," *The American School and University* (1939), 235-40.

"Indoor Winter," *Time* (21 December 1936), 31-2.

John Kieran, "The Skis the Limit," *The American Magazine* (February 1937), 28-9, 93-5.

John Kieran, "A Good Skate," *The American Magazine* (March 1938), 46-7, 71-2.

Leonard L. Knott, "Canada's New Winter Thrill," *Liberty* (20 February 1937), 26-7.

Richard Lewis, "Why Hibernate. Skiing is Golf's Brother," *Esquire* (February 1936), 66, 118, 121.

Ruth Senfel, "Belles on Their Toes," *Collier's* (5 February 1938), 20, 50.

"Skating. Sonja Henie Whirls and Spins in Paris Dresses," *News-week* (17 March 1934), 24.

R. S. Stephens, "Skiing over America," *Sportsman* (November 1936), 40-2, 74.

Frank White, "Soop, Mon! Soop! The Scotch Game of Curling," *Esquire* (March 1940), 56-7, 120.

"Will Sonja Henie Change American Styles in Beauty?" *Liberty* (27 February 1937), 22-4.

## SECONDARY SOURCES

## CHAPTER 1

Dave Berkman, "Long Before Arledge...Sport & TV. The Earliest Years, 1937-1947—As Seen by the Contemporary Press, *Journal of Popular Culture* (Fall 1988), 49-61.

Susan K. Cahn, *Coming on Strong. Gender and Sexuality in Twentieth-Century Women's Sport* (New York, 1994).

Pamela J. Creedon, ed., *Women, Media and Sport. Challenging Gender Values* (Thousand Oaks, California, 1994).

Judith Davidson, "Sport for the People. New York State and Work Relief 1930's Style," *Canadian Journal of History of Sport* (May 1988), 40-51.

Foster Rhea Dulles, *America Learns to Play. A History of Popular Recreation, 1607-1940* (New York, 1952).

Charles Fountain, *Sportswriter. The Life and Times of Grantland Rice* (New York, 1993).

Ellen Gerber, "The Controlled Development of Collegiate Sport for Women, 1923-1936," *Journal of Sport History* (Spring 1975), 1-28.

Allen Guttmann, *Women's Sports. A History* (New York, 1991).

John Hoberman, *Darwin's Athletes. How Sport Has Damaged Black America and Preserved the Myth of Race* (Boston, 1997).

Maxwell L. Howell, Reet A. Howell, eds., *History of Sport in Canada* (Champaign, Illinois, 1981).

Reet Howell, ed., *Her Story in Sport. A Historical Anthology of Women in Sports* (West Point, New Jersey, 1982).

Bruce Kidd, *The Struggle for Canadian Sport* (Toronto, 1996).

Don Morrow, "Lou Marsh. The Pick and Shovel of Canadian Sporting Journalism," *Canadian Journal of History of Sport* (May 1983), 21-33.

Benjamin G. Rader, *American Sports,* 4th ed. (New Jersey, 1999).

Benjamin G. Rader, *In Its Own Image. How Television Has Transformed Sports* (New York, 1984).

Lisa Smith, ed., *Nike Is a Goddess. The History of Women in Sports* (New York, 1998).

Thomas G. Smith, "Outside the Pale. The Exclusion of Blacks from the National Football League, 1934-1946," *Journal of Sport History* (Winter 1988).

Mary Vipond, "London Listens." The Popularity of Radio in the Depression," *Ontario History* (March 1996), 47-63.

Evelyn Janice Waters, "A Content Analysis of the Sport Section in Selected Canadian Newspapers, 1927 to 1935," (MA. The University of Western Ontario, 1981).

David Welky, "Viking Girls, Mermaids, and Little Brown Men. U.S. Journalism and the 1932 Olympics," *Journal of Sport History* (Spring 1997), 24-49.

**AERONAUTICS**

Don Dwiggns, *They Flew the Bendix Race. The History of the Competition for the Bendix Trophy* (Philadelphia, 1965).

Reed Kinert, *American Racing Planes and Historic Air Races* (New York, 1952).

S.H. Schmid, Truman C. Weaver, *The Golden Age of Air Racing. Pre-1940* (Random Lake, Wisconsin, 1991).

**BASEBALL**

Colin Howell, *Northern Sandlots. A Social History of Maritime Baseball* (Toronto, 1995).

William Humber, *Diamonds of the North. A Concise History of Baseball in Canada* ((Toronto, 1995).

Robert V. Leffler, "Boom and Bust. The Elite Giants and Black Baseball in Baltimore, 1936-1951," *Maryland Historical Magazine* (Summer 1992), 171-86.

Peter Levine, *Ellis Island to Ebbetts Field. Sport and the American Jewish Experience* (New York, 1992).

William B. Mead, *Low and Outside. Baseball in the Depression, 1930-1939* (Virginia, 1990).

Robert Obojski, *Bush League. A History of Minor League Baseball* (New York, 1975).

James Overmyer, *Queen of the Negro Leagues. Effa Manley and the Newark Eagles* (Lanham, Md. 1998).

Benjamin G. Rader, *Baseball. A History of America's Game* (Urbana, 1992).

Lorne W. Rae, "It Was Real Baseball," *Saskatchewan History* (Winter 1991), 16-20.

Steven Riess, "Professional Sunday Baseball. A Study in Social Reform, 1892-1934," *The Maryland Historian* (Fall 1973), 95-108.

Harold Seymour, *Baseball. The People's Game* (New York, 1990).

David K. Wiggins, "Wendell Smith, the *Pittsburgh Courier-Journal* and the Campaign to Include Blacks in Organized Baseball, 1933-1945," *Journal of Sport History* (Summer 1983).

## BASKETBALL

"Basketball," Arthur Ashe, *A Hard Road to Glory. A History of the African-American Athlete, 1919-1945* (New York, 1988), 44-58.

Jan Beran, "The Story. Six-Player Girls' Basketball in Iowa," in Reet Howell, ed., *Her Story in Sport. A Historical Anthology of Women in Sports* (West Point, NY, 1982), 552-63.

Susan K. Cahn, *Coming on Strong. Gender and Sexuality in Twentieth-Century Women's Sport* (New York, 1994).

Elaine Chalus, "The Edmonton Commercial Graduates. Women's History. An Integrationist Approach," in Elise A. Corbet, Anthony W. Rasporich, eds., *Winter Sports in the West* (Calgary, 1990), 69-86.

Helen Gurney, "Major Influences on the Development of High School Girls' Sport in Ontario," in Reet Howell, ed., *Her Story in Sport. A Historical Anthology of Women in Sports* (West Point, NY, 1982), 472-9.

Joan S. Hult, Marianna Trekell, eds., *A Century of Women's Basketball. From Fraility to Final Four* (Reston, Virginia, 1991).

Neil D. Isaacs, *All the Moves. A History of College Basketball* (Philadelphia, 1975).

Peter Levine, *Ellis Island to Ebbets Field. Sport and the American Jewish Experience* (New York, 1992).

Robert W. Peterson, *Cages to Jump Shots. Pro Basketball's Early Years* (New York, 1996).

Paula Welch, "Interscholastic Basketball. Bane of Collegiate Physical Educators," in Reet Howell, ed., *Her Story in Sport. A Historical Anthology of Women in Sports* (West Point, N.Y., 1982), 424-31.

## BRITISH BALL GAMES

Gary Ross Mormino, "The Playing Fields of St. Louis. Italian Immigrants and Sports, 1925-1941," *Journal of Sport History* (Summer 1982).

Colin Jose, William Rannie, *The Story of Soccer in Canada* (Lincoln, Ontario, 1982).

David Waldstein, Stephen Wagg, "UnAmerican Activity. Football in US and Canadian Society," in S. Wagg, ed., *Giving the Game Away. Football, Politics and Culture on Five Continents* (London, 1995).


## COMBAT SPORTS—BOXING, WRESTLING, FENCING

Arthur R. Ashe, Jr. *A Hard Road to Glory. A History of the African-American Athlete, 1919-1945* (New York, 1988) 7-24, 70-72.

Dominic J. Capeci, Martha Wilkerson, "Multifarious Hero. Joe Louis, American Society and Race Relations During World Crisis, 1935-1945," *Journal of Sport History* (Winter 1983).

Anthony O. Edmonds, "The Second Louis-Schmeling Fight—Sport, Symbol, and Culture," *Journal of Popular Culture* (Summer 1973), 42-50.

Arthur S. Evans, "The Jim Braddock-Max Schmeling Affair. An Assessment of a Jewish Boycott of a Professional Prizefight," *Journal of Sport and Social Issues* (Fall/ Winter 1982), 1-12.

Peter Levine, *Ellis Island to Ebbets Field. Sport and the American Jewish Experience* (New York, 1992).

Glynn A. Leyshon, *Of Mats and Men. The Story of Canadian Amateur and Olympic Wrestling from 1600 to 1984* (London, Ontario, 1984).

Don Morrow, "With Craft and Guile. Canada's Jimmy McLarnin and the Business of Welterweight Boxing During the Great Depression," *Canadian Journal of History of Sport* (May 1935), 40-51.

Jeffrey T. Sammons, *Beyond the Ring. The Role of Boxing in American Society* (Chicago, 1990).

Jeffrey T. Sammons, "Boxing as a Reflection of Society. The Southern Reaction to Joe Louis," *Journal of Popular Culture* (Spring 1983), 23-33.

William H. Wiggins, "Boxing's Sambo Twins. Racial Stereotypes in Jack Johnson and Joe Louis Newspaper Cartoons, 1908 to 1938," *Journal of Sport History* (Winter 1988).


## FIELD SPORTS—LACROSSE, FIELD HOCKEY, SPEEDBALL

Susan K. Cahn, *Coming on Strong. Gender and Sexuality in Twentieth-Century Women's Sport* (New York, 1994).

Anne Lee Delano, *Lacrosse for Girls and Women* (Dubuque, Iowa, 1970).

Alexander M. Weyand, Milton R. Roberts, *The Lacrosse Story* (Baltimore, 1965).


## FOOTBALL—CANADIAN

Frank Cosentino, "Football," in Don Morrow, et al., *A Concise History of Sport in Canada* (Toronto, 1989), 140-68.

Frank Cosentino, *Canadian Football. The Grey Cup Years* (Toronto, 1969).

Gordon Currie, *100 Years of Canadian Football* (Don Mills, 1968).

Ronald S. Lappage, "Sport as an Expression of Western and Maritime Discontent in Canada between the Wars," *Canadian Journal of the History of Sport and Physical Education* (May 1977), 50-71.

**FOOTBALL—US COLLEGE**

Jack Falla, *NCAA. The Voice of College Sports. A Diamond Anniversary History, 1906-1981* (Mission, Kansas, 1981).

Hal A. Lawson, Alan G. Ingham, "Conflicting Ideologies Concerning the University and Intercollegiate Athletics. Harper and Hutchins at Chicago, 1892-1940," *Journal of Sport History* (Winter 1980), 37-67.

John McCallum, Charles H. Pearson, *College Football U.S.A., 1869-1971* (Canton, 1971).

David M. Nelson, *The Anatomy of a Game. Football, the Rules and the Men Who Made the Game* (Newark, 1994).

Donald Spivey, "'End Jim Crow in Sports.' The Protest at New York University, 1940-41," *Journal of Sport History* (Winter 1988).

Richard Stone, "The Graham Plan of 1935. An Aborted Crusade to De-emphasize College Athletics," *The North Carolina Historical Review*, 64 (July 1987), 274-93.

John R. Thelin, *Games Colleges Play. Scandal and Reform in Intercollegiate Athletics* (Baltimore, 1994).

**FOOTBALL—THE NFL**

Carl M. Becker, "The 'Tom Thumb' Game. Bears vs. Spartans, 1932," *Journal of Sport History* (Fall 1995), 216-27.

Kevin Britz, "Of Football and Frontiers. The Meaning of Bronko Nagurski," *Journal of Sport History* (Summer 1993), 101-27.

Richard M. Cohen, et al., *The Scrapbook History of Pro Football* (Indianapolis, 1976).

Robert W. Peterson, *Pigskin. The Early Years of Pro Football* (New York, 1997).

Thomas G. Smith, "Outside the Pale. The Exclusion of Blacks from the National Football League, 1934-1946," *Journal of Sport History* (Winter, 1988).

**GOLF**

Arthur R. Ashe, Jr. *A Hard Road to Glory. A History of the African-American Athlete, 1919-1945* (New York, 1988), 65-9.

James Barclay, *Golf in Canada. A History* (Toronto, 1992).

Marvin P. Dawkins, "African American Golfers in the Age of Jim Crow," *The Western Journal of Black Studies*, 20 (1996), 39-47.

Herb Graffis, *The PGA. The Official History of the Professional Golfers' Association of America* (New York, 1975).

**HOCKEY**

Joanna Avery, Julie Stevens, *Too Many Men on the Ice. Women's Hockey in North America* (Toronto, 1997).

Jack Batten, *The Inside Story of Conn Smythe's Hockey Dynasty* (Toronto, 1969).

Todd Christie, "The Eddie Shore-Ace Bailey Incident of 1933. One of the Greatest Tragedies in Canadian Sports History," *Canadian Journal of the History of Sport* (May 1988), 63-76.

David Cruise, Alison Griffiths, *Net Worth. Exploding the Myths of Pro Hockey* (Toronto, 1991)

Dan Diamond, ed., *Total Hockey. The Official Encyclopedia of the NHL* (New York, 1998).

Ken Dryden, *The Game. A Thoughtful and Provocative Look at a Life in Hockey* (Toronto, 1983).

Richard Gruneau, David Whitson, *Hockey Night in Canada. Sport, Identities and Cultural Politics* (Toronto, 1993).

Bruce Kidd, *The Struggle for Canadian Sport* (Toronto, 1996).

Wayne Simpson, "Hockey," in Don Morrow, et al., *A Concise History of Sport in Canada* (Toronto, 1989).

Conn Smythe (with Scott Young), *Conn Smythe. If You Can't Beat 'Em in the Alley* (Markham, 1981).

Scott Young, *Hello Canada! The Life and Times of Foster Hewitt* (Toronto, 1985).

Scott Young, *Stanley Cup Fever. 100 Years of Hockey Greatness* (Toronto, 1992).


**INDOOR SPORTS—BOWLING, BILLIARDS**

Henry Fankhauser, Fank Micalizzi, *The Book of Duckpin Bowling* (New York, 1969).

A.W. Karcher, *WIBC. The First 75 Years* (Columbus, Ohio, 1991)

Willie Mosconi and Stanley Cohen, *Willie's Game. An Autobiography* (New York, 1993.

*WIBC History. A Story of 50 Years of Progress, 1916-17 to 1966-67* (1967).


**INTERNATIONAL GAMES—OLYMPICS, EMPIRE GAMES**

Cleve Dheensaw, *The Commonwealth Games. The First 60 Years, 1930-1990* (Toronto, 1994).

George Eisen, "The Voices of Sanity. American Diplomatic Reports from the 1936 Berlin Olympiad," *Journal of Sport History* (Winter 1984), 64-78.

Moshe Gottlieb, "The American Controversy Over the Olympic Games," *American Jewish Historical Quarterly* (March 1972), 181-213.

Wendy Gray, Robert Barney, "Devotion to Whom? German-American Loyalty on the Issue of Participation in the 1936 Olympic Games," *Journal of Sport History* (Summer 1990), 214-31.

D.A. Kass, "The Issue of Racism at the 1936 Olympics," *Journal of Sport History* (Winter 1976), 223-5.

Bruce Kidd, "Canadian Opposition to the 1936 Olympics in Germany," *Canadian Journal of Sport History* (December 1978), 20-40.

Erik Kjeldsen, "Integration of Minorities into Olympic Sport in Canada and the USA," *Journal of Sport and Social Issues* (Summer-Fall 1984), 30-44.

Glynn A. Leyshon, "An Empire in Competition. 'The Friendly Games,'" *The Beaver* (August-September 1994), 14-21.

Richard D. Mandell, *The Nazi Olympics* (New York, 1971).

Carolyn Marvin, "Avery Brundage and American Participation in the 1936 Olympic Games, *Journal of American Studies* (April 1982), 81-105.

Katharine Moore, "A Divergence of Interests. Canada's Role in the Politics and Sport of the British Empire During the 1920s," *Canadian Journal of History of Sport* (May 1990), 21-9.

Barbara Schrodt, "Canadian Women at the Olympics. 1924 to 1976," in Reet Howell, ed., *Her Story in Sport. A Historical Anthology of Women in Sports* (New York, 1982), 273-81.

Barbara Schrodt, "Canadian Women at the Commonwealth Games. 1930 to 1978," in Reet Howell, ed., *Her Story in Sport. A Historical Anthology of Women in Sports* (New York, 1982), 284-90.

David B. Welky, "Viking Girls, Mermaids, and Little Brown Men. U.S. Journalism and the 1932 Olympics," *Journal of Sport History* (Spring 1997), 24-49.

Stephen R. Wenn, "A Tale of Two Diplomats. George S. Messersmith and Charles H. Sherrill on Proposed American Participation in the 1936 Olympics," *Journal of Sport History* (Spring 1989), 27-43.

**MARKSMANSHIP—ARCHERY, SHOOTING**

J. Boa, "Thirty Years in the D.C.R.A., 1920-1950," *Canadian Marksman* (1951).

E. Burke, *The History of Archery* (1958).

Desmond Burke, *Canadian Bisley Shooting. An Art and a Science* (Oakville, 1970).

C.E. Chapel, *Field, Skeet and Trapshooting* (New York, 1949).

Judith Jenkins, "Women's Riflery Teams. A Collegiate Anomaly of the Post World War I Period," *Canadian Journal of HIstory of Sport,* 23 (May, 1992), 32-45.

P.E. Klopsteg, *Bows and Arrows. A Chapter in the Evolution of Archery in America* (Smithsonian, 1962).

**RACING ON LAND—BICYCLES, AUTOMOBILES**

Allan E. Brown, ed., *The History of the American Speedway. Past and Present* (Marme, Michigan, 1985).

Richard Browne, "The Concept of the 6-Day Cycling Show-Circus in the 1930s. The Star Showman, 'Torchy' Peden, *Canadian Journal of History of Sport* (December 1986), 85-96.

Stanley L. De Geer, *Pikes Peak is Unser Mountain. A History of the Pikes Peak Auto Hill Climb, 1916-1990* (Albuqueque, 1990).

Edward Harper, *Six Days of Madness* (Stroud, Ontario, 1993).

William Humber, *Freewheeling. The Story of Bicycling in Canada* (Toronto, 1986).

Peter Nye, *Hearts of Lions. The History of American Bicycle Racing* (New York, 1988).

Ivan Rendall, *The Checkered Flag. 100 Years of Motor Racing* (London, 1993).

Henry Roxborough, "King of the Six-Day Cyclists," *Great Days in Canadian Sport* (Toronto, 1957), 149-59.

*Seventy Years of the American Motorcyclist Association, 1924-1994* (Westerville, Ohio, 1994).


**RACING ON WATER—YACHTS, MOTOR BOATING, ROWING**

Gerald Guetat, *Classic Speedboats, 1916-1939* (Osceala, Wisconsin, 1997).

John Parkinson, Jr., *The History of The New York Yacht Club* (New York, 1975).


**RACKET SPORTS**

Allison Danzig, Peter Schwed, eds., *The Fireside Book of Tennis* (New York, 1972).

Oliver H. Durrell, ed., *The Official Guide to Platform Tennis* (New York, 1971).

Larry Engelmann, *The Goddess and the American Girl. The Story of Suzanne Lenglen and Helen Wills* (New York, 1988).

U.S.L.T.A., *Official Encyclopedia of Tennis* (New York, 1972).


**RECREATIONAL SPORTS—VOLLEYBALL AND SOFTBALL**

Merrie A. Fidler, "The Establishment of Softball as a Sport for American Women, 1900-1940," in Reet Howell, ed., *Her Story in Sport. A Historical Anthology of Women in Sports* (New York, 1982), 527-30.


**TRACK AND FIELD**

Arthur Ashe, "Track," in *Hard Road to Glory. A History of the African-American Athlete, 1919-1945* (New York, 1988), 73-91.

Susan K. Cahn, "'Cinderellas of Sport. Black Women in Track and Field," in *Coming on Strong. Gender and Sexuality in Twentieth-Century Women's Sport* (New York, 1994) 110-39.

Susan E. Cayleff, *Babe. The Life and Legend of Babe Didrikson Zaharias* (1995).

Tom Derderian, *Boston Marathon. The History of the World's Premier Running Event* (Champaign, 1994).

Roberto L. Quercetani, *Athletics. A History of Modern Track and Field Athletics (1860-1990)* (Milan, Italy, 1990).

Louise Mead Tricard, *American Women's Track and Field. A History, 1895 through 1980* (Jefferson, North Carolina, 1996).

David K. Wiggins, "'Great Speed But Little Stamina.' The Historical Debate over Black Athletic Superiority," *Journal of Sport History* (Summer 1989), 158-85.

**TURF, HORSE RACING, EQUESTRIAN EVENTS**

Gene Brown, ed., *The Complete Book of Horse Racing/Automobile Racing* (New York, 1980).

Louis E. Cauz, *The Plate. A Royal Tradition* (Toronto, 1984).

Kristine Fredriksson, *American Rodeo. From Buffalo Bill to Big Business* (Texas A&M, 1985).

James H. Gray, *A Brand of Its Own. The 100 Year History of the Calgary Exhibition and Stampede* (Saskatoon, 1985).

Mary Lou LeCompte, *Cowgirls of the Rodeo. Pioneer Professional Athletes* (Urbana, 1993).

Mary Lou LeCompte, "Wild West Frontier Days, Roundups and Stampedes. Rodeo Before There Was Rodeo," *Canadian Journal of the History of Sport* (December 1995), 54-67.

Mary Lou LeCompte, "Colonel William Thomas Johnson, Premier Rodeo Producer of the 1930s," *Canadian Journal of the History of Sport* (May 1992), 61-86.

Mary Lou LeCompte, "Home on the Range. Women in Professional Rodeo. 1929-1947," *Journal of Sport History* (Winter 1990), 318-45.


**WATER SPORTS—SWIMMING, DIVING, WATER POLO, SYNCHRONIZED SWIMMING**

David Armbruster, et al., *Swimming & Diving* (St. Louis, 1973).

Gladys Bean, *The History of Synchronized Swimming in Canada* (Ottawa, 1975).

Peter C. Conrad, *In the Winning Lane. A History of Competitive Swimming in Saskatchewan* (Regina, 1996).

Buck Dawson, *An Era to Remember. Weismiller to Spitz. The First 21 Years of International Swimming* (Fort Lauderdale, 1986).


**WINTER SPORTS—SKIING, FIGURE SKATING, CURLING**

E. John B. Allen, *From Skisport to Skiing. One Hundred Years of an American Sport, 1840-1940* (Amherst, 1993).

Lynn Copley-Graves, *Figure Skating History. The Evolution of Dance on Ice* (Columbus, Ohio, 1992).

Morris Mott, John Allardyce, *Curling Capital. Winnipeg and the Roarin' Game, 1876 to 1988* (Winnipeg, 1989).

Bob Weeks, *The Brier. The History of Canada's Most Celebrated Curling Championship* (Toronto, 1995).

# INDEXES
## INDEX OF NAMES

## INDEX OF SUBJECTS

# INDEX OF INSTITUTIONS

New York University, 75, 133
*New York World-Telegram,* 30-1, 74, 113
*New Yorker,* 227, 229
New Zealand All-Blacks, 108
Ninety-Nines Women's Aviation Organization, 34
Non-Sectarian Anti-Nazi League, 118
North Atlantic Fishermen's Trophy, 324-5
North Shore Indians, 137
Northern League (baseball), 71
Northwestern University, 75
Notre Dame, 82, 162-3, 178-9, 192
Nova Scotia Cricket Association, 96
Nuremberg Laws, 266

Oakland Athletics, 46,
Ohio State University, 75, 98, 383, 385-6, 421
Oklahoma A&M University, 117
Ontario Athletic Commission, xv
Orange Bowl, 162
Original Celtics, 76, 87
Ottawa Rough Riders, 150
Ottawa Senators, 224

Pacific Coast Conference, 75, 87
Pacific Coast Football League, 193
Pacific Coast League, 66
Paddle Tennis Association, 342
Parker Brothers Inc., 362-5
Penn State, 97-8, 162
Philadelphia Eagles, 191
Philadelphia Phillies, 46
Philadelphia Quakers, 224
Philadelphia Stars, 50
*Philadelphia Tribune,* 59, 61, 205, 274
Philadelphia Tribune Girls, 78
Philadelphia Warriors, 73
*Pittsburgh Courier,* 51, 59
Pittsburgh Homestead Grays, 50, 61
Pittsburgh Pirates, 56
Pittsburgh YMHA, 76
Polo Grounds, 196-7, 203-4
*Popular Aviation,* 39
Porstmouth Spartans, 191, 193
Port Arthur Bearcats, 230, 270

President's Cup, 318, 325-6
Preston Rivulettes, 2, 230
Princeton University, 96, 98, 103, 105-6, 135, 140, 332
Professional Golf Association, 208-10
Professional Racing Pilots Association, 32, 42
Public Parks Playground Association, 349
Public Works Administration, xv, 9, 54, 73, 87, 320
Purdue University, 74, 82, 84
PWA, see Public Works Administration

Quebec Senior Hockey League, 249
Queen's University, 108, 147, 244

*Reader's Digest,* 2,
*Recreation,* 373, 375
Red Deer Amazons, 230
Regina Roughriders, 148, 160-1
*Research Quarterly,* 17, 209, 336
*Review of Reviews,* 445
*Ring (The),* 113, 115, 125
Rodeo Association of America, 399-400, 414-6
Rolls Royce, 41
Rose Bowl, 162
Royal Canadian Golf Association, 210
Royal Henley, 320
Rubenstein Cup, 96
Rugby Union of Canada, 97, 108
Rutgers University, 135
Ryder Cup, 212

San Jose State College, 105
*Saturday Evening Post,* 6, 51, 237, 347
St. Andrews College, 95
St. John's University, 74-5
St. Louis Browns, 4, 46, 48, 54, 56, 66, 69
St. Louis Cardinals, 4, 48, 52, 66-7
St. Louis Eagles, 224, 235-6
St. Louis Gashouse Gang, 49, 53, 57
St. Louis Giants, 50
Sargent School of Physical Education for Women, 89
Sarnia Imperials, 148-9, 161

## INDEX OF GEOGRAPHIC AND PLACE NAMES

# FROM ACADEMIC INTERNATIONAL PRESS*

## THE RUSSIAN SERIES

1 S.F. Platonov History of Russia **
2 The Nicky-Sunny Letters, Correspondence of Nicholas and Alexandra, 1914-1917
3 Ken Shen Weigh Russo-Chinese Diplomacy, 1689-1924
4 Gaston Cahen Relations of Russia with China...1689-1730
5 M.N. Pokrovsky Brief History of Russia
6 M.N. Pokrovsky History of Russia from Earliest Times
7 Robert J. Kerner Bohemia in the Eighteenth Century
8 Memoirs of Prince Adam Czartoryski and His Correspondence with Alexander I
9 S.F. Platonov Moscow and the West.
10 S.F. Platonov Boris Godunov
11 Boris Nikolajewsky Aseff the Spy
12 Francis Dvornik Les Legendes de Constantin et de Methode vues de Byzance
13 Francis Dvornik Les Slaves, Byzance et Rome au XIᵉ Siecle
14 A. Leroy-Beaulieu Un Homme d'Etat Russe (Nicholas Miliutine)...
15 Nicolas Berdyaev Leontiev (In English)
16 V.O. Kliuchevskii Istoriia soslovii v Rossii
17 Tehran Yalta Potsdam. The Soviet Protocols
18 The Chronicle of Novgorod
19 Paul N. Miliukov Outlines of Russian Culture Vol. III Pt. 1. The Origins of Ideology
20 P.A. Zaionchkovskii The Abolition of Serfdom in Russia
21 V.V. Vinogradov Russkii iazyk. Grammaticheskoe uchenie o slove
22 P.A. Zaionchkovsky The Russian Autocracy under Alexander III
23 A.E. Presniakov Emperor Nicholas I of Russia. The Apogee of Autocracy
24 V.I. Semevskii Krestianskii vopros v Rossii v XVIII i pervoi polovine XIX veka
25 S.S. Oldenburg Last Tsar! Nicholas II, His Reign and His Russia
26 Carl von Clausewitz The Campaign of 1812 in Russia
27 M.K. Liubavskii Obrazovanie osnovnoi gosudarstvennoi territorii velikorusskoi narodnosti. Zaselenie i obedinenie tsentra
28 S.F. Platonov Ivan the Terrible Paper
29 Paul N. Miliukov Iz istorii russkoi intelligentsii. Sbornik statei i etiudov
30 A.E. Presniakov The Tsardom of Muscovy
31 M. Gorky, J. Stalin et al., History of the Civil War in Russia (Revolution)
32 R.G. Skrynnikov Ivan the Terrible
33 P.A. Zaionchkovsky The Russian Autocracy in Crisis, 1878-1882
34 Joseph T. Fuhrmann Tsar Alexis. His Reign and His Russia
35 R.G. Skrynnikov Boris Godunov
36 R.G. Skrynnikov The Time of Troubles. Russia in Crisis, 1604-1618
38 V.V. Shulgin Days of the Russian Revolutions. Memoirs From the Right, 1905- 1907. Cloth and Paper

39 A.E. Presniakov The Formation of the Great Russian State.
40 J.L. Black "Into the Dustbin of History"! The USSR From August Coup to Commonwealth, 1991. A Documentary Narrative
41 E.V. Anisimov Empress Elizabeth. Her Reign and Her Russia, 1741–1761
42 J.K. Libbey Russian-American Economic Relations, 1763–1999
43 Nicholas Zernov Three Russian Prophets. Khomiakov, Dostoevsky, Soloviev
44 Paul N. Miliukov The Russian Revolution 3 vols.
45 Anton I. Denikin The White Army
55 M.V. Rodzianko The Reign of Rasputin—An Empire's Collapse. Memoirs
56 The Memoirs of Alexander Iswolsky

## THE CENTRAL AND EAST EUROPEAN SERIES

1 Louis Eisenmann Le Compromis Austro-Hongrois de 1867
3 Francis Dvornik The Making of Central and Eastern Europe 2nd edition
4 Feodor F. Zigel Lectures on Slavonic Law
10 Doros Alastos Venizelos—Patriot, Statesman, Revolutionary
20 Paul Teleki The Evolution of Hungary and its Place in European History

## FORUM ASIATICA

1 M.I. Sladkovsky China and Japan—Past and Present

## REFERENCE SERIES

The Modern Encyclopedia of Russian, Soviet and Eurasian History 60 vols.
The Modern Encyclopedia of East Slavic, Baltic and Eurasian Literatures 50 vols.
The Modern Encyclopedia of Religions in Russia and the Soviet Union 30 vols
Russia & Eurasia Military Review Annual
Russia & Eurasia Facts & Figures Annual
Russia & Eurasia Documents Annual
USSR Calendar of Events (1987- 1991) 5 vol. set
USSR Congress of Peoples's Deputies 1989. The Stenographic Record
Documents of Soviet History 12 vols.
Documents of Soviet-American Relations
Gorbachev's Reforms. An Annotated Bibliography of Soviet Writings. Part 1 1985–1987
MilitaryEncyclopedia of Russia and Eurasia 50 vols.
China Facts & Figures Annual
China Documents Annual
Encyclopedia USA. The Encyclopedia of the United States of America Past & Present 50 vols.
Sports Encyclopedia North America 50 vols.
Sports in North America. A Documentary History
Religious Documents North America Annual
The International Military Encyclopedia 50 vols.
Nationalities and Ethnicity Terminologies. An Encyclopedic Dictionary and Research Guide

## SPECIAL WORKS

S.M. Soloviev History of Russia 50 vols.
SAFRA Papers 1985-

*Request catalogs. Sample pages, tables of contents, more on line at www.ai-press.com